Management Perspectives in Retailing

The Wiley Marketing Series

WILLIAM LAZER, Advisory Editor
Michigan State University

Management Perspectives in Retailing

Ronald R. Gist
Associate Professor of Business Administration
Oregon State University

John Wiley & Sons, Inc.   NEW YORK · LONDON · SYDNEY

Preface

Education for business is in the process of fundamental change. A spirit of experimentation is reflected in the literature of the professional journals and in the program content of professional meetings. Similar ferment is apparent in almost every aspect of the business curriculum. Clearly, the challenge of developing classroom materials which pose greater intellectual challenge for the student of business administration has been accepted.

Education for marketing has also undergone significant change. A "management perspective" pervades many of the course offerings in marketing. Much of the traditional content of marketing has been discarded or deemphasized. But marketing education has undergone another, much less obvious kind of change. This latter change is manifest in a new approach to the issues and problems which comprise the discipline. The use of concepts, abstraction, and formal reasoning processes represents highly significant progress.

One of the traditional areas of marketing which has been slow to effect change is retailing. It is hoped that this collection of readings may suggest direction for retailing education. The work of preparing the collection was undertaken because of a conviction that the literature of retailing and the issues which are pertinent to the subject constitute a challenge which is appropriate for advanced study.

The articles in this collection are organized into ten parts. Parts I, II, and III deal with retail institutions. These parts include consideration of several theories of retail institutional development, an examination of some of the important existing and evolving institutional forms and a brief consideration of some foreign institutional characteristics. Part IV examines the principal dimensions in which retail competition is manifest, including an elaboration of the "retailing mix." The remainder of the collection is given to problems in the management of the retail enterprise.

More specifically, Part V examines some recent research techniques which have particular applicability toward the solution of management problems in retailing. This section includes techniques for the measurement of store "image" and an approach which permits the use of "early adopters" in fashion buying. Part VI is concerned with the role of spatial competition in retail management, including materials on trade area conceptualization, delineation, and evaluation as well as matters of site analysis and store layout. The section also has a computerized application for trade area delineation and appraisal.

Part VII focuses on problems in retail promotion, including an examination of the recent status of trading stamps, a study of the role of retailers or "dealers" brands, and a consideration of the likely consequence of mass preselling activities by manufacturers on the promotional activities of retailers. Part VIII considers the strategy of price competition in retail management. Part IX examines the use of "services" as an aspect of retail competition and as an important element in the retailing mix. Finally, Part X identifies some traditional and recent approaches to effective retail management through internal control.

Thus the first three parts of the collection provide a foundation for the understanding of change in retail institutions—a foundation often slighted, but one which has important implications for retail planning and management. The remainder of the book is organized around the problem areas and issues which represent the principal elements in the retailing mix.

The selections were chosen on the basis of three criteria. First, an article ideally should involve concepts or ideas which are fruitful but which have not yet become well integrated in retailing textbooks. Second, where possible, the article should encourage argumentation and student involvement in the classroom. This criterion suggests that some of the articles were selected because they embody a controversial or speculative position regarding some issue in retailing. In large part, the learning process is an exposure to different points of view; it comprises, to some extent, the sifting through many views and opinions in order to develop an opinion of one's own. Avoidance of the controversial denies students one of the most satisfying aspects of exposure to formal education. Finally, some of the articles were selected because they reflect recent views or "progress reports" on some long-standing problem in retailing. The selections included were chosen with the student in mind: hopefully, they convey some of the excitement, risk, and reward of a career in retailing.

Some topics have been intentionally omitted because they either receive consideration in other courses or generate slight current interest. These omissions include such matters as organizational arrangements, problems in managing retail personnel, handling insurable risk, and the receiving and marking of incoming merchandise.

Discussion questions are provided for each article. Several types of questions are included. In working with "readings" as a teaching device in the past, students have expressed the feeling that articles frequently do not provide the point-by-point structure which a text format may involve. Some of the questions are intended to provide structure of this type; these questions direct the attention of the student to particular matters within a given selection. A second type of question identifies more general discussion topics, and may encourage the student to evaluate the contents of the article against his or her own experiences and observations. A third type of question urges the student to speculate on the future forms which institutions and operational procedures in retailing may take.

My gratitude should be expressed for the encouragement and guidance provided by a number of people. Professor Fred M. Jones of the Department of Marketing, College of Commerce of the University of Illinois, is largely responsible for my interest in retailing. Much of the work of preparing these materials was facilitated and expedited by a research grant received while a faculty member of the University of Southern California. Professor Taylor W. Meloan, Chairman of the Department of Marketing and Business Communications, School of Business Administration of the University of Southern California, encouraged the development of these materials in every possible way. My expression of gratitude is obviously due the many authors and publishers whose works are represented in this book. Limitations on the length of the collection prevented the use of many equally valuable articles. Finally, my appreciation is due Mrs. Barbara Turner whose excellent typing assistance was invaluable.

Ronald R. Gist

Oregon State University
December 1966

Contents

*Management Perspectives
in Retailing*

The Dynamics of Retail Institutions

The universe of American retail institutions is in a perpetual process of change. This institutional universe both adapts to its environment and causes its environment to adjust to it. Some retail institutions serve us effectively over long periods of time—others flounder and disappear. A better understanding of the processes through which retail institutions evolve and develop and an identification of the forces which engender change in such institutions lies at the very base of success in retail management.

This section includes materials which might be best described as theories or hypotheses of retail institutional change. In this instance, however, "theory" should not be construed to mean "impractical." A careful consideration of these theories will provide valuable insight into the nature of the causes which produce perpetual change in our retail universe.

1. Responses of Selected Retail Institutions to Their Changing Environment

DELBERT J. DUNCAN*

Tremendous changes have taken place since World War II in the social, economic, and technological environment within which retailers operate. This article reviews some of the major responses which traditional department stores, developers of shopping centers, supermarkets, and discount stores have made to these dynamic developments.

INTRODUCTION

Any discussion of the "Responses of Selected Retailing Institutions to Changes in Their Environment" within the time limits at our disposal requires considerable selectivity and judgment in choosing the environmental factors to be examined, the types of retail institutions to be analyzed, and the particular responses that are of significance.

Moreover, one encounters considerable difficulty in judging the extent to which the marked changes that have taken place in retail distribution during the past five decades or so constitute responses of retail management to the changing social and economic environment or the degree to which entrepreneurial activities of retailers themselves have contributed to these environmental changes. A case in point, for example, is the growth and development of the discount house. Few informed observers would attribute this significant development merely as a response to a changing environment.

Perhaps it is merely a question of semantics, but in any case the difficulty of selecting and appraising important developments remains present. In this connection the writer makes no claim to divine guidance, but has relied on his own knowledge and experience and the judgment of respected colleagues whose advice he has sought.[1]

All of us are aware, also, of the environmental changes taking place in technology, in governmental regulations, and even on the political front. And, although progressive retailers must adapt their policies and practices to such changes if they are to survive, time and space limitations force us to restrict our discussion primarily to some selected social and economic environmental factors.

This restriction is justifiable because the market for retailers is people—people with money to spend. Success in retailing is dependent on the ability to provide merchandise at reasonable prices with the kind and extent of service customers require to maintain or to improve their standards of living. Consequently, retailers need to be informed about people, including such factors as the growth and changing characteristics of the population, the geographical shifts taking place among regions, states, cities and sections of cities, the suburbs and our rural areas, and changes in modes of living. Similarly, to be successful they must have knowledge of personal income and its distribution among members of our society, and the opportunities afforded by the tremendous increase in discretionary income since World War II.

Some of the major developments in both of

* SOURCE: Reprinted by permission from the American Marketing Association, in *Marketing and Economic Development*, Peter D. Bennett, Editor, 1965, pp. 583–602.

* Professor of Marketing, University of California.

[1] I am indebted, particularly, to my esteemed colleagues Malcolm P. McNair and John W. Wingate.

these areas are discussed later in this paper. But a long standing axiom in retailing should be emphasized at this point. No retailer can be everything to all people; he, like every successful marketer, should define his market and cater to it. And, in the case of fashion merchandise, he should decide on his place in the fashion cycle and not attempt to serve all levels of taste or preference.

With this brief prologue, let us turn to some of the more significant social and economic forces in the United States which have played and are continuing to play an important part in shaping the policies and methods of traditional retail institutions and their more modern counterparts. For discussion purposes, let us attempt to consider each group of forces separately, although it is quite evident that they are closely related. We shall then examine the responses of selected types of retail institutions to these developments.

THE SOCIAL ENVIRONMENT
AFFECTING RETAILING

A multitude of social forces has influenced the conduct of retail enterprises over the years, and these forces have been particularly strong since World War II. Only a few of them may be mentioned here, but they are indicative of the broad spectrum of developments with which retailers must cope in our growing, dynamic economy.

Population Growth, Characteristics, and Mobility

In the fifty-year period between 1910 and 1960 the population of the continental United States grew from 91,972,266 to 178,464,236 persons. If we include the newly admitted states of Alaska and Hawaii, the latter figure becomes 179,323,175, an increase of almost 28 million or more than 18 percent in the last census decade alone. More recent years have witnessed a continuation of this "population explosion."

By 1963 it is estimated that our total population reached 188,616,000, and on May 1, 1965 about 193,473,000, an increase in five years of more than 14 million or 7.9 percent.[2] Projections for the next two decades indicate

continued population growth—225.1 million in 1965 and 265.6 million in 1985.[3] It is possible, of course, that these projections may require some revision if the growing "birth-control" measures continue to gain momentum and gain increasing acceptance.

Closely related to the rapid growth of our population is the formation of households and families, since these constitute buying units to the retailer. The number of households has been increasing recently at a rate of about 900,000 a year, and it is probable that before this decade is over the rate will be one million. By 1975, the total number is expected to reach 70 million or more,[4] and this growth trend is likely to continue especially in the age group of 18–25 and among people over 65 years of age.

A multitude of data is available to the retailer on population characteristics. They include geographical distribution among regions, states, standard metropolitan statistical areas, counties, and cities as well as between urban and rural areas. Information is available, also, concerning such factors as age, sex, race and color, education, marital status, employment status, and occupation, all important to the retailer in choosing locations, defining his market, and establishing his merchandise, service and promotional mixes. Only two significant developments need be mentioned here.

First, there is the tremendous growth of the teenage group. Between 1960 and 1964, the 14–17 age group in our country increased 27.3 percent while the 18–24 age group gained 17.2 percent. One out of 12 people in the United States is in the 14–17 category. And by 1970 it is expected that there will be 99 million persons under 25 years of age out of a projected total of 208 million.[5] Truly we are now in a "youth-oriented" economy and may well be for some time.

The second noteworthy development is occurring in the "over 65" age group. This segment of our population continues to grow rapidly and, in fact, is projected to show the second highest gain, about 50 percent, between 1960 and 1985. By the latter year, there

[2] *Population Estimates,* Current Population Reports, Series P-25, No. 309, June 11, 1965, 1. (Washington, D.C.: U.S. Department of Commerce).

[3] *Ibid.,* No. 301, February 26, 1965, p. 4.
[4] Conrad Taeuber, Assistant Director, Bureau of the Census, "Projected Composition of the U.S. Population by 1975," *Commercial and Financial Chronicle, September* 24, 1964, p. 62.
[5] "Will Markets Develop as Hoped?" *Business Week,* May 15, 1965, p. 32.

may well be over 25 million of these "old sters." [6]

Another important characteristic of our population of interest to retailers is its mobility. Our nation has experienced this phenomenon since our Colonial Days. Shifts from cities to new agricultural lands, from rural to urban areas, from major cities to suburbs, and, more recently, a return of many suburbanites to city living—not to mention movements from one region or state to another in our large country —furnish ample evidence of the "gypsy" traits within us. In the decade of the 1950's alone, 85 percent of our total increase in population took place within metropolitan areas and most of it in the suburbs.[7]

Significantly, also, our farm population has declined steadily since the 1930's; and during the 1950's the net migration from farms to metropolitan areas averaged one million persons per year. The growing concentration of population in metropolitan areas has simplified the task of retailers in serving people's needs in merchandise and services.

Suburban Living

The movement of people to the suburbs has brought about important changes in their modes of living, in their buying behavior, and in their future expectations as members of our affluent society. These changes are influenced mainly by such factors as greater leisure, better highways, and more automobiles (in fact our increasing dependence on such transportation is revealed by the 72 million passenger cars licensed in 1964). Many parts of our great middle class have, as one of my colleagues has expressed it, "suddenly experienced a widening horizon of the 'economic good life:' [these people want] a better house, . . . better education for their children, improved health and medical care, opportunity to develop all kinds of personal interests and hobbies, vacations, travel, sports, a second car, and all the expensive household conveniences of the modern age." [8] Although this "widening horizon" is not confined to residents of our suburbs, it is probably most pronounced in these areas.

Life in the suburbs, likewise, has contributed to more casual living with increasing sophistication evidenced in clothing, food, and housing. An appetite for better things, partially generated by social emulation, has created desires for better quality merchandise and improved retailer services. This "trading up" by consumers, and again certainly not restricted to the suburbs, accompanied by better education and a growing culture, has created demands which, in many instances, have exceeded current income and stimulated the growing of "buying on time." As a result, consumer credit now outstanding is at the highest level in our history.

One other development in suburban living deserves brief mention. This is the "do it yourself" movement now prevalent in both suburbs and cities in all sections of our country. Unable or unwilling to pay the high labor costs involved in repairs, improvements and other services, an increasing number of people are doing the necessary work themselves. As a consequence, many service institutions have been established to meet the growing demand.

Other Changes in the Social Environment

The growth of our suburbs has contributed in large degree to the significant changes that have taken place in the downtown areas of our large cities. And, despite some evidence of a downtown rebirth in certain major cities encouraged by numerous low-cost housing projects, dissatisfaction with suburban living, and other reasons, the effects of the movement to the suburbs have been rather severe on retailing institutions in central downtown shopping areas since World War II and will likely continue to be felt in the future.

Yet attempts are being made to improve the situation. Greater attention is being given by retailers to the problem of "over-storing," that is, the existence of more stores of particular types in certain locations than are needed to meet effective customer demand. And, as one observer notes in reviewing this problem, "one of the earmarks of the new downtown rebirth is the location of stores in sub-metropolitan areas, not necessarily suburbs, but 10, 15, 20 miles from the main drag." [9]

Another factor in the social environment of retailers is the increasing proportion of con-

[6] Ibid.

[7] Taeuber, op. cit., p. 63.

[8] M. P. McNair, in an address in New York City on October 5, 1964, entitled "Change and Challenges in the Department Store Industry."

[9] "The Merchant's Point of View," New York Times, June 13, 1965, p. F11.

sumer income being spent for services. Increased leisure has resulted in a marked growth
in recreation activities—boating, bowling,
swimming, and others, in travel, and in the
leasing of "do-it yourself" equipment. In addition, the purchase of insurance and other similar services continues to expand.

And finally, in our consideration of social
forces, let us emphasize the fact that the
"growth in education, literacy, and culture
have combined with leisure-time to enhance
the scope and sway of fashion" [10] in this country. And fashion developments will likely be
influenced most by teenagers and the under-
25-year-old group now comprising almost 50
percent of our population!

THE ECONOMIC ENVIRONMENT
AFFECTING RETAILING

The economic forces influencing the policies
and methods of retailing institutions, although
not as numerous perhaps as the social ones, are
nonetheless of equal importance. Let us examine some of them.

Personal Income and Its Distribution

Personal income, providing essential spending capacity for consumers and strongly affecting retail sales volume, has shown a sharp rise
in the United States especially since World
War II. Without detailing this growth, let it
suffice to concentrate on the present situation.
For the country as a whole, individual incomes in 1964 totaled $488 billion, an increase
of some $26 billion or 6 percent over 1963.[11]
In the four-year period, 1961–1964 inclusive,
the increase amounted to 22 percent. On a
per capita basis, personal incomes in 1964
amounted to $2548 or $100 more than in 1963
—an increase of 4 percent. And more importantly perhaps, from the point of view of the
retailer, *disposable* income continues to expand
substantially. In 1964 it was 7 percent greater
than in 1963. The effects of changes in Social
Security benefits and the proposed increases
in minimum wages cannot be fairly judged at
this time.

Like population growth, this expansion in

total personal income and in disposable income
has varied among different regions and states.
Available data reveal, for example, a clear
long-term trend of income to move from the
northern and eastern sections of our country
to the southern and western ones. This is true,
particularly, of disposable income. Since 1929,
for example, the four southern and western regions have increased their *share* of our country's disposable income by almost 50 percent
with the four northeastern and central regions
sustaining the loss.[12] More specifically, in New
England disposable income increased from $6.9
billion in 1929 to $25.7 billion in 1963. During
this same period the Far West area (California, Nevada, Oregon, and Washington) increased from $7.2 billion to $56.6 billion while
the disposable income for the country as a
whole grew from $83 billion to $398.2 billion.
As we have noted, this expansion continued in
1964 with a further substantial gain of 7 percent. Similar variations both in total personal
income and disposable income exist among the
states and even areas within states.

Turning briefly to per capita figures for disposable income, government data reveal an
increase for the country as a whole from $575
in 1940 to $2,122 in 1963. And, here again,
wide variations prevail among geographical regions and states. Among the former, per capita
income in 1963 ranged from $1,823 in the
southwest to $2,491 in the far west. Among
states, the range was from $1,266 in Missis-
sippi to $2,781 in Nevada. The highest in any
area in 1963 was in the District of Columbia,
amounting to $2,787.

The reasons for the geographical differences
in total personal income and disposable income
that we have mentioned are familiar to most
of us and need not be repeated here. But one
of these is of sufficient importance, perhaps, to
warrant restatement. Changes in population
have a strong influence on the growth of income; in fact, much of the redistribution of income on a geographic basis that has taken
place over the years is the result of net interstate migration.

The Redistribution of Income

No discussion of personal and disposable
income would be complete without emphasis

---

[10] McNair, *op. cit.*, p. 3.
[11] These figures, and others given in this paragraph,
are taken from E. A. Trott, Jr., "Personal Income
by States, 1964," *Survey of Current Business*, April,
1965, pp. 13, 15.

[12] "Disposable Personal Income by States in Current and Constant Prices," *Survey of Current Business*, April, 1965, p. 16.

on the redistribution of income that has taken place, particularly in the past two decades, and the consequences of this development. In 1960 families with annual incomes between $5,000 and $15,000 constituted 53.6 of the total,[13] and a further increase has taken place since that time.

This growth in middle-class income is important to retailers because it represents a gain in discretionary income that has been reflected in considerable "trading up" in both merchandise and services. One aspect of this change is the patronizing of stores which have an aura of social status.

Credit

Still another significant factor in the economic environment affecting retailing is credit. Since 1945 private debt has increased more than 500 percent and continues to increase 10 percent annually.[14] Our personal debt now exceeds $264 billion—70 percent accounted for by mortgages—or $4,700 for the average American family. This amount equals 60 percent of our annual income after taxes, and toady we are typically spending 14.3 percent of our income to pay off our debts.

Particularly pertinent to our discussion are the facts that revolving credit in department stores alone is about $2.5 billion, more than double that of 1961, and that credit cards account for $633 million. The use of these cards, however, is increasing 20 percent each year.[15] In the field of consumer installment credit alone—which reached $744 million in April of this year, an all time high—the fastest growing area is automobile credit, now at a $25.4 billion level. The credit-mindedness of consumers creates great opportunities and responsibilities for retailers.

TECHNOLOGICAL DEVELOPMENTS

Very recent years have witnessed a real revolution in technology and the concomitant development of management science. With all business operations, including retailing, become more complicated in our dynamic economy, these changes are welcomed by all progressive managements. Full employment of the newer tools and techniques is required to improve decision-making in a wide variety of situations. Electronic technology, for example, has created a number of information-handling tools that are altering the processes of business management. And, "the swift evolution of commercial electronic computers and data-processing systems" accompanied by devices for communicating data from system to system, have opened horizons to the retailer considered impossible only a few years ago.

Despite the adoption by many firms of these and other new tools and techniques, a growing gap exists between the capabilities of the equipment and systems and their use in American business. The obvious need, therefore, is for the adoption of programs designed to equate management functions and electronic systems capabilities. These programs, states one qualified student of this subject, should include two large areas: (1) ". . . the quest for new and improved devices and techniques to increase further the speed, capacity, reliability, and operating economy of computing and data processing systems;" and (2) ". . . a conceptual approach which seeks to develop new programs and new thinking that will take greater advantage of what the systems already offer as a direct aid to management." [16]

Developments related to business electronics are but one significant factor in the technological environment affecting retailing. Other forms of automation useful in the physical handling of merchandise in warehouses and distribution centers are available, and mechanization of various activities proceeds at an increasing rate. Some of the applications of these technological developments to retailing are discussed in a subsequent section although it is not possible to assess them full at this time.

The important and continuous changes in the various environments affecting retailing which we have discussed have provided, and will continue to provide, challenges and opportunities for progressive institutions, but they will involve obligations as well. History reveals that traditional retailers are reluctant to make changes; they respond slowly to the opportunities available. This slow response to new conditions may be due either to lethargy or

---

[13] U.S. Department of Commerce, Bureau of the Census, 1960 *Census of Populations*, Vol. I, *Characteristics of the Population*, Part 1, U.S. Summary, p. LXXX.

[14] *Time,* June 18, 1965, p. 82.

[15] *Ibid.*

---

[16] Elmer W. Engstrom, "New Concepts in Business Electronics," *Retail Control*, October, 1963, Part II, p. 45.

to the unwillingness of management to assume new obligations created by the changing time. Regardless of the reason, however, management's failure to act more quickly and courageously has opened wide the door for discount houses, house-to-house sellers, and others to meet the needs of a growing population with money to spend.

Let us now examine the responses of four types of retail institutions to changes in their social and economic environments: the traditional department store; the supermarket; the discount house; and the mail-order company. Note, please, that chain stores are not included, although their evolution constitutes, perhaps, the most significant development since our association was founded. The very breadth of this development and the implications involved, however, preclude even scanty reference to this type of institution since justice cannot be given to it in the time and space available. It deserves and will receive, later, a full measure of justice in treatment.

SOME MAJOR RESPONSES OF RETAILERS TO ENVIRONMENTAL CHANGES

A. The Traditional Department Store.

No retail institution in this country has reached the degree of maturity attained by the traditional department store. This institution was the original exponent of the "wide-variety-of-merchandise-under one-roof" concept and sought to provide maximum convenience to its customers. Moreover, for many years it enjoyed a monopoly on central downtown locations and, with other stores of the same type located close together, furnished a hub of activity unmatched elsewhere. Secure in its belief that customers had no shopping alternatives, it was content to prolong policies and methods that had proved successful in the past. As a result, its proportion of total retail sales declined in comparatively recent years until arrested by a departure from traditional practices by such measures as the establishment of branch stores and improvements in organization.

The rapid growth of the suburbs following World War II and the widespread dependence on the private automobile for transportation, together with the very substantial increase in the number and purchasing power of a strong "middle class" to which most department stores

catered, forced them ". . . to sally forth from [their] protective downtown walls and join the battle in the open plains. . . . The whole terms of the retail contest were changed . . . [yet relatively few] managements perceived this potential disadvantage and dragged their feet in the establishment of suburban branches." [17] Some of the oldest and best-known stores in all sections of the country have paid the ultimate price—failure—for this lack of foresight and judgment. Established in their "ivy towers," they probably considered themselves impregnable to the great social and economic changes swirling around them.

Those firms whose management did recognize the challenge of the changing social and economic forces, however, and established branches of various sizes and types to serve these new markets, made the necessary shifts in organization structure to accommodate multi-unit operation, and adopted other innovations, have been richly rewarded. Moreover, in doing so they helped to pioneer the development of the regional shopping center, one of the most important retailing developments of the past two decades.

Yet the measures adopted by the traditional department stores to meet the changing social and economic scene brought them face to face with problems not wholly anticipated. Moving from their long-established fortresses in downtown areas, they became vulnerable to the sharply increasing competition of other retailers quick to make innovations in policies and practices. The discount house, discussed in the following section, was one such innovator.

But other problems also required close attention. These included, among many others, the following: choice of a suitable location and whether to choose a site in a shopping center or elsewhere; deciding on the size of the suburban store and the breadth and depth of merchandise assortments; fixing responsibility for the buying and the control of stocks in the branches; selecting and training the managerial and other personnel; and adopting appropriate accounting methods and financial records.

Finding satisfactory solutions to these problems, and the many others of equal or greater importance, has proved, and is continuing to prove, a difficult task. At present, with executive obsolescence increasing because of mental

---

[17] McNair, *op. cit.*, p. 4.

and physical deterioration, advances in technology, and the increasing complexity of doing business, the need is great for young men with the requisite qualifications to provide stimulating and intelligent leadership. A major responsibility of top management today is planning for the future, both on a short- and long-term basis. And this planning involves the creation of a "climate" in which good performance is encouraged, recognized and rewarded—where management development takes place continuously on a day-to-day basis! The future of the department-store business depends on the quality of its management!

Before attempting to assess the probable future of the traditional department store, let us look backward briefly. Professor McNair reports the following "great strengths and . . . accomplishments" of this institution: "it has shown great stability; it has successfully made the transition to multi-unit operation required by the profound changes in the social and economic patterns of our cities and . . . created a significant innovation . . . the planned regional shopping center; it continues to command the strong allegiance of those shoppers for whom fashion, quality, reliability, and service are paramount considerations; it has pioneered in the development and great expansion of consumer credit; it has led the way in . . . important accounting developments— the Retail Inventory Method, LIFO, expense center accounting, production unit accounting, and so on; it has formed alliances with education at both the high school and university levels; it has furnished frequent civic leadership in our cities; and it has carried the brunt of the battle for all of retailing in matters of governmental regulation and taxation." [18]

Certainly, the future of this venerable institution appears bright if it continues to make appropriate and timely innovations required by the dynamic environment in which it operates. But, as noted, there must be greater management alertness, quicker adjustment to change, and the courage to depart unhesitatingly from past policies and methods when conditions dictate. Only through decisive action based on evaluation of all relevant facts can it be successful under the highly competitive conditions in the years ahead.

Some encouraging signs of management's awareness of its changing responsibilities and its willingness to do something about them are present. One is the creation of new images of fashion merchandising through the promotion of younger modes aimed at teenagers and the under-25-year olds. As we have noted, this group now comprises about 50 percent of our total population. As a part of this development management is giving increasing attention to merchandise imports, to more effective window displays, to improved store layouts, to better methods of soliciting charge accounts, and to more efficient coordination of all aspects of the sales promotional "mix."

A second evidence of management's alertness is the adoption of automated devices designed to improve operations and reduce costs. Despite an early seeming reluctance to explore the possibilities these technological developments afforded, the "profit squeeze" and the aggressive tactics of manufacturers of equipment, plus the increasing number and variety of new consumer products entering the market, forced acceleration in the automation of retailing operations. Today, data capturing and data processing equipment, used in connection with appropriate systems designed to provide essential information for prompt decision-making, are being used increasingly by many retailing organizations, particularly the larger ones. "Total electronic systems," involving extension of "the data-processing system from original entry at the sales register, through computer processing, to final reports with a minimum of intermediate data handling," [19] have been adopted by stores in all sections of the country.

Automation in department stores has not been restricted, however, to the handling of retail transactions. Systems have been developed for merchandise planning and control, pricing, checking credits, accounting for receivables and payables, improving turnover; and for payroll and accounting and sales audit and analysis. Let us take computers as an example. Since 1960 their use in department stores and departmentalized specialty stores has grown from about 4 to 78 in 1962 and to 120 at present. [20]

Comparable data for all retailing institutions are not immediately available. We do know, however, that the total computers in use or on order by retailers grew from some 10 in 1960

[18] *Ibid.*, p. 6.

[19] B. L. Trippet, "The Automation of Retail Transactions," *Retail Control*, January, 1965, p. 35.

[20] These figures were supplied by Touche, Ross, Bailey & Smart, an accounting firm.

to 483 in 1962. Since that time the growth has been phenomenal, especially among the larger firms, as electronic data processing is used for an increasing number of purposes and the costs of the necessary equipment are being reduced. As one retailer expressed it— "People are costing more, the machines are costing less, and we have to keep up with our competition." [21] Despite this attitude, which the growth of EDP reflects, a wider and more productive utilization of it in retailing activities can come only through greater knowledge that will narrow the gap between retail management and the electronics people regarding what the machines can achieve in solving day-to-day operating problems.

Shopping Centers

Mention has been made of the part played by the department store in the development of regional shopping centers. Real estate developers and architects also contributed importantly to this development. And, although these centers are composed of a complex of retail institutions, they deserve at least brief attention here because they do represent a response of some importance by retailing institutions, especially department stores, supermarkets, and variety chains, to their social and economic environments.

Probably the first institution to recognize the need for shopping areas of this type was Sears, Roebuck and Company in the late 1920's. Although the depression of the Thirties retarded their growth, their expansion has been phenomenal since World War II. Providing one-stop shopping in convenient locations outside the traffic congestion and parking difficulties of the central downtown shopping districts, furnishing free parking space for large numbers of automobiles, and enabling automobile traffic to move more freely, they have filled a genuine need as evidenced by their wide acceptance by customers of all social and income strata.

Moreover, responding to such influences as shorter work weeks, greater leisure, and "family" shopping, they have adjusted store hours to include more night and Sunday openings. Let us note quickly, however, that this re-sponse is by no means restricted to shopping centers or one type of store.

Proof of the fact that shopping centers met a real consumer need is evidenced by their rapid growth. In the United States and Canada combined, their number grew from 1,000 in 1955 to some 7,800 in 1964 with an additional 800 scheduled for completion in 1965.[22] In the United States alone their sales volume reached $65 billion at the end of 1964, comprising 33 percent of our total retail trade of $197.167 billion (excluding automobiles and building materials). The projected increase for 1965 is $8.4 billion, or an increase to 35 percent of our total retail business. When viewed in the light of the claims of "over-building" and "super-saturation" of these centers in many areas, this continued growth seems fantastic. Only the future can determine the accuracy of the estimates.

Two additional points of interest should be mentioned before we leave shopping centers. First, regional shopping centers appear to be increasing more rapidly than other types, and sales volume in these centers is increasing much more rapidly than retail sales as a whole. Second, some $9 billion in sales, or more than 40 percent of the volume of department stores, now come from such stores located in shopping centers.[23]

The Supermarket

The evolution of the supermarket as a response to social and economic change is an interesting phenomenon. It is the culmination of the changes that saw the independent grocery and the independent meat store (or their chain store equivalents) merge into the combination food store, and finally the supermarket. Contributing factors, of course, were the "distress merchandise" and the vacant, low-rent buildings available during the depression of the 1930's.

Today the vast supermarket field is basically one of chain store operation and mass merchandising, reflecting the tremendous increase in new products constantly being developed. The growth of "convenience" foods in wide variety is but one example. In addition, supermarkets are doing a growing proportion of

[21] Richard Rosenthal, "Sprawling Grade of EDP Captures Retailers' Eyes," *Women's Wear Daily,* June 28, 1965, p. 15.

[22] "Shopping Center Trends," *Chain Store Age* (Executive Edition), May, 1965, p. E 23.
[23] Andrew Murphy of Allied Stores, quoted in *ibid.,* p. E 18 h.

their business in nonfood lines, and their self-service feature has been widely accepted by consumers.

Although satisfactory statistics on the early period of supermarket growth are not available, we do have enough to reveal the general trend. As early as 1938 annual sales were $1 billion and by 1948 had grown to $7.8 billion. Regarding later years, *Super Market Merchandising* reports that the number of supermarkets increased from 24,151 in 1960 to 30,339 in 1964. In this same period sales grew from $34.6 billion to $43 billion.[24] Of these sales, about 7 percent consisted of general merchandise. *The Progressive Grocer*, which includes as supermarkets only those food stores with annual sales of $500,000 or more, reports that they numbered 28,400 in 1963 with total sales of $40.5 billion. If superettes are included— those stores with sales of $150,000 to $500,000 —27,100 stores and $7.8 billion in sales are added, or a total for both types of 55,500 stores with some $48 billion sales. This combined sales total amounted to 82 percent of food store sales in this country in 1963.[25]

It is noteworthy that supermarkets associated with discount stores are making steady progress in recent years, reflecting a growth in sales from $410 million in 1960 to $2.8 billion in 1964. During this period, their share of total supermarket volume increased from 1.2 percent to 6.5 percent. Indications are that this trend will continue since "discounting" has become an accepted and respectable method of retailing in our nation. Let us examine the "discounting" phenomenon in more detail.

The Discount House

It has been noted that it is a question of semantics as to whether the growth of the discount houses and some other retail institutions constitutes a response to the changing environments in which they operate or whether the entrepreneurial activities of retailers themselves have contributed to such changes. In any case, the discount house represents an important development in the retailing revolution of the past few decades and warrants some attention.

Discount retailers of various types, recognizing the opportunities afforded by sweeping changes in the social and economic environment and encouraged by the failure of department stores and others to take prompt and constructive action to meet the challenge, in a relatively few years have built a sales volume of more than $10 billion. All of the factors responsible for this rapid growth cannot be mentioned here, but the more important ones include self-service, strong price appeal, convenience in location, effective sales promotion, and the management foresight shown in adapting merchandising efforts to the changing needs of consumers. "Rising income and rising economic well-being, accompanied by a substantially heightened interest in bargain merchandise . . . combined to create a jackpot . . . which the discounters have hit."

Some indication of the "gold" in this jackpot is the widespread acceptance of this institution as reflected in its spectacular growth in numbers as well as in sales volume. Although completely reliable figures are not readily available, those that are will serve our particular purpose. During the period 1960 to 1964, "discount sales rose from $2 billion to almost $11 billion, an increase of over 440 percent and an average annual growth rate of more than 40 percent. This represents a gain in their share of the total retail market from 2.1 percent to 9.4 percent."[26] Among some 20 discount chains for which data are available, sales increased from $2.2 billion in 1963 to $2.8 billion in 1964, a gain of some 25.8 percent.[27] At the close of 1964, the number of discount houses in operation was 2,730, an increase of 221 units or 8 percent over 1963.[28] And, significantly, tardy recognition of the value of discounting is the entry into the field of such established organizations as F. W. Woolworth, A & P, J. C. Penney, Jewel Tea Company, Allied Stores Corp., S. H. Kress, and many others. Despite some recent setbacks, which are characteristic of all retailers, the list is likely to grow in the future.

Our discussion of supermarkets and discount houses should not be concluded without noting

[24]"The True Look of the Super Market Industry, 1964," *Super Market Merchandising*, April, 1965, p. 50. Other figures in this and the following paragraph are from the same source.

[25] *Progressive Grocer, Grocery Business Annual Report* 1964, p. F7. Later data are not available as this is written.

[26] Bernard Kessler, "Discount Surge Will Continue," *Discount Store News*, May 31, 1965, p. 9.

[27] *Discount Store News*, July 12, 1965, p. 2.

[28] "New Phase for Discount Chains," *Financial World*, March 17, 1965, p. 6.

one of the strange anomalies of our era, that is, the growing practice of consumers to seek bargains and values in their purchases and thus increase the spread of their disposable income over goods and services, at a time when spending power is the highest and most widely distributed in our history. In other words, the strong desire of consumers to improve their standard of living is exceeding their growth in income, a socio-economic phenomenon of considerable significance. Small wonder that discount houses and supermarkets are thriving under present conditions.

Retail Mail-Order Companies

These organizations were among the first to recognize the significance of the changes taking place in the environments affecting retailing and in adopting measures to benefit from these changes. Moves into chain-store operations by Sears and Ward's in the late 1920's, with stores classified into "A," "B," and "C" categories according to the variety and type of merchandise handled, evidenced their awareness of the need for new policies and methods. Ward's opened a "display store" in Maryville, Kansas in 1926 and in 1927 followed with its first "sale-on-the-spot" store. Sears opened its first over-the-counter store in its Chicago mail-order plan in February, 1925. On January 31, 1965, this company had 777 stores in operation; and on February 3, 1965, Ward's had 502. Other, and smaller, companies have also established stores.

But the responses of the mail-order companies to environmental changes were by no means restricted to establishing new stores! Over the years they have also revolutionized selling through their catalogues. These alert merchandisers have "traded up" the quality and variety of goods offered for sale, demonstrated an appreciation of the growth of culture in our economy, increased and improved their sales promotional efforts, placed greater stress on their own brands of merchandise, continued to stress "value" along with price, and, above all, maintained a policy of complete satisfaction or money refunded. But they did not stop here. Catalogue stores or sales offices have been established in increasing numbers (Sears and Ward's operated 1,944 such stores at the close of fiscal 1964), solicitation of catalogue customers by telephone has been intensified, and the sale of services such as insurance and mutual funds have been added. It is impossible to foresee the wide diversity of merchandise and services that the mail-order companies of the future will offer. If, however, we can judge their future by their past prompt responses to changes in our dynamic economy, one may predict with some confidence that they will react in a similar fashion in the future.

As we conclude our discussion, let us be reminded of the continuing, recurring pattern of competitive changes evident among retailing institutions, often referred to as the "revolving wheel of retailing." Professor McNair, probably the first to suggest this hypothesis, explains it this way:

A daring and imaginative enterpriser, typically outside the ranks of existing retailing top management, conceives the idea for an innovation in retailing, commonly an innovation that will reduce costs and permit lower prices; he starts operations on a shoe string, scorned by the conventional sources of capital, utilizing make-shift premises, dispensing with accustomed services, avoiding high overhead, handling goods of lower than top quality, concentrating on fast movers, taking narrow margins, hammering away at price appeal, and realizing fractional profits on sales (though often a respectable return on equity capital). His competition is with the established channels of distribution, by whom he is initially ignored. If successful (and not all such ventures do succeed), he soon has imitators, and he and his life are no longer ignored. Then his competition gradually becomes increasingly with others of his kind, and a trading up process begins—better quality, more variety, improved plant and fixtures, greater extension of services, a little slower stockturn, a somewhat higher margin to cover higher expenses, and an increase in capital in relation to sales. Now, however, he is no longer spurned by the bankers, he can obtain wanted lines of merchandise with less difficulty, and is no longer necessarily excluded from good locations. In the meantime traditional channels have had to modify their methods of doing business to some degree, and perhaps to borrow some leaves from the innovator's book. [This pattern continues to repeat itself.] For, as the innovator gradually becomes the accepted 'legitimate' or 'normal' channel of distribution, he often takes on characteristics of maturity—complacence, defensiveness, and lethargy, accompanied by higher expenses, higher margins, and a lower rate of return on capital; and then he becomes vulnerable to the next successful innovator.[29]

---

[29] *Op. cit.*, pp. 1–2.

Although the McNair hypothesis probably needs more refinement and testing over a period of time, evidence of the recurring pattern of competitive change in retailing is plentiful. And, with the rapidly shifting socio-economic forces in the environment within which retailers must operate, further changes in policies, methods, and even in competitive patterns, may be expected.

DISCUSSION QUESTIONS

The suggestion that retail institutions live and die according to their ability to adjust to environmental change is a "survival of the fittest" explanation of institutional change.

1. What are the most important elements in this retailing environment? Are some of these elements you identify more important than others? Are some of these elements likely to change more quickly than others?
2. If "environmental shifts" or changes can kill a retail market, how might a retailing organization develop a system of continuous feedback which would provide early warning of detrimental environmental shifts?
3. What environmental changes are in process today which may seriously alter the nature of retailing institutions in the future?
4. The ability to adjust quickly to environmental change is a desirable attribute in retailing. What organizational attributes hinder a rapid adjustment to environmental circumstances?

2. Schumpeter, the "Big" Disturbance and Retailing*

PERRY BLISS

Some retail organizations operate in such a manner that their influence on retailing in general goes far beyond what could be conveyed by a simple listing of their number, or their sales volume, or their total employment—the three measures typically used to indicate size and influence in the retail field. The institutions we have reference to have the characteristics of innovators in whose wake come imitators and whose presence so colors the competitive picture that they require special analysis. Such organizations create what Schumpeter called a "big" disturbance because they ". . . disrupt the existing system and enforce a distinct process of adaptation." [1]

For Schumpeter the usual method of competition in which *familiar* types of organization compete for the patronage of a given market by *familiar* methods is not the competition that counts. Rather, if there is to be "competition that matters," new institutions must enter the market place with new ways of organizing things, new sales-cost relationships, new methods of selling. Concerning competition in the retail trades, Schumpeter said:

In the case of retail trade the competition that matters arises not from additional shops of the same type, but from the department stores, the chain store, the mail order house and the supermarket. . . .[2]

In the early part of the present century, the period which Schumpeter very likely had in mind, the department stores such as Macy's and Wanamaker's, the mail order houses such as Sears' and Ward's, the supermarkets of King Kullen and Big Bear, and chain store organizations such as F. W. Woolworth and the A & P, furnished the "competition that matters;" they indeed caused a "big" disturbance and compelled a "process of adaptation." It is the point of this paper that today we also have in the retail market place institutions that offer competition that matters and that are a source of a big disturbance.

The present day supermarkets by their disruptive effect on the service structure of *non-food* retailers, the discount houses by their impact on the retail price structure (especially consumer durables), and the planned regional shopping centers by their destructive effect on the location values of older retailers are innovating institutions in the Schumpeterian sense given above; they enter the market place with new types of organization, new cost-price relationships, and they compel imitation and/or adaptation on the part of the older forms of retail institutions.

SUPERMARKETS AND THE SERVICE STRUCTURE

The revolutionary effect supermarkets have had the last decade or two on the *food* industry has been nothing short of phenomenal. And their force is still being felt. Today they do something over 60 percent of all food business,

---

◆ SOURCE: Reprinted by permission from the editors of *Social Forces*, in the October, 1960, issue, pp. 72–76.

* The author wishes to thank his colleague, Professor Forest Hill, for helpful comments.

[1] Joseph Schumpeter, *Business Cycles* (1st ed.; New York: McGraw-Hill Book Company, 1939), I, p. 101 (italics Schumpeter's).

[2] Joseph Schumpeter, *Capitalism, Socialism and Democracy* (2nd ed.; New York: Harper and Brothers, 1947), p. 85. This paper is concerned chiefly with Schumpeter's notion of a "big" disturbance and the imitation and adaptation which follow. Schumpeter was also greatly concerned with a larger system of analysis in which much weight

was given the fact that innovating institutions were started by new men in the field, with new money and new organizations. Although it is beyond this paper, the retail institutions we will be discussing were initiated by new men, in new firms with new capital. Especially is this true in the case of discount houses and shopping centers; it is less the case in supermarkets.

and the overwhelming number of new food outlets being established are of the supermarket type. While supermarkets are apparently still increasing their share of the food dollar, the food industry has more or less learned to live with them; and so the supermarket revolution in the food field, as important as it was for Schumpeter, is not our present concern. Rather our interest here is centered on what the supermarket industry is doing to *non-food* stores such as department stores, variety and drug stores, retail lumber yards, clothing stores and hardware stores, to name a few.

While the method of operation of supermarkets has a tendency to bring a downward pressure on the price and margin structure of any non-food merchandise it handles, and we will comment on this again, it is the supermarkets' part in forcing a reduction in the *service mix* of stores which traditionally were *full service* outlets that is being emphasized here. The apparent willingness or even eagerness of consumers to purchase a long list of non-food items (toys, beauty aids and drugs, small hardware items, women's hosiery, women's and children's soft goods, paper products, books, magazines, housewares, and so on) without the aid of salespeople and without the services and amenities of the traditional outlets has caused the older stores selling these categories of goods to adopt all, or part, of the supermarket technique of self-service, open display, check out stations, and cash and carry policies.

Just how far supermarkets will go in stocking non-food lines is difficult to say. Supermarket operators differ among themselves. Lansing P. Shield, president of the Grand Union Company, had this to say when asked about the trend toward operating a wider variety in supermarkets:

. . . I'd say it probably will increase. Food stores now rival drug stores in the sale of many non-prescription medicines. For example, 37.9 percent of total aspirin sales are made through supermarkets. Also more than 31 percent of shaving products move through supermarkets.

This year, Grand Union will open nine so-called "super general stores," with up to 90,-000 square feet of selling space and as many as 25,000 non-food items. These stores will offer refrigerators, TV sets and wearing apparel for the entire family. In the near future, a considerable number of centrally located supermarkets will really be complete shopping centers in themselves.[3]

All supermarket operators, however, are not this enthusiastic. Safeway Stores and A & P, among others, have not adopted non-food items to such an extent.[4] And undoubtedly there are limits to the addition of non-food items to food store inventories. Presently it is felt that, in order to qualify readily for supermarket acceptance, goods must have such characteristics as high turnover, low price per unit, routine reordering procedures, adequate margins, quick identification, and high sales per square foot.[5] Over time these requirements may change.[6]

The pressure of food store competition is not the sole reason for less service in retailing. There are other pressures of a general economic nature, such as increasing costs of labor and the difficulty of attracting sales help from the apparently more attractive factory, clerical, governmental and other jobs, which also force the retailer to the economies of self-service where feasible. Nonetheless, supermarkets have thus far been sufficiently successful in selling a wide enough variety of non-food lines to bring about a significant change in the service mix of a broad area of non-food retailing and have forced competition *to imitate the supermarket type of selling by omitting many of the services which had previously been the operating strength of these outlets.* The important thing about this is that the removal of services, and hence the removal of the costs incident to these services, should have the effect of bringing about, over time, a downward trend in the price structure of the goods handled. The extent and depth of the price

---

[3] *U. S. News & World Report* (June 20, 1958), p. 56.

[4] The Chairman of the Board of Safeway Stores, Inc., looks at the matter this way: "The trend to huge markets of 50,000 or 100,000 square feet has slowed down. Our present and future plans for Safeway Stores, with only a few exceptions, are under 23,000 square feet with most of our new stores arund 14,000 square feet. The huge markets tend to get into completely new fields and nearly complete lines of merchandise: soft goods, furniture, etc. That's not for us. It's a question if you are in the food business or running a department store."

[5] Milton Alexander, "Where We Stand in Non-Food Merchandising," *Progressive Grocer* (Oct. 1952), pp. 197 ff.

[6] The large volume of sales of non-food items through food stores has caused a revision in the estimates of expenditures for food. See Marguerite C. Burk, "Revised Estimates of Food Expenditures," *Journal of Marketing* (July 1949), pp. 31–35.

reductions in the future will depend on the degree of competition present. Inasmuch as supermarkets traditionally are highly promotional, low margin institutions, pressures to reduce margins in non-food outlets will be present to a much greater degree than had the supermarkets not decided to enter the non-food area.

DISCOUNT HOUSES AND THE PRICE STRUCTURE

The growth and popularity of those retail firms which operate their stores in such a manner that expense margins are at about 14–20 percent level on consumers' durables (and some soft lines) which traditionally called for 30–40 percent margins, and cut prices accordingly, have been among the really revolutionary forces in modern retailing.

It is not easy to define a discount house even though most people are familiar with both the term and the institution. Many retailers "sell at a discount," yet are not thought of as a discount house. Perhaps it is best to think of them in terms of the way they operate their business. They are characterized by

. . . a large selection of merchandise, emphasis on fast-turning national brands, price as the main sales appeal, inexpensive buildings, a minimum of stock, limited customer services, low rent locations, extensive advertising, inexpensive and limited fixtures, for less use of merchandising and accounting controls than exist in the typical chain, or department store, and frequently a willingness to bargain on price.[7]

There are several reasons why these low-margin, low-price discounters now loom so large. For one thing the capacity of manufacturers of consumer durable goods has increased greatly since World War II and these manufacturers are apparently capable of producing larger quantities of merchandise than traditional channels can dispose of at current prices. This pressure of capacity has made many suppliers, especially of highly promoted national brands, eager to utilize these new price cutting outlets which can move their products in large

quantities, even though the result is antagonism of the older retailers.

This need of suppliers for high volume outlets is not, however, sufficient cause alone to account for the tremendous success of the discount houses. There are also other reasons such as ". . . manufacturer preselling of brand merchandise, the umbrella hoisted by fair-trading retailers, the heightened interest of consumers in stretching their dollars, and the possibilities of cutting many cost corners in the handling of big-ticket hard goods."[8]

The success of the discount type of retailing has been rather dramatic. Polk Bros. of Chicago had sales in 1955 in the neighborhood of $40,000,000, carried an inventory of some $2,500,000, allocated $1,500,000 for advertising, and utilized over 450 salesmen.[9] Korvette, Inc., of New York, in 1956 claimed sales of over $70,000,000 with an inventory mix composed of 60 percent hard goods and 40 percent soft.[10]

While these are admittedly giants of the field, the impact of the total array of discount houses in the retail system has been strong enough to bring readjustments from many types of competitors. The greatest readjustment is occurring in those outlets selling consumer durables such as appliance stores, hardware stores, sporting goods outlets, furniture stores, and in the sections of department and variety stores selling appliances and "big ticket" items. Soft lines are currently being affected as the discount houses add apparel items to their inventories.

The adaptation of the older retailers has taken several forms. Some stores, such as Marshall Field and Carson Pirie Scott, have inaugurated "warehouse sales."[11] In such instances goods are retailed from the organization's warehouse at cut prices and with very

---

[7] Delbert J. Duncan and Charles F. Phillips, *Retailing: Principles and Methods* (Homewood, Illinois: Richard D. Irwin, 1959), pp. 446–447. A full discussion of both discount houses and discount selling is given in S. C. Hollander, "The One-Price System —Fact or Fiction," *Journal of Retailing* (Fall 1955), pp. 127–144.

[8] Malcolm P. McNair, "Significant Trends and Developments in the Postwar Period," *Competitive Distribution in a Free High-Level Economy and Its Implications for the University*, ed. by Albert B. Smith (Pittsburgh, Pa.: University of Pittsburgh Press, 1958), p. 13.
[9] Daniel Seligman, "Chicago's Red Hot Merchandiser," *Fortune* (September 1955), p. 130 ff.
[10] For an interesting account of Korvette's history see "The Spectacular Rise of E. J. Korvette," *Fortune* (November 1956), p. 122 ff.
[11] Charles Silberman, "Retailing: It's a New Ball Game," Fortune (August 1955) p. 80. This article contains many instances of the devices used to combat discounters.

limited services offered. (Even Sears has adopted these warehouse special events.) Other stores, especially department stores, have dropped those appliance, radio and TV lines that are subject to discount house promotion; still others have continued the lines but lowered their prices appreciably and continued to handle the merchandise with their traditional services and/or charged extra for credit, guarantees, etc.

What is significant for those who wish to analyze retailing is that discount houses compelled a reëxamination not only of the pricing policies and practices of manufacturers and distribution but *compelled a very broad range of retailers to lower their margins and adjust prices downward to adapt to this new type of competition.*[12]

SHOPPING CENTERS AND THE LOCATION STRUCTURE

The third retail institution which has been selected as one of the innovating forces in retailing today is the shopping center—specifically, the *controlled centers.* Not a retail establishment, but rather a clustering of establishments, the controlled center of today is one that is in important ways (store selection, architectural design, etc.) planned, operated, and promoted as *a unit.* And the public tends to look upon these centers as units, as single places to shop. For example, Northland Center in Detroit or the Cross Country Center in Yonkers, to name just two, have a much greater market impact than a mere cluster of similar stores would have. The centers themselves are as well known as the big stores that happen to dominate these centers.

The presence in the centers of such giants of retailing as Penny's, Woolworth, A & P, Macy's, Marshall Field, Sears, Bullocks, etc., results in a "pull" of such a volume of consumer traffic that many smaller local independent hardware, drug, men's and women's wear stores, bakery shops, sporting goods and auto appliance outlets are drawn to the centers or to locations on their fringes.[13] Those that remain in the older neighborhood shopping areas have been forced to band together into "main street" associations to act *as a unit* to offset the draw of these new centers. And the downtown merchants are "fighting back" in a similar way—by promoting "downtown days" and by replanning the city center to imitate the "mall" idea of many of the new controlled shopping centers.[14]

This does not mean that the older neighborhood clusters of stores, the string street outlets or the center-of-town locations are obsolete. Far from it. Just as the supermarkets do not by any means take all non-food business, nor the discount houses force price reductions on all other retailers, so the shopping centers, controlled and otherwise, do not make all other locations second class.[15] Nonetheless, shopping centers are a strong enough innovating force to bring about basic changes in older location values; they have compelled large numbers of retailers *to "join them" or adopt the planning and coordinating techniques of these new controlled centers.*

The institutions discussed here—the modern supermarket selling non-foods, the discount house and the controlled centers—illustrate what the author believes is the essence of Schumpeter's innovating institutions: institutions that force imitation and adaptation. The competitive situation is never the same after such institutions enter the market place; they are institutions which seem to differ not only in degree, but in kind.

---

[12] It's interesting to see the spread of the discount idea. "Paris Says Oui Oui to Discount Houses," *Business Week* (February 2, 1957), pp. 47–48. Also, discount houses are "upgrading" themselves. See Claire M. Gross, "Services Offered by Discount Houses in Metropolitan New York," *Journal of Retailing* (Spring 1956), p. 1 ff. Malcolm McNair has an interesting thesis that in retailing market forces compel innovating institutions to upgrade themselves. McNair, *op. cit.*

[13] The impact on location choice of shopping centers is well illustrated by these figures: "Most new stores being opened today are in shopping centers. They account for 50 percent of the new grocery stores, 77 percent of the drug stores and 85 percent of shoe stores." *U. S. News and World Report* (June 20, 1959), p. 56.

[14] See Catherine Bauer, "First Job: Control New-City Sprawl," *Architectural Forum* (September 1956), pp. 105–112; Victor Gruen, "How to Handle This Chaos of Congestion, this Anarchy of Scatteration." *Ibid.*

[15] Apparently, for the big retailers there is not as much freedom as for smaller retailers. Earl Puckett, head of Allied Stores, states that if you attempt to "go it alone" others will follow and cluster around you. Hence, the choice is to go into a planned center or become the center of an unplanned one. See Earl Puckett, "Planned Growth for Retailers," *Stores* (January 1956), p. 9 ff.

DISCUSSION QUESTIONS

This article suggests that retail institutional innovation which has an immediate and profound influence on one type of retailing may have important secondary or tertiary effects on some other parts of the retailing system. These innovations normally involve the elimination of some economic "bottleneck" which up to the time of the innovation stood in the path of further economies.

1. What are some economic "bottlenecks" in retailing today? That is, what are some activities or processes whcih are seemingly *unavoidable* and *costly* which, if eliminated or modified significantly, could substantially reduce the cost of retailing? How about check-out procedures?
2. Are there remote techniques or methods which may one day find application in retailing but which, at present, are excessive in cost? How about television receivers with "shopping" channels on which local retailers continuously show new merchandise?

3. The Retailing Cycle

EDWARD A. BRAND

Retailing in North America began with the general store. A community was fortunate to have one retail outlet for groceries and general merchandise. One of the best known names of this era, The Hudson Bay Company, began as a trading post—taking furs and other items, as well as money, for merchandise. These early stores were all the one-stop shopping centers at which the people gathered to talk, exchange gossip, and, before departing, shop for anything needed that was available. They were not called shopping centers—this is a new term—but general stores. Variety, especially style merchandise, was limited.

The general store owner stocked any items he believed his customers would buy. Merchandise stayed on the shelf until it was sold. There was no turnover problem, likewise no special sales or promotion—people just shopped at the general store.

The limitations of the general store created a vacuum; people wanted more style and variety. This vacuum was filled by the mail-order house. To people in small rural communities, the mail-order catalog opened new vistas of shopping.

The mail-order business flourished, and a few giants developed. A few names from the early mail-order days that are still giants in retailing are Sears, Montgomery Ward, and Aldens.

Buying by mail is not a substitute for personal shopping. Therefore, as retail stores opened, offering the people an opportunity to shop, the mail-order business declined. The aggressive mail-order houses joined the advance of progress and opened retail stores; the others dropped out of the picture.

The move to specialty stores spread rapidly; and as towns and cities grew, more stores opened. During this period the butcher operated a butcher shop, the baker a bakery, the grocer a grocery store and the druggist a drug store. The dry goods store, the forerunner of the department store, came into being. The department store trade association was called the National Retail Dry Goods Association until a few years ago. (The name was changed to the National Retail Merchants Association.)

The early specialty store operator was a specialist. For example, the butcher did his own slaughtering, sold fresh meat, made sausage, and cured and smoked meats. The grocer stocked a limited number of staple items and bought his merchandise for the year during the processing season. He was both wholesaler and retailer. The produce stand flourished when local items were in season even though many people had gardens. He stored hard produce items and brought in a few items, such as bananas and citrus fruit, whenever these items were available. Thus, the era of specialization evolved.

The small, specialized retailer soon learned that the limited lines stocked also limited expansion and profit potential. The service features, such as telephone order and delivery service, made combining of similar lines, such as groceries, produce and meats, into one store economically desirable. This was accomplished by forming partnerships, or the grocer or butcher simply began stocking other food lines. The grocery store became a complete food store. This is not to imply that the specialty store was eliminated; some of them continue to operate. Some aggressive operators developed complete stores while a few developed chains of butcher shops, bakery shops, etc. Also during this period, the dry goods store evolved into the department store.

Some retailers had no closely allied specialty stores with which to merge. The druggist is the classic example of this type of specialty retailer. The early druggist needed additional lines in order to expand. Since there were no related stores with which to merge, he selected items with high volume potential and added

* SOURCE: Reprinted by permission from the Book Division of Fairchild Publications, a chapter from *Modern Supermarket Operation,* 1963, pp. 242–244.

these items to his stock. As lines added were successful, other lines were added. Thus, the drug store, as we know it today, emerged. "Creaming" the merchandise of specialty retailers, which the druggists started, became a retailing practice. "Creaming" refers to selecting the traffic or volume items that most people buy frequently and stocking them, leaving the handling of the complete line to the specialty store. For example, the variety store stocks the leading tooth paste items, perhaps six, while the drug store stocks 20 to 30 items. The variety store is "creaming" the tooth paste line. "Creaming" permits the store to stock added lines without changing the basic risk pattern. The "creaming" of merchandise lines gains sales and profits without changing the basic pattern of operation. The specialty store stocking the full line loses sales of volume items while sales of the remainder of the line remains constant. The risk pattern changes— sales are lost, and costs remain unchanged. This, in turn, forces the specialty store to look for items to "cream" from some other retailers. Thus, the cycle of expansion is accelerated by the pressure for more sales and profits.

Expansion of merchandise lines was followed by expansion of stores, and the chain store system evolved. The local retailers resisted the expansion of chain competition. This opposition took many forms, but the enactment of special per-store taxes in an attempt to make chain stores unprofitable received the greatest effort. "Support local merchants" and "Keep the money in the community" promotions did not deter shoppers. The more efficient retailers survived, and the opposition subsided. Many chain store taxes have been repealed, and the chains are considered residents.

The first change in retail operation was the development of the self-service supermarket. Beginning during a depression period in available buildings such as garages and warehouses with crude fixtures and opened cases of merchandise stacked on the floor, the supermarket grew into today's luxury store. The concepts of reduced costs, high turnover rates, variable margins based on "cents" margin instead of "per cent" margins were supermarket innovations. The early supermarket was a good store. However, costs increased, stores become more luxurious, competition increased, and profits decreased. This situation again activated the expansion cycle, and supermarket operators began to "cream" health and beauty aid items from the drug store, household items and housewares from hardware and variety stores,

etc. Thus, sales and profits were increased without changing the basic risk pattern.

The high cost of service retailers compared to the lower cost supermarket type of retailing created another vacuum in retailing, which was filled by the discount house. The early discount house sold well-known manufacturer brands at reduced prices, thereby "creaming" the specialty and department store merchandise lines. At first, durable goods constituted the main merchandise lines. Later, discount houses expanded into soft goods. Thus, the discount house became the low-cost operator in durable goods and, to some extent, soft goods.

Aggressive retailers looking for expansion opportunities moved their stores to the suburban areas. During the early years of the expansion to suburbia, the supermarket was the first store to open. As the population of suburbia increased and the problems of getting downtown multiplied, other retailers became interested in expanding; the shopping center concept became a reality. During the last ten years, nearly every major trading area has experienced the development of at least one shopping center.

The shopping center concept flourished on the basis of convenience which meant easy-to-reach and complete shopping facilities. In theory, shopping centers were planned to provide convenient and complete shopping. Actually most centers were more accidental—just grew—then planned. Nevertheless, they were easier to reach than downtown, they provided free parking close to the stores and the stores were close together and offered convenient shopping facilities. Therefore, most centers were successful.

During this period the supermarket offered more non-foods. Two factors made this expansion attractive: the first store in suburbia found a need for an outlet for non-food volume items, and the cost-profit squeeze forced stocking high-margin non-food items. Thus, the expansion by supermarkets into non-foods was encouraged by shoppers and needed by opeartors.

Competition between shopping centers forced planners to devise ways of providing greater convenience in order to compete advantageously with older centers that just grew. The enclosed, air-conditioned mall permits shoppers to shop the various stores without going "outside." Shoppers are able to shop the entire center as easily as the various departments of a large store. The enclosed mall shopping center became a very sophisticated general store.

Since expansion occurs as a result of aggressive merchants seeking areas into which to expand and operators tend to expand in the direction of higher spendable income levels, a vacuum was created in the low income shopping facility area. The low income (under $5,000 per year) shopper was restricted to the variety store and the bargain basements in the local department stores. This vacuum was filled by the low income department store, commonly referred to as the discount department store. These operators followed the pattern established by the low cost operators—the supermarket and the discount house.

The discount department store originated in vacant factory and warehouse buildings, much the same as the first supermarkets, and progressed to new buildings designed to house their vast assortments of merchandise. To draw traffic, a few discount department store operators started using food as leader items. This put them into the supermarket business. Having learned from both supermarket and discount operators, they reduced costs by streamlining inventories and reducing expenses. Thus, they have become serious competitiors of the supermarket.

The first low-price department stores have been highly successful. The combining of the department store and the supermarket was even more successful. The obvious occurred—the discount department store operators are optimistically predicting that the store of the future is a 200,000 square foot monster that is a complete shopping center with a 5 to 1 parking ratio and stocking over 200,000 items. A complete supermarket is included to build weekly store traffic.

The first discount shopping centers have been successful with the result that supermarket operators are getting into the discount department store and discount shopping center business.

The cycle is now complete; the discount shopping center is the present-day version of the old general store. It is more sophisticated, much larger, has greater merchandise variety, etc., with nearly everything the customer wants to buy under one roof. Low-cost operation results from cheaper building costs. Walls are eliminated since it is one large store. Lower overhead is made possible by one giant checkout area with tremendous flexibility of operation.

Strenuous competition is forcing supermarket operators to investigate the potential in the discount department store area. Currently, many supermarket operators are buying or building large stores and becoming discounters. However, obvious limitations of the discount, or low-price, department store should be noted. The number of shoppers, and the total expenditure for the merchandise offered, limits the volume potential. Also, the current consumer image of these low-price stores is poor, and few shoppers acknowledge that they shop in them. Maintaining the favorable image of the supermarket may become a major problem. The large trading area required to support a 100,000 or 200,000 square foot store increased the vulnerability to traffic cut off by competitors. Thus, the optimism of successful operators in areas of limited competition should be evaluated before a decision regarding expansion into this area is made.

The discount shopping center completes the cycle from a single unit general store to a single unit sophisticated general store called a discount shopping center.

The specialty store, department store, supermarkets, and small stores will not be replaced. The competition from the giant stores operating at low cost in relation to sales will force changes and economies in operation.

Retailing has completed a full cycle. Expansion will continue to be an important factor in the shaping of the retailing structure. Estimates and guesses of future developments should be based on an understanding of the past as a basis for forecasting.

DISCUSSION QUESTIONS

If the cycle which Professor Brand identifies is truly a cycle; i.e., repeats itself many times over, we can expect a shift back to the "specialty" dominated retail system within the present century.

    1. Do you perceive any such shift back to "specialty" retailing today? What form(s) is it taking?

A satisfactory explanation of some phenomenon does more than simply describe that phenomenon: a thorough "explanation" indicates why the phenomenon under scrutiny occurs.

    2. Does this article establish a reason or reasons why the "retailing cycle" occurs? Why, in your opinion, has the general-specific-general portion of the cycle occurred?

4. The Wheel of Retailing

STANLEY C. HOLLANDER*

New types of retailing frequently start off with crude facilities, little prestige, and a reputation for cutting prices and margins. As they mature, they often acquire more expensive buildings, provide more elaborate services, impose higher margins, and become vulnerable to new competition.

The author examines the history of numerous retailer institutions to determine if this process really constitutes a "natural law of retailing."

"The wheel of retailing" is the name Professor Malcolm P. McNair has suggested for a major hypothesis concerning patterns of retail development. This hypothesis holds that new types of retailers usually enter the market as low-status, low-margin, low-price operators. Gradually they acquire more elaborate establishments and facilities, with both increased investments and higher operating costs. Finally they mature as high-cost, high-price merchants, vulnerable to newer types who, in turn, go through the same pattern. Department-store merchants, who originally appeared as vigorous competitors to the smaller retailers and who have now become vulnerable to discount house and supermarket competition, are often cited as prime examples of the wheel pattern.[1]

Many examples of conformity to this pattern can be found. Nevertheless, we may ask: (1) Is this hypothesis valid for all retailing under all conditions? (2) How accurately does it describe total American retail development? (3) What factors cause wheel-pattern changes in retail institutions?

The following discussion assembles some of the slender empirical evidence available that might shed some light on these three questions. In attempting to answer the third question, a number of hypotheses should be considered that marketing students have advanced concerning the forces that have shaped retail development.

TENTATIVE EXPLANATIONS OF THE WHEEL

Retail Personalities

New types of retail institutions are often established by highly aggressive, cost-conscious entrepreneurs who make every penny count and who have no interest in unprofitable frills. But, as P. D. Converse has suggested, these men may relax their vigilance and control over costs as they acquire age and wealth. Their

* SOURCE: Reprinted by permission from the American Marketing Association, in the *Journal of Marketing*, July 1960, pp. 37–42.

* Stanley C. Hollander (Ph.D., University of Pennsylvania) is Professor of Business Administration at Michigan State University. He is editor of a recent book of readings in retailing theory, "Explorations in Retailing" (Bureau of Business Research, Michigan State University, 1959), and was a panelist on retail pricing before the Joint Economic Committee, U.S. Congress, in 1958.

His previous work in marketing history has included several studies of discount retailing, one of which M.S.U. recently published as "The Rise and Fall of a Buying Club." He compiled the American Marketing Association's "Bibliography on Discount Selling" (1956) and has published articles and monographs on other aspects of retailing and marketing.

The author is indebted to the participants in the 1959 Marketing Theory Seminar at Boulder, Colorado, for many penetrating comments on an earlier draft of this paper.

[1] M. P. McNair, "Significant Trends and Developments in the Postwar Period," in A. B. Smith (editor), *Competitive Distribution in a Free, High-Level Economy and Its Implications for the University* (Pittsburgh: University of Pittsburgh Press, 1958), pp. 1–25 at pp. 17–18.

successors may be less competent. Either the innovators or their successors may be unwilling, or unable, to adjust to changing conditions. Consequently, according to this view, deterioration in management causes movement along the wheel.[2]

Misguidance

Hermann Levy has advanced the ingenious, if implausible, explanation that retail trade journals, seduced by profitable advertising from the store equipment and supply industry, coax merchants into superfluous "modernization" and into the installation of overly elaborate facilities.[3]

Imperfect Competition

Although retail trade is often cited as the one type of business that approaches the Adam Smith concept of perfect competition, some economists have argued that retailing actually is a good example of imperfect competition. These economists believe that most retailers avoid direct price competition because of several forces, including resale price maintenance, trade association rules in some countries, and, most important, the fear of immediate retaliation. Contrariwise, the same retailers feel that service improvements, including improvements in location, are not susceptible to direct retaliation by competitors. Hence, through a ratchet process, merchants in any established branch of trade tend to provide increasingly elaborate services at increasingly higher margins.[4]

Excess Capacity

McNair attributes much of the wheel effect to the development of excess capacity, as more and more dealers enter any branch of retail trade.[5] This hypothesis rests upon an imperfect competition assumption, since, under perfect competition excess capacity would simply reduce margins until the excess vendors were eliminated.

Secular Trend

J. B. Jefferys has pointed out that a general, but uneven, long-run increase in the British standard of living provided established merchants with profitable opportunities for trading up. Jefferys thus credits adjustments to changing and wealthier market segments as causing some movement along the wheel. At the same time, pockets of opportunity have remained for new, low-margin operations because of the uneven distribution of living-standard increases.[6]

Illusion

Professor B. Holdren has suggested in a recent letter that present tendencies toward scrambled merchandising may create totally illusory impressions of the wheel phenomenon. Store-wide average margins may increase as new, high-markup lines are added to the product mix, even though the margins charged on the original components of that mix remain unchanged.

DIFFICULTIES OF ANALYSIS

An examination of the actual development of retail institutions here and abroad does shed some light on both the wheel hypothesis and its various explanations. However, a number of significant difficulties hinder the process.

(1) Statements concerning changes in retail margins and expenses are the central core of the wheel hypothesis. Yet valid information on historical retail expense rates is very scarce. Long-run changes in percentage margins probably do furnish fairly reliable clues to expense changes, but this is not true over short or intermediate periods. For example, 1957 furniture-store expense rates were about 5 percentage points higher than their 1949–1951 average, yet gross margins actually declined slightly over the same period.[7]

(2) Historical margin data are somewhat more plentiful, but these also have to be dredged up from fragmentary sources.[8]

[2] P. D. Converse, "Mediocrity in Retailing," *Journal of Marketing,* Vol. 23 (April, 1959), pp. 419–420.

[3] Hermann Levy, *The Shops of Britain* (London: Kegan Paul, Trench, Trubner & Co., 1947), pp. 210–211.

[4] D. L. Shawver, *The Development of Theories of Retail Price Determination,* (Urbana; University of Illinois Press, 1956), p. 92.

[5] Same reference as footnote 1.

[6] J. B. Jefferys, *Retail Trading in Great Britain,* 1850–1950 (Cambridge: Cambridge University Press, 1954), various pages, especially p. 96.

[7] Cited in Fabian Linden, "Department Store Operations," *Conferences Board Business Record,* Vol. 14 (October, 1958), pp. 410–414, at p. 411.

[8] See Harold Barger, *Distribution's Place in the American Economy Since 1869* (Princeton: Princeton University Press, 1955).

(3) Available series on both expenses and margins merely note changes in retailers' outlays and receipts. They do not indicate what caused those changes and they do not report changes in the costs borne by suppliers, consumers, or the community at large.

(4) Margin data are usually published as averages that may, and frequently do, mask highly divergent tendencies.

(5) A conceptual difficulty presents an even more serious problem than the paucity of statistics. When we talk about "types" of retailers, we think of classifications based upon ways of doing business and upon differences in price policy. Yet census categories and other systems for reporting retail statistics are usually based upon major differences in commodity lines. For example, the "pineboard" druggists who appeared in the 1930s are a "type" of retailing for our purposes. Those dealers had cruder fixtures, charged lower prices, carried smaller assortments, gave more attention to turnover, and had less interest in prescriptions than did conventional druggists. Yet census reports for drugstores necessarily included all of the pineboards that maintained any sort of prescription department.

Discount houses provide another example of an important, but amorphous, category not reflected in census classifications. The label "discount house" covers a variety of retailers. Some carry stocks, others do not. Some have conventional store facilities, whereas others operate in office buildings, lofts, and warehouses. Some feature electrical appliances and hard goods, while other emphasize soft goods. Some pose as wholesalers, and others are practically indistinguishable from all other popular priced retailers in their fields. Consequently discount dealers' operating figures are likely to be merged into the statistics reported for other appliance, hardware, or apparel merchants.

EXAMPLES OF CONFORMITY

British

British retailing provides several examples of conformity to the wheel pattern. The grocery trade has gone through several wheel-like evolutions, according to a detailed analysis made by F. G. Pennance and B. S. Yamey.[9] Established firms did initiate some changes and some margin reductions, so that the pattern is obscured by many cross currents. But the major changes seem to have been due to the appearance and then the maturation, first, of department-store food counters; then, of chain stores; and finally, of cut-price cash-and-carry stores. Now supermarkets seem to be carrying the pattern through another evolution.[10]

Jefferys also has noted a general long-run upgrading in both British department stores and chains.[11] Vague complaints in the co-operative press and a decline in consumer dividend rates suggest that wheel-like changes may have occurred in the British co-operative movement.[12]

American

Very little is known about retail margins in this country before the Civil War. Our early retail history seems to have involved the appearance, first, of hawkers, walkers, and peddlers; then, of general stores; next, of specialty stores; and finally, of department stores. Each of these types apparently came in as a lower-margin, lower-price competitor to the established outlets, and thus was consistent with the wheel pattern. We do not know, however, whether there was simply a long-run decline in retail margins through successive improvements in retail efficiency from one type to another (contrary to the wheel pattern), or whether each of the early types was started on a low-margin basis, gradually "up-graded," and so provided room for the next entrant (in accordance with the pattern).

The trends toward increasing margins can be more easily discerned in many branches of retailing after the Civil War. Barger has described increases over the years 1869–1947 among important retail segments, including department stores, mail-order firms, variety stores, and jewelry dealers. He attributes much of the pre-World War I rise in department-store margins to the absorption of wholesaling functions. Changes in merchandise mix, such as the addition of soda fountains and cafeterias to variety stores and the upgrading of mail-

---

[9] F. G. Pennance and B. S. Yamey, "Competition in the Retail Grocery Trade, 1850–1939," *Economica*, Vol. 22 (March, 1955), pp. 303–317.

[10] "La Methode Americane," *Time*, Vol. 74 (November 16, 1959), pp. 105–106.

[11] Same reference as footnote 6.

[12] "Battle of the Dividend," *Co-operative Review*, Vol. 36 (August, 1956), p. 183; "Independent Commission's Report," *Co-operative Review*, Vol. 38 (April, 1958), pp. 84–89; "£52 Million Dividend in 1957," *Co-operative Review* (August, 1958), pp. 171–172.

order merchandise, seem to have caused some of the other increases. Finally, he believes changes in customer services have been a major force in raising margins.[13] Fabian Linden has extended Barger's observations to note similar 1949–1957 margin increases for department stores, variety chains, and appliance dealers.[14]

Some other examples of at least partial conformity to the wheel pattern may be cited. Many observers feel that both discount-house services and margins have increased substantially in recent years.[15] One major discount-house operator has stated that he has been able to keep his average markup below 12%, in spite of considerable expansion in his facilities and commodity mix.[16] However, the concensus seems to be that this probably is an exception to the general rule.

A study of gasoline pricing has pointed out how many of the so-called "off-brand" outlets have changed from the "trackside" stations of pre-war days. The trackside dealers typically maintained unattractive and poorly equipped installations, at out-of-the-way locations where unbranded gasoline was sold on a price basis. Today many of them sell well-promoted regional and local brands, maintain attractive, efficient stations, and provide prompt and courteous service. Some still offer cut prices, but may have raised their prices and margins up to or above national brand levels.[17] Over time, many of the pineboard druggists also seem to have become converted to fairly conventional operations.[18]

NON-CONFORMING EXAMPLES

Foreign

In underdeveloped countries, the relatively small middle- and upper-income groups have formed the major markets for "modern" types of retailing. Supermarkets and other modern stores have been introduced in those countries largely at the top of the social and price scales, contrary to the wheel pattern.[19] Some nonconforming examples may also be found in somewhat more industrialized environments. The vigorous price competition that developed among Japanese department stores during the first three decades of this century seems directly contrary to the wheel hypothesis.[20] B. S. Yamey's history of resale price maintenance also reports some price-cutting by traditional, well-established British merchants who departed from the wheel pattern in the 1880s and 1890s.[21] Unfortunately, our ignorance of foreign retail history hinders any judgment of the representativeness of these examples.

American

Automatic merchandising, perhaps the most "modern" of all American retail institutions, departed from the wheel pattern by starting as a high-cost, high-margin, high-convenience type of retailing.[22] The department-store branch movement and the concomitant rise of planned shopping centers also has progressed directly contrary to the wheel pattern. The early department-store branches consisted of a few stores in exclusive suburbs and some equally high-fashion college and resort shops.

Only in relatively recent years have the branches been adjusted to the changing and more democratic characteristics of the contemporary dormitory suburbs. Suburban shop-

---

[13] Same reference as footnote 8, p. 82.

[14] See footnote 7.

[15] D. A. Loehwing, "Resourceful Merchants," *Barron's*, Vol. 38 (November 17, 1958), p. 3.

[16] S. Masters, quoted in "Three Concepts of Retail Service," *Stores*, Vol. 41 (July–August, 1959), pp. 18–21.

[17] S. M. Livingston and T. Levitt, "Competition and Retail Gasoline Prices," *The Review of Economics and Statistics*, Vol. 41 (May, 1959), pp. 119–132 at p. 132.

[18] Paul C. Olsen, *The Marketing of Drug Products* (New Brunswick: Rutgers University Press, 1948, pp. 130–132.

[19] H. S. Hettinger, "Marketing in Persia," *Journal of Marketing*, Vol. 15 (January, 1951), pp. 289–297; H. W. Boyd, Jr., R. M. Clewett, & R. L. Westfall, "The Marketing Structure of Venezuela," *Journal of Marketing*, Vol. 22 (April, 1958), pp. 391–397; D. A. Taylor, "Retailing in Brazil," *Journal of Marketing*, Vol. 24 (July, 1959), pp. 54–58; J. K. Galbraith and R. H. Holton, *Marketing Efficiency in Puerto Rico* (Cambridge: Harvard University Press, 1955), p. 35.

[20] G. Fukami, "Japanese Department Stores," *Journal of Marketing*, Vol. 18 (July, 1953), pp. 41–49 at p. 42.

[21] "The Origins of Resale Price Maintenance," *The Economic Journal*, Vol. 62 (September, 1952), pp. 522–545.

[22] W. S. Fishman, "Sense Makes Dollars," *1959 Directory of Automatic Merchandising* (Chicago: National Automatic Merchandising Association, 1959), p. 52; M. V. Marshall, *Automatic Merchandising* (Boston: Graduate School of Business Administration, Harvard University, 1954), pp. 108–109, 122.

ping centers, too, seem to have appeared first as "Manhasset Miracle Miles" and "Ardmores" before reaching out to the popular price customers. In fact, complaints are still heard that the regional shopping centers have displayed excessive resistance to the entry of really aggressive, low-margin outlets.[23] E. R. A. Seligman and R. A. Love's study of retail pricing in the 1930s suggests that pressures on prices and margins were generated by all types of retailers. The mass retailing institutions, such as the department and chain stores, that had existed as types for many decades were responsible for a goodly portion of the price cutting.[24] As McNair has pointed out, the wheel operated very slowly in the case of department stores.

Finally, Harold Barger has described the remarkable stability of over-all distributive margins during the years 1919–1947.[25] Some shifting of distributive work from wholesalers to retailers apparently affected their relative shares of the total margins during this period, but this is not the type of change contemplated by the wheel pattern. Of course, the stabiltiy Barger notes conceivably could have been the result of a perfectly smooth functioning of the pattern, with the entrance of low-margin innovators providing exactly the right balance for the upcreep of margins in the longer established types. But economic changes do not come in smooth and synchronized fashion, and Barger's data probably should indicate considerably wider oscillations if the wheel really set the mold for all retailing in the postwar period.

CONCLUSIONS

The number of non-conforming examples suggests that the wheel hypothesis is not valid for all retailing. The hypothesis, however, does seem to describe a fairly common pattern in industrialized, expanding economies. Moreover, the wheel is not simply an illusion created by scrambled merchandising, as Holdren suggests. Undoubtedly some of the recent "upcreep" in supermarket average margins is due to the addition of nonfood and other high margin lines. But in recent years the wheel pattern has also been characteristic of department-store retailing, a field that has been relatively unreceptive to new commodity groups.[26]

In some ways, Jefferys' secular trend explanation appears most reasonable. The tendency of many established retailers to reduce prices and margins during depressions suggests also that increases may be a result of generally prospering environments. This explanation helps to resolve an apparent paradox inherent in the wheel concept. Why should reasonably skilled businessmen make decisions that consistently lead their firms along seemingly profitable routes to positions of vulnerability? Jefferys sees movement along the wheel as the result of sensible, business-like decisions to change with prospering market segments and to leave the poorer customers to low-margin innovators. His explanation is supported by the fact that the vulnerability contemplated by the wheel hypothesis usually means only a loss of market share, not a loss of absolute volume. At least in the United States, though, this explanation is partially contradicted by studies showing that prosperous consumers are especially prone to patronize discount houses. Also they are equally as likely to shop in supermarkets as are poorer consumers.[27]

The imperfect competition and excess capacity hypotheses also appear highly plausible. Considerably more investigation is needed before their validity can be appraised properly. The wheel pattern developed very slowly, and very recently in the department-store field. Yet market imperfections in that field probably were greater before the automobile gave the consumer shopping mobility. Major portions of the supermarket growth in food retailing and discount-house growth in appliance distribution occurred during periods of vastly expanding consumption, when excess capacity probably was at relatively low levels. At the moment there is little evidence to suggest any clear-cut correlation between the degree of market imperfection and the appearance of the

[23] P. E. Smith, *Shopping Centers* (New York: National Retail Merchants' Association, 1956), pp. 11–12; M. L. Sweet, "Tenant-Selection Policies of Regional Shopping Centers," *Journal of Marketing*, Vol. 23 (April, 1959), pp. 399–404.
[24] E. R. A. Seligman and R. A. Love, *Price Cutting and Price Maintenance* (New York: Harper & Brothers, 1932).
[25] Same reference as footnote 8, pp. ix, x.

[26] R. D. Entenberg, *The Changing Competitive Position of Department Stores in the United States by Merchandise Lines* (Pittsburgh: University of Pittsburgh Press, 1957), p. 52.
[27] R. Holton, *The Supply and Demand Structure of Food Retailing Services, A Case Study* (Cambridge: Harvard University Press, 1954).

wheel pattern. However, this lack may well be the result of the scarcity of empirical studies of retail competition.

Managerial deterioration certainly must explain some manifestations of the wheel, but not all. Empires rise and fall with changes in the quality of their leadership, and the same thing seems true in business. But the wheel hypothesis is a hypothesis concerning types of retailing and not merely individual firms. Consequently, the managerial-deterioration explanation holds true only if it is assumed that new people entering any established type of retailing as the heads of both old and new companies are consistently less competent than the first generation. Again, the fact that the wheel has operated very slowly in some fields suggests that several successive managerial generations can avoid wheel-like maturation and decay.

DISCUSSION QUESTIONS

This article suggests a cycle in retailing, but one which differs from that in the preceding article. The wheel thesis might be "pictured" as follows:

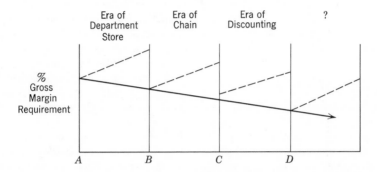

Note that each new institution begins its life at a relatively low point on the "% gross margin requirement" axis (point A is the Department Store's birthday, point B is the Chain's birthday, etc.); and as it matures, its gross margin requirements increase. The dashed and upward sloping line *within* each era reflects this tendency.

1. What forces produce this increasing gross margin requirement?

Note also that from era to era, the lowest gross margin requirement for each institution is *lower* than for preceding institutions. The downward sloping red line connecting the low points in each era reflect this tendency.

2. What factors account for this downward slope in gross margin requirements?

5. The Roots of Large Scale Retailing

M. S. MOYER

The most momentous developments in North American retailing have been institutional innovations—and all of them large scale. The department store, the mail order house, the chain store, the supermarket, and the discount house have been "the dynamic leavening" [1] of distribution.

What factors have bred this parade of large scale innovations in retailing?

EXTERNAL CAUSES

Clearly, one prerequisite of the large retail enterprise is a market capable of supporting sizeable merchandising operations.

It was the burgeoning farm population that followed the thrust of the Union Pacific system west of the Mississippi which spawned the mail order house.

The department store is the product of urban markets—those which arose on the Atlantic seaboard and then in the American Northwest, the St. Lawrence Valley, and in the lower Great Lakes region in the last half of the nineteenth century.

Like the department store, the chain unit has required an urban market of at least moderate size, since there its competitive strengths are most telling and its competitive weaknesses least damaging. Consequently, even today the chain remains a creature of the large city and its surrounding metropolitan areas, and tends to give ground to the small independent in the western states and in the Canadian prairies and maritime provinces. Competition among supermarket chains now turns importantly on control of adequate urban sites. In Canada, the necessity (and scarcity) of sizable markets is underlined by the vigorous westward expansion of Eastern food chains and discount house organizations.

But the appearance of new retail forms cannot be explained in terms of market size alone, for populous markets awaited for some decades before each new type of large scale retailing actually made its appearance. Qualitative as well as quantitative changes in markets have played an important part in the success of large retailing institutions.

The department store could not have thrived without a public readiness to accept a one-price policy: "If the entrepreneur himself does not sell, he has to have one price; he cannot trust clerks to bargain successfully." [2] The mail order house would have been impossible had its market not been prosperous, literate, and ready to trust in the unprecedented promise, "Your Money Back if You Are Not Satisfied." The chain owes part of its dramatic success of the 1920s to the extreme price consciousness of consumers during that period, and their willingness to accept standardized merchandise. Conversely, the limited success of the consumers' cooperative on this continent can be partly traced to the mobility, prosperity and cosmopolitan quality of the North American market.

The rise of the discount house also illustrates the importance of qualitative changes in the market in giving rise to large new retailing forms. By the 1950s important sectors of the American market had learned to view household durables as reliable and essential rather than unreliable and pretentious. Manufacturers' list prices had become convenient benchmarks of value. New family formation was high. Many knew depression only as a word. Self-serve had been tried and accepted in the supermarket. In these ways the market

♦ SOURCE: Reprinted by permission from the American Marketing Association, in the *Journal of Marketing*, October, 1962, pp. 55–59.
[1] Peter F. Drucker, *The New Society* (New York: Harper & Brothers Publishers, 1950), p. 29.

[2] C. Wright Mills, quoted in H. Pasdermadjian, *The Department Store: Its Origins, Evolution and Economics* (London: Newman Books, 1954), p. 22.

had become qualitatively "right" for the discount house and the later "soft lines supermarket."

Thus, the development of markets of suitable size and quality has been a requirement of large scale retailing.

Tapping Potential Markets

No market exists, however large and rich, unless it can be effectively tapped. That means that the seller must be able to communicate with prospective buyers in terms of both goods and ideas.

To the small retailer, communications in terms of goods usually presents no particular problems. In fact, proximity to his markets may be his most important single competitive advantage—but not so for the large retailer. Almost by definition, large scale retailing means large assortments. Such assortments are possible and feasible only if devices are available for assembling goods from many scattered sources, and for embracing substantial markets for these assortments. For this reason, mail order houses were "children" of the postal system and the early railways centering in Chicago. For the same reason, the department store would have been quite inconceivable without the railroad and steadily improving forms of interurban transportation. Similarly, the decade of the chains' most dramatic growth coincided with the first widespread use of the automobile.

Especially for the large scale enterprise, it is necessary to communicate with potential markets in terms of ideas as well as goods. The department store and chain found their most suitable medium in the newspaper, and the mail order catalogue has been called the greatest salesman in the world. Given suitable technical refinements, television could lead to "buy-while-you-watch" retailing.[3]

Marshaling Capital Resources

The ability to muster substantial capital funds effectively is another prerequisite of the large scale firm.

While markets remained local, demand unsophisticated, and production processes simple and discrete, the personal means of a resourceful individual might support a viable commercial enterprise. Elaborate facilitating agencies for mustering capital resources were unnecessary. It was appropriate, then, that the classical economists should describe a capital market based largely on face to face contact and individual negotiation.

The broadening of markets during the nineteenth century made it possible and sometimes necessary to operate on a scale which far outstripped such limited financial resources. Consequently, some more facile means was needed for the pooling of capital. Thus, despite early hostility to it, the limited company became "one of the major innovations of all time in business organization."[4]

The invention of the corporate form has promoted large scale operations in other important ways. The separate existence of the corporation implies continuity, and its unlimited life implies growth. The legality of earnings retention means that a corporation may own exclusive access to the means of its own expansion, free in part from the scrutiny of the capital market. The separation of ownership from control provides both the means and the motive for the professional manager to seek re-employment of, rather than distribution of, such accumulations.

Finally, the invention of corporate shares, readily transferable through a stock market, introduces capital gains as a motive for investment; and capital gains are rooted in the expectation of continued corporate growth.

Favorable Ideological Climate

"There is a moral and religious, as well as a material environment which sets its stamp upon the individual, even when he is least conscious of it."[5] This moral and religious environment shapes behavior in the market place. This means that to explain large scale business activity fully, one must take note of the ideological climate in which it flourishes.

The modern business enterprise, geared to the rational, continuing, and systematic seeking of profit, would have been quite inconceivable in the ideological climate of an earlier

---

[3] See for example "Buy While you Watch is Pay-TV's New Angle," *Business Week*, No. 1,634 (December 24, 1960) p. 62; and Daniel Seligman, "Chicago's Red Hot Merchandiser," *Fortune,* Vol. 52 (September, 1955), pp. 130–134, 156.

[4] Richard Eells and Clarence Walton, *Conceptual Foundations of Business* (Homewood, Illinois: Richard D. Irwin, Inc., 1961), p. 29.

[5] R. H. Tawney, *Religion and the Rise of Capitalism* (New York: The New American Library of World Literature, Inc.), p. 19.

age. "The spirit of capitalism . . . had to fight its way to supremacy against a whole world of hostile forces. A [capitalist] state of mind would both in ancient times and in the Middle Ages have been proscribed as the lowest sort of avarice . . ." [6] Thus, the large scale business enterprise is possible partly because a revolution of monumental proportions has taken place in accepted thought as to the place and purpose of economic activity.

It was the Reformation which prepared a favorable ideological climate for the rise of capitalistic business enterprise. Protestantism, and especially Calvinism, taught men that the accumulation of wealth was not perilous to the soul but indispensable to divine grace; that unremitting labor in one's calling, and not idle contemplation, was the mark of the chosen; and that the taking of every profit was not avarice but obedience to a God who so favors his elect. "We must exhort all Christians to gain all they can, and to save all they can; that is in effect to grow rich." [7]

This Christian asceticism has been the ideological heritage of business in North America. Its logic is the rationale of the businessman, including the trader. Its practical consequence is capitalism and large scale business enterprise. It has offered an unusually hospitable ideological climate for the growth of retailing on a large scale.

INTERNAL CAUSES

Many observers have noted that a business enterprise seems to be possessed of a propensity for growth that is not fully explainable in terms of economic advantage or even of human ambition. Note the formation of business units "larger than those necessary to permit the most economical means of production." [8] "A system may operate over a long period of time as if it has a destiny of its own and as if it were guided by inherent goals of survival and growth." [9] How can one explain this tendency?

The Propensity for Growth

While a firm remains small, it may be the shadow of a man. Its dominant characteristics may be a reflection of his character; its growth rate may be largely attributable to his own ambition and drive.

But as a firm expands, and as its founder passes, this drive seems to stem less from individuals than from relationships between them. With size, an enterprise develops a character "quite beyond the people who work for it at any given time." [10] At this point, the impersonal fact of size itself seems to generate the impetus for its further attainment. This is seen when in the large manufacturing firm retention of market share becomes not a measure of achievement but achievement itself, and when in the large retailing organization each period's efforts are typically directed toward "beating last year's figures." Then, too, "the prospect of growth is one of the principal means by which a firm can attract vigorous recruits. Thus, management in a typical firm is caught in a cycle in which growth is essential even though management may not have an intense desire for expansion." [11]

Another reason for this preoccupation with growth is that more relevant criteria of achievement are difficult to apply, particularly in the large firm. In the large organization, responsibility for the attainment of profit objectives must be apportioned and reapportioned many times. Staff activities tend to multiply. Costs tend to become nontraceable. Consequently, in a large complex organization it becomes increasingly difficult to calculate the effect on profits of any individual's activities. Under these conditions, it may be expedient to focus on sales growth. Therefore, although the retailer's maxim that "sales will cure anything" is not intellectually impeccable, it is a workable truth for the salesfloor.

Altogether, it does not seem fanciful to suggest that the rise of large scale retailing organizations is partly the product of an inherent propensity for growth, and one that becomes more compelling as sizeable operations are achieved. These pressures are reflected in the widely held view that "companies, like men

[6] Max Weber, *The Protestant Ethic and the Spirit of Capitalism* (London: George Allen & Unwin, Ltd., (1948), p. 56.
[7] John Wesley, quoted in Weber, (footnote 6), at p. 175.
[8] Arthur Robert Burns, *The Decline of Competition* (New York: McGraw-Hill Book Co., Inc., 1936), p. 9.
[9] Wroe Alderson, *Market Behavior and Executive Action* (Homewood, Illinois: Richard D. Irwin, Inc., 1957), p. 54.

[10] William H. Newman, "Basic Objectives Which Shape the Character of a Company," *The Journal of Business of the University of Chicago*, Vol. 26 (October, 1953), pp. 211–223, at p. 211.
[11] Same reference as footnote 9, at p. 59.

must either grow, or shrivel. They can't stand still . . ."[12]

Competitive Advantages of Scale

The large scale retail firm may enjoy a number of advantages not fully available to its smaller rival. Commonly mentioned are the expertise that can be brought to bear in all areas but especially in buying; the ability to make economic use of such media as radio, television, and newspapers; the more advantageous buying prices that go with relatively large purchases and a strong financial position; and the operating economies which may result from the integration of wholesaling and manufacturing activities with retailing.

Several less celebrated advantages bear mention. Analyses of the causes of the high mortality rate among small retailers suggests that there has been a tendency to undervalue the large retailer's ability to enlist superior managerial talent. Note also that the cumulative quality of most promotional effort enhances the effectiveness of the large retailer's advertising budget simply because it *is* large. Then, too, high volume retailing offers the possibility of conducting marketing research at a low level of cost to sales—an opportunity which has not been widely exploited.

Another important advantage of the large retail organization is its capacity to hedge against those unfortunate individual decisions which could cripple a smaller firm. The chain extricates itself from a badly chosen store location with little difficulty and with no enduring ill effects; for the independent, the same bad decision can be irrevocable and fatal. In the crucial area of merchandise selection, the large retailer can spread the risk of error over a wide number of lines and over a variety of trading areas; this hedge is not available in the same degree to the smaller merchant.

Finally, as Galbraith points out: "In the large organization, even the risks associated with the selection of leadership are reduced. Organization replaces individual authority; no individual is powerful enough to do much damage. Were it otherwise, the stock market would pay close attention to retirements, deaths, and replacements in the ranks of the large corporations. In fact, it ignores such details in tacit recognition that the organization is independent of any individual."[13]

Taken together, the advantages of scale in retailing are impressive.

Overcoming Internal Problems of Scale

In any growing organization, increasing scale gives rise to vexing administrative problems. Inability to master these difficulties can restrict the scale of operations attainable. This is especially so in retailing. Therefore, the fact that large scale retailing operations have been achieved is partly due to the success of retail management in solving these problems.

Growth is a process of qualitative as well as quantitative change. An expanding organization is something more than the multiple of its previous parts, for the addition of every new member to an organization compounds the number of potential lines of communication within a group. Thus, the very growth of a firm can be the source of its own paralysis. Means must be found to push back "the point at which further expansion runs into increasingly unfavorable internal structure."[14]

The "schedule system" did just that for the mail order house; indeed, without it the growth of mail order operations would have been seriously hampered.[15] Boulding reminds us of the more general contributions of mechanical aids, from the telephone to the computer, which have facilitated the recording, communication, and interpretation of information.[16] He has also underlined the power of conceptual aids including accounting and statistics, for abstracting and condensing information.[17]

These techniques have their weaknesses. Most important is their inability to deal with information which cannot meaningfully be reduced to abstract quantitative terms. This has been a special source of difficulty for the re-

[12] Russell B. Robins, "New Products by Proxy," *Marketing's Role in Scientific Management,* Robert L. Clewett, editor, (Chicago: American Marketing Association, 1957), pp. 74–82, at p. 74.

[13] John Kenneth Galbraith, *The Affluent Society* (Boston: Houghton Mifflin Company, 1958), p. 120.

[14] Kenneth E. Boulding, *The Organizational Revolution* (New York: Harper & Brothers Publishers, 1953), p. 25.

[15] See Boris Emmet and John E. Jeuck, *Catalogues and Counters* (Chicago: University of Chicago Press, 1950), pp. 129–136.

[16] Same reference as footnote 14, at p. 26.

[17] Same reference as footnote 14, at p. 135.

tailer. The outstanding merchant must have "a great eye, a sense of color, and a sense of sell," so that some of the most crucial decisions in even the largest retail organization can best be made not by perusing written reports but by "feeling the cloth."

This means that in retailing, as opposed to branch banking or insurance, for example, the scattered raw data of decision making are not readily reduced to abstract numerical form for transmission to other parts of the organization. Nevertheless, even in retailing the development of planned information and control systems has been an important means of pushing back the limits to further growth imposed by cumbrous internal structures.

Clarifying and Enhancing Personal Status

Man needs to have the approval of his fellows. In earlier centuries his status was protected or at least clarified through membership in such stable groups as the tribe, the city state, the feudal manor, the chartered town, or the craft guild.

These earlier social underpinnings were broken by the march of the factory system and the industrial state. Industrialization "uproots . . . the individual from the social soil in which he has grown." [18] Especially in the New World, geographic mobility and the setting aside of tradition and heredity rendered personal status ambiguous. The industrial community required new groupings in which status could be rooted.

One basic social grouping in a job-oriented society is the large business corporation, and it fills the need for status fairly well. It has not been entirely adequate, of course; the labor union in particular is in part a reflection of the inability of the large business enterprise to satisfy the status needs of all its members. Still, the capacity of the large firm to clarify and protect the personal status of its membership has been an additional source of its strength.

This can be seen in retailing. The large retail firm has offered "respectable" employment for much labor unable or unwilling to associate

itself with the factory, farm, or mine. This is particularly true as one moves from retailing jobs which involve the processing of assortments and toward retailing jobs which involve consultation with shoppers, that is, as one moves from the mail order house and the food chain toward the department store and the departmentized specialty store.

But "honour makes a great part of the reward of all honourable professions. In point of pecuniary gain, all things considered, they are generally under-recompensed." [19] Thus, some retail managements have found it possible to substitute psychic wages for some payroll dollars.

This reasoning partly explains the relatively low salaries at nonsupervisory levels in the field. No doubt this asset will depreciate as the retail outlet tends toward the "factory of distribution." [20] Nevertheless, in retailing especially, the growth of the large scale firm seems to have been reinforced by its ability to offer status to its members.

IMPLICATIONS

The rise of large scale retailers appears to be the result of a rather large number of factors, most all of which can be expected to operate in the future. Therefore, we can expect to see the continued appearance of new forms of large scale retailing—a pattern which has existed for a century in North America.

This should be a welcome prospect. The distributive trades are particularly liable to ossification in thinking, practice and structure. We need the "perennial gale of creative destruction" [21] stirred up by successive innovations in large scale retailing.

---

[18] Same reference as footnote 1, at p. 7.

[19] Adam Smith, *An Enquiry Into the Nature and Causes of the Wealth of Nations,* Vol. 1 (London: J. M. Dent & Sons, Ltd., 1920), p. 89.

[20] E. B. Weiss, "Salespeople Can't Be Trained and Shouldn't Be," in George H. Brown, editor, *Readings in Marketing* (New York: Henry Holt and Company, 1955), pp. 101–104, at p. 104.

[21] Joseph A. Schumpeter, *Capitalism, Socialism, and Democracy* (New York: Harper & Brothers Publishers, 1950), p. 84.

DISCUSSION QUESTION

This article will help you answer question 2 concerning the "wheel" of retailing. Specifically, what factors account for the economies in operation achieved by American retail institutions?

6. The Interaction of Consumer Behavior and Market Competition on the Store of the Future

ROBERT D. ENTENBERG*

The changing competitive market position of any store, product or service is one of the key indicators of how consumers value these offerings. The development of a consensus numerical value system should be a major goal for marketing managers and researchers inasmuch as the manner in which the "why" of consumer choices are measured and evaluated by executive management determines the evolving patterns of market competition. The author looks beyond the present and presents a series of predictions as to the store of the future and the accompanying patterns of market competition.

For some years now, in order to improve business effectiveness and executive performance, we, in marketing education, have been analyzing the factors and motivations underlying managerial purchasing decisions. To the same end, we have also been analyzing consumer motivations and behavior in the market place—unfortunately, without really pinpointing the quantitative value scale which actually "triggers" consumer purchases.

By and large, the decision-making processes as to whether "to buy" or "not to buy" at both the consumer and the industrial levels flow in relatively the same procedural chains. The consumer weighs alternatives in much the same manner as the retail store buyer, the commercial purchaser or the industrial agent. What does differ are the underlying value scales and motivations.

In the case of the business firm, the purchasing decision is only one of several types needed to attain organizational goal objectives. At the consumer level, the purchasing decision results in the actual fulfillment of a personal or family objective in terms of direct satisfaction and well being.

Again, consumer decisions in the market place can be classified as either rational or irrational in nature. The business decision, on the other hand, can generally be classified as rational or strategic. For the purposes of this paper, I am defining a rational buying decision as one where the purchaser can give a definite reason for buying.

When consumers, as a group, give a consensus of similar rational reasons for either individual or various combinations of purchases, the determination of the most effective promotional and advertising appeals is not too difficult a task. In such cases, merchandise offerings tend to become uniform in character. Further, market competition based on rational reasoning by consumers tends to become severe, with price cutting a common feature.

When consumers, as a group, cannot give definite reasons for the purchase of specific products or for buying in particular stores, or for shopping in a specific trading area, then the motives underlying these purchasing decisions can be classified as irrational or emotional!

In such cases, store maangement and consumer goods manufacturers generally have to maximize their sales promotion and competi-

* SOURCE: Reprinted by permission from the American Marketing Association, in *Marketing Precision and Executive Action,* Charles H. Hindersman, Editor, 1962, pp. 571–579.
* Robert D. Entenberg is Louis D. Beaumont Professor of Marketing and Business Administration, University of Denver.

tive efforts through subjective value judgments. These value judgments are, more often than not, based on qualitative factors. This is simply not enough. As a result, market competition in these latter areas tends to become haphazard in character with relatively little price cutting taking place.

Fortunately, almost all trading areas at the retail level have and will continue to have strong mixtures of both price and non-price competition. Market competition has become so complex that even often bought, low-priced convenience goods may present complicated purchasing decisions for the rationally minded consumer. For example, if any of you look at the mass array of grocery store advertising in your mid-week newspapers, you will find that the consumer can maximize his dollar purchases price-wise only by shopping at several different stores.

It seems that food store price setters do their utmost to compete on non-competitive items to which they add "gifts" in the form of stamps of various kinds. The consumer in evaluating these promotional efforts generally adds convenience costs in the form of alternative amounts of time that they must spend in mazes of shelf space exposures and checkout stand delays. Faced with many inescapable disutilities in the midst of desired alternatives makes it almost impossible for the consumer to make a rational purchasing decision. All the consumer really looks for is a net "pleasant" utility appeal based on a personal value scale.

Each consumer has a built-in, culturally adjusted, biological decision maker through which he automatically weighs alternatives in terms of potential satisfactions. When a consumer purchases a product, or patronizes a store or shopping area for the first time, a learning pattern is initiated. This learning pattern is either reinforced or lessened through "trial and error" experiences with the product. If the intrinsic satisfactions derived from the product or the shopping process itself is satisfactory, then the learning experience can be reinforced by advertising and sales promotion efforts.

It is common knowledge that sales promotion and advertising efforts could achieve maximum effectiveness if advertising appeals could be based on a specific quantitative value system underlying consumer motivations. Regardless of whether or not consumers act rationally or irrationally, marketing managers must forecast on the basis of the empirical "whys" of consumer choices. The manner in which the "whys" are measured and evaluated by executive management determines the evolving patterns of market competition and the store of the future.

QUANTITATIVE EVALUATIONS

The term "value" as used within the content of this paper will refer to a consensus value scale of desirabilities in terms of monetary equivalents of dollars and cents. Thus, the monetary amounts paid for merchandise or services by customers in a competitive market place automatically rate the desirabilities of various kinds of purchases. All purchasing decisions, whether business or personal, intuitive or scientific, are generally based on a sort of "pain-pleasure" utility concept.

The Utilitarians such as Bentham and J. S. Mill suggested numerical measurements more than a century ago. However, only recently have serious attempts been made to measure desirabilities quantitatively in terms of dollars and cents market prices.

Numerical measurements of intelligence are commonplace; in addition, heuristic programs whose values are essentially subjective are being fed into computers for quantitative evaluation. Why, then, should the assignment of numerical values to consumer motivations be so surprising? By this means, every product, service, or location can be assigned definite numerical values in terms of monetary equivalents.

For example, if we pass a pastry shop, the satisfaction of potential enjoyment plus the disutility of adding unwanted calories may determine the decision "to buy" or "not to buy." The quality of the pastry might be a secondary consideration as would the price of the pastry itself. The effort needed to purchase would represent another "value" factor. All told, however, the decision alternatives can be quantitatively measured.

Certainly there are differences as to what a good cup of coffee is worth to different individuals, or for that matter, a Brooks Brothers suit or Christian Dior dress. Despite its complexities, a dollar and cents consensus value system can be the basis for a prediction market planning system—except where monopolistic or oligopolistic conditions may exist.

Thus, intuitively, the consumer sets up purchasing alternatives on a personal utility scale based on necessity, preferences, and spendable income. If the net result is favorable, the purchase is made; if it is not, the opportunity is bypassed. Also, what is automatically true at a particular point in time does not mean that it will be true at another point in time. Often, particular types of market promotions or innovations are unsuccessful because of improper timing. When similar techniques are tried out at a later time, they may succeed. Witness the "Keedozle" and other automated ventures that failed in the past.

The actual amount of money spent by consumers for specific merchandise and services in a competitive market is an indisputable numerical preference system. In effect, the money allocated for these purchases registers desirabilities in terms of consumer satisfactions. Another problem of measurement is that of evaluating optimum market share for a single product or brand. In such cases, techniques developed by psychologists in measuring public opinion preferences and individual attitudes can be applied.

In experimental techniques used to measure the monetary value equivalents of trading stamps, supermarket customers at checkout counters were given the choice of a 3 per cent cash discount or the trading stamps due for the amount of the purchase. On the basis of preliminary findings, it was found that in transactions of less than $5, stamps were generally preferred. In transactions above $5.00, customers preferred the 3 per cent cash discount. When the rate of discount offered was gradually reduced from a high of 3 per cent to a low of 2.3 per cent of the transaction price, it was found that a point of indifference was reached at 2.6 per cent of the transaction prices falling between $5.01 and $10. In transactions over $10, the point of indifference centered around 2.5 per cent. The indifference points measure the face value of the stamps in terms of cash equivalents. Of course, differing amounts of discounts had to be extended to various customers who might have reacted differently had their purchases been greater or smaller in amount.

Irrespective of difficulties, the development of a consensus numerical value system should be a major goal objective for marketing managers and researchers.

PREDICTIONS FOR THE FUTURE

The changing competitive market position of any store, product or service is one of the key indicators of how consumers value these offerings. The store of the future will be located, designed, and stocked on the basis of preference trends indicated by changing relative competitive positions in the market place.

There will be a slowing acceleration of the suburban movement and a resurgence of migration into urbanized, centrally located rebuilt residential zones.

In a modern economy there is no such thing as a status quo: be it social, economic or technical. Economies of scale at the retail level will continue to be briefly enjoyed before being absorbed without any appreciable reduction in operating expenses. In a competitive economy, regardless of the size of any particular store or firm, an artificial price level cannot be maintained. Nor can any firm continually and generally undersell all its competitors!

Among others, Sears, A & P, and Federated are today the reflections and brain children of other men. These men in past years were not afraid to innovate and operate contrary to the then existing traditional forms of competition. In a like manner, the stores of the future are now being conceived by young men today and men who are youthful in their thinking and outlook. Now, let us review what is happening.

Last year for the first time in any recovery period, total consumer expenditures and retail sales failed to reflect increases in personal income. These decreases in expenditures continued from the last quarter of 1960 up to the first quarter of 1962. Of greater significance, there has been a continuing decrease in consumer allocations for goods, primarily in the non durable categories. It is evident that consumer expenditures can no longer be regarded as a comparatively stable function of income.

Consumer expenditures can and do change both as to direction and amount and not necessarily with any advance notice. Service expenditures today account for more than 42 per cent of total consumer spending; this is an increase of more than 17 per cent during the last ten years.

Accompanying this increasing demand has been an upward rise of wage rates in the service industries. These wage rate increases parallel the gains in the manufacturing sectors of our economy, with little, if any, accompanying increases in improved productivity. As a result, the cost of services has increased almost 50 per cent since 1946. During the same period of time the price of commodities at the retail level has risen only 18 per cent. Thus, services have become much more costly relative to goods. Further, there is nothing to indicate any trend reversals in this direction.

The store of the future will offer fewer "free"

services and will have to charge more for whatever services that they do offer. In addition, as service expenditures continue to expand, innovators will introduce new concepts in "service departments" just as we have continuing innovations in "merchandise departments." Also, combination service-convenience stores will be part of the future scene.

The decline in the proportion of consumer spending for non durables has not yet resulted in any significant changes in the stores handling these merchandise lines. This is because total dollar sales in these areas are continuing to show increases due to population growth and rising incomes.

Generally, the greater discretionary income, the larger the amounts spent for expensive durables, visible material possessions, and the greater the tendency to maximize total satisfactions in the service areas.

The real income of consumers will continue to rise. During the past 15 years, subsistence level families have been fast disappearing from the American scene. As a result, consumer spending in the aggregate is becoming more typical of the spending patterns of the higher income families of the past.

The actual behavior of retail firms in the market place will continue to be competitive in a "workable" sense with greater ease of entry than exists today. Further, inter-firm competition at the retail level will continue to be greater than that existing in any other segments of the economy.

The market framework, of course, is always determined by the availability of goods and services, and the facilities available. Exclusives on "really differentiated" merchandise categories will continue to be rare attributes for most stores. Even discount and promotional department stores can now buy well-known nationally advertised prestige brands. Witness Korvettes' merchandise line offerings in their new Fifth Avenue store.

Consumer patronage motives as to brand and store preferences will have to be maintained or improved.

Many stores will continue to go all out into "non price" as well as price competition. Whether based on service, selections, more convenient locations, or better prestige surroundings, the projection of the store image as the better place to shop will become an increasingly important part of the retail scene.

The larger stores will continue to strive to be all things to all people. This means that the large store of the future will have to offer new combinations of merchandise and variations in store operations now extended by variety, specialty, prestige, and discount stores. There will be more manufacturer and wholesale sponsored retail operations.

Based on present trends, the number of retail establishments should not greatly exceed 1,800,000. The key to the successful store of the future will be in the extent to which its management can evaluate the services and conveniences which customers want and are valuing at higher utility levels. Also, the stores and locations which offer the most in total conveniences will stand to achieve the greatest measures of success. The successful store of the future will have to offer services, rentals, and lease equipment.

The department store will not disappear, but instead will change in form and approach on departmental and unit levels and become a more firmly fixed institution than ever before.

There is no reason to predict that the operating expenses of retail establishments in the aggregate will decrease—automation and checkouts notwithstanding. To date, most savings effected by innovation and E.D.P. systems seem to disappear.

Food, gasoline, garden supplies, hardware, and children's apparel, etc. will continue to be bought primarily at stores located immediately adjacent to zones of residence while specialty and shopping goods such as apparel and home furnishings, will continue to be bought primarily downtown where selections are more complete.[1]

The greater the income level of the people in a trading area, the further they are willing to travel in order to get specific items of apparel, specialty, or home goods.

As a competitive weapon, the popularity of stamps will again show cyclical declines and gains. The greatest growth in department and specialty stores will be specialty areas geared to the "senior" customer. The older members of our society will get more fashion conscious and enterprising—especially in their purchasing. You will see a return of the cut-rate drug chains in many states, supported in a great measure by the older members of our society.

Gross margins in the aggregate will not be very different from what they are today.

The stores of the future will have to actively

---

[1] Robert D. Entenberg, *The Changing Competitive Position of Department Stores in the United States by Merchandise Lines* (Pittsburgh: University of Pittsburgh Press, 1961), p. 117.

support and in some cases subsidize newspapers as well as mass transportation facilities. In some cases, stores will choose to promote through the use of handbill circulars and flyers.

As more and more shopping centers are built in marginal areas, there will be an increasing array of empty stores "for rent."

The store of the future will have to place greater reliance on resident buying offices. Geographical dispersions have become so great that it has become uneconomic for consumer goods manufacturers to reach many retailers.

Shopping centers will get bigger and more inconvenient. The problem of "walkathons" involved in any diversified shopping will have to be solved. Perhaps the answer lies in moving sidewalks, moving sidewalks with chairs, or continuous customer shuttle transportation. There may be a decline of the one stop shopping centers of the regional variety because of inconvenience attendant with parking and shopping. Free standing stores conveniently located will become more important in suburban areas.

A greater proportion of sales volume will be generated in stores by means of catalogue, mail, and telephone orders.

Mergers and combinations will not "kill off" the independent, because size of firm and scale of plant at the retail level is apparently not resulting in appreciably lower operating expenses.

The larger stores are furnishing "umbrellas" rather than "floors" on pricing. The aggressive independent will continue to compete through time, personal service, and convenience as well as price competition. There is a firm future for the progressive independent. However, estate and tax planning will have to be integrated with business planning—not just as an afterthought.

Service competition both as to price and extent of offerings will become more important. Retailing is and will be local in character. However, locational monopolies, for the most part, are aspects of the past.

In conclusion, here are some present projections based on research in process at the University of Pittsburgh.

The store of the future will benefit in added volume from the increase of acceptance of in-home, catalogue, and telephone order selling. There will be a resurgence in food sales on a full service basis featuring delivery and credit.

There will be further revitalization in secondary shopping districts along with central business districts.

Leased department syndicates will increase in volume through larger independent and corporate chain stores.

Department stores with sales of $40 million annually or over will continue to have an increased proportion of their sales generated by branches.

Supermarkets in the future will be smaller in size as many of those being built today are proving uneconomic for both the operator and the customer.

Less efficient retailers will continue to disappear with new hopefuls taking their place.

The term "discount" will lose much of its present day connotation and other promotional identities will replace it.

The major competition at the retail level will continue to be between one-stop regional shopping centers and central business districts. Further:

Many of the retail firms which we know today as discount houses will continue to grow through mergers, acquisitions, or expansions. Their operating expenses, contrary to much popular belief, will probably go up, not down, with increasing size. This is because of built-in cost factors that accumulate over time. This means that the prices charged must increase also. As this happens, these organizations become less and less discount houses and more and more promotional and conventional departmentalized stores.

As to discount selling, this will persist in one form or another long after the discount house matures, gains respectability, and ceases to be a "bogey" on the retail scene.[2]

---

[2] Robert D. Entenberg, "The Discount House,—Panic or Panacea," *Georgia Business* (Bureau of Business Research, University of Georgia, Oct., 1961).

DISCUSSION QUESTIONS

Professor Entenberg suggests that the size of regional shopping centers will get so large that a real inconvenience in movement within the center will be likely.

1. What do you think is a realistic answer to this problem? Moving sidewalks? Shuttle services between major stores within the center? Perhaps the de-

sign of centers in the future should make greater use of vertical space! A *column* of specialty shops might replace the *row* of such shops which prevails now.

It is also suggested that the discount house will undergo a gradual change such as that suggested in the "wheel" thesis. Entenberg predicts that the supermarket of tomorrow will be smaller.

2. Is it possible to facilitate the shopping process within the store by more efficient use of vertical space? Could merchandise be placed on shelves which would move up and down (as miniature elevators) at the will of the shopper?

American Retail
Institutions

The nature of the retail institutions which comprise our retailing system is determined by the size of the market such institutions can serve. Retailing is thus a particular form of specialization and division of labor which produces a great variation in the size and character of the individual stores which we see. If markets for stores offering large assortment exist, stores having such a trait will develop. If markets exist for a retail store offering few "services"—that is, if enough of us want to perform some of the traditional functions and services of retailers *for ourselves*—stores having that characteristic will develop. If markets demand locational convenience, an institution will offer that dimension of service.

In this section, several of the American retail institutions which are of growing importance are examined. These institutions include *individual* stores as well as *clusters* of stores. These clusters or shopping centers are as surely retailing institutions as are individual stores—indeed the same basic forces which produce specialized individual stores work to produce specialized groupings or clusters of stores. Specifically, the low-margin high-turnover philosophy of retail enterprise is examined carefully in the article by E. B. Weiss. "Closed door" discount houses, "planned" shopping centers, franchise retailing, and the "discount department store" are scrutinized. In another article, Professor Entenberg argues that the need exists for a new classification system for our retail institutions since few of the traditional classes of stores can be found in a pure form today.

1. Low-Margin Retailers Forging Ahead with Explosive Growth, Innovation, Shifting Income Sources

E. B. WEISS[*]

PREDICTIONS: WHAT LOW-MARGIN RETAILING WILL ACHIEVE IN 1961—AND BY 1965

Stephen Masters, president of Masters Inc., one of the original discount houses and one of the more successful, estimated discount store values in 1960 at over $5 billion. This is, of course, a guess-estimate, and perhaps a bit biased—there is no complete list of discount outlets, and many discount outlets keep their figures confidential. Moreover, it is really quite misleading to create the impression that only low-margin outlets price off list. Almost every retailer, at least periodically, cuts his margin.

In any event, that estimate of over $5 billion in 1960 volume for the low-margin outlet, even if it over-states the case by a billion dollars, clearly underscores the fantastic growth of true low-margin outlets. If it is a reasonably accurate figure, it would mean that, in 1960, the low-margin outlet had achieved a dollar volume equal to about *one-third* of total department store sales! Since the low-margin outlet really got started only after World War II, this is a remarkable achievement. . . .

The low-margin form of retailing is in a stage of not merely dynamic growth—but *explosive* growth. Without question, its jump in *dollar* volume in 1961 will make that year its year of greatest expansion to date. It may also achieve, in 1961, a greater *dollar increase* than its *total volume* in 1956—just five years ago! . . .

If we point out that the low-margin outlet in

1961 probably will move about *one-third* of all appliances (major and traffic) sold at retail—then we begin to see this outlet in its true enormous dimensions. And, if Sears' and Ward's appliance volume is removed from the calculation, then it is probable that the low-margin outlets accounted for 40% of all appliance volume!

There are some 53,000,000 families in this nation. By the end of 1961, close to 5,000,000 families—almost 10% *of all families*—will be card-holding members of closed-door discount chains. This is almost unbelievable when it is understood that the closed-door discount chain, as it exists today, really is not much over five years old!

When all low-margin outlets are lumped together, it is entirely probable that *one out of four families* shops in these outlets in 1961 with some regularity. This, too, is an amazing achievement.

Sees Appliance Industry Selling 90% of Volume Off List in 1961

In some merchandise classifications, the low-margin outlet will probably account for close to 50% of the nation's total volume! Toys would be an example—there is little doubt that nearly 50% of the toy industry's total volume will be moved through low-margin outlets in 1961. Moreover, and this certainly underscores the marketing significance of the discount outlet, all other major retailers—department stores, mail-order chains, variety chains, drug chains, food chains, etc.—have been compelled to meet the low-margin outlet's prices on toys. As a consequence, the toy industry will be moving perhaps 90% of its total volume in 1961 at prices that are *off list!*

♦ SOURCE: Reprinted by permission from the editors of *Advertising Age,* in the August 7, 1961, issue, pp. 86–94.

* Vice-President and Director of Special Merchandising Service, Doyle Dane Bernbach, New York.

This has happened also in appliances—both traffic and major. It would be reasonably correct to conclude that something like 75% of the total volume on appliances in 1961 will be priced off list! And the actual figure may be much higher.

In one merchandise classification after another, this same situation either has happened, is happening, or is about to happen. The phonograph record industry is clearly caught up in this situation. Even such a category as foundation garments finds that the low-margin outlet may account, in 1961, for about 10% of its total volume—and from 15% to 20% of total volume on certain types and price lines of foundation garments. Moreover, several manufacturers in this classification may, in 1961, do considerably more than 20% of their volume through low-margin outlets . . .

The early discount chains—Korvette, Masters, etc.—were primarily hard-goods chains. Today, their aim is to become at least 70% to 80% soft goods, home furnishings, food, drugs. They are even turning to old-line department store buying offices for soft-goods aid! And they have forced some food supers to curtail their soft-line selling.

The newer low-margin outlets—especially closed-door and mill chains—started out with major emphasis on soft goods; today, their object is to present a complete department store inventory—plus food.

This is the new 1961 look of the low-margin outlet—a *full-line department store*, including food and drugs. And by 1965, these low-margin outlets may have *as many full-line department store* units as do the traditional department stores! (And they will have vastly more food departments than the traditional department stores.) . . .

Low-Margin Outlets to Rival Top Department Stores in Floor Space

Right now we would like to make the point that, by 1965, the low-margin outlets will have at least 500—at least 500!—store units with from 100,000 sq. ft. to 200,000 sq. ft. of floor space, which will be stocked with an inventory capable of supplying almost *all* the wants of our affluent society. This will give them a *larger total* floor space than the 800 also-ran traditional department stores—and will bring them within hailing distance of the total floor space of the 200 top department stores!

Dynamic progress of that kind, by a new *low-margin* retailer, must inevitably shake the world of marketing right down to its toes. *And it will.*

Too many marketing men *still* think of the low margin outlet in terms of hard goods. This is like thinking of the food outlet in terms of food, the variety outlet in terms of 5 and 10-cent merchandise, the drug outlet in terms of drugs. . . .

The president of National Bellas Hess, which operates closed-door low-margin outlets under the GEX name, stated that "We now carry everything from aspirin to automobiles." (Apparently, GEX has made arrangements with auto dealers so its card-holding members can receive a special discount.)

These outlets will make astounding gains in food. Almost every new department-store type store opened by low-margin retailers now includes a *large* food department. They will also make astounding gains in drugs—the drug chains are opening leased departments rapidly in the low-margin outlets.

Incidentally, the newer low-margin outlets lean *heavily* on the leased department; the older discount outlets are now turning to the leased department.

The low-margin outlets are exerting a major impact in areas where they have bunched their stores. For example, Houston, Texas, will have some 15 large new low-margin stores ringing the city by the end of 1961. Traditional chains in that area report tumbling volume. Somewhat the same situation is developing around Boston. In one city after another, by 1965, they will control a *substantial* percentage of total retail floor space. Moreover, their stores will be in top locations; the stores will be completely modern—and they will be full-line department stores.

Incidentally, some owners of closed-door discount chains insist that they are not a discount store. For example, a vice-president of GEM Inc., Washington, makes the point that it is not a discount store. It contends it is not a discount store because it does not sharpshoot at prices. It doesn't move a particular price up and down. It does not engage in newspaper advertising. It asserts it has found a way to operate at a much lower cost than conventional stores and it insists it should pass these savings on to member-customers in the form of a lower price. Once having established its price, *it leaves these prices alone.* In short, it doesn't discount. But it *is* low-margin retailing.

And this is the *crux* of this new marketing situation.

The low-margin outlet is, indeed, a low-margin retailer. The National Retail Merchants Assn.—which, since it represents department stores, wasn't too pleased to report what follows—studied some closed-door chains in the West and found their average margin was between *22% and 24%!* This is remarkable—bear in mind that the food super today requires a 21% margin *on food!* Also bear in mind that department stores, variety chains, drug chains require a margin of from 30% to 40% (and higher)—the department store figure is in the area of 37%. The Fed-Mart closed-door chain claims its margin is under 18%.

Low-Margin Retailers Getting 100% to 1,000% Return on Investment

Yet, despite its low margin, the low-margin outlet manages to show an extremely high return on investment—the true guide to store performance. No other mass retailer equals its performance. GEM, one of the big closed-door discount chains, reports a 30% to 35% return on investment. (GEM leases almost all departments and declares that it can open a 100,000-sq.-ft. unit for an unbelievably low investment of $125,000—which is another staggering element in this retail revolution.) In general, the low-margin retailer shows a percentage return on investment that is from 100% to 1,000% larger than that of most traditional department stores and most traditional chains (with a few notable exceptions such as J. C. Penney).

The low-margin outlet is now being invited into some shopping centers from which it was formerly barred. However, more important, some of these low-margin chains are now big enough to open their *own* shopping centers. Korvette, for example, will be opening a 42-acre shopping center near Trenton, N.J. Korvette will have three of its own stores on the site—a department store, a furniture store, and a super market. The three stores will total about 300,000 square feet—making the threesome about as large as all but maybe a dozen of our largest department stores.

That trend toward shopping centers owned by low-margin outlets will move ahead fast. These will be strikingly *new types* of shopping centers and will include huge amusement areas, because the low-margin outlet is bringing fun back into shopping . . .

The low-margin outlet has come of age. It is now an adult.

But it is a *young* adult.

It will stub its toes. It will make serious errors. It will, in some instances, over-expand. In other instances, it will accumulate too much overhead—which may be true right now of several of the older discount outlets.

But it is on the march—and it is marching not merely double-time, but *triple* time.

And it has made such tremendous progress that the older forms of retailing are no longer able to view its progress with equanimity. To the contrary, practically every major retailer in the country right now is planning to meet the competition of the low-margin outlet. Even Sears is opening an "outlet" store as a test, despite its tending to down-talk the discount operation. This could be the start of a new form of low-margin retailing by Sears. And chains that are not opening discount outlets are turning to trading stamps as a competitive substitute.

The food chain, the drug chain, the variety chain and the department store were all turning in an extremely poor net profit percentage and an even poorer return on investment—*before* they had to compete with the two new types of discount chains. This has been particularly true of the new one-stop store units of the traditional chains. The older chains simply do not know how to merchandise many of their new merchandise categories profitably—even at markups of 40% and more!

Yet, if they are to compete with the new low-margin outlets, they *must* take lower margins on many old and new classifications. They can't do this safely with their high costs—if they match prices with low-margin outlets, their tiny net profit will disappear.

As a consequence, they are planning other moves. They are no longer trying merely to meet price with price; they really *can't*. They are opening low-margin stores of their own. They are merging or affiliating with low-margin chains. They are opening leased departments in low-margin stores. They are inviting low-margin operators to open leased departments in their stores.

All this, when toted up, clearly means not only that most manufacturers must now look more realistically at the low-margin store as an outlet—but must also take another look at their prices, their price lining, their trade discounts and margins.

We have been moving out of a *one-price* era

for well over a decade. Oddly, it was advertising that presumably would establish the one-price concept for all time. But it was the pre-sold brand that made the low-margin retailing concept feasible. Today, only a minor percentage of brands are retailed under a one-price philosophy. By 1965, the total will be much smaller.

Moreover, trade margins will be re-examined. After all, a brand that moves with a *minimum* of effort at retail does not require the trade margin that was established when that brand needed—and got—*specialty* selling of a high order in the retail store.

Weaknesses of Department Stores, Chains Invite Low-Margin Retailing

The big weakness of the established department stores and chains stems from the fact that in their stores, they did less and less intelligent selling, less and less merchandising, less and less promotion. They also permitted the manufacturer to do, not merely more and more of the pre-selling, but also more and more of the actual floor selling, of the store advertising and of the store promotion. *Yet, they have asked for larger and larger margins!*

They simply were unable to *pass on to the public* the savings made possible by the pre-sold brand and by self-service; they insisted on *larger margins* than in the era when pre-sold brands and self-service were unknown. They moved their margins and demands for allowances up and up, at exactly the time that brands were more and more strongly pre-sold and self-service was becoming paramount!

This held open an umbrella for a new type of retailing—*low-margin* retailing. And the low-margin operators moved in!

They are here to stay. They will compel other retailers to go through vast changes—and they will compel manufacturers to revise distribution programs, pricing programs, discount and margin programs.

The public is about to get more of the benefits of an era in which it not only buys pre-sold brands, but buys them via self-service and self-selection. The traditional retailer has passed on to the public more and more of the retailer's function—and has charged the public more and more for this "privilege." That, too, held open an umbrella for a retail concept that would "pay" the public when the public performed traditional retail functions.

CLOSED-DOOR AND MILL CHAINS SPEARHEAD LOW-MARGIN RETAILING CHANGES

It is odd to talk of "old" and "new" groups of low-margin retailers. After all, low-margin retailing, in its present-day forms, is really a development of only the last decade. In 1950, the "discount house" was just emerging.

Yet, during the single decade of the 1950's, low margin retailing has moved so dynamically that the Korvette's, the Master's, the Polk Bros. have become the *oldsters,* and the GEM's, the GEX have become the *newer* forms.

This is not said to disparage the older discount houses. They are old only with respect to their newer discount rivals. In almost every other respect, they continue to display all of the drive of youth—Korvette, for example, is moving ahead at a remarkable pace.

In 1961, Korvette will open four new department stores. *Each* will boast floor space of 240,000 square feet, bigger than the largest stores being built by Sears, Ward's, and larger than 90% of department store branches. Korvette now has 12 discount department stores in addition to some smaller specialty operations . . .

Low-Margin Retailers Will Force Manufacturers to Re-Shape Marketing

Between them, the older and the newer forms of low-margin retailing are, today, rolling up a total volume that makes them potent factors on the retail scene. Early in 1961, there were probably well in excess of 2,000 discount store units of all types (insofar as it is possible to clearly identify a discount store). By the early part of 1962, there will be perhaps 2,400 of these low-margin outlets of all types. This will represent, in one year, an increase of about 25% in store units. But, since then, new stores will tend to run between 50,000 square feet and 150,000 square feet, the increase in floor footage will be on the order of perhaps 35%.

It is probable that, by the early part of 1962, those 2,400 low-margin store units will be moving merchandise at *an annual rate of over $4 billion!*

That $4 billion would represent a low-margin volume equal to about *one-third* of total department store volume. It would nose out the total volume of our variety chains. It would considerably exceed the volume of the drug chains. It would exceed the non-food volume of the food chains!

And it will include practically every merchandise classification from food to drugs, from beauty aids to soft goods, from hard goods to home furnishings, furniture, sports goods, etc. Clearly, retailing of this scope must have two major effects:

1. It must compel most mass retailers to reshape some of their policies and practices.

2. It must compel most manufacturers to reshape some of their marketing policies.

What Low-Margin Retailers Won't Do

This is the point where we might very well pause in order to make some necessary reservations concerning the fast-moving low-margin outlets.

1. Low-margin retailing will *not* take over *all* mass retailing.

2. Even though most of our traditional department stores and chains will not be able to meet discount margins of 22% to 24%, these older forms of mass retailing will continue to operate, will even continue to grow (although perhaps at a slower rate).

3. Some of the low-margin retailers, like their more traditional elders, will acquire a haunch, a paunch and a jowl. They will accumulate overhead. They will have to lift their margins. This has already happened in some instances. Whether they will *ever* require margins of 36% to 40% and more, is certainly debatable; it could happen in time. But it is reasonably certain that even those that become "soft" fastest will not get up to 36% margin for a number of years.

4. The death rate among the low-margin retailers will mount. This is *inevitable*. Amateurs are rushing in. Some are poorly heeled; shoe-string operators are clearly coming in. In some areas, too many low margin outlets have been opened too fast. (This is true, for example, in several areas in California.)

5. It is possible that, over a decade or more, the present crop of low-margin outlets may no longer be low-margin retailers at all. The mail-order chains, the food chains, the drug chains, *all* started out as *low*-margin retailers. They are all *high*-margin retailers today. It is not impossible that the existing low-margin operators will go through the same cycle. But manufacturers must plan their merchandising basically for the next several years—and, for the next five years at least, the dominant development

in mass retailing will be the *low-margin* requirements of these new forms of retailing.

6. Most traditional mass retailers will *try*, in various ways and in various degrees, to meet low margins with low margins. This has already happened in some merchandising classifications in department stores, variety stores, drug stores, food stores. It will happen in additional merchandise classifications in these outlets.

Thus, the $4 billion dollar total of the low-margin outlets must, at least, be *doubled* if we are to get a true picture of the scope of low-margin retailing. Perhaps it should be *tripled*.

In brief, more retail volume, in more classifications, is today being moved at low-margins by retailers of every description than at any previous period in the history of modern retailing!

The trend in this direction will not merely continue; it will accelerate. We are coming into an *age of low-margin retailing*—the inevitable end result of the pre-sold brand.

And that, too, must have a profound impact on the total marketing policies of innumerable manufacturers.

"Closed-Door" Chains Cut Costs

The "older" forms of discount retailing are well known. It is interesting to note that these older discount chains are, themselves, taking steps to meet the challenge of the newer forms. The "established" discount chains:

1. Are turning to the closed-door concept—a concept, by the way, which they really pioneered in a different form and then dropped (although they rarely actually charged for a membership card or limited membership to unions, etc.).

2. Are expanding by the merger route. These mergers involve both other discount chains and other forms of retailing.

The *newer forms* of low-margin retailing involve primarily the "closed-door" retailers and the "mill" outlet. While both of these terms are pretty well comprehended, some confusion still exists with respect to each of these two new types of low-margin retailing. We offer, therefore, the following brief description of each:

The closed-door discount chain is a "membership" form of retailing. The customer buys a membership card—the usual price is about $2. (This may be an annual fee or a lifetime fee.)

Presumably, only card-holding members may shop in a closed-door store. In some of these closed-door stores, the shopper must actually insert her card in a device that opens the entrance turnstile. Others unquestionably are not quite so fussy in this respect. But the majority definitely insist on the membership card.

It aspires to be, and usually is, a complete department store of a new type. It usually includes a large food department. Its stores now tend to occupy over 100,000 square feet.

In many closed-door discount chains, membership is limited to specific segments of the population. Some sell only to employes of the federal government; others only to employes of state, county or city governments. Some sell only to union members or to employes of specifically-listed large corporations.

Because it is a "closed door" operation—its doors closed to non-members—the closed-door chain rarely advertises in newspapers. Its advertising is usually limited to direct-mail to its members—a considerable savings in advertising costs and therefore a distinct competitive cost advantage.

Also, it unquestionably obtains a degree of shopper *loyalty* from its members that perhaps no other form of mass retailing can equal. Shopper disloyalty lifts retailing costs—so here is another low-cost advantage enjoyed by the closed-door discount chain.

The closed-door discount store enjoys still other competitive advantages. For example:

1. Government and union workers, and workers in some giant factors, are in a fixed income group, showing earnings on a continuity income basis not subject to drastic employment-unemployment cycles.

2. Because such workers generally have similar incomes and consumption habits, the store can carry a narrower, but deep assortment of merchandise, primarily in the popular-priced category, thus maintaining rapid turnover and lower rate of markdowns.

3. The economic solidarity of this customer group is such that extension of credit and check cashing services can be offered with less than normal risk.

Now, let's turn to the mill chain.

Mill Chains Use 30% Concessionnaire

While the closed-door concept was getting off the ground on the West Coast, the "mill" chain, another type of low-margin operation, was getting started on the East Coast. (Interestingly, it is spreading west while the closed-door is spreading east—and, before long, these two types of chains will meet head-on. The "mill" store is so called because it actually started in abandoned New England textile mills.

These low-margin chains started primarily as soft-goods outlets—but now are branching out into much the same categories as the closed-door outlets. (Their turnover on soft goods averages a remarkable *14 times* annually —a figure that the variety chains, for example, on their soft goods, cannot even approach.) Today, their dollar sales mix would be, roughly 70% soft goods—30% hard goods. In soft goods, their emphasis is on women's and children's apparel.

Their gross margins range between 20% and 30%. That would be substantially under the margins of the traditional chains and department stores. It has been estimated that their selling prices for comparable soft goods lines are about 15% lower, on the average, than established competitors.

Their new stores are modern in every respect. They tend to hover around the 100,000 square-foot mark. Their competitive threat to established merchants is underscored by the fact that, when two of these mill stores opened near a large Massachusetts suburban shopping center, volume in the shopping center fell off by some 30%!

The mill store, like the closed-door store (the mill store does *not* use the paid membership concept) leans heavily on the leased department operator. Over-all, perhaps 30% of total dollar volume in the mill chain is done by concessionaires—with the individual figure running from 10% to well over 50%. Moreover, as the mill stores add more non-soft-goods departments, these departments tend to be leased.

The mill stores (like the closed-door stores) are essentially self-service; even shopping carts and turnstiles are used in some. Because of self-service, their wage costs tend to total a low 6% to 8% of sales—which would be on the order of one-half to one-third the payroll cost in department stores. This, plus their high turnover rate, are two competitive weapons which enable them to give established mass retailers virile rivalry.

Even some manufacturers are opening discount chains. For example, Spartan Industries is a popular priced apparel manufacturer. It is a leading manufacturer of low-priced apparel for men, women, and children. It recently entered the retail field through the establishment of two discount centers. Further expansion in this direction is anticipated in the near future and this venture could become comparable in size to its apparel manufacturing business.

Each unit carries the name of Spartan Department Store. They will average 75,000 square feet in size and are expected to attain sales of $4 million per unit. The establishment of the stores is similar in operation to many other chains as neither the land nor the buildings are owned by the company. Both are leased and, therefore, the operation can be initiated and carried through to completion with a minimum cash outlay. It is anticipated that 20% or 25% of the products sold by these outlets will be manufactured by Spartan Industries. Lines by other manufacturers will also be displayed and a portion of each store will be leased. Both soft and hard goods will be sold.

New Developments in Discount Area

Here are some additional straws in the discount wind:

C. D. Kaufman, president of Kay Jewelry Stores, Washington, D.C., had this to say:

Alert to the vast merchandising changes that are currently developing, and after considerable study, it was concluded that it would be advantageous to the company, in the long run, to enter the field of the so-called discount department stores that are currently opening all over the United States. From published figures, we know that they have done billions of dollars worth of volume during the past 12 months; therefore, we felt it incumbent to be certain we were not missing the advent of a new merchandising vehicle.

Embarking on an aggressive campaign to enter the retail discount field, Franklin Stores Corp. acquired Barker's, Inc., in Connecticut.

"Franklin's future lies in discounting," Albert Rubenstein, president of the 179-store women's and children's apparel chain told Fairchild News Service . . .

Arthur Rubloff & Co. is one of the nation's foremost developers of shopping centers. Zayre Corp. is a New England based soft-goods discounter. Eagle Foods is an aggressive Illinois-Iowa food chain. All three have gotten together for the construction of a 120,000-square-foot shopping center to open on a 12-acre tract at Lincoln Hwy., U.S. 30 and Western, in the Greater Chicago area. The Zayre unit will occupy 60,000 square feet while Eagle will be alongside with a 22,500-square-foot super market. The remaining footage will be occupied by drug and variety stores, a restaurant, and a gasoline service station.

Another developer is planning to open a center with a 180,000-square-foot unit, Korvette unit, an 80,000-square-foot J. C. Penney unit, and a 40,000-square-foot unit for F. W. Woolworth Co. When completed, this center will contain about 500,000 square feet of retail space.

This is a fascinating development—Korvette, Penney and Woolworth actually bedding down together in a shopping center!

National Bellas Hess, Inc., was weighing plans for two more Government Employes Exchange (GEX) closed-door stores in addition to three additional units already under construction last spring.

Each of the three GEX stores in operation in early 1961 was running at an annual volume rate of $8 million to $10 million, the president disclosed. The Oklahoma City unit has approximately 51,000 members, the Atlanta unit 39,000, and the Norfolk store 40,000 members.

For the six months ended January 31, 1961, the first half of National Bellas' fiscal year, GEX accounted for about 15% of the firm's net earnings of $863,000. Only two or three currently operating GEX stores were in business throughout the entire six month period.

While there is no definite number of units set for the GEX expansion program, the president said, if the present rate of store openings continues, this subsidiary could account for about 50% of the parent company's earnings in three or four years.

A sidelight on the GEX operation is that the stores are operating in the black almost from the point of opening. The membership fees received during the first 60 days are practically enough to wipe out the pre-opening expenses, the president said. . .

News reports such as those just quoted are appearing in the press regularly.

Clearly, the low-margin retailers of all types are stepping as high as a major-domo!

They will, in some instances, stub their toes. They will have their problems. They are even now becoming so numerous that they are beginning to compete *with each other* as well as with traditional retailers.

But there is no question that they are finally

ushering in an era of low-margin retailing that will be of so large a dimension as to compel innumerable manufacturers to re-study major areas of their marketing policies.

LOW-MARGIN RETAILERS AIM FOR NON-MERCHANDISING

Traditionally, retailing has looked to the *merchandising* function for its net profit. But now—the giant retailer is beginning to find that other sources of income can become exceedingly attractive. These "other" sources of income are *non*-merchandising sources.

In at least a few sizable traditional retail organizations, the non-merchandising function will contribute, in 1961, from 10% to 20% of the total net profit!

Will non-merchandising some day account for 50% of total net profit for some large retail organizations? It surely will—and that day is not 'way off in 1975 or even off to 1965. In fact, it is here right now—because the closed-door discount chains account, in some instances, for almost 100% of their income from non-merchandising functions.

The number of large retail organizations in which this will happen will multiply—rapidly! It will become a *competitive* necessity. *Discount chains* with large non-merchandising income will compel *other* large retailers to follow suit.

Ultimately, the *non*-merchandising functions will contribute a larger percentage of the total net profit of an *increasing number* of giant retailers than will the *merchandising* functions.

The head of one closed-door discount chain underscores its non-merchandising role in this way: "We operate something like a shopping center. We are *landlords and management consultants*, although we obtain the rights to *control personnel and costs within each department*."

Get Income from Closed-Door Memberships, Concessionaire Rentals

The closed-door chain's income from memberships furnishes a cash flow of enormous importance. Thus, one closed-door discount chain reported total memberships in six stores of 370,000! It charges a $2 membership fee. On an annual basis, this represents a cash flow of some $740,000! *And that, in turn, would represent the net profit on gross volume of a food super chain of no less than $74,000,000!*

In the case of variety chains, drug chains and department stores, the comparative figure would be equally startling. With this cash flow, there is not too much difficulty in opening one store after another. This is low-cost money-management of an extremely high order—and *money* management today is, if anything, *more* important in modern mass retailing than *merchandising* management!

In addition, there is another source of cash flow, for the closed-door chain and for many other discount chains—income from rentals to concessionaires. In many instances, concessionaires pay several month's rent *in advance*.

Add cash flow from memberships to cash flow from payments on rentals—and it is clear that the closed-door discount chain enjoys a money-management competitive advantage that poses real problems for traditional, high-cost chains and department stores.

That is a phrase of non-merchandising operation that is relatively new. It is bound to compel other mass retailers either to find parallel sources of non-merchandising income, or to find other sources of non-merchandising income, or to strengthen their present sources of non-merchandising income. Very likely, all three approaches will be used by most traditional mass retailers because, very clearly, the retailer with the largest non-merchandising income enjoys a powerful competitive advantage.

More Profit, Less Risk in Real Estate Income for Retailer

In an editorial *Chain Store Age* remarked:

Chains that go into the shopping-center development business usually do so primarily to lock up desirable sites for their own stores.

As they get into the complex real estate operation, however, they can lose sight of the prime objective. So far as the shopping-center development is concerned, the chain runs a risk of becoming a *developer* first and a *retailer* second.

If the current thinking of some giant retailing management executives is correct, this editorial observation misses a fundamental point, to wit: There may not only be *greater net profit* for the large retailer as a real estate promoter than as a merchant—there may also be *less risk*.

Mass retailing's net profit percentage from inventory turnover tends to be microscopic; moreover, it simply cannot be *dramatically* increased. But a successful real estate promotion can throw off a handsome net on the invested dollar.

Right here is the genesis of the retail move toward non-merchandising income. Inventory turnover no longer offers *dynamic* net profit growth; but non-merchandising functions are fully capable of juicy net profit growth.

This same chain-store trade publication remarked:

Developing your own shopping centers may be the best solution for some chains in certain situations, but it is probably still true that the money and effort a retailer puts into bricks and mortar could be more profitably utilized in merchandise and merchandising.

Some giant retailers currently dispute that conclusion. More—and still more—giant retailers will dispute that conclusion. And the low-margin chains, with their brilliant exploitation of new *and* old non-merchandising sources of income, will prod the established mass retailers toward real estate and other non-merchandising functions.

Giantism in *any* field ultimately leads to a mounting emphasis on real estate, on securities, on corporate maneuvers, on tax factors. This has been true of *manufacturers*. It is now becoming true of *retailers*.

Finance Surpassing Merchandising as Retail Management Skill?

Indeed, it is entirely probable that, more and more, the top heads of these giant retail organizations will be selected more for their knowledge of real estate procedures, taxes and corporate securities than for their retail merchandising knowledge.

There is every reason to expect that the investment banker, the real estate consultant, transportation and warehouse experts, the financial consultant (as well as assorted security market specialists) will play increasingly important roles in the policies of giant retailers. This will hardly raise the importance of the merchandising functions of these organizations.

As more of the retailer's total dollar went into real estate, warehousing, financing, taxes and other non-merchandising functions, it was inevitable that these requirements would, in time, challenge the traditional spot of merchandising as the prime focus of retail executive attention. This, in turn, required changes in the organizational blueprint—changes that inevitably down-graded the merchandising function from its former dominant spot on the organizational chart.

When top retail management concerns itself increasingly with non-merchandising functions —then this attitude must, inevitably, be reflected right down the executive line. And, in some large retail organizations this is happening—right now.

The management of *finances* is becoming more important, to some retail giants, than the management of *merchandising*. The promotion of *real estate* is becoming more important than the promotion of *merchandise*. The acquisition of *other companies* for corporate profit is becoming more important than the acquisition of merchandise for resale. Naturally, the executives responsible for these non-merchandising functions move up on the organizational chart.

The capital requirements of large retail businesses are now a prime problem. Expansion objectives and the cost factor combine to bring this about. The mass retailer who does a superb job of merchandising but a mediocre job of financial management will not move ahead fast.

Of course, our retail giants have been getting a growing percentage of total net profit from a spreading variety of allowances. At least some large retailers earn a larger net profit from allowances than from floor merchandising.

But allowances are by no means the largest single source of non-merchandising income for giant retailers. *Other* and *newer* sources of non-merchandising income are beginning to assume respectable totals in the net profit figures of some big retailers. Some of these other sources provide retail giants with a larger non-merchandising income than all allowances combined!

For example, there is the growing practice among some large retailers of buying up other organizations (not necessarily retail) with an attractive tax loss position. One drug chain bought out an apparel chain which was attractive because it had a $5 million tax loss. This might be called the corporate routine—pieces of paper, in the form of an exchange of securities, become important sources of income. This means that corporate or financial management, as distinguished from merchandising management, may be destined to become more important in the management functions of more large retailers—and, of course, this is already the case in a number of instances.

One of the giant food chains, in a report to stockholders, states that its real estate subsidiary—which builds complete shopping centers —is now the *largest shopping center developer in the nation!* Isn't it reasonable to conclude that some of the chief executive officers of this food chain may spend as much time in *real estate* as they do in merchandising?

Incidentally, this same food chain reported that approximately 10% of its net profit for the last fiscal year came from "other sources." This is a healthy percentage of total net profit—and it is obvious that "other sources" means sources other than the merchandising function but not including allowances.

It would not be astonishing were this same food chain to report, say in two years, that 20% of its total net profit comes from "other sources." And since these "other sources" would not include allowances, it is clear that when allowances are added to "other sources," as should be done—(allowances definitely are *not* merchandising)—then this food chain may soon be getting the *major share* of its total net profit from non-merchandising functions.

A small drug chain builds office space above some of its store units and rents this space to doctors as a professional building! The office space rental may challenge the net profit on operations of the store!

And yet, another example involves the growing practice by some large retailers of setting up subsidiary organizations to service other retailers. In the food field, for example, several food chains have set up subsidiaries to centralize the non-food function. In a few instances, these non-food subsidiaries are actually servicing other food retailers as well as their own stores; they are becoming a new form of service jobber.

Clearly, this will, in time, provide a new source of income that is not what tradition would define as a *retail merchandising* source of income. Certainly this income does not come from the movement of merchandise on the floor of the stores of the parent retailer.

Right here is the basic point involved. For generations, the basic—*if not the exclusive*—source of net profit for the retailer came from the movement of merchandise *on the retail floor*. Manufacturer's trade margins have been premised on this function. Now this situation is in the process of change.

The development of the holding company concept in mass retailing—which is a strong trend—involves corporate maneuvers that can throw off extraordinarily large net profit primarily through the exchange of pieces of paper. This is a non-merchandising function.

The leased department represents non-merchandising income. It is currently enjoying a substantial boom in most major chains. It is a non-merchandising income for the retail landlord because the merchandising is done by an outsider.

Manufacturing, Warehousing Become Source of Income for Retailer

Retailers are going into manufacturing. This promises to become a powerful trend, particularly as giant retailers concentrate on their own brands. Profits from the *manufacturing* operation are *not retail* merchandising profits. So here is another source of non-merchandising income for a retail organization.

The store-controlled brand, in still other of its aspects, provides non-merchandising income. Since the store-controlled brand is, right now, being almost feverishly expanded by large retailers, it promises to become a substantial contributor to non-merchandising income. (In some instances, retailers will sell their controlled brands to non-competing outlets—this, obviously, will throw off net profit that cannot be classified as *retail* merchandising profit.)

The wholesale-warehousing function performed by many retailers is not a *retail* merchandising operation, strictly speaking. It is only indirectly related to the movement of merchandise on the retail floor. In some instances, this function is lodged in a subsidiary organization which means it receives its own accounting analysis. So here too is a source of non-merchandising income.

Credit retailing involves financial aspects that are not strictly retailing merchandising. The trend is for retailers to form a credit financing subsidiary. Since all mass retailing is turning to credit, the astute management of the financial aspects of the retail credit function is expected to throw off a net profit *apart* from the merchandising operation. (Department stores were recently urged by a store controller to separate income from credit operations from other income because it has become a *major source* of income in some departments, yet it never has been separately accounted.)

In 1958, May Department Stores Co. established the May Stores Shopping Centers, Inc., a wholly owned real estate subsidiary, to which it transferred ownership of present and future May shopping centers. Future expansion in particular is to be financed principally through this new wholly owned real estate subsidiary. Stockholders were told:

"It is contemplated that ownership or control of various present and future suburban shopping centers and single store properties will be transferred to the subsidiary. It will hold or control stores leased to The May Department Stores Co. and stores leased to other tenants in May shopping centers. New construction of stores and shopping centers will be financed primarily by loans on these properties.

"The new real estate subsidiary will also provide a more precise and convenient method for our management to separate our retail store operations from our real estate operations and financing."

The hands-off attitude of many merchants with *respect to real estate operations* was labeled an "illusion" by Frank Clark Jr., vp of May, in a talk before the New York Society of Security Analysts.

Mr. Clark said: "Many retailers say: *'We are merchants—not* real estate men—and, therefore, will not invest in brick and mortar.' We feel that this attitude is an illusion . . .

"A department store operator is in the real estate business whether he likes it or not. We happen to like it, and as a result of our real estate policies, we are very substantially adding to the value of our stock for our stockholders."

Mr. Clark referred in this talk to the recent organization of May Stores Corp., with departments for negotiation, construction, property management and research.

"In the last 10 years, the major population shifts both within and between metropolitan areas *have created a constantly increasing real estate opportunity for the department store operator,"* Mr. Clark stated.

The head of Food Fair stated that real estate is the *number one* requirement of successful food super operation!

Trend Is to Big Expansion, Requiring Big Financing

The J. L. Hudson Co. owns Shopping Centers Inc., which in turn owns two huge centers now operating and which will ultimately own four giant centers. That should provide substantial non-merchandising income.

Three of Chicago's large retailers developed and operate a suburban shopping center. The $18 million project in Mount Prospect, about 29 miles northwest of the Loop, is owned equally (via the formation of the Randhurst Corp.) by Montgomery Ward & Co., Carson Pirie Scott & Co., and Wieboldt Stores. Here

we see an indication of the innumerable forms that real estate development by large retailers will take.

The race to build retail volume was never so swift. And, over the next three to five years, its present swift pace will be considerably accelerated. But expansion is *no longer* to come primarily through *merchandising*—expansion is to come through acquisition, through merger, through such corporate developments as the holding company.

Expansion must be financed. *Big* expansion demands *big* financing.

And expansion by our retail giants will be big: *very* big.

Consequently, the management of finances *in total* becomes a major preoccupation of giant retailers. One manifestation of this fundamental requirement is the establishment of accounts receivable subsidiaries—a non-merchandising function.

However, even more important is the entire range of functions in retailing that come under the head of "financial management"—a non-merchandising subject. The expansion era of retailing puts a premium on the management of finances such as retailing never before contemplated. *A good banking connection may be more important than good suppliers!*

Given a choice between astute *financial* management and astute *merchandising* management—and there is little doubt that the giant retailer whose management of *finances* is tops will run competitive circles around the giant retailer whose *merchandising* is tops.

Management attention necessarily gravitates toward the major management problem. Today and tomorrow, in giant retailing, the major management problem will revolve around the management of finances, *not* around the management of merchandising!

This does not imply that merchandising is to be neglected. But it does suggest, indeed it *dictates*, that merchandising be delegated to a secondary position.

And this, in turn, means secondary not only to the management of money—but also secondary to the management of real estate; and secondary, too, to the collective host of other non-merchandising functions that we have charted.

Allowances Big Income Source

Then there is the matter of allowances—a substantial source of non-merchandising income.

It is impossible to compile a complete list of the allowances giant retailers get. But the following very incomplete list is long enough to make self-evident the flight of large retailers from their traditional merchandising functions:

1. Cooperative advertising allowances.
2. Payments for interior displays, including floor fixtures, shelf-extenders, dump displays, "A" locations, extra facings, aisle displays, overhead banners, general promotional cooperation, etc.
3. Payments for window display space—plus installation costs.
4. P.M.'s for salespeople.
5. Contests for buyers, salespeople, etc.
6. Allowances for a variety of warehousing functions.
7. Payments for seasonal inventories.
8. Demonstrators.
9. Label allowance.
10. Coupon handling allowance.
11. Free goods.
12. Guaranteed sales.
13. Local research work done through retailer.
14. Delivery costs to individual stores of large retailers.
15. Payments for mailings to store lists.
16. Liberal return privileges.
17. Contributions to favorite charities of store personnel.
18. Contributions of infinite variety to special store anniversaries and to store openings. (The great hoopla at the opening of giant new stores is largely financed by manufacturers, brokers, sales agencies, wholesalers.)
19. Payments for use of special fixtures owned by the store.
20. Payments for store improvements—including painting.
21. An infinite variety of promotional and merchandising allowances.
22. Payment of part of salary of retail salespeople.
23. Trade deals of innumerable types.
24. Time spent in actual selling on retail floor by manufacturers' salesmen.
25. Inventory adjustments of many types.
26. Transportation allowances.

That's a pretty impressive list. But it's far—very far—from being complete.

However, allowances have been around for decades; they simply have been multiplying. The *newer* aspects of the non-merchandising role of the mass retailer involve the aspects that we have summarized here from our previous deep study on this subject.

And the *newest* aspects of this total area of non-merchandise as a major source of income for large retailers have been furnished by the closed-door discount chain. Its ability, by its unique concept, to open huge stores with a minimum investment (even the land and the building may not be owned) results in a new form of retail *financial competition* that is, if anything, destined to be *more* troublesome to at least some of our major traditional retailers than the low-margin *merchandising* competition of the closed-door chains.

For example, the GEM closed-door chain shows a 30% return on investment. Since it leases all departments, it claims it can open a 100,000 square foot unit for $125,000, which is fantastic. Income from membership could cover that sum! *That* is modern retail non-merchandising.

Moreover, it must be understood that it is these new and old sources of non-merchandising income that account, in considerable measure, for the ability of the closed-door discount chain in particular, and for the other forms of discount chains only to a somewhat lesser extent, to operate profitably at low-margins.

In other words, their low-margin operation rests *at least as much on non-merchandising skills as on merchandising skills!*

And their ability to show an amazing return on investment without question stems from their new financial and other non-merchandising concepts which enable them to open new stores with a minimum investment.

So the low-margin outlets will not only *compel* many mass retailers to reform their *merchandising* operation—but will also compel them to improve upon, to broaden, to strengthen their non-merchandising functions.

DISCUSSION QUESTIONS

Mr. Weiss, who has been associated with the mass communications industry for many years, pictures the "low margin retailers" as a kind of shark-in-the-pool who have disturbed the peace and tranquility of American retailing. Most "low margin" retail operators depend in part for their success upon the proclivity of the American public to buy with the aid of little in-store personal selling.

1. Specifically, how does "low-margin" retailing owe part of its success to mass communications?

It is normally assumed that certain types of products, notably those which require skill in demonstration and involve intricate mechanisms in their operation are not amenable to sale through mass communications techniques, and therefore are not likely to be sold in low-margin high-turnover types of retail stores. Some products, however, which were thought to be "too complex" for mass pre-selling techniques have become standard fare for low-margin operations.

2. What products are still being sold principally with *personal selling* efforts which might actually be sold *impersonally* with mass communications?

2. Franchising—New Scope
for an Old Technique

WILLIAM P. HALL

... which can be a lifesaver for the independent wholesale and retail merchant, in the face of increasing competition from corporate chains and discount operations.

- Why are well-run franchise programs the most complete answer to the critical problems of independent wholesalers and retailers?
- In the particular case of voluntary wholesaler-retailer franchising programs, what does the experience of leading companies show about the financial advantages obtainable?
- What are the most important services, requirements, and other features of wholesaler-retailer franchise programs?
- What problems must be solved to make franchising successful?

Franchise selling has rapidly evolved since the 1930's into an important and dynamic force in American merchandising. And today, for example, in food merchandising, wholesaler-retailer organizations using either the voluntary or cooperative form of franchising are battling toe-to-toe with corporate chains whose percentage of retail food sales has remained practically unchanged in recent years. Meanwhile, retailers affiliated with franchise programs have rapidly expanded their share of retail food sales from 29% in 1947 to almost 50% at present.

Yet not until the last few years has much attention been given to this subject. Only as recently as 1960 the International Franchise Association was formed—the one true measure of arrival on the U.S. economic scene.

As we shall see, franchise programs take many forms. It is not possible to cover them all adequately in one article. In this discussion

I shall focus on programs that assist the independent retailer and his independent wholesaling counterpart to remain independent, profitable, and competitive in the face of the growth of corporate chains and discounters in U.S. merchandising.

The wholesaler-retailer franchising concept combines the economies and strengths of centralized buying and merchandising with the vigor and resourcefulness of local, private retail ownership. Even though franchising arrangements vary widely, as illustrated by examples in this article, the success of any program is dependent on the maintenance of a sensitive and workable balance between strong centralized wholesaler direction and local retailer incentive.

INDEPENDENTS' PLIGHT

Today, independent retailers and wholesalers share the same problems in more or less the same degree and for the same causes.

Dun & Bradstreet, in its summary of wholesaling results for 1961, commented: "It has been said that the only difference between a rut and a grave is one of dimensions. To many a wholesaler, unable or unwilling to pioneer new approaches to changing markets and faced with rising costs, the rut has indeed become long and deep." [1] This study of 24 wholesale lines showed that median net profits on net sales were lower in 11 of 24 lines than in the

---

♦ SOURCE: Reprinted by permission from the editors of the *Harvard Business Review*, in the January–February, 1964, issue, pp. 60–72.

[1] "14 Important Ratios in 24 Wholesale Lines," *Dun's Review and Modern Industry*, November 1962, p. 94.

recession year of 1960. Meanwhile, failures reached a postwar peak in number and dollar liabilities.

And what about retailers? Comparing the financial ratios for 12 retail lines in 1961, Dun & Bradstreet stated, "The figures aptly show how the discounter is taking the measure of his conventional competitor." The majority of retailers "merely are maintaining an above-water position on profits, inventory, and debt." [2]

To be sure, the expansion of mass discount merchandising is a contributor to the plight of many independent retailers and wholesalers, but there are other factors. These include:

1. Continued growth of corporate chains.
2. Growth of shopping centers whose lease requirements shut out many smaller independents.
3. Decline of the population of small, country towns and the concurrent decline of independent stores serving these communities.

Compounding these economic, external problems are the historical shortcomings of doing business which are common to small independent retailers. The typical retailer learns "the hard way." He has little sophistication in inventory management, accounting, or merchandising. In recent field interviews with 24 small Midwestern dry-goods and variety retailers, I found not one with a regular local advertising program.

The house of the typical wholesaler serving such a group of independents is built on shifting sands. His credit costs are high because of the personnel required to handle hundreds and often thousands of accounts, bad debt experience, and high capital commitment to slow accounts. Inventory turnover is slow. Worst of all, multiple solicitation of the small retailer by competing salesmen is a gross economic waste paid for by the retailer and his customer. In one Des Moines store last spring the manager complained. "You are the fifth person to come into the store this morning, and each has been a salesman!"

Attempts to Innovate

In this competitive economy, independent merchants are clearly faced with the proposition that they must innovate or die.

Wholesalers and retailers are trying various alternatives to eliminate some of the shortcomings mentioned. For example:

Cash-and-Carry. In 1958, Anderson Mercantile Company in Omaha, Nebraska, was faced with losses on its variety wholesaling business. "After considering various alternatives," said the president, W. N. Bailey, "we decided to go cash-and-carry. It was a tough decision, taking careful planning of break-even costs and potential volume." Anderson made the move in 1959, dropping all salesmen, eliminating the credit department, and putting all merchandise in marked bins to be picked up by store owners. The basement layout is like a supermarket, with shopping carts and a cash checkout counter. (To overcome the disadvantages of a strictly pickup business, Anderson offered to ship merchandise with an added 5% charge for handling and shipping.)

Although volume did not respond immediately, sales turned up sharply in 1961, and a modest profit was shown in the same year. A number of retailers in the area comment that Anderson's lower prices have helped them to stay in business.

Cooperative Groups. Another approach taken by retailers is to turn cooperative. Allied Clothiers in Kansas City is a small, retail-owned cooperative, serving independent dry-goods stores. Retail members are limited to better accounts; sales efforts are limited to supervision and new member solicitation; and buying is by order blank, with periodic merchandising displays in Kansas City. From its modern warehouse Allied serves its members at a gross margin of about 8%, a figure well below the marking required by many conventional wholesalers competing in the vicinity.

On July 10, 1963, an article in *The Wall Street Journal* [3] pointed out that "a growing number of independent appliance retailers around the country have been pooling their buying power in cooperatives." As an answer to discounters and department stores, the co-ops offer such benefits as buying concessions, larger inventory selection, common warehousing, and joint delivery service.

Wholesaling Specialists. The answer of some wholesalers has been to specialize in a limited number of lines and to serve largely the high-volume accounts. Heyman Distributing Com-

---

[2] "14 Important Ratios in 12 Retail Lines—1961," *Dun's Review and Modern Industry,* October 1962, p. 64.

[3] Scott R. Schmedel, *"Rivaling Discounters:* More Appliance Dealers Join Buying Co-Ops to Cut Costs, Vary Stock," p. 1.

pany in Chicago has concentrated on a few well-established popular, soft-goods lines such as Buster Brown and Hanes (hosiery and underwear). According to Bureau of Census data, growth of wholesalers in soft goods and general merchandise appears to be concentrated among specialists (shoes, hosiery, and the like), while general-line wholesalers showed a sharp drop in numbers from 1954 to 1958.

Common Shortcomings

All of these approaches have achieved some degree of success. However, the programs often have one important shortcoming. They fail to offer the means to strengthen merchandising weaknesses found in varying degrees among most independent retailers. Some, such as the cash-and-carry operations, have passed on cost savings but offer no merchandising help at all. Others, such as the co-ops, offer varying degrees of assistance. As for the wholesaling specialists, they may offer strong support on the lines they carry, performing a function very close to that of a leased department operator, but they usually make little or no contribution to over-all store merchandising programs.

Something more is needed.

MOST COMPLETE ANSWER

It is through well-run franchise programs that independent wholesalers and retailers have found one of the most complete answers to their problems. This movement offers the retailer a broad merchandising program which completely equips him to take on all forms of retail revolutions.

In its early, historical application, a franchise was "a system under which a manufacturer granted to certain dealers the right to sell his product or service, in generally defined areas, in exchange for a promise to promote and merchandise the product in a specific manner." [4] As franchise selling has evolved to encompass a wider segment of the economy, the definition has broadened to include "any contract under which independent retailers or wholesalers are organized to act in concert with each other or with manufacturers to distribute given products or services." [5] Typically,

the franchise agrees to operate his business within certain prescribed limitations and in keeping with agreed-on buying and merchandising programs.

In short, franchise programs now include all levels of manufacture and distribution, not simply the manufacture-retailer relationship.

Types of Programs

Four types of franchising have evolved. In each type, retail volume through franchised outlets represents a significant portion of merchandise volume.

Manufacturer-Retailer. In this category, manufacturers may franchise (a) the entire retail outlet, (b) a single department, or (c) a line within a department in particular retail outlets.

Manufacturers who franchise entire retail outlets include producers of passenger cars and trucks, farm equipment, earth-moving equipment, petroleum, shoes, and paint. Franchising may be a significant factor in these industries. Virtually all new passenger cars and trucks are sold through a franchise dealer system. And an estimated 90% of all gasoline is sold through franchised, independently operated, retail service stations. Curiously, the leading trade association in the petroleum industry declares that it has no publicly available data on the importance or practices of franchising within its industry.

Turning to the more specialized programs, an example of a manufacturer operating franchise departments in a store is Mode O'Day Corporation, a California soft-goods manufacturer. Mode O'Day, under a franchise arrangement begun in 1933, consigns merchandise to some 756 stores, mostly specialty shops dealing in reasonably priced style apparel. By not owning the merchandise, the store owner avoids the inventory risks inherent in style goods, but makes a good living on the normal selling margin.

As for the practice of franchising lines within one department of a store, this is most prevalent with appliance, radio, and television manufacturers. It means that the retailer sells products of competing makers. With the exception of the highly selective distribution policies used by companies such as Magnavox, the manufacturer-dealer relationship in this type of franchise program appears to be far less secure than that in which the dealer works almost exclusively with one manufacturer.

Manufacturer-Wholesaler. The most outstanding example of this type of franchising is

[4] Charles M. Hewitt, "The Furor Over Dealer Franchises," *Business Horizons*, November 1958, p. 81.

[5] Leonard Knopa, "What Is Meant by Franchise Selling?" *Journal of Marketing*, April 1963, p. 37.

the soft drink industry. Most national manufacturers of soft drink syrups, including Coca-Cola, Pepsi-Cola, Royal Crown, and Seven-Up, franchise independent bottlers who, in turn, serve retail and institutional outlets of all types. Historically, automotive and appliance manufacturers have also signed up distributors under franchises to cover restricted territories, but this practice is changing. In recent years automotive sales have been more commonly made direct from factory to dealer, and factory branches have replaced the independent distributor in the appliance field (notable exceptions are Zenith and Whirlpool, which continue to use independent distributors).

Service Sponsor-Retailer. Probably the fastest growing category of franchising, this type was well described in Harry Kursh's, *The Franchise Boom.*[6] These programs generally are built around a service sponsored by the franchiser. A product, most likely a food or drink, may be involved. Sometimes the franchiser performs a manufacturing and/or wholesaling function for all or a part of the products.

Most members of the International Franchise Association are in this category. The association estimates that "in 1962 over 400 companies in 80 different fields franchised over 100,000 people."[7]

Included in this category are such industries and businesses as:

- Soft ice cream drive-ins (Tastee Freez).
- Food drive-ins (McDonalds, Do-Nut King).
- Restaurants (Howard Johnson, Aunt Jemima Kitchens).
- Motels (Holiday Inns).
- Auto rental (Avis, Hertz, National).
- Part-time help (Manpower, Kelly Girl).

The above list is far from all-inclusive, but it is representative of some of the leading names. Through a franchise system, Howard Johnson has become the largest national chain of restaurants; Tastee Freez has the largest drive-in program. Also, franchise systems are dominant in the auto-rental and part-time help industries. To the reader with a financial bent, a review of the revenue records and return on capital of the publicly owned companies in the group above will reveal some of the fastest growing performance figures in the United States. (Tastee Freez has had financial prob-

lems, as some know, but these have resulted largely from its manufacture and financing of mobile truck units rather than from any basic fault in its soft ice cream program.)

Wholesaler-Retailer. There are two types of franchise programs in this category:

In *cooperative* programs retailers band together to form or buy wholesaling organizations that set standards under which new members may join in the cooperative. Members, in effect, "own" the wholesaling business and share in its profits. This type of cooperative becomes a franchise operation when it ceases to be merely a loose buying federation and adopts contractual merchandising obligations for its members. Two of the larger cooperative organizations in the food field are Associated Grocers and Certified Grocers of America.

In *voluntary* programs the wholesaler is a privately owned, for-profit company which signs up independent retailers on a "voluntary" franchise basis. This movement includes both national franchise sponsors and wholesaler sponsors. National sponsors, such as the Independent Grocers Alliance, have national headquarters which franchise regional wholesalers, establish national standards, and may select merchandise for the group. These wholesalers, in turn, franchise IGA or NAPA retailers in their regions. The National Automotive Parts Association is a national sponsoring organization similar to IGA, franchising warehouse distributors of automotive parts; these distributors in turn franchise jobbers who then supply NAPA-approved parts to retail outlets.

Wholesaler sponsors are both national and regional in scope. Among the "nationals" are Butler Brothers, Walgreen Co., and Western Auto Supply Company, while among the "regionals" are Super Valu Stores, Inc., and Ace Hardware Corporation.

Selecting a Focus

From this discussion, it is apparent that franchise selling now takes many forms. Indeed, certain forms overlap since some wholesalers and service franchisers are active in manufacturing. Also, many voluntary wholesalers operate their own retail outlets and qualify, to a greater or lesser degree, as chains.

For the balance of this article, I will discuss only the wholesaler-retailer type of franchising. Within this category, the voluntary, for-profit wholesaler will receive the most attention. He is especially deserving of attention because his

---

[6] Englewood Cliffs, New Jersey, Prentice-Hall, Inc., 1962.

[7] *Ibid.,* p. 35.

growth has been more vigorous than that of the cooperatives and his programs are generally more forceful.

EXAMPLES OF SUCCESS

Successful voluntary wholesaler-retailer franchising programs have been developed for a wide range of products, including food, variety goods, hardware, drugs, tobacco, and automotive supplies.

Within various categories of merchandise, five of the largest Midwestern voluntary wholesalers were studied in some detail, both as to the extent of their business and as to the nature of their franchise programs. These companies are listed in Exhibit I.

Although not comparable in size to some of the very largest corporate chains, the first four of these companies are, nonetheless, among the 50 largest U.S. merchandising companies. Moreover, the profit performance of all five in terms of return on investment is among the best of all merchandising companies, regardless of size.

Walgreen Co.

Walgreen of Chicago is an example of a franchising organization with heavy company store commitments as well as manufacturing operations. The nation's largest drug chain,

Exhibit I. Five Companies Studied

Company	Merchandise	1962 Sales Volume (in millions)
Walgreen Co.	Drugs	$353
Western Auto Supply Company	Automotive parts, appliances, & hardware	304
Super Valu Stores, Inc.	Food	302
CityProducts Corporation (Butler Brothers)	Variety goods	295*
Ace Hardware Corporation	Hardware	40†

* About 50% of sales are to independent, affiliated (franchised) Ben Franklin stores.
† Estimated.

Walgreen has also moved into the manufacturing, wholesaling, and franchising of independent drug stores. Today, Walgreen operates some 470 retail drug stores in 36 states, and it serves over 1,900 "Walgreen Agency Drug Stores."

The franchise program of Walgreen greatly strengthens the retail base for its manufactured drugs, toiletries, and household items, which are sold only to company-owned or franchised stores. At the same time, the franchised retailer benefits from a well-advertised name, a protected territory, an exclusive product line, and group merchandising, advertising, store planning, employee training, and other programs.

Walgreen sales have increased from $182 million in 1953 to $353 million in 1962. Although return on equity has declined in recent years, the 11.2% return in 1962 compares favorably to the median return of 7.7% for 77 drug wholesalers covered by the Dun & Bradstreet survey in 1961.

Western Auto Supply Company

Originally a mail-order operation, Western Auto, based in Kansas City, was a pioneer in the franchise field, selling its first dealer store in 1935. The number of dealers has increased as follows:

Year	Dealers
1935	37
1940	1,728
1950	2,599
1962	3,851

Western Auto will have reached store number 4,000 well before the end of 1963. It also has 431 company-owned units. The stores are located in all states except one and are served from 16 strategically located warehouses and several service centers. The company also operates its own fleet of approximately 425 trucks and trailers.

In 1962 retail sales by company-owned stores were $118.7 million, an increase of 3.7% over 1961. Wholesale sales to associated stores and agencies were $184.9 million, an increase of 10.3%. Volume grew from $178 million in 1953 to $304 million in 1963. Now owned by Beneficial Finance Company, Western Auto's earnings were a reported $9.4 million in 1962, representing a return of 17.3% on equity. Listed by *Fortune* magazine as 38th in sales volume among the top 50 U.S. merchandising companies in 1962, Western Auto was third in return on equity.

Super Valu Stores, Inc.

Super Valu, with headquarters in Hopkins, Minnesota, is one of the oldest and largest of the franchising wholesalers. Faced with the impact of the corporate food-chain movement, Super Valu in 1930 started its voluntary operation. Today, it serves over 1,100 affiliated independent food stores in 12 north central states from 8 modern warehouses. The company works on a "blank check with order"

basis, offers an aggressive program of merchandising assistance, and operates on a low 4% gross profit margin.

The record of Super Valu in its changeover from a full-service wholesaler to the present voluntary program is a financial classic. As Exhibit II shows, since 1927 Super Valu's management has, on a gross profit margin reduced to less than 4%, increased capital turnover more than 20 times, while return on equity grew to more than 15% in 1962 (among the highest for all U.S. merchandising firms). Two major acquisitions of Midwestern wholesalers in 1963 will put Super Valu volume over $400 million.

Exhibit II. Selected Financial Statistics of Super Valu Stores, Inc.

Year	Net Sales (in millions)	Gross Profit	Capital Turnover	Return on Net Worth	Average Days Outstanding Receivables
1927	$ 6.2	12.2%	$ 3.4	(Loss)	46
1937	5.7	8.6	4.0	3.7%	21
1947	26.0	5.6	15.0	9.2	2
1957	152.1	4.2	21.6	13.2	5
1962	302.2	3.8	21.3	15.3	3

Butler Brothers

Now a part of City Products Corporation, Butler Brothers operate from its Chicago headquarters a successful franchise program in variety goods merchandise. About 2,400 franchised Ben Franklin Variety Stores, located in every state except Nevada and served by 8 large regional warehouses, belong to this voluntary group. For an average annual franchise fee running close to 1%, Butler offers its members aggressive merchandising programs, close supervision, and operating assistance.

Butler's financial figures are now included in City Products' results; also included as part of Butler operations are certain retailing operations. Even before acquisition by City Products in 1960, Butler's sales increased from $122 million in 1954 to $196 million in 1959, and return on capital was high. City Products' return on equity in 1962 was 10.7%.

Ace Hardware Corporation

Ace Hardware is a privately owned wholesaler serving 550 affiliated stores in 27 states from its single, modern, 450,000-square-foot

Chicago warehouse. Like Super Valu, Ace operates with a very low wholesaling cost (a 2% to 9% charge over cost, depending on factory or warehouse shipments). It also offers merchandising aids and inventory control plans.

Based on Dun & Bradstreet figures, Ace sales will exceed $40 million in 1963. Volume increased a reported 21% in 1962 over 1960 and was running 28% over 1962 in the first few months of 1963. Taking the change in net worth from 1961 to 1962 as a measure of profit, Ace showed a 16.7% return on net worth, compared to a median of 4.3% for 200 hardware wholesalers as reported by Dun & Bradstreet for 1961.

In all cases, the financial results of these wholesalers substantially exceed the average results for typical wholesalers in their merchandise fields. For none of them is there the evidence of grief common to their old-line contemporaries. The reason lies in the nature of the programs they sponsor.

FEATURES AND REQUIREMENTS

All successful voluntary wholesaler-retailer franchise programs incorporate the key idea of centralized buying and merchandising. To this degree, they function much as do corporate chains, but there the comparison ends. Unlike the corporate chain, the sponsoring wholesaler and his franchised retailer live together in a contractual, "voluntary" relationship. Many elements of this relationship are common from one voluntary group to another, but others show marked differences in structure and philosophy.

Franchise Fees

Of the five companies earlier described, three (Super Valu, Walgreen, and Western Auto) have no franchise fees and two (Ace Hardware and Butler Brothers) charge fees:
- Ace has an initial fee of only $300.
- Butler Brothers charges an annual fee representing a percentage of sales. The percentage declines as volume increases, as shown by these selected examples:

Volume Range	Annual Fee	Percent of Sales
$ 50,000–$ 59,999	$ 660	1.32%–1.10%
90,000– 99,999	950	1.05 –0.95
140,000– 159,999	1,275	0.91 –0.80
180,000– 199,999	1,425	0.75 –0.71

Except for Butler Brothers, most voluntary wholesalers do not appear to look on franchise fees as a significant revenue source. This policy is notably different from service franchisers whose franchise fees often form an important part of income.

Territorial Restrictions

Whether written into contracts or merely adhered to as a matter of policy, franchise programs generally provide some type of restriction on the location of franchises. The only written specification among the five examples is Walgreen's Retailer Agreement which guarantees the retailer "the exclusive right to sell Walgreen products in the [location described] . . . , at retail only."

Territorial restrictions in manufacturer-retailer franchises are currently under attack in federal courts. The Supreme Court in March 1963 returned for trial to the Federal District Court of Northern Ohio a test case in which the government challenged White Motor Company's franchise agreements with its dealers. According to The Wall Street Journal, Justice

William O. Douglas wrote that a vertical territorial limitation (an agreement like White Motor's between a manufacturer and its own dealers and distributors) "may or may not have the purpose or effect of stifling competition. We don't know enough of the economic and business stuff out of which these arrangements emerge to be certain." [8] In order to find out more about franchise agreements, the article reported that "both the Justice Department and the Federal Trade Commission are investigating franchises in several fields, including autos, air conditioning, hardware and shoes."

Buying Requirements

In the five examples of franchise programs, the only specific requirement for a retailer to buy a determined amount of merchandise from the wholesaler is found in the Walgreen contract, which sets a moderate annual minimum dollar purchase of its products by an agency store. However, the Walgreen agency stores are not limited in their purchases of any other products, including competitive lines.

In commenting on this subject, T. G. Harrison, chairman of the board of Super Valu, states:

"Nowhere in Super Valu Stores' relationship with its affiliated dealers, either in its franchise agreements or otherwise, are the retailers required to purchase a given percentage of their needs from Super Valu warehouses. In the first place, we think that such a requirement would be a violation of the Clayton Act as it would be a restraint of trade. In the second place, we do not think it is a good trade relationship, for we feel that Super Valu Stores, Inc., must earn its right to serve its stores. As a matter of actual results, Super Valu enjoys 60% to 65% of its affiliated retail stores' business, which would be 70%–72% of its retail stores' purchases."

Similarly, C. M. Wilson, Jr., treasurer of Western Auto, comments:

There is no restrictive covenant in it [franchise agreement] or otherwise which says he must buy all, or a given per cent of his merchandise from us. This means to us that we must be competitive in our prices and services, otherwise the dealer will take his business somewhere else.

Providing a high percentage of the needs of its retailers is one of the fundamentals of a

---

[8] March 5, 1963, p. 2.

good franchise program. Whether backed by some form of written agreement or not, successful programs are predicated on capturing 60% to 100% of each affiliated retailer's purchases. Rather than putting this objective in writing, most successful voluntary wholesalers achieve it by maintaining low competitive wholesaling costs, through supervisory programs, and through inventory control programs provided by the wholesaler. One independent (nonvoluntary) wholesaler summed it up by saying, "We do some business with affiliated stores, but we always reach a point where the store manager says he doesn't want to buy any more or he may get into trouble on his franchise."

Merchandise Pricing

Pricing policies vary widely among the five companies discussed, but all have the objective of providing wholesale costs to retailer group members which are below conventional wholesale costs. Low costs have been achieved by elimination of salesmen, by reduction of credit through concentration on better accounts, or by being virtually on a cash basis (like Super Valu) through improved purchasing power and modern, well-located warehouses. Salesmen's expenses may add 3% to 7% to typical wholesaler costs. With the franchisee buying all, or substantially all, of his requirements from his franchising wholesaler, sales contacts are reduced to order forms and the occasional calls of supervisors. As for specific store policies:

M. R. Kephart, Agency Division vice president of Walgreen, stated.

Pricing on Walgreen branded products normally allows the retailer to work on a 50%–5% discount, compared to about 32% allowed by other wholesale sources. Twice a year, during our one-cent sales, the structure changes to 50%–20%–5%. We also give quantity discounts on sundries which may run as high as 10%.

Ace Hardware operates on a cost-plus basis with markups over manufacturer prices running from 2% for factory shipments to 9% for shipments from its warehouse. According to one Ace franchise store owner, "With our merchandise costs, we can compete with any discounter in the country."

According to Harrison of Super Valu:

[Our company], for the most part, sells merchandise to its affiliated stores at its cost, to which a fee is added. The amount of the fee varies, depending upon the type of merchandise handled and the amount of merchandise purchased during a given week. Fee charges for the supplying of perishable merchandise, such as fresh fruits and vegetables, frozen foods, and so on, are higher than for supplying nonperishable merchandise, such as canned goods and packaged groceries. For example, the fee schedule for so-called dry groceries is 3% for the first $1,500 per week purchased, 2½% for the next $500, 2% for the next $500, and 1% for everything over $2,500.

Where Super Valu has arrangements for other suppliers to service its affiliated stores directly and bill the merchandise through Super Valu for rebilling to retail stores, Super Valu charges a fee of 2% of manufacturer's invoice less a cash discount which that manufacturer may offer.

In regard to Western Auto pricing policies, Wilson commented:

Our prices are generally the same for one item as for 1,000. This was something which was started at the very first in order to get the dealer to get the turnover and at the same time reduce chances of obsolescence and have capital to buy new items which might be brought into the line.

At the retail level, it is customary for some of the voluntaries to suggest retail prices, but the dealer is usually left on his own in pricing. However, it is at the retail level that the federal government is taking an increasing interest in pricing policies of franchise operations, particularly the manufacturer-retailer types:

— This year the Federal Trade Commission ruled that Brown Shoe Co. illegally restrained competition by requiring independent franchised dealers to adhere to its established resale prices and to refuse to handle competing shoes from other manufacturers.

— In the White Motor case referred to earlier, the federal government attacked as illegal White Motor's arrangement with its franchisees to establish fixed prices at which wholesale distributors could sell White trucks to franchised dealers.

Undoubtedly, more legal attention will be given in the future to the subject of pricing in franchise programs.

Merchandising Assistance

As indicated earlier, one of the outstanding contributions made to the retailer by a strong voluntary organization is extensive, professional merchandising assistance. Some cooperative organizations and a small but growing number of independent wholesalers offer effective merchandising programs to retailers, but the voluntary programs have generally set the standard in terms of abundant professional assistance. All five companies provide help of great depth and variety. Included are such items as:

Store Openings. All major franchisers offer assistance to the new franchisee in store location, lease arrangements, store layout, opening stocks, and grand opening sales. Practices in this area are quite similar. Strict controls of store appearance, store fronts (always featuring the voluntary logo), and store layout are insisted on in all well-run programs. Many times in smaller towns the store front of a franchised retailer will stand out like a sore thumb among the drab exteriors of local independent retail stores.

Advertising. Inability to prepare and to pay for effective advertising is a major weakness of many independent retailers. Franchised retailers, on the other hand, benefit from strong regional or national programs. For example:

• Some programs, such as those of Butler Brothers, Walgreen, and Western Auto, use both local and national media.

• Western Auto runs advertising in national magazines such as *Life, Saturday Evening Post,* and *Progressive Farmer* for which no charge is made to the dealer.

• The programs of Ace and Super Valu are primarily local or regional in nature. These programs generally include newspaper mats, direct mailing pieces, and in-store display material of various types.

One of the great benefits to franchises, particularly in larger cities where more than one store is present, is the spreading of costs among stores to permit full-page newspaper advertising, competitive in size and impact with corporate chain advertising.

In all five companies, participation in advertising programs is optional. National advertising is typically supplied free of charge, but in most instances retailers pay for the direct costs of other advertising services.

In the case of Super Valu, some of these direct costs may be absorbed by manufacturers who are supplying merchandise under special merchandise contracts.

Promotions. Central promotion departments plan special and seasonal promotion programs for affiliated stores. Typically, these programs are also on an optional basis. Wilson of Western Auto comments:

Sales events are planned throughout the year, and the dealers are asked to cooperate in them, for it has been found that these promotions are what keeps the dealer store from being 'just another' independent operator. I certainly do not mean to imply that you will not find successful independent operators, but I think it is agreed that when a person follows an integrated plan, his chances of success are much better inasmuch as our plan tries to eliminate the pitfalls the average individual runs into when starting a business of his own.

Retail Training

Training of store management and operating personnel is another key to the success of franchise programs:

Butler Brothers point out in its literature to prospective franchisees: "The program is so complete that retail experience is not necessary to successfully operate a Ben Franklin Store."

In its booklet, *How to Step Forward,* Super Valu tells its prospects:

Super Valu Stores, Inc. was one of the first in the voluntary field to make these training programs available. A considerable amount of money has been spent in obtaining the best information possible for training of retail personnel, and periodically all Field Representatives are brought up to date as to new methods and procedures.

Western Auto conducts five training centers throughout the country on a permanent basis. According to Wilson:

These are staffed by trained men who run such classes all year long, not only for new dealers, but for retaining older dealers and for training our own company store managers. Subjects covered are credit, selling, product knowledge, bookkeeping, display, purchasing, and so on. It should be recognized that during a two-week period only the basics can be covered . . . a man can come out of a training class equipped to keep a set of books even though he had no previous knowledge of bookkeeping.

Supervision

All five wholesalers have men on the road regularly contacting affiliated stores. Walgreen uses the term "sales representative"; Butler Brothers and Ace use the name "zone manager"; Super Valu, "field representative"; and Western Auto, "representative."

Whatever they are called, the function of these men is much broader than the selling and order-taking role typical of many a wholesale salesman in companies where management has not seen the need to train its people in modern merchandising. A former Butler Brothers' zone manager in Iowa relates:

I had 14 stores to call on, which meant I was in a store for a full day about once every three weeks. While in the store I spent 50% of my time in reviewing inventories and assisting in ordering, and the other 50% of the time I devoted to merchandising assistance."

Western Auto's Wilson puts it this way:

While these men [representatives] will not turn down an order and do promote merchandise, their chief purpose is that of a business counselor. The way I put it in talking with a prospect is that the representative does what he can to help the dealer move the merchandise out of the front door so we can move it in the back door.

Two notable differences between the voluntary's supervisory program and the typical wholesale sales effort are that under the former (a) the men devote a large percentage of time to merchandising, and (b) the cost is well below the typical field sales cost. For example:

• Ace is reported to have only six men, or about one salesman per 100 stores. They contact the better stores so infrequently that the manager of a large Ace store said that he thought Ace had no salesmen because he had never been contacted.
• Western Auto has about 200 representatives dedicated to assisting dealers.
• Super Valu engages 40 to 42 general store supervisors serving from 15 to 25 affiliated stores, depending on the size of the stores, complexity of merchandise lines handled, and distances traveled. In addition to general supervision, Super Valu engages special field representatives for meat, produce, and bakery departments.

As an example of typical supervisory costs, I have estimated what a Ben Franklin country zone manager's sales and expenses might be, based on the assumption that his retail stores on the average buy 90% of their needs from Butler Brothers:

Average retail sales per store	$120,000
Total purchases per store	72,000
Purchases from Butler (90%)	65,000
Purchases by 14 stores in zone	910,000
Estimated zone manager expense	15,000
Zone manager expense ratio	2.3%

This expense ratio of 2.3% compares to a 5% to 7% field selling expense for some variety and soft-goods wholesalers. Of course, supervisors covering larger stores will develop a much lower expense ratio. Also, Ace, Super Valu, and Western Auto cover more stores per supervisor, further reducing expenses. At the same time that expenses are lower, the dealer has the substantial additional benefit of merchandising assistance and general counsel.

Store Operations Assistance

In addition to merchandising assistance, headquarters provides all the necessary assistance for store operations, including merchandise control systems, accounting methods and procedures, personnel practices and training. To illustrate:

• The Ace inventory control system includes catalogs of merchandise, preprinted order blanks, a checklist of all items furnished, and preprinted bin and price tickets.
• Butler Brothers has a well-developed merchandise control system consisting of a basic stock checklist and seasonal listing records. These records are printed forms in alphabetized, loose-leaf binders listing items by department and telling the store manager when to count, when to buy, how much to buy, and which related items are displayed together.

Most voluntary programs also provide store owners with operating manuals and monthly publications, such as Butler Brothers' "Idea Service" and Super Valu's "Profit Builder."

Financial Assistance

It is not customary for voluntary wholesalers to lend direct financing assistance to dealers for working capital purposes. Butler Brothers' attitude is typical: "We do not make loans to new affiliated store owners, but we have worked an arrangement with a major bank to finance fixtures." Super Valu's attitude is that financing retailers is purely a banking function, although the company offers substantial low-cost financing of fixtures and equipment to its affiliated stores.

On the other hand, Western Auto does extend credit to its group members. As Wilson explains:

"Fixtures are sold to the dealer at about cost plus freight, and these can be purchased on a payment plan. In addition to this type of credit, Western Auto also offers other types of financial assistance through floor planning of certain types of merchandise, dating plans, and trade acceptances." (There is no carrying charge or interest charge on the trade acceptance program.)

"Further financial assistance is given in the discounting of paper on major items which the dealer might sell on the installment plan. In this case, the dealer gets the full cash price plus a portion of the handling charge, and thus he does not tie up his working capital in accounts receivable."

Another facet of financing where policies differ is the leasing of stores. Some wholesalers, such as Butler Brothers, will lease store properties in their own name and sublease to franchisees. Super Valu holds approximately 150 retail store leases where the stores are subleased at a nominal override to its affiliated members. In this way, Super Valu retailers are able to occupy prime locations, both in and out of shopping centers, which they as individuals would be unable to obtain because the property owners quite logically prefer a corporate lessee rather than an individual.

Others, such as Western Auto, insist that the lease be in the store owner's name, the belief being that this makes the store more of an "owner's" store than if the wholesaler made the lease and subleased to the retailer.

Private Brands

All five voluntary wholesalers offer private branded merchandise. Because of its manufacturing interests, Walgreen's franchise program has as a major objective the sale of the company's brands. To this end, the agreement states that the retailer shall, at all times, use his "best efforts and facilities to establish, maintain and increase the sale of . . . Walgreen products."

Ace has a broad line of private-label items, prominent among which are paint products, Ace private-label products must be carried by the franchise dealer.

Super Valu has numerous private labels and, like Walgreen, has moved into manufacturing. Some of the products Super Valu processes or packs are baked goods, coffee, candies, and nuts. In 1960 Harrison told The Investment Analysts Society of Chicago, "We have a small research group that is constantly putting together figures as to the possibility of getting more and more into manufacturing."

Company Stores

Among the five companies, only Ace does not own and operate retail stores. Retail operations are of major importance to Walgreen and Butler Brothers. Butler owns the T G &Y store and Scott variety store chains, concentrated in the Southwest and Midwest; Walgreen stores are located all across the country. As for Western Auto, a company salesman has stated:

We believe the stronger we can make our retail organization and the more we learn about retailing, the better our advice and counsel will be for our dealer organization.

In commenting on the 12 retail stores owned by Super Valu in 1960, Harrison said:

We own them for two reasons: first, to get close to the retail operation, to learn more about it . . . the other is to enter a market where we do not find independent retailers with sufficient capital. . . . I don't think—and there is some disagreement within our organization—that we should own and operate a large number of stores.

RETAILER REACTIONS

Of the thousands of retailers who are now a part of voluntary programs, some will not succeed and others will become disenchanted. I have visited with a number who have dropped out of the voluntary movement because they felt "too regimented," believed the wholesaler's supervisor "didn't know my local problems," or thought "the lease arrangement was too stiff."

Some retailers have not performed according to the spirit of their franchise or were marginal in size. Butler Brothers prefers to franchise new stores with at least $75,000 of annual volume; Ace prefers new stores with $100,000 or more volume. Older stores with volume significantly below these levels may eventually become too small to be served economically. Thus, in 1962, Butler Brothers discontinued 104 franchises.

The greatest mortality among many types of retail stores is in those with sales under $50,-000 annually. One reason is that many of the larger voluntary wholesalers have not geared their programs to this size of store. In effect, the voluntary movement generally is not available to many thousands of small retail establishments.

In spite of these shortcomings, a large and growing number of independent retailers have benefited from the voluntary programs. Financial figures of affiliated retailers are not easy to come by since all are privately owned and their results are usually lost in the combined annual retail studies published by Dun & Bradstreet and others. However, some data are available. In its franchise brochure, "Owning A Ben Franklin Store," Butler Brothers has published the following composite results for 1,068 Ben Franklin stores using the Ben Franklin Optional Accounting Service:

Sales	$88,776,169
Net income (before taxes)	$9,617,723
Net income (as percent of sales)	11.62%
Average sales per store	$83,200

These profit results are well above the median figures published by Dun & Bradstreet for variety goods retailers. What is more, they reflect operations of stores very modest in size.

In a recent interview, officers of Super Food Services, Inc. (an IGA voluntary wholesaler) pointed out that an attainable rate of return on investment for an independent with a store of under 10,000 square feet would be 25%–30% after a reasonable salary rate, and allowing for financing repayments. Some of the better IGA and Super Valu retailers have shown returns on invested capital substantially in excess of this.

A typical Super Valu store owner in Iowa summed up his opinion of membership in the voluntary group by saying, "We feel that we have the best all-around program for an independent operator that there is in this country."

PROBLEMS & OPPORTUNITIES

Although a strong case can be made for the five voluntary wholesalers, starting and maintaining a successful franchising program has many problems and pitfalls. For all of its success in variety goods, Butler Brothers, a few years ago, abandoned its franchise program in soft goods under the "Federated Stores" name. Also, Hibbard Spencer Bartlett & Co., a major hardware wholesaler in the Midwest that undertook a hardware franchise program, has recently sold out its business. In the opinion of trade spokesmen, part of the reason for the program's failure was that it was late. Many of the better Midwestern hardware retailers were already franchised by Ace and others. Another possible reason was that the company straddled the fence, selling to both franchised and nonfranchised stores. By contrast, the five wholesalers described sell only to affiliated and company-owned stores.

Some of the difficulties faced by wholesalers in initiating franchise programs include:

The need to supply more than 50% of a retailer's requirements — With certain types of merchandise, this problem may be quite real. For example, in dry goods, the 50% objective, becomes difficult because of the retail tendency to buy more goods directly from factory sources as store volume grows.

The independence of independents — Characteristic of many independents is their desire to go their own way without help. I interviewed a dry-goods wholesaler in Nebraska who had made an attempt to start a joint merchandising program with 100 retailers. All members paid a fee to join, although they did not sign a franchise contract. Effective advertising and promotion programs were developed. However, only a half dozen of the members ever participated, and the program fell apart.

The slim pickings in some merchandise fields — The food industry is an example where the unaffiliated share of retail store sales has dwindled to an estimated 9%. Voluntaries and cooperatives are finding few independent retailers left to franchise. Again, an executive of Western Auto commented to me: "In many large sections of the country, it would be impossible to add an additional dealer store because of complete saturation."

The resurgence of progressive, independent wholesalers — Aware of the techniques developed by franchising wholesalers, a growing number of independent wholesalers are offering programs which incorporate many features of franchise programs. For example, a number of large independent drug wholesale houses have about ten telephone salesmen, up to ten outside salesmen, and ten or more people in advertising, promotion, store layout and location, and management training. Outside salesmen operate less and less as order takers and more and more as detail men with capabilities in displays, promotions, inventory control, and so forth.

Historically, most of the major franchise programs have been built on the smaller, independent dealer, particularly the kind in country towns. It is doubtful today that this base can be extended very far, both because of the decline of country towns and because better independents in many lines of merchandise have already joined some type of franchise program. Nevertheless, franchise selling appears to offer further opportunities for well-managed programs. City Products Corporation, of which Butler Brothers is a part, continues to see opportunities. Two possibilities mentioned in the City Products 1962 *Annual Report* are:

1. *Variety goods franchising in super markets* — "The Division [Ben Franklin] has continued to work toward expansion of its franchising techniques into the distribution of variety type merchandise within super markets. Units have been introduced in several parts of the country and results have been most encouraging. We are confident that the franchising technique can be substantially developed in this field."

2. *Furniture and home furnishings* — "A pilot franchise operation will be developed in 1963 to test its possible application on a broad scale in furniture and home furnishings retailing. The experience City Products Corporation has accumulated in the general field of franchising will be important in developing this program."

Other fields which may hold promise for expansion of franchising activities include drugs, jewelry, liquor, photographic equipment, and a variety of other merchandise. Such lines have a wholesaling function of importance and a wide retail base. Both factors lend themselves to franchising.

Aside from competitive factors, the most significant unknown in franchising is the attitude of federal agencies now examining the field. To date, their efforts have been directed largely at manufacturer-retailer franchises, but their inquiries appear to be broadening into wholesaler-retailer franchises as well as the other types described.

CONCLUSION

Now just over 30 years of age, the wholesaler-retailer voluntary franchise movement is today a mature and vigorous merchandising phenomenon. It is founded on the principle of entrepreneurship at both the wholesale and retail levels.

As stated most aptly in the 1962 *Annual Report* of City Products Corporation, "The appeal to the franchisee is the opportunity to build a profitable enterprise for himself and his family with the name, buying power and professional back-up of a national organization." What makes Ben Franklin and other similar voluntary programs successful, according to the report, is "the incentive inherent in individual proprietorship, the sensitivity of local ownership to community characteristics and demands, teamed with quality standards, continuity of merchandising, professional store operation and promotional techniques."

In formulating their programs, voluntary wholesalers have learned to "think retail." No longer just a middleman-peddler of merchandise, the modern wholesaler has become an expert in retailing concepts and techniques.

It may be that by joining a collective movement, the independent retailer sacrifices some of his independence. Yet therein lies for many the best practical means of salvation. Recognition of this is the key to the future of the franchise idea. How much further it can spread in the economy can only be answered by that dynamic, resourceful, competitive entity—the independent American merchant.

DISCUSSION QUESTIONS

Franchising is by no means new, though its growth in recent years has been spectacular. Many of the retail operations which appear to be "chains" or some other common form are actually franchise arrangements.

1. What accounts for the recent renewal of interest in franchising?
2. What is the economic contribution of the franchiser?
3. What is likely to be the future for franchise retailing?

3. Retail Innovations Challenge Manufacturers

GERALD B. TALLMAN and BRUCE BLOMSTROM

In 1965 over 25% of the retail business in many lines of trade will move to consumers through stores which did not carry these products ten years earlier. The present rate of change in store locations, in the scrambling of retail lines, and in the development of new types of retail operations and of new shopping opportunities for consumers is probably as great as in any decade of our country's commercial history.

This relocation and reorientation of retail outlets represents a catching-up of retail institutions with the vast changes that have taken place in consumer living habits, locations, and buying power since World War II. These changes have generated a major revolution in the kinds and quantities of goods purchased by consumers, and in the type and location of shopping which is convenient and attractive to them.

For manufacturers, the great growth and shift in retail stores now underway presents serious problems in the choice of outlets. Most manufacturers of consumer products practice some degree of selective distribution in order to secure desired qualities in retail presentation of their products and to meet retailer requirements for some protection against excessive brand competition in the products carried. Though consumer acceptance of the combination of brands which the retailer carries may be a major factor in determining the customer pulling power of a store, few individual manufacturers enjoy strong enough consumer preference for their brands to assure that a high proportion of potential buyers will be deflected from customer-preferred shopping locations. Thus, the manufacturer must place his products in enough of the right kind of stores and locations if he is to achieve desired market goals.

On the other hand, for most products it is important that manufacturers be sufficiently selective in the number and compatibility of outlets used in order to gain retailer support for the brand.

Manufacturers have little problem in adapting their selling efforts to normal changes of ownership and management of stores, or the relocation or increase in numbers of familiar kinds of stores which are accepted as normal competition within the retail community. *But the emergence of a new kind of outlet has always presented a problem of major magnitude, particularly if the outlet is oriented to lower margins and lower retail prices.* This was true with the development of variety chains, of large general-merchandise, mail-order operations, of food chains, and of food supermarkets. The problem has been particularly acute with the development of discount selling of appliances following World War II and the current development of self-service supermarkets in the soft-goods field.

The decisions made will have a major effect on future sales and profits for manufacturers. We suspect that manufacturers' decisions will have considerably less effect on the rate of change in the retail marketplace. The growth and survival of stores in new types of locations with new combinations of product offerings and new balancing of convenience, service, and price appeals will depend more on the response of consumers, and on the skill with which retailers present themselves and adjust to consumer response, than on the choices made by manufacturers.

In this article, we shall document the growth of the discount department store and compare the development of this type of outlet with past innovations in retail institutions. We shall then report on the findings of a research study conducted among soft-goods manufacturers to determine their reactions to the growth of discount outlets. Finally, based on our conclusions from this research, we shall offer suggestions

◆ SOURCE: Reprinted by permission from the editors of the *Harvard Business Review,* in the September–October 1962, issue, pp. 130–134.

for manufacturer analysis in making decisions as to type of outlet.

DISCOUNT DEPARTMENT STORE

The development of self-service supermarket selling of soft goods (initiated in New England) and of "closed door" discount stores (on the West Coast) was first identifiable in about 1954. It is currently estimated that by the end of 1962 there will be 2,100 to 2,300 of these stores (with those built after 1959 averaging about 70,000 square feet of selling space each), doing an aggregate volume of about $6 billion to $7 billion in retail sales. The early growth and emergence into significance of this new type of retail operation was reported in the September–October 1960 HBR.[1]

The growth of this type of retailing has continued; it is clearly the most dynamically changing force in retailing today. Its effect is seen not only in the continued rapid establishment of stores following this new pattern, but also in operational changes being adopted by traditional retailers. Though less readily measurable, it is apparently accompanied by a shrinking of activities for the few remaining general merchandising wholesalers and a loss of sales for small stores carrying women's and children's apparel, particularly in low- and medium-quality lines.

The "discount department stores," as they are commonly described, are of two general types:

1. The closed-door stores allow only "members" access to the store through membership eligibility as defined by rather broad classifications of government employees, teachers, union members, or employees of government contractors. They carry a wide range of soft goods and apparel, but also give major attention to furniture, appliances, food, and automotive supplies. Several of the closed-door operations have recently opened their doors to the general public. Among the better known names under which closed-door stores operate are GEM, GEX, Fedco, and Fed Mart.

2. The discount department stores, which first developed self-service for soft goods in New England and have subsequently spread across the country on an open-door basis, typically derive substantially more than 50% of their sales from apparel items. They use supermarket-type self-service, shopping carts, and central check-out for all but a few departments. The income class to which their merchandising appears to be directed is somewhat lower than for the closed-door stores.

Low operating margins achieved through volume sales and limited service expenditures for clerks, delivery, credit, and so on have allowed prices which average about 15% below those of the department stores and specialty shops with which discount stores compete in the sale of soft goods. Full-size food supermarkets are being established within many of the new large discount stores. Because of consumers' long experience in comparing food values between stores and because of the frequency of food store visits by the average family, these food departments are attractive to the soft-goods stores as traffic builders, and are frequently operated with planned narrow margins (or even planned losses) to maximize their drawing power.

The closed-door stores depend primarily on word of mouth and on mail promotion to their members to publicize the attractive values offered. The open-door discounters, however, make extensive use of local advertising media and special values which they offer. Because their low prices are more apparent to both consumers and competing retailers, the open-door stores represent a thornier problem for manufacturers faced with the decision of whether or not to sell through these new type stores in competition with established dealers. The problem is especially acute in the case of well-known brands.

PAST INNOVATIONS

Retail innovations of importance comparable to that now found in the discount department stores have been the development from 1870 to 1890 of the early forms of the now "traditional" department stores, of general merchandise mail-order selling (1890–1910), of the variety and food chain stores (1910–1930), and of the food supermarkets after 1930.

Each of these major retail innovations, when first developed, offered consumers lower prices than were generally available through previously existing retail outlets. Each, with time, has traded up the quality of its service, and with this its operating expenses and margins. This has been particularly true of department stores with the development over the years of more elaborate services and a greater emphasis on style merchandise.

---

[1] Gerald B. Tallman and Bruce Blomstrom, "Soft Goods Join the Retail Revolution," p. 133.

Each innovation, however, offered the consumer something new besides lower prices:

• The department store offered a broader selection of kinds of merchandise under a single roof, the convenience and assurance of a fixed price, and the grouping of like goods into departments for more effective merchandising.

• The mail-order houses offered, particularly to rural patrons, a wider selection of merchandise than was available from local stores.

• Chains, particularly in the variety and apparel fields, brought the consumer a standardization of merchandise and a faster availability of new developments and styles from market centers.

• The supermarkets brought all kinds of food products into a single store, thus eliminating the necessity of visiting several specialty food stores in order to complete a shopping list, and, perhaps most important, introduced the consumer to the convenience and pleasures of self-service shopping.

The self-service soft-goods supermarkets, which are currently the most rapidly growing segment of retailing, have offered to consumers significantly lower prices for standard (not deluxe) quality merchandise. They have also adapted to the marketing of soft goods features which consumers have tried and liked in the food field, namely, convenient access by automobile, ample parking, evening shopping hours, and the opportunity for browsing or buying at a pace determined by the customer rather than by the availability or attitude of clerks. One sees far more family groups shopping in these discount department stores than is typical of the department stores and the specialty shops with which they primarily compete.

In each period of innovation, established retailers have failed to realize that the new type of store was finding consumer acceptance on other than a price basis. This characteristic failure to comprehend the reasons for favorable consumer response has slowed the adjustment on the part of existing merchants to meeting the new competition, and has allowed the new institutions to secure a firm foothold.

At present, many consumers appear to like the shopping freedom provided by the soft-goods self-service outlets just about as much as they like the low prices. A dramatic confirmation of the appeal of self-service is developing in Dayton, Ohio, where a department store branch operation offers main-store quality and prices on a self-service basis. Volume is reported to be very satisfactory—although results are uneven as between types of merchandise.

The expansion of discount department store sales is proceeding at a pace unequalled by other major retail innovations during the period of their own most rapid expansion. In Exhibit I we have plotted the sales growth of discount department stores during the slightly less than ten years since they emerged as a recognized new type of retail institution and have compared this growth with the sales of food supermarkets in the years 1932–1941, and the sales of grocery chains during 1919–1928. In Exhibit II the growth of open-door, soft-goods supermarkets in New England is compared with that of variety chains and mail-order sales. Exhibit III shows the growth of selected individual firms in several of the types of retail innovations discussed.

It seems unreasonable to expect that the growth of self-service supermarkets in the soft-goods field can continue to expand as equivalent operations in the food field have done during the second and third decades of their development. In the food field the total volume is substantially larger, and products are to a much greater extent standardized. By contrast, in apparel and soft goods, greater diversity of product, ever-changing fashions, the need for counseling, fitting, and other personal services, and higher average unit product price all suggest that there is much greater opportunity for continuance of service operations and for specialty store operators offering products of better or more distinctive style and faster styling turnover (at higher prices) than are feasible in large-scale, low-margin operations.

RETAILER RESPONSE

The past century has seen several dramatic innovations in retail operations which have had an impact on manufacturers and have raised the necessity for difficult choices in the selection of outlets. Each major innovation in retailing has threatened the existence or continued growth of some established retailers. A characteristic response to the threat has been for established retailers to use whatever dissuasive power was available to limit manufacturers' sales to the upstart operation. The threat and the reaction have been strongest when the retail innovation has allowed retail margins below those at which established re-

EXHIBIT I. Early Sales Growth of Retail Institutions
(All sales in 1947–1949 dollars)

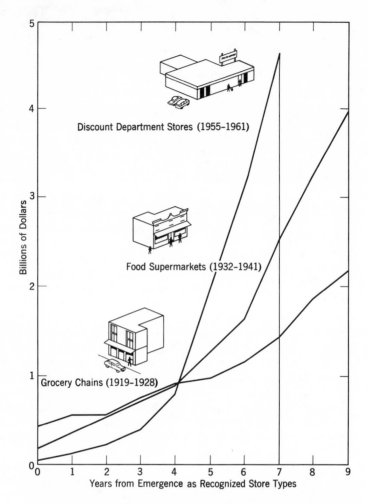

SOURCES: Discount department stores—estimated by us; food super-markets—F. S. Charvat, *Supermarketing* (New York, The Macmillan Company, 1961), p. 3; grocery chains—U.S. Department of Commerce, *Survey of Current Business* (Washington, D.C., U.S. Government Printing Office, February 1928, p. 119 and February 1929, p. 117). Sales figures in 1928 are for 34 firms having 29,433 stores. Actual number of firms was less than 34 in prior years, but sales have been adjusted by the Department of Commerce to reflect these changes.

tailers felt they could profitably survive. For example:

The trade response to chain stores illustrates the conflict which low-cost innovation generates. The rise of chain stores was accompanied by shrunken volumes or the actual demise of thousands of independent retailers. Wholesalers and retailers had no doubt that the competition of the chain stores was the principal cause of their difficulties.

And so pressures were brought to bear against chain stores. Many suppliers were forced to boycott chain stores in order to retain independent stores as customers; national brands available to chain as well as independent stores were partially displaced by wholesaler brands, or by manufacturers' brands available only to "legitimate" dealers. Particularly in the smaller towns and cities, families whose economic welfare depended on the good will of their neighbors were pressured to stay

EXHIBIT II. Early Sales Growth of Selected Outlet Types
(All sales are in 1947–1949 dollars)

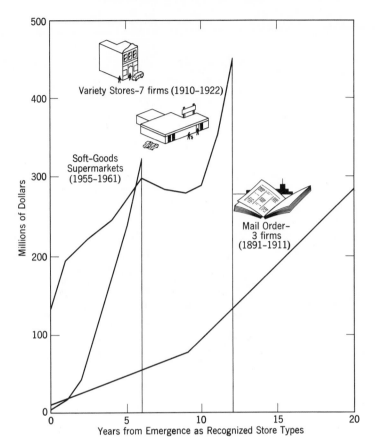

SOURCES: Soft-goods supermarkets in New England—estimated by
us; variety stores—Godfrey M. Lebhar, *Chain Stores in America,
1859–1959* (New York, Chain Store Publishing Corp., 1959), pp. 35,
38, 368–373, 385; mail order—P. H. Nystrom, *Economics of Retailing*, Volume I (New York, The Ronald Press Company, 1930), pp.
178–179, and B. Emmett and J. Jeuck, *Catalogues and Counters* (Chicago, University of Chicago Press, 1950), pp. 172 and 301.

away from the chain stores. Even the force of
government was brought to bear when, under
the prodding of independent retailers and
wholesalers, anti-chain store legislation was
passed by a majority of the state legislatures.

Licensing ordinances were instituted, differential taxation of multiunit retail operations
was adopted, and fair trade (price maintenance) and loss leaders (unfair sales practices)
laws were enacted to reduce the chain stores'
advantages. At the national level the Robinson-
Patman Act restricting the price differentials
that manufacturers could offer to various
classes of competing customers went through
Congress as an "anti-chain store bill."

Another example, not quite so vivid, was the
reaction to aggressive mail-order retailing.
Though the effect of mail-order houses was
more diffuse than the more immediate competition which the chain store offered to individual competitors, the retailing community
brought significant pressure to bear against
manufacturers who sought to serve *both* retail
stores and mail-order houses. Furthermore, in
many towns the municipal employees,
teachers, preachers, and local bankers were
led to understand that the receipt of parcels
from mail-order houses could be a source of
embarrassment to them.

The early supermarkets faced attempts to

EXHIBIT III. Initial Sales Growth of Leading Firms During Periods of
Major Retail Innovations
(All sales are in 1947–1949 dollars)

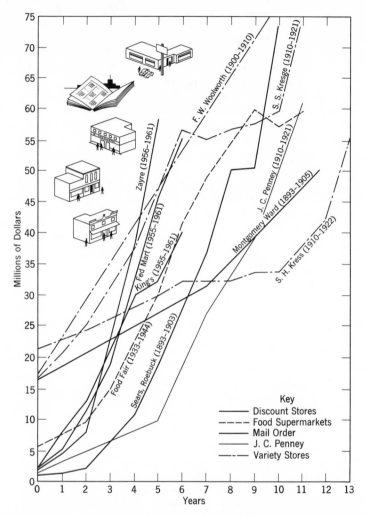

limit their store hours and their access to advertising media and to products. Eventually the entry of established chains into this field turned competitive efforts toward emulation rather than obstruction.

Understandably, the full history of pressures exerted on manufacturers by established retailers and wholesalers is not adequately recorded. In view of recent occurrences, however, it is not difficult to imagine that in their early years even the department stores felt pressure on their suppliers from the then-established wholesalers and retailers who feared the new type of competition that they represented.

MANUFACTURERS/RETAILERS

The development of new retail institutions, and the consistent reaction of consumers to

them, has affected the nature of manufacturer-retailer relations. Traditionally, the manufacturer has taken the lead in getting products designed, manufactured, distributed, and sold across retail counters. He has usually acted as "captain" of the marketing team and as such has determined the product, its price, and the method of distribution. He has solicited the cooperation of subsequent members of the distribution chain to get these products into the hands of consumers.

By contrast, two retailing institutions—i.e., mail-order houses and, to a lesser extent, chain stores—have frequently taken this leadership role away from the manufacturer. In these instances they have expected of the manufacturer only efficient production of the goods which they (as captains, subject always to confirmation by consumer purchase action) would sell. Under these conditions the retailer, rather than the manufacturer, held the "consumer franchise" and was in a position to draw down most of the profit from successful product design and promotion.

The contest between manufacturers and large retailers for the dominant role in the marketing sequence becomes more intense as retailer buying power is increasingly concentrated in large organizations. The manufacturer's chances of retaining his traditional role and independence of action are greatly enhanced if he has a brand which consumers will prefer to buy by name and if he has the support of outlets that will provide favorable retail representation to his brand. It is concern over losing this support, as well as the loss of specific orders, that has made manufacturers sensitive to the complaints of established retailers whose sales are threatened by new types of retail operations.

MANUFACTURERS' REACTIONS

Manufacturers of convenience goods (food products, housewares, drugs and cosmetics, notions, and so on) and others who have generally practiced extensive, rather than selective, distribution have had few qualms about making their products available through the new discount department stores, although some brand-name manufacturers have insisted that their regular retail prices be maintained. The discount stores have also found appliance dealerships generally available. In the soft-goods field, however, many manufacturers, particularly those with branded lines, have refused to sell their products to the self-service supermarkets.

In the summer of 1961, we interviewed 78 major companies manufacturing products typically sold in the soft-goods departments of discount department stores (men's, women's, and children's apparel and domestics). About one half of the firms interviewed have brands with some degree of national advertising support. In conducting the interviews, we investigated both manufacturers' selling policies toward discount department stores and the ways in which manufacturers' operations have been affected (either voluntarily or involuntarily) by the burgeoning importance of the discount outlets. The key results of these interviews are discussed here.

Selling Policies and Sales

Of the firms interviewed, 61 reported that they offer some or all of their products to discount stores, while 17 stated that they were not then selling to discount stores. Exhibit IV indicates the general selling policies of these manufacturers classified as to whether or not the firms have some type of consumer-advertised brand.

A truly representative sampling of soft-goods manufacturers would presumably report a higher proportion of small firms which do no consumer advertising and sell freely to discounters. In a few instances manufacturers who claim not to sell to discounters find their goods being transshipped by traditional customers.

Soft-goods manufacturers, who have in the past carefully franchised their products to avoid undue competition among their customers and to secure maximum retail merchandising support, have generally refused to sell

EXHIBIT IV. Selling Policies of Soft-Goods Manufacturers

	Manufacturers Who Sell to Discounters		Manufacturers Who Refuse to Sell to Discounters	Total
	Without Limitation	With Limitation*		
Manufacturers with consumer-advertised brands	1	22	13	36
Manufacturers without consumer-advertised brands	6	32	4	42
Total manufacturers interviewed	7	54	17	78

* Limitations include area restrictions, product disguise through changing or removing labels or changing style or fashion, selling a different price line, or changing the quality of goods sold.
SOURCE: Author's survey date.

identical merchandise to discount operations. Only one of the manufacturers with an advertised brand makes all of his products available to discount stores. That manufacturer reports a very encouraging sales trend.

A number of the firms (48 of 61) that sell to discounters were willing to indicate the *share of their business* going to such customers. Of this number, 8 report that about 50% of their sales are to discounters; 14 report 20%; 15 report 5% to 15%; and 11 state that less than 5% goes to discounters. Manufacturers report that both the size of individual orders and the frequency of reorders is substantially greater from self-service stores than from the average or traditional customers. For many manufacturers, sales to discount stores result in an increased concentration of business among a few customers. In the contest for dominance this is a source of worry.

Subject to Pressures

Whether or not they sell freely to discounters, most manufacturers report serious concern over the conflicting interest of their older customers, on the one hand, and the low-margin, low-price discounter, on the other.

About 75% of the manufacturers (45 of the 61) who reported selling to discounters say that at the time they began such selling they were subjected to pressure from established customers to discontinue the practice. Of these, 32 report that they suffered a temporary loss of volume; but they note a tendency for their old retail customers to renew the purchase of attractive merchandise once it has been clearly established that withhold purchases will not be effective in keeping the manufacturer's products out of the hands of discounters. Without exception, these 32 firms reported total volume to be at least as big as it was before they began selling to discounters, and most reported it to have grown.

None of the manufacturers interviewed would admit to an over-all reduction in sales; but the most enthusiastic claims of sales growth were made by firms that sell to the new self-service retailers. All of the firms presently selling to discounters expect this part of their business to grow in importance.

Reducing Conflict

A majority of the firms interviewed seek to restrict the effects of competition between dis-

counters and their traditional customers by limiting the geographical areas in which they sell to discounters or by making some modification in products.

One pattern has been that of selling to discounters in areas like New England, the West Coast, and parts of the Middle West, where discounters already account for too large a part of the soft-goods volume to be ignored, while refusing to sell to discounters in other parts of the country, such as the South, where the development of self-service operations in soft goods has been relatively slow.

Another way of avoiding the conflict has been to sell to discounters only in areas where the manufacturer has had little or no prior representation. Area restrictions are becoming less manageable because the discount stores are so often parts of chains which are rapidly expanding into new territories. This makes selective distribution more difficult than when dealing with individual department or specialty stores. Chain operators of discount stores, or leased departments with outlets in several parts of the country, are increasingly unwilling to carry product lines on a restricted area basis.

Nearly three-fourths of the manufacturers who do sell to discounters report that, by one means or another, they differentiate the product made available to discounters from that sold to retailers following traditional markup policies. About half of these manufacturers state that they merely change the labels on their products. Since in soft goods so few brands have any meaningful degree of consumer recognition or preference, the mere change of label is not likely to affect consumer evaluation of the goods offered. The other half introduce some variation in style, fabric, or packaging when selling to discounters. In this process, some firms reduce the quality level from that sold to traditional outlets, but most state that they modify characteristics without changing quality level. Three report selling higher quality to discounters than to traditional customers.

Buying Relations

We find little evidence that discount-store buyers have yet abused the power which they may have by virtue of the fact that they represent a large part of manufacturers' total output, but the possibility is always there. Faced with rapidly expanding consumer patronage, on the one hand, and a degree of manufacturer reluctance, on the other, the discount-store buyers are considered by manufacturers to have been very "reasonable" customers. A common statement from manufacturers interviewed is that "discounters pay top dollar for merchandise and are less demanding than department stores in their bargaining relationships." Manufacturers say that the buyers for discount stores operate under less tightly organized merchandise control systems, are less frequently handcuffed by "open-to-buy" controls from store management, and are generally more flexible in dealing with the manufacturer. An interesting sidelight of the interviews is the reflection of a deep-seated antagonism against what are considered to be the arbitrary and high-handed buying practices of department stores.

There is, however, some evidence that the discount-store buyers are beginning to flex their muscles as buyers. We think the time may not be far off when discount-store buyers will become as unreasonable and hard to live with as "normal" customers.

Moreover, we believe the time is also coming when manufacturers who have refused to sell to discounters at a time when discounters were more or less humbly seeking sources of supply may well face some reverse discrimination. Some discounters, well entrenched with consumers and with acceptable sources of supply, are beginning to put into force their often stated intention to favor vendors who have supported them in their time of need and to refuse belated offers of previously unavailable brands. This may be particularly hurtful to the manufacturer whose brand has relatively little drawing power with consumers. However, we think it unlikely that discounters will allow old antagonisms to stand in the way of handling merchandise which can be bought under acceptable terms and which will have ready acceptance by consumers.

Effect on Operations

About half of the manufacturers state that they have had no major problems in servicing discount stores. Those who do have problems point most frequently to the fact that discounters seem to "want their goods yesterday." The heavy initial orders and frequent reorders, sometimes closer to the season than the manufacturers have been accustomed to, make the delivery of goods a major problem. More specifically, manufacturers report on the effect of discounters on inventory, costs, and sales-service:

- *Inventory* — One fourth of the manufacturers state that discounters have caused them additional storage problems, principally because of the duplication of lines to avoid identity with traditional customers. On the other hand, two manufacturers point out that they actually carry less inventory for discounters than for their regular customers because the discounters buy fewer different items.

- *Costs* — Only one fourth of the manufacturers interviewed mention that their costs have changed because of discounters, and these are evenly divided among those who claim cost increases and those whose costs have declined. Increased volume is the principal reason for a fall in costs. Changes in packaging and labeling, mainly to disguise the product, are the major causes of cost increases.

- *Sales Organization* — Barely 25% of the manufacturers note that they have made any changes in their sales organization as a result of discounters, but another 17% are considering one. Most changes were through the addition of personnel rather than a basic shift in the method of handling discounters.

Two manufacturers, both reporting dramatic sales increases, have begun to service the stock in discount stores, including taking inventory, writing the order, and setting up displays. Their sales to discount department stores are now about 50% of their total volume. Both expect their future growth to come primarily from the discount trade, while one states that the volume of business done by these stores is so great that what he is able to deliver to them every three to four weeks is actually sold within a period of one week. Three other manufacturers service the stock of discounters, but also have done so with their older customers; they report the same magnitude of sales success to discounters. All five of these manufacturers sell popular price merchandise, four of them having staple lines like men's or women's undergarments or hose.

One manufacturer who provides in-store servicing for all major customers and whose business with discounters now amounts to $15 million per year finds that such a complete merchandising program results in discounters buying primarily from one source, rather than from the large number of different suppliers typical for department stores. Moreover, he has been able to set up a plan for upgrading the stock carried in discount department stores and has just added, to his surprise, goods which sell at the fourth price level above those he originally sold to discounters. We believe that the success which these manufacturers have achieved through the adaptation of old and new selling practices to the discount department store trade is evidence of the potential which exists in this field.

DETERMINING POLICY

Whatever have been the manufacturers' decisions to date—to sell freely to discounters, to sell selected products only, or to refuse entirely—the decisions seem to have been made on an expediential basis with little systematic analysis of the long-run potential for low-margin, self-service soft-goods retailing. Though the application of supermarket methods in soft goods has been growing spectacularly for almost a decade, most manufacturers have remained uncertain as to its long-run future and how to adjust their own sales and operating policies.

The absence of orderly analysis is due in part to the division of the soft-goods manufacturing industry into a large number of relatively small firms whose success has depended more on their ability to keep abreast of style changes and to sell on a personal contact basis than on their ability to plan and develop long-range market representation. In neglecting long-range distribution analysis, the soft-goods manufacturers have not been alone. In marketing research, both academic and business attention has been focused more on problems of product innovation, promotion, and price response than on the adjustments in distribution required to accommodate changes in consumer income, living patterns, and shopping preferences.

The interrelated commitments and "choosing up of sides" implied in a manufacturer's choice of type of retail representation (particularly when selective distribution is used) make it impractical for either manufacturers or retailers to adjust channels of distribution as frequently as is common with promotional methods, product design, or price. This infrequency of opportunity for change carries with it the implication of longer range effects from major adjustments when they *are* made. Major retail innovations such as the development of mail-order houses, variety chains, food chains,

food supermarkets, and soft-goods supermarkets have appeared infrequently; but when they do occur, the effect can be devastating on the distributors or manufacturers who do not accommodate their operations to the innovation.

Framework for Analysis

Even the fastest growing of these major retail innovations has taken a period of several years to achieve market significance. The dynamic growth of self-service supermarkets in soft goods has been available for observation over an eight-year period. Thus, there is more opportunity for an orderly analysis of future distribution prospects than there is, for example, for an analysis of changes in product fashions or promotion appeals.

Yet only one of the manufacturers interviewed appears to have made a thorough analysis of ways best to adapt its operational methods, products, price lines, packaging, inventory, and delivery system in order to serve the special requirements of large-volume self-service stores and to minimize the cost of moving the product from factory to consumers via these institutions.

Our direct contact with manufacturers in the soft-goods field, supplemented by numerous conversations with discounters themselves and with trade editors in the field, leads to the conclusion that both those manufacturers who are actually jumping on the discount-outlet bandwagon and those who are standing to one side are following the dangerous course of *making expediential decisions based on current surface indications without probing into the long-range soundness of the new operations.*

Major retail innovations involve an "invention" of new means of performing the retailing function. They may be dependent on concomitant developments in products, in physical handling technology, and in organization at the wholesale supply level; but, *most important of all, they are dependent on changes in the income, location, and style of life of consumers.* Thus, it is important to make a detailed analysis of consumer action patterns and of the vulnerability/survival prospects of established outlets. Here are some specific suggestions:

1. *Test against consumer buying patterns —* A manufacturer seeking to appraise the potential significance of a new form of retailing should first probe its appropriateness from the

consumer viewpoint. Is the new innovation compatible with developments in consumer income, location, and living patterns as these may affect shopping patterns? Early in the development of self-service for soft goods, such inquiry might have indicated, for example, that:

• A large portion of the population, formerly at a low income level and with relatively little available discretion in both the kind of goods purchased or the place of purchase, had achieved a new freedom.

• These newly prosperous consumers were being poorly served by the small specialty shops in low income areas, and they had developed little affinity for department stores oriented to the already established middle- and upper-class consumers.

• Suburban locations, easy automobile access, ample parking, and long store hours would prove convenient for large numbers of consumers increasingly oriented to the automobile as a mode of transportation, and frustrated by the crowding of downtown shopping areas.

• Consumer acceptance of self-service in food products represented a positive preference for self-service and not merely a desire for the lower prices associated with elimination of the costs of clerk "service."

Such a study might also consider the increasing physical and social mobility within our population. A useful portrayal of this mobility was given a decade ago in a series of articles by William H. Whyte.[2] This mobility may have an influence on loyalty to familiar retail establishments and on the willingness to sample the wares and methods of new kinds of stores.

2. *Study the customers of pioneer stores* — There appears to have been remarkably little study of the types of consumers buying in discount department stores, the development of repeat-purchasing, interstore shopping, or the extent to which individual families take advantage of the wide range of products available in these stores.

There has also been little study of the aspects of these new stores which have positive pulling power to bring in consumers versus those aspects which customers merely tolerate in their search for bargains. Both manufacturers and retailers have a real stake in learning more about the consumers who patronize

the new stores, where they previously bought similar products, and the share of total buying which consumers appear willing to do in these stores after they have had some experience with them. Only one of the 78 manufacturers interviewed is undertaking a direct study of consumer shopping as affected by self-service soft-goods supermarkets.

3. *Study areas of highest saturation* —It is of greatest importance to manufacturers, to store operators, and to the financial community to identify more accurately the point at which the building of new discount department stores will saturate the market for this type of operation. In many areas in Southern New England, self-service soft-goods supermarkets are thickly enough established to make possible some measurement of the saturation point. Detailed analysis of sales trends in individual product lines and of the level at which long-exposed customers stabilize the share of their patronage given to the new type stores could provide useful information long before information on saturation becomes apparent in total store sales experience. Springfield, Massachusetts, and Lowell, Massachusetts, would be good locations for such saturation studies inasmuch as each has had a heavy concentration of stores for several years.

4. *Appraise the survival potential of customers* — The growth of discount department stores has occurred during a period when consumer income and buying have been increasing in total. However, since 1958 or 1959, the annual increase in sales of the new-type stores has exceeded the average rate of total market growth ($1.0 to $1.25 billion a year) for the "general merchandise" and "apparel" classifications of stores. As a result of this transfer of volume, some older stores will go out of business and others will fail to achieve planned growth. Some of the traditional outlets will stagnate. Others will redirect their operations in order to serve some selected part of the market less directly affected by self-service competition. Still others will find some means of adaptation to offer consumers many of the advantages which they have recognized in the new self-service soft-goods stores. It appears reasonable to say that most of the volume of almost any manufacturer in the soft-goods field (except those in the very high-style and high-price lines) will move through stores whose operations are materially affected by this major retail innovation.

Few soft-goods manufacturers have made

---

[2] *Fortune*, May, June, July, and August 1953.

an orderly analysis to identify that share of their total business which is going through established retailers who are subject to direct competitive inroads from low-margin, self-service operations compared with those retailers who by virtue of operating methods or location are relatively insulated from such competition.

Obviously, much of the information necessary for the above kinds of analysis cannot be developed feasibly by individual firms. However, some of it exists from government-developed and/or industry-developed research. And for most manufacturers analysis of their own situations in the context of generally available information will yield bases for judgments far more sound than those presently employed.

CONCLUSION

The original self-service soft-goods supermarkets established in New England from five to eight years ago, located in an existing warehouse or mill building and frequently some distance from major traffic arteries and established shopping centers, were highly successful, but they represented a pattern from which the constructive evolution which has occurred could have been expected. The majority of new stores offering soft goods on a low-margin, self-service basis have been substantially upgraded from the original prototypes in terms of store buildings and facilities, convenience and prominence of location, quality and completeness of merchandise offerings, and supporting services offered. A modest increase in expenses, margins, and prices has been associated with this upgrading, but there still exists a substantial—10% to 20%—gap between the prices offered in these self-service stores and those of the traditional retailers with which they principally compete.

Along with the improvement of store characteristics, locations, and merchandise, there has been an upgrading in the type of customer drawn into the store. The early stores were planned to appeal mainly to the working-class family. More recently, the self-service operations in soft goods have become established in, or adjacent to, first-class shopping centers in higher income suburbs.

We think that the evolutionary process within the self-service selling of soft goods, housewares, and related items will continue. Additions to store services and merchandise (automobile care centers for tires, realignment, lubrication, etc., would be an example) may increase substantially the sales level at which general-merchandise, self-service stores will saturate a community.

Until now, these stores have been located primarily in the Pacific Coast, Southwest, North Central, Northeast, and Middle Atlantic sections. From the success achieved in these areas, there would appear to be substantial opportunity for hundreds of new stores in other parts of the country. Development has also been largely in major metropolitan areas. It is reasonable to expect that some further development of self-service, general-merchandise operations will be found in the smaller towns and cities throughout the country.

We believe that the intrusion of low-margin, self-service retailing (other than in foods) has to date accomplished considerably less than half of its eventual growth. In the light of our research into manufacturer decision making thus far in this dynamic field, we would conclude that there is little assurance that the right decisions are being made with regard to product, price, promotion, and type of distribution outlet. Much fundamental information, as well as sophisticated analysis, has been lacking. Most neglected by manufacturers has been investigation of trends in the income, location, and style of life of consumers. How well do their present outlets fit changing distribution patterns?

By the past record of one new major retail innovation every decade or so, the next "retailing revolution" may already be in incubation. Will manufacturers and existing retailers be ready to appraise its potential? If past records foreshadow the future, the established firms will again allow a group of brash new innovators to sweep past them and to capitalize on the new approach.

DISCUSSION QUESTION

This article identifies the "discount department store" as an emerging retail innovation, and presents an interesting historical discussion of the process of growth and acceptance traced by earlier "innovations" in retailing. The argument advanced is that retail institutions represent a universe of continual change and manufacturers must develop the skill to distinguish the institutional "fad" and the true institutional innovation.

Is the "discount department store" an innovation in the sense that it involves a significantly different approach to retailing than existing institutions? Is the "discount department store" more nearly a synthesis of existing institutions? Which institutions does it synthesize? Are there other existing retail institutions which might reasonably synthesize?

4. Closed Door Discount Stores

FRANK MEISSNER*

The wheel of American retailing is taking another turn.

When, after World War II, the discount house originally caught on, many of the stores operated on a closed-door or membership basis. This was in part an attempt to avoid litigation on fair-traded merchandise.[1] For instance, Master's, one of the first major postwar discount houses, issued "membership cards in its early days in an effort to protect itself from fair trade snoopers and similar annoyances. It soon found it could cut prices with impunity, and dropped the cards." [2]

As time wore on, fair trading died a slow death. The "classic" discounters began to open their door to the general public, and gradually came to look more and more like the old-line retailers.

In the early 1960's the closed-door discount house staged a come-back.

It looked as if the closed-door store was soon to be a historical phenomenon only. Yet there was already at least one exception to the disappearing "courtesy card:"

discount houses that are connected with labour unions and associations of government employees or professional people. In this respect discount house privileges are becoming a new and very important type of fringe benefit. This arrangement is getting to be known as closed shop retailing. On the West Coast this trend is particularly strong.

Now it looks as if close-door discount houses are staging a come-back far beyond the modest original expectations. What is behind this trend? Where are we heading?

The Western States are the major breeding ground for the closed-door revival. In 1961 out of 35 leading closed-discount organizations no less than 22 had units in the 11 Western States.

In 1952 in Los Angeles, a group of government employees decided to try to save money by shopping at wholesale prices directly from distributor catalogues. The venture proved so popular that the group decided to go into the store business, and set up FEDCO (Federal Employees Distributing Co.). By mid-1961 FEDCO had become a 5-unit Southern California chain with three stores in Los Angeles, and one each in San Diego and San Bernardino.

Other closed-door stores are springing up along the Pacific Coast: MORE with five stores in Los Angeles; SAVECO in San Diego; AGE in Oakland and Valejo; GET in San Francisco; General Sales in Portland and Salem, Oregon; Gov-Mart in Seattle and Tacoma, Washington. The membership concept is spreading throughout the country. Fed-Mart Corp., which started in San Diego, has branched out into Arizona and Texas; a merchandiser known as SAGE operates stores in Houston and Dallas. GEX (Government Employees Exchange), a subsidiary of National Bellas Hess, has opened up in Oklahoma City, Atlanta and Norfolk, Va.; FAME Inc. has stores in Cleveland, Columbus and Dayton, Ohio.

♦ SOURCE: Reprinted by permission from the editors of *Cartel*, in the January, 1961 issue, pp. 15–26; January, 1962 issue, pp. 34–40.
* Associate Professor of Marketing San Francisco State College.

[1] Unlimited amounts of imagination have gone into evasion of Fair Trade laws on both sides of the Atlantic. Thus, when early in 1961, Grandways—a Leeds, England discount department store—ran afoul of the legislation permitting price maintenance (which can be enforced by any one manufacturer) it started to draw up instalment agreements which do not require the customer's signature. Purchasers are given the normal receipt which the firm regards as acceptance of its unique hire terms—quarterly payments of one penny for 21 years "if demanded."

[2] James C. Cumming, "Closed Door Discounters Are on the Move," Sales Management, August 19, 1960, p. 46.

GEM International is rapidly becoming a national closed-door chain. At the end of 1961 it operated units all the way from Hilo, Hawaii to Virginia, Alexandria. CMA, Consumer Mart of America, is a relatively new, but very aggressive entrant into the race. It opened its first store in 1959 in Chicago; its second in 1960 in Oaklawn, Illinois, and invaded California in 1961.

In late 1961, there were perhaps as many as 100 closed-door discount stores in the United States. About two-thirds of them have joined together in the National Association of Consumer Organisations (NACO), which represented a "membership" of almost 2 million and sales of perhaps $300 to $400 million.[3]

RECRUITING MEMBERS

"Members" of the store are recruited initially from amongst "eligible" occupational groups- Federal, State and local government employees. Eligible membership usually soon widens, however, to include trade unionists, servicemen, factory workers engaged on defence contracts, employees of banks. "Members carry a card costing them $2–$3. The stores operate a strict non-admission for non-members policy, and try to build up loyalty amongst the membership by selecting advisory committees from among "card-holders."

Stores are situated in low rent areas, resemble large warehouses and have a minimum of fixtures. Services are kept to a minimum and cash sales are encouraged. Because of the members-only policy, advertising and promotional costs are kept down. Floor space is let to concessionaires who must give an agreed discount from normal retail prices. Discounts range from 10–35 per cent.

Food, dry goods and even motor cars are sold by membership stores.

The concession setup is being advocated because it minimises the operators' risks. The concessionaire owns the fixtures, the inventory, and pays his personnel. It all adds up to low costs and better profits. Even more important in this way the operator buys built-in management.

For the concessionaire, the licence brings a larger captive audience than he would pull in if he were working on his own. Low prices mean fast turnover. Since April 1960, the National Association of Consumer Organisations has thus had a close tie-in with a separate organisation, Co-operating Marketing, Inc., which buys in bulk for concessionaires of membership companies. Getting good concessionaires seems no problem; they allegedly stand in line at NACO headquarters seeking appropriate landlords.

However, both UNIMART and FEDCO on the West Coast claim that the fewer concessions a store has, the better off it is. The reason lies in control. GEM controls concessionaires by working on short 30 day contracts. As a company grows, it attracts merchants better.

MORE THAN A MATTER
OF DEFINITION

There is considerable confusion about what distinguishes a closed-door store from a "conventional" discount house. NACO (National Association of Consumer Organisations) draws a fine distinction. It maintains that conventional discounters take the *manufacturer's price* and cut it. In contrast, closed-door stores take the *wholesale price,* and add to it a smaller than normal markup. This low margin is made possible because membership houses have low cost of doing business. They are not located in expensive downtown areas or shopping centres but rather on vacant lots on the outskirts of cities. There they erect austerely functional buildings with exterior decoration limited to the store name, and possibly an elevated neon sign. Most units depend on self-service, and keep employees to a minimum. Robert L. Wolfson, Chairman of GEM, likes to call this the "no-gloss-no-floss" policy.

Some operators lease departments to concessionaires for a fee or share of the profits on the ground that such specialisation pays off in earnings. Others prefer to keep the whole operation under their own control, to maintain quality and eliminate the expenses of the middleman. Either way, closed-door retailers feel they have a valuable edge; by limiting their customers to specified groups, they have a pinpointed, homogeneous, market. "We can forget the bargain-basement crowd and the mink-coat crowd," one executive says. This means concentrated buying in price ranges pretty well fixed by income—and akin in taste.

Limited promotion—again pinpointed to its market—also cuts costs. Self-service simple fixtures, payment for services—all help to make a low-margin setup profitable.

---

[3] The headquarters of NACO are at 1411 K Street, Washington, D.C.

Closed-door merchants do not rely heavily on loss leaders. Rather, they profess a "sustained overall low markup." Across the board, we save members from 15 per cent to 20 per cent every day of the year," claims an official of GEM. Most open door discounters claim the same thing, of course.

Profits come primarily from direct sales and from concessions. Proceeds from membership fees are usually used for promotion.

The rationale behind the closed-door concept was well described recently by E. T. Ageno, Controller of the Fed-Mart in San Diego, California.

According to Ageno, "Membership fees are not collected for the sake of the income they produce; this is actually very little in the end. The membership idea, however, brings a homogeneous type of customer to the store, making the merchandising far simpler. It also has a psychological effect upon the customer, creating a feeling of belonging and loyalty to the store. It makes for minimal credit losses, partly from the feeling of loyalty, and partly because the selection of members is in the area of good risks. A monthly mailing to members constitutes advertising, and there are no loss leaders or promotional sales." [4]

It must be emphasized that the paid-card system give the store an excellent mailing-list —and they all use this list as the basis for most of their promotional effort. MORE, for example, publishes the *Buyer's Digest*, a monthly house organ, which goes to all its members. It carries editorial material as well as advertising—articles written to interest its customers, most of whom are Government workers. FAME, in Columbus, puts out a monthly magazine. All of them use conventional direct mail advertising material, and some use newspaper advertising as well. Most of them direct their newspaper advertising at getting new membership applications, rather than direct sales.

Under these circumstances most of the closed-door discounters keep their promotional expense in the neighbourhood of 1½ per cent, with very few going as high as 3 per cent. While these stores are self-service stores, they all offer plently of parking space and convenient hours. Usually they are open seven days a week, and six nights. Their credit policies are liberal with 30-day revolving charge accounts and instalment plans.

Perhaps this sort of philosophy makes closed-door discounters less vulnerable to the impact of the business cycle. In fact, some of the operators felt that the 1960–61 recession actually tended to encourage sales. For instance, Save-Co Veterans in San Diego, a "depressed area" with over 8 per cent unemployment, actually expected an improvement in 1961 profits. Similarly, 1961 sales of the widely-scattered units of GEM International, some of which are also in areas of high unemployment ran ahead of 1960. The company expects to issue about 250,000 additional membership cards during 1961, bringing its total to around 750,000.

RESPECTABLE PROFIT RECORD

So far, only a few of the closed-door discounters have offered common stock to the public. Among them are Save-Co Veterans, Fed-Mart and GEM International, General Sales, Gemco and GEX. More are planning to issue equities.

In 1960 the publicly owned companies turned in impressive performance records. For instance, Fed-Mart Co. scored a 45 per cent gain in sales during its fiscal year ended August 31, to $58.3 million; net rose by over 30 per cent to $1.3 million, equal to 86 cents a share. Both figures were new records. Last year, the company raised its semi-annual cash payment to 12½ cents from 10 cents; it will pay a 2 per cent stock dividend on March 1, as it did in 1960. Since 1954, when Fed-Mart opened its first store in San Diego, sales have soared 20-fold and net, 17 times.

GEM International reported a 43 per cent increase in sales during 1960, to $47.6 million. Net rose by 50 per cent to $650,000, or 57 cents a share, from $432,995, or 38 cents. Robert L. Wolfson, chairman, says that sales are running "substantially ahead of average retail figures, both on local and national levels."

WHO IS AFFECTED?

Conventional downtown retailers are keenly feeling the pinch of closed-door discount competition. The long opening hours are particularly bothersome. A Dayton retailer remarks, "It was bad enough when food markets and some neighbourhood furniture stores remained open on Sundays. When the major discount houses started keeping Sunday hours, our backs were broken."

[4] *Sketches of Two Discount Set-Ups,* Stores, July–August, 1961, p. 29.

The reaction of the department stores is the same as it would be toward any other discounter or unorthodox retailer: they either try to ignore them, retaliate or join them. Thus, in St. Louis, where GEM is the big closed-door discount store, one department store has tried to strike back. In a newspaper advertisement illustrated with a kitten and a skunk, the store said, "You can tell a cat by his stripe, just as you can tell a bargain from a discount deal. There's a difference, as there is between a polecat and one of the feline variety. Of course, you can find items at so-called discount prices, but what is behind those prices? The confidence that the store will back you 100 per cent should something go wrong? How about delivery to your door and credit terms? Here you pay no registration fee: you need no card. Regardless of where you are employed or whom you know, everyone can take advantage of everyday low prices at Stix, Baer & Fuller."

This sort of "competitor knocking" can lead to serious boycotts of the closed-door discounters. Thus, Consumer Mart of America, a Chicago-based store, suddenly found the local newspapers refused its advertising copy.

When checked, the *Tribune* admitted that it wouldn't accept the store's advertising for policy reasons, the *Daily News* and the *Sun-Times* said Consumer Mart did not qualify for local rates, and *The American* stated that it had never turned down the advertising.

However, a good idea cannot be boycotted out of existence. The success of the closed-door stores depends on their ability to win and hold the loyalty of large groups of customers. No attempt is made to attract the general public; in fact, non-members are barred from the premises by a security system which rivals that of defence plants. Shoppers must have a certifying membership; however, the cost is nominal, ranging from $2 to $3.

Because at most stores employees of federal, state and local governments form a nucleus of the membership—the word "government" or its abbreviations occur in many company titles. Other typical card holders are members of labour unions, of the armed services and veterans, employees of companies which do a substantial volume of defence business and employees of non-profit organisations. Normally cards may be used not only by members but also by their families and guests.

The success of closed-door discount houses tends to dissipate some of the traditional Employee Product Purchase Plans (EPPP) that have for years been in effect in many corpora-

tions. Thus early in 1961 General Electric modified its EPPP because a "company study has shown that changes in retailing practices in recent years have lessened the effectiveness of the old Plan and that it is no longer working to full advantage for most employees." The modified EPPP makes it possible for GE employees to make trade-ins as part of the purchase arrangement. This is because the new plan places an employee in the same position in the market place as any other customer— free to negotiate the most favourable terms and conditions of purchase with the franchised General Electric or Hotpoint dealer of his choice.

Courtesy discounts for employees range from $10 to $75 on major appliances, audiophonographs and television receivers, and are being applied against the purchase price— "thus guaranteeing that employees will pay less for their General Electric and Hotpoint appliances than the general public in the community." [5]

DIVERSIFICATION

In 1961 many of the closed-door discounters were able to boost sales by broadening their merchandise assortment and increasing the number of departments. Some stores have thus added drugs, and specialised services such as life insurance, optometry, and filling stations where members can get petrol at a discount.

In the process, the corporate structure (or organisational charts) can become a rather confusing maze. For instance, Fed-Mart, by far the most highly diversified firm in the industry, reflects largely the mergers and acquisitions leading to its formation. Among its other activities, it wholesales petroleum products, through a 50 per cent-owned subsidiary, Reid International Petroleum: the latter not only supplies Fed-Mart stations but also sells to outside customers. As a result of a merger with Rifco, Inc., in 1958, Fed-Mart acquired investments in two shopping centers in San Antonio, a 50 per cent interest in a third in Austin, 17 acres (partially occupied by a company-owned bowling alley) and three other parcels of land outside San Antonio. Fed-Mart also owns a half-interest in 15 acres in San Diego, occupied by a new department store. A subsidiary, the Fed-Mart Life Insurance Co., is licensed to do business in Texas, Arizona and California. De-

---

[5] See: *The Temp Orbit*, General Electric-Santa Barbara, California, March 17, 1961, p. 1.

spite this broad diversification, however, 85 per cent—90 per cent of total income still come from its Fed-Mart membership stores.

Part of the diversification effort is focused on foods. For instance, in mid-1961 Safeway, the second largest supermarket chain in the United States (A & P is first) became tenant of the grocery departments of GEM International (Government Employees Market) in the Omaha, Nebraska and Denver, Colorado stores. GEM is a 14 unit closed-door discount chair with over 700,000 "members" and a 1962 hoped-for volume of $150 million, or about $200 per member.

WHERE DO CONSUMERS CO-OPERATIVES FIT IN?

After some setbacks closed-door discount stores are going strong again. Why this development should sprout and prosper at this time is, frankly, something of a mystery. After all, Fair Trade no longer seems the key. Although California is still a Fair Trade stronghold, strong membership houses flourish where the law has been crippled or thrown out. Thus, closed-door stores are moving eastwards, and are now operating in Arkansas, Florida, Kentucky, Maryland, New Jersey, New York, Rhode Island, Virginia, and Washington, D.C.

The explanation might in part be found in the similarity between the closed-door store and consumer co-operatives.

There are, of course, important differences. Most closed-door concerns run their firms for profit like any businessman would. Yet the "co-operative halo" may still be part of the picture. Many closed-door operators have advisory councils of local businessmen, who "represent the consumer's viewpoint," as one company rather vaguely puts it. The successful operators make their members feel they are on the consumers' side. GEM, for example, puts much of its promotion money into scholarships. Planning such outlays is a function of the advisory council.

Membership carries a strong appeal, thinks John W. Martin, psychologist and consultant for Ward J. Jenssen, who helped Unimart set up its organisation. People like the feel of exclusiveness that membership brings. The fact that they have paid to belong convinces them they are getting a bargain to which they are entitled. Perhaps this might come closer to the heart of the matter. The relatively few consumer co-operatives in the United States, some

exceedingly successful, others less so—might heed this clue.

WHAT OF THE FUTURE?

In spite of the recent success of the closed door houses, their membership requirements put some inherent limitations on future growth. Too many stores is a distinct danger. In San Diego, where at one time there were seven closed-door houses, by Fall 1960, there were only three.

The closed-door revival has not had everything its way. In soft goods, especially some suppliers still refuse companies that would like to sell their wares. This has helped to push private labels in some lines. In a few cases, newspapers have balked at carrying their advertising. Fair Trade is still a headache to some, as it is to other low-markup operators.

Weaker operators can, of course, decide to discard the membership requirement. Some have already done so. In fact, the loosening of requirements or total abolition of membership is already disturbing the National Association of Consumer Organisations; NACO has a rigid set of by-laws, which refuse membership to any store that admits customers without "privilege cards." Thus, Mr. Dickson, President of GEX recently emphasised that the opening in the near future of a number of open-door, low mark-up department stores by GEX was a complete departure from the company's present membership department store operations. The new stores will be an entirely separate division of National Bellas Hess Inc., and certainly none of them are planned for communities in which a GEX store will be operating. "This Management," stated Mr. Dickson, "has been the severest critic of those so-called membership department stores whose eligibility rules include just about everybody . . . in our concept there is room for both bonafide membership department stores such as GEX and for similar low-markup stores that are open to the general public." [6]

Perhaps the most balanced view of the future should have some sort of regional stratification to it. "While competition among the various closed-door firms is getting keen in certain sections of California, throughout the rest of the country the potential customer list has barely been scratched. In fact, only about two million people now hold membership cards

[6] *Modern Retailer,* October 13, 1961.

—less than one-tenth of the number who are eligible." [7]

And when the East and the Midwest get saturated, perhaps the day will indeed come when closed shopes open up. The United States will then be ready for another "new" turn in the wheel of retailing. In the meantime let us prudently abstain from putting a date on this forecast.

[7] Norris Willcott, *Closed Shops: Members Only Discount Houses are the Latest Thing in Retailing,* Barron's, February 27, 1961, p. 12.

DISCUSSION QUESTION

The "closed door" discount operation has not had spectacular success in the United States. The concept of "closed doors" does, however, enjoy some advantage from the psychological appeal of membership restrictions. If the task of securing and holding a *regular* clientele gets much more difficult, it may be that a club-like atmosphere could provide the *esprit de corps* among customers which is all but non-existent in retailing today.

> What advantages might there be to selecting your clientele formally, and expressly (by omission) excluding others? What difficulties would a firm experience in formal market segmentation of this kind? Is it possible that, with increasing consumer affluence, a highly selective or "snob appeal" store might find an enthusiastic market segment?

5. Planned Shopping Centers

FRANK MEISSNER[*]

This paper is largely based on data collected for a study originally commissioned by the Consulate General of the Federal Republic of Germany, San Francosco. I am grateful to the Consulate for permission to use the material.

The post-war growth of American suburbs has brought about quick and profound changes in the pattern of living. Exodus from central cities shifted the concentration of potential buyers from downtown to suburbia. Since people make markets, the structure of the retail trade had to change in order to satisfy the needs of the suburban residents. The concept of the "planned shopping centre" fills this need admirably.

A Shopping Centre is an "area in which a number of stores of various types are located and in which the large majority of the consumer's wants may be satisfied. In this sense there is nothing new about the concept. For centuries shopping centres have been developing more or less accidentally in many towns, as stores tended to gravitate towards each other. In fact, already in Greek antiquity merchants spread their wares under the colonnades of the Stoa, which was an integral part of the Agora, the city square.

The adjective "planned" is new, however. It refers to the "premeditated" concentration of different types of stores, conceived as a unit and located in outlying sections of metropolitan areas or in suburbs. The centres are usually developed by an individual, a real estate promoter, a retail chain store, or consortia of often widely differing interests. Victor Gruen, the outstanding authority in the field, suggests the following twelve yardsticks that ought to qualify a development as a "true" shopping centre:

(1) The planning function should be based on careful research of existing shopping facil-ities, and evaluation of the sales potential of the area from which the centre is to draw business. (2) The centre should be easily accessible to shopping traffic. (3) The physical characteristics of the site should be suited for mass retailing: the area should not be a leftover from housing developments or a public road strip. (4) Mass parking of highest quality is required, to provide ample space for opening of car doors, loading, manoeuvering of cars, and good circulatory roads. (5) The type of stores should be balanced and systematically arranged so as to encourage purposeful traffic flow between them. (6) Customer traffic should be separated from service traffic. (7) Even the remotest parking places ought to be at a convenient walking distance from the stores. (8) Weather protection for window shoppers is highly desirable. (9) The overall architectural layout and sign control should offer variety without confusion and gaiety without vulgarity. (10) To offer high quality service and shopping convenience consistantly, the buildings should be air conditioned, provided with escalators, and with enough pickup stations so that shoppers should not have to carry heavy parcels. (11) As part of careful planning of a shopping centre, provision for enlargement of the facilities ought to be made, so as to meet the demands of anticipated growth in business. (12) The centre should be integrated with the surrounding area, so as not to reduce the desirability of residential developments in its vicinity.

In summary, a planned centre makes shopping a worthwhile and pleasurable experience, rather than a tiresome chore. It provides convenience of location, ample parking space,

[*] San Francisco State College.

freedom from congestion, reasonable variety of goods and values, and opportunity to shop at leisure.

TYPES OF CENTRES

Shopping centres are usually classified into three groups: neighbourhood, community, and regional.

The neighbourhood centres vary in size from 30,000 to 100,000 square feet and serve populations from 5,000 to about 40,000. They pro-vide shopping facilities for convenience goods. The principal tenant is usually a supermarket. Such centres are most numerous.

Besides size, there are no clear-cut criteria for distinguishing between community and regional centres. However, a shopping centre that has more than 400,000 square feet draws customers from a ten to fifteen mile radius, and in which one or two full-line department stores are the principal tenants, will usually be classified as regional. The classification criteria are summarized in Table 1:

TABLE 1. Attributes of Different Types of Shopping Centres

Type	Centre (thousands) of sq. ft.)	Size of Marketing Area (thousands of people)	Type of Goods Carried	Principal Tenant	Comments
Neighbour-hood	30– 100	5– 40	Convenience	Supermarket	Large walk-in traffic, small parking facilities
Community (intermedi-ate, accommodation, district)	100– 250	40–150	Convenience and comparison shopping goods in the "soft" line (apparel and dry goods)	Junior department store or a strong specialty store occupying an area of 25,000 to 75,000 square feet	Often includes a bank, a post office, possibly a theatre and professional offices for physicians, lawyers and accountants
Regional	250–1,000	150–400	Comparison shopping facilities attracting customers from within a 10 to 15 mile radius of the centre Also carries furniture and hard goods	Full line department store occupying from one-third to one-half of the entire area	A "satellite downtown," which provides facilities for complete one-stop shopping. Ample parking facilities for drive-in trade

Source: Victor Gruen and Larry Smith, *Shopping Town USA*, New York, Reinhold Publishing Company, 1960, pp. 277 and 278; and Gordon H. Stedman, *The Rise of Shopping Centers*, Journal of Retailing, Spring 1955.

The superstore is a rather recent variation on the theme. In essence, it is a shopping centre under one roof and under one management. It might cover between 50,000 and 200,000 square feet and needs 25,000 to 100,000 people for support. The superstore carries roughly the same type of merchandise as supermarkets and discount houses, plus such other services as laundries, beauty shops, and shoe repair shops. Superstores are owned and managed by a single company. This permits greater speed in the planning, organization and construction than is possible for conventional shopping centres, where a number of occasionally opposed interests must be reconciled.

So far the experience with superstores has

been too limited to warrant treatment as a retailing form separate from shopping centres. In this report superstores are therefore considered to be identical with shopping centres.

FLIGHT TO SUBURBIA

Growth and redistribution of U.S. population characterizes the changes that occurred in the last decade. The 178 million persons counted in April 1960 by the Bureau of the Census represents an increase of about 26 million or 17.5 per cent over April 1950. About 109 million people, or 61 per cent, of the national total, live in 189 standard metropolitan areas. It is in the suburbs of these areas that most of the population gain occurred. Thus, between 1950 and 1960 the population in metropolitan areas outside the central cities grew by over 17 million people, or 47 per cent, accounting for nearly two-thirds of the overall national population increase of 26.4 million persons during the decade. This is in contrast with a gain of only 8 per cent in the central cities. Four of the five United States cities with a million inhabitants or more, lost population—New York, Chicago, Philadelphia and Detroit. Only Los Angeles registered an increase of 24 per cent.

Traditionally urban purchasing power and retail sales were concentrated in the central city. Thus in 1947, although only 35 per cent of the total U. S. population lived there, central cities accounted for 48 per cent of all disposable income and 50 per cent of retail sales. In the suburbs the relationships were opposite: 23 per cent of population, 21 per cent of disposable income, and only 18 per cent of retail sales (see Table 2).

The fact that suburban retail sales lag behind the purchasing power of suburban residents is primarily due to a historical lack of adequate suburban shopping facilities and the habit of consumers to shop downtown.

However, shifts in purchasing power and growth of shopping centres are rapidly changing the situation.

Thus, figures in Table 2 indicated that between 1947 and 1958 population in central cities of standard metropolitan areas decreased from 35 to 32 per cent of the national total. The central cities' share of the total U.S. disposable income decreased from 48 to 37 per cent, or by almost one-fourth. This is because the character of the downtown population changes as well. Usually the "emigrants" are

white middle-income families with young children. They are being replaced by low-income "immigrants" who belong to minority groups such as Negroes, Puerto Ricans, or Mexicans.

In the suburbs the opposite trend is noticeable. Primarily due to the recent growth in shopping centres, suburban retailers are getting more than their share of the buying power that the ex-urbanites are bringing along with them. Thus, while in 1947 only 18 per cent of total national retail sales were made by suburban shops, the proportion rose to 25 per cent in 1958. There was a corresponding decline in downtown retail sales from 50 per cent of the national total to 43 per cent. (see Table 2).

GROWTH OF SHOPPING CENTRES

The recent growth in the "shopping centre movement" is phenomenal. To be sure, in the 1920s one or two groupings of stores were put in such a manner as to warrant the shopping centre designation. Yet, as recently as twenty years ago developers of suburban residential real estate considered inclusion of stores as a relatively unprofitable and unimportant service fringe-benefit that could occasionally be offered to would-be clients. Today the wheel has come around a full turn: a residential subdivision is unthinkable unless there is convenient access to a shopping centre. And so, from a mere 75 centres in 1949, the number soared to 1,800 in 1956, and doubled in three years to 3,600 in 1959. If all goes according to existing blueprints, U.S. shopping centre developers will put into operation another 900 units in 1960. The 4,500 centres expected by the end of 1960 will be doing $45 billion of business, accounting for about one-fifth of the total of $225 billion of retail sales. If the present trend continues, by 1970 some 10,000 shopping centres will be in existence.

The truly fantastic growth in shopping centres is clearly reflected by the fact that perhaps 70 to 85 per cent of the new supermarkets, drug stores, and department stores are now being located in shopping centres. For instance, in 1960 chain drug stores anticipate opening about 700 new units, of which about 550, or almost 80 per cent, are planned to locate in shopping centres. This will bring to 3,400 the total number of chain drug store units operating in shopping centres, or 34 per cent of the 10,175 chain drug stores. In 1958 "only" 27 per cent of these chain drug store units were in shopping centres (see Table 3).

TABLE 2. Share of Urban and Rural Locations in the National
Population, Disposable Income and Retail Sales, United States,
1947 and 1958. (Percent of U.S. total)

| Year | Standard Metropolitan Areas | | | |
	Rural	Central Cities	Suburbs	Total
	%	%	%	%
(A) Population				
1947	42	35	23	100
1958	38	32	30	100
(B) Disposable Income				
1947	31	48	21	100
1958	30	37	33	100
(C) Retail Sales				
1947	32	50	18	100
1958	32	43	25	100

SOURCE: *Sales Management:* Survey of Buying Power, May 10,
1959.

DEFINITIONS: *Standard Metropolitan Area* comprises a county or
a group of counties within which there is a city or combination of
cities with a population of at least 50,000.

Central Cities are used for defining Standard Metropolitan Areas.

Suburbs are those parts of Standard Metropolitan Areas that lie
outside the limits of the central cities.

Rural areas include all counties not included in Standard Metropolitan Areas.

TABLE 3. Chain Drug Stores in U.S. Shopping Centres,
1958–1960

| Location | Number of Stores | | |
	1958	1959	1960[1]
New Openings			
In shopping centres	300	450	550
Total	425	550	700
Stores in shopping centres as percent of total	70%	82%	79%
Stores in Operation			
In shopping centres	2,400	2,850	3,400
Total	8,925	9,475	10,175
Stores in shopping centres as percent of total	27%	30%	34%

SOURCE: "Chain Drug Stores," *Chain Store Age Magazine* (2 Park
Avenue, New York 16, New York), Special Release 0460—6M/708,
1960, p. 4.

[1] Estimated.

In California and other fast growing western states the growth of shopping centres is even more fantastic. Take, for instance, the booming Santa Clara County, which is located in the southern part of the San Francisco Bay Area. Between 1958 and 1959 the number of community and regional shopping centres increased from 31 to 39 and sales went up from $84.5 million to $111.8 million or by 38 per cent.

This compares to an increase in total taxable retail sales of 23.5 per cent in Santa Clara County, or from $502 million to $620 million. In other words, in a span of one year shopping centres were able to increase their share of taxable retail sales from 16.8 to 18.0 per cent (see Table 4).

PLANNING AND OPERATION

To put together a shopping centre requires capital, lots of it. For instance, in its final form, Westchester Terminal Plaza in New Rochelle, New York, would call for an investment of

TABLE 4. Share of Community and Regional Shopping Centres in Taxable Sales of Retail Outlets in Santa Clara County, California, 1958 and 1959

Area	(Sales in $ million)[3]		Percent 1959 Is Above 1958
	1958	1959	
	$	$	$
Shopping centres[1]	84,504	111,672	138.0
Other stores	417,412	507,947	121.8
Total[2]	$501,916	$619,619	123.5%
Shopping centres as percent of total	16.8%	18.0%	—

[1] "1960 Shopping Center Study," San Jose, California, *Mercury and News*, p. IV.
[2] Retail Sales Trends in Metropolitan San Jose—Annual Summary 1959 vs 1958," San Jose, California, *Mercury and News*, Table 1, p. 1.
[3] Includes all taxable sales reported in tax returns; excludes taxable sales disclosed by the State Board of Equalization through its audit program.
Tax-exempt retail sales (principally food for off-premises consumption and gasolene) are not included. Such sales were conservatively estimated at $5,475,000,000 in the entire state during 1958, or over and above the total taxable sales figures reported.

approximately $40 million. Only extremely careful planning and operation can result in profitable returns on such a large venture.

Although much has been written about the different business aspects of shopping centres, only a few rules of thumb have been developed. Planning and management of shopping centres still remains primarily an art, rather than a science. Let us review some of the major stages customarily followed in developing American shopping centres.

Economic Analysis

Having spotted a likely looking area, a shopping centre company, regardless of its associa-

tion, starts with a location survey. This study usually focuses around population data broken down by Census tracts, or the smallest relevant land division for which statistics are readily available. The quality of the potential customer is then described in terms such as age, income, number of spending units, nationality, occupation, driving time on the several roads to various parts of the area, estimates of the distance that these shoppers would be willing to drive for each kind of merchandise, traffic density at different times of the day, and the competitive "climate" both in downtown shops and nearby shopping districts or centres.

Developers usually hire consultants on marketing research and traffic engineering to carry out the necessary surveys. It is a highly technical job for which new methods are being evolved practically every day. Regardless of how much subjective judgment still remains as an inevitable part of the research approach, surveys are a "must." Most financial institutions are today unwilling to consider even tentative negotiations with a promoter unless a survey has been made. In fact, the lack of an adequate appraisal before development is generally considered to be the main reason for past failures of shopping centres.

Selection of Site

Once the market potential of a certain area is ascertained, a specific location for the centre must be found. As the number of shopping centres increases, it is becoming more and more difficult to find suitable locations. The following factors must be taken into consideration:

(1) Local land zoning, municipal regulations, and attitudes of residents of the immediate vicinity; (2) availability of power (voltage capacity and reliability of supply), water and gas and sewer connections; (3) drive-in and walk-in access to site from nearby highways and streets; (4) availability of "buffer strips" around the centre should permit future expansion, prevent fly-by-night retail shops to settle on the periphery, and provide landscaped strips for effective and attractive separation of commercial and residential areas.

Choosing Tenants

Selection of the principal tenant is crucial, because this store tends to be the major attraction of the centre. Leases for smaller tenants therefore normally are being negotiated only after the supermarket has been secured for the neighbourhood centre, the variety store for the community centre, or the department store for the regional centre.

The search for the tenant is an exceedingly delicate, and by no means painless process. On the one hand financial interests generally prefer 65 to 70 per cent of the tenants to be branches of well-known, well-established chain stores with AAA credit ratings. The large traffic generating stores know their bargaining strength. In order to get the principal tenants signed up the developer therefore has to make considerable rate concessions. This means that small stores are usually charged higher per square foot (fixed) rentals, as well as higher

percentage of sales (flexible) rentals. Once the centre gets going the small stores therefore frequently become the main source of the developer's income. Yet he can lease only 30 to 35 per cent of his space to them.

The small stores readily concede that they could not exist without the big stores drawing power. In spite of that they tend to complain that the leases are "rigged" in favor of the large and powerful principal tenants. The recent announcement of the formation of Lease Guaranty Company provides some hope that this situation could be alleviated. L.G.C. intends to insure leases of small retailers; this should make their papers acceptable to financiers looking for tenants with AAA credit ratings.

Be that as it may, we can use the Stanford Shopping Centre as an example of the "mix" of stores that one can find in a rather typical regional centre. Stanford Shopping Centre is located about 35 miles south of San Francisco and is the largest centre in Santa Clara County. It has 51 stores which in 1959 generated taxable sales of about $23,625,000. The land on which the centre stands is owned by Stanford University, which also owns the buildings and manages the centre on its own account.

The core of the centre is The Emporium, a department store belonging to the Associated Merchandising Corporation. It occupies practically half of the available 500,000 square feet. Next in importance is the Purity supermarket belonging to a local California chain. It has 23,400 square feet, or 47 per cent of total area; third is the Woolworth variety store with 15,800 square feet or 3.2 per cent of the total area.

However, apparel stores are the most numerous. There are eleven of them with a total of almost 127,000 square feet, representing over one-fourth of the total area.

All in all then the eighteen department, apparel, food, shoes, and variety stores occupy almost 85 per cent of the total store area. The rest of the retail, service, and commercial establishments are supplementary to the core. Shortly, the dominance of the department stores will become even more pronounced, because Macy's is planning to open a store with about 75,000 square feet.

Promotion and Advertising

Good developers are recognizing that their job does not cease when the centre opens. In order to generate and maintain satisfactory sales volume a favourable "image" has to be created for the centre. Different arrangements are being used for financing in promotional and advertising efforts.

"Increasingly, leases require tenants to join the merchant's association and contribute to overall centre promotion on a pro-rated basis. The big stores are more apt to come around if developers contribute to the promotion themselves. And some recognize the necessity for paid centre officials to direct the centre's promotion. Allied Stores Corporation, for one, has a full-fledged corporate management team to run its four large centres."

The advertising industry has also responded to the specific needs of tenants in shopping centres. In 1959 the Minnesota Mining and Manufacturing Company (makers of Scotch Tape) set up a subsidiary called Shopping Centre Network (SCN)—a national organization of over 200 major shopping centres with an estimated audience of 53 million adult exposures per month. Shopping Centre Network uses the parking area as medium for advertising. In return for a percentage of the advertising revenue, the co-operating centres allow ads to be displayed on light poles in their parking areas. Shopping Centre Network also plans to put up shoppers' showcase directories "consisting of permanent pylons installed along sidewalks in shopping centre malls. Each directory will include seven internally-illuminated ads, plus a directory of stores, a map of principal roads serving the centre, a clock, thermometer and weather vane.

The uniqueness of the Shopping Centre Network advertising is in its alleged ability to reach an audience in an ideally receptive situation. It is almost a point-of-sale medium. In contrast, most major media—such as newspapers, magazines and television—reach their audience at home, where no shopping action actually can take place.

FINANCING

Shopping centres come in assorted sizes and shapes. Some are tailor-made to fit the requirements of their trading areas. Others are run up on a standard pattern and then taken in here and let out there until they seem to fit. Still others are poorly stitched together of shoddy materials and are intended for quick sales rather than for lasting wear.

Up to the middle 1950's "poorly stitched together" centres were quite important on the scene. Actually, shopping centres were generally shunned as outlets for investment of financial and real estate experts. Lately the industry has gained in stature. Tight money and stiffer demands from lending institutions have driven out of business most amateurs and "flight-by-nighters." The industry is now dominated by professionals, American and foreign. Thus, for instance, many of the leading department stores and supermarket chains own centres: Stop and Shop, Allied Stores, Macy's, J. L. Hudson, Sears and Roebuck, Steinberg's (Montreal)—to name a few. Among the real estate firms are such giants as Realty Equities Corporation of New York and the British owned Dollar Land Holdings, which acquired in early 1960 the $23 million, 71-acre Cross Country Shopping Centre in Yonkers, New York, with such blue chip tenants as Woolworth, John Wanamaker, Gimbel Brothers and First National Stores.

Superstores are usually set up as logical extensions of discount houses (Two Guys from Harrison). Some food and drug retailers have also started such establishments (Grand Union of New Jersey, Giant of Washington, D.C., and Schwegman's of New Orleans).

Often one finds apparently "unlikely" parent enterprises to have a few eggs in the shopping centre basket. For instance, Utah Construction and Mining Company, a Rocky Mountain builder of dams and factories, operates a 65-acre shopping centre in Alameda, an islands city in the San Francisco Bay. Then there is Sunset International Petroleum, which owns 4,000 acres of land in San Diego, California; part of this huge acreage is being set aside for the development of a shopping centre. The Stanford Shopping Centre is controlled by the Stanford University. Roosevelt Field of New York is owned by Webb and Knapp, the leading American real estate company of which the illustrious William Zeckendorf is president. Similarly, Giant Food Properties are controlled by the privately owned Giant Food Supermarkets, while one-third of Eastern Shopping Centres of New York is owned by Grand Union, the chain of combined supermarket-discount houses.

Like many a baby, a shopping centre often starts as a gleam in a developer's eye. From then on the realization of the dream becomes a matter of ability to find land, tenants and money, and to translate them into bricks and mortar. The translation requires skill in handling figures by addition, subtraction, multiplication and division.

DISCUSSION QUESTION

Much of the sales volume which the central business districts in the United States have lost has been lost to large shopping centers of the "community" and "regional" size. These centers are, for the most part, the "planned centers" about which Professor Meissner writes.

The success of these centers in general attests to the need for them. But there are certain types of merchandise which one rarely sees offered in these centers.

> What are some of these neglected types of merchandise? Does this neglect constitute an opportunity in retailing which has been overlooked? How do you explain the absence of these merchandise lines?

6. Suggested Changes in Census Classification of Retail Trade

ROBERT D. ENTENBERG*

The field of retail distribution is so complex and dynamic that any method used to compile and class its statistics should be reviewed for possible improvement.

The purpose of this article is to review analytically the present retail-trade classifications, and to suggest changes that would improve the usefulness of the data. The changes suggested probably would result in more pertinent criteria for improving retail efficiency and productivity.

The classifications included in the *Census of Business, Retail Trade* include some 1,721,-000 diverse, complex, and highly competitive establishments generating an annual sales volume in excess of $200 billion. Compared with other fields of endeavor, retail distribution can be further characterized by comparative "ease of entry," high failure rates, and predominantly small size of most of its establishments.

Unfortunately the Bureau of Census classi-

♦ SOURCE: Reprinted by permission from the American Marketing Association, in the *Journal of Marketing*, January, 1960, pages 39–43.

* Robert D. Entenberg is Louis D. Beaumont, Professor of Marketing and Business Administration, University of Denver. He was formerly Professor of Retailing of the Graduate School of Retailing, University of Pittsburgh, and Chairman of the Retailing Department of the University of Georgia. He has wide experience as a business executive, speaker, and consultant. He received his M.B.A. from Washington University in St. Louis, and his Ph.D. from the Department of Business Organization of The Ohio State University where he also taught.

Professor Entenberg's essay won a $500 award in their open competition on "Problems in American Economic Development." He has authored numerous articles on market analysis and management, shopping centers, and forecasting. His book *The Changing Competitive Position of Department Stores in the United States by Merchandise Lines* (University of Pittsburgh Press, 1957) is now in its second printing.

fications underemphasize specific trading areas while far too much emphasis is placed on artificial geographical and political divisions. Yet in no other segment of the economy are trading areas of such vital importance. They determine the ease and extent of customer accessibility, a basic prerequisite for successful operation.

Among the many *Retail Trade* classifications are those of total sales—volume size by geographical and political subdivisions, kind-of-business, legal form of organization, number of paid employees, etc. The resulting data offer varying degrees of usefulness for scientific analysis and application. In effect, these data form the basic marketing tools used in determining the relative efficiency, productivity, and sales trends of the many diverse forms of enterprise making up the retail structure.

But far greater degrees of usefulness would result were the various types of retail establishments pinpointed and classified by specific trading areas such as Central or Secondary business districts; neighborhood or "string-street" locations; planned or unplanned regional, sectional, or local shopping centers. The introduction of these kinds of data by the Bureau of Census would provide far better evaluative criteria than now exist.

PRESENT RETAIL-STORE CLASSIFICATIONS

Present retail census data are compiled on an "establishment" basis and grouped into

94

categories classified according to predetermined structure characteristics.

Kind-of-Business

The "kind-of-business" grouping of stores is based on general-commodity group sales by merchandise lines. The extent and relative importance of the specific lines carried and sold cannot be evaluated very accurately because of the wide overlapping of similar merchandise classifications handled by separate intra-store departments and groupings. However, the "kind-of-business" classification does point out in broad general terms the type of information available in census data, and this information is basic to any projected conceptual changes in the collection of the data.

Ownership Classes

This grouping should be expanded to include subclassifications of "affiliated" as well as "non-affiliated" independent stores. Such as expansion would refer to whether the independent store worked co-operatively in promotion, merchandising, and operation through the sponsorship of manufacturers, wholesalers, or through "joint" efforts with other retailers. This change would be of particular significance to many consumer-goods manufacturers and distributors—especially those in grocery, automotive, accessory, variety, and drug businesses.

Sales-Volume Size

Retail establishments are grouped according to comparative sales size and by geographical areas. Basic trends concerning market concentrations, competitive conditions, and general types of consumption expenditures made can be determined from this grouping.

Classifications by Functions Performed

The value of the grouping by functions performed becomes a useful analytical tool when the relative operating costs of stores handling similar merchandise and offering similar services can be compared. If this grouping could be further subdivided according to type of shopping locale, its usefulness would be considerably enhanced.

Extent and Nature of Merchandise Lines Handled

The extent and nature of the product lines handled are greatly influenced by the size of trading areas, degree of population concentration, and the location of stores within the trading area. Selected "kind-of-business" groupings —such as food stores, general merchandise stores, and drug stores—are combined according to the nature and extent of the lines handled—into general stores, single-line stores, specialty stores, departmentalized specialty stores, department stores, variety stores, etc.

The shortcoming of these groupings is that the same or similar lines, as well as the varieties and assortments offered, are not carried by all stores within each group. No clear lines of demarcation exist; and broad-line classifications of merchandise offerings invariably involve extensive degrees of "value-judgment" interpretations.

Because the number of retail establishments carrying complementary or supplementary commodity lines is likely to increase rather than to decrease, the analytical usefulness of such classifications tends to be limited.

Classification by Location

Present criteria are set up for classifications according to size of geographical and political subdivisions without regard to "natural" or "planned" shopping areas. This imposes severe limitations on the usefulness of this grouping.

The encompassing trading area of large concentrations of population represents only a "first approximation" for scientific market analysis. There are so many different types of "shopping" and "buying" areas within "Standard Metropolitan Areas" that determination of markets is too often the result of educated guesswork. Purchase motivations, services, functions performed, types of goods offered, prices charged, and the extent of lines carried are almost completely interrelated with specific shopping-area location. Census data compiled according to geographical and political subdivisions leave much to be desired.

Further Problems

Lack of any specific trading-area identity is much more acute when marketing analysis is needed with reference to "shopping" goods and "specialty" goods. On the other hand, marketing analysis of widely distributed "convenience" goods is less dependent on correlations to particular types of shopping locales.

Again, the field of retailing is so dynamic and complex that data which would furnish optimum market measures will probably always represent broad generalizations and compromises.

Another widely used generalization that tends to be applied too broadly is the term "credit." "Credit" in itself is incomplete for purposes of setting up standards of comparison for this type of sales transaction. A credit sale may involve a 30-day charge account; a "revolving," "delayed," a "straight" installment sale; a combination of any of these; or still other types of deferred payment plans. Every type of credit offered has a direct bearing on size of store, frequency of purchase, amount of sale, price lines, clientele, functions performed, capital needed, and nature and extent of the lines handled. The economic groups residing in an establishment's trading area represent another important determinant of the type and the extent of credit offered.

Changes Indicated

A valid workable basis for a practical classification of retail establishments can be developed with the present "kind-of-business" groupings as a base. To be entirely comprehensive, the suggested changes and expansions should also include present groupings in terms of significant and contiguous population segments. Such segments could then be further subdivided into various trading-area classifications as detailed below. Each trading area, district, or center, in turn, would have a "kind-of-business" classification by size (as pointed out above), with further subdivisions by ownership status and by the kind of services offered.

In this manner, Census data enumerating similar types of stores with like volumes in similar trading areas, in similar types of shopping centers, handling similar lines, and offering similar groups of services would provide much more scientific bases for meaningful comparisons and analyses.

SUGGESTED REVISIONS

Accordingly, the following expansions and additions to present Census classifications are suggested:

Group I. Consisting of four broad divisions:

This group would include, as a first step, the listing of establishments by sales, according to kind-of-business classification *and* according to specific shopping-district locations by area segments as shown below. Suggested shopping-district classifications and subdivisions are listed and defined under Group II.

(a) The 184 largest cities.
(b) Cities of 25,000 inhabitants or more, exclusive of those included with "a."
(c) Cities of 10,000 to 24,999.
(d) Rural areas under 2,500 to cities with population up to 9,999.

Regarding Group I-a, a total of 178 cities were listed as "Standard Metropolitan Areas" in 1954. These metropolitan centers included 56.5 per cent of the country's total population, and accounted for almost $110 billion (approximately 64.7 per cent) of all retail-store sales. A "standard metropolitan area" has been defined by the Bureau of the Census as consisting of counties containing a city of 50,000 or more population as a basic framework.

Group II. Consisting of five locational subdivisions:

This group would represent the first subdivision for each category of Group I. The initial grouping would be by geographical area. A second regrouping could then be carried out according to comparable shopping district locations, irrespective of geographical areas. This would form a cohesive central core of *like* retail units in *similar* external settings as follows:

(a) *Central business districts*—This would include the sections within a town or city where all or mostly all communications, streets, and transportation converge, and where the principal shopping and specialty goods stores are concentrated. Their radii would be determined by population concentrations. Extremely large cities are quite likely to have more than one such district, while smaller cities, especially those adjacent to or contiguous with larger cities, may not have such a "district."
(b) *Regional shopping centers*—These would consist of "planned" centers that may have as many as 100 retail units, consisting of shopping, specialty, and convenience stores of all kinds. Such regional centers usually have a minimum total area of approximately forty acres and parking provisions for more than 4,000 cars.

(c) *Sectional, suburban, and intra-city secondary shopping locations*—These would include any sections where important segments of a town's or city's communications and transportation facilities emanate in conjunction with close proximity to extensive residential areas. Both "controlled" and "sporadic" secondary shopping districts would be in this category; this would include planned centers of approximately thirty-five to fifty stores on the order of the regional centers in II-b, but on smaller scales.

(d) *Neighborhood "string streets" and "convenience" centers*—These areas generally consist of contiguous "convenience" goods stores with only minimum differences between them (food, drug, bakery, etc.). Such store groups are generally developed along main traffic arteries. "Planned" shopping plazas of six to twelve convenience stores would be included in this subdivision.

(e) *Small clusters and scattered stores*—These would include all types, sizes, and varieties of establishments not classified elsewhere.

In the case of Group II-c, a "controlled" shopping-center classification would indicate those centers sponsored by private or collective efforts, and so planned that all developments benefit both the surrounding community and itself. A "sporadic" classification would be one where stores have evolved naturally into a full-blown secondary shopping district or section in response to locational needs.

"House-to-house" sales could be enumerated properly only if an established sales office is maintained. Where "selling effort" areas are undefined, location of main offices would be the determining factor of locational area. Mail-order sales which are solicited and processed through identifiable local offices would be considered as having originated in that "establishment." Mail-order and vending machines are also grouped in a "non-store" category in the present Census. All such sales would be more realistically grouped if included with total sales of the originating retail establishments.

Group III. By kind-of-business, ownership classes, co-operative affiliations, and service function type

(A) INDEPENDENTS

   (1) *Non-affiliated*—(By kind-of-business)

      (1a) *Full service* (where 50 per cent or more of total sales are made on a full-service basis—includes credit and delivery).

      (1b) *Limited Service* (where 50 per cent or more of total sales are made on a simplified, self-selection, self-service, and/or cash-and-carry basis).

   (2) *Affiliated* (By kind-of-business as 1-a or 1-b) for co-operative efforts through:

      (2a) Manufacturer-sponsored voluntary chains

      (2b) Wholesale-sponsored voluntary chains

      (2c) Ownership-group activities

      (2d) Joint buying, merchandising, etc., with other retailers

(B) *Multi-units*—(By kind-of-Business as 1-a or 1-b above)

   (1) Chains

   (2) Ownership groups

   (3) Independents with three or more satellite branches

(C) *Utility, government, and consumer-operated stores* (including permanently leased stalls in public or farmers' markets)

FINAL RECOMMENDATIONS

Unquestionably retail distribution will remain largely a local and personal type of business. And smaller stores will continue to represent a major portion of the retail structure both in numbers and sales volume. Census classifications should continue to reflect such characteristics.

Unfortunately, however, the smaller retail organizations are generally not in any position to develop their own evaluative criteria to improve their operating performance. More often than not, these smaller firms are the ones that need "guiding" data the most.

On the other hand, the larger retail organizations which can afford to channel funds into scientific research either fail to do so or merely make "token" explorations in this direction.

Because price lines, merchandise offerings, and operating procedures are determined in a great measure by external economic settings as well as entrepreneurial direction, store policies must be flexibly set and quickly responsive to the changing requirements of these settings. The suggested groupings above not only would indicate policy changes when needed, but would also provide more valid and pertinent standards of institutional comparisons.

Far more meaningful standards result when the basic data consist of statistical groupings of similar kinds of stores doing the same approximate volume, located in similar types of shopping centers, offering the same types of services, and having the same type of competitive advantages due to similar kinds of group affilia-tions. On the other hand, only limited usefulness can be derived from comparisons of similar stores located in completely different types of shopping centers with varying degrees of other competitive differences.

If the final stage in the distributive process is to achieve greater efficiency, more useful and greater applications of statistical compilations of the Bureau of Census must be developed.

DISCUSSION QUESTIONS

American retail institutions have been in a constant state of change particularly since the end of World War II. Though the Bureau of the Census still recognizes what are essentially "pure" classes of retail stores, the fact is that virtually every class has undergone some measure of "adulteration."

1. What are the major ways in which each of the following institutions have changed since 1945:
   (a) the supermarket?
   (b) the department store?
2. What are the emerging institutions which appear to be stable in spite of all of the apparent shifting about among and between older classes of retail store?

International Retailing Perspectives

In recent years, interest in marketing opportunities in foreign countries has increased. The concept of the multi-national business enterprise is reality for many firms. Retailing in foreign countries should be of interest to us for two reasons. First, many foreign countries hold great opportunity for the application of modern techniques of retail distribution. Secondly, retailing systems in foreign countries are fascinating laboratories for the study of alternative schemes for performing the retailing functions.

The readings in this section include an examination of some of the types of retail enterprise confronted in the U.S.S.R. and those to be found in France. It is generally believed that Europe has led the United States in vending machine retailing. An article is included which reflects some of the most recent developments in "automatic" retailing in Europe. An article by Professor Cundiff suggests some characteristics which are common to all retailing systems and which may permit a more systematic study of retailing on an international basis.

1. Concepts in Comparative Retailing

EDWARD W. CUNDIFF

The marketing systems that have evolved in different parts of the world clearly share certain common characteristics, but they also differ from each other in many important ways. Little is known about the degree and magnitude of these differences, and the degree, if any, to which they follow a logical, predictable pattern.

An understanding of such a pattern would be of great value to businessmen who wish to enter new markets or to predict developments in their own markets. At present, it is necessary to make a detailed study of each new market the businessman may propose to enter, because only rudimentary bases have been devised for comparing and generalizing about marketing systems.

These systems are at different stages of development throughout the world; and just as there are underdeveloped economies, there are underdeveloped marketing systems. By comparing economic systems at various stages, economists have attempted to devise ways of predicting future development in underdeveloped economies.[1] No equally comprehensive attempt has been made to explain the development of marketing systems.

Despite the lack of a theory of marketing development, marketing scholars have sometimes found it necessary to make predictions about foreign marketing systems by generalizing from their own systems.

An analysis of marketing in Finland indicated that, "Socio-economic conditions in Finland and the United States are sufficiently

similar that our past is Finland's present and our present is seen evolving as Finland's future." [2] In their predictions for future retailing in Europe, Jefferys and Knee do little more than project existing American development.[3] To improve the value of such predictions, a better understanding of the evolution and development of marketing systems is needed.

Bartels has made an important preliminary contribution to this problem, by suggesting alternative methods of approaching the comparative study of marketing.[4] However, the preparation of a comprehensive explanation of the interrelationships among comparative marketing systems is a major job. One way of contributing to such an explanation is the development of hypotheses concerning specific aspects of marketing which may ultimately help to fill in the total picture. Since retailing is important in all systems, the hypotheses described herein were developed to help explain the comparative evolution and adaptation of retailing practices.

EVOLUTION AND ADAPTATION IN RETAILING

An orderly process of evaluation and adaptation of important retailing innovations in separate marketing systems seems to exist. An explanation of this process requires four postulates:

1. Innovation takes place only in the most highly developed systems. The retailers in

♦   SOURCE: Reprinted by permission from the American Marketing Association, in the *Journal of Marketing*, January 1965, pages 59–63.
[1] W. W. Rostow, *The Stages of Economic Growth: A Non-Communist Manifesto* (Cambridge, England: The University Press, 1960), p. 4; Colin Clark, *The Conditions of Economic Progress*, 1st edition (London: Macmillan and Co., Ltd., 1940), pp. 337–338.

[2] A. J. Alton, "Marketing in Finland," *Journal of Marketing*, Vol. 27 (July, 1963), pp. 47–51.
[3] James Jefferys and Derek Knee, *Retailing in Europe, Present Structure and Future Trends* (London: The Macmillan Company, 1963).
[4] Robert Bartels, *Comparative Marketing: Wholesaling in Fifteen Countries,* sponsored by the American Marketing Association (Homewood, Illinois: Richard D. Irwin, Inc., 1963), pp. 1–6.

other systems have more to gain from the adoption and adaptation of developments already tried and tested in the most highly developed systems.

2. The ability of a system to adapt innovations successfully is related directly to its level of economic development. Certain minimum levels of economic development are necessary to support anything beyond the most simple retailing methods.

3. When the economic environment is favorable to change, the process or adaptation may be either hindered or helped by local demographic-geographic factors, social mores, governmental action, and competitive pressures.

4. The process of adaptation can be greatly accelerated by the actions of aggressive individual firms.

The following discussion is a test of these hypotheses, by measuring the stages of adoption of some retailing innovations in a selected group of marketing systems.

OPERATING METHODS VERSUS INSTITUTIONS

New retailing institutions would seem to be a logical kind of retailing innovation to study, since new institutions, such as supermarkets, are found in many nations. Yet such institutions are often too different from each other to justify comparison, having little in common beyond a name.

For example, there is little value in comparing American supermarkets with European supermarkets. Even a casual examination of the newly-developed "supermarkets" in Italy or England shows that the European institution is usually smaller, has a much more limited selection of merchandise, places far less emphasis on price appeals, makes less use of advertising, and makes no provision for parking.

American retailers themselves have used the term so loosely that it is necessary to define "real" supermarkets in terms of physical and operating criteria. Although *institutions* may evolve so differently as to preclude comparison, the basic retail *operating methods* are often the same in all marketing systems. The term "supermarket" may have different meaning in different markets; but a basic method of retail operation, such as self-service, has the same meaning everywhere. For this reason, the four hypotheses will be tested against new methods of retail operations, not against new institutions.

Identification of New Retail Operating Methods

For the purposes of this analysis, a new retailing development may be described as a new method of operating retail establishments, something that could be adopted by existing or newly-developed institutions, but that in no sense describes specific institutions. In this analysis it is necessary to confine attention only to *recent* innovations, because there is not enough historical information available about marketing methods in other nations to trace the pattern of adoption of earlier innovations.

At least four really new retail operating methods have evolved in the past half century. The best known and most widely adopted of these is self-service, which involves the displaying of merchandise in a manner so that the customer may, if he wishes, examine it and make his purchase selection without the help and supervision of store employees. The aspect of self-service that is really new is not the open display of merchandise (which is as old as retailing itself), but the provision for customers to handle and select the merchandise themselves *without* supervision.

A second innovation is the use of unusually low markups made possible by strict limitation of inventories and strong emphasis on high stockturn. The new development here is the price-inventory-stock-turn relationship, and should not be confused with price reductions resulting from other improvements in efficiency, such as increasing productivity of personnel.

A third development is the placement of large retail outlets or groups of retail outlets in suburban locations away from city congestion, as exemplified by planned shopping centers in the United States.

The fourth new development is automated retailing, providing the substitution of machines for people in the process of paying for and delivering possession of merchandise.

Selection of Marketing Systems of Comparison

The paucity of information on marketing in other nations limits the comparison that can be made. Census data are available for a large number of countries, but statistical information on retail operating practices is very limited. For this reason, it is necessary to rely to a large extent on descriptive material about foreign marketing institutions published by Americans who have visited and worked abroad.

Twenty nations were selected for comparison, including eleven European nations (Belgium, Denmark, Finland, France, Germany, Italy, the Netherlands, Spain, Switzerland, and the United Kingdom); four American nations (Canada, Mexico, the United States, and Venezuela); three Asian nations (India, Japan, and the Philippines); Australia; and the U.S.S.R. Unfortunately comparable economic information was not available for the U.S.S.R., and so it is not placed in rank order with the other nations.

TESTING THE HYPOTHESES

Of the four new developments, self-service has been the most widely adopted in marketing systems around the world, so it provides the best information for comparison between systems. For this reason it will be considered first as a means of testing the four hypotheses. To the extent that information is available, the other three innovations will be used to check the experience with self-service.

Evolution and Adaptation of Self-Service

Self-service, as an accepted method of retail operation, evolved in the United States primarily during or after the 1920s. Its development and dissemination in most of the highly-developed marketing systems throughout the world provides some support for the four hypotheses stated previously.

Hypothesis 1. The development of self-service supports the hypothesis that *retailing innovations evolve only in highly developed marketing systems.* On a purely *a priori* basis, the American marketing system is widely accepted as the most advanced in the world today, and was at least among the most advanced in the 1920s when self-service was first widely introduced.

Furthermore, there is no evidence of subsequent independent evolution of this method of operation in other marketing systems. The method appears to have spread primarily through adaptation of the original American idea.

Hypothesis 2. The spread of self-service into other marketing systems seems to support the hypothesis that *the ability to adapt innovations is related directly to the level of economic development of a system.* However, the identification and classification of stages of economic development is a problem challenging a number of economists today. A further complication is the wide variation in economic development that occurs within an economy. Just as the stage of economic development differs widely between New England and the Appalachian Mountain regions of the United States, so does it vary between the Amazon regions and the Rio de Janeiro-Sao Paulo areas in Brazil, and between the Piedmont and Sicilian areas of Italy. Thus, statistics on average economic development ignore the importance of highly developed subareas that may offer great potential for retail innovation.

Although it is beyond the scope of the present article to solve this problem of describing economic development, it is in order to have some basis for relating changes to economic differences, a number of factors for which comparable international data were sought. Only two factors were found—other data which showed promise of relating to economic development were not available on a current basis for all or most nations.

The first factor is an index of per-capita industrial productivity—percentage of value added in world industry divided by percentage of world population. The second is a measure of a nonessential semi-luxury good (telephones). These two economic factors, although offering promise as parts of a complex measure which may some day be devised to identify stages of economic development, are presented in this instance only as indicators of levels of economic development. Table 1 shows the measures of production and consumption, and the percentage estimates of self-service retail stores in all countries where information is available.

When the nations are ranked with respect to industrial production and with respect to telephones per capita, the similarity in order is fairly close; in most instances where the change in rank order is more than two or three, the differences can be explained in terms of noneconomic factors. For example, the United Kingdom, which drops from second place on the production ranking to seventh place in telephones per capita, has a tradition of heavy reliance on mail and telegraph in situations where other nationals might more likely use the telephone. Also, the nationalized telephone system provides unusually extensive public telephone facilities.

A comparison of the data on production and consumption with self-service in the 20 coun-

TABLE 1. A Comparative Ranking of Selected Nations with Respect to Economic Indices and Percent of Self-Service Stores[a]

Country	Index of production Per capita	Rank	Telephones in use Per capita	Rank	Self-service stores % of Total	Rank
United States	7.7	1	.42	1	>10.0	1
United Kingdom	6.8	2	.16	7	1.3	8
Switzerland	6.7	3	.32	3	2.4	5
Canada	5.6	4	.315	4	6.0	2
Germany	5.3	5	.12	11	3.6	4
Sweden	4.4	6	.36	2	5.35	3
Denmark	4.3	7	.245	5	1.4	6
Australia	4.1	8	.215	6	1.0	10
Belgium	3.7	9	.133	10	0.13	12
France	3.2	10	.101	12	0.24	11
Netherlands	3.0[b]	11	.1495	8	1.35	7
Venezuela	2.8[c]	12	.0285	16	0.005	16
Italy	1.9	13	.0805	13	0.02	13
Finland	1.6	14	.1464	9	1.1	9
Spain	1.05	15	.062	15	0.014	14
Japan	1.0	16	.065	14	(NA)	—
Mexico	0.7	17	.016	17	0.1	15
Philippines	0.05	18	.004	18	(NA)	—
India	0.03	19	.001	19	None	19
U.S.S.R	—				< 0.1	—

[a] SOURCES: Production and Telephone usage data data were from *Statistical Yearbook, 1962*, Fourteenth Issue, Statistical Office of the United Nations, New York, 1963. Data on self-service penetration were collected from 16 sources.

[b] Production data understate level of economic development in this primarily trading nation.

[c] Production data overstate level of economic development because of the large production of oil for export.

tries shows a relationship between these factors. For example, 5 of the 6 leading nations in production are also leaders in penetration of self-service, or, to move further down the list, 11 of the top 12 are leaders in both. It would also be useful to know what level of productivity constitutes an absolute minimum below which there will be no self-service; but since this list comprises almost entirely highly developed or developing nations, there are insufficient data to locate a possible cutting point.

Hypothesis 3. The spread of self-service also provides some support for the hypothesis that *noneconomic factors may affect the level of marketing development that might otherwise have been predicted in terms of economic factors.* At least some of the variance between rank in production and consumption and rank in use of self-service can be explained by such factors. For example, the United Kingdom, second in value added in industry, is only eighth in penetration of self-service. The British gov-

ernment maintained rigorous restrictions on consumption long after the end of World War II, which served as a barrier to the introduction of new methods of retailing. Credit restrictions, for example, were not removed until 1958. The wide variance between production and consumption (as measured by installation of telephones) would appear to support this view.

As another example, Australia, which ranks sixth on the consumption index and eighth on the production index, is only tenth in adoption of self-service. This discrepancy can be explained at least partly by social pressures against strong business competition, and a history of cooperative action among retailers and manufacturers to oppose changes that might affect the status quo.

Hypothesis 4. As long as a marketing system has reached the minimum stage of development necessary to support retailing innovations, it seems likely that this process can be hastened by the actions of aggressive individuals or firms.

For example, Sears Roebuck has dramatically influenced the retailing climate in Mexico since World War II, and may partially be responsible for the development of self-service in that nation at a more rapid rate than might be expected.

Also, in those instances where strong noneconomic forces may operate to prevent or delay the introduction of retailing innovations, an individual or firm may at least partially counteract these forces. Switzerland is a case in point where Gottlieb Duttweiler, through his Migros cooperative, worked almost single-handedly to overcome the organized opposition to change by entrenched retailers and wholesalers. Self-service has not developed as rapidly as might be expected in Switzerland, as indicated in Table 1; but might be nearly non-existent without the Migros retail outlets and the examples set by Migros.

The Price-Inventory-Stockturn Relationship

The discount house provides the best example of an application of the price-inventory-stockturn relationship in most marketing systems, since it is by definition a price promoter. Other institutions, such as supermarkets, which emphasize price appeals in the United States, do not use this appeal consistently in different nations. Thus, the discount house provides a better basis for measuring the spread of the price-inventory-stockturn method of operation in *all* marketing systems.

Subjective descriptions of the development of retailing in other marketing systems provide evidence that discounting and the price-inventory-stockturn appeal has been adopted in the same manner as self-service—in a direct relation to the economic factors mentioned before. In those markets where it has met with almost no success thus far, there seem to be either legal, competitive, or social barriers to its adoption. In Melbourne, Australia, for example, new discount houses that were operating successfully were forced out of business by conventional retailers who were able to bring pressure on manufacturers and wholesalers to shut off their supplies of goods.

Decentralized Locations

The decentralized location of retail stores also appears to be related to the stage of eco-nomic and marketing development. But it may be more strongly affected by noneconomic factors than the other retailing innovations.

For example, there seems to be a relationship between population concentrations, land costs, and the development of planned shopping centers. In Belgium, high population density and land cost have restricted the availability of parcels of land large enough for planned shopping centers. In addition, most decentralized retail locations are strongly dependent on the automobile as a means of transportation for the patrons. In those nations where excessive government taxes and restrictions have discouraged widespread ownership and use of automobiles (such as in Great Britain until recently) planned shopping centers have been slow to develop.

Automated Retailing

Since an important end-result of automated retailing is the reduction of labor costs, it is potentially more valuable in those systems where labor is costly relative to capital. Also, it will flourish best in those systems where the level of consumption is high enough that there is a high priority on consumer convenience.

Australia provides an example of a situation where noneconomic factors can hasten the adoption of new developments. Union pressures for shorter working hours have resulted in legislation forbidding operation of retail stores on Saturday afternoons, Sundays, and evenings; and so retailers have turned to automatic vending of certain convenience goods (such as gasoline), to serve the needs of customers when stores must be closed.

CONCLUSIONS

Retailing institutions provide a part of the environment in which marketing decisions must be made. A better understanding of their evolution in different marketing systems helps to provide a framework for generalizing about comparative marketing systems. One factor, however, has been consciously ignored in this simplified explanation of retailing innovations. Retailing and the broader field of marketing are not only affected by the total economic environment, but, in turn, they may themselves affect this environment.

In societies with high discretionary income and abundant goods there are pressures for improvement in retailing efficiency. The degree to which these economic pressures result in the evolution and adoption of new methods of retailing operation depends on the total environment. Cultural acceptance of or resistance to change, demographic and geographic influences, the political and legal framework, the strength of pressure groups such as business competitors and unions—all of these may have an effect on retailing innovations. When these pressures are negative, the actions of aggressive individuals or firms may do much to achieve and hasten change.

DISCUSSION QUESTIONS

Leadership in retail innovations gives the American retailer a perspective and insight into retailing in foreign countries which is often superior. Many foreign countries have retailing systems today which closely parallel that of the United States several decades ago. Many of these foreign countries are adopting retailing innovations which came originally from the United States—having had experience with these methods may qualify the American retailer for retailing in some foreign countries.

1. Which foreign countries offer the best retailing opportunity? What sources help to answer this question?
2. What environmental considerations are important in selecting a foreign country in which to do a retail business?

2. Retailing in the Soviet Union

MARSHALL I. GOLDMAN*

> How does the consumer shop in the Soviet Union? What kind of stores are there in Russia?
> The following article describes the Soviet retail network and the pattern of merchandising. It also examines some new if not "revolutionary" innovations in trade and distribution.

The simple but perplexing question—how do goods reach the Soviet consumer?—is an elementary but inadequately understood matter in the West. The purpose of this article is to generalize the complex channels of Russian consumer-good distribution into a slightly simplified description of Soviet retail trade.

While there are immense variations, the basic pattern of consumer-good distribution in the United States is from factory to wholesaling agency to retailer to consumer. There may be direct selling from factory to retailer (Jonathan Logan dresses), the wholesaler may be a subsidiary of the manufacturer (General Electric) or of the retailer (A & P), or all three may be commonly owned (Sears Roebuck). Orders and sales estimates originate at the retail level, and the goods are passed to the lower echelons with almost no intervention by governmental agencies.

A similar generalization about the organization of trade in the Soviet Union may be useful, but this does not imply such a model to be the one and only method of distribution existent in the Soviet Union. Very seldom are classifications actually neat and precise, even in the controlled Soviet state.

Although the variety of forms and patterns is in no way as complex as those in the United States, there is nonetheless considerable heterogeneity in the organizational structure. Essentially there are three main trade networks in the Soviet Union: government or state stores, co-operative stores, and *kolkhoz* (collective farm) markets. The relative share of sales of each is presented in Table 1.

The government and co-operative trade networks have their own administrative, wholesale, and supply systems. As in the United States, the basic pattern of distribution is from factory to wholesale agency to retailer to consumer. There is a major difference, however, in that normally the wholesale and retail organizations are not independent of one another, but are controlled by the same parent organization. For the most part, the manufacturing enterprises are under the jurisdiction of unrelated government organizations, but occasionally there may be direct selling from factory to retailer, as well as common control of all three links. In such cases, the manufacturing link is usually little more than a workshop. Finally, of course, it is only on the most rare occasions that there is insignificant intervention by governmental agencies. The government not only owns all the trading facilities, but it administers and controls distribution functionally at the wholesale stage and geographically at the city, regional, and republic levels.

Despite some overlapping of jurisdiction, the government trade network, which is the largest,

◆ SOURCE: Reprinted by permission from the American Marketing Association, in the *Journal of Marketing*, April 1960, pages 29–35.
* A member of the Economics Department of Wellesley College, Marshall I. Goldman has written several articles about various aspects of marketing and economics in the Soviet Union. Part of the present article is based on a 1959 visit to the major Russian marketing centers where the author had extensive interviews with marketing officials. He would like to acknowledge the facilities provided him by the Russian Research Center, Harvard University.

TABLE 1. Retail Sales Volume of the Three Main Networks in the Soviet Union[a]

(In billion rubles—prices of given year)

	1940	1950	1955	1956	1957	1958
Government (state) stores	128.1	261.1	347.3	379.6	432.9	
						677.2
Co-operative stores	47.0	98.5	154.6	167.8	193.1	
Kolkhoz markets	29.1	49.2	48.9	41.4	40.0	
TOTAL	204.2	408.8	550.8	588.8	666.0	

[a] SOURCES: 1940, 1950, 1955: Tsentral'noe Statistichskoe Upravlenie, *Sovetskaia Torgovlia* (Soviet Trade), Gosstatizdat, Moscow, 1956, p. 19. 1956: Tsentral'noe Statisticheskoe Upravlenie, *Narodnoe Khoziaistro SSSR v 1956 Godu*, Gosstatizdat, Moscow, 1957, p. 233, and Tsentral'noe Statisticheskoe Upravlenie, *SSSR V Tsifrakh*, Gosstatizdat, Moscow, 1958, p. 427. 1957: *Vestnik Statistiki* #8, 1958, p. 81. 1958: *Vestnik Statistiki* #5, 1959, p. 90.

is limited almost solely to urban areas and is run and supervised through the governmental Ministries of Trade, formerly at an all-union level, now at a republic level. The co-operative system in turn caters basically to the rural populace and has its own co-operative hierarchy, though ultimately it is also under the Republican Ministries of Trade. Collective farm or *kolkhoz* markets sell only agricultural products and are found in both cities and villages. While the government through the Ministry of Trade may be said to control the activities of the *kolkhoz* market, it does so to a much smaller degree than in either the government or co-operative stores.

THE GOVERNMENT STORE NETWORK

Because it is the most important trade sector, this article focuses primarily on the urban retail trade facilities. For the most part, this means government stores, both food and nonfood outlets. Since the *kolkhoz* market is an important source of food for urban consumers, it too will be considered. Except for the new phenomenon of commission sales, the co-operative stores are administered, structured, and operated in the same manner as the government store network.

The Soviet urban consumer has a relatively wide selection of stores from which to make his purchases. For nonfood goods, there are specialized stores which sell only a particular type of good such as clothing, as well as the department stores which provide an assortment of various goods. By far the largest and finest stores are in the centers of the large cities, especially such Moscow department stores as GUM (*Glavnvi Universalnyi Magazin*, or *Univermag*),

with a staff of about 4,300; Ts-Sum (*Tsentralnyi Univermag*) with approximately 2,300 employees; and the Leningrad department stores, *Gorodskoi Passazh* and *Dom Leningradskaia Torgovlia*, with staffs of over 900 each. Reconstruction of Leningrad's *Gostinyi Dvor* will be completed in 1960, making it the largest department store in the Soviet Union. Another type of department store different from anything in the West is the relatively new *Detskii Mir*, Children's World. It is a new and very large specialized department store devoted entirely to children. With a staff of 3,200, it combines the sale of toys and clothes as well as almost all other children's products from toiletries to furniture.

The neighborhood outlets of the specialized stores are often located on the street floor of the larger multi-story apartment house units. Moreover, there are a few department stores in residential neighborhoods, such as *Dzerzhinskii Univermag* in Moscow, and the *Kirovskii* and the *Fruzenskii Univermagy* in Leningrad.

When shopping for groceries, the Soviet urban consumer may also select from a wide variety of government stores. The central city placement of the largest and most spectacular food stores in Russia contrasts sharply with the United States and its automobile-oriented outlying supermarkets. The Soviet locational pattern of food stores is very similar to that of nonfood stores in the Soviet Union, with the largest stores in the center of the city.

The largest and best multi-product grocery stores in Russia are called *Gastronoms*. Appropriately enough, one of the largest occupies the first floor of GUM. There is also a wide selection of specialized stores—dairies, butcheries, bakeries, vegetable shops, and delicatessens—in which to shop. Usually the housewife can find a wider selection of a given specialty in these shops than in the traditionally smaller conglomerate type grocery store, the *prodmag*. The latter resembles what used to be known in the United States as the corner grocery store. In any event, the size of the typical food outlet, specialized or unspecialized, is relatively small, with only one or two sales clerks.

In 1955, The Russians reversed an earlier trend and began to emphasize the specialized type of outlet. Russian marketing experts argued that increased specialization not only would provide the Soviet consumer with a wider selection of goods, but would also improve services and labor productivity and decreaes costs of distribution. Nonetheless, the number of multi-variety grocery outlets has grown in recent years. This development, however, has come as a by-product of the expansion of self service rather than as a separate movement.

Initially, existing specialty grocery stores were converted to the new system of self service as specialty store operations continued to grow. Gradually, however, stores were opened with a more general selection of goods in the *Gastronom* tradition, but with self service. These new stores were not necessarily in the center of the city. The main stimulus for self service seemd to be the desire to make the *Gastronom* type of operation more efficient and thereby reduce costs of distribution. The fact that the consumer is better served by being able to purchase under one roof all the various items he needs for his meals seems to have come as a fortunate by-product.

OTHER GOVERNMENT STORES

Such are the main characteristics of what is usually referred to as the urban government store system, which in turn constitutes the trade network of the Ministry of Trade. Within the general category of government stores, however, there are some special organizations which deal with both food and nonfood items.

In numbers almost as large as the official Ministry of Trade network, but much less significant in terms of sales volume, the ORS (Workers Supply Departments) are a peculiar Soviet institution. Although they are administratively classed as government stores, their closest counterpart in the United States is the factory cafeteria. There is a considerable difference, however, between an American factory cafeteria and the ORS. In addition to the provision of food and meals the latter also sells nonfood consumer goods. Nonetheless, food sales and meals are relatively more important. Quality and price are usually better than average, especially for industrially processed items. The suppliers are often provided from the factory's own farm or vegetable plots, a questionable division of labor.

Actually the ORS are also comparable to U. S. military PX's, which sell food and manufactured goods to military personnel. However, since there is also a PX system for military personnel in the Soviet Union, it may not be wise to make too much of this analogy. Information available about Soviet military PX's is not too plentiful, but one of the largest Moscow department stores, the central department store of the ministry of defense of the USSR, had 563 employees as of 1957, and a sales volume about half that of the *Gorodskoi Passazh* department store in Leningrad.

Drugstores are the most important component in the specialized trade network. There are almost 7,000 drugstores and over 4,000 smaller type outlets in the Russian Socialist Federated Soviet Republic.

The distribution of periodicals is carried out by the Ministry of Communication. Although there are few stores, there are over 6,000 newspaper stands in the RSFSR. Naturally, as is true for the other two classes of specialized stores, the share of periodicals in government store retail sales is very low. Books are sold through the Ministry of Culture bookstore network. Recently many of the outlets were transferred to the complete control of either the Ministry of Trade or the co-operative societies. The rural bookstores were merged into the co-operative trade network in 1957.

There are other miscellaneous Government enterprises, including pawn-shops, second-hand shops, and commission trade stores for industrial goods, where personal possessions and handicraft items may be sold at a commission to the state. However the Ministry of Trade network, the ORS, the specialized stores, and the restaurants essentially represent what are known as government stores. It is in these stores that urban consumers purchase all of their manufactured goods and the bulk of their groceries.

It is also possible to have home delivery of certain food commodities such as milk and bread. While government stores are providing more and more of these services, for the most part they have been performed by individual peasants on a private basis, much as the local egg man continues to sell eggs from door to door in the United States.

THE KOLKHOZ MARKET

Despite urbanization and suburbanization, farmers' markets continue to thrive in many European and American cities. They are also found in the Soviet Union. However, the collective farm or *kolkhoz* market plays a much more important role in Russian retailing. While their share of total retail sales (shown in Table 1) is not now significant, their share in food sales alone, which is almost the only thing sold on such markets, is much more impressive. It was as high as 20 per cent in 1940, although it has fallen to 10 per cent since then.

In certain areas, *kolkhoz* market sales are very important, and in Odessa *kolkhoz* markets accounted for 60 per cent of the food sales in 1955 and 42 per cent of the food sales in 1956. A fairer picture of the role of *kolkhoz* markets, however, is obtained by considering the share of sales of only those varieties of foods actually sold on the *kolkhoz* markets, in comparison with the sales of these same goods in government and cooperative trade. This excludes canned goods and alcoholic beverages and includes mainly fresh vegetables, grain and livestock products, meat, and milk. Here the role of the *kolkhoz* market is greater and was as high as 31 per cent in 1940, although it had fallen to 19 per cent in 1957.

The *kolkhoz* markets are primarily outlets for the surplus produce of the *kolkhoz* farms and farmers. Such surpluses accumulate after fulfillment of delivery contracts to the state, formerly obligatory quotas. If a city resident has a garden of his own and wishes to sell any of his surplus, he may do so. The Russians refer to the *kolkhoz* market as a free market, and within limits feel that the prices are determined by interaction of the free forces of supply and demand.

There are a considerable number of such markets. In the larger cities they abound near railroad stations and other points of natural population flow. Moscow has at least thirty, and Odessa eight. *Kolkhoz* markets are located in both rural and urban areas and are divided about equally between them, although the largest and best are located in the cities where they also have the greatest sales volume. As of January, 1959, there were about 9,000 throughout the country, although the growth in the number of *kolkhoz* markets has slackened in the last few years.

Generally, prices on the *kolkhoz* markets are above those in the government stores. This is contrary to Western experience where farmers' market prices are usually below those of supermarkets and groceries. In the past this has been largely due to poor pricing policies in the government stores. Prices have been set too low relative to the inadequate supplies. However, part of the price difference is in a sense a premium paid for the better quality and freshness of the *kolkhoz* market products, a further indication of the unsatisfactory service of government stores.

The *kolkhoz* markets are administered by a branch of the local city trade organization. In addition to seeing that the market runs smoothly, this branch is responsible for attracting the outlying collective farms to their particular markets and signing contracts and providing transportation and stalls for the goods of both the peasants and the farms. Advertisements are periodically placed in the local press to attract both supplies and customers. The market administrators are also responsible for providing sanitary marketing facilities and living accommodations for the users. Finally, the administration levies a daily franchise tax on all sellers who desire to use the market facilities. It also maintains the price and quantity statistics of the market sales.

COMMISSION TRADE

In order to complete the description of retail trade facilities in the cities, it is necessary to mention a relatively new phenomenon in the Soviet system—commission trade. To some extent this is the reason for the decline in the absolute and relative role of *kolkhoz* markets.

Commission-trade stores are under the control of the cooperative trade organizations. They were first authorized in 1953 and are located predominantly in urban areas, either in special urban shops of the co-operative trade organization or in a section of the *kolkhoz* market. They are encouraged to accept, on a commission basis, agricultural commodities either from the *kolkhoz* farms or the peasants. Upon delivery, the producer receives 50 per cent of the estimated sales price in advance and the remainder upon the completion of the sale. The farm or peasant retains the title and bears the risk in the meantime.

As one might expect, such a system has been subject to considerable abuse, and there have been many calls for various reforms. Despite serious shortcomings, however, commission trade permits an increased division of labor and allows the peasant to market his surplus without having to leave his fields. It also serves as a competitive pressure on the *kolkhoz* market. Although commission trade prices are higher than those of the government stores, they are lower than prices on the *kolkhoz* market and have accompanied the slow decline of the latter.

Commission-trade sales have shown a remarkable growth. By January 1, 1957, there were 5,165 stores and 6,135 stalls selling food on commission. The decision to permit the return of co-operatives to the city and to allow commission-trade sales of agricultural surpluses seems to be a major development.

In summary, when the urban housewife does her grocery shopping, she really has a choice of three basic types of trade outlets. She purchases the bulk of her goods in government stores and the remainder in either the *kolkhoz* market or through commission-trade. Almost all prepared and processed foods are sold only in the government stores, while fresh or raw foods are also sold on the *kolkhoz* market and through commission-trade. The commission-trade stores sell relatively more meat, milk, and butter—foods requiring some additional preparation other than harvesting: and the *kolkhoz* market sells relatively more vegetables and eggs.

THE TRADITIONAL
PURCHASING PROCEDURE

Having selected the outlet which is most accessible or which promises to have the best assortment of goods, the consumer chooses a convenient day and goes shopping. To accommodate the urban worker, Soviet stores are open Sundays and also most secular holidays when the factory workers are free and able to shop. Most retail stores are then closed Mondays and the day after any holiday.

Upon entering the store, the urban customer typically finds a line of people before him. In due time it is his turn. Often with a cold, unsolicitous tone, the salesclerk inquires of his needs. If the customer finds something that suits him, all he can do at this stage is to ask the price and permission to examine the goods. He then leaves the salesclerk (without the merchandise) and enters a new line in front of the *kassa* or cashier. Here he pays the cashier the ruble amount of the price just quoted to him by the salesclerk, and in return receives a receipt *(chek)*. With his receipt in hand, the shopper moves to a third line. After turning in his receipt to the *kontroler*, he finally receives his package. Unless the typically crowded Russian store is empty, this means he has had to queue up three times before being able to walk out with his purchase. The Russians call this the "*kassa* system."

SOME MARKETING INNOVATIONS

Clearly the *kassa* system has been costly in terms of both time and money. To expedite the purchasing routine, a number of so-called "progressive methods of trade" have been introduced. The first to be considered is *bez prodavtsa*, literally service without the aid of salesclerks. The temptation is to describe this as self service, but it is not the same. The Russian version of sales without a salesclerk means that the customer enters the store but does not need to stand in line to ask the salesclerk what is available and the price. Instead, the goods and their prices are displayed on the wall or in glass cases. The customer can therefore walk in, choose an item, and find its cost without having to wait in line. He must still stand in two queues, however, to pay the cashier and pick up his goods. The goods he examines are locked in the cases or securely anchored. There have been one or two experiments in which the salesclerks have been allowed to receive cash and personally hand over the goods, but this has not been widespread and usually is permitted for items of very small cost only.

Self service *(samo obsluzhivaniia)* as it is known in the West is a relatively new phenomenon in the Soviet Union. It was first introduced in late 1954 by a Leningrad food store. Although it has been most widely adopted in the selling of food, it is also being used in nonfood type outlets.

As with all daily operations, self service in the Soviet Union varies from store to store. As of January, 1959, there were approximately 1,500 self-service stores in operation.

On entering a store, the customer must first check all her parcels. The American system of the manager's reserving the right to check all packages is inadequate. While this inconvenience seems bothersome enough, at one time there were even more obstacles confronting the Soviet consumer. Initially, only a few customers were allowed in the store at a time. This was mainly to prevent shoplifting. Consequently, as late as July, 1957, there were complaints published about the long lines outside the stores, and the fact that often there were as many store personnel inside as customers.

Having passed all the entrance requirements, the customer finally is able to select her groceries and place them either in a little handbasket often provided by the store or in a little handbag carried by most Soviet housewives. A few stores have the customary western carts, but this seems a little too costly, especially in retail trade where capital is short. Because of their showpiece nature, commodity selection in the supermarkets is fairly wide, and the newer stores may even have open refrigerated cabinets. Most of the stores, however, still have a poor assortment of products.

With her selection completed, the shopper moves to the check-out counter. The *kassa* system has even had an imprint here. Originally one first had to go to a *kontroler*, who computed the total of the purchases. Then, following the same old scheme, the customer had to go to the cashier to pay and receive a receipt; and only then could she return to the *kontroler* and walk out with the goods and the parcels previously checked.

However, it was discovered that one person, the *kontroler-cashier*, could simultaneously determine the total and collect the money. The calculation of the total cost of the purchases is made on an abacus and the result entered on a cash register. As yet the Russians do not have cash registers which also add. Although some stores still retain an additional *kontroler* at the exit to insure that packages and checked parcels belong to the proper person, the over-all operation of self service—especially its more recent improvements—is more satisfactory and efficient than the older method.

In addition to the improved sales procedures, several other innovations have been introduced. A state mail-order service, *Posyltorg*, was formed a few years ago and now has an annual sales volume of almost 700 million rubles. A Soviet citizen can now order any one of 5,000 articles from a 99-page illustrated catalogue. Vending machines for soft drinks, milk, beer, sandwiches, and hard goods have now become commonplace throughout the Soviet Union. A machine has been developed which sprays essence of Soviet cologne over the consumer's hair for 15 kopecks. Operational problems are many, however; and, aside from complaints about the unprofitable location of various machines, the service is poor and the machines are often inadequately supplied. It is not an uncommon sight to see a row of soda-pop vending machines adjacent to a woman vendor selling the same thing from her portable stand. In some instances, the vendor is not just adjacent to the vending machines, but in front of them.

Two other more radical (one would think a good Marxist would say reactionary) developments are the formation of a State advertising agency, *Torgreklama,* and the introduction of installment credit. Organizations are aided in preparing their advertising copy, making their window displays and preparing attractive packaging with the purpose of making their commodities or stores more attractive or differentiated. Television commercials are also prepared.

Installment sales are as yet on a limited basis. This is partially because the Marxist theoreticians have suddenly been given the task of justifying a practice they condemned as late as 1959, and partially because most consumer goods are still in short supply. Installment sales would only worsen the situation. Consequently, consumer credit and other forms of sales promotion are used only in certain areas and on certain overproduced items such as television sets, cameras, and watches. Regardless of the scale of these activities, the fact that such phenomena have been officially introduced into a Communist state seems significant.

CONCLUSION

On the whole, it appears that trade in the Soviet Union is cumbersome and service is poor. Largely due to the inattention devoted to marketing in the past, Russian consumers must suffer numerous inconveniences in making even the simplest purchase. Although by Western standards service and efficiency are poor, Soviet attitudes toward retail trade have improved.

Now not only is the volume of trade growing, but there has also been an increase in the number and variety of retail outlets. Many new improvements and innovations are being introduced. From self service to advertising to commission trade, the nature of retail trade in the Soviet Union is changing.

BRIEF BIBLIOGRAPHY

1. Gogol', V. I., editor, *40 Let Sovetskoi Torgovli* (40 Years of Soviet Trade), Gostorgizdat, Moscow, 1957.

2. Goldman, Marshall I., "Marketing—A Lesson for Marx," *Harvard Business Review*, **38** (January-February, 1960), p. 79.

3. Serebriakov, S. D., *Organizalsiia i Teknika Sovetskoi Torgovli* (Organization and Technology of Soviet Trade), Gostorgizdat, Moscow, 1956.

4. *Sovetskaia Torgovlia* (Soviet Trade), a monthly journal and a tri-weekly newspaper.

5. Tsentral'noe Statisticheskoe Upravlenie, *Sovetskaia Torgovlia* (Soviet Trade), Gosstatizdat, Moscow, 1956.

6. Tsentral-noe Statisticheskoe Upravlenie, *Sovetskaia Torgovlia v RSFSR* (Soviet Trade in the Russian Republic), Gosstatizdat, 1958.

DISCUSSION QUESTIONS

"Kassa," "bez prodavtsa," and "samo obsluzhivaniia" are all terms which designate some type of Russian retailing. The "Kolkhoz" market is still another retail institution of importance in Russia.

1. Which *American* retail institutions most nearly embody the characteristics suggested in each of these terms?
2. Contrast the "kassa" purchasing sequence with that in a typical American supermarket.

3. French Retailing and the Common Market

S. WATSON DUNN

What is the role of the retailer in France? Most analysts overlook the retailer when they assess the chances for success of such well-publicized arrangements as the European Common Market (inner six) and the European Free Trade Association (outer seven). They seem to assume that somehow he will accommodate his operation to the demands of such probable developments as the invasion of strong foreign brands, an increase in consumer advertising by manufacturers, and the relatively free movement of goods from one country to another.

France is of special interest from the retailing standpoint. For one thing, it has reversed its traditional isolationism and has, along with Germany, exercised leadership in speeding up provisions of the Rome (European Common Market) treaty, such as the lowering of internal tariffs. Also France is associated with the earliest developments of modern retailing techniques. For example, Bon Marché in Paris is generally considered one of the world's first department stores. However, the French retailer has been notoriously slow in adopting such recent innovations as self-service supermarkets and national brands. Most Americans tend to consider French retail stores either exasperating anachronisms or quaint reminders of old France.

Two questions need to be answered. First, is the structure of French retailing adaptable to the needs of expanding, dynamic markets? In other words, are there enough of the right types of outlets, too many of the wrong? Second, to what extent are the retailer and his customers adaptable psychologically to the demands of the future? Is he willing and able to make needed changes?

FRAGMENTATION OF RETAIL TRADE

By U.S. standards, the French retailing system is highly fragmented. France has approximately 60 per cent more retail shops per 10,000 population than the United States. Even in wholesaling, the typical organization is a small one.

There are far too many outlets for certain types of merchandise and service. A good example is the café which exists in surprisingly large numbers in almost all sections of every French city. Also one finds in France many small specialized stores which in America would be combined into one. For example, the American supermarket equals the French *épicerie* (groceries), plus *crèmerie* (dairy products, eggs), plus *charcuterie* (specialty meats), plus *boulangerie* (bread), plus *pâtisserie* (pastries), plus *droguerie* (household cleaning supplies), plus *poissonnerie* (fish), plus *boucherie* (fresh meat), etc.

In a middle-class section of Lyons there is one bakery for every 800 inhabitants. As David S. Landes points out, "The small shop is a sort of caricature of the family firm . . . with the objective of high profits on a limited turnover carried to an astonishing degree. There are haberdashers who try to live on the sale of three shirts a day, restaurants which serve six meals at noon." [1]

According to INSEE (French National Council of Commerce), the official French gatherer of statistics, the average French independent food store in 1958 had a gross volume of approximately $23,000. In one random sample of 108 food stores, 27 were found to have an annual volume of less than $10,000.

♦ SOURCE: Reprinted by permission from the American Marketing Association, in the *Journal of Marketing*, January 1962, pages 19–22.

[1] David S. Landes, "French Business and the Businessman: A Social and Cultural Analysis," in *Modern France*, Edward Mead Earle, editor (Princeton: Princeton University Press, 1951), p. 342.

The INSEE divides the French retailing structure into the following major categories:

Multiple businesses. These include such well-known department stores in Paris and the provinces as Aux Galéries Lafayette and Au Printemps, and the popular variety stores misleadingly called "one-price stores" (such as Monoprix and Prisunic). There are approximately 1,000 of these, with about 550 accounted for by the popular variety store. They represented approximately 4.5 per cent of the total retail volume in 1958.

Chain stores. There were in 1958 about 37,-000 retail shops which were owned by chains having four or more branch stores. Approximately 58 per cent of these were food chain stores. Chain stores accounted for about 6 per cent of retail sales in 1958.

Co-operative societies. Consumer co-operatives are popular and well-established in France. In 1958 there were over 3 million members in approximately 800 co-operative societies. There were 11,000 shops, but 6,500 were run by the 50 largest societies. Part of the remainder were included in the 2,700 co-operatives of shops in private business firms and government services. Co-operative societies, mainly in food, accounted for slightly more than 2 per cent of retail sales in 1958.

Supermarkets. Still a rarity in France are supermarkets. Unlike neighboring Switzerland and Germany, France has only a handful of what most American marketers would accept as supermarkets.

Non-sedentary retailers. There are approximately 95,000 retailers without a fixed place of business (of these, 44,000 handle foodstuffs who account for about 3 per cent of the nation's retail volume).

Sedentary independent retailers. The independent retailer is the perennial backbone of retailing in France. He accounts for approximately 92 per cent of all stores and 84.5 per cent of the total retail sales in France. In the food field the independent retailer is losing a little ground, but the INSEE estimates that the independent food retailers (sedentary and non-sedentary) still handle about 83 per cent of food volume.

What the INSEE calls the "concentrated" form of retail distribution (department stores, chains, co-operatives, and supermarkets) accounts for only 12.5 per cent of the national retail sales. The 95,000 non-sedentary retailers are responsible for about 3 per cent, and the traditional independent shopkeepers handle the remaining 84.5 per cent.

LOW PRODUCTIVITY IN RETAILING

Although the number of retail outlets is decreasing at the rate of more than 6,000 a year, there are too many small outlets, and productivity per worker is low. Table 1 summarizes some productivity statistics.

This table indicates that not only in France but in most of the countries of western Europe the typical store is too small to take advantage of large-scale operation (mass buying, mass advertising, etc.). Productivity per worker, as indicated by employees per million dollars of volume, is much lower than in the United States. Edouard LeClerc, a young Frenchman who is trying to introduce mass retailing and discount selling in France, claims that approximately 21 per cent of the French labor force is engaged in food distribution, as compared with 7 per cent in the United States.[2]

WHAT ABOUT THE FUTURE?

To solve the problem, one must go behind the statistics of French retailing and delve into somewhat imponderable human factors. One must find out what motivates the retailer and his customer.

The retailer presents certain interesting paradoxes. For example, he is more of an individualist than his American counterpart. Most Americans are impressed by the individuality of the average French store. The arrangement of the merchandise, window displays, interior decorations—all tend to reflect the personality, feelings, and prejudices of the owner and even of the family of the owner.

But one finds the French retailer going to all odds to avoid competition as we know it—particularly price competition. He is likely to join a "syndicat" to fix prices and many of the rules of doing business. A few years ago Maurice Gottegno opened two American-style discount houses in Paris; but he encountered strong pressure from groups of his competitors and eventually was forced to go out of business.

Another apparent contradiction stems from the typical Frenchman's great reverence for

---

[2] "Cut-price Grocer Stirs France," *The New York Times*, November 8, 1959, Sec. IV, p. 8.

tradition, but along with this his proven ability to adapt his *modus operandi* to needed changes.

This contradiction has fascinated many historians. In 1915 J. R. Moreton wrote, "The truly remarkable way in which, under the present trial, France has purified herself of her traditional vices and developed virtues which were supposed to be quite alien to her character drives one to the conclusion, not only that the temperamental qualities of nations change more rapidly than we have been accustomed to think, but also that they are often only qualities which have been foisted on nations by noisy minorities." [3]

Forty years later another specialist in French history, Henry Bertram Hill, emphasized France's recuperative power in the face of the French Revolution, the Franco-Prussian War, and the two World Wars and its continuity as a great power.[4] France's adaptability is shown also by her switch from economic isolationism to full participation in the ECM.[5]

Thus, when we note the French retailer's reluctance to make use of modern merchandising techniques, keep in mind that the French retailer may, like his fellow countrymen, eventually change his methods when he is faced by the challenge of international markets.

In the meantime, the retailers are slow to adopt even such standard retailing procedures as advertising and self-service. A department store in Orléans which spends 0.4 per cent of sales for advertising is known as a big advertiser. A large and rapidly-growing food chain in south and central France which spends 0.3 to 0.5 per cent for advertising (all of it in newspapers) is considered by its competitors to be overly aggressive. These percentages would, of course, be considered quite low in the United States for these store types.

Net profit and accumulated surplus are less important to the French retailer than his American counterpart. Instead he is influenced by such considerations as keeping control of his firm within his family, and in maintaining his status within the community. Landes says: "The word *maison* has retained business con-

notations long since lost by our word 'house.' It is this bond that accounts for astonishing solidarity shown by French families when the integrity or the stability of the firm is imperiled; even today, the social register or family tree is often a better credit reference than the most profitable series of annual statements." [6]

Many French retailers resist expansion because it may weaken family control of the firm. More often than in the United States they let their merchandise stagnate rather than sell it at a "face-losing" reduction. Even when French retailers install self-service, they frequently overlook cutting prices to compensate for this innovation.

WHAT ABOUT THE CONSUMER?

In all fairness, it should be noted that the French retailer has to satisfy a difficult, hard-to-predict customer who is somewhat different from his or her counterpart in other countries. His store is something of a social institution, with many of the attributes of a "club." The proprietor is sometimes as much a social director as a businessman. He must keep his members (his loyal customers) happy, and is often relatively unconcerned about enlarging his circle of customers. Naturally this is more true of the small store than the large one.

An investigation by École Supérieure de Commerce in one of the heavily populated sections of Lyons indicated that many people patronized a certain store because they felt they were thereby members of a privileged group. Buying was a sort of reinforcement of membership rites. The housewives were quite conscious of how they should dress to go to the store (no pin curls, no shorts, no slacks for this venture into the outside world). The daily shopping expedition is an important part of the housewife's routine, bringing her contacts with the outside world. Since she has no P.T.A. meetings, and few social or bridge clubs as a substitute, she is not likely to welcome weekly shopping in bulk, even though it might bring certain savings.

One of the most formidable barriers to marketing progress is the reluctance of the French consumer to accept the standardization implicit in mass production and mass marketing. Even when the French housewife has a refrigerator in which to store her food, even when she has

[3] J. R. Moreton MacDonald, *A History of France* (London: The Macmillan Company, 1915), p. 6.
[4] Henry Bertram Hill, "The Reliability of France in the European System" in Earle, *Modern France.* Same reference as footnote 1, p. 475.
[5] Edgar S. Furniss, Jr., *France, Troubled Ally* (New York: Frederick Praeger, 1960), Chapters 5 and 7.

[6] David S. Landes, same reference as footnote 1, pp. 336–337.

a car to transport the entire week's food supply, she will still harbor considerable wariness toward packaged, processed, or canned foods and continue to make daily rounds of her stores. Canned soups have been a failure in France in spite of the fact that soup is a staple item in the French cuisine. It is not feasible to mass-produce fabrics or dresses, because even the most overworked housewives take time to select their own fabrics and sew their own garments, or find a couturière whom they like.

Also, consumption patterns vary substantially from those in the United States. The American is likely to spend the money he or she has left after taking care of food, clothing, shelter, and an automobile . . . for such items as appliances and home furnishings. In France, good wining and dining, along with clothing and shelter, are considered part of basic living costs. What is left is more likely to be spent for services or a vacation than for appliances or other durables.

IMPLICATIONS

The French retailer could well be a real "stumbling block" to successful achievement of European Common Market aims. The retailing system is overly fragmented; and efficiency is handicapped by retailer acceptance of inefficient practices handed down from the isolationist past, a sometimes irrational disregard for maximizing profits, and concerted action on the part of some store managers designed to stem the tide of retailing innovations. The danger is compounded by such consumer characteristics

as suspicion of mass-produced items and reluctance to change established shopping habits.

Retailing is being modernized, but the pace is still slow. One encouraging sign is the growth of co-operative chains. These are independently owned and thus not so objectionable to the Poujadists (or other restrictionists) as corporate chains. At the same time they provide the advantages of group buying and merchandising.

A second sign of progress is the success of certain intelligently-run discount houses, supermarkets, and corporate chains. Most of these are managed by people who have studied mass marketing in other countries, yet who know the pitfalls of imposing too quickly foreign retailing methods on the French consumer. Supermarkets have been developing, although progress has been slow and those established so far are more like the Swiss and German types than those in America. However, a genuine American-type supermarket was opened in 1961 on the outskirts of Paris. Several American chains have become quite interested in France, and we may soon see them opening outlets there. Also, it is quite possible that the entry of Great Britain into the Common Market may spur development of more modern retailing methods. As Table 1 indicates, Britain has a higher sales volume per store and a lower number of stores per million dollars of sales than the present ECM countries.

A third encouraging sign is the growth of marketing education. Although university-level courses are but a few years old, some of the graduates are already active in retailing, put-

TABLE 1. Retailing Productivity in Western Europe and the United States[a]

Country	Stores		Employees	
	Sales Volume per Store	Number of Stores per Million $	Sales Volume per Employee	Employees per Million $
France	$15,430	65	$ 8,385	119
Germany	13,970	72	5,415	185
Italy	12,980	77	7,300	137
Low Countries	10,810	93	5,140	195
Belgium	10,980	91	7,080	141
United Kingdom	24,760	40	6,075	164
United States	75,270	13	15,285	65

[a] SOURCE: Andre Anstett, *Opportunities et Exigencies du Marché Commun pour l'Entreprise* (Paris: J. Walter Thompson Company, 1959), p. 17.

ting into practice what they have learned. Also, marketing conferences and short courses have helped retailers to find out why some are more successful than others. They are discovering that marketing research and advertising really pay.

DISCUSSION QUESTIONS

The typical French retail outlet is a prototype of the high-margin/low-turnover philosophy of retail enterprise. A much greater percentage of the total economic base of France is devoted to retailing than is true in the United States.

What particular problems would an American retailer who planned to introduce a self-service, "discount" type of operation located in France encounter? Be as specific as you can! Are some of these problems virtually insurmountable?

4. Latest Developments in Automatic Retailing in Europe

GIANFRANCO MOLINARI

Despite tremendous improvements in retailing—particularly self-service—such problems as personnel shortage and higher pay, profit squeeze, and restrictions on opening hours, still have to be reckoned with. "Automatic vending" —self-service extended to its logical goal—may offer a chance to solve these problems satisfactorily.

The oldest known vending machine already existed about 2,000 years ago in Egypt, offering wine in exchange for a coin. Today automatic vendors are operating all over the world. It is anticipated that sales through automatic vending in the United States alone will exceed $4 billion in 1965. Automatic retailing in Europe undoubtedly also will show an encouraging expansion during the next few years. Present shortcomings of different automatic systems cannot hinder but only slow down the trend toward greater vending units and broader sales mix.

AUTOMATIC SHOPS

In most European countries, vending machines quite commonly are operated.
- at suitable locations some distance from the shops, running 24 hours a day;
- or outside the store for food and nonfood items, after closing hours and on holidays.

Even in Russia the era of robot retailing has begun. A largely automatic department store of small size has been opened in Moscow, where a multitude of vending apparatuses replace most shop assistants and cashiers. The articles for sale are described in folders and are on display.

But the latest automatic shops do not necessarily operate as a large battery of vending machines. Various examples of other types of automated stores can be found in the United States and in Europe.

Punch-card System

Much has been written about a hardware store in Dayton, Ohio, as a fascinating experiment of unattended retailing. Similar stores can be found in France, as well as in Sweden. These types of automated food stores make use of punch-cards for identifying the brand, price, and weight of an article.

The first automatic food store in Sweden—opened in the center of Stockholm in August, 1963—displaye only one sample of each of the 800 food articles and the other 600 daily necessities. The store looks like a modern self-service department, covering only 850 square feet of selling space and 1,950 square feet of stock space. Instead of an article, the customer takes a punch-card, which is sorted by color— each color representing a merchandise category. An electronic computer establishes two copies of a list of articles—one as a bill for the customer and the other for the stockroom, where packaging and delivery take place.

Reports from this store and similar ones in France indicate that the punch-card system needs little space, minimizes personnel and stock costs, and offers great advantages to the owner with regard to stock control and accountancy. But is there an advantage for the customer who in peak hours has to queue twice, once to pay for and once to receive the goods?

Dial System

Another type of automatic shopping, based on a dial system, is operated in a few cities of Northern Germany, and with one in Holland and another in Finland. A merchandise catalog or exhibited samples indicate a number to be dialed. Any number of coins can be inserted—

♦   SOURCE: Reprinted by permission from the American Marketing Association, in the *Journal of Marketing*, October, 1964, pages 5–9.

the surplus coinage is returned. An illuminated text informs the customer as to the functioning of the robot. A conveyor belt connected with a lift guarantees quick service. Thanks to separate installations for checkout, an electronic center, money changer, and stockrooms, up to 1,000 articles can be sold on a front space of only 100 square feet.

Shoppers still seem to feel uncertain about handling the rather complicated apparatus. Only time will tell whether or not this concept will be accepted by the public.

Push-button System

One of the most recently developed systems of automatic retailing has been developed in Switzerland.

Zirobot is the name of a self-computing fully automatic Swiss vending machine, consisting of three main sections.

While the *article selector* with push buttons and the *computer group* with coin slots are located in the actual control unit, the *delivery section* is separate and can be adapted to local conditions. One standard vending machine set —and several of them can be converted to a completely automatic supermarket—carries 50 different articles.

According to Mr. E. Zindel, the inventor, *Zirobot* is the only vending machine in the world that will sell—in the same vending process and against a total sum payment—any number of compact, liquid, frozen, or fragile articles in packs of different kinds and sizes. An astonishing fact is that this machine will compute automatically, check the turnover, and facilitate immediate price adjustment; it will also take different size coins in any sequence, verify, and add them up. Furthermore, *Zirobot* gives exact change through visual indication and replenishes the coin reserve automatically.

If supervision of the vending capacity in another part of the building is desirable, a remote indicating panel transmits the turnover and shows the stock in hand. If an article is sold out, or if an irregularity such as current failure occurs, then the vendor is given visual as well as alarm signals. As all control components are plug-in units, elements can immediately be replaced so that long interruptions of the vending operation are avoided.

For discount trading it is useful to add a discount stamp machine. Another unit may be required to issue credit vouchers, gift vouchers, publicity articles, or a leaflet with the goods.

Two prototypes now are in use in Switzerland—one, with two units, in Zurich; and the other, with only one unit, in Berne. A third *Zirobot* was exhibited at the Swiss National Fair in Lausanne from April to October, 1964.

The two Zurich units operated experimentally by a Swiss supermaket chain since July, 1963, reveal certain inadequacies. Problems of various kinds crop up unexpectedly. Even if the technical failures could be completely conquered, there still remain other problems to be solved, such as store architecture, preselling techniques, and seasonal sales mix. Furthermore, it is still useful to have an attendant or a hostess present, in order to familiarize customers with the system and to prevent errors in usage.

Mr. Zindel is convinced that the well-considered combination of electronic, electromechanical, and mechanical functions requires only minimal maintenance, while ensuring trouble-free continuous service. On the other hand, he is desirous of improving his system further. For example, he expects to be able to invent a note selector on a new principle. His actual coin selector verifies the coins inserted by means of an electronic system, thereafter by mechanical testing for thickness, diameter, weight, magnetic properties, and alloy, thus guaranteeing that the money inserted is genuine.

A complete *Zirobot* unit, including turnstile-enclosed display area, delivery area, delivery equipment, merchandise storage, and electronic payment-computing system with discount stamp machine, costs about $25,000. It is possible that mass production can reduce the unit price to $20,000 or even lower.

The total annual cost per unit—including depreciation, location rent, insurance and fees, supervisor salary, lighting and utilities, maintenance and repair, and payment of interest— will amount to about $10,000. Assuming that such articles can be sold with an average profit margin of 20%, a minimum turnover of $50,-000 a year or almost $140 per day is needed.

Thus, problems of investments and profitability may hinder manufacturers in developing and operators in promoting these and other new types of automatic retail stores.

TECHNICAL AND PSYCHOLOGICAL TENETS

Automatic selling has developed over the years from smaller units to larger ones, from single articles to a shoplike supply. Through numerous experiments it has become quite clear that problems in automatic vending do not arise from the technical and mechanical angle only, but that the psychological aspect has also to be taken into serious consideration.

Why Do Customers Mistrust Vending Machines?

Many persons, because of failures in their application, or various prejudices, show a negative and reticent attitude towards "selling robots." It is a fact that the location of automatic machines is not always favorable, and that the sales mix does not necessarily accord with customers' requirements. Furthermore, the lifeless robots sometimes look empty and dirty; others offer old stock or tainted goods. Once a shopper has been disappointed—either from the technical reliability of the apparatus or from the quality, price, or hygienic point of view—he not only will avoid further purchase but, by negative comments, will prevent other potential clients from experimenting with vending machines.

Consumers' buying habits cannot be changed from one day to another. Most shoppers are used to being advised and served by other persons. Purchase without the possibility of personal attendance may leave an empty feeling; and furthermore the action of buying becomes confused by the necessity for complicated know-how about the systems. Technical failure and the impossibility of returning goods chosen, even if the error is the robot's and not the customer's, are further obstacles to the popularization of automatic selling.

Why Do Customers Like Vending Machines?

Experience has shown that younger people in particular like to make use of coin-operated machines that dispense cigarettes, chocolate bars, tinned foods, ice cream, pastries, candy, fresh fruit, hot and cold drinks, sandwiches, or even complete meals—as well as nylon stockings, books, newspapers, records, films, flowers, toys, men's clothing, and pharmaceutical products. Also, dry cleaning and insurance policy machines, amusement games, and even coin-operated pumps for gasoline are becoming more and more popular.

A well designed and attractively-operated automatic retail store can have its own rational and emotional appeal, just as the old marketplace and modern supermarket have theirs. For retailers, potential impulse buying on an even larger scale than in other types of outlets may be an important factor.

Apart from the restrictions on opening hours of traditional stores, the increasing number of housewives going to work, as well as people with irregular or limited shopping time in general, may provide an increasing clientele to automatic retail outlets. The convenience of buying round-the-clock and seven days a week could lead to automatic vending machines being used not only as a standby when traditional stores are closed, but also during normal working hours.

SOME MARKETING ASPECTS

It is false to consider automatic stores as an interesting complement to a nearby traditional or self-service shop only. The high cost of acquiring new-fashioned vending machines and the considerable operating expenses—such as location rental payments, depreciation over three to five years, interest of 5% to 7% on invested capital, maintenance cost, all types of insurance, taxes, and other expenses—require unusually accurate marketing analysis before going into business.

The turnover, the gross profit margin, and the total cost determine the profitability. The turnover particularly varies with the location. Vending machines tend to be set up in places with much traffic, such as railway, bus, and underground stations; air terminals; amusement parks; camping areas; factories; department stores and shopping centers; motorways and filling stations; large apartment and business houses; military camps; hospitals; schools and universities; hotels; clubs; and theaters.

Of course, density of population is of the greatest importance. Nevertheless, additional conditions influence profitability. For example, the technical equipment must be adequate for the services provided, and be foolproof for both operator and shopper.

Experience in Europe shows that it is easier to achieve liberal operating hours for automatic stores with little or no staff than is the case with traditional outlets. Automatic stores will become more prevalent as the number of sizes, selection and combinations of articles, form and presentation of products, price policy, and advertising are "tuned" more carefully to the consumer's wants.

IN CONCLUSION

Far from being perfect, the *Zirobot* and other up-to-date robot store concepts (and perhaps better ones have already been designed on drawing boards or tested behind the scenes) represent real technical progress compared with existing traditional vending machines.

Robot retailing not only may revolutionize the physical setup of stores but also will require a continuous search for novel practical marketing ideas that will satisfy the wants of both retailers and customers.

New problems will arise with regard to merchandising, product design, packaging, point-of-purchase advertising, and displays. Efforts must be made to change the disadvantages of a "coldly automated mood" into a warm, impulse-buying situation.

DISCUSSION QUESTIONS

Visualize a battery of "Zirobots" aligned shoulder to shoulder, as it were, offering hundreds of different items of merchandise of varying sizes, shapes, and values under a single roof.

1. Would this type of store be substantially more efficient than a typical supermarket operation? Why? Why not?

Suppose stocks which were used to fill orders came not from the machine itself, but from a larger storage and stock area behind the Zirobot.

2. How would that system compare with the efficiency of the typical supermarket? Why?

Research: Understanding the Customer and the Store

The value of formal research procedures is widely recognized by the management of manufacturing businesses. Retailing management has traditionally relied less upon formal research activities. In a general way, research performed by the manufacturer serves as a substitute for similar research at the retail level. Thus, the more carefully the manufacturer recognizes the nuances of consumer preferences in product design and engineering, the less is the retailer likely to encounter the need for similar research.

There are, however, research areas in which the retailer cannot depend upon the manufacturer. One of these areas is in the measurement of customer perceptions of the store. This type of research problem has been popularized in the term "store image." Another such area is in the identification of fashion preferences which are to some extent peculiar to the particular market being served. The manufacturer cannot be of help in matters which involve fashion preferences which are virtually unique to a particular locale.

Researching the store image can identify facets of the store personality which require modification and such research may therefore provide a basis for directing the promotional efforts of the store. The buying of fashion merchandise has traditionally been a high-risk activity with intuition and a "feel for values" being the essential skill required for success. The concept of the market "influential" or "early adopter" suggests a means through which the effectiveness of fashion buying may be enhanced. This section includes articles which relate to these two basic areas of research in retailing.

1. A Conceptual Model for Studying Customer Image

GEORGE FISK

Since everything about a store, from its odor to its merchandise handling, either attracts or repels a certain segment of the market, image research can identify a store's actual and potential customers. It can also suggest changes in the marketing mix, decor, service features, price range, etc., to increase the appeal to this particular segment. Image research succeeds to the degree that it increases the proportion of people entering the store in a state of being ready, willing, and able to buy. Thus image research performs a "gate keeper" function: nothing more.

THE RESEARCH TASK

To measure the influence of store image on customer states with fidelity, a number of customer state determinants have to be measured simultaneously. In tracing the interaction between these other determinants and store image, a researcher must: (1) express these determinants in a mathematical system of equations or inequalities; (2) test the mathematical model against the criterion of predictive effectiveness; and (3) use it (if it tests out reasonably well) to predict the outcomes of simulated executive decisions under a variety of assumptions.

The purpose of this paper is happily confined to step one: presentation and explanation of the conceptual model required to measure the influence of image. The usefulness of this model in shaping the research program will vary, of course, with the size of the firm. Even for small firms, however, it should provide a superior method of organizing records already available as aids in balancing elements in the store's marketing mix.

* SOURCE: Reprinted by permission from the editor of the *Journal of Retailing*, in the winter 1961–62 issue, pages 9–16.

THE MODEL

The model consists of two parts shown in Figures 1 and 2 respectively. Figure 1 shows the relationship between image and other customer state determinants. Figure 2 shows major measurable determinants of retail store image as revealed by the Wharton Studies in Retailing.[1]

The first and most basic observation about the patronage determinant model is that it is a model of dynamic interaction in which the end result is capable of modifying input variables as well as the other way around. In this model image interacts with other predispositions as well as other determinants of customer state. Without a precipitating circumstance to trigger a drive state, however, image remains latent as a guiding force. Thus image is but one of a number of influences governing the consumer's actions. If customer behavior is sometimes contrary to what would be predicted from favorable store image responses, the answer may easily be found in the relative strength of image determinants, not the least of which is the operation of the principle of least effort operating through locational convenience. Or there may be frame of reference considerations such as income limitations that establish boundaries on the kinds of customer behavior deemed appropriate to a particular purchasing act.

It is highly important to recognize the inter-

[1] Correspondence with the author is invited concerning a bibliography of the Wharton Studies in Retailing along with code books that will enable interested persons to gain access to IBM cards for a number of mail, telephone, and personal interview sample surveys covering a wide range of shopping behavior. Inquiries may be directed to the author at the Wharton School of Finance and Commerce, University of Pennsylvania, Philadelphia 4, Pa.

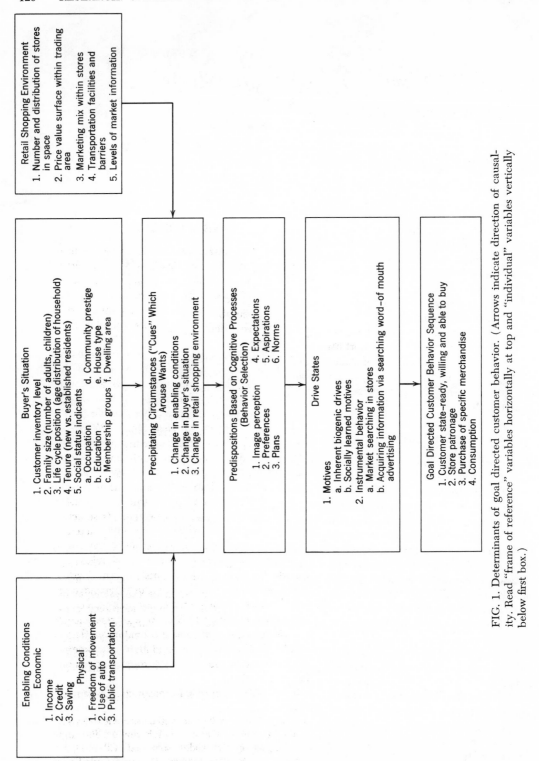

FIG. 1. Determinants of goal directed customer behavior. (Arrows indicate direction of causality. Read "frame of reference" variables horizontally at top and "individual" variables vertically below first box.)

action of store image with what are termed "frame of reference" variables in Figure 1.[2]

Too often motivation researchers pose a problem as amenable to solution either by analysis of psychological typologies or by what is derisively called "nose counting," which is supposed to be inferior as an explanatory and predictive technique.

[2] See William A. Mindak, "Fitting the Semantic Differential to the Marketing Problem," *Journal of Marketing*, April 1961, p. 33.

Cognitive Dimension	Determinants
Locational Convenience	Access routes
	Traffic barriers
	Traveling time
	Parking availability on arrival
Merchandise Suitability	Number of brands stocked
	Quality of lines stocked
	Breadth of assortment
	Depth of assortment
	Number of outstanding departments within store
Value for Price	Price of particular item (Z) in a particular store
	Price of item (Z) in competing store
	Price of particular item (Z) in particular store on sale day
	Prices of substitute products in substitute stores
	Trading stamps and patronage discounts in kind
Sales Effort and Store Services	Courtesy of sales clerks
	Helpfulness of sales clerks
	Advertising, reliability, usefulness
	Billing procedure, adequacy of credit arrangements
	Delivery promptness and care
	Restaurant, eating facilities
Congeniality of Store	Store layout
	Store decor and attractiveness of merchandise display
	Class of customers
	Store traffic and congestion
Post Transaction Satisfaction	Satisfaction wtih merchandise in use
	Satisfaction with returns and adjustments
	Satisfaction with price paid
	Satisfaction with shopping experience in store
	Satisfaction with accessibility to store

FIG. 2. Thirty determinants of cognitive dimensions of store image.

As Figure 1 shows, the choice is not between psychological methods or sociodemographic analysis but between numerous possible mathematical expressions which include *both* groups of variables. To look at psychological or economic considerations only is to reduce needlessly the accuracy of the predictions which could be made on the basis of more complete information about both. Figure

1 stresses the study of changes in all of these states if changes in patronage behavior are to be understood and predicted. To the extent that researchers do not employ dynamic interaction models they are making the hidden assumption that income, age, and shopping environment, customer inventories, and a host of other frame of reference variables are constant for *all* consumers. This is clearly nonsense, but nowhere in papers urging psychological research published by the behavioral scientists is this difficulty explicitly analyzed.[3]

A second distinguishing characteristic of the model in Figure 1 is the concept of customer state introduced originally by operations research analysts. It is especially helpful because the expected values of the outcomes can be measured empirically by a number of indicators which can then be built into prediction models. To be in a customer state an individual must be *ready to buy* due to precipitating circumstances. She must be *willing to buy* from a particular store because of certain expectancies embedded in her memory image. She must be *able to buy* due to economic and physical enabling conditions and other frame of reference variables.

Empirical measurement of customer state takes many diverse forms. First, are the verbal statements of intention to buy. Second is the record of frequency of visits to a particular store during some reasonable shopping interval. Third are the amounts of money spent in one store compared with its rivals. These and related measures can be examined to determine the degree of agreement among them before selecting the indicant or indicants to be used in actual field studies.

In addition to measures of persons "entering a customer state," measures should be made of persons "leaving a customer state" because of some action. For example, adding more store clerks and delivery trucks enables a store to take care of customers' orders more speedily. Yet it may force a rise in price that may, in turn, induce some customers to "leave the customer state." Many operations research analysts are content to measure customer birth and death rates as indicants of customer state. In dealing with so intangible a determinant as store image, however, psychological measures are needed at comparable levels of consciousness.

A third distinguishing feature of the model

[3] See for example Ernest Dichter, "Seven Tenets of Creative Research," *Journal of Marketing*, April 1961, pp. 1–4.

is the adaptation of Clark Hull's systematic behavior theory of learning within an environment of long-run determinants. These establish the limits within which image is operative. Such determinants include economic, sociological, and physical characteristics, fixed in the short run, but subject to long-run changes due to new precipitating circumstances.[4]

Reduced to its simplest form, the Hull behavior system postulates that an individual wants something (goal object), sees something (image), does something (instrumental behavior), and gets something (reward, reenforcement, and habit formation, or nonreward and discouragement from repeating the practice). This learning behavior must be carried on within the frame of reference supplied by the three classes of variables at the top of the diagram in Figure 1.

Among the frame of reference determinants is the retail shopping environment. Included here are the "marketing mix" variables subject to direct manipulation by the merchant who seeks to induce consumers to enter "customer states." Store location is perhaps the most powerful dimension of image and of patronage alike. Other shopping environment variables are treated as if each retailer had full independence of action. It is the clustering of stores at a location, however, plus the difference among competing stores in prices and merchandise assortments, that directs trade between areas and stores. These macromarket environmental variables are measurable. They present little difficulty to the retailer seeking to appraise his own performance as long as he is aware that while they are beyond his ability to control, they also influence customer behavior with respect to his store. Thus they must be explicitly introduced in functional equations describing customer behavior.

What about using image as a predictive variable within the conceptual model just described? Here we distinguish between the dimensions of image that *are* responsible for inducing a customer state and those which are not. Much psychological research has focussed on irrelevant dimensions that have little, if any, influence on patronage.[5] Even if we succeed in identifying the relevant dimensions, we are confronted with the further task of specifying their relative importance or interaction.

Researchers have not yet accomplished the first part of this task. Much of the literature reveals the delight of discovery of new variables which have a bearing on store image. However, management cannot wait for research to provide the answers. Management must daily subject its intuitive predictions to the test of the market place. Consequently, however imperfect their answers may be, researchers must provide *some* information on the relative importance of each image dimension as well as on the identity of the relevant determinants. Otherwise they cannot give guidance to retailers seeking to employ this concept in decision making. The purpose of the concluding section is to provide a foundation for such analyses.

DETERMINANTS OF IMAGE

Research findings of the Wharton Studies indicate that six dimensions of image are relevant to customer patronage: locational convenience, merchandise suitability, value for the price paid, adequacy of store services, congeniality of the store, and satisfaction with the purchase after the transaction is completed. It is not easy to determine the relative importance of, or interaction between, these variables. Only a few low-level-generalizations can be ventured. Figure 2, however, shows thirty determinants of each of the image dimensions contributing to the desired customer state.

Figure 2 is intended to portray the relationship between cognitive dimensions of image and the determinants of these dimensions. Hopefully these will be useful in constructing questionnaires and observational forms for the collection of data. From the data, in turn, acceptance threshold levels can be calculated.

Once the preference threshold level has been reached for the relevant image variables, they can be expressed as expected values for population samples drawn from each distinct segment of the total market. The expected value, it will be remembered, is simply the proportion of persons indicating some behavior or other characteristic. It is a measure of average behavior. As for the influence of image determinants on customer states, preference thresholds vary among market segments. That is, customers exist in relatively different circumstances as measured by frame of reference

---

[4] For a recent restatement, see E. R. Hilgard, *Theories of Learning*, Second Edition (New York: Appleton-Century-Crofts, Inc., 1956), Chapter 5.
[5] Proceedings of the Fourteenth Annual Conference, American Association for Public Opinion Research, *Public Opinion Quarterly*, Fall, 1959, p. 426.

variables. Thus the expected values of the image determinants shown in Figure 2 must be measured empirically for each market segment. Only in this way can they be used to develop predictive models.

Figure 3 shows expected values of the preference thresholds for the six dimensions of store image. To provide a contrast we chose the working man's store and the carriage trade store. As it happens, this illustration is based

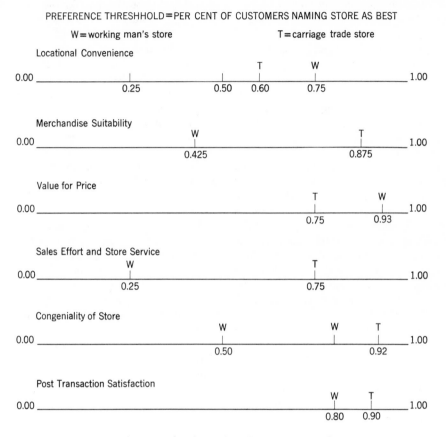

FIG. 3. Comparison of expected values of preference thresholds for customers who spent the most money and the working man's store and the carriage trade store, and who considered store "best." (Percentages have been changed to conceal store identity.)

on department store patrons. However, we could have used discount houses, supermarkets, or any other retail establishments.

The data in Figure 3 are calculated from patronage in the store in which the most money was spent in the year preceding the date of interview. Our measures of stores that people say they are ready, willing, and able to shop in are at variance with stores that they do enter. Thus the entry of consumers into customer states is difficult to infer from behavioral measures, and customer-state statistics are difficult to verify. It is particularly hard to obtain stable measures of psychologically antecedent states. This difficulty might be sur-

mounted if we were able to convert to a personal interview consumer panel operation—provided, of course, that the costs involved would justify the expenditure of effort.

Customer "death rate" information is more easily obtainable. People tell quite accurately not only the stores that they stopped patronizing in the past year, but are quite articulate in explaining why. "I shopped in ————'s for twenty years until I bought a girdle that wasn't right. I took it back and they wouldn't exchange it. I haven't been back there since."

Suggested here is a fresh approach to the measurement of transitional states involved in "birth-death" relationships. We have in the design stage a predictive model using all the determinants of image in Figure 2. This should tell us indirectly, by structured nondisguised techniques, whether the consumer seems to be entering a customer state for a store she has not previously patronized, even if she herself is unable to predict what she will do.

Also on the agenda of unfinished business is the weighting of the contribution of each of the determinants of the cognitive dimensions shown in Figure 2. Rather than delay our research program we have acted as if the measures we have are reasonably close approximations to situations of consumer choice. In Figure 3 location is prepotent among the perceptions guiding shoppers to one store or another.

Our research has shown some interesting variations in the determinants of locational convenience. For example, we find that people in the extreme suburban communities regard suburban communities closer to the core of the city as central shopping places. Similarly, the people living near these suburban centers look to the downtown store for the same kinds of merchandise. Thus judgments of the "best assortment of women's clothing" are made relative to the distance between the nearest shopping facilities and those at a distance that does not involve passing through a second shopping center. Clearly a "Reilly's Law" relationship holds here.

However, a second determinant of locational convenience is the access route to a store. We have found numerous well-to-do New Jersey shoppers bypassing our center city stores because turnpikes will carry them directly into a swanky cluster of high fashion suburban stores on the outskirts of Philadelphia. In contrast to the residents of outer suburbs who must pass through a more centrally located suburban shopping center, the New Jersey residents have the opportunity to bypass center city traffic lights, congestion, and parking problems for travel time assumes relatively less importance than does ease of access.

How should one weight these determinants of locational convenience for the two different groups of suburbanites? Predictions based on Reilly's Law might be less accurate than guesses because locational convenience is an image determined largely by sign expectancies posed by traffic barriers, physical congestion, and access routes not immediately measurable in spatial or temporal terms.

Similar problems appear with merchandise suitability and value for price. (Adequacy of promotion effort and store services are further variables which have muddied our efforts at understanding thus far.) Nevertheless we are progressing in understanding the dynamics of "birth-death" processes and the importance of each of the major image dimensions in interactions under varying frames of reference. We have mapped the major dimensions of store image and we know a good deal about their determinants. On an item-by-item basis we can predict with some accuracy the types and exact locations of stores people will enter when shopping. There is much that we do not know, of course, and we have a long road to travel before we can meet the management challenge of image. Yet it was only a few years back, in 1959, that conferees at a round table on corporate image timidly concluded that there really was such a thing—because people were able to make distinctions between companies.[6]

---

[6] Proceedings of the Fourteenth Annual Conference, American Association for Public Opinion Research, *Public Opinion Quarterly*, Fall, 1959, page 427.

DISCUSSION QUESTIONS

This article is of particular value because of the concept of "customer state" and because of the discussion of cognitive dimensions of store image.

Using the 0 to 1 continua in Figure 3, place each of the following stores at an appropriate point for each of the seven dimensions represented:
(a) Sears
(b) Nieman Marcus
(c) Marshall-Fields
(d) May Company Department Stores

2. Communicating with the Innovator in the Fashion Adoption Process

CHARLES W. KING*

Can the marketer communicate with the fashion innovator? In this paper, the communication characteristics of the early buyer of a particular fashion product are presented. The implications of the data are discussed in terms of adoption theory and fashion marketing strategy.

The consumer fashion adoption decision is the product of a complex procedure of information processing. To develop a contemporary theory of fashion adoption, the marketer must understand the dynamics of fashion communication on the time-of-adoption continuum. The innovator or early buyer represents a discrete market segment and a key consumer change agent in the diffusion process. The central question is, what are the communication characteristics of the fashion innovator? How can the marketer communicate with the fashion innovator or early buyer?

COMMUNICATING WITH THE FASHION INNOVATOR

The Role of the Fashion Innovator or Early Buyer in the Adoption Process—An Overview

In earlier research, fashion adoption has been treated as a specific type of innovative behavior within the broader context of social change. Fashion adoption has been defined as "a process of social contagion by which a new style or product is adopted by the consumer after commercial introduction by the designer or manufacturer.[1]" The consumer adoption decision is made within the time dimension of a season. The buying and wearing of a particular season's new fashions by the mass consumer market involve a shift from the styles appropriate the previous year to the current season's fashion offerings. Consumers across socio-economic classes adopt new styles early in the season, and the contagion spreads horizontally within social strata and to a more limited extent, vertically across strata. Consumers may select from a wide range of styles in the current season's inventory and be "in fashion."

In this adoption process, the innovator or early buyer plays a key role as a consumer change agent. The early buyer initiates the adoption cycle within the season through her early purchase and is the earliest visual communicator of the new season's styles to the mass of fashion consumers. Fashion retailers and manufacturers monitor the early buyers' selections and make major decisions regarding the season's fashion trends and inventory based on the early buyers' purchase patterns.

Among the mass fashion consumers, the early buyers give legitimacy to the season's styles through displaying the season's offerings to their social networks in various social settings. In some social networks, the early buyer may also be a fashion opinion leader and may define broad fashion standards for the group as well as display the season's inventory.

* SOURCE: Reprinted by permission from the American Marketing Association, in *Marketing and Economic Development*, Peter D. Bennett, editor, 1965, pages 425–439.
* Assistant Professor in Industrial Management, School of Industrial Management, Purdue University.
[1] For a detailed critique of the fashion adoption process, see Charles W. King, "Fashion Adoption: A Rebuttal of the 'Trickle Down' Theory", in Stephen A. Greyser (Ed)., *Toward Scientific Marketing*, Proceedings of the Winter Conference of the American Marketing Association, 1963, Boston, Massachusetts, pp. 108–125.

The Fashion Innovator as a Discrete Market Segment

Empirical research focusing on the early buyer in the millinery product category has suggested that the early buyer may be a discrete market segment.[2] Comparative analysis of early buyers and other consumers has indicated that the early buyers are differentiated from other consumers by consistent differences in demographic and life style characteristics rather than by isolated idiosyncracies. More specifically, the early buyers were found to be higher in social status, more psychologically compatible with fashion involvement, more gregarious and involved in social activities where fashion consciousness would be appropriate and more interested in personal grooming and hat wearing per se.

Communicating with the Fashion Innovator

The fashion innovators or early buyers represent a prime sales target for the fashion merchandiser because of their key position in the adoption process and because of their sales potential as a major market segment. The central question is, how can the fashion marketer communicate with the early buyer?

Communications Variables as Discriminants of Innovative Behavior. In previously reported multiple discriminant analysis of the early buyer and other consumer groups to be studied in depth in this paper, ten selected communications variables were analysed as an independent predictive battery of measures. The resulting linear discriminant function was not significant at the .05 level and accurately classified only 65 percent of the respondents.[3] While these data suggest that differences between these groups on these variables were not pronounced, there may be subtle differences between adopter groups that were not detected by the variables used or the linear analysis.

Other Research on Fashion Communication. Other published empirical research on fashion communication has not included time of adoption as a dimension of analysis. Barber and Lobel performed a content analysis of fashion

copy in leading fashion journals from 1930 to 1950 but did not consider differential communication processes within the fashion market.[4] Rich generated a body of evidence on communication behavior and information usage in fashion but did not pursue communication in the time of adoption context.[5]

Fashion journalists and media researchers have segmented the fashion market into socioeconomic groups, and various fashion journals focus on particular segments. Each journal typically testifies to reaching *the* "fashion leader," but media research has focused on reader profiles rather than on the dynamics of fashion communication within the adoption process.[6]

Hypotheses from Other Adoption Research. Research on innovative behavior in other contexts, particularly by rural sociologists, indicates that early adopters tend to differ from later adopters in terms of communication behavior.[7] Early adopters tend to rely more on impersonal rather than personal sources of information concerning the innovation adopted. Early buyers use more "cosmopolite" sources (sources external to the adopters' social system). In turn, the early adopters utilize more technical sources, e.g., agricultural scientists, county agents, agricultural extension service bulletins, etc. and report more involvement with all kinds of information sources. In the area of social interactions and communications, early adopters are more gregarious and have more contacts outside their immediate social system. In turn, the early adopters appear to be more active as personal communicators within their social system. Though these conclusions have been drawn from adoption contexts markedly different from the fashion environment, do similar communication pat-

---

[2] Charles W. King, "The Innovator in the Fashion Adoption Process", in L. George Smith (Ed.,), *Reflections on Progress in Marketing*, Proceedings of the Winter Conference of the American Marketing Association, 1964, Chicago, Illinois, pp. 324–339.

[3] Ibid., p. 331–332.

---

[4] Bernard Barber and Lyle S. Lobel, "Fashion in Women's Clothes and the American Social System", *Social Forces*, 31 (1952) pp. 124–131.

[5] Stuart U. Rich, *Delivery Service and Telephone Ordering: Department Store Policies and Consumer Demand*, Division of Research: Harvard Graduate School of Business Administration, 1963.

[6] Based on interviews with fashion editors, journalists and researchers. For a simplified report on the marketing strategies of leading fashion journals, see "The Fashion Beat", *Time*, 86:7, August 13, 1965, p. 58.

[7] For a review of research dealing with communication behavior in the adoption process, see Everett M. Rogers, *Diffusion of Innovations*, New York: Free Press, 1962, pp. 98–105, 178–188, 217–247.

terns characterize the innovator in fashion adoption?

The objective of this paper is to explore the communication characteristics of the innovator or early buyer in the category of women's millinery. More specifically, the following issues have been studied:

1. What are the communication characteristics of the early buyer in comparison with other consumers?

2. What are the implications of these findings in terms of fashion adoption behavior and in terms of fashion merchandising strategy?

THE RESEARCH METHODOLOGY

The Data

The data analyzed in this paper were collected in an exploratory consumer survey of the innovator or early buyer and the influential or opinion leader within the product category of women's millinery. The research design was built around defining the time of adoption as the critical variable. Respondents were qualified on a time of adoption continuum based on their Fall, 1962, hat buying behavior. Time of adoption was defined as the month of first purchase of a hat during the Fall season. The adoption decision was not defined as the purchase of any specific style, because the consumer can purchase a wide range of styles *within the current season's merchandise* and be "in style" regardless of the specific style selection.

Adopter Groups Analyzed

In this paper, two adopter groups have been analyzed in depth:

1. Innovators or early buyers—late August or September buyers representing the first 35% of the Fall, 1962, season's millinery buyers.

2. All other consumers—later buyers and consumers that did not buy in the Fall, 1962 season.

THE DYNAMICS OF COMMUNICATION BEHAVIOR IN FASHION ADOPTION

Do the dynamics of communication behavior differ among adopter groups on the time of adoption continuum? The communication characteristics of the early buyer and other consumer groups have been studied on four major dimensions:

1. Exposure to mass communications.

2. Involvement in general social communications and specific social activities.

3. Social communications about fashion and hats.

4. Preferred fashion information sources.

Exposure to Mass Communication

Fashion theory and adoption research in other contexts suggest the early buyer group should have higher mass communication exposure than other consumers. The early buyer and other consumer groups, however, report very similar exposure to print and broadcast media based on the data presented in Table 1, though the direction of the differences does favor the hypothesis of higher exposure of the early buyers.

The early buyers' lower TV viewing and higher general interest and total magazine readership reflected the only statistically significant differences from the exposure patterns of the other consumers. More subtle support for the hypothesis is found, however, when the *direction of difference* is noted on each communication dimension. With the exception of TV viewing, the early buyer group reported higher exposure to each of the 6 other media suggesting a non-random distribution of the direction of the differences that is significant and supports the hypothesis.

Involvement in General Social Communications and Specific Social Activities

Involvement in general social communications and specific social activities reflects consistent and fundamental differences in the dynamics of the communication process among early buyers compared with other consumers. The data presented in Table 2 have been confined to those activities on which the groups reported statistically significant differences using the 5 percent significance criterion. The complete array of activities measured also included telephone conversations with women, family visiting with friends, church-synagogue attendance, pleasure driving, shopping in neighborhood centers, wedding attendance and traveling by public transportation (subway, bus, etc.).

The early buyer group is more involved in general social communications and specific social activities in which the communication of fashion cues is an integral part of the personal

TABLE 1. Exposure to Mass Communications by Adopter Category

Mass Communications Variable	Early Buyers	Other Consumers	X^2 Test of Significance
Radio Listening:			
Low	48%[a]	51%[a]	p<.70[a]
High	52	49	
Total	100%	100%	
TV Viewing:			
Low	56%	44%	p<.02
High	44	56	
Total	100%	100%	
Newspaper Readership:			
Low	61%	67%	p<.20
High	39	33	
Total	100%	100%	
General Interest Magazine Readership:			
Low	28%	42%	p<.05
Medium	41	35	
High	31	23	
Total	100%	100%	
Fashion Magazine Readership:			
Low	41%	48%	p<.20
High	59	52	
Total	100%	100%	
News Magazine Readership:			
Low	65%	71%	p<.50
High	35	29	
Total	100%	100%	
Total Magazine Readership:			
Low	43%	56%	p<.02
High	57	44	
Total	100%	100%	
BASE SAMPLE SIZE	112	395	

[a] Read: 48% of the early buyers and 51% of the other consumers reported "low" radio listening. The difference was not statistically significant at the 5% level based on X^2 analysis.

interaction process. The early buyers' higher frequency of social visiting with other women provides the setting for oral exchange of fashion information. In turn, the greater frequency of downtown shopping may enable the early buyer to canvass a wider inventory of current fashion merchandise.

Higher participation in more formal and fashion oriented activities such as cocktail parties, teas, club meetings, etc. gives the early buyer a role in a complex fashion information exchange network. The early buyer monitors the fashion standards and preferences of the social environment and contributes the display of her fashion selections to the network. While oral exchange of cues may occur, visual monitoring is typically a continuous activity of all participants.

The early buyer is also more exposed to fashion cues from outside her immediate social environment as indicated by her higher attendance at conventions, professional meetings, etc. This coincides with the greater "cosmopoliteness" of early adopters noted in farm practice adoption.

In turn, the early buyer is generally more gregarious as measured by total organization membership and the total activities index. Further analysis of the direction of the differences on all 17 measures of social communications and activities indicated that the early buyers reported higher involvement on every measure except use of public transportation. As in the case of the exposure to mass media, the consistency of the direction of the differences is significant and supports the higher gregariousness of the early buyer.

Social Communications About Fashion and Hats

The traditional "trickle down" theory of fashion adoption and other adoption research suggest that the early buyers would be high transmitters while the other consumers would be high receivers of person-to-person communications about fashion and hats. The data presented in Table 3 challenge that hypothesis. The early buyers and other consumers *have essentially identical involvement* in information receiving (talking to someone to get ideas about fashion) and information transmission (respondent's advice requested or respondent offered information).

The similarity in personal communication patterns across adopter categories is due in part to the level of interest in fashion throughout the population. Approximately 50 percent of the total sample reported "high" interest and less than 7 percent of the total population reported no interest in fashion.[8] While more early buyers (60 percent) reported high fashion interest compared with other consumers (46 percent), the topic has high relevance to the attitudes of both groups.

The *level of information seeking* within both groups attests to the initiative of the adopters

in information gathering. The information seeking by the early buyer may make the task of communicating with this market segment easier for the fashion marketer.

Preferred Fashion Information Sources

Fashion information sources selected as "helpful" and "most helpful" in keeping informed about fashion are presented in Table 4. In general both adopter groups reported using a variety of types of fashion information. Technical fashion sources, such as fashion shows, fashion magazines and newspaper fashion ads and shopping in the stores, clearly rank as the most important categories.

In turn, the adopter groups differ somewhat in their information preferences. In general, early buyers tended to prefer technical sources more than did the other consumers. In turn, the other consumers reported greater usage of in-store shopping.

A Profile of the Early Buyers' Communications Characteristics

A broad profile of the early buyers' fashion communications characteristics emerges from the data analysis. Compared with other consumers, the early buyers report:

1. Moderately higher exposure to the mass communications media;

2. Markedly higher involvement in general social communications and specific activities where fashion communication is an integral part of the social interaction;

3. higher general gregariousness as measured by organization membership and total activities;

4. higher exposure to communications from outside the immediate social environment as measured by attendance at professional meetings, etc. and attendance at formal activities where new fashion concepts might be introduced by "visitors" to the environment;

5. preferences for different kinds of fashion sources over others. Though both the early buyer and other consumer groups assigned greater importance to technical fashion sources and shopping in stores, the early buyers placed significantly greater emphasis on the technical sources than did the other consumers and less importance on shopping in the store;

6. equally high involvement in person-to-person information seeking and information transmission about fashion and hats.

---

[8] Somewhat similar data have been reported by Rich, *op. cit.* p. 67 using the same measure of fashion interest.

TABLE 2. Involvement in General Social Communications and Specific
Activities by Adopter Category

Social Activities Variable	Early Buyers	Other Consumers	X^2 Test of Significance
Frequency of Social Visiting with Women:			
Low	49%	66%[a]	p<.01[a]
High	51	34	
Total	100%	100%	
Shop Downtown:			
Low	31%	46%	p<.01
High	69	54	
Total	100%	100%	
Eat Lunch or Dinner Out at a Restaurant:			
Low	26%	44%	p<.01
High	74	56	
Total	100%	100%	
Attend Cocktail Parties And Open Houses:			
Low	52%	66%	p<.01
High	48	34	
Total	100%	100%	
Attend Night Clubs:			
Low	71%	81%	p<.05
High	29	19	
Total	100%	100%	
Attend Conventions, Business And Professional Meetings:			
Low	69%	80%	p<.02
High	31	20	
Total	100%	100%	
Attend Morning or Afternoon Teas:			
Low	65%	79%	p<.01
High	35	21	
Total	100%	100%	
Attend PTA, Fraternal and Club Meetings:			
Low	32%	46%	p<.01
High	68	54	
Total	100%	100%	

[a] Read: 49% of the early buyers and 66% of the other consumers reported "low" frequency of social visiting with other women. The difference was statistically significant at the 1% level based on X^2 analysis.

TABLE 2. Continued

Social Activities Variable	Early Buyers	Other Consumers	X² Test of Significance
Attend Theatrical Play, Concerts, Lectures:			
Low	46%	60%	p<.02
High	54	40	
Total	100%	100%	
Organization Membership:			
Low	52%	67%	p<.01
High	48	33	
Total	100%	100%	
Total Activities Index:			
Low	20%	36%	
Medium	38	38	p<.02
High	42	26	
Total	100%	100%	
BASE SAMPLE SIZE	112	395	

IMPLICATIONS FOR ADOPTING THEORY AND FASHION MARKETING STRATEGY

The analysis of the dynamics of the communications process among the early buyers and the other consumers supports two major conclusions:

1. The innovator or early buyer in the fashion adoption process within the millinery context appears to differ in communication characteristics compared with other consumers.

2. The innovator or early buyer is differentiated from the other consumers by consistent though subtle differences in communication exposure and usage rather than by particular idiosyncracies in communication behavior.

What are the implications of these findings to adoption theory and to fashion marketing strategy?

Implications for Adoption Theory

The analysis of the communication behavior of the fashion early buyer and other consumer groups has significant implications for adoption theory across product categories. The bulk of research in product adoption and diffusion has been conducted within the context of farm practices adoption. A basic question of concern to marketers is, how applicable are the generalizations derived from farm practices adoption research to consumer product adoption in the mass market?

Communication Behavior Across Adoption Contexts. The findings regarding fashion communication behavior are relevant to this question. Despite the diversity of the environments and adoption contexts, i.e., farm practices adoption among farmers in rural farming communities versus fashion adoption among women in Boston, Massachusetts, *a consistent pattern of communication behavior on the time-of-adoption continuum appears to exist across adoption contexts.*

The fashion early adopter and the farm practices early adopter both have similar communication exposure and usage patterns. The early adopters from both contexts report higher exposure to communication in general, are more gregarious and are more exposed to communication from outside their immediate social environments. In terms of communication source preferences and usage, both early adopter sets report greater preferences for impersonal sources than their later adopter counterparts. Both early adopter groups prefer technical information sources over other types of communication.

Adaptive Communication Behavior. Though consistent patterns of communication behavior appear to exist across adoption contexts, the

TABLE 3. Social Communications About Fashion and Hats
by Adopter Category

	Early Buyers ("Yes" Answer)	Other Consumers ("Yes" Answer)
"Generally like to talk to someone to get ideas about fashion before going shopping . . ."	34%[a]	33%[a]
"Talked to someone recently to get ideas about fashion . . ."	24%	21%
"Know someone in particular you generally like to talk to about fashion . . ."	30%	30%
"Someone recently asked your advice about fashion . . ."	33%	27%
"Recently offered someone suggestion about fashion . . ."	23%	23%
"Talked with someone recently to get ideas about hats . . ."	7%	8%
"Know someone you generally like to talk to about hats . . ."	12%	11%
Placed "high" dependence on millinery saleswoman when buying a hat.	20%	24%
BASE SAMPLE SIZE	112	395

[a] Read: 34% of the early buyers and 33% of the other consumers reported they generally like to talk with someone to get ideas about fashions before going shopping for clothes. None of the differences are statistically significant at the 5% level based on X^2 analysis.

fashion personal communication data indicate that *communication behavior is adaptive to the adoption context.* Rural sociologists have reported that personal influence and person-to-person information exchange are more important in the adoption decisions of later adopters. In contradiction to this conclusion, however, the fashion early buyer was as involved in person-to-person information seeking as her other consumer counterpart.

The difference in communication patterns is explained in part by the differences in the adoption environments. In the farm practices adoption context, few expert personal sources may be available to early adopters since their relatives, friends and neighbors are unlikely to have expertise regarding the innovation at the time of the early adopter's evaluation and trial decisions. In the fashion adoption context, however, interest in keeping informed about

fashion is high and early buyers and other consumers have substantial exposure to fashion cues via mass media, shopping and visual and oral information exchange. Therefore, at the evaluative stage in her adoption decision, the early buyer may get valuable information from personal communication within her social network.

The Functions of Communication Sources. The fashion communication patterns suggest that *different information sources may perform different and complementary functions.* The early buyer prefers technical sources for keeping informed about fashions yet also shops in stores and actively seeks information in the social network. An analysis of the functions of the various sources might indicate that technical sources are used to maintain general awareness, while shopping in stores focuses on fashion trends within the early buyer's shop-

TABLE 4. Preferred Fashion Information Sources by Adopter Category

	Fashion Sources Designated "Helpful"			Fashion Sources Designated "Most Helpful"		
	Early Buyers	Other Consumers	X² Test of Significance	Early Buyers	Other Consumers	X² Test of Significance
Specialized Fashion Sources	42%[a]	34%[a]	p<.05[b]	40%	31%	p<.10[b]
Going Shopping in Stores	22	26	p<.30	33	45	p<.05
General Mass Media	18	20	p<.50	14	12	p<.80
Personal Communications	18	20	p<.50	13	12	p<.80
Total	100%	100%		100%	100%	
BASE	273[c]	893[c]		112	395	

[a] Read: 42% of the early buyers and 34% of the other consumers designated specialized fashion sources such as fashion shows, fashion magazines and newspaper fashion ads as "helpful" in keeping informed on fashion trends.
[b] X² analyses based on differences by individual information source.
[c] Total number of sources mentioned. Multiple answers accepted.

ping environment and affords a basis for evaluation through trying on styles, matching colors with the existing wardrobe, etc. The social network may provide information on the fashion norms and attitudes of the network relevant to the early adopter's fashion behavior.

Implications for Fashion Marketing Strategy

As noted earlier, the early buyer and other consumer groups appear to represent discrete market segments. The different life styles of the early buyers and the other consumers suggest that the groups may have different millinery style preferences for functional and aesthetic reasons. The early buyers may have more current and high fashion wardrobes with which new millinery styles must be coordinated. In turn, the early buyers and other consumers may have learned different fashion "rules" and style preferences in their respective social environments.

To integrate the unique market segment notion into the marketing strategy of the fashion industry, specific marketing programs involving product line, promotion and retail selling tactics should be directed at the individual market segments. Given the role of the early buyer as a prime sales target and as a consumer change agent, at least one objective should be to accelerate the first purchase by the early

buyer group to initiate the season and to maximize the time for repeat purchases by the segments during the season.

To implement these strategies, the fashion marketer must improve his communication with the market segments. The differential communication behavior of the early buyers and other consumers reinforces the discrete market segment notion and has basic implications for fashion industry promotion and retail selling tactics.

Communication Source Selection and Market Segmentation. How can the early buyer of the other consumer set be reached most efficiently by fashion marketers? The research findings indicate that *no single fashion source can be used to reach either market segment.* The optimum communication program should include a combination of technical fashion sources such as fashion shows, fashion magazines and newspaper fashion ads and in-store promotion display and personal selling, general mass media and personal communications. The data indicate that *individual information sources are not used to the exclusion of others but in conjunction with one another.*

The communication program should differ *in emphasis and in message content* over the fashion season. The season's styles and major fashion themes should be introduced through the technical sources with reinforcement by the in-store retailing effort. Later in the season, emphasis should shift to more localized communication centered around the in-store shopping experience in conjunction with factual newspaper advertising.

The Communication Message. Given that an optimum combination of information sources is selected, what kinds of fashion information do the market segments need? Though these data have not probed content preferences per se, the demographic and life style profiles of the early buyer and later buyer groups suggest that the segments' information needs may differ. The more fashion conscious and informed early buyer group may need more technical information on new styles, silhouettes, etc. while later buyers may need more detailed fashion "rules" to guide their fashion behavior and reduce perceived risk. The communication preferences of the market segments suggest that the early buyers and other consumers do seek different types of information. If the information needs do differ, promotional copy and retail selling tactics should be planned accordingly over the season.

The Information Seeking Function. The high level of information seeking and information transmission about fashion and hats should be integrated into the broad communication program. Though the complexities of message transmissibility and rumor networks are inadequately understood, the high level of information seeking suggests that the formal communication effort need not seek to reach all consumers in each segment. The introduction of instructive information relevant to the segments' particular environments will travel through social networks as a result of the purposive information seeking activity among consumers.

SUMMARY

To develop a contemporary theory of fashion adoption, the marketer must understand the dynamics of fashion communication on the time-of-adoption continuum. The analysis of the communication characteristics of the early buyer and other consumer groups in the millinery product category has indicated that consistent though subtle differences exist in communications exposure and usage between the early buyers and the other consumers.

The differences in communication behavior for the two groups give additional support to the concept that the early buyer and the other consumer groups represent discrete market segments. The differential communication characteristics of the adopter groups have implications for generalizations regarding adoption behavior in fashion and in other product categories. To the fashion marketer, the communication patterns of the early buyers and the other consumers suggest marketing strategies that may improve the marketer's communication with the market segments on the time-of-adoption continuum.

While this analysis has been confined to the fashion category of millinery, the concept of market segmentation by time-of-adoption and the concept of differential communication behavior across market segments have applicability across fashion categories. While the characteristics of the market segments may change by fashion category, understanding the dynamics of communication behavior by market segment is essential to the fashion marketer.

DISCUSSION QUESTIONS

Fashion influentials or innovators hold the key to important advances in our understanding of fashion adoption and diffusion. This article has particular implications for the retail fashion merchandiser.

1. What are the important behavioral characteristics of early fashion adopters?
2. How can the retailer use an understanding of early fashion adopters to increase profits and reduce the risks in fashion retailing?

3. The "Imageries" of Department Stores

STUART U. RICH and BERNARD D. PORTIS

Postwar migration to the suburbs, increasing traffic congestion in the cities, and new suburban shopping centers, have greatly reduced the popularity of downtown shopping.

In the last few years several large downtown department stores in many major cities—including Boston, New York, Philadelphia, Baltimore, Pittsburgh, and Cleveland—have been forced to close their doors. Despite this decline in downtown shopping, however, there are still many profitable downtown stores which not only serve city dwellers but also attract customers from the suburbs.

What is it that has enabled these remaining downtown stores to stay in business? One view is that these downtown stores have appealed to the fashion shoppers and the bargain hunters.[1] A similar explanation is that the successful downtown store is one with a "high prestige image of quality and fashion" or one with an "image of complete stocks and very wide range of selection," and that the "more or less faceless department store" is likely to be in trouble.[2]

This idea of the successful store as one with an "image" of one type or another is an important concept. Department stores may need to upgrade their fashion image, to strengthen their private brand image, to improve their service image, and so on. The tone of store newspaper advertisements, the type of lighting used, and the voice of the telephone sales clerk are important "image-builders."

What is it that really constitutes a department store's "image"? Is this concept a useful one for department stores? Or is a firm's image just a meaningless stereotype?[3]

THE CONCEPT OF STORE IMAGE

Pierre Martineau defined store personality or image in the following way:

Clearly there is a force operative in the determination of a store's customer body besides the obvious functional factors of location, price ranges, and merchandise offerings. I shall show that this force is the store personality or image —the way in which the store is defined in the shopper's mind, partly by its functional qualities and partly by an aura of psychological attributes.[4]

Martineau has described the many different intangible traits which constitute a store's personality: store layout and display, styling, character of sales personnel, advertising tone, service facilities, and store reputation. Although retailers must be concerned with the more concrete factors of location, price, and merchandise, nevertheless these intangible features play a crucial role in attracting customers to particular stores.

In keeping with their different personalities, stores attract different types of clientele; and women may choose the type of store whose overall image best fits the image they hold of themselves. Women who identify themselves with different social classes, for instance, may

♦ SOURCE: Reprinted by permission from the American Marketing Association, in the *Journal of Marketing*, April 1964, pages 10–15.

[1] George Sternlieb, *The Future of the Downtown Department Store* (Cambridge, Massachusetts: Joint Center for Urban Studies of the Massachusetts Institute of Technology and Harvard University, 1962), p. 180.

[2] Malcolm P. McNair, "The Changing Retail Scene and What Lies Ahead," speech delivered to the annual convention of the National Retail Merchants Association, New York, January 8, 1962, reported in *Women's Wear Daily*, January 9, 1962, p. 1.

[3] W. T. Tucker, "How Much of the Corporate Image Is Stereotype?" JOURNAL OF MARKETING, Vol. 25 (January, 1961), pp. 61–65, at p. 64.

[4] Pierre Martineau, "The Personality of the Retail Store," *Harvard Business Review*, Vol. 36 (January-February, 1958), pp. 47–55, at p. 47.

choose to shop at stores of differing status from others. Martineau concludes that ". . . there is no such thing as a store image with equal appeal for all income groups, all social classes, all ages, all types." [5]

It was the downtown stores to which Martineau gave most of his attention. However, referring to the expansion of suburban branches, he also noted that branch stores took on the personality and character of the big downtown store, even though quite different in appearance and merchandise offerings from the main store.

THE PRESENT STUDY

The data in the present study are based on interviews conducted in the spring of 1962 with 4,500 randomly selected women shoppers. The interviews lasted approximately one hour and were conducted in person by interviewers furnished by the Psychological Corporation of New York. They were conducted in the New York—northeastern New Jersey metropolitan area, and in the Cleveland metropolitan area.[6]

Three Types of Appeal

An important part of the study dealt with the reasons which prompted women to do more of their shopping in one particular store than in any of the others. Nine major department stores in the New York City area and in Cleveland were mentioned most frequently by respondents. The stores fell into three groups: high-fashion appeal, price appeal, and broad appeal.

Table 1 shows the attractions of these three types of appeal. The stores which present the strongest 'image" are the high-fashion ones. The style and quality of their merchandise, their sales clerk service, and their reputation and reliability put them well above the stores in the other two groups. Their store layout and merchandise displays also give them an "edge" over most of the other stores.

In contrast with the high-fashion stores, the price-appeal stores receive very little customer mention for fashion or quality merchandise or for sales clerk service, but considerably more mention for low prices and bargains. Except

in the case of store C, however, price appeal is not the dominant attraction.

In another part of the study, there were indications that the discount stores have the strongest price image, whereas the department stores are mentioned more for their merchandise, reliability, and services.[7]

Also, note that the price-appeal stores receive greater mention than the fashion-appeal stores for their services other than from sales clerks—that is, delivery, telephone orders, charge accounts, and ease of returning merchandise.

There are two possible explanations. One is that these services may just be taken for granted by the fashion-store patrons, but really appreciated by the price-appeal customers. A second reason may be that although the fashion-appeal stores give special attention to the quality of their sales clerk service, they do not attempt to provide anything extra in other services.

Stores in the broad-appeal group fall in between the fashion-appeal stores and the price-appeal stores in the sort of image they present to customers. They offer some degree of attraction in both fashion merchandise and bargains. They are strong on selection and variety of merchandise, although not ahead of the price-appeal stores in this regard.

The broad-appeal stores also rank about equal with the price-appeal stores in reputation and reliability, but ahead of them in sales clerk service and in store layout and display (except in the case of Store H). Their accessibility gives them an advantage over both the other types of stores.

Customer Characteristics

What about the types of customers attracted by the stores with images of fashion, price, or broad appeal? The income groups, life cycles, and types of residence of the women mentioning these three types of "favorite" stores are given in Table 2, and are related to the types of stores preferred by the women with these different characteristics.

The stores with a high-fashion image in the minds of customers are the ones most favored by the high-income women, whereas the price-appeal stores attract very few of these customers.

[5] Same source as footnote 4, at p. 50.
[6] For a full report on the project, see Stuart U. Rich, *Shopping Behavior of Department Store Customers* (Boston, Massachusetts: Division of Research, Harvard Business School, 1963).

[7] Stuart U. Rich and Bernard Portis, "Clues for Action From Shopper Preferences," *Harvard Business Review*, Vol. 41 (March–April, 1963), pp. 132–149.

TABLE 1. Types of Attraction of Nine Downtown Department Stores

| Reasons for Store Preference[b] | "Favorite" Downtown Stores[a] | | | | | | | | |
| | High-Fashion Stores | | Price-Appeal Stores | | | Broad-Appeal Stores | | | |
	A	B	C	D	E	F	G	H	I
Merchandise:									
Fashion or quality merchandise	46%[c]	44%	28%	23%	23%	19%	17%	15%	14%
Selection and variety of merchandise	11	34	40	41	40	50	46	48	36
Store reputation and reliability	28	38	18	23	29	11	21	24	20
Price appeal (lower prices, bargains, good values)	9	12	16	20	24	16	54	22	20
Shopping convenience:									
Accessibility and parking	19	5	37	16	23	45	13	14	16
Sales clerk service	37	37	22	15	14	24	8	10	5
Other services (delivery, phone orders, charge accounts, ease of returning merchandise)	14	12	19	39	13	18	17	37	39
Efficient store layout and display	16	19	17	13	1	8	4	6	5
(Sample size)	(56)	(41)	(185)	(157)	(196)	(62)	(24)	(134)	(44)

[a] Women were asked at which store they did most of their shopping for various categories of merchandise. Stores A through I were those downtown department stores in Cleveland, Manhattan, Brooklyn, and Newark most frequently mentioned as being the stores most often patronized.

[b] Reasons for preferring favorite stores total more than 100% because respondents commonly gave multiple reasons in explaining their choices.

[c] This means that 46% of those women whose "favorite" store was Store A (that is, did more shopping at A than at any other store) mentioned fashion or quality merchandise as a reason for preferring Store A.

The middle-income women represent the largest group for all three types of stores.

The low-income women go mainly to the broad-appeal and the price-appeal stores, although some patronize the fashion-appeal stores.

As for the relationship between life cycle (age and children) and store preference high-fashion stores attract mainly the women 40 or over, especially the ones without children at home. These women presumably have more money to spend and are more demanding of the type of service found in these stores.

As to both the broad-appeal and the price-appeal stores, women under 40 with children are the most important single customer group, although women in over-40 groups are also numerous.

Younger women with no children at home are not an important group of shoppers for any of the stores.

Of the women whose favorite store is a downtown fashion-appeal store, 41% live in the suburbs. This is in contrast with the broad-appeal and the price-appeal stores, whose customers are much more likely to live in the city. The belief that the large downtown store with "more of everything" (the broad-appeal store),

TABLE 2. Downtown Store Types and Customer Characteristics[a]

Customer characteristic	Store types		
Income group:	High fashion	Price appeal	Broad appeal
High income over $10,000 annually	40%	8%	20%
Middle income: $5,000–$10,000 annually	43%	60%	53%
Low income under $5,000 annually	17%	32%	27%
(Sample size)	(97)	(202)	(600)

Customer characteristic	Store types		
Life cycle:	High fashion	Price appeal	Broad appeal
40 and over, and children at home	23%	21%	29%
No children at home	52%	31%	25%
Under 40, and children at home	12%	39%	36%
	13%	9%	10%
(Sample size)	(97)	(202)	(600)

Customer characteristic	Store types		
Type of residence:	High fashion	Price appeal	Broad appeal
Suburbs	41%	27%	21%
City	59%	73%	79%
(Sample size)	(97)	(202)	(600)

[a] Characteristics are averaged for all stores in the same category in order to describe clientele of average stores in that category. (For example, 30% of shoppers at store A and 49% of shoppers at store B have incomes over $10,000. The average figure for these two stores in the high-fashion store category is $\frac{30 + 49}{2} = 39.5\%$, presented here as 40%.)

[b] This means that 40% of the women whose "favorite" store is in the high-fashion category are in the over-$10,000 income group.

and the downtown price-appeal store "pull in" the suburban shoppers does not appear to be as valid today as perhaps was true a few years ago.

Customer Shopping Behavior

Related to these three socio-economic characteristics are three shopping behavior traits. These are the degree of interest shown in the changing fashions in women's clothing by the respondents, the amount of bargain hunting they do, and whether or not they shop at discount stores. These shopping-behavior traits are shown in Table 3, as related to types of stores most often patronized.

The fashion-type stores are the ones most likely to attract the fashion-conscious shoppers, although the broad-appeal stores are nearly as popular with this group. Even the price-appeal stores attract a sizable number (38%) of the fashion-conscious shoppers, taking into account the total purchases which these women make.

Among the bargain hunters, the fashion-appeal stores have some attraction, although not necessarily for bargains. These shoppers are more likely to favor the broad-appeal or the price-appeal stores.

Probably related to bargain hunting is discount shopping, and the broad-appeal and the price-appeal stores are more likely to attract the discount shoppers.

Of the women favoring the high-fashion stores, 42% also shop at discount stores on occasion. Another part of the study reveals that 70% of women in the New York sample and 60% of the women in the Cleveland sample did at least some of their shopping in discount stores. Many of the higher-income women, whose favorite stores are fashion-appeal ones, still go to discount houses for merchandise such as children's clothing and appliances.[8]

The customers of the fashion-appeal stores are most likely to be in the middle-income and upper-income brackets, in the 40-and-over age group, often without children at home, and living in the suburbs. These women are quite

---

[8] Rich and Portis, same reference as footnote 7, at p. 132.

TABLE 3. Downtown Store Types and Customer Shopping Behavior[a]

Customers shopping behavior	Store types			Customer shopping behavior	Store types			Customer shopping behavior	Store types		
Fashion interest:	High fashion	Price appeal	Broad appeal	Look for bargains:	High fashion	Price appeal	Broad appeal	Shop at discount stores:	High fashion	Price appeal	Broad appeal
High	54%	38%	50%	Often	24%	37%	33%	Yes	42%	53%	57%
				Occasionally	36%	37%	43%				
Low	44%	60%	43%	Never	40%	24%	24%	No	58%	43%	37%
(Sample size)	(97)	(202)	(600)		(97)	(202)	(600)		(97)	(202)	(600)

[a] As in the case of Table 2, behavior characteristics are averaged for stores in the same category.

[b] This means that 54% of the women whose "favorite" store is in the high-fashion group are women who register a high degree of interest in fashions. Because of a few "don't knows," the percentages in this table do not always total 100%.

interested in fashion, and less interested in bargain hunting.

The price-appeal stores, on the other hand, attract the middle-income and lower-income women, both old and young, both with and without children, mainly from the city. These customers are also likely to be bargain hunters and to shop at the discount houses.

Finally, the broad-appeal stores fall in between the other two store categories as to the types of shoppers they attract. Although the majority of their customers are in the middle-income group, they also attract sizable numbers of both high-income and low-income women; and their customers are predominately city dwellers, representing all age groups both with and without children. They are interested both in fashions and in bargains, and are likely to shop in the discount stores.

Suburban Branches

Martineau's belief that the branch stores take on the personality and characteristics of their downtown units was borne out to some degree in the present study. However, the store images are weaker in the suburbs; and there is considerable similarity among the suburban branches of different types of downtown stores. See Table 4.

Although the fashion-image stores are still recognizable as distinct types in the suburbs, their major attractions of quality merchandise, sales-clerk service, store layout and display, and store reputation are less than in the case of the downtown stores. Not only do the suburban fashion stores receive less mention for their possession of these traits, but they also show less strength than their downtown units when compared with the broad-appeal and the price-appeal stores. For example, merchandise quality was emphasized by 45% of the customers of the downtown fashion-appeal stores, but with only 15% of the customers of the downtown price-appeal stores; but in the suburbs these two percentages are 37% and 22% respectively.

The price-appeal stores in the suburbs do not show the contrasting picture of strength in price and relative weakness in quality merchandise apparent in their downtown units. Price appeal is less, and the attraction of quality mer-

TABLE 4. Attractions of Downtown and Suburban Department Stores

Reasons for Store Preference[a]	Favorite-Store Category and Location					
	High-Fashion Stores		Price-Appeal Stores		Broad-Appeal Stores	
	Downtown	Suburban	Downtown	Suburban	Downtown	Suburban
Merchandise:						
Fashion or quality merchandise	45%	37%	23%	22%	15%	22%
Selection and variety of merchandise	23	38	43	48	43	50
Store reputation and reliability	33	15	18	10	22	6
Price appeal (lower prices, bargains, good values)	11	15	19	12	32	28
Shopping convenience:						
Accessibility and parking	12	30	30	38	14	26
Sales-clerk service	37	28	20	14	8	10
Other services (delivery, phone orders, charge accounts, ease of returning merchandise)	13	18	22	21	31	19
Efficient store layout and display	18	8	10	15	5	6
(Sample size)	(97)	(95)	(600)	(360)	(202)	(181)

[a] Reasons given are averaged for all stores in the same grouping in order to describe attractions of average store in the grouping. (For example, 46% of shoppers at downtown store A and 44% of shoppers at downtown store B cite fashion or quality merchandise as a reason for shopping these stores, as described in Table 1. The average figure for these two stores is $\dfrac{46 + 44}{2}$ 45%.)

chandise is higher. The suburban price-appeal stores also have less distinctiveness in the "other-services" category; they are at the same level as the other two types of stores, probably due to the lessening importance of delivery and phone orders in the more accessible suburban branches.

As for the broad-appeal stores, their suburban branches have less of a price-attraction advantage, relative to the fashion-appeal stores, than do their downtown units. Furthermore, when compared with the price-appeal stores, the suburban branches of the broad-appeal stores do not have the strong image of sales-clerk service enjoyed by their downtown units. In the case of store layout and display, however, the broad-appeal suburban stores surpass both the price-appeal and the fashion-appeal stores.

All three types of stores in the suburbs receive greater mention for the selection and variety of their merchandise than the city stores. The traditional belief that downtown stores attract suburbanites for their wide selection of merchandise may no longer be valid today.

On the other hand, the downtown stores are still ahead of suburban stores in terms of overall store reputation and reliability. This advantage is noticeable in all three types of stores—the high-fashion stores, the price-appeal stores, and the broad-appeal stores.

IMPLICATIONS

Those downtown stores which present a fashion image are undoubtedly in the strongest position of the three groups. Not only do they stand out more sharply than the others in the attractions they offer their customers, but they also have a strong following among suburbanites, who are still willing to come downtown to shop when buying fashion merchandise.

However, one important weakness of the fashion stores is their failure to attract many younger women. These stores need to reexamine their merchandise lines, store layout, advertising, and so on, to see whether they are inadvertently presenting themselves as stores for older women. They may also be missing a lucrative market among younger, fashion-conscious, career women working downtown.

Since the downtown price-appeal stores must rely mainly on city dwellers for their clientele, they probably will be in a less tenable position as migration to the suburbs continues. They may be able to offset this loss of customers to some degree, however, by catering to the downtown office workers.

The traditional role of the downtown broad-appeal stores has been to offer both fashion and price, and such wide assortments of merchandise that women will come in from the suburbs to get what they cannot find locally. Note, however, that the suburban branches are mentioned more often for their merchandise assortments than the downtown stores. These broad-appeal stores should emphasize their fashion merchandise more, since assortment alone will no longer attract women from the suburbs.

These stores and all classes of department stores should capitalize on their assets of service, reputation, and reliability in order to keep their customers from shopping at discount houses.

Of major interest is the fact that the imagery of suburban department stores is so much less clearcut than it is in the case of downtown department stores. The branches first built in the early 1950s were designed to appeal to the huge new middle-income class living in the suburbs, a more homogeneous group than was found in the cities. The price-appeal stores left their bargain basements downtown; and the high-fashion stores toned down their wearing-apparel offerings for fear of frightening away the suburban housewives shopping in "non-city" attire.

The result has been a fairly high degree of sameness among the suburban branches of department stores. Unless these stores want to compete almost entirely on merchandise selection and store location, serious consideration should be given to their imagery. Now that the suburban population has greatly increased, it seems likely that there will be places for more distinctive types of stores which will project the fashion appeals, price appeals, and broad appeals of their downtown "parents."

DISCUSSION QUESTIONS

The creation of an "image" is one of the important steps in competition of an *ecological* kind in which some particular market segment is sought as the clientele of the store.

1. How can retail management *measure* its store image?
2. Can retail management consciously and systematically alter its image? How?
3. What is to be gained from effective control of store image?

4. The Creation of a Store Image

STANLEY MARCUS*

It starts with clear and consistent management objectives and policies. These make the image definite. To make it attractive as well requires something more—and that, in a word, is style.

There are fashions in ideas, in words and phrases. A few years back the phrase "trading-up" was *the* fashionable word at NRMA conventions, but since everybody has "traded-up" the phrase has gone out of fashion. No store would ever want to admit that it needed to trade up during this era of prosperity!

Now the fashionable word is "image" and the fashionable phrase is "image projection." It sounds very mystical, but actually "image" is just another way of saying "reputation." We used to refer to a merchant as having a good reputation in one field or another. Now we would say that a particular store has projected an image of friendliness, or corporate integrity, or alertness, or what not.

I've jested a bit with this newly-fashionable word, "image," but perhaps it is a more accurate way of describing an institution's total appearance. The word "reputation" suggests "hearsay" while the word "image" suggests a "picture." Since our folkways have long held the idea that "seeing is believing," then the picture our public sees is more credible than the words it hears about us.

I should define this word "image," in the retail connotation, as the way a store appears to be in the eyes of any fairly large group of the people with whom it does business. Thus, a store might project one image to its customers, another to its employees, another to its vendors, and still another to its stockholders.

TRUTH PLUS TECHNIQUE

It seems to me that good merchants were *always* aware of their reputation with their

♦ SOURCE: Reprinted by permission from the editors of *Stores,* in the January 1960 issue, pages 17–18.
* President, Neiman-Marcus.

customers, but today's merchant or industrialist recognizes that the good customer image is not enough by itself and that the well-balanced image to employee, vendor and stockholder is of equal importance. Formerly, a good merchant earned a good reputation by his conduct in and out of business, but in most cases he alone controlled all of the major actions of his business. Today, with multiple stores, with greater numbers of employees, with diverse markets, the techniques for reputation building or image projection grow more complex.

Store images aren't any more alike than people are, nor should they be alike. A good store image is an honest reflection of what the store actually is—not a phony collage put together by a publicist. It should accurately mirror what the store stands for in services, value, quality, assortments, taste, aggressiveness, and citizenship.

Many stores project a muddled image to their public because their managements don't always have a clear-cut idea of what they do stand for; or because their ideas change with the months of the year or, more likely, with the ups and downs of business. When business is 10 per cent ahead, they emit a sound of leonine courage, but when it runs five per cent behind, they run like the proverbial mouse. Consequently, the picture the public is apt to get is that of a lion with the head of a mouse or vice-versa.

The great retail institutions of this nation, small or large, in the East or the West, have had a clear-cut idea of what they wanted to be and how they wanted to perform their jobs. They have been progressive enough to change course from time to time but never guilty of erratic steering. Their pictures have come over "loud and clear," as they say on the air waves.

Thus, a clear-cut definition of store character

is the first step in image projection. The next steps are those of the proper utilization of the devices of projection. Every store has them in varying degrees of strength—advertising, display, publicity or public relations, special events —but the trick is to use these devices with maximum coordination and with style. The word "style" can have numerous meanings, but the best description I've seen is one that Kenneth Tynan, that master of English prose who does the theater reviews for The New Yorker, gave when he wrote: "Style is the hammer that drives in the nail without bruising the wood, the arrow that transfixes the target without seeming to have been aimed. It makes difficult things . . . look simple. When a strenuous feat has been performed without strain, it has style."

The N-M Truth

And now I should like to describe to you in a general way our approach to image projection at Neiman-Marcus, for actually that's the only case of image projection that I really know anything about first hand. Our business is 52 years old and was founded by my father, Herbert Marcus, and his sister and brother-in-law, Mr. and Mrs. Neiman, in the belief that Dallas, then a thriving metropolis of 86,000 inhabitants, would support a shop which would specialize in the finest, most carefully selected ready-to-wear in the world, and which would sell its goods with the conviction that no sale was a good sale for Neiman-Marcus unless it was a good buy for the customer. That was the reputation they succeeded in earning and which my brothers and associates have inherited.

There was oil in Texas when they started Neiman-Marcus, but the founders didn't know it at the time, and as a matter of fact, it was some 15 years later before oil became a factor in the economy of Texas and 25 years later before it became an important influence on our business. Our image projecting had been pretty much of a local affair until that day in 1932, in the depths of the depression, when my father approved of an idea my brother and I had for advertising in the national fashion publications, Vogue and Harper's Bazaar.

That doesn't sound like anything today, but in 1932 there were few if any advertisers in those magazines outside of New York City, and the idea of vendor participation had not yet been discovered. These advertisements created great attention because of the novelty, and even audaciousness, of a store in Texas advertising nationally. The news value of those ads became the topic of articles written in Colliers and Life. Then Fortune discovered both Neiman-Marcus and Texas in 1937, and every year since that time, Neiman-Marcus has been the subject of one or more magazine articles.

The N-M Technique

About this time, we established a department of public relations, as many stores had done previously, but we completely disassociated it from our advertising department. Its director reported to top management, and she was charged with the responsibility of helping us to create news and to make the most of the unusual, interesting things that happened in the store. Because there is never any advertiser pressure brought to bear upon our newspapers or other media, I think we've earned the respect of people who handle news.

We haven't been at all bashful about sending out newsworthy stories of actual happenings in our stores, but I hope also that we haven't been brash. Just as our advertising, our display, our fashion shows and special events are directed towards impressing the customers with Neiman-Marcus's fashion leadership, its alertness, its sense of perfection, its gift wrappings, its taste that marks a $35,000 chinchilla coat bought by a movie star or a $3.50 silver thimble sent to a reigning princess—so does our public relations department capitalize on interesting events and anecdotes that occur in the course of a day's business and make them available to writers in search of interesting copy.

We are beaming our image projection to a national and now an international audience. We want to be sure that any man who comes to Dallas for a convention or on business will have instructions from his wife to visit that "fabulous" store and to bring back a Neiman-Marcus gift-wrapped package. And they do!

Newspaper Relations

Newsmen use to have a jaundiced view towards stores, for they felt that all news about a store was tantamount to "free advertising." Because all of our press releases are based on bona fide news stories, because we've played straight with the press, because we have a sense of humor about our mistakes and humility about our successes, we've helped many newspapermen realize that "store" news is as good news for its human interest value as any other similar news stories.

One of the favorite stories of this nature regarding Neiman-Marcus occurred during the Christmas season several years ago. The store usually employs several hundred extra gift wrappers during this season to handle the overflow of wrapping. Things do get rather frantic, and one day a woman wrapper accidentally packaged up her lunch in a gay Neiman-Marcus wrap instead of the elegant gift she had been instructed to wrap.

She discovered her mistake too late for retraction. The store management waited until after Christmas, thinking the unhappy recipient of a week-old ham sandwich and orange would demand retribution. We were wrong. To this day, we haven't heard a word from the person who received the package, and I doubt that we ever will. We thought the story was so funny—that it was such a good joke on us—we had to tell the press. They in turn, thought we were good sports for admitting we had made an error.

Just this past Christmas, another Neiman-Marcus error became the subject of a page one column in the Dallas Morning News. This is it:

"Everybody knows that Neiman-Marcus is 99.9 per cent perfect. It takes the low mind of a newspaper columnist to find that other .1 per cent, and here it is.

"Early in the week Katherine Altermann ordered some bath oils as a present for a friend. At 4 P.M. Tuesday, when the delivery hadn't been made, she checked by telephone. She told the lady in the toiletries department that she had ordered some bath oils and had asked that they be delivered to her office on the 12th floor of the Southland Center.

" 'Southland Center?' said the lady in toiletries. 'Is that in Dallas?'

" 'It is,' said Mrs. Altermann.

" 'Then you'll have to check with Local Delivery,' said the lady.

"Local Delivery didn't have her package but did find out it had been gift-wrapped. ' I suggest you try Gift-Wrapping,' suggested local delivery.

"At Gift Wrapping, nobody had seen the bath oils either, but the lady there was undismayed. 'I'm sorry that we have no record of it,' she said, 'but it is bound to come here sooner or later.'

" 'But I can't wait. It's a gift and I need it now!'

" 'Then I would suggest that you call the superintendent's office,' said the woman pleasantly.

"The superintendent's office had never heard of the package. 'Let me suggest,' said the spokesman, 'that you call Adjustments.'

"At each of these calls, Mrs. Altermann had had to repeat the whole story, and the story, of course, was growing like the verses of Old MacDonald Had a Farm.

" 'Oh, no,' she said. 'I'm so tired.'

"The superintendent's office expressed its regret but assured her that Adjustments would clear everything up if she would only check it. When she called Adjustments, she had to wait a while. It seemed like 10 years. Finally, a man's voice was on the phone, and she was telling her story again.

" 'Look,' she said, 'I'm so tired. Would you please just listen to my sad story?' She told it while he listened politely.

" 'Let me suggest . . .' he began, and she broke in, 'Oh, no.'

"He went on to say he wished he could help her but that he couldn't.

" 'Why not?'

" 'I'm in Stemware,' said the man.

" 'Why did you listen to my story?,' wailed Mrs. Altermann.

" 'You asked me to,' said the man, 'and the longer I listened, the sadder it got. I didn't have the heart to stop you.' Somehow that made everything seem a lot pleasanter.

"A few hours later, the whole thing began to get funny. And next morning the package, which hadn't been anywhere in the Neiman system, showed up at her desk."

All of this contributes to the Neiman-Marcus image, but in addition, our executives contribute to the image by participating in a wide variety of community affairs and political activities of their own choice.

The N-M Employee

To our employees we say, and we mean it: "We want to provide the most pleasant working conditions for you to be found in any retail establishment in the world. Our most important rule is the Golden Rule, and we want you to practice it and apply it in all of your relationships with our customers."

To the end of being sure that we are maintaining the most pleasant working conditions possible, we operate continuous round table discussion groups consisting of employees from all departments of our stores, to discuss problems that affect their happiness. It would be impossible to build a store image without the help of its employees. For they represent to the public what the store stands for. They project its image. They buy and sell the merchandise in the store, and they provide all of those services which make a store special in the eyes of its customers. Employees can make a store alive and human or dull and unpleasant. We constantly remind our employees of the image we are attempting to create. It makes them feel they are very much a part of the image.

Each new employee entering the Neiman-Marcus Company is given a booklet about the store which begins with these words:

"So glad you're here . . . your smart appearance, your warm friendliness, your interested efficiency . . . these are Neiman-Marcus. They make up what is referred to as 'the Neiman-Marcus Personality,' a compelling quality that causes many of our customers to call Neiman-Marcus simply 'The Store,' as if there were no other. The Neiman-Marcus personality is expressed in: a porter's welcoming smile . . . a salesperson's interested concern . . . a fitter's pleasant understanding of figure problems . . . an executive's personal greeting . . . a credit man's interest in a family's budgeting . . . a packer's loving care of merchandise . . . a delivery man's extra courtesy . . . and in you, our newest staff member. You are now 'what we're famous for.'"

Wider Public

Just recently, we made a public offering of our stock, so now we are vitally concerned with what our stockholders think we look like. Not all of them are like an oil man who called up at the time of the stock issuance and asked what sort of profits retailers generally made. We told him that the national average was about two per cent after taxes and that ex-ceptional store operation yielded about three per cent.

He was silent for a moment and then he asked, "Did you say three per cent?" I said, "Yes."

"Well," he replied, "you're in the wrong business. We spill that much!"

We want our stockholders to see us much as our customers do, for just as the customer has pride in the mink coat with the Neiman-Marcus label, so we want our stockholders to have similar pride in possessing a stock certificate with that same label.

During this past Christmas season, our Christmas catalogue probably received more publicity than any catalogue in recent history, because we devoted two pages to the kind of fabulous gifts we've become famous for. One was the black Angus steer which we offered to deliver on the hoof to any place, with a roast beef cart, and the other was a Willys Beach Jeep together with a chinchilla jacket, and emerald necklace, etc., for $151,580.70. These pages made news. They were reported in papers all over the world because they were *right* for Neiman-Marcus to run. Because of our previous image projecting, the press and the public were prepared for these items from Neiman-Marcus. They might well have been a flop if another store with a different type of public image had run the same pages.

All of this adds up to the fact that each store, each individual, must have its own individuality and its own method of expression. No person ever became great by copying someone else, and no store has reached immortality by imitation. Every store, large or small, should seek to tell its own story honestly and forcefully. Its image must always be a true reflection of the ideals, aspirations and accomplishments of the store and its management.

5. The Revolution in Interior Store Design

PETER COPELAND*

Within the last 20 years a distinct change in interior store design has been slowly evolving. This has produced a "New Look" in store interiors which has gradually emerged in stores all over the country. Suddenly, in the space of a year or two, this new and different look has spurted ahead so far and so fast that it is no longer accurate to refer to it as "new."

It is a look that is "in," one that has arrived and is now revolutionizing interior store planning. The retailing merchant cannot afford to ignore it for it is no passing vogue. It is the logical development of an enormous change in merchandise that occurred in the post-war period and is still under way.

What is this great change in merchandise? What brought it about?

It involves many things: A sharp upswing in luxury goods and goods slanted to leisure-time activities; a greatly expanded market for imports; and the constant growth of new materials and new inventions designed to streamline modern living. Of course, when one seeks to discover the reasons for the change, it is apparent that it stems from the fact that we, as a nation, have changed.

We live now in an affluent society. We have greater leisure and greater interest in leisure-time pursuits. We are part of the jet age and so we are more widely traveled, with greater knowledge of Old World culture and greater appreciation of the beauty of Old World goods and designs.

More and more of us are better educated, with a wider range of interests and hobbies, and a greatly improved taste. We live in a time in which servants have all but disappeared. To replace them we need appliances, tools, gadgets, and work-saving devices.

To sum it up, our pocketbooks are fatter, our time is freer, our taste is better. We want the good life and the comfortable one. Because of this we look to the merchant to provide the wares that help us to pursue it. Not only do we want him to provide those wares—we want him to present them in a manner that attracts us and makes it possible for us to select and purchase them with a minimum of time and effort, and some enjoyment to boot.

How can the merchant capitalize on a situation which is so much to his advantage?

He must change the interior of his store as drastically as his wares have changed. Today's colorful merchandise cannot merely be enclosed in glass cases, placed routinely on racks, or even piled on gondolas or table tops. Its range is so vast that to display it effectively it must be coordinated, with related items grouped together.

Some progressive merchants were astute enough to recognize this some years ago. They experimented with merchandising groupings that were a drastic departure from the display methods of the past. Then merchandise was rigidly grouped according to the dictates of the buyer.

The new groupings assembled items of merchandise that had a natural affinity for each other and, consequently, had a much greater display impact. They also resulted in making it much easier for customers to locate them and much quicker for them to make their selection.

The customers immediately indicated an enthusiastic response to the idea. It is not difficult to discover their reasons.

The woman who carefully selects a shower curtain for her bathroom resents being forced to go to another floor and department to buy towels and other bathroom accessories. She wants them all in one place so that she can formulate a coordinated color plan for the bathroom, make all her purchases according to that plan, and be able to do it with ease.

When she selects her china she desires to select, at the same time and place, the table

---

* AIA, founding partner, Copeland, Novak and Israel.

152

linens that will be the best foil for it, and crystal and silverware that will properly coordinate with both china and linens.

The same is true of bedding. With the new vogue for color and floral designs in sheets and pillow-cases, it is important that blankets, comforters, bedspreads, even bedroom curtains, be grouped together. As a consequence we now have Bath Shops, Dining Shops, Sleep Shops. We have actually a store that is, in effect, a series of shops. We have learned the lesson that store planning must be carried out so that it is the buyer who walks, not the customer.

We have also learned that the shop or the boutique approach can lend itself to endless variations. It is limited only by the imagination of store planners.

On the surface, cameras and records may appear to be totally unrelated items. But when an imaginative store designer coins the phrase "Leisure World," a shop immediately comes into being. This shop not only includes those items, but sports goods, art supplies, radios, TV, Hi-Fi, health equipment, playing cards and bridge accessories, adult games and puzzles.

When he eliminates the men's wear department and replaces it by a "Man's World," he creates a shopping area that includes not only wearing apparel but a smoke shop, a gift shop where the man can find presents for mothers, wives and sweethearts, a greeting card corner, and even a "Meeting Corner" with a coffee bar and a TV set.

So it will readily be grasped that, while we have accustomed ourselves to Sleep Shops, Closet Shops, Sewing Centers and Leather Shops, these are only the beginning and that the future holds many more intriguing possibilities.

In other words, one of the key words in the revolution now taking place in store design is "coordinate."

In some cases this may result in the elimination of time-honored departments. But if the aim of coordination destroys some traditional small areas of the store, it also opens up other areas to far greater expansion and improvement.

In home furnishings departments one of the most exciting new developments in store design is beginning to take place. Model rooms, and separate areas for tables, chairs and other items of furniture are giving way to a large area that simulates an entire house. This is accomplished by the use of walls, not of ceiling

Macy's, Colonie Shopping Center, Colonie, New York. One of Copeland, Novak and Israel's recent interior designs.

height, but high enough to create room effects and give a "look-through" effect.

This attracts the customer and induces her to wander through the entire area. (Naturally the walls should be flexible enough to accommodate the frequent changes that are required.)

It will be immediately apparent what a range of possibilities this presents for attractive furniture groupings. Gone will be the "warehouse look" of the past, with its dreary arrays of sofas, chairs and tables. In its place customers will enjoy the pleasant illusion of strolling through several lovely homes—perhaps one modern, one traditional, one Early American.

They can wander from living room to dining room, to bedroom—even out on the patio. They will see furniture at its best. The trained taste of the decorating and display departments will be of help in visualizing how they can arrange and coordinate it in their own homes. It is obvious that this new, modern interior planning has a far greater sales potential than the dull, unimaginative methods of the past.

Another facet of the revolutionized interior planning is the active display of practically all merchandise.

The stiff, formal look imposed on the store by the standardization of fixtures is completely eliminated. It is replaced by a casual, lived-in appearance that has far greater beauty and (from a practical standpoint) much greater effectiveness in inducing the customer to browse and indulge in impulse buying.

How is the casual look achieved?

By placing the emphasis on the merchandise and giving it a background that dramatizes it to the fullest extent possible.

Any number of techniques can be utilized. Some of them that come readily to mind include:

Breaking up the floor plan to get away from the "regimented" look and permit the customer to wander through a department rather than walking in rigid aisles; generating excitement by a circulation plan leading the customer from one department to another through the use of imaginative and dramatic displays; making greater use of high walls, and greater use of spotlighting for feature displays; a more definite color change from one department to another; a gift-shop approach that emphasizes the beauty and originality of individual items; exciting "table-top" presentations to the entrance of departments.

Still another technique in achieving the casual look is to accessorize in the modern manner. This means, again, an active manner. For example, in home furnishings, where lamps, pictures and mirrors are shown in a natural home setting, or in the Rain Shop, where a mannequin wears one of the new vinyl raincoats accessorized with visor cap, boots and umbrella.

Actually, the modern store designer should never think of accessories in separate terms. In his mind they should be viewed only as an integral part of the whole.

While it is true that duplication may be involved (the same accessories may appear in the junior department as in the sportswear department, for instance) this does no harm. The important thing is that the accessories accompany the merchandise and are part of its successful presentation.

This manner of accessorizing has an impressive sales potential. Obviously the customer finds it much more interesting and stimulating to purchase a lamp, a mirror or a picture, posed against a natural, attractive setting, than she does to engage in the boring and confusing task of selecting these items in separate departments.

Whatever the techniques used to achieve the casual, lived-in look, they should all aim at the same end result. That is to make the customer aware of the vast array of merchandise available to her.

Today, when she enters a store she should get an immediate feeling of adventure. The purchase she is seeking may be mundane, but on her way she should be given a glimpse of beautiful objects, displayed with charm and taste, that will captivate her. These will often persuade her to make other purchases in addition to the article which prompted her visit.

Fortunately for the merchant, the new approach to store design need not involve large expenditures. In many respects the new design approach is no more costly than the old. The concentration on the merchandise rather than the fixturing permits using inexpensive types of fixtures.

Also, greater use of high walls for merchandise presentation makes less fixturing necessary. Popular design techniques, such as wood valances that can be covered by the display department to effect changes in design from one season to another, can produce savings.

Of course the new method of interior design involves other changes in the store.

A system of fluorescent lighting throughout

the entire store is now giving way to more of a combination of fluorescent and incandescent, with the latter preferable for individual shops. And floor covering is now broken up, with a wide use of scatter rugs.

Various changes in store operation are required also. A much greater coordination between the display department and the various merchandising departments is essential to achieve the utmost effect in the active display of merchandise. In fact, the display department must assume a much more active role in every way. This is especially true during the early planning stages when it is important to include provision for flexibility in changing the decor each season.

Since the new method of merchandising presentation calls for more selectivity, there must also be a more careful study of forward and reverse stock, and a greater "behind the scenes" activity. But this should not present a great problem, since with automation progressing, stock control is simpler and the movement of merchandise faster.

From what has already been stated, it will be clear that the two most important factors in the modern approach to interior planning are the grouping of coordinated merchandise to form individual shops or boutiques, and the emphasis on the active display of merchandise.

This, however, is far from the whole story. Other important factors enter into the over-all plan.

There is the necessity of making provision for an area that can be used for special promotional purposes. With imports, for instance, an Italian Week, a Spanish Fiesta, a Salute to Ireland, a Portuguese Antiques Fair. These are marvelous attention-getting devices that can send a surge of buying excitement throughout the whole store. Interior planning should not fail to take them into consideration.

While it is true that many of these promotions will be store-wide, usually they need a focal point where the interest reaches a peak.

For instance, recently in Paris I was fortunate enough to stumble on a promotion of Hungarians imports at Printemps. Hungarian arts and crafts and Hungarian-produced goods of all descriptions were on display throughout the entire store. But in one area there was a concentration of the most colorful merchandise, with a full Hungarian orchestra playing the tuneful music of native composers, to the great delight of the store's customers.

The lesson is clear, I believe. While Hungarian goods could easily find their way into any and all departments, finding space for a full orchestra might have presented a problem if the store's management had not had the foresight to plan ahead for such a contingency.

And finally, there is the most important factor of all, the evolution of a clear-cut plan to give the store a stamp of individuality, to define its personality, or perhaps the more accurate word to use is "character."

This is an intangible asset but it is one which can be achieved by tangible means. It is the facet of store design which presents the greatest challenge to store designers. It is one which requires all of their ingenuity and talents. To accomplish it, there must be a keen understanding of the type of clientele which the store has or seeks, the area in which the store is located, and the range and quality of its merchandise.

Naturally the store's exterior is a significant element in conveying the character of the store. If the merchant is building a new store, this should receive serious consideration in the over-all planning. The entrance to the store also plays a crucial role, and this is another element that should be carefully considered.

Of course part of the character of any noteworthy store of today is a "World's Fair feeling." With merchandise easily available from all over the globe, the customer must get the same pleasant sensation in visiting the store that she had when she toured a number of World's Fair exhibits.

But it should not be overlooked that the store should also convey an "area impression." A store in Jacksonville, Florida, for instance, might have a lighthearted, summery air, with gay, light colors and fabrics used as background. It would express the relaxed, outdoor feeling of that community, with its leisurely pace of living. Its impact would be heightened by this expression.

To inject a New York sophistication into that atmosphere would considerably lessen this desirable impact. On the other hand, it would be equally inappropriate to stress a southern, outdoor feeling in a wintry, northern city, where indoor pursuits take precedence and urban sophistication is paramount.

All in all, it will be seen that the revolution that has occurred in interior planning for stores has not simplified the task of the designers—or of the retailer. It has, in fact, made it much more complex. The challenge is great, but it can be met. Many of today's top merchants have solved it, and it will not be too difficult for others to follow suit.

DISCUSSION QUESTION

This article identifies a technique for creating warmth and personality within the context of large, and potentially impersonal, retail stores. The type of intimacy which Copeland's "shoppe" concept may create does not, however, find equal usefulness for all types of stores.

Specifically, which types of retail operations would not be well advised to consider the "shoppe" concept as a technique for interior design and space utilization?

The Nature of
Competition in Retailing

The nature and strength of competition in retailing has been the subject of many thousands of words. The subject is of fundamental importance, for as final consumers we have a vested interest in the effectiveness of our retailing system. As students of business administration we should have an intellectual interest in the effectiveness of our retail system. And as students of retailing management, we must understand the nature of such competition if we are to fully appreciate the challenge of a career in retailing.

This section includes an examination of the most significant dimensions of retail competition. The article by Professors Lazer and Kelley identifies and elaborates the nature of the retailing "mix." The article by Mr. Mallen suggests some dimensions of retail competition not usually explored in a discussion of this kind. Professor Hollander provides some historical perspective for the subject of retail competition, and reveals some interesting "gimmicks" which have been employed in seeking to gain and hold customers. The article by Professor Sweet identifies a form of "institutional discrimination" which has been a part of retailing competition for over one hundred years.

1. The Retailing Mix: Planning and Management

WILLIAM LAZER and EUGENE J. KELLEY

The retailing mix is comprised of three sub-mixes: a goods and service mix, a communications mix, and a distribution mix. Consumer satisfaction is achieved through optimal sub-mix blending.

Some retail managers have been observing the rapid growth of the marketing management concept in manufacturing firms with considerable interest. This concept of marketing is resulting in the acceptance of a new perspective for business activities in which marketing is viewed as the basis of an integrated system of business action. Adaptation of the marketing management approach has significance for retail managers concerned with designing a total retail capability to achieve realistic and attainable objectives.

The marketing management concept in retailing is characterized by:

1. Planning. An emphasis on planning to achieve clearly defined retailing targets, this is the key concept. It stresses that retailing objectives can be identified and that an integrated program of action be designed to achieve these objectives through orderly retail planning.

2. Customer Orientation. The customer orientation is adopted as the focus for retail decision making. A philosophy of customer orientation is more important than any body of retailing techniques, personnel policies, or organizational arrangements. It ensures that retail decisions are viewed through the consumer's eyes.

3. Systems Approach. The systems perspective of retailing action is used. In this approach, a retail organization is viewed as a total system of retail action. The interaction between the components of the retailing system is stressed as is the functioning and structure of the whole organization. This approach focuses on the integrated use of all retail resources to satisfy current market needs and future opportunities.

4. Change. Change is recognized as the "constant" in planning, organizing, and controlling retailing activity. The prime managerial responsibility is seen as that of adapting retailing organizations creatively to conditions of accelerating change. Retailing leadership's charge becomes that of planning for and managing change.

5. Innovation. There is a new emphasis on research and innovation. Innovation is seen as the basis for retailing action. The important fact is that innovation is becoming programmed and a basic part of the retail management process. In short, research, a system of commercial intelligence, and innovation are becoming standard factors in modern retail action. This is resulting in the application of findings from the behavioral and quantitative sciences to retailing. The effect is new techniques of retail control, better management of inventories, improved communications, and a greater awareness of the usefulness of theory in understanding and solving retailing problems.

The crucial factor for retail management to recognize is that socioeconomic developments are operating so as to stimulate the emergence of more accurate and intelligent planning on the part of retail executives. Retailing executives are operating in an economy which is characterized by rapid change and explosive cultural and economic developments. The increasing degree of competition from both

♦ SOURCE: Reprinted by permission from the editor of the *Journal of Retailing*, in the Spring 1961 issue, pages 34–41.

downtown and suburban areas, the impact of population shifts, trends in income and expenditures, the degree of innovation in both areas of products and services, the availability and utilization of more information about customers and markets, are examples of forces which require retail management to accept change as a normal way of life and to assign high priorities to developing creative adaptations to change. It is in such a climate that the marketing management movement, with prime emphasis on planning, has made its greatest headway.

To manage retailing effort effectively in such an environment requires planning. Yet retail planning is more than just a tool of growth. It is a rational means of achieving continuing profitable adjustment of the retail system to current and future marketing conditions.

Retailing planning, in its broadest terms, may be thought of as the utilization of analysis and foresight to increase the effectiveness of retail action. Planning retailing effort, therefore, is necessarily concerned with the objectives and goals that the retailing organization seeks to attain, the development of retailing systems, the operating system, through which retail management is attempting to achieve these goals, the availability of capacity and resources within the firm and existing facilitating agencies to exert the quantity and quality of effort necessary for their achievement.

Retail plans must be conceived as functioning within an external framework determined by various forces beyond the control of the management of a given retail enterprise. This is one reason why it is becoming increasingly important in retail planning to consider environmental business factors as well as to identify the many retailing inputs, their interactions, and expected outputs.

The retail planning process involves at the first level three actions on the part of executives: analysis, evaluation, and prediction. The analysis of available information, and an evaluation of trends and relationships will give retail management the frame of reference from which to perceive current and future problems. It will afford executives a perspective of the future. Past data is useful to management mainly as it helps predict the future.

RETAILING MIX

The analysis and evaluation of data and the predictions made place executives in a position of being able to program total retailing effort. Retail programming is achieved through the determination of a retail store's retailing mix. Such a mix becomes the total package of goods and services that a store offers for sale to the public. The retailing mix, then, is the composite of all effort which was programmed by management and which embodies the adjustment of the retail store to its market environment.

The retailing mix, as such, is comprised of three sub-mixes: a goods and service mix, a communications mix, and a distribution mix. Consumer satisfaction is achieved through optimal sub-mix blending. It is through the achievement of a high customer satisfaction that a store prospers and grows. Some of the components of each of these sub-mixes are depicted in Chart I.

In Chart I the consumer is presented as the focus for all market planning and programming. The retail program is designed specifically to bring the offerings of a retail organization into line with the wants and needs of its customers and the natural market areas. The established program, therefore, sets the tone for all retailing activity.

The sub-mix that is most apparent in retailing is the GOODS AND SERVICE MIX. Retailers are often well aware of the impact of the variety and assortment of goods offered for sale and the customer services that are extended. Other components of the goods and service mix are various credit plans that are offered, the price lines that a store will adhere to, the guarantees that are made and exchanges, alterations and adjustments, the image of the store and the goods it offers for sale, delivery, sales service, and parking facilities. The total goods and service mix should be so integrated that it will tie in with the store's own marketing goals. For example, if the image of the store is one of high quality then the customer lines offered, the price lines offered, and the types of service offered should be such that they will blend in with this concept, rather than clash with it.

The PHYSICAL DISTRIBUTION MIX essentially has two components: a channel of distribution component and a physical distribution component. The channels of distribution component is concerned with the number and type of retail outlets that comprise the total retailing complex. For example, the number and type of branch stores that are part of the retail enterprise, and the types of suburban stores that are members of the organization, are part of the mix. The physical distribution part of the distribution mix is concerned with integrating the warehousing, handling, and transporting of goods. It is evident, therefore, that the distribution mix is concerned with such factors as store location, the establishment of distribution centers, breaking bulk, warehousing, transporting, physically handling the goods, and packing them. This group of activities has been traditionally grouped under the authority of an operations manager or a store operations manager.

The COMMUNICATIONS MIX is the third sub-mix. The retailer is separated in time and space from the ultimate consumer. He attempts to overcome these barriers by obtaining information about the market and by communicating information to it. The provision of information about the retail store and the goods and services available for sale constitute the crux of the communications mix. The retailer has a variety of tools for communicating with the market place. Included among these tools are personal selling, advertising, window displays, internal displays, public relations efforts, store layouts, catalogues, and telephone sales.

The communications mix is extremely important in adjusting the goods and services that are offered for sale to consumer demand. It can convince consumers that the retail store's program is primarily satisfactory to the consumer. The communications mix should be such that it ties in with the image and reputation of the store and the goods that are offered for sale.

It should be noted that the consumer is separated in Chart I from the retail program. A gap exists that must be bridged by the total retailing mix. Here marketing research helps management to adjust the mix and become aware of future trends in order to plan and make rational decisions. As retail organizations grow larger, develop more branches and become more decentralized, the existing gap between top retail management and consumers becomes wider. Therefore, more pertinent and readily available marketing information becomes a requisite for proper programming and control of retailing effort.

Chart I

THE RETAIL MANAGEMENT SYSTEM

Planning an optimal retailing mix involves viewing a retailing operation as an integrated action system affected by both internal and external forces. The success of a retail system depends not only on proper selection of each element and sub-mix but on the interaction between them.

The retail management system can be perceived as an input-output system. All of the ingredients of the retailing mix may be viewed as the inputs which flow through the retail organization and attain the outputs realized by the retailing organization. Hopefully, the outputs achieved match the accepted objectives of the organization. The response of consumers in the market place ultimately determines whether or not the store actually achieves its objectives, or the outputs planned by the programmer. In this sense, consumers hold the veto power over the entire retail system.

The retail management system, as an organization, has been studied in various books and research studies. It is composed of various levels of managers. The department manager is concerned with management and cultivation of a particular market area. He is immediately concerned with selling and sales tactics. The group manager co-ordinates the departmental marketing effort of several departments. Therefore, his is an integrative function to alleviate dysfunctioning between the departments. The division manager has a higher-level integrative point of view and is concerned with co-ordinating the store marketing effort with the marketing effort of a number of departments. The merchandise manager is more concerned with integrated corporate policy and action as it relates to the total marketing effort within the store. Top management, of course, is concerned with the broader corporate issues including store adjustment to non-controllable environmental forces.

The consumer reactions to the retailing mix determines the profits that are achieved by the organization, its volume, its share of market, its image as an industry leader, its status in the community, and the degree of channel control that retail management earns. If the proper planning has taken place, the outputs that are achieved through consumer behavior will be in line with the retailing objectives originally planned by management. If this alignment does not occur, then retail management has three alternatives:

1. Alter the objectives of the retail organization,
2. Adjust the retailing mix
3. Combine the two

The systems view also has implications for manufacturers who are concerned with developing a retailing-customer orientation. The systems view of retail planning and management is more likely to foster a genuine customer-retailer orientation by manufacturers than the product or process orientation typical of many manufacturers selling through retailers today.

CONCLUSION

The marketing management approach assigns high importance to planning. This philosophy of business, when applied to retail operations, requires that retail managements place heavy emphasis on planning and developing a total retailing strategy. Only then will they program a retailing mix which achieves predetermined objectives.

Sound retail planning, in other words, becomes the basis for developing co-ordinated and goal-directed systems of retail action. Fundamentally the main functions of retailing leadership are similar to those of other business areas. Retail management must plan, organize, actuate, and control market and customer-related factors to achieve clearly defined market and organization objectives. They must view their retailing operations as a total system of action comprised of the goods and services, communication and distribution mixes, geared to the satisfaction of consumers' wants and needs, and be willing to adjust quickly to the demands of market change. Only through such enlargement of perspective can the profit thrust of a retail organization be maximized.

DISCUSSION QUESTIONS

One form of competition which is encountered in retailing involves serving a particular market segment better than other retail operations and, through this superior "service," securing and retaining the patronage of that segment. This is competition in which the retailer finds a niche for himself—the "niche" being a market segment—and has been called "ecological" competition.

Note that the battery of tools which the retailer uses involves *not just price* but other dimensions of value to consumers.

Regarding Chart I, how does the retailer determine the particular emphasis to be placed on each of the three sub-mixes which are identified? Having determined that, how does he determine the relative effort to give to each individual element in each sub-mix?

2. Conflict and Cooperation in Marketing Channels

BRUCE MALLEN

The purpose of this paper is to advance the hypotheses that between member firms of a marketing channel there exists a dynamic field of conflicting and cooperating objectives; that if the conflicting objectives outweigh the cooperating ones, the effectiveness of the channel will be reduced and efficient distribution impeded; and that implementation of certain methods of cooperation will lead to increased channel efficiency.

DEFINITION OF CHANNEL

The concept of a marketing channel is slightly more involved than expected on initial study. One author in a recent paper [1] has identified "trading" channels, "non-trading" channels, "type" channels, "enterprise" channels, and "business-unit" channels. Another source [2] refers to channels as all the flows extending from the producer to the user. These include the flows of physical possession, ownership, promotion, negotiation, financing, risking, ordering, and payment.

The concept of channels to be used here involves only two of the above-mentioned flows: ownership and negotiation. The first draws merchants, both wholesalers and retailers, into the channel definition, and the second draws in agent middlemen. Both, of course, include producers and consumers. This definition roughly corresponds to Professor Breyer's "trading channel," though the latter does not restrict (nor will this paper) the definition to actual flows, but to "flow-capacity." "A trading channel is formed when trading relations, making possible the passage of title and/or possession (usually both) of goods from the producer to the ultimate consumer, is consummated by the component trading concerns of the system." [3] In addition, this paper will deal with trading channels in the broadest manner and so will be concentrating on "type-trading" channels rather than "enterprise" or "business-unit" channels. This means that there will be little discussion of problems peculiar to integrated or semi-integrated channels, or peculiar to specific channels and firms.

CONFLICT

Palamountain isolated three forms of distributive conflict.[4]

1. Horizontal competition—this is competition between middlemen of the same type; for example, discount store *versus* discount store.

2. Intertype competition—this is competition between middlemen of different types in the same channel sector; for example, discount store *versus* department store.

3. Vertical conflict—this is conflict between channel members of different levels; for example, discount store *versus* manufacturer.

♦ SOURCE: Reprinted by permission from the American Marketing Association, in *Reflections on Progress in Marketing*, L. George Smith, editor, 1964, pages 65–85.

[1] Ralph F. Breyer, "Some Observations on Structural Formation And The Growth of Marketing Channels," in *Theory In Marketing*, Reavis Cox, Wroe Alderson, Stanley J. Shapiro, Editors. (Homewood, Illinois: Richard D. Irwin, Inc., 1964), pp. 163–175.

[2] Ronald S. Vaile, E. T. Grether, and Reavis Cox, *Marketing in the American Economy* (New York: Ronald Press, 1952), pp. 121 and 124.

[3] Breyer, *op. cit.*, p. 165.

[4] Joseph C. Palamountain, *The Politics of Distribution* (Cambridge: Harvard University Press, 1955).

The first form, horizontal competition, is well covered in traditional economic analysis and is usually referred to simply as "competition." However, both intertype competition and vertical conflict, particularly the latter, are neglected in the usual micro-economic discussion.

The concepts of "intertype competition" and "distributive innovation" are closely related and require some discussion. Intertype competition will be divided into two categories; (a) "traditional intertype competition" and (b) "innovative intertype competition." The first category includes the usual price and promotional competition between two or more different types of channel members at the same channel level. The second category involves the action on the part of traditional channel members to prevent channel innovators from establishing themselves. For example, in Canada there is a strong campaign, on the part of traditional department stores, to prevent the discount operation from taking a firm hold on the Canadian market.[5]

Distributive innovation will also be divided into two categories; (a) "intrafirm innovative conflict" and (b) "innovative intertype competition." The first category involves the action of channel member firms to prevent sweeping changes within their own companies. The second category "innovative intertype competition" is identical to the second category of intertype competition.

Thus the concepts of intertype competition and distributive innovation give rise to three forms of conflict, the second of which is a combination of both: (1) traditional intertype competition, (2) innovative intertype competition, and (3) intrafirm innovative conflict.

It is to this second form that this paper now turns before going on to vertical conflict.

Innovative Intertype Competition

Professor McCammon has identified several sources, both intrafirm and intertype, of innovative conflict in distribution, i.e., where there are barriers to change within the marketing structure.[6]

Traditional members of a channel have several motives for maintaining the channel status quo against outside innovators. The traditional members are particularly strong in this conflict when they can ban together in some formal or informal manner—when there is strong reseller solidarity.

Both entrepreneurs and professional managers may resist outside innovators, not only for economic reasons, but because change "violates group norms, creates uncertainty, and results in a loss of status." The traditional channel members (the insiders) and their affiliated members (the strivers and complementors) are emotionally and financially committed to the dominant channel and are interested in perpetuating it against the minor irritations of the "transient" channel members and the major attacks of the "outside innovators."

Thus, against a background of horizontal and intertype channel conflict, this paper now moves to its area of major concern; vertical conflict and cooperation.

A supplier may force a product onto its resellers, who dare not oppose, but who retaliate in other ways, such as using it as a loss leader. Large manufacturers may try to dictate the resale price of their merchandise; this may be less or more than the price at which resellers wish to sell it. Occasionally, a local market may be more competitive for a reseller than is true nationally. The manufacturer may not recognize the difference in competition and refuse to help this channel member.

Resellers complain of manufacturers' special price concessions to competitors and rebel at the attempt of manufacturers to control resale prices. Manufacturers complain of resellers' deceptive and misleading price advertising, nonadherence to resale price suggestions, bootlegging to unauthorized outlets, seeking special price concessions by unfair methods, and misrepresenting offers by competitive suppliers.

Other points of price conflict are the paperwork aspects of pricing. Resellers complain of delays in price change notices and complicated price sheets.

Price Theory. If one looks upon a channel as a series of markets or as the vertical exchange mechanism between buyers and sellers, one can adapt several theories and concepts to the channel situation which can aid marketing

---

[5] Isaiah A. Litvak and Bruce E. Mallen, *Marketing: Canada* (Toronto: McGraw-Hill of Canada, Limited, 1964), pp. 196–197.

[6] This section is based on Bert C. McCammon, Jr., "Alternative Explanations of Institutional Change And Channel Evolution," in *Toward Sci-* *entific Marketing*, Stephen A. Greyser, Editor. (Chicago: American Marketing Association, 1963), pp. 477–490.

theory in this important area of channel conflict.[7] For example, the exchange mechanism between a manufacturer as a seller and a wholesaler as a buyer is one market. A second market is the exchange mechanism between the wholesaler as a seller and the retailer as a buyer. Finally, the exchange mechanism between the retailer as a seller and the consumer as a buyer is a third market. Thus, a manufacturer-wholesaler-retailer-consumer channel can be looked upon as a series of three markets.

The type of market can be defined according to its degree of competitiveness, which depends to a great extent on the number of buyers and sellers in a market. Some possible combinations are shown in Table 1.

TABLE 1. Classification of Economic Markets

Suppliers (Sellers)	Middlemen (Buyers)	Market Situation
Pure competitor	Pure competitor	Pure competition
Pure competitor	Oligopolist	Oligopoly
Pure competitor	Monopolist	Monopoly
Oligopsonist	Pure competitor	Oligopsony
Monopsonist	Pure competitor	Monopsony
Oligopsonist	Oligopoly	Bilateral oligopoly
Monopolist	Monopsonist	Bilateral monopoly
Monopolist	Monopolist	Successive monopoly

A discussion of monopoly in a channel context may show the value of integrating economic theory with channel concepts.

If one channel member is a monopolist and the others pure competitors, the consumer pays a price equivalent to that of an integrated monopolist; and the monopolist member reaps all the channel's pure profits; that is, the sum of the pure profits of all channel members. Pure profits are, of course, the economist's concept of those profits over and above the minimum return on investment required to keep a firm in business.

Assume that the retailer is the monopolist and the others (wholesalers and manufacturers) are pure competitors, as for example, a single department store in an isolated town. Total costs to the retailer are composed of the total cost of the other levels plus his own costs. No pure profits of the other levels are included in his costs, as they make none by definition (they are pure competitors).

The retailer would be in the same buying price position, so far as the lack of suppliers' profits are concerned, as would the vertically integrated firm. Thus, he charges the same price as the integrated monopolist and makes the same profits.

If the manufacturer were the monopolist and the other channel members pure competitors, he would calculate the maximizing profits for the channel and then charge the wholesaler his cost plus the total channel's pure profits—all of which would go to him since the others are pure competitors. The wholesaler would take this price, add it on to his own costs, and the result would be the price to retailers. Then the retailers would do likewise for the consumer price.

Thus, the prices to the wholesaler and to the retailer are higher than in the first case (retailer monopoly), since the channel's pure profits are added on before the retail level. The price to the consumer is the same as in the first case. It is of no concern to the consumer if the pure profit elements in his price are added on by the manufacturer, wholesaler, or retailer.

Thus, under integrated monopoly, manufacturer monopoly, wholesaler monopoly, or retailer monopoly, the consumer price is the same; but the prices within the channel are the lowest with the retailer monopoly and the highest with the manufacturer monopoly. Of course, the nonmonopolistic channel members' pure profits are not affected by this intrachannel price variation, as they have no such profits in any case.

Vertical Conflict—Non Price

Channel conflict not only finds its source in the exchange act and pricing, but it permeates all areas of marketing. Thus, a manufacturer

---

[7] Bruce Mallen, "Introducing The Marketing Channel to Price Theory," *Journal of Marketing*, July, 1964, pp. 29–33.

may wish to promote a product in one manner or to a certain degree while his resellers oppose this. Another manufacturer may wish to get information from his resellers on a certain aspect relating to his product, but his resellers may refuse to provide this information. A producer may want to distribute his product extensively, but his resellers may demand exclusives.

There is also conflict because of the tendency for both manufacturers and retailers to want the elimination of the wholesaler.

One very basic source of channel conflict is the possible difference in the primary business philosophy of channel members. Writing in the *Harvard Business Review*, Wittreich says:

In essence, then, the key to understanding management's problem of crossed purpose is the recognition that the fundamental (philosophy) in life of the high-level corporate manager and the typical (small) retail dealer in the distribution system are quite different. The former's (philosophy) can be characterized as being essentially dynamic in nature, continuously evolving and emerging; the latter, which are in sharp contrast, can be characterized as being essentially static in nature, reaching a point and leveling off into a continuously satisfying plateau.[8]

While the big members of the channel may want growth, the small retail members may be satisfied with stability and a "good living."

ANARCHY [9]

The channel can adjust to its conflicting-cooperating environment in three distinct ways. *First,* it can have a leader (one of the channel members) who "forces" members to cooperate; this is an autocratic relationship. *Second,* it can have a leader who "helps" members to cooperate, creating a democratic relationship. *Finally,* it can do nothing, and so have an anarchistic relationship. Lewis B. Sappington and C. G. Browne, writing on the problem of internal company organizations, state:

The first classification may be called "autocracy." In this approach to the group the leader determines the policy and dictates or assigns the work tasks. There are no group deliberations, no group decisions . . .

The second classification may be called "democracy." In this approach the leader allows all policies to be decided by the group with his participation. The group members work with each other as they wish. The group determines the division and assignment of tasks . . .

The third classification may be called "anarchy." In anarchy there is complete freedom of the group or the individual regarding policies or task assignments, without leader participation.[10]

Advanced in this paper is the hypothesis that if anarchy exists, there is a great chance of the conflicting dynamics destroying the channel. If autocracy exists, there is less chance of this happening. However, the latter method creates a state of cooperation based on power and control. This controlled cooperation is really subdued conflict and makes for a more unstable equilibrium than does voluntary democratic cooperation.

CONTROLLED COOPERATION

The usual pattern in the establishment of channel relationships is that there is a leader, an initiator who puts structure into this relationship and who holds it together. This leader controls, whether through command or cooperation, i.e., through an autocratic or a democratic system.

Too often it is automatically assumed that the manufacturer or producer will be the channel leader and that the middlemen will be the channel followers. This has not always been so, nor will it necessarily be so in the future. The growth of mass retailers is increasingly challenging the manufacturer for channel leadership, as the manufacturer challenged the wholesaler in the early part of this century.

The following historical discussion will concentrate on the three-ring struggle between manufacturer, wholesaler, and retailer rather than on the changing patterns of distribution within a channel sector, i.e., between service wholesaler and agent middleman or discount and department store. This will lay the necessary background for a discussion of the present-day manufacturer-dominated *versus* retailer-dominated struggle.

---

[8] Warren J. Wittreich, "Misunderstanding The Retailer," *Harvard Business Review*, May–June, 1962, p. 149 .

[9] The term "anarchy" as used in this paper connotes "no leadership" and nothing more.

[10] Lewis B. Sappington and C. G. Browne, "The Skills of Creative Leadership," in *Managerial Marketing*, rev. ed., William Lazar and Eugene J. Kelley, Editors. (Homewood, Ill.: Richard D. Irwin , Inc., 1962), p. 350.

Early History

The simple distribution system of Colonial days gave way to a more complex one. Among the forces of change were the growth of population, the long distances involved, the increasing complexity of new products, the increase of wealth, and the increase of consumption.

The United States was ready for specialists to provide a growing and widely dispersed populace with the many new goods and services required. The more primitive methods of public markets and barter could not efficiently handle the situation. This type of system required short distances, few products, and a small population, to operate properly.

19th Century History

In the same period that this older system was dissolving, the retailer was still a very small merchant who, especially in the West, lived in relative isolation from his supply sources. Aside from being small, he further diminished his power position by spreading himself thin over many merchandise lines. The retailer certainly was no specialist but was as general as a general store can be. His opposite channel member, the manufacturer, was also a small businessman, too concerned with production and financial problems to fuss with marketing.

Obviously, both these channel members were in no position to assume leadership. However, somebody had to perform all the various marketing functions between production and retailing if the economy was to function. The wholesaler filled this vacuum and became the channel leader of the 19th century.

The wholesaler became the selling force of the manufacturer and the latter's link to the widely scattered retailers over the nation. He became the retailer's life line to these distant domestic and even more important foreign sources of supply.

These wholesalers carried any type of product from any manufacturer and sold any type of product to the general retailers. They can be described as general merchandise wholesalers. They were concentrated at those transportation points in the country which gave them access to both the interior and its retailers, and the exterior and its foreign suppliers.

Early 20th Century

The end of the century saw the wholesaler's power on the decline. The manufacturer had grown larger and more financially secure with the shift from a foreign-oriented economy to a domestic-oriented one. He could now finance his marketing in a manner impossible to him in early times. His thoughts shifted to some extent from production problems to marketing problems.

Prodding the manufacturer on was the increased rivalry of his other domestic competitors. The increased investment in capital and inventory made it necessary that he maintain volume. He tended to locate himself in the larger market areas, and thus, did not have great distances to travel to see his retail customers. In addition, he started to produce various products; and because of his new multi-product production, he could reach— even more efficiently—these already more accessible markets.

The advent of the automobile and highways almost clinched the manufacturer's bid for power. For now he could reach a much vaster market (and they could reach him) and reap the benefits of economics of scale.

The branding of his products projected him to the channel leadership. No longer did he have as great a need for a specialist in reaching widely dispersed customers, nor did he need them to the same extent for their contacts. The market knew where the product came from. The age of wholesaler dominance declined. That of manufacturer dominance emerged.

Is it still here? What is its future? How strong is the challenge by retailers? Is one "better" than the other? These are the questions of the next section.

Disagreement Among Scholars

No topic seems to generate so much heat and bias in marketing as the question of who should be the channel leader, and more strangely, who is the channel leader. Depending on where the author sits, he can give numerous reasons why his particular choice should take the channel initiative.

Authors of sales management and general marketing books say the manufacturer is and should be the chief institution in the channel. Retailing authors feel the same way about retailers, and wholesaling authors (as few as there are), though not blinded to the fact that wholesaling is not "captain," still imply that they should be, and talk about the coming resurrection of wholesalers. Yet a final and compromising view is put forth by those who believe that a balance of power, rather than a general and prolonged dominance of any channel member, is best.

The truth is that an immediate reaction would set in against any temporary dominance by a channel member. In that sense, there is a constant tendency toward the equilibrium of market forces. The present view is that public interest is served by a balance of power rather than by a general and prolonged predominance of any one level in marketing channels.[11]

John Kenneth Galbraith's concept of countervailing power also holds to this last view.

For the retailer:

In the opinion of the writer, "retailer-dominated marketing" has yielded, and will continue to yield in the future greater net benefits to consumers than "manufacturer-dominated marketing," as the central-buying mass distributor continues to play a role of ever-increasing importance in the marketing of goods in our economy. . . .
. . . In the years to come, as more and more large-scale multiple-unit retailers follow the central buying patterns set by Sears and Penneys, as leaders in their respective fields (hard lines and soft goods), ever-greater benefits should flow to consumers in the way of more goods better adjusted to their demands, at lower prices.[12]

. . . In a long run buyer's market, such as we probably face in this country, the retailers have the inherent advantage of economy in distribution and will, therefore, become increasingly important.[13]

The retailer cannot be the selling agent of the manufacturer because he holds a higher commission; he is the purchasing agent for the public.[14]

For the wholesaler:

The wholesaling sector is, first of all, the most significant part of the entire marketing organization.[15]

. . . The orthodox wholesaler and affiliated types have had a resurgence to previous 1929 levels of sales importance.[16]

. . . Wholesalers have since made a comeback.[17] This revival of wholesaling has resulted from infusion of new management blood and the adoption of new techniques.[18]

For the manufacturer:

. . . the final decision in channel selection rests with the seller, manufacturer and will continue to rest with him as long as he has the legal right to choose to sell to some potential customers and refuse to sell to others.[19]

These channel decisions are primarily problems for the manufacturer. They rarely arise for general wholesalers. . . .[20]

Of all the historical tendencies in the field of marketing, no other is so distinctly apparent as the tendency for the manufacturer to assume greater control over the distribution of his product. . . .[21]

. . . Marketing policies at other levels can be viewed as extensions of policies established by marketing managers in manufacturing firms; and, furthermore, . . . the nature and function can adequately be surveyed by looking at the relationship to manufacturers.[22]

Pro-Manufacture

The argument for manufacturer leadership is production oriented. It claims that they must

[11] Wroe Alderson, "Factors Governing The Development of Marketing Channels," in *Marketing Channels For Manufactured Products,* Richard M. Clewett, Editor. (Homewood, Richard D. Irwin, Inc., 1954), p. 30.

[12] Arnold Corbin, *Central Buying in Relation To The Merchandising of Multiple Retail Units* (New York, Unpublished Doctoral Dissertation at New York University, 1954), pp. 708–709.

[13] David Craig and Werner Gabler, "The Competitive Struggle for Market Control," in *Readings in Marketing,* Howard J. Westing, Editor. (New York, Prentice-Hall, 1953), p. 46.

[14] Lew Hahn, *Stores, Merchants and Customers* (New York, Fairchild Publications, 1952), p. 12.

[15] David A. Revzan, *Wholesaling in Marketing Organization* (New York: John Wiley & Sons, Inc., 1961), p. 606.

[16] *Ibid.,* p. 202.

[17] E. Jerome McCarthy, *Basic Marketing* (Homewood, Illinois: Richard D. Irwin, Inc., 1960), p. 419.

[18] *Ibid.,* p. 420.

[19] Eli P. Cox, *Federal Quantity Discount Limitations and Its Possible Effects on Distribution Channel Dynamics* (Unpublished Doctoral Dissertation, University of Texas, 1956), p. 12.

[20] Milton Brown, Wilbur B. England, John B. Matthews Jr., *Problems in Marketing,* 3rd ed. (New York: McGraw-Hill Book Co., Inc., 1961), p. 239.

[21] Maynard D. Phelps and Howard J. Westing, *Marketing Management,* Revised Edition. (Homewood, Ill.: Richard D. Irwin, Inc., 1960), p. 11.

[22] Kenneth Davis, *Marketing Management* (New York: The Ronald Press Co., 1961), p. 131.

assure themselves of increasing volume. This is needed to derive the benefits of production scale economies, to spread their overhead over many units, to meet increasingly stiff competition, and to justify the investment risk they, not the retailers, are taking. Since retailers will not do this job for them properly, the manufacturer must control the channel.

Another major argumentative point for manufacturer dominance is that neither the public nor retailers can create new products even under a market-oriented system. The most the public can do is to select and choose among those that manufacturers have developed. They cannot select products that they cannot conceive. This argument would say that it is of no use to ask consumers and retailers what they want because they cannot articulate abstract needs into tangible goods; indeed, the need can be created by the goods rather than vice-versa.

This argument may hold well when applied to consumers, but a study of the specification-buying programs of the mass retailers will show that the latter can indeed create new products, and need not be relegated to simply selecting among alternatives.

Pro-Retailer

This writer sees the mass retailer as the natural leader of the channel for consumer goods under the marketing concept. The retailer stands closest to the consumer; he feels the pulse of consumer wants and needs day in and day out. The retailer can easily undertake consumer research right on his own premises and can best interpret what is wanted, how much is wanted, and when it is wanted.

An equilibrium in the channel conflict may come about when small retailers join forces with big manufacturers in a manufacturer leadership channel to compete with a small manufacturer-big retailer leadership channel.

Pro-Wholesaler

It would seem that the wholesaler has a choice in this domination problem as well. Unlike the manufacturer and retailer though, his method is not mainly through a power struggle. This problem is almost settled for him once he chooses the type of wholesaling business he wishes to enter. A manufacturers' agent and purchasing agent are manufacturer-dominated, a sales agent dominates the manufacturer. A resident buyer and voluntary group wholesaler are retail-dominated.

Methods of Manufacturer Domination

How does a channel leader dominate his fellow members? What are his tools in this channel power struggle? A manufacturer has many domination weapons at his disposal. His arsenal can be divided into promotional, legal, negative, suggestive, and, ironically, voluntary cooperative compartments.

Promotional. Probably the major method that the manufacturer has used is the building of a consumer franchise through advertising, sales promotion, and packaging of his branded products. When he has developed some degree of consumer loyalty, the other channel members must bow to his leadership. The more successful this identification through the promotion process, the more assured is the manufacturer of his leadership.

Legal. The legal weapon has also been a poignant force for the manufacturer. It can take many forms, such as, where permissible, resale price maintenance. Other contractual methods are franchises, where the channel members may become mere shells of legal entities. Through this weapon the automobile manufacturers have achieved an almost absolute dominance over their dealers.

Even more absolute is resort to legal ownership of channel members, called forward vertical integration. Vertical integration is the ultimate in manufacturer dominance of the channel. Another legal weapon is the use of consignment sales. Under this method the channel members must by law sell the goods as designated by the owner (manufacturer). Consignment selling is in a sense vertical integration; it is keeping legal ownership of the goods until they reach the consumer, rather than keeping legal ownership of the institutions which are involved in the process.

Negative Methods. Among the "negative" methods of dominance are refusal to sell to possibly uncooperative retailers or refusal to concentrate a large percentage of one's volume with any one customer.

A spreading of sales makes for a concentrating of manufacturer power, while a concentrating of sales may make for a thinning of manufacturer power. Of course, if a manufacturer is one of the few resources available and if there are many available retailers, then a concentrating of sales will also make for a concentrating of power.

The avoidance and refusal tactics, of course, eliminate the possibility of opposing dominating institutions.

Suggestives. A rather weak group of dominating weapons are the "suggestives." Thus, a manufacturer can issue price sheets and discounts, preticket and premark resale prices on goods, recommend, suggest, and advertise resale prices.

These methods are not powerful unless supplemented by promotional, legal, and/or negative weapons. It is common for these methods to boomerang. Thus a manufacturer pretickets or advertises resale prices, and a retailer cuts this price, pointing with pride to the manufacturer's suggested retail price.

Voluntary Cooperative Devices. There is one more group of dominating weapons, and these are really all the voluntary cooperating weapons to be mentioned later. The promise to provide these, or to withdraw them, can have a "whip and carrot" effect on the channel members.

Retailers' Dominating Weapons

Retailers also have numerous domination weapons at their disposal. As with manufacturers, their strongest weapon is the building of a consumer franchise through advertising, sales promotion, and branding. The growth of private brands is the growth of retail dominance.

Attempts at concentrating a retailer's purchasing power are a further group of weapons and are analgous to a manufacturer's attempts to disperse his volume. The more a retailer can concentrate his purchasing, the more dominating he can become; the more he spreads his purchasing, the more dominated he becomes. Again, if the resource is one of only a few, this generalization reverses itself.

Such legal contracts as specification buying, vertical integration (or the threat), and entry into manufacturing can also be effective. Even semiproduction, such as the packaging of goods received in bulk by the supermarket can be a weapon of dominance.

Retailers can dilute the dominance of manufacturers by patronizing those with excess capacity and those who are "hungry" for the extra volume. There is also the subtlety, which retailers may recognize, that a strong manufacturer may concede to their wishes just to avoid an open conflict with a customer.

VOLUNTARY COOPERATION

But despite some of the conflict dynamics and forced cooperation, channel members usually have more harmonious and common interests than conflicting ones. A team effort to market a producer's product will probably help all involved. All members have a common interest in selling the product; only in the division of total channel profits are they in conflict. They have a singular goal to reach, and here they are allies. If any one of them fails in the team effort, this weak link in the chain can destroy them all. As such, all members are concerned with one another's welfare (unless a member can be easily replaced).

Organizational Extension Concept

This emphasis on the cooperating, rather than the conflicting objectives of channel members, has led to the concept of the channel as simply an extension of one's own internal organization. Conflict in such a system is to be expected even as it is to be expected within an organization. However, it is the common or "macro-objective" that is the center of concentration. Members are to sacrifice their selfish "micro-objectives" to this cause. By increasing the profit pie they will all be better off than squabbling over pieces of a smaller one. The goal is to minimize conflict and maximize cooperation. This view has been expounded in various articles by Peter Drucker, Ralph Alexander, and Valentine Ridgeway.

Together, the manufacturer with his suppliers and/or dealers comprise a system in which the manufacturer may be designated the primary organization and the dealers and suppliers designated as secondary organizations. This system is in competition with similar systems in the economy; and in order for the system to operate effectively as an integrated whole, there must be some administration of the system as a whole, not merely administration of the separate organizations within that system.[23]

---

[23] Valentine F. Ridgeway, "Administration of Manufacturer-Dealer Systems," in *Managerial Marketing*, rev. ed., William Lazer and Eugene J. Kelley, Editors. (Homewood, Ill.: Richard D. Irwin, Inc., 1962), p. 480.

Peter Drucker [24] has pleaded against the conceptual blindness that the idea of the legal entity generates. A legal entity is not a marketing entity. Since often half of the cost to the consumer is added on after the product leaves the producer, the latter should think of his channel members as part of his firm. General Motors is an example of an organization which does this.

Both businessmen and students of marketing often define too narrowly the problem of marketing channels. Many of them tend to define the term channels of distribution as a complex of relationships between the firm on the one hand, and marketing establishments exterior to the firm by which the products of the firm are moved to market, on the other. . . . A much broader more constructive concept embraces the relationships with external agents or units as part of the marketing organization of the company. From this viewpoint, the complex of external relationships may be regarded as merely an extension of the marketing organization of the firm. When we look at the problem in this way, we are much less likely to lose sight of the interdependence of the two structures and more likely to be constantly aware that they are closely related parts of the marketing machine. The fact that the internal organization structure is linked together by a system of employment contracts, while the external one is set up and maintained by a series of transactions, contracts of purchase and sale, tends to obscure their common purpose and close relationship.[25]

Cooperation Methods

But how does a supplier project its organization into the channel? How does it make organization and channel into one? It accomplishes this by doing many things for its resellers that it does for its own organization. It sells, advertises, trains, plans, and promotes for these firms. A brief elaboration of these methods follows.

Missionary salesmen aid the sales of channel members, as well as bolster the whole system's level of activity and selling effort. Training of resellers' salesmen and executives is an effec-

tive weapon of cooperation. The channels operate more efficiently when all are educated in the promotional techniques and uses of the products involved.

Involvement in the planning functions of its channel members could be another poignant weapon of the supplier. Helping resellers to set quotas for their customers, studying the market potential for them, forecasting a member's sales volume, inventory planning and protection, etc., are all aspects of this latter method.

Aid in promotion through the provision of advertising materials (mats, displays, commercials, literature, direct-mail pieces), ideas, funds (cooperative advertising), sales contests, store layout designs, push money (PM's or spiffs), is another form of cooperation.

The big supplier can act as management consultant to the members, dispensing advice in all areas of their business, including accounting, personnel, planning, control, finance, buying, paper systems or office procedure, and site selection. Aid in financing may include extended credit terms, consignment selling, and loans.

By no means do these methods of coordination take a one-way route. All members of the channel, including supplier and reseller, see their own organizations meshing with the others, and so provide coordinating weapons in accordance with their ability. Thus, the manufacturer would undertake a marketing research project for his channel, and also expect his resellers to keep records and vital information for the manufacturer's use. A supplier may also expect his channel members to service the product after the sale.

A useful device for fostering cooperation is a channel advisory council composed of the supplier and his resellers.

Finally, a manufacturer or reseller can avoid associations with potentially uncooperative channel members. Thus a price-conservative manufacturer may avoid linking to a price-cutting retailer.

E. B. Weiss has developed an impressive, though admittedly incomplete list of cooperation methods (Table 2). Paradoxically, many of these instruments of cooperation are also weapons of control (forced cooperation) to be used by both middlemen and manufacturers. However, this is not so strange if one keeps in mind that control is subdued conflict and a form of cooperation—even though perhaps involuntary cooperation.

---

[24] Peter Drucker, "The Economy's Dark Continent," *Fortune*, April 1962, pp. 103 ff.

[25] Ralph S. Alexander, James S. Cross, Ross M. Cunningham, *Industrial Marketing*, rev. ed., (Homewood, Ill.: Richard D. Irwin, Inc., 1961), p. 266.

TABLE 2. Methods of Cooperation as Listed[27]

1. Cooperative advertising allowances	20. Studies of innumerable types, such as studies of merchandise management accounting
2. Payments for interior displays including shelf-extenders, dump displays, "A" locations, aisle displays, etc.	21. Payments for mailings to store lists
3. P.M.'s for salespeople	22. Liberal return privileges
4. Contests for buyers, salespeople, etc.	23. Contributions to favorite charities of store personnel
5. Allowances for a variety of warehousing functions	24. Contributions to special store anniversaries
6. Payments for window display space, plus installation costs	25. Prizes, etc., to store buyers when visiting showrooms—plus entertainment, of course
7. Detail men who check inventory, put up stock, set up complete promotions, etc.	26. Training retail salespeople
8. Demonstrators	27. Payments for store fixtures
9. On certain canned food, a "swell" allowance	28. Payments for new store costs, for more improvements, including painting
10. Label allowance	29. An infinite variety of promotion allowances
11. Coupon handling allowance	30. Special payments for exclusive franchises
12. Free goods	31. Payments of part of salary of retail salespeople
13. Guaranteed sales	
14. In-store and window display material	32. Deals of innumerable types
15. Local research work	33. Time spent in actual selling floor by manufacturer, salesmen
16. Mail-in premium offers to consumer	
17. Preticketing	34. Inventory price adjustments
18. Automatic reorder systems	35. Store name mention in manufacturer's advertising
19. Delivery costs to individual stores of large retailers	

Extension Concept is the Marketing Concept

The philosophy of cooperation is described in the following quote:

The essence of the marketing concept is of course customer orientation at all levels of distribution. It is particularly important that customer orientation motivate all relations between a manufacturer and his customer—both immediate and ultimate. It must permeate his entire channels-of-distribution policy.[26]

This quote synthesizes the extension-of-the-organization system concept of channels with the marketing concept. Indeed, it shows that the former is, in essence, "the" marketing concept applied to the channel area in marketing. To continue:

The characteristics of the highly competitive markets of today naturally put a distinct premium on harmonious manufacturer-distributor relationships. Their very mutuality of interest demands that the manufacturer base his distribution program not only on what he would like from distributors, but perhaps more importantly, on what they would like from him. In order to get the cooperation of the best distributors, and thus maximum exposure for his line among the various market segments, he must adjust his policies to serve their best interest and, thereby, his own. In other words, he must put the principles of the marketing concept to work for him. By so doing, he will inspire in his customers a feeling of mutual interest and trust and will help convince them that they are essential members of his marketing team.[28]

SUMMARY

Figure I summarizes this whole paper. Each person within each department will cooperate, control, and conflict with each other (notice arrows). Together they form a department (notice department box contains person boxes) which will be best off when cooperating (or cooperation through control) forces weigh

[26] Hector Lazo and Arnold Corbin, *Management in Marketing* (New York: McGraw-Hill Book Company, Inc., 1961), p. 379.

[27] Edward B. Weiss, "How much of a Retailer Is The Manufacturer," in *Advertising Age*, July 21, 1958, p. 68.

[28] Lazo and Corbin, *loc. cit.*

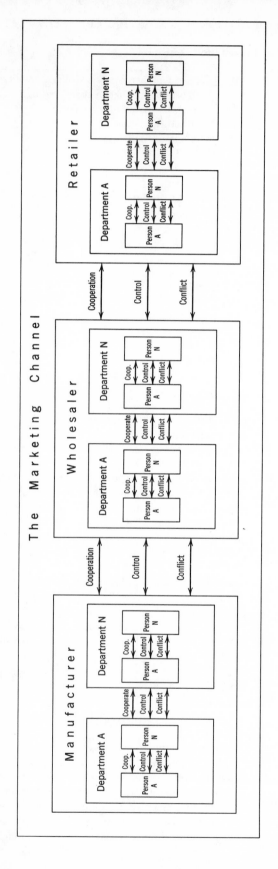

FIG. 1. Organizational extension concept.

heavier than conflicting forces. Now each department cooperates, controls, and conflicts with each other. Departments together also form a higher level organization—the firm (manufacturer, wholesaler, and retailer). Again, the firm will be better off if department cooperation is maximized and conflict minimized. Finally, firms standing vertically to each other cooperate, control, and conflict. Together they form a distribution channel that will be best off under conditions of optimum cooperation leading to consumer and profit satisfaction.

CONCLUSIONS AND HYPOTHESES

1. Channel relationships are set against a background of cooperation and conflict; horizontal, intertype, and vertical.

2. An automatic relationship exists when one channel member controls conflict and forces the others to cooperate. A democratic relationship exists when all members agree to cooperate without a power play. An anarchistic relationship exists when there is open conflict, with no member able to impose his will on the others. This last form could destroy or seriously reduce the effectiveness of the channel.

3. The process of the exchange act where one member is a seller and the other is a buyer is the basic source of channel conflict. Economic theory can aid in comprehending this phenomenon. There are, however, many other areas of conflict, such as differences in business philosophy or primary objectives.

4. Reasons for cooperation, however, usually outweigh reasons for conflict. This has led to the concept of the channel as an extension of a firm's organization.

5. This concept drops the facade of "legal entity" and treats channel members as one great organization with the leader providing each with various forms of assistance. These are called cooperating weapons.

6. It is argued that this concept is actually the marketing concept adapted to a channel situation.

7. In an autocratic or democratic channel relationship, there must be a leader. This leadership has shifted and is shifting between the various channel levels.

8. The wholesaler was the leader in the last century, the manufacturer now, and it appears that the mass retailer is next in line.

9. There is much disagreement on the above point, however, especially on who should be the leader. Various authors have differing arguments to advance for their choice.

10. In the opinion of this writer, the mass retailer appears to be best adapted for leadership under the marketing concept.

11. As there are weapons of cooperation, so are there weapons of domination. Indeed the former paradoxically are one group of the latter. The other groups are promotional, legal, negative, and suggestive methods. Both manufacturers and retailers have at their disposal these dominating weapons.

12. *For maximization of channel profits and consumer satisfaction, the channel must act as a unit.*

DISCUSSION QUESTIONS

This excellent article suggests that competition of different kinds exists between (a) retailer and similar retailer, (b) retailer and dissimilar retailer, and (c) retailer and other channel functionaries. Mallen also argues that "the 'mass' retailer (is) the natural leader of the channel for consumer goods."

1. Provide an illustration of each of the three basic classes of competition indicated above. Which of these types of competition has been responsible for the most substantial consumer benefits over the last 100 years?
2. Why is the mass retailer the "natural" leader of the channel under the "marketing concept"?

3. Competition and Evolution in Retailing

STANLEY C. HOLLANDER

It is 11:15 A.M. on the warm morning of July 21, 1899, in Lowell, Mass. The Subcommittee on Manufactures and General Business of the United States Industrial Commission is investigating economic changes that are disturbing the public, including the recent entry of department stores onto the distributive scene. Mr. Joseph L. Chalifoux, a merchant of substance who owns department stores in Lowell and in Birmingham, Alabama, has just taken the stand. Chairman Smyth asks him whether he thinks these giant stores have benefited the public.

Mr. Chalifoux: It is so. No one store could sell goods at the small margin on the average practiced by the larger department stores. The fact is they are not popular with the people, and yet the people buy their entire wants in these stores simply because they look after their own personal pocketbooks.

Later, in Chicago, the Commission will hear Mr. R. D. Goudie, a small merchant, condemn the department stores as "one of the worst and strongest trusts in existence . . . restricting the peoples' opportunity for making a living," while Mr. Roth, editor of The Retailers' Journal, will argue for government control of these vicious institutions. Mr. Otto Young, general manager of The Fair, will testify that his firm is not making any effort to force small retailers out of business, but that his lower prices and larger assortments are bound to have such an effect.

Sixty years later, of course, the big department store problem is no longer one of unpopularity, of low standing in the community, or of opposition from the small merchant. Today the department store executive is more likely to worry about expense and margin rates that have climbed about 10 percentage points

from 1900 levels, and is more likely to be concerned about the competitive inroads of the discount houses.

But the difference in the competitive situation between 1900 and 1960 is similar to the changes in pattern that appear in a Persian rug. The lines move up and down, and the colors shade and shift from one segment to another. However, the over-all effect is one of repetition, and from a distance it takes an experienced eye to notice the changing role of the different figures. The movement of the department stores in the competitive medley of retail distribution is part of a pattern that Professor McNair of Harvard calls "the wheel of retailing," a pattern that has been the experience of most of the innovating institutions in retailing in this country during the last century.

In examining changes in retail competition during the last 50 years, we shall first look at the repetitive patterns that have shown so much persistency. Then we shall divert ourselves with minor eddies and whirls in the pattern that demonstrate the rich ingenuity and variety of merchandising approaches. Finally, we will turn to the fundamental trends that truly alter the retailing picture.

Before we proceed to our examination, however, readers of STORES may be relieved to know that the five Senators, five Representatives and nine other public-spirited citizens President McKinley appointed to the Industrial Commission finally decided that they liked department stores. To quote their final report: "In the absence of monopoly, which in general seems to be the situation today, the establishment of department stores must be regarded as being on the whole advantageous to the consuming public."

THE RECURRING PATTERN

A few crude figures will help illustrate American retailing's amazing tendency towards

◆ SOURCE: Reprinted by permission from the editors of Stores, in the September 1960 issue, pages 11–24.

stability and repetition. Detailed analysis is difficult, if not impossible, since historical statistics on retail trade in the United States and in other countries are surprisingly limited. The first census of retail trade was taken in 1929, and the latest one for which full information has been released occurred in 1954. The various censuses and other enumerations really are not comparable because of differences in definitions, classifications, and methodology.

Nevertheless, we have pretty good estimates that in 1920 the American population was served by about 1.2 million stores, or approximately one store for every 90 people. Throughout the 1920s and 1930s the number of stores increased far more rapidly than the total population, so that in 1939 we had about one store for every 73 persons in the country. This trend reversed itself during the period 1940 to 1954. Population increased much more rapidly than the number of stores, and adjusted census figures for the end of that period indicate roughly the same ratio of stores to population as existed in 1920. We cannot be certain, as yet, whether this ratio persisted from 1954 to 1959; but in all probability the new census figures will not show too much change.

The Wheel of Retailing. Harold Barger has assembled and analyzed all of the available material on retail and wholesale margins in this country from 1869 to 1947.[1] His figures show many changes, including both increases and declines in individual trades. The sum of wholesale and retail margins, though, has remained astonishingly constant, rising less than one percentage point from 36.5 per cent in 1909 to 37.4 in 1947. Godfrey Lebhar has reported a similar stability, over the years 1929 to 1954, in the chain store's share of the total retail market.[2] After an early spurt, the chains seem to have stabilzed at about 22 per cent of total retail sales.

The most striking and persistent theme we will note, however, concerns the way in which individual types of retailers have evolved within the total pattern. New manufacturing industries often first appear as relatively high cost firms producing for "class" markets and then gradually work their way down the price

and status scales to mass production for mass markets. New types of retailers, on the other hand, usually have had the opposite experience. In greater or lesser degree, mail order houses, department stores, and chain stores (three types of retailing that accompanied the industrial expansion of the later 19th century) appeared first as low service, low status, low margin distributors, encountered vigorous opposition, and then gradually moved up in both respectability and in expense, thereby becoming exposed to new, lower margin competition.

Mail Order Houses

The large mail order houses faced violent condemnation during the final quarter of the 19th century, and again around 1912, when the introduction of parcel post service made them formidable competitors to country merchants. Rural storekeepers tried to organize boycotts against the mail order firms, school boards fired teachers who dared to buy from Chicago, and country bankers were critical of farmers who sent out of town for their supplies. Emmet and Jueck, the able historians of Sears, Roebuck and Company, describe how local merchants would conduct great public bonfires in the village parks, paying 10 cents for each catalogue contributed to the flames.[3]

In time, the public learned that the mail order firms were not going to drive all other retailers out of business. The development of the automobile and the paved highway, along with concomitant improvements in shopping facilities, imposed limitations upon catalogue business. The mail order companies, in turn, adjusted by providing increased services, offering guarantees and credit, increasing merchandise selection and, eventually, entering the chain store and department store business with vigor and skill. From 1899 on, their margins increased very slowly, but equally steadily, according to Barger's study.

Department Store Rise

Many department store founders, such as Wanamaker, Palmer and Field, soon came to be regarded as men of considerable standing in their communities. As a general thing, though, their branch of retailing did not enjoy the same public esteem. Some leaders in the

[1] Harold Barger, *Distribution's Place in the American Economy Since 1869*. Princeton University Press, 1955.

[2] Godfrey M. Lebhar, *Chain Stores in America*. Chain Store Publishing Corporation, New York, 1959.

[3] Boris Emmet and John E. Jueck, *Catalogs and Counters*. University of Chicago Press, 1950.

trade felt that the term "department store" carried so little prestige that they stoutly, but vainly, insisted upon "consolidated" or "general store" as a designation for their enterprises. Department store, they maintained, was a proper name only for those establishments in which each department was under separate ownership, much like the so-called "farmers' markets" of today. The public, however, was not interested in the distinction and consistently referred to all of the big stores as department stores.

However, a major shift in attitude seems to have occurred just about the time our story opens. The report of the Industrial Commission, which we have already noted, reflected that change and also may have helped foster it. In 1899 The Arena, a liberal magazine of the period, published a set of laudatory articles on department stores in the major cities of the country. It noted that social workers, who 10 years previously had regarded the stores as a means of exploiting female labor and as hotbeds of immorality, were now revising their opinions. The accusations of immorality were false, and the magazine applauded "the spectacle of Mr. White, of the R. H. White Company, chartering a Boston theatre and going with his hundreds of clerks to witness a meritorious play." This rise in public esteem was accompanied by fairly large increases in average department store percentage margins from 1899 to 1919, and again from 1929 to 1939.

Chains Survive Discrimination

Although chain organizations developed during the 19th century, their first great flowering came during the years from World War I to the depths of the great depression. Again their growth incited the hue and cry that the fabric of independent retailing was being destroyed. This time the opposition was more vigorous and, at least superficially, more successful than before.

Chain stores, as a group, had obtained a larger share of total retail business than had either department stores or mail order houses; small retailers were ready to blame the chains for all the misery of the depression; changing social and economic climates made legislators more amenable to restrictive legislation; and the anti-chain movement attracted colorful and ingenious advocates. In Shreveport, La., "Old Man" W. K. Henderson used his Radio Station KWKH to sell "Hello World" Coffee at $1.00 per pound and to recruit members for his anti-chain "Merchants' Minute Men." Frank R. Wilson, who had been national publicity director for the 3rd, 4th and 5th Liberty Loan campaigns, prepared a film, called Forward America, that used "all the sure-fire movie tricks to dramatize the downfall of the independent retailer and to drive home with simple graphs all the arguments used against chains." In some cities merchants bought tickets for the picture at 10 cents each and gave them to their customers, in other places local retail groups simply hired a theatre and opened it to the public free. Either way, Business Week noted, "chains don't like it."

Discriminatory chain store taxes that were bothersome but relatively ineffective appeared in a number of states. More fundamental influences upon retail competition were exerted by the Robinson-Patman Act (1936) and resale price maintenance laws (1937) that were passed largely under an anti-chain guise. By the mid-1930s, however, the chains had learned some important lessons in public relations, some of the worst economic pressures of the depression had lessened, and some of the steam went out of the anti-chain movement.

Supermarkets and Discount Stores

Meanwhile, in the grocery trade, the chains had to fight the competition of the new, very low service and very low margin independent supermarkets. In deference to the time honored principle of "if you can't lick 'em, join 'em," the major grocery chains somewhat reluctantly switched to supermarket operation. The early supers, sometimes called "cheapy jacks," often located in abandoned factories and ramshackle buildings, in turn, gave way to conveniently located, glossy, modern structures, equipped with attractive fixtures and well maintained parking lots, offering a wide variety of staple and gourmet foods and many non-food specialties. Recently supermarket expenses have begun to climb, and some grocery executives are worried about the possible competitive inroads of discount houses selling packaged foods in case lots at bedrock prices. But the discount houses, which have slowly begun to climb in public esteem, are worried as to how they can offer all the merchandise assortments as well as the credit, delivery and installation services their customers seem to want, and still operate on the low margin that is their supposed major attraction. And so the wheel continues to turn.

Two types of retailing in our recent history have proven exceptions to this rule. One is automatic vending, which right from the start was a high convenience, high margin operation. The other is composed of the department store suburban branch and its ultimate concomitant, the planned shopping center. This type of retailing seems to have started with the swankiest shops, largely because the suburbs were originally an expensive place of residence for the wealthy. As the suburbs changed to an expensive place of residence for all mankind, this type of retailing trickled down to the popular priced stores. Interestingly enough, the wheel of retailing also seems to have been reversed in the underdeveloped countries, where modern supermarkets are first welcomed as status symbols for the ruling groups.

Intense Price Competition

Economists sometimes seem to picture the world of retailing as a peaceful place, where no one ever disrupts established percentage markons. Nostalgic merchants, faced with the competitive onslaughts of aggressive new distributors, often think this picture may have been true in father's day, even if it is a laughable distortion of the present. Discount selling, for example, may seem to be a feature of modern life that was unknown or unimportant in the good old days. But, actually, almost any point in our pattern of retail competition during the last half-century will show the sharp clashes of vigorous price warfare. The history of discount selling exemplifies this.

For example, we usually think of industrial stores as necessary establishments in remote mining and lumbering camps, or possibly as devices to exploit mill workers. Yet immediately after World War I many industrial firms opened commissaries to supply their workers with the necessities of life at discount prices. In 1926, three such stores that Henry Ford had established in his Detroit area plants were officially opened to the public and did $12 million volume. Protests from merchants around the country threatened a national boycott of Ford cars and delivery trucks, and in early 1927 the stores were, at least officially, restricted to Ford workers and their families. By 1941 four states had passed laws prohibiting such retail ventures. Employers who did not operate stores frequently allowed their purchasing departments to make wholesale purchases for some or all of their staff, and in 1938, Business Week estimated that some seven to 10 thousand large industrial firms were supplying their employees with names and addresses of discount houses.

Only Saps Pay Retail

A pre-war military officers' uniform cooperative burgeoned out in 1919 into a veterans' buying club called The Association of Army and Navy Stores, Inc. This organization, which sold almost 300,000 memberships before its liquidation in 1953, managed to obtain discounts for its members in leading department and specialty stores throughout the country. The early success of the Association led the American Legion to flirt with the thought of its own discount buying club for its members, but the idea was finally abandoned as politically inexpedient.

United Fraternal Buyers seems to have been formed in Philadelphia in 1926 to coordinate the efforts of various lodges, including the Moose, Eagles, Elks, Shriners, Red Men and Veterans of Foreign Wars, in soliciting discounts from local merchants. All during the 1920s many branches of the A.A.A. obtained discounts on gasoline, tires and automotive supplies for their members. Only the war, and the 1930–1940 trade association campaigns against trade diversion, ended customary department store discounts to the theatrical profession, to registered nurses, to teachers, to dressmakers and to professional shoppers.

Manufacturers and wholesalers made "back door" sales to consumers. Two 1932 Federal Trade Commission actions finally resulted in rulings that leading firms in the so-called wholesale catalogue jewelry and giftware industry were really making retail sales, though perhaps at discount prices, through their "counter books." Showrooms, supposedly designed as wholesale centers to provide extra display space for small furniture retailers, made more and more sales directly to consumers during the 1930s, and the "open showroom" became a center of controversy in the furniture industry. In fact, so many deviations from the "one-price" system existed in the supposedly halcyon years before World War II, that a leading law journal published an article in 1937 entitled "The Fiction of the Quoted Price." At the same time, Mrs. Hannah Lees, a well-known journalist, debated in the pages of The American Mercury with Mr. Ira Hirschmann of Bloomingdale's as to whether "only saps pay retail," or "only saps buy at 'wholesale.'"

Stamps and Coupons

In 1890, the Larkin Company, a soap manufacturer of Buffalo, New York, embarked on a plan that was to make it a leading supplier of rocking chairs to parsonages throughout the country. Ecclesiastical furniture may seem far removed from toilet soap, but the connection was simply a form of a merchandising device that occurs, recurs, and persists in our distributive fabric. Larkin sold its soap through consumer clubs that earned premium points for every bar purchased. Many of the club groups were church organizations that used their points to buy furniture for the minister's study or living room. The plan was so successful that Larkin soon concentrated mainly upon manufacturing the premiums. One of the first commercial buildings ever designed by Frank Lloyd Wright was erected in Buffalo as Larkin's headquarters.

At the same time trading stamps were obtaining their first burst of popularity, evidenced by the fact that between 1888 and 1915, 26 states and the Territory of Hawaii passed laws restricting or regulating the devices. The percentage of total retail sales that was accompanied by trading stamps declined steadily from 1916 to a low point in 1934, then increased, and of course, expanded rapidly after World War II. The United Profit Sharing Corporation was established in 1914, more or less in affiliation with the United Cigar Stores Corporation, to supply retailers with "profit-sharing coupons" that could be redeemed for merchandise prizes. Later Schulte Cigar Stores responded with its own mutual coupon system. In 1929 both Schulte and United Cigar dropped their coupon plans, but resumed again in 1932. This time Schulte was the leader, and it was the one that signed up with United Profit Sharing.

Adolph O. Goodwin, a Chicago advertising man added a short but bright splash of excitement and controversy to our pattern of redeemable stamps and coupons. In 1936 he started the Goodwin Plan, under which members of church groups and Ladies Aid Societies became "oral broadcasters" for 55 manufacturers who participated in the scheme. The oral broadcasters collected labels from packages of the brands included under the plan and mailed them to Goodwin, who in turn forwarded them to the manufacturers in return for 3½ per cent of retail value.

The Goodwin Corporation retained one per cent, the Goodwin district representative received one-half of one per cent, and the church was rewarded with the remaining two per cent. In the first flush of excitement, many leading brands, including Du Pont paint, BVD underwear, Burnett's extracts, Barbasol shaving cream, Van Camp's spaghetti and Dictograph hearing aids, were brought into the plan, and Goodwin claimed 265,000 broadcasters. His organization soon encountered difficulties, and was declared bankrupt in 1936. Goodwin next appeared with a plan to promote union label goods, but his church stamp idea was not dead. Many other groups, including the Religious Press Association of Philadelphia, the National Good-Will League Guild, Inc., and individual retail stores developed similar plans in the late 1930s.

Scrambled Merchandising

The most consistent change in the warp and woof of retail competition has been the constant shifting of merchandise assortments, as each retailer tried to find the particular bundle in goods on which he could specialize most effectively, and at the same time enjoy all the profits and attractions inherent in offering his customers a wide choice.

Widening markets provided profitable opportunities for specialization, but the traffic the specialization drew also presented a chance to sell a few extra items, and so commodity lines were broadened and changed again and again.

Drugstore history provides a very clear example of this. The early druggists in many parts of the country did not have enough potential customers to support a specialized trade. Besides, much of the business in medicine was siphoned off by physicians who dispensed their own drugs. Consequently, up to and even after the Civil War, druggists relied upon house paints, dyestuffs for domestic use, and various oil products, for a substantial portion, if not the bulk, of their volume. After the Civil War, pharmacy gradually broke loose as a separate profession, distinct from medicine on the one hand and general storekeeping on the other. The preparation of sodas and similar drinks had a long history of association with the more medicinal aspects of the business. After 1900 local, and then national, prohibition threw much of the refreshment traffic to the soft drink counters. This traffic, plus the trade the pharmacist generated during the evening hours, provided a perfect outlet for a wide assortment of general merchandise, and so the typical drugstore began its evolution into the miniature variety shop we know today.

While the druggist was broadening his own assortments, he painfully lost some highly profitable merchandise to his grocery competitors. Prepared baby foods, originally considered a highly specialized item, moved into the grocery store when the manufacturers decided high traffic was more important than specialized attention. More recently a wide range of health and beauty aids have wandered into the supermarket mix, where their markups make them especially attractive to margin-starved grocers.

Diversification for Profit

Scrambled merchandising was a significant aspect of early department store growth. Samuel Hopkins Adams, writing in Scribner's Magazine in 1897, attributed the foundation of the department store to the dry goods merchants' desire for new opportunities and larger fields. Because of competition, growth along established lines seemed impracticable, and the more progressive stores began to reach out for other lines of trade in which the opportunities for profit seemed greater. As usual this trend encountered severe opposition. The ministers of Philadelphia preached sermons of condemnation when the dry goods stores in that city added umbrellas, canes and parasols to their stock. But diversification and scrambling continued until:

Today, within those capacious stores, can be bought orchestrions and toothbrushes, instruction on the bicycle and the latest patent liniments; while it is but a short trip from the photograph gallery with its "north light" to the hothouses on the roof.

Ralph Hower, who studied Macy's history in great detail, believes that store reached its limit in diversification about 1902.[4] The same thing seems to be true of department stores in general. Grocery departments played an im-

portant role in the early stores, but have gradually dwindled to insignificance in today's merchandise mix. Adams gives the department store a large share of the credit for the popularization of the bicycle in America. The automobile, on the other hand, has been far less significant as a direct source of sales volume. John Wanamaker was one of the first Ford dealers in the country: some stores prematurely anticipated the compact car movement with Crosley departments in the 30s; Army surplus trucks moved into a few stores in the 1940s; and Sears tried to sell a version of the Kaiser during the same decade. Private planes also crept into the merchandise mix at about the same time, and flew right out again. From 1929 to 1953 department store sales of tires and automotive accessories did increase rather sharply, according to Entenberg's study,[5] but not nearly enough to maintain anywhere near the 1929 share of the market. In fact, since 1930 department store attention seems to have been concentrated increasingly upon textile products. But even though it has seldom been part of the merchandise inventory, the automobile has had profound effects upon the giant stores, as we shall note a little later on.

Sales Promotion

We cannot talk of the pattern of retail competition in this country without mentioning advertising or sales promotion. A later article in this series will trace their development and evolution; all we can do now is to notice their constant presence. Adams' 1897 description of the department store credits two departments with supplying much of the institution's originality:

These are the advertising department and the window-dressing department. One is the literature of the great store; the other its art. . . . Frequently the head advertising man is the general manager of the store. . . . Every day he holds consultations with heads of departments to find out what particular lines of articles they want "boomed," and about those articles he writes alluring statements for the shopping public to read, sometimes arranging for illustrations with them. The amount of money spent for advertising is appalling when looked upon as an expense. One great store in Philadelphia spends on an average of $1,000

---

[4] Ralph Hower, *History of Macy's of New York, 1858–1919.* Harvard University Press, 1943.

[5] Robert D. Entenberg, *The Changing Competitive Position of Department Stores in the United States by Merchandise Lines.* Published by the University of Pittsburgh Press, 1957.

every day in the year, and a good many spend $500. . . . It is pretty safe to say that every good advertising man earns his salary, and the best man in this country at this work is said to receive $15,000 a year.

Advertising men also seem to have been the first comparison shoppers. Macy's, for example, did not formally establish a shopping operation until sometime between 1910 and 1915. This led Adams to comment:

One of the bitternesses of life to the hard-working buyer is to have the advertising man (who keeps track of the other stores as well as his own, and is a sort of general information bureau) tell him, after he has set his price on a particularly promising line of goods, that the rival establishment down the street has cut under him by 10 per cent.

As the French say, "The more things change, the more they are the same."

VARIATIONS ON A THEME

Economists love to talk of competition, and have classified it into many varieties, such as "pure," "perfect," "imperfect," "monopolistic," and "oligopolistic competition." Some of these are abstractions, found only in the textbooks, but one realistic concept is the idea of "workable competition." Workable competition requires, among other things, that the consumer have a wide variety of alternatives among which to make her selections. American retailing, over the years has met this test by presenting its customers with many different types of stores and many different bundles of services, to be accepted or rejected as consumer taste dictated.

Cooperatives

Neither this issue of STORES nor a whole year's volume would provide sufficient space to recount all of the experiments and all of the innovations in retailing that have been presented to the American consumer during the last 50 years. Hundreds of books have been written on the consumer cooperative movement alone. Heralded with much fanfare in the 1920s and 1930s, that movement seems to have reached its apex in the Edward A. Filene Good-Will Fund's attempt to establish a cooperative department store in the Washington suburbs in the late 1940s. Although the co-operatives attracted much attention among

both merchants and students of marketing, they never really found a way to improve upon the chain stores. Consequently the movement's successes were limited to some rural areas and to some branches of banking and public utility services.

Subscription Buying

In April, 1926 a fledgling author, Sylvia Townsend Warner, had her first book, a novel called *Lolly Willowes*, selected by an equally untested organization, The Book-of-the-Month Club, and a new chapter in publishing history opened. The fantastic success of this venture inspired literally hundreds of similar subscription plans. Today other book clubs cater to the specialist in Civil War history, or business, or science. Record clubs, fruit clubs, and cheese clubs flourish. On the other hand, necktie-of-the-month, fish-of-the-week, and gadget-of-the-month clubs stimulated less consumer enthusiasm.

Frozen Food Stores

Rising acceptance of frozen foods after World War II led to a wave of highly specialized stores that were really giant refrigerators equipped with display cases and sales counters. However, the consumer decided that she wanted to buy her frosted foods along with the rest of her meals in traditional supermarkets and delicatessens, and so the specialized stores disappeared, along with many a GI loan.

On Wheels

We are all familiar with the profound effects the automobile has exerted upon all phases of American life, including retailing. We all know how it enabled the farmer to get to the city for his shopping, and how it moved the urbanite and his trade out of the city to the suburban store and the planned shopping center. We know of the congestion it induced downtown, of the delivery problems it solved and created, and of the retail industry that developed for its distribution, care and maintenance. But one of the most interesting things about the automobile is the effect it did not have.

The historian who reads either the retailing or the automotive literature of the 1920s constantly encounters predictions that the traveling store, built upon a truck body, will soon replace the sedentary establishment. The "Motorteria" of Detroit, 22 feet long, 7½ feet wide, with a shopping aisle down the center and a plate glass display window at the rear, was a typical example of attempts to develop mobile stores. One ingenious entrepreneur experimented with rolling gasoline stations, really modified tank-trucks, that cruised the highways looking for customers. Somewhat similar thoughts were advanced after World War II; one plan, described with considerable enthusiasm in the trade press, called for the use of giant trailer trucks that would park in residential neighborhoods (undoubtedly to the great delight of the zoning authorities). Salesmen equipped with little pushcarts and walkie-talkie radios would fan out from the trucks, while motorcycle couriers would deliver special orders from the same points in response to radioed instructions. More serious attempts were made to capitalize upon the motoring habits of the nation by converting gasoline stations into one-stop shopping centers. An Illinois filling station chain and a Chicago mail order firm experimented with catalogue order desks next to the pumps, but the idea did not work out.

Vending Machines

Automatic vending, the coin-in-the-slot method of retailing, has enjoyed enormous growth. Trade circles estimate present volume in the billions. But the machines have had their failures as well as their successes. Sometimes the consumer has been delighted to buy from the machines, in other cases he has resisted them.

At about the end of the first World War, Clarence Saunders pioneered in the establishment of self-service grocery stores, and founded the Piggly Wiggly chain. His innovation led to a rash of organizations called Helpy-Selfy, Nifty-Jifty, Handy-Andy and the like, to great success for his own venture, and eventually, to financial battles that removed him from control of Piggly Wiggly. His ingenious mind then turned to a truly automatic store, called the Keedoozle. The first Keedoozle opened in Memphis in spring, 1937. Each item in the store was displayed in its indivdual, glass-enclosed niche. The customers carried long wooden rods equipped with keys that were inserted in slots underneath the niches to select their merchandise. Each time the key was inserted in a slot, a crystal at the other end of the rod lit up, and one can or box was sent on its way to a central assembly point. Prices were totalled as the products came off the conveyor belt, and the customer found her order and her bill waiting for her. The electro-mechanical system soon broke down, and in 1939 was replaced by an improved version. The customer's key was now designed to look like an automatic pistol, and was equipped with its own adding machine tape upon which prices were registered as items were selected. This new system promised to work well, but it too soon collapsed. A model of a somewhat similar store, called "Auto-Serv," was demonstrated to the Society for the Advancement of Management in 1939. In this version the customer selected punched cards from racks under the display niches and gave them to a cashier who actuated conveyor belts to draw the merchandise from a central stockroom.

The Home Humidor, i.e., a piece of walnut furniture that hid a small cigarette vending machine designed to foil borrowing friends, placed in 2,000 test homes in 1934, represented another attempt to extend the traditional boundaries of automatic vending. So too were Soundies, 1940s' little individual movie viewing machines designed to show travelogues and short subjects at 10 cents for each three minutes or eighth of a reel. Vending machines were installed in street cars and buses in Birmingham, Dallas, Detroit, Oakland, Pittsburgh, San Diego, and Milwaukee at various times between 1920 and 1940; but customers tripped over them, bumped into them, broke them, cheated them with slugs, and littered the cars with their debris. In 1950 the Filene Store tried U-Serv-U centers in the Boston airport, Greyhound bus station and Back Bay railroad station to vend lingerie, gloves, hosiery, and men's shirts. The venture proved quite unsuccessful, and the installations were soon closed.

But innovations usually require considerable trial and error. Many failures are needed for every success. Experimentation improves methodology and equipment, while each venture acclimates the public to new techniques. The future of automatic vending, and of many other innovations, cannot help but be bright. Many experiments that seem visionary today, or even silly, will prove to be the forerunners of tomorrow's successes.

LOOKING AHEAD

The pattern we have been looking at repeats itself again and again, exhibits all sorts of minor variations that come and go, and yet, somehow winds up being different from what it was at the start. The merchant, who has to plan for the future, is entitled to ask: "What are the fundamental trends that can be projected into that future?" Several tendencies can be discerned.

Systematizing Retailing

The pulpwood forests of the United States and Canada have supported the most significant single transformation in American retailing during the past 50 years. The retail enterprise of 1960 runs on paper, and occasionally is choked by paper, to an extent undreamed of in 1910. Conventional double-entry bookkeeping and some rudimentary stock records were the only tools the average merchant of 1910 had available to supplement his impressions of his store and his market. The retail method of inventory was just beginning to attract attention in most stores. Expense center and production unit accounting, merchandise management accounting, M.O.R. reports, market research, sales analyses, trade association reports and operations research were all unknown. Today we are on the brink of an era in which mark-sensing machines will transform sales checks into instantaneous inventory and sales reports. We may even reach the ultimate stage of perfection, when some genius finds a way to insure that the writing on the sales check will be legible to machines, to clericals, and to deliverymen.

Although the retail executive sometimes complains that he can only dimly perceive customers and merchandise hidden behind a veil of reports, all of these analytical techniques have enabled him to operate and compete in entirely different fashion from his predecessors. Nationally coordinated chains, operating relatively homogeneous units from coast to coast, would be impossible without modern control devices. The techniques of accounting and cost analysis used have naturally influenced the pricing policies retailers have selected. Merchandise management accounting, to cite one example, seems to have intrigued some retailers mainly as a means of improving their pricing posture vis a vis the discount house.

To date, electronic data processing itself does not seem to have altered the general nature of retail competition significantly. It has replaced some hard-to-secure clericals, permitted some retailers to develop a few more conventional reports, and, perhaps most significantly, facilitated stock control improvements for some mass merchandisers. However, the greatest impacts may well be in the future when merchants have learned all the potentialities inherent in the expensive new gadgets. For example, 20 years ago R. H. Whitman tried to construct statistical demand curves (measures of the changes in sales that would result from small changes in price) for staple merchandise in Macy's housewares basement.[6] He concluded that the project was completely feasible, but hardly worth the cost. Ultimately data processing machinery should make this sort of analysis quite economical, and so may well influence price decisions. Similarly, improved motivational research techniques may finally illuminate the most fundamental question in competitive strategy: why customers select one particular store in preference to its competitors.

Government Regulation

To the newspaper reader, government regulation of business means a fight between the steel industry and the Department of Justice. To the merchant, it means the pervasive effects of decisions reached in city, state and federal councils. Local zoning boards may control his choice of location; state sales taxes must be collected from his customers; and federal regulation influences all phases of his operations. For example, the retail inventory method, fundamentally a device for internal control, could not become really popular with retailers until the Internal Revenue Service grudgingly accepted it.

Two trends in government regulation, one potential, the other already present, appear important. The development of the suburbs and the disappearance of the open spaces between cities have created vast economic interurbias. Eventually the logic of the situation probably will break down the current balkanized system of villages, towns, counties, small cities, and overlapping administrative districts. If so, retailers will have to deal with fewer, but stronger, local jurisdictions.

The other trend, which has been clear for the last 30 years, is one of increased state and

---

[6] Roswell H. Whitman, *Demand Functions for Merchandise at Retail,* in Oscar Lange (ed.), *Studies in Mathematical Economics and Econometrics in Honor of Henry Schultz.* University of Chicago Press, 1942.

federal legislation affecting retailing. The abortive chain store taxes, the influential Robinson-Patman Act, and the currently withering resale price maintenance laws marked the start of the trend in the 1930s. FTC campaigns against misleading pricing, labeling laws for woolens, furs and synthetic fibers, the Automobile Dealers' Franchise Act, and similar legislation suggests the trend's continuance. Perhaps this is part of a larger pattern that repeats itself over 100- or 150-year cycles. In 1860 and 1870, for example, wholesaling interests in cities and states throughout the country attempted to keep traveling salesmen from calling on local retailers through restrictive ordinances and prohibitive license fees. But, in general, the second half of the 19th century and the earliest part of the 20th were pretty well committed to laissez-faire in distribution. Now the pendulum is swinging the other way.

Self-Regulation

While certainly individual merchants will differ in their opinions of specific laws, the retail trade has been distinguished by a desire for enlightened self-regulation. About 1911 the publisher of Printer's Ink magazine advanced the idea of a model statute for advertising regulation. The real strength of the movement developed, however, out of the joint work of the Associated Advertising Clubs and the retailer-oriented Better Business Bureaus that were operating in 40 cities by 1924. Since then the movement has spread to virtually every major city, and many smaller towns, throughout the country. Improvements in technique have been the work of both individual retailers and their trade associations. Improvements in retailing standards appear, almost necessarily so, as the work of retail associations.

The New Market

Changes in both retail techniques and retail standards rest upon fundamental changes in the markets American retailers serve. In spite of ups and downs, despite the vicissitudes of war and depression, long-run changes in American consumption have been most encouraging to retail development. We have more consumers than ever before, they are better educated and more prosperous than they have ever been, and they are willing to express their confidence in the future at the retail counters of the country. High level consumption usually means an interest in goods for their own sake as well as in goods as a means to an end. The hungry man simply wants food; it takes abundance to produce gourmets. With increasing consumption, small differences become important. Style, variety and taste take on a new significance. Convenience and comfort are prized. The merchant faces continual problems in adjusting supply to fickle demand, but at the same time his opportunities increase in geometric fashion.

One of the surprising things about prosperity is that it does not necessarily lessen interest in price. Every analysis of discount selling suggests that high income consumers are more prone to shop discount sources than are low income consumers. At the same time, markets for luxuries and for extras expand enormously.

Changing Concept of Service

The change in the market has caused vast changes in the services that the consumer expects from the retail trade. In spite of open display, cash-and-carry, self-selection and self-service, we cannot say that the consumer of 1960 wants less service than the shopper of 1910; in fact, she (or he) wants more. But a different type of service is demanded, and perhaps the difference can best be summarized by the distinction between the words "shopper" and "consumer."

Leisure and elegance were the keynotes of service at the beginning of the century. A 1901 textbook on department store retailing noted that floor managers and ushers:

. . . . should see that all customers are properly served, and the greatest courtesy and politeness shown them, whether buying or simply looking at goods. Strangers from out of town visiting the store should be made to feel at home, and particular attention paid them. Should they desire to be shown through the store, it should be arranged. They should be impressed with the manner of doing business and this effect is best secured where consideration is shown them. It is better to answer the inquiries of customers by accompanying them to the department asked for and requesting a salesperson to wait on them, rather than pointing to that department, and much better to name the salesperson than to use the word "forward."

Stores were designed as imitation palaces. Furniture and fixtures that hid the merchandise from view turned each transaction into a sort of social call between shopper and salesperson.

In fact, some of the older customers objected to the department system because it upset their friendly visits with favorite salespeople. In many stores, "check boys" carried bundles and money from sales counters to cashiers and back to customers, while the customers remained at the counters. The few who could afford to buy, and could afford the time, were treated like visiting potentates in many establishments.

On the other hand, today's consumer is so busy using his possessions that he hasn't time for leisurely strolls through marble corridors, with or without the company of a frock-coated floorwalker. The service he demands is primarily convenience; convenience of location, of easy parking, of good selection, of quick sale and checkout, of freedom from worry about quality or value, of easy payment. He wants the service of abundant credit, and he gets it. At times he seems to want to disassociate himself from the nuisances of ownership of goods, and rental plans permit even that high level of convenience.

Fundamentally, then, the basic change in retailing results from the fact that while shopping may be a pleasure for some consumers, for many others purchasing is primarily a means to a more pleasant life. And merchants inevitably will display increasing skill in helping people obtain that objective.

DISCUSSION QUESTION

Professor Hollander identifies several dimensions in which competition or rivalry in retailing is felt. Note that competition occurs between old and new firms—this is the threat of the innovator to the established. Note also that competition occurs between existing firms, but this is competition of a different sort than that assumed in courses in economic theory. This competition between existing firms features variations in price, promotion, merchandise, location, service, and other parts of the total competitive effort.

> Appraise retailing in terms of its competitive strength. What factors can you identify which suggest the existence of strong competition? What evidence suggests some non-competitive elements in retail rivalry?

4. Tenant-Selection Policies of Regional Shopping Centers

MORRIS L. SWEET

In the development of the regional shopping center, a policy of tenant selection is evolving that favors the traditional retailer, the department store, and the national chain. By giving these outlets more favorable rental terms and a veto power over prospective tenants, many successful low-margin mass retailers are put into a marginal category.

Is this policy in the best interests of the regional shopping center's future? Is it likely to lead to the lowering of distribution costs? The answers are analyzed in this article.

The current development of regional shopping centers and their prospects for future growth raise critical questions about policies that determine the selection of retailers as tenants. What is the effect of present tenant-selection policies on distribution costs? Are present tenant-selection policies likely to contribute to the longevity of these new retailing institutions? Do their current selection policies assist or hamper the distribution of consumer goods? Do they expand or limit consumer choice? Can excluded retailers survive outside regional centers? The importance of these questions is enhanced by the possible application of selection criteria developed in regional centers to the planned redevelopment of downtown shopping areas.

TENANT-SELECTION POLICY

This article is concerned with selection criteria related to the merchandising character and practices of retail tenants—that is, mass retailers, rather than merchants selling luxury goods of limited appeal. It assumed that the basis of unacceptability is not lack of financial stability or managerial competence and integrity.

♦ SOURCE: Reprinted by permission from the American Marketing Association, in the *Journal of Marketing*, April 1959, pages 399–404.

The Present Policy

An important factor in current tenant-selection programs is the emphasis on planned or limited competition, protection against undue competition from new tenants, and limitation of the introduction of new merchandise lines by existing tenants. Retailers who are too aggressive or unorthodox in their merchandising policies are not wanted. The common result of such tenant-selection procedures is the exclusion of successful low-margin mass retailers from regional shopping centers. If possible, a buffer zone is established around the center to keep these retailers at a distance.

This policy stems from the procedure followed in planning a center. When a desirable site is found, the developer obtains an option to buy the land. He then attempts to secure long-term leases from prospective tenants as a basis for financing the construction of the center. Leases with "prestige" tenants facilitate his efforts to secure the necessary funds. The most desirable "prestige" tenant is a large traditional department store. The next most desirable tenant is a national chain.

Thus the department store and the national chain are in a strong bargaining position, and they can hold out until the developer accedes to their demands. Tight money-market conditions have made it even more necessary for the developer to grant concessions to those retailers considered blue-ribbon tenants by the lending agency. One result is the more favorable rental arrangements given to the department store. These arrangements are such that "most department store deals are of the loss leader type." [1] The reason for the preferential treatment is the drawing power of the favored retailer from which other less favored tenants benefit.

An extremely important concession to be observed in tenant-selection policy is the creation of "certain types of restrictive covenants protecting the tenant against certain types of competition." [2] This gives selected retailers the right to veto any prospective tenant.

Gimbel Bros. has the right to approve all prospective tenants at the Cross County Center, Yonkers, N. Y. Macy's was unable to take over the John Wanamaker store at this center. The rental asked may have been too high, or key tenants in the center may have disapproved of Macy's as a fellow retailer. If Macy's was vetoed, the action is paradoxical in the light of later developments at the Roosevelt Field Shopping Center in Long Island.

In addition to getting free land upon which to erect its own building, Macy's was also given a veto privilege over other tenants at the Roosevelt Field Shopping Center. All other stores were to be leased on a minimum guarantee and percentage basis. [3] The poor showing of this center, one of the country's largest, has been well publicized. [4] A major factor appears to have been too much dependence on the department store. When Macy's did not provide sufficient drawing power at the center, the developer and other tenants wanted an additional heavy-traffic pulling retailer, preferably Ohrbach's. The success of a nearby discount department store made this type of retailer the logical tenant. But Macy's is believed to have demanded additional concessions before surrendering its veto against an Ohrbach type tenant.

Effects of Present Policy

The poor earnings record of many shopping centers has encouraged investors to reexamine the potential of shopping centers. [5] Against this skepticism should be noted the optimism of such statements as the following. According to Theodore Berenson, a leading shopping-center developer, "our centers are planned for a fifty-year business cycle, and once a regional gets in they are suicide to compete with." An Urban Land Institute Report states: "Even those regional centers without the best locations or stores will nevertheless be successful because their heavy capital investment will deter any competitor from attempting to set up a better designed center in the same trading area." [6]

But does the present tenant-selection policy warrant any such confidence in the future of the regional shopping center? Is the regional center strengthening its competitive position by linking its future development to that of the department store and other traditional retailers? In the years since World War II many department stores have experienced difficulty in adapting to changing conditions and to new forms of competition. As a result of conventional merchandising methods, many national chains have also found themselves in a vulnerable position. [7]

The Innovator

Historically the innovating entrepreneur has been considered a disturbing element by those whose equilibrium he upsets. Within the center the customary resistance exists toward innovistic competition. This type of competition is a "dynamic which threatens the status quo, puts all known goods and methods potentially out of date, and makes hazardous all investment in specific production equipment and distribution alignments. It is the antithesis of

---

[1] A. L. Alcorn, "Problems of Tenant Selection and Rental Determination in Shopping Centers," *Journal of Property Management* (Fall, 1956), pp. 29–35, at p. 33.

[2] "CAUGHT IN TIGHT MONEY PINCH Independents Lost in Shuffle as Centers Seek Big Names," *Women's Wear Daily* (October 19, 1956), pp. 1, 29.

[3] Eugene J. Kelley, "SHOPPING CENTERS Locating Controlled Regional Centers," *Eno Foundation for Highway Traffic Control* (Saugatuck, Connecticut, 1956), pp. 107–108.

[4] "WEAKNESSES POP UP Roosevelt Field Misses First Year Sales Goals," *Women's Wear Daily* (September 27, 1957), pp. 1, 26.

[5] David Hoddeson, "CRACKED FACADE Shopping Centers Have Lost Their Glamor for Investors," *Barron's* (August 12, 1957), p. 17.

[6] "Shopping Centers Here En Masse," *New York Times* (October 21, 1956), Section 3, pp. 1, 11.

[7] Faye Henle, "NEW LOOK IN WOMEN'S WEAR Self-Service, Discount Merchandising Pay Off for Apparel Chains," *Barron's* (October 7, 1957), pp. 5, 6.

handicap competition which aims deliberately to preserve existing channels of distribution and to give security to competitors rather than to maintain competition." [8]

If the center is successful in freezing local retailing into a mold which is immune to change, new retailing forms or concepts will probably develop outside the center. Such changes are socially desirable since they result from increased efficiency which generally brings merchandise to consumers at lower prices.

However, the established retailer is reluctant to adopt changes which disturb his smoothly functioning organization. For example, starting on a self-service basis differs from conversion to a self-service basis because it does not involve the discharge of employees or changing the physical layout of the store. The innovator does not have the problem of preserving what may have taken years to build; he utilizes innovation without concern for existing methods. Retailers of this type have enjoyed the greatest growth since World War II. Their thinking has consistently been in terms of a high turnover-low margin policy and not in terms of higher markups.

If regional centers follow a policy of excluding such retailers, their competition will only be intensified. Competition not only emanates from other regional centers, and it does not knock at the center gate and wait to be admitted. Outside retailers will have to compensate the shopper for giving up the conveniences of the center. They can do this and survive only by performing the retailing function more efficiently. In this rivalry the center merchant may find himself at a disadvantage, with higher costs than the excluded retailer who is not subject to center controls and higher rents.

The degree of control a center can exercise over a particular trading area is limited by the automobile and the availability of alternative retailing facilities. These facilities are rapidly coming into existence in the form of farmers' markets, mill outlets, smaller shopping centers dominated by discount houses and supermarkets, and retailers in free standing locations. Certain of these retailers using austere or primitive facilities seem to have gauged consumer preferences better than the developers of many elaborate shopping centers.[9]

THE PUBLIC INTEREST

Does the regional shopping center have any responsibility to the public in its selection of tenants? The answer would seem to depend upon its economic importance as a regional retailing center. The center attempts to reach its goal of beçoming the area's major retailing institution by developing into the civic, cultural, and social center for the region—as integral a part of modern life as were the Greek, Roman, and medieval markets and fairs. If the center reaches this goal, it might find itself vested with substantial public responsibility and subject to some degree of public control. Thus present tenant selection procedures could play an important role in determining the extent of public responsibility.

Legal Aspects

Much of the common law affecting trade emanated from the medieval markets which later developed into retail centers and were most influential from the twelfth to the fifteenth centuries. Legislation derived from these markets may become even more meaningful when applied to their lineal descendants, today's shopping centers.

. . . But when persons hold themselves out as dealing with the public, when persons desire to enter a trade or calling of their own choice, and when exchange (trading) is publicly conducted, property and persons become subject to the overriding law of the market. Under Anglo-Saxon law (which is the basis for the Sherman Act), everyone has of common right the liberty of coming to market to buy in competition with others. Everyone has of common right the liberty of access to the market, to buy or to sell, without monopoly control, concerted action or other restraints on competition . . .[10]

Power of Exclusion

Does the shopping center begin to assume the characteristics, importance, and responsibility of the medieval market if it is the civic,

[8] Edward M. Barnet, "Showdown in the Market Place," *Harvard Business Review* (July–August 1956), pp. 85–95, at p. 89.

[9] Morris L. Sweet, "Will Today's Farmers' Markets Become Tomorrow's Super Market?" *Printers' Ink* (October 12, 1956), pp. 28–31.

[10] Report prepared by Dr. Vernon A. Mund for the Select Committee on Small Business, U.S. Senate, 85th Congress, 1st Session, *The Right to Buy and Its Denial to Small Business*, Document No. 32 (1957), p. 74.

cultural, and social center of the community? Its economic importance may be the result of municipal assistance in rezoning, which enables the center to occupy the most strategic location in the region. Does an excluded retailer then have grounds for demanding admission to the center on the basis of common or statutory law? Obviously, physical limitations preclude the acceptance of all who might wish to become tenants. But does the center have a unilateral right to select and exclude prospective tenants? Several decisions, although not directly concerned with the shopping center as such, suggest the difficulties that could arise from arbitrary use of such a power. These rulings also point out the need for continued administrative review of tenant-selection procedures by the center management.

The Sherman Act

In *Gamco, Inc. v. Providence Fruit & Produce Building, Inc.* (194 F.2d 484, 1952), the Providence Fruit and Produce Building controlled the building and surrounding land where retail buyers habitually congregated and which had the best shipping facilities in Providence. Gamco, a wholesaler, leased space in the Produce Building, and upon affiliation with a Boston wholesale fruit and produce dealer was refused renewal of its lease. The State Supreme Court upheld a suit for trespass and ejectment, but the U.S. Circuit Court overruled the decision; the Supreme Court (97 L. Ed. 636) upheld the Circuit Court ruling.

The defendants contended that the availability of alternative sites precluded any charge of monopoly, but the court held that the availability of substitute sites was not an adequate defense. It was only at the Produce Building at which buyers gathered and which had the most economical transportation facilities; it was thus a monopolist's advantage to impose upon the plaintiff the work of developing another site.

The court further stated:

Admittedly the finite limitations of the building itself thrust monopoly power upon the defendants, and they are not required to do the impossible in accepting indiscriminately all who would apply. Reasonable criteria of selection, therefore, such as lack of available space, financial unsoundness, or possibly low business or ethical standards would not violate the standards of the Sherman Antitrust Act. But the latent monopolist must justify the ex-

clusion of a competitor from a market which he controls. . . . The conjunction of power and motive to exclude with an exclusion not immediately and patently justified by reasonable business requirements established a prima facie case of the purpose to monopolize. . . . (p. 487, 488)

The final judgment in this case (*U.S. v. Providence Fruit & Produce, Inc.*, C. A. 1533, District of Rhode Island, February 6, 1953) contained the following provision with implications for the limitation of center control over the operations of existing tenants.

IV. The company is enjoined and restrained from: . . .

(B) Interfering with or restricting any tenant in the conduct of its business; provided, however, that the Company shall have the right to promulgate reasonable, uniform and non-discriminatory rules and regulations relating to the physical operation of the Produce Building.

Another pertinent case is *American Federation of Tobacco Growers, Inc. v. Neal* (183 F.2d 869, 1950). The plaintiff, a farmers' cooperative, was refused selling time at tobacco auctions controlled by the defendant, a tobacco board of trade, and which was a prerequisite to doing business in the Danville, Virginia, market. The court held that the Sherman Act had been violated.

. . . A restraint of trade involving the elimination of a competitor is to be deemed reasonable or unreasonable on the basis of matters affecting the trade itself, not on the relative cost of doing business of the persons engaged in competition. One of the great values of competition is that it encourages those who compete to reduce costs and lower prices and thus pass on the saving to the public; and the bane of monopoly is that it perpetuates high costs and uneconomic practice at the expense of the public. (p. 872)

Another legal factor which might be considered is that of the state interest involved. Federal legislation may not necessarily apply to an intrastate shopping center, but most states have legislation comparable in many respects to the federal Sherman and Clayton Acts. "Some twenty-seven states have adopted constitutional provisions which condemn monopoly, restraint of trade, restraint of competition, price fixing, and in some cases, concerted action to limit output. . . . Some forty-one states, moreover, have enacted statutory provisions against such offenses."[11] There has been limited activity under the provisions of this type of legislation. Since there is no need for new legislation to be enacted, they may serve to facilitate action by interested parties.

CONCLUSIONS

The pertinent question at this point is what would occur if the philosophy of the regional shopping center were to change, and if those tenants now considered marginal were admitted to the center. The need for such change is foreshadowed by the incipient development of a new type of retailer, a combination of the supermarket and discount house. Supermarkets are expanding even further into nonfood lines to the extent of duplicating the merchandise lines of the discount house, and discount houses are expanding into food lines. The competitive problems of the regional shopping center would be accentuated because the combined supermarket and discount house offer more intense competition in all merchandise lines. The merchants in the center, besides being subject to higher costs which limit their competitive ability, were selected on the basis of a center philosophy of limited or planned competition. This orientation would contribute little in a struggle for survival.

The advantages of admitting presently unacceptable tenants are demonstrated by the increase in the shopper appeal of downtown areas when these retailers have moved into buildings formerly occupied by traditional department stores. Further proof is suggested by the consideration given to such retailers when

---

[11] Vernon A. Mund, *Government and Business* (New York: Harper and Bros., 1955), 2nd edition, p. 446.

the regional shopping center fails to meet its sales goal. If these tenants were admitted to the regional center at its inception, its drawing power would be strengthened by providing the shopper with a more representative and desirable selection of merchandise and prices.

There would be a favorable reaction on marketing costs as other center tenants are stimulated to reduce costs and are prevented from becoming complacent. The center could then absorb and utilize innovation instead of being threatened by it. Problems could arise for the developer, with the likelihood of retailers questioning the suitability of present rental arrangements which are based on the costs of building and operating the center.

The absence of the low-margin mass retailers makes the center attractive largely to the shopper seeking goods of limited appeal or regarding the center as a showplace. With the passage of time another type of regional shopping center may be planned without frills for the low-cost retailer, or some of the existing centers under pressure may be reoriented toward the low-cost retailer. The use of the automobile and the increased availability of comparative price information limit the power derived from location and distance. If the center is successful, outside retailers will demand changes in admission policies; and legal controls are a possible concomitant of a closed door policy.

A modified open-door policy that gives equal consideration to those retailers now considered unacceptable or marginal is necessary; the center cannot thrive as the citadel of the *status quo*. The regional shopping center can assure itself of a healthy and continued existence and make a contribution toward lowering distribution costs by encouraging the innovating entrepreneur.

DISCUSSION QUESTIONS

Professor Sweet is concerned with an "institution discrimination" which tends to work against the low-margin/high-turnover type of retail institution. If the planned regional shopping center is thus reducing price competition within the Center, it will probably not continue in its present form. Competing centers featuring the low-margin/high-turnover philosophy may evolve. Existing regional centers may (as some are) admit the types of institutions previously *not* permitted.

1. How has the discount operation grown and prospered in spite of discrimination against it in shopping centers?
2. How would you explain the policy of regional centers in not permitting discount operations within the center?
   (a) From the point of view of a consumer?
   (b) From the point of view of a member of the shopping center management?

Spatial Competition in Retailing

Spatial competition in retailing is competition which involves (a) the choice of a trade area or community within which to operate, (b) the selection of a specific site upon which to conduct a retail business, and (c) the arrangement of merchandise or "layout" of merchandise within the store. Each of these elements of spatial competition is an important part of the total competitive effort exerted by a retail store management.

This section examines methods and techniques for the conceptualization, estimation and evaluation of such trading areas. It examines principles or guides for the evaluation of particular retail sites. Included are materials which identify computerized techniques for the process of trade area delineation and materials which deal with the theory of trade area concepts and estimation. Trade area and locational problems which are of particular interest to shopping center and super-market management are considered.

1. Defining and Estimating a Trading Area

DAVID L. HUFF

Market analysts have long speculated about the nature and scope of trading areas. Such speculations have been based primarily upon conclusions drawn from empirical studies.

However, except for the "gravitationalists," few analysts, if any, have formulated their conclusions into propositions that are capable of being verified or refuted by empirical test. As a consequence, the conceptual properties of a trading area are extremely vague and perhaps in error. Furthermore, existing techniques for estimating trading areas are limited and subject to question.

The objectives of the present article are threefold: (1) to appraise the principal techniques used to delineate retail trading areas; (2) to enumerate significant conclusions derived from empirical studies using such techniques; and (3) to advance an alternative technique, believed to be better conceptually and superior predictively.

ESTIMATING TECHNIQUES

The methods employed to delineate trading areas, particularly retail trading areas, generally involve surveys or the use of empirically derived mathematical formulations.

Survey Techniques

Typically, in the case of survey techniques, a sample of individuals representing either households or firms are interviewed at their places of origin or at the particular firm or center for which the trading area is being estimated.

Such interviews are designed primarily to determine the kind or kinds of products that are purchased by each respondent, the frequency of patronage, and the home-base location of each respondent. These data can then be used to prepare a map from which inferences can be drawn concerning the nature and scope of the trading area.

As a result of trading area studies using survey techniques, a number of important empirical regularities have been shown to exist:

1. The proportion of consumers patronizing a given shopping area varies with distance from the shopping area.

2. The proportion of consumers patronizing various shopping areas varies with the breadth and depth of merchandise offered by each shopping area.

3. The distances that consumers travel to various shopping areas vary for different types of product purchases.

4. The "pull" of any given shopping area is influenced by the proximity of competing shopping areas.

A number of market analysts have attempted to generalize about the nature and scope of trading areas by citing *specific* conclusions drawn from such empirical studies. For example, it is often maintained that the trading area for a certain size of retail facility offering a particular class of products will encompass a radial distance of some specified number of miles, of which the primary trading area will involve a certain proportion of the total area, etc., etc.

But generalizations of this kind may be subject to a great deal of error because of differences among regions with respect to transportation facilities, topographical features, population density, and the locations of competing firms.

Mathematical Techniques

A few analysts have attempted to formalize some of the general conclusions drawn from empirical studies. They have expressed their ideas in terms of mathematical propositions that are capable of being tested empirically.

♦ SOURCE: Reprinted by permission from the American Marketing Association, in the *Journal of Marketing*, July 1964, pages 34–38.

The work that has been done in this area is limited primarily to the so-called "retail gravitationalists."

Notable among these is William J. Reilly who made a significant contribution by formalizing a number of empirical observations concerning consumer shopping movements between cities.[1] The nature of his formal construct is shown below:

$$(1) \qquad \frac{B_a}{B_b} = \left(\frac{P_a}{P_b}\right)\left(\frac{D_b}{D_a}\right)^2$$

where $B_a =$ the proportion of the retail business from an intermediate town attracted by city A;

$B_b =$ the proportion of the retail business from an intermediate town attracted by city B;

$P_a =$ the population of city A;

$P_b =$ the population of city B;

$D_a =$ the distance from the intermediate town to city A; and,

$D_b =$ the distance from the intermediate town to city B.

The extensive empirical tests of Reilly's model that were made by P. D. Converse are also noteworthy.[2] In addition, Converse is to be credited for making a significant modification of Reilly's original formula.[3] This modification made it possible to calculate the approximate point between two competing cities where the trading influence of each was equal. As a consequence, a city's retail trading area could be delineated by simply calculating and connecting the breaking points between it and each of the competing cities in the

region (see Figure 1). The breaking point formula derived by Converse is: [4]

$$(2) \qquad D_b = \frac{D_{ab}}{1 + \sqrt{\dfrac{P_a}{P_b}}}$$

where $D_b =$ the breaking point between city A and city B in miles from B;

$D_{ab} =$ the distance separating city A from city B;

$P_b =$ the population of city B; and

$P_a =$ the population of city A.

Limitations. The significance of the pioneering efforts of both Reilly and Converse to provide a systematic basis for estimating retail trading areas cannot be denied. The variables employed, the functional relationships advanced, and the estimated parameters provide precise and meaningful hypotheses that can be tested empirically.

However, there are several important conceptual and operational limitations associated with the use of the "Reilly-type" model.

First, the breaking point formula, as it now exists, is incapable of providing graduated estimates above or below the break-even position between two competing centers. See Figure 1. As a consequence, it is impossible to calculate objectively the *total* demand for the product(s) or service(s) of a particular distribution center.

Second, when the breaking point formula is used to delineate retail trading areas of several shopping areas within a given geographical area, the overlapping boundaries that result are inconsistent with the basic objective of the formula's use; to calculate the boundaries between competing shopping areas where the competitive position of each is equal. Furthermore, in the case of multi-trading area delinea-

---

[1] William J. Reilly, *Methods for Study of Retail Relationships* (Austin: The University of Texas, Bureau of Business Research, Research Monograph, No. 4, 1929).

[2] P. D. Converse, *A Study of Retail Trade Areas in East Central Illinois* (Urbana: University of Illinois, Bureau of Economic and Business Research, Business Studies, No. 2, 1943); and *Consumer Buying Habits in Selected South Central Illinois Communities* (Urbana: University of Illinois, Bureau of Economic and Business Research, Business Studies, No. 6, 1948).

[3] This modification as well as other changes that Converse made of Reilly's original model is well summarized in P. D. Converse, "New Laws of Retail Gravitation," *Journal of Marketing*, **14** (January, 1949), pp. 379–384.

[4] Converse did not demonstrate how he derived the breaking point formula from Reilly's equation. However, the proof of such a derivation is simply:

(i) $\dfrac{B_a}{B_b} = 1$ (v) $\dfrac{D_b}{D_{ab} - D_b} = \sqrt{\dfrac{P_b}{P_a}}$

(ii) $\left(\dfrac{P_a}{P_b}\right)\left(\dfrac{D_b}{D_a}\right)^2 = 1$ (vi) $\dfrac{D_{ab}}{D_b} - 1 = \sqrt{\dfrac{P_a}{P_b}}$

(iii) $\dfrac{D_b}{D_a} = \sqrt{\dfrac{P_b}{P_a}}$ (vii) $\dfrac{D_{ab}}{1 + \sqrt{\dfrac{P_a}{P_b}}} = D_b$

(iv) $D_a = D_{ab} - D_b$

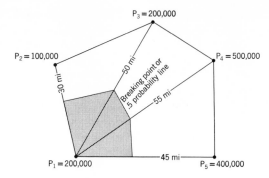

Calculation of Breaking Points:

$$D_2 = \frac{D_{12}}{1 + \sqrt{\dfrac{P_1}{P_2}}} = \frac{30}{1 + \sqrt{\dfrac{200,000}{100,000}}} = 12.4$$

$$D_3 = \frac{D_{13}}{1 + \sqrt{\dfrac{P_1}{P_3}}} = \frac{50}{1 + \sqrt{\dfrac{200,000}{200,000}}} = 25.0$$

$$D_4 = \frac{D_{14}}{1 + \sqrt{\dfrac{P_1}{P_4}}} = \frac{55}{1 + \sqrt{\dfrac{200,000}{500,000}}} = 33.0$$

$$D_5 = \frac{D_{15}}{1 + \sqrt{\dfrac{P_1}{P_5}}} = \frac{45}{1 + \sqrt{\dfrac{200,000}{400,000}}} = 26.3$$

FIG. 1. Estimating a trading area with the breaking point formula.

tions derived from using the breaking point formula, there may be areas that are not even within the confines of any shopping area's trading area. Such a development is certainly not very realistic. A visual exemplification of these conditions is shown in Figure 2.

Finally, the parameter which was originally estimated empirically by Reilly should not be interpreted as a constant for all types of shopping trips as so many analysts have assumed. It seems quite logical to hypothesize that such an exponent will vary, depending on the type of shopping trip involved. As a result, a distribution center may have several different trading areas corresponding to the different classes of products that it sells.

AN ALTERNATIVE MODEL

An alternative model will now be presented which overcomes the limitations described above.

The principal focus of the model is on the consumer rather than on the firm. It is, after all, the consumer who is the primary agent affecting the trading area of the firm. The model describes the process by which consumers choose from among acceptable alternatives, a particular distribution center (a firm or group of firms) to obtain specific goods and services. A formal expression of the model is:

$$(3) \qquad P_{ij} = \frac{\dfrac{S_j}{T_{ij}^{\lambda}}}{\displaystyle\sum_{j=1}^{n} \dfrac{S_j}{T_{ij}^{\lambda}}}$$

where P_{ij} = the probability of a consumer at a given point of origin i traveling to a particular shopping center j;

S_j = the size of a shopping center j (measured in terms of the square footage of selling area devoted to the sale of a particular class of goods);

T_{ij} = the travel time involved in getting from a consumer's travel

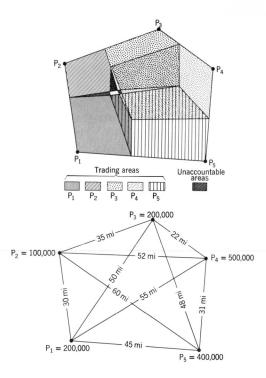

FIG. 2. Estimating multiple trading areas with the breaking point formula.

base i to a given shopping center j; and

λ = a parameter which is to be estimated empirically to reflect the effect of travel time on various kinds of shopping trips.

The *expected* number of consumers at a given place of origin i that shop at a particular shopping center j is equal to the number of consumers at i multiplied by the probability that a consumer at i will select j for shopping. That is,

$$(4) \qquad E_{ij} = P_{ij} \cdot C_i$$

where E_{ij} = the expected number of consumers at i that are likely to travel to shopping center j; and

C_i = the number of consumers at i.

In many respects the preceding model resembles the original model formulated by Reilly. It differs, however, in several important respects.

First, the alternative model is not merely an empirically contrived formulation. It represents a theoretical abstraction of consumer spatial behavior. As a result, mathematical conclusions can be deduced from the model which, in turn, can be interpreted in terms of their behavioral implications.[5]

Second, the alternative model estimates the likelihood of a consumer (P_{ij}) or the number of consumers (E_{ij}) patronizing a particular shopping area by taking into consideration *all* potential shopping areas simultaneously.

Third, the parameter λ is not assumed to be to the second power. Rather, it is assumed to vary with different types of product classes. For example, in an initial pilot study λ was found to be 2.723 for shopping trips involving furniture and 3.191 for trips involving clothing purchases.[6] The respective magnitudes of these estimates simply reflect the comparative amounts of time that consumers are willing to expend for each of these two product classes. The larger the estimated value of λ, the smaller will be the time expenditure. Similarly, the

larger the estimated value of λ, the more restrictive will be the scope of the trading area.

Finally, equations (3) and (4) enable a retail trading area to be graduated in terms of demand gradients. These gradients are expressed as probability contours ranging from $P < 1$ to $P > 0$. An illustration of how these contours look when mapped is illustrated in Figure 3, in which a partial retail trading area has been calculated for shopping center J_1.

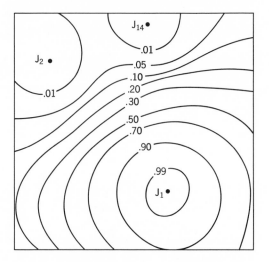

FIG. 3. A retail trading area portrayed in terms of probability contours. Source: David L. Huff, *Determination of Intra-urban Retail Trade Areas* (Los Angeles: University of Colifornia, Real Estate Research Program, 1962).

If the retail trading area of shopping center J_2 and J_{14} had also been calculated and superimposed over the trading area of J_1, it would be seen that parts of each shopping center's trading area envelop parts of the others. Furthermore, where these envelopments occur at intersections of contours having the same probability values, it would be possible to determine the breaking points between each of these competing centers.

GENERAL CONCLUSIONS

The following general conclusions can now be drawn concerning the nature and scope of a trading area:

1. A trading area represents a *demand surface* containing potential customers for a specific product(s) or service(s) of a particular distribution center.

2. A distribution center may be a *single firm or an agglomeration of firms*.

[5] For a discussion of the theoretical aspects of the model, see David L. Huff, "A Probabilistic Analysis of Consumer Spatial Behavior," in William S. Decker, Editor, *Emerging Concepts in Marketing* (Chicago: American Marketing Association, 1963), pp. 444–450.

[6] David L. Huff, *Determination of Intra-urban Retail Trade Areas* (Los Angeles: University of California, Real Estate Research Program, 1962).

3. A demand surface consists of a series of *demand gradients* or zones, reflecting varying customer-sales potentials. An exception to the condition of demand gradients would be in the rare case in which only one distribution center existed in a unique geographical setting, thus representing an absolute monopoly in providing products and/or services that are of an absolute necessity. Under these conditions, no gradients would exist but rather a single homogeneous demand plane.

4. Demand gradients are of a *probabilistic* nature, ranging from a probability value of less than one to a value greater than zero (except in the complete monopoly situation in which the probability value equals one).

5. The total potential customers encompassed within a distribution center's demand surface (trading area) is *the sum of the expected number of consumers from each of the demand gradients.*

6. Demand gradients of competing firms overlap; and where gradients of like probability intersect, *a spatial competitive equilibrium position is reached.*

Final Definition

Accordingly, a trading area can be defined as: *A geographically delineated region, containing potential customers for whom there exists a probability greater than zero of their purchasing a given class of products or services offered for sale by a particular firm or by a particular agglomeration of firms.*

This definition can be expressed symbolically as:

$$(5) \qquad T_j = \sum_{i=1}^{n} (P_{ij} \cdot C_i)$$

where T_j = the trading area of a particular firm or agglomeration of firms j, that is, the total expected number of consumers within a given

region who are likely to patronize j for a specific class of products or services;

P_{ij} = the probability of an individual consumer residing within a given gradient i shopping at j; and

C_i = the number of consumers residing within a given gradient i.

By comparison, the currently accepted definition of the term "trading area," as expressed by the Committee on Definitions of the American Marketing Association, is: "A district whose size is usually determined by the boundaries within which it is economical in terms of volume and cost for a marketing unit to sell and/or deliver a good or service." [7] This definition provides little insight concerning the nature and scope of a trading area. Furthermore, this definition implies that a trading area does not encompass the entire region within which potential demand exists, but rather only that portion which a marketing unit finds it economical to sell and/or deliver a good or service.

It is obvious, however, that in order for a marketing unit to determine the specific region that it finds economical for distribution purposes, it first has to assess the demand in the entire potential trading area. In addition, no matter what cost variable is considered, for example, delivery or promotion, it is very likely that the cost of the service under consideration will not turn out to be a very satisfactory determinant of any precisely bounded trading area as suggested by the Committee's definition. Finally, this definition conveys the image that it is the marketing unit that determines the trading area rather than the consumer.

---

[7] Committee on Definitions of the American Marketing Association, *Marketing Definitions: A Glossary of Marketing Terms* (Chicago: American Marketing Association, 1960).

DISCUSSION QUESTIONS

Why is it important to measure the boundaries of "trading areas"? Is your answer any different for "proposed" stores than for existing stores?

How would you expect the trading areas for each of the following types of retail stores to differ in terms of their size? Why?

1. An antique shop offering great and unusual assortments?
2. A super market?
3. An isolated discount operation serving an essentially rural area?
4. A large department store?

2. The Use of Credit Accounts and Computers in Determining Store Trading Areas

MANUEL D. PLOTKIN*

The store trading area—the geographic area from which a store draws its customers—is a fundamental concept in store location research. Basic principles for measuring store trading areas were first conceived more than three decades ago. Indeed, William Applebaum published an excellent article on this subject 25 years ago.[1] Many of the principles described in that article are still being employed by most professional location researchers. More recent advances in store location research have included contributions from a number of disciplines—geography, demography, economics, psychology, sociology, statistics, and mathematics. Nevertheless, store analysis—at the present stage of development—is still based more on empirical research than on accepted theory. And much of this empirical research is centered on the measurement, delineation, and analysis of trading areas.

This paper describes how one large retail organization successfully used samplings of customer credit accounts, an optical scanner, and a digital computer in a major empirical research program designed to delineate the trading areas of its stores and to obtain summary profiles of credit customer characteristics. Significant features of this research were that no customer contacts were made, key punching of data was not necessary, nor were extensive manual computations and tabulations required. Yet trading areas were determined for each of approximately 700 retail stores and major

demographic-economic characteristics of over 10,000,000 retail credit customers were summarized by store, by metropolitan area, by territory (or region), and nationally.

SAMPLING CREDIT ACCOUNTS TO DETERMINE TRADING AREAS

Before discussing the specific procedures employed in conducting the research program just outlined, it is appropriate to review briefly some findings from previous surveys of credit accounts for the purpose of delineating trading areas. Experimental surveys in several markets showed that carefully selected samples of customer credit accounts, when tabulated by census tract, postal zone, or other small geographic segment, could provide accurate data for the determination of store trading areas. These surveys indicated that although the distribution of customer installment accounts usually under-represents high-income segments and over-represents low-income segments of the trading area, revolving charge accounts have the opposite effect by over-representing the former and under-representing the latter. Simple arithmetic means of the percentage frequency distributions for the installment and revolving charge account samples were found to be good approximations of the distribution of the total customer population. This was confirmed by subsequent personal interview surveys which demonstrated that distributions of non-credit customer locations were indeed very similar to arithmetic means of the two kinds of credit account distributions.

Moreover, there are certain important advantages to the determination of store trading areas from a sampling of credit accounts over more conventional methods, i.e. in-store personal interview surveys or parking lot license plate surveys. These are:

* SOURCE: Reprinted by permission from the American Marketing Association, in *New Directions in Marketing*, Frederick E. Webster Jr., editor, 1965, pages 271–282.
* Manager, Market Research Division, Sears, Roebuck and Co., Chicago.
[1] William Applebaum, "How to Measure the Value of a Trading Area," *Chain Store Age*, Vol. 16 (November, 1940), pp. 14–16, 37–40.

a. No customer need be contacted—this eliminates any respondent bias that may result from customers that refuse to cooperate in personal interview surveys; at the same time interviewer selection bias is eliminated.

b. Store and parking lot surveys often are of short duration—usually a week or less—and thus are subject to biases that may result from special promotions, major holidays, or extreme temperatures that alter normal shopping habits.

c. Sampling from credit accounts gives each credit customer an equal opportunity of being considered in the trading area tabulation, no matter how often she visits the store. Store or parking lot surveys introduce a frequency bias; e.g., the customer who visits the store an average of once a week has a 5 to 1 greater probability of being included in the survey than the customer who visits the store once a year. Although personal interview surveys confirm that frequent shoppers have larger annual purchases than infrequent ones, total annual purchases per customer are not in direct proportion to frequency of shopping or anywhere near this ratio.

The purpose of the above discussion is not to argue that the data necessary for adequate descriptions of trading areas cannot be obtained by in-store personal interviews or by parking lot license plate surveys, but only to show that in some cases a sampling of customer credit accounts may be preferable.

COLLECTION OF DATA FROM CUSTOMER CREDIT ACCOUNT FILES

The experimental surveys referred to in the preceding section also confirmed that, given adequate instruction and an uncomplicated sampling procedure, credit department personnel at retail stores could be relied on to provide accurate customer credit account information for the research program outlined earlier. With this in mind, the following procedure was employed for the collection of data for this research project.

The credit department manager of each retail store was given the responsibility for the data collection from the customer credit account files of his store. He received a letter of instruction for the conduct of the survey, survey forms which were designed to be read by an optical scanner, and directions for the recording of the data. All survey procedures and forms were pretested by the corporate market research division.

Through systematic sampling techniques, representative samples were selected from the installment and revolving charge accounts of each store. The size of the sample selected from each type of account ranged from 500 to 1,500 depending primarily on the class of store (or assortment of merchandise carried) and the number of accounts held by the store. Individual store samples were later consolidated into an all-store sample of more than 700,000 accounts. This large number of accounts in the total sample was necessary to obtain representative samples of both types of accounts for each store.

OPTICAL SCANNER TO FEED DATA TO MAGNETIC TAPE

As noted earlier, special survey forms were designated to be read by an optical scanner or high-speed electronic document reader. The Docutran System—used extensively by Science Research Associates of Chicago in the educational field to score student test results—was employed to collect and transcribe the information from the source document to magnetic tape. Important features of the optical scanning device of this system were that it could (a) handle standard size, 8½ x 11 inch forms, (b) read both sides of the forms with only one pass through the machine, and (c) feed the data through a computer directly on to magnetic tape. Moreover, it was not necessary to use electrographic pencils to record the data on the survey forms; any soft lead pencils would do the job adequately.

A portion of the survey form—for the recording of information from one account—is shown in Figure 1. The survey forms were set up so that data from eight accounts could be entered on each sheet, four accounts on each side. Circles to be filled-in were spaced with no overlap of those on the front with those on the back of the survey form so that both sides could be read simultaneously by the optical scanner.

Name, address, employment, and occupation data were printed in the spaces provided as shown in Figure 2. The balance of the form was filled in by blackening the proper circles under each item. Information was recorded by blackened circles to show when the account was opened, whether the customer had moved since the original contract data, length of time

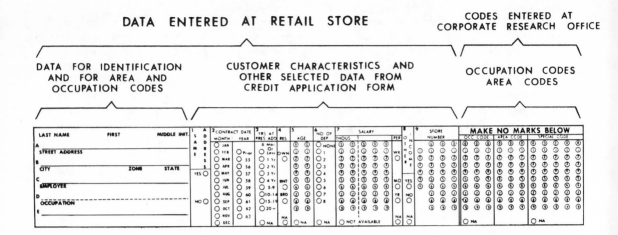

FIG. 1. One of the eight segments of survey form designed to be read by optical scanner. (This segment of form has been reduced to about 60% of its original size for this illustration.)

at present address, whether the customer owned his home, age, number of dependents, salary, whether there was other family income, and store identification number. All of the above information was entered by credit department personnel at the retail store.

The corporate research office reviewed the survey forms and completed the coding of data. Occupations were coded by means of a three position code consistent with Bureau of Census occupational groupings. Coding for residential locations of customers was accomplished by an eight position numerical code, with two positions representing state, three for county, and the remaining three for segment of the county—postal zone, suburb, or city. Although detailed analyses of city postal zone and census tract maps were required to develop the geographical codes, this work was essential to achieve the major purpose of the survey. These location codes became the basis for obtaining computer tabulations of the trading areas for each store in the survey.

COMPUTER TO PROCESS AND TABULATE DATA

An IBM 1401 Computer was programmed to produce an array of statistics and tabulations describing store trading areas and credit customer characteristics:

Trading Area Tabulations for Each Store

Tabulations were prepared to show the distribution of credit customers for each store by place of residence. The computer print-out listed the geographic segments of the store's market and recorded for each segment:

- the number of accounts and percentage to total store sample for installment accounts,
- the number of accounts and percentage to total store sample for revolving charge accounts, and
- the average percentage of the two types of accounts and accumulative total of this percentage.

The market segments together with the above information for each segment were ranked in descending order of average percent.

Subtotals were shown for the *primary trading area*, defined as the top accumulated group of market segments in which 75% of the store's credit customers reside, and the *secondary trading area*, or those segments which comprise the next 15% of the store's customers. The remaining 10% of the sample was defined as the fringe or *tertiary trading area*.

Credit Customer Characteristics

Frequency distribution tables were also produced by store for each customer characteristic listed in the form. In addition to the number of responses in each category, the computer printed the percentage of each response caption to the total number of responses. Here again, separate tabulations were reported for installment accounts and for revolving charge accounts. Summaries of these customer char-

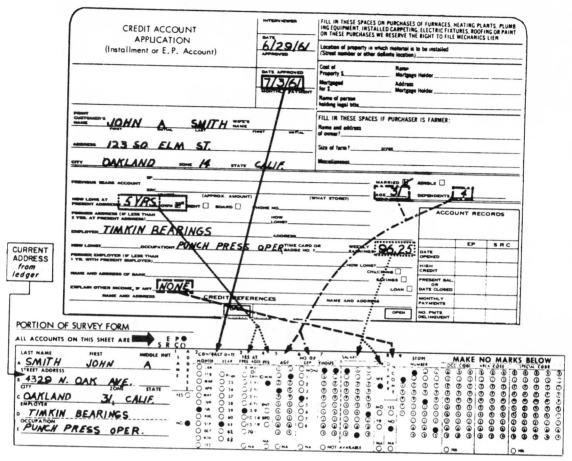

FIG. 2. Recording customer characteristics information from the credit account application form and the current ledger card to the survey form.

acteristics were prepared for metropolitan areas, regional territories, and national totals, by type of account and by class of store.

SALES PENETRATION DATA REQUIRED FOR COMPREHENSIVE ANALYSIS

The computer tabulations provide valuable information as to the approximate trading areas of several hundred individual stores. This furnishes the researcher with an important tool for the quick review of large numbers of markets and highlights areas of apparent weakness in market coverage.

However, in appraising sales potential and examining possible new store locations for a specific market, the corporate research department requires more data on present store trading areas than is provided by the computer tabulations. For a comprehensive study of a market, each of the following three factors are considered in the delineation and analysis of primary, secondary and, tertiary trading areas of present stores:

a. *percent of the store sales* attained in each segment of its market,

b. *geographic proximity* of each segment to the location of store, and

c. *sales penetration* of each segment expressed as per capita sales, percent of total consumer expenditures, etc.

As described earlier, the computer print-outs include estimates of percent of store sales obtained in each market segment. Adjustments for geographic proximity are easily made by reference to area codes and maps. Estimates of sales penetration require additional data and computations, but are necessary for an appraisal of the effectiveness of an individual store location.

The importance of reliable estimates of sales penetration to good store location analysis would be difficult to overemphasize. Descriptions of store trading areas can actually be misleading when used without knowledge of the sales penetration attained within segments of the market. Perhaps this can be illustrated by a simple hypothetical example—not remote from an actual market situation investigated recently. Figures 3 and 4 show the outline of the central city, the distribution of population, the location of stores, and the trading area boundaries of these stores in this hypothetical metropolitan area.

The trading area of a large department store located near the center of the city is depicted in Figure 3. This trading area is extensive, including virtually all major population concentrations, and gives the appearance of excellent coverage of the entire market. However, further analysis indicates that sales penetration obtained by this store is quite low and that no segment of its market is served effectively. This is largely due to the store's poor location in a deteriorating industrial belt; although only a few blocks from downtown, it is not in a pleasant or convenient area for shopping.

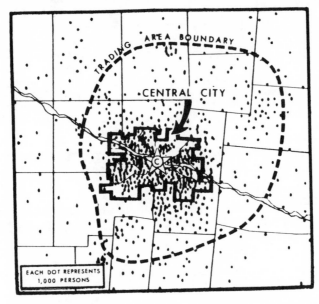

FIG. 3. The trading area of this centrally located store is extensive and gives the appearance of excellent coverage of the entire metropolitan area market. However, sales penetration was found to be quite low with no segment of the market served effectively.

A comprehensive analysis of the market resulted in a store location strategy which recommended closing the present store and opening three new stores in outlying locations as illustrated in Figure 4. The combined estimated trading areas of the three new stores is only moderately greater than the trading area of the one centrally-located store. However, substantially higher sales penetration would be achieved by each new store within its local market. Sales potential estimates indicate that total metropolitan area sales would rise to more than three times the present volume.

A number of different methods and techniques for measuring sales penetration and potential are employed by location researchers. The scope of this paper does not permit a detailed appraisal of these techniques, some of which in the author's view lack the necessary precision for sound store location analyses. One of the best discussions on the subject of sales penetration estimates is included in an article published a few years ago by Applebaum and Cohen.[2] As suggested in that article, and confirmed by our experience, a breakdown

---

[2] William Applebaum and Saul B. Cohen, "The Dynamics of Store Trading Areas and Market Equilibrium," *Annals of the Association of American Geographers*, Vol. 51 (March, 1961), pp. 73–101.

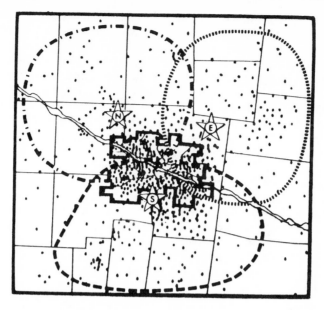

FIG. 4. By closing the present store and opening three new stores in outlying locations substantially higher sales penetration would be achieved within each local market. Sales potential estimates indicate that total metropolitan area sales would rise to more than three times the present volume.

of the trading area into relatively homogeneous market segments is usually essential for a perceptive analysis.

SUMMARY OF RESEARCH FINDINGS AND APPLICATIONS

The major applications of the computer tabulations and other findings of the research program described in this paper were as follows:

1. The markets for each of 700 stores were defined and the primary, secondary, and tertiary trading areas for each store delineated. Moreover, the importance of each market segment to the sales of the stores serving that market were determined.

2. Sales penetration estimates were developed which reflected how well each store achieved potential by segment of its market. These estimates provided a sound basis for the determination of potential for expansion of retail facilities in the same market and/or in similar markets.

3. Trading area tabulations were employed in estimating the amount of sales that would be transferred from present facilities if a new store were to be built in the market.

4. Valuable information was obtained on the characteristics of credit customers as to where

they reside, their occupations, ages, income levels, and other significant factors related to their shopping habits.

5. Important differences in the characteristics of installment customers versus revolving charge customers in terms of ages, incomes, home ownership, etc. were quantified.

6. Information on the characteristics of present credit customers also served as a base in interpreting national trends and changing markets and in determining implications of these changes to future retailing opportunities.

The results of this research proved to be of significant value at the local retail store level as well as to the corporate research department. Copies of individual store reports containing computer tabulations of trading areas and credit customer characteristics were distributed to the managers of all stores that participated in the survey. These reports thus provided additional knowledge to store managers about their local markets and helped many of them take effective action to improve market penetration and boost store sales.

Studies are now underway using the computer tabulations for more comprehensive analyses of trading areas to determine differences in the patterns of trading areas in markets where the company has one store, two stores, three stores, and four or more stores. No uniform patterns have yet been discovered, and none may result since a trading area is determined by many forces including the size of the store, the dominance of the shopping center in which it is located, topography and highway access, location and strength of major competitors, etc. However, some useful generalizations concerning trading areas in different kinds of markets have been developed and others appear to be emerging.

As a result of the research program described in this paper, and the continuing "long-range" research that we are now conducting, our store location analytical techniques have improved markedly. In addition, a better framework has been established for other major market research projects including customer surveys and product marketing research.

CONCLUSION

The trading area study described in this report is somewhat unique because of three factors: (1) the use of samplings from credit customer accounts is a variation from the usual methods of collecting data for trading area analysis; (2) the large scope of the project; and (3) the use of an optical scanner and computer for a trading area study. Nonetheless, the basic underlying principles are quite simple: (A) a wealth of useful research information is already on hand in company records; and (B) procedures must be adapted to fit the project.

There have been several occasions recently to re-appraise individual markets in order to evaluate the performance of stores opened since the original large-scale survey. In these particular instances a simple hand tallying of a sampling of credit customer addresses has proved to be the most efficient means of getting the necessary information. This would seem to indicate that a company of any size, large or small, can find a practical procedure for applying similar methods to an examination of its company records to define trading areas and summarize the characteristics of its own customers. This information should prove helpful in pointing to marketing opportunities which previously may have been overlooked.

DISCUSSION QUESTIONS

1. Is the basic approach that one might use to the estimation of store trading area boundaries different for the going concern than for the proposed operation?
2. How might one employ internal records to measure store trade areas?
3. Knowing where customers reside is one clue to action, and knowing what the socioeconomic characteristics of those customers are is another clue to action. Illustrate the way in which each of these "clues" may provide some competitive advantage!

3. Projecting Sales Potentials for Department Stores in Regional Shopping Centers

HAROLD R. IMUS

Since 1948, the planned regional shopping center has had tremendous growth as a major merchandising and investment vehicle. Projecting the sales potentials for department stores in such centers is becoming an increasingly more critical task in both department store and shopping center planning.

For purposes of this discussion, regional shopping centers are defined as planned projects usually under single ownership and having as principal tenant at least one department store branch with a store size in excess of 150,000 square feet of gross store area. These projects range in floor area size from 350,000 square feet to over 1,200,000 square feet. While this discussion relates to planned regional centers, the same general approach is applicable to calculating sales potentials for any branch store in any location.

BASIC MATERIALS

Development of sales potential projections for branch department stores in regional shopping centers utilizes as basic data readily-available information. The essential materials include the Census of Business, the Census of Population, highway access and location data, statistics as to the amount and kinds of competition in the area, and aerial photographs. Beyond these essentials, three other factors have major bearing on department store planning:

1. The share of the market which a particular parent store proposing a branch is already obtaining in its market area;

♦ SOURCE: Reprinted by permission from the editor of *Economic Geography,* in the January 1961 issue, pages 33–51.

2. The corporate image of the store as a merchandising vehicle, particularly if the store specializes in either very high- or low-quality merchandise.

3. Management's attitude to merchandising. This is important in determining minimum store size. A management may feel that a branch store below a certain size cannot be representative of the parent company.

SALES POTENTIAL PROJECTIONS

The procedures for projecting sales potential are based on the simple equation "Store Sales Potential Equals Total Market Minus Competition." Eleven steps are involved:

The Determination of a Trade Area for the Proposed Branch Store

Determination of a trade area is at least partly based on judgment. A number of observable factors must be considered. Primary among these are:

a. The arterial pattern.

b. The distribution of competition, both suburban and downtown.

c. The distribution of population.

d. The influence of physical or cultural barriers.

e. The strength of the parent department store, in terms of its share of the market and its ability to be dominant over other facilities of a similar character.

f. The distribution and levels of income.

g. The results of actual branch store operation in analogous situations.

Where the department store proposing a new branch intends to join an existing regional shopping center in which another department store already operates a branch, the trade area can be approximated on the basis of distribution of the present customers of the operating store. However, even this information may not be completely conclusive because there may be a substantial difference in the types of markets which the two stores are proposing to serve.

A correctly defined trade area will encompass the concentrated population contributing approximately 85 per cent of the sales volume of the branch unit after it opens. The remaining 15 per cent will come from widely scattered areas, even from as far as several hundred miles away.

Subdivision of the Trade Area into Sectors

The trade area may be divided into two to five segments for purposes of determining the relative contribution of the various population groupings to the proposed branch unit. Population living beyond the proposed location for the branch on the side away from the central business district is likely to contribute at least twice as much sales volume per capita as the population living between the proposed project and the central business district.

The sales per capita curve has a skewed distribution. The curve tends to be relatively flat at the top, falls off rapidly in the vicinity of the 10–12 minute driving time zone, and then flattens out with a gradual slope to about 20 to 25 minutes' driving time. Driving time distance will vary somewhat depending on type of arterial access and city size. Trade areas tend to be more extensive for larger shopping centers in larger metropolitan areas, and smaller in the smaller centers that serve smaller cities.

Determination of Population, both Existing and Future, for Each Segment of the Designated Trade Area

Projections based on Census material or other data are developed for the segments as a whole rather than by Census tract. The tracts having the greatest growth at any particular time are likely to be filled quickly as housing developers complete their projects. Growth then moves on to the advancing suburban perimeter.

Determination of Income Characteristics

Family and unrelated individual income information is ordinarily developed by using Census tract material where available, or by house value or other indicator where Census data are not available. Per capita income determined by this method is useful primarily as an index of the extent to which the population in a particular portion of a trade area differs in department store expenditure characteristics from other areas and from the metropolitan area as a whole.

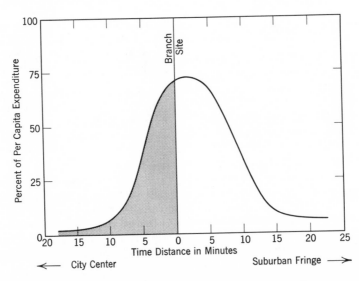

FIG. 1. Schematic distribution of department store spending at a branch store.

Establishment of Per Capita Department Store Expenditures

Per capita expenditures for department store-type merchandise are determined on the basis of Census of Business reports of department store sales adjusted by Federal Reserve Board index information for years subsequent to the Census. There are many pitfalls inherent in using these kinds of data, but they are about the only reasonably reliable data available.

Using the per capita income figures for the trade area and comparing them with the metropolitan area average, adjustment may be made in per capita expenditures for the trade area in question. Ordinarily, the markets which new branches propose to serve have per capita expenditures which are higher than the metropolitan area average.

The Bureau of Labor Statistics has published consumer expenditure data for ten selected cities in 1948 through 1949,[1] and in a subsequent study on 90 cities.[2] Studies were also done by *Life* magazine in developing basic data on consumer expenditure characteristics by type of merchandise.[3] All of these studies indicate that per capita expenditures vary with income, but not necessarily directly as income varies. In other words, high-income families may spend proportionately less in department stores than middle-income families. Low-income families may make practically no department store purchases because their orientation is toward local, low-priced general merchandise, variety, and apparel stores.

Estimation of Total Trade Area Department Store Sales Potential

Total sales potential is simply the product of population times per capita expenditures. Total trade area sales potential indicates the amount of sales volume originating in the trade area to be divided among downtown stores, existing suburban branches, and the proposed new facility.

Estimation of Sales Potential Available to Suburban Stores

At this point in the analysis, it is necessary to determine the probable proportion of total sales potential which suburban branch facilities can obtain.

The suburban store proportion of total department store potential varies from almost zero in many cities to as much as 70 per cent to 85 per cent in some parts of the New York metropolitan area, where nearly all major stores have developed significant branches. In cities of between 200,000 and 400,000, the suburban retention approximates 35 per cent to 45 per cent and in cities with population in excess of 1 million, the figure approaches 50 per cent to 65 per cent. The suburban retention estimates of sales potential are applied on a trade area segment basis (Table I).

TABLE I. Sample Department Store Sales Potential Calculation—1960

	Primary Zone	Secondary Zone
Trade area population	50,000	50,000
Per capita expenditures	$150	$100
Total expenditure potential	$7,500,000	$5,000,000
% Suburban share	50%	50%
Suburban potential	$3,750,000	$2,500,000
Effective competition	1,300,000	300,000
Unsatisfied potential	$2,450,000	$2,200,000
Branch store share	50%	50%
Branch store potential	$1,225,000	$1,100,000
Total branch potential— two zones combined		$2,325,000
Desired volume per sq. ft.		$50
Estimated store size in sq. ft.		46,500 sq. ft.

Estimating Competition and Its Effect on New Branches

Sales potential available to a proposed new branch is further reduced by the effects of both existing and proposed suburban competition.

---

[1] *Family Income, Expenditure & Savings in 10 Cities,* The U. S. Department of Labor, Bureau of Labor Statistics, Bulletin No. 1065.

[2] *Family Income, Expenditure & Savings in 1950,* The U. S. Department of Labor, Bureau of Labor Statistics, Bulletin No. 1097, revised.

[3] *Life* Survey of Consumer Expenditures, Volume I, 1957. Published by *Time,* Inc.

Existing facilities are measured in the field, and a sales figure of between $40 and $70 per square foot is applied to the gross floor area to arrive at an estimate of the effectiveness of the competition. Competing department store facilities are not likely to close their doors simply because another department store management announces its intention to expand. On the other hand, existing suburban stores are likely to face some decline in volume as the market is divided among all those stores capable of competing for a share of the total potential.

Estimating Branch Store Sales Volume

If the department store proposing the branch is weak, compared to its competitors, and all probable competitors are represented, then subtracting the total sales capacity of the competitors from total trade area suburban sales potential is likely to determine the maximum sales potential of the new branch, and its size. If, on the other hand, the store proposing the branch is strong, perhaps dominant, and its competitors are weak, or are not represented by branches of their own, the proposed branch will be able to obtain its reasonable share of the market almost without regard to competitors' present capacity and willingness to serve the needs of trade area residents. A strong store can obtain somewhere between its present share of the metropolitan market and double that share of the suburban sales potential at a well-located branch, provided the store is large enough to be representative of its parent store downtown.

Not all department stores present in a market are necessarily able to develop branch stores, no matter what the wishes of their management. Some of the stores in the larger metropolitan areas have such a small share of the market that if they should attempt development of branches, any such branches would be so insignificant in size as to function more as specialty stores than department stores, and would serve primarily the apparel market. In markets where one or two of the smaller downtown department stores find themselves in this position, it is probable that the stronger stores' branches will serve the sales potential to which they are entitled and, in addition, will absorb the suburban sales volume which the weaker department stores are unable to serve in the suburbs.

Determination of Branch Store Size

Store size is calculated by dividing sales potential by the proposed design sales volume factor. In most instances, this factor is approximately $60 per square foot of gross area, although it may range from $40 to $75 per square foot, depending upon management intent and the necessity to maintain or increase dominance and accommodate future growth potential in the area.

Checking the Conclusions

Having determined probable store volume and size, the question then remains of deciding whether or not the store size capable of support by the trade area is sufficiently strong to influence the area which it is proposing to serve. In smaller metropolitan areas, the total population which can be served in any one suburb is likely to be relatively small, so that the branch store will similarly be small. It is a matter of management decision as to whether the branch is worth pursuing, taking into account effects on the downtown store (the transfer of sales volume), and also the capital requirements and diversion of management's attention.

In many cities of less than 300,000 population, department store managements reach a negative conclusion and postpone branches, at least temporarily. This is especially the philosophy of the stronger stores, whose branches are usually their downtown parent stores' strongest competition. Frequently, the initiator of rapid branch expansion is a nondominant store, possibly the second or third store in terms of rank based on sales volume. Such a store might attempt to improve its position at the expense of the dominant store. The latter in turn might permit such competitive action without retaliation until such time as the competitor's branch units make substantial inroads into its sales volume. Then a major branch facility might be undertaken by the dominant store for defensive purposes. Dominant store management strategy in such cases emphasizes the fact that continued loss of position to competitors is worse than transfer of sales volume from the parent store to the branch store.

With respect to the transfer of sales volume from parent to branches, strong stores will face transfer in early years of branch operation of as much as 25 per cent to 40 per cent of suburban branch sales volume. However, with the passage of time and growth in the market as a whole, the transfer effect of branches disappears.

It is probable that in cities in which department stores are aggressively defending their position against the specialty houses and chain stores, there will be an increase in the department stores' share, collectively, of the total market. In this manner, the way may be opened for additional branch expansion and development of still more regional shopping centers.

A CASE STUDY

An actual case study, with the area involved and the name of the department store withheld, is included in this paper to illustrate the principles discussed throughout. The basic questions raised by the department store management for whom this study was prepared were:

1. How much sales potential is available in the trade area of the proposed branch?
2. How much sales volume would the proposed branch achieve in that location on opening and on maturity?
3. How large should the store be?
4. What will be its effect on the parent store downtown?

A SUMMARY OF DEVELOPMENT OPPORTUNITIES FOR STORE X AT RIVER PLAZA SHOPPING CENTER

The location being considered by *Store X* is the River Plaza Shopping Center property currently occupied in part by an existing shopping center development whose major tenant is a 200,000 square foot Store Y unit, and which is apparently capable of expansion to accommodate a *Store X* unit of comparable size, as well as some additional other retail facilities.

Access to the existing shopping center is adequate from all parts of the trade area. The development has a typical suburban shopping center characteristic in that over 90 per cent of the customers at the project reach the center by automobile. Public transportation is of little importance to the River Plaza Center. This is of special significance in view of the depend-ence of *Store X*'s other unit, which will be influenced by River Plaza, upon public transportation to bring customers to the store.

Trade Area and Population

The trade area which is tributary to the existing River Plaza center is relatively extensive, covering all of southern Bowman and a portion of southwestern Harris County, as shown in Figure 2. The existing project shows a high degree of dependence upon the primary zone of the trade area for its sales volume. A recent customer survey indicated that over 71 per cent of the total River Plaza customers resided within the primary zone of the trade area as it has been drawn here. An additional 14 per cent of the customers resided within the secondary zone, and the remaining 15 per cent resided outside of any logical trade area borders which could be drawn.

Trade area population at the present time is very high, totalling approximately 986,600, with 355,500 of these persons residing within the important primary zone. Population growth since 1950 in the trade area has been at a relatively high rate—8900 per year—but it is expected that this growth rate will decrease in future years, due mainly to the approach of population saturation in Bowman, and to a lesser extent in southwestern Harris County. It is expected that by 1960, the primary zone of the trade area will have a population of 373,300, increasing by 1965 to 400,000 and, by 1970, to 417,700. It is expected that the total trade area will have a population by 1970 of somewhat over 1,050,000.

Income and DSTM (Department store-type merchandise) Expenditures

Income levels in the trade area are relatively high, averaging approximately $2500 per capita in the primary zone and $2425 per capita in the secondary zone. The trade area average is somewhat over $2450 per capita.

It is estimated that approximately $370 per capita would be spent for major DSTM items by residents of the primary zone of the River Plaza trade area. Of this total, approximately $135 per capita would be spent in department stores, with the remaining amounts being divided among variety, apparel, and furniture and appliance outlets. In the secondary zone, DSTM expenditures would be only slightly

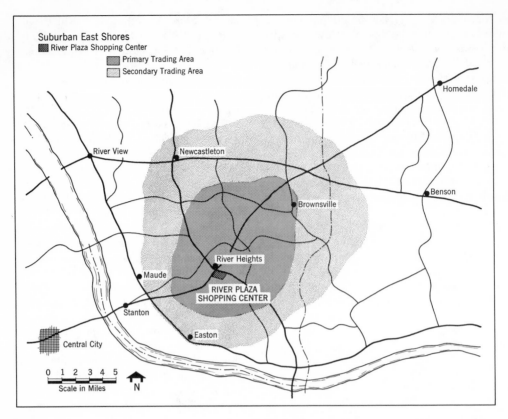

Fig. 2.

Sales Potential

less—$360 per capita—with the department store expenditures again approximating $135 per capita.

Sales Potential

As a result of the very high trade area population, the total department store potential generated within the trade area in 1960 is estimated at approximately $125,300,000, increasing by 1965 to $136,300,000. Of this total department store potential, it is estimated that about 70 per cent would be retained by *suburban* department store facilities. Thus, in 1960 the total suburban potential would amount to about $87,700,000, increasing to $95,400,000 by 1965. This potential would, of course, be available not only to the proposed store, but also to all of the other existing department store facilities in River Heights, Stanton, Brownsville, Newcastleton, and other retail areas in this portion of East Shores (Fig. 2).

It is estimated that the existing department store facilities (exclusive of those at River Plaza) which influence the River Plaza trade area comprise an effective competition for approximately $49,300,000 of suburban department store potential. Exclusive, then, of the volume which would continue to be available to existing stores, the unsatisfied department store potential from within the entire River Plaza trade area is estimated at approximately $38,400,000 in 1960, and $46,100,000 in 1965. It is estimated that the entire River Plaza project, including the proposed unit of *Store X*, could expect to obtain approximately 80 per cent of this total unsatisfied potential from within the primary zone and an additional 40 per cent from within the secondary zone. Thus, by 1960 the total development would have a department store potential of about $23,100,000, increasing by 1965 to $27,200,000. At a stabilized sales level of $60 per square foot, the 1965 department store volume would warrant approximately 455,000 square feet of department store space at River Plaza. Thus it is apparent that there would be adequate opportunity for a unit of *Store X* of approximately 200,000 square feet to be added to existing department store facilities at River Plaza.

TABLE II. Major DSTM Sales Potential (000's)

	Per Capita Expenditure	Total Sales Potential			% Suburban Share	Suburban Potential			Effective Competition	Unsatisfied Potential			% Center's Share	Center's Share		
		1960	1965	1970		1960	1965	1970		1960	1965	1970		1960	1965	1970
Primary Zone																
Population		373,300	400,000	417,700												
Dept. store	$135	$ 50,396	$ 54,000	$ 56,390	70	$ 35,277	$ 37,800	$ 39,473	$ 15,869	$ 19,408	$ 21,931	$ 23,604	80	$15,526	$17,545	$18,883
Variety	35	13,066	14,000	14,620	85	11,106	11,900	12,427	5,818	5,288	6,082	6,609	55	2,908	3,345	3,635
Apparel	130	48,529	52,000	54,301	75	36,397	39,000	40,726	17,622	18,775	21,378	23,104	60	11,265	12,827	13,862
Furn. and appl.	70	26,131	28,000	29,240	80	20,905	22,400	23,392	10,089	10,816	12,311	13,303	50	5,408	6,156	6,652
Total	370	$138,122	$148,000	$154,551		$103,685	$111,100	$116,018	$ 49,398	$ 54,287	$ 61,702	$ 66,620		$35,107	$39,873	$43,032
Secondary Zone																
Population		554,800	609,600	637,000												
Dept. store	$135	$ 74,898	$ 82,296	$ 85,995	70	$ 52,429	$ 57,607	$ 60,196	$ 33,467	$ 18,962	$ 25,140	$ 26,729	40	$ 7,585	$ 9,656	$10,692
Variety	30	16,644	18,288	19,110	85	14,147	15,545	16,244	11,077	3,070	4,468	5,167	35	1,074	1,564	1,808
Apparel	125	69,350	76,200	79,625	75	52,012	57,150	59,719	30,931	21,081	26,219	28,788	35	7,378	9,177	10,076
Furn. and appl.	70	38,836	42,672	44,590	80	31,069	34,138	35,672	20,448	10,621	13,690	15,224	35	3,717	4,792	5,328
Total	$360	$199,728	$219,456	$229,320		$149,657	$164,440	$171,831	$ 95,923	$ 53,734	$ 68,517	$ 75,908		$19,754	$25,189	$27,907
Total Trade Area		$337,850	$367,456	$383,871		$253,342	$275,540	$287,849	$145,321	$108,021	$130,219	$145,528		$54,861	$65,062	$70,936

The Share of the Market Available to Store X

In combination with *Store X* units in other parts of East Shores, the River Plaza unit could probably influence its trade area sufficiently to increase the over-all *Store X* share of the suburban market from 30 per cent to as much as 40 per cent. At the mid-point of this range—35 per cent—about $30,700,000 would be available to the *Store X* organization in 1960, rising to $33,400,000 by 1965. Of this total, *Store X* in River Plaza could expect about 75 per cent from the primary zone and 25 per cent from the secondary zone. In 1960 this could afford a volume of about $13,800,000 to *Store X* in River Plaza, rising by 1965 to over $14,900,000.

On the basis of a stabilized sales level of $60 per square foot, this volume would warrant a unit of *Store X* at River Plaza of about 230,000 square feet in 1960.

All of these calculations that have been described are summarized in Table II.

Conclusions

From the above, it is apparent that there is an opportunity for *Store X* to develop a major branch unit of a size at least comparable with the existing unit of Store Y, or 200,000 square feet, in the River Plaza Shopping Center at River Heights. This analysis of the volume potential available has indicated, however, that the problem of volume transfer from existing *Store X* units at other East Shores locations will be important in this situation. This is due primarily to the fact that there is some duplication of coverage of trade areas between existing *Store X* units and the proposed unit at River Heights. (In the complete version of this report, the question of the extent of volume transfer was considered in detail.)

DISCUSSION QUESTION

This is an excellent step-by-step discussion of the process of estimating trade area potentials for department stores. The "Case Study" is especially valuable.

What are the important steps in estimating trade area sales potentials?

4. The Logistics of Retail Location

BERNARD J. LA LONDE

In recent years much attention has been focused on the changing structure of the metropolitan area. These changes have been presented mainly in terms of shifting population concentrations. However, the impact of such population shifts in turn initiates a whole series of secondary adjustments designed to meet the needs of the changing population concentrations.

One of the most significant adjustments occurs in the retail structure of the community. The retail structure exists to serve the population of the area; and since it serves a definite need, it shifts in response to a change in that need. Many studies have indicated that the retail structure of a community arranges itself functionally, so as to best serve the needs of the community. Systematic patterns of functional relationships have been empirically established for the retail structure of the community.

The decentralization of the urban population within the metropolitan area has caused a similar decentralization in the retail structure of the community. Probably the outstanding symptom of decentralization has been the rapid growth of the suburban shopping center. Just as significant, though not as obvious, has been the growth of the retail structure along suburban streets and highways.

The retailer, in adjusting to the pressure toward larger-scale retailing and population moves to the suburbs, has been faced with a great variety of problems. Not the least of these problems has been what types of stores to build and where to build new stores. The suburban market, the suburban customer, and the suburban retail structure were new and unfamiliar arenas of competition for many merchants with traditional roots in the downtown commercial districts.

During the post-war decentralization of retail business, most firms at one time or another probably faced the following questions:

1. Where can I best locate to serve potential customers without weakening present market position?
2. What type and size store should be built consistent with merchandising policy and long-range planning for market development?
3. Within the framework of the preceding two questions, from where will our customer come? Will the downtown location lose volume to the suburban store?

THE RETAIL LOCATION PROBLEM

The continued growth of the shopping center movement, along with increased emphasis on large-scale retailing, has given rise to a number of retail location problems.

Saturation

The absolute amount of consumer expenditures for any segment of retailing is relatively fixed within any given trading area. This amount is fixed by: 1) the parameters of the trading area, and 2) the expenditure pattern of the consumers within the trading area. When the amount of retail facilities allow the retail segment to earn a reasonable average return on investment, the market is probably over-saturated (over-stored). It is, of course, entirely possible that a trading area might be unsaturated in one segment of retailing (e.g. drug stores) and over-saturated in another segment of retailing (food retailing).

Growth Potential

A retail facility is established not only on the basis of presently existing potential, but also in many cases on the anticipation of future growth. As the more densely populated areas

◆ SOURCE: Reprinted by permission from the American Marketing Association, in *The Social Responsibilities of Marketing*, William D. Stevens, editor, 1961, pages 567–575.

become saturated with retail facilities, more consideration is directed toward growth areas. Retail facilities are constructed, in many cases, far ahead of the market necessary to support the proposed facilities. This problem itself would not be a major consideration, in that many chains follow a policy of attempting to secure prime market position in anticipation of growth. However, careful analysis indicates that the typical situation is one where all retailers anticipate growth and all retailers establish facilities in the growth area. It is not unusual for this type of policy to result in permanent retail over-saturation prior to growth area maturity.

Market Myopia

A unique type of myopia affects many retail operations and developers. This weakness is particularly prevalent in chain operations and shopping center developers. The symptom of this problem is the conviction that everyone else is building too many stores or shopping centers, but he is just keeping pace with his share of the market or capitalizing on a real economic need. When this particular form of myopia is present in all of the competitors in the market area, over-saturation is usually the result. There is also strong tendency in this case to blame competitors for poor performance of both new and existing facilities.

THE RETAIL LOCATION DECISION

The retail location problem can be subdivided into two distinct tasks. The first task involves a general evaluation of the potential available in a competitive market. The question must be asked: Does the market contain enough potential to profitably support an addition to currently existing retail facilities? In other words, is the market presently saturated with retail facilities?

The second task involves the specific delineation of the potential market in terms of the exact location for the retail facility. The question may be posed as: Given sufficient potential, where is the best location to serve the available potential?

An additional problem is faced by the retailer with several units in the same general market area. The multi-unit retailer must evaluate a specific site, based on both the site's potential volume and its place in a multiple store network. The development of a retail unit for the multi-unit operation, then involves the question of individual site profitability and optimum network expansion.

Marketing contributions to the retail location decision revolve largely around a checklist of significant factors or gravitational models. While both the checklist and gravitational methodology can be useful in narrowing the range of the location decision, both methodologies rely heavily upon the subjective judgment of the researcher.

The gravitational model, based upon a variation of the principle of comparative advantage, was originally developed by William J. Reilly in 1929.[1] Professor Converse has suggested significant alterations to the "law," making it more applicable in specific situations.[2] During the past several decades new applications have been proposed to extend the usefulness of the gravitational principle to small retail clusters.[3]

The checklist methodology for the retail location decision has its roots in the early development of retailing. In 1885, Samuel H. Terry discussed those factors considered important in locating a store.[4] Included in his discussion were considerations of: the type of town, traffic volume and flow, city growth, store decentralization, acquisition, etc. Modern versions of the checklist approach are strikingly similar to Terry's presentation of significant factors.

A third approach to retail location has been generated outside the field of marketing. The third approach might be termed the "clinical" approach to the location decision. The methodology of the clinical approach is directed toward the empirical study of existing retail location patterns. The empirically established characteristics of existing retail locations provide a basis for generalization and prediction for proposed location decisions. The clinical

---

[1] William J. Reilly, *Methods for the Study of Retail Relationships Research,* Monograph No. 4, Bureau of Business Research, Austin, the University of Texas, 1929.

[2] Paul D. Converse, Harvey W. Huegy, and Robert V. Mitchell, *Elements of Marketing,* 6th Edition. New York, Prentice-Hall, 1958. See Appendix B pp. 746–750.

[3] Leon W. Ellwood, "Estimating Potential Volume of Proposed Shopping Centers," The Appraisal Journal, Vol. No. 4 (October, 1954), pp. 581–589.

[4] Samuel H. Terry, *How to Keep a Store,* 12th Edition. New York, Fowler and Wells Co., 1887. Chapter III "On the Choice of a Locality," pp. 40–50.

approach has been developed and presented in a discipline termed Economic Geography.[5] The methodology has been developed, and the research is being conducted largely by professionally trained geographers. To date the "clinic" for the research has been mainly the supermarket industry.[6] However, there are some indications in the literature that an increasing number of retail segments are in the process of being subjected to the clinical type of analysis.

In summary, it would seem that the field of marketing has not contributed significantly during the past several decades to the formulation of efficient methodology for the retail location decision. A new and promising area of investigation is being opened by the clinical approach to the retail location decision. However, the clinical approach to the development of store location methodology also has some serious weaknesses, as it is presently applied. One weakness involves a lack of operational definition in research methodology which makes independent research validation difficult, if not impossible. A second weakness is the heavy dependence of the clinical approach on the skill of the diagnostician. That is, there remains a good deal of subjective interpretation of results in the clinical methodology.

A MARKETING APPROACH

Elements of traditional market analysis and the clinical approach can be combined into a methodology for providing marketing insights into the location problem. A program combining elements of these two approaches would provide objective guidelines for the retail location decision. A proposed program of this type would require consideration of both the general evaluation of potential and the specific location decision.

In the following sections an attempt is made to provide a marketing framework or approach to the location decision. It is intended as a tentative guide, or proposal, for retail research, rather than a solution to the retail location problem. It should be noted that the examples used to illustrate the marketing approach are drawn from the supermarket industry. While the supermarket industry represents a fairly specialized segment of retailing, tentative research findings indicate that the proposed methodology with appropriate alterations can be applied to most forms of retailing.

The Index of Retail Saturation

The utility of measurements of market potential has long been recognized by alert marketing management. It is equally well recognized that the probability of success in obtaining a share of any given market must be carefully weighed against the resource investment necessary to obtain a share of available market potential.

A similar situation exists in the area of retailing. Any given geographic market contains a relatively fixed amount of market potential in terms of consumer dollars. The resources necessary to secure a share of the retail market will show wide fluctuations in different areas. While this fluctuation could be due to other causes, it is most frequently caused by the intensity of competition for the available market potential.

In the retail segment it is possible to calculate the amount of retail sales available in any geographic area with reasonable accuracy. It is also possible to quantify certain characteristics of retail facilities in any geographic area. These two factors can be combined to form an index of retail saturation. This index could be defined as: An index number providing a relative measure of retail facility saturation in any given trading area. Expressed as a functional relationship:

$$IRS = \frac{C_1 \times RE_1}{RF_1}$$

Where: IRS_1 = Index of Retail Saturation for area one

C_1 = Number of Consumers in area one

RE_1 = Retail Expenditures per consumer in area one

RF_1 = Retail Facilities in area one

Consider the following example in analyzing supermarket potential in Market A:

The one-hundred thousand consumers in Market A spend an average of $5.50 per week in food stores. There are 15 supermarkets

[5] William Applebaum and Saul Cohen, "The Dynamics of Store Trading Areas and Market Equilibrium," *The Annals of the American Association of Geographers*, Vol. 51, No. 1 (March, 1961) pp. 73–101.

[6] Saul B. Cohen, Ed. *Store Location Research in the Food Industry*, New York, N. Y., National-American Wholesale Grocers Association, 1960.

serving Market A with a total of 144,000 square feet of selling area.

$$IRS_A = \frac{100,000 \times 5.50}{144,000} = \frac{550,000}{144,000} = \$3.82$$

The \$3.82 per square foot of selling area measured against the dollars per square feet necessary to break even would provide the measure of saturation in market A. The \$3.82 figure would also be useful in evaluating relative opportunity in different market areas.

The sales per square foot calculation is a common measurement tool in the supermarket industry. However, the inputs into the system and the measurement of saturation would vary with the segment of the retail structure being analyzed. For example, in the case of the service segment of motels, "RF" might be calculated by available rooms during a given time period.

There are several problems of methodology that are immediately evident. Chief among these problems are: 1) the operational definition of terms and 2) the delineation of the market area. Careful development of methodology should either eliminate or minimize the above problem areas. It should also be recognized that the index of retail saturation is a static type of analysis and can be calculated for only one point in time.

The development of an index of retail saturation could have both practical and theoretical significance. The practical significance of the index would stem from its usefulness as a decision-making guide for the location analyst. From a theoretical point of view, the index could be used to study the relationship between retail saturation and characteristics of retail operation and competition. The relationship between saturation and price competition would constitute an important area of research investigation. Another tentative research hypothesis might revolve around the relationship between saturation and return on investment.

The index of retail saturation would provide valuable insights for the retailer into the evaluation of available potential in any market. It would provide a superior measurement to the simple analysis of market potential, since it would take into account both the demand side (potential) and the supply side (retail facilities) in evaluating a market.

The Store Location Type

After the construction of the index of retail saturation the retailer would still face the

problem of specific site selection. Borrowing from the methodology developed by the clinical approach, distinctive store location types can be developed. A store location type can be defined as a distinctive classification of stores possessing certain measurable location characteristics. The usefulness of the approach is probably best illustrated by presenting the results of a pilot research project concerning supermarket store location types. The complete methodology is beyond the scope of this paper. The purpose of presentation of this research is to illustrate the validity and usefulness of the store location type concept.

Fifteen supermarkets, all operated by the same chain, were selected in six different store location types. The store location type categories were established on the basis of: 1) the number and type of retail stores surrounding the survey store, 2) population density, 3) planned versus unplanned retail centers, and 4) traffic artery configuration.

The in-store interviewing was done in late 1959 and 1960. A quota type of sample with store sales as the criterion was used, resulting in 5300 customer interviews. The customers were asked a series of questions including their home addresses, and this information was plotted on a map of the area. Using 1960 Census Tract data and sample data, per capita sales were calculated for each of the survey stores. The per capita sales were calculated for three distance zones: 1) ½ mile radius from the store; 2) ½ to 1¼ mile radius from the store; and 3) 1¼ to 2 mile radius from the survey store. A mean average of distance traveled to the survey store by the nearest seventy and ninety per cent of the store's customers provided a measure of drawing power.

Tables I and II illustrate distinctive patterns of drawing power and per capita sales by store location type. The data were analyzed using Analysis of Variance and Correlation Analysis. The statistical tools indicated significance at the ninety-five and ninety-nine cent level in most cases. The factors of store size, competition, and population density were statistically analyzed in relation to the finding. No significant relationship between per capita sales and the above factors was in evidence.

SUMMARY AND CONCLUSIONS

In summary, this paper proposes a new method of approaching the retail location de-

TABLE 1. Drawing Power at 70 and 90 Percent Customer
Levels by Store Location Type

Store Location Type (Supermarket)	Drawing Power	
	70 Percent[a]	90 Percent[b]
Urban Strip	.38 Miles	.52 Miles
Urban Cluster	.43	.62
Small Town	.79	1.38
Neighborhood Shopping Center	.79	1.05
Community Shopping Center	.87	1.22
Regional Shopping Center	1.95	2.53

[a] Mean average distance traveled by nearest 70 percent of survey store customers.
[b] Mean average distance traveled by nearest 90 percent of survey store customers.

cision. The two elements of the method correspond to the two tasks (i.e. general evaluation of potential and specific delineation) involved in the retail location decision. The approach presented can have both pragmatic usefulness to the location analyst, and provide a theoretical framework for location research in marketing.

In the opinion of the writer, the location decision has been a neglected area in the development of effective marketing methodology. Retail research should receive increased emphasis for the following reasons:

1. Poor location practice results in economic waste, for which the consumer ultimately pays the cost.

2. The small retailer and the uninformed retailer are often the cause of disrupted or over-saturated markets. It would seem that the field of marketing could render a valuable service if practical methodology could be developed which would aid in the stabilization of the market place.

3. The rapid growth of cities and sprawling suburbs have compounded the problem of the city planners. The field of Marketing could provide a valuable service to the city planner in effectively planning retail service districts.

TABLE 2. Per Capita Sales by Store Location Type at ½, 1¼,
and 2-Mile Distance Intervals

Store Location Type (Supermarket)	Per Capita Sales[a]		
	½-Mile Interval	1¼-Mile Interval	2-Mile Interval
Urban Strip	$1.55	$0.21	$0.02
Urban Cluster	1.89	0.28	0.06
Small Town	2.46	2.64	1.64
Neighborhood Shopping Center	1.70	0.71	0.23
Community Shopping Center	1.58	0.62	0.20
Regional Shopping Center	0.45	0.27	0.16

[a] Per week.

DISCUSSION QUESTIONS

An extremely important consideration in the evaluation of a trading area is to estimate the strength of competition which exists or *will* exist in the area. Professor LaLonde's Index of Retail Saturation offers great promise in this regard. The concept of standard "location types" is equally promising.

1. Does the Index of Retail Saturation have equal applicability for all types of stores? Why or why not?
2. What is the most difficult element in the saturatoin index to estimate?
3. In Table I, there are some "standard" trade areas for some common "location types." What factors would serve to alter these figures in a particular situation? Be as thorough as possible.

5. A Realistic Division of Downtown Retailing

LOUIS C. WAGNER

The present Census definition of central business districts is too restrictive.

By confining "downtown" to areas of most intensive retailing use, presently designated boundaries tend to exclude many centrally located retailing establishments located on the fringe of the downtown area, appealing to city-wide or metropolitan area trade.

THE "CORE" AND "FRAME" CONCEPT

Recently studies analyzing the nature and composition of the central business districts (CBD) have advanced the "Core" and "Frame" concept.

The central business district *"Core"* is defined as an area of intensive land use characterized by offices, retail sales outlets, consumer services, hotels, theaters, and banks. This area is generally very compact and tends to be limited by pedestrian walking distances. This part of the downtown area is the hub of a city's mass transportation facilities, and tends to be more adequately served by mass transportation than any other section of the city.[1]

The horizontal size of the core does not increase with the growth of the metropolitan area. As population increases, there is a tendency for the area to grow vertically rather than horizontally. Land-use studies indicate that the core area generally covers a region not more than one square mile and tends to average about 30 square blocks.[2]

As applied to retailing, the downtown core contains establishments able to support maximum rentals and to achieve highest sales per square foot. This area contains mainly downtown department stores and all types of major apparel shops.

In Seattle, Washington, for example, the central business district retailing *"Core"* is a region of 18 square blocks located in the northern half of census tract M-1.[3]

On the other hand, the central business district *"Frame"* is an area surrounding the core and involving less intensive land use. While the core includes the hub of a city's mass-transportation facilities and while its horizontal area tends to be restricted by walking distances, the frame area is spread out horizontally because movements of people are mainly vehicular. Since adequate parking can be provided, this area has greater appeal to automobile users than the core area. In addition to containing a wide variety of retail establishments appealing to city-wide trade, the frame contains wholesalers, warehouses, intercity transportation terminals, light manufacturing plants, medical services, and multi-family dwellings. The differences between these two subdivisions of the downtown area are given in Table 1.[4]

From a retailing standpoint, the downtown frame contains types of retailing and service establishments not able to command the high rentals necessary to secure locations in the core. Due to lower land values, retailers in the downtown frame are generally able to provide more adequate parking than competitors located in the downtown core. The outer boundaries of the central business district frame are more difficult to determine than the boundaries

♦ SOURCE: Reprinted by permission from the American Marketing Association, in the *Journal of Marketing*, July 1964, pages 34–38.

[1] Raymond E. Murphy and J. C. Vance, Jr., "Delimiting the CBD," *Economic Geography*, Vol. 30 (October, 1954), pp. 189–222; Raymond E. Murphy, J. C. Vance, Jr., and Bart J. Epstein, "Internal Structure of the CBD," *Economic Geography*, Vol. 21 (January, 1955), pp. 21–46.

[2] Raymond E. Murphy and J. C. Vance, Jr., "A Comparative Study of Nine Central Business Districts," *Economic Geography*, Vol. 30 (October, 1954), pp. 302–330.

[3] *Seattle Central Business District: A Land Use Study* (Seattle: Seattle Planning Commission, 1958).

[4] Based on Edgar M. Horwood and Ronald R. Boyce, *Studies of the Central Business District and Urban Freeway Development* (Seattle: University of Washington Press, 1959), pp. 9–22.

TABLE 1. Primary Differences Between CBD Core and Frame

| | Primary Characteristics | |
Factor	In CBD Core	In CBD Frame
Land utilization	Intensive	Semi-intensive
Site utilization	Fully built on	Partially built on
Building types	Similar	Dissimilar
Growth	Upward	Outward
Business linkages	Internal	External
Parking space	Very limited	Generally adequate
Transportation mode	Pedestrian	Vehicular
Transportation foci	Intracity	Intercity
Boundary determinants	Internal factors	External factors

of the core. However, from a retailing standpoint the frame should include areas surrounding the core, in which the majority of retail outlets appeal to city-wide trade rather than to neighborhood or community shopping.

Beginning with the 1954 Census of Business, the Bureau of the Census has published central business district retail trade statistics for all cities over 100,000 in population. In 1958 these data were made available for 109 CBDs in 97 standard metropolitan statistical areas. In most cities the delineation of the central business districts was accomplished with the cooperation of a local Census Tract Committee, meeting with a variety of local interests.

Although the Bureau of the Census does not set up rigid specifications for defining a central business district, it does provide committees with specific guides to be followed when designating the scope of the area. It defines a central business district as "an area of very high land valuation, an area characterized by a high concentration of retail businesses, offices, theaters, hotels, and service businesses, and an area of high traffic flow."

In addition, it recommends that the central area normally be defined to follow existing census tract lines, by consisting of one or more tracts.[5] The Census designates Seattle's central business district (core) as census tracts M-1 and M-2.

By specifying that the central business district should be confined to areas of "very high land valuation," "high concentration of retail business," and "high traffic flow," the Bureau of the Census is in fact instructing local committees to include in the central business district primarily the "core" area.

As a result, it is of interest to examine retail sales in an area located on the fringe of the downtown core area. Special tabulations of the 1954 and 1958 Census of Business for Seattle permit separation of the central business district "frame" retail sales from retailing statistics normally published for a city. These special tabulations permit three different kinds of analysis:

1. Relative importance of the frame area in total, and by major categories of stores.
2. Distribution of sales by kind of store.
3. Changes in sales volume between 1954 and 1958.

COMPARISON OF THE SEATTLE CBD CORE AND FRAME

The central business district frame for Seattle, as defined by the author, includes census tracts L-1, L-2, L-3, L-5, M-3, M-4, M-5, O-1, O-2, and O-3.

Relative Importance of the Frame Area

In 1958 the Seattle central business district core accounted for 24.8% of the city's retail sales. Retail stores in the core area have shown moderate growth during the past decade; sales increased 5.1% between 1948 and 1954, and an additional 5.8% between 1954 and 1958. Seattle CBD core area stores experienced larger sales increases than most other western cities, partly because of an aggressive program of store modernization and expansion.[6]

---

[5] Central Business District Bulletins, U. S. Bureau of the Census, U. S. Census of Business, 1958 (Washington, D. C.: Department of Commerce, 1961).

[6] Louis C. Wagner, "Geographic Distribution of Retail Trade in Seattle Metropolitan Area, 1954–1958," Occasional Paper No. 15 (University of Washington, College of Business Administration, 1962).

Seattle CBD core area stores were relatively strongest in the shopping goods categories; core area stores accounted for over 60% of the city's sales in the apparel and general merchandise categories. Core area retailers also obtained from 25 to 30% of the city's volume in furniture, home furnishings and equipment, eating and drinking places, drug and proprietary stores, and in the other retail stores (largely other specialty establishments) categories.

Table 2 shows that the central business district frame, with nearly 20% of the city's total in 1958, was nearly as important as the core in volume of retail sales. However, the composition of retail sales in this area differed from that found in the core. Due to disclosure problems, special frame area tabulations were restricted to the 10 major categories of retail stores listed in Table 2. While less than 1% of the city's automotive sales were found in the core area, the CBD frame accounted for 41.4% of Seattle's sales.

In addition, while lumber, building material, and hardware dealers in the core area obtained only 7.6% of the city sales, frame area retailers secured 30.7% of the city's business.

A further examination of 1958 figures shows that CBD frame area retailers in the eating-and-drinking categories and in "other" retail store categories accounted for nearly as much business as did core area retailers. Retailers located on the fringe of the CBD core also contributed a substantial percentage of city sales in two other shopping lines, furniture and home furnishings, as well as general merchandise.

Further analysis of CBD frame sales in Seattle indicates justification for including this area as part of downtown. As is true of the CBD core area, CBD frame retailers in most convenience categories obtain a relatively small percentage of city sales.

TABLE 2. Retail Sales, Seattle Central Business District Core and Frame, 1958

	Retail Sales ($1,000)				CBD Core as % of City	CBD Frame as % of City	CBD Core & Frame as % of City
	Seattle	CBD Core[a]	CBD Frame[b]	CBD Core & Frame			
Total retail stores	898,750	223,109	174,095	397,204	24.8	19.4	44.2
Lumber, building materials, hardware	36,634	2,783	11,258	14,041	7.6	30.7	38.3
General merchandise group	172,729	103,959	29,754	133,713	60.2	17.2	77.4
Food stores	204,402	7,614	15,880	23,494	3.7	7.8	11.5
Automotive dealers	115,793	649	47,925	48,574	0.6	41.4	42.0
Gasoline service stations	48,749	1,897	8,037	9,934	3.9	16.5	20.4
Apparel, accessory stores	51,818	32,923	2,724	35,647	63.5	5.3	68.8
Furniture, home furnishings, equipment	48,654	14,714	9,160	23,874	30.2	18.8	49.0
Eating, drinking places	83,143	24,245	22,517	46,762	29.2	27.1	56.3
Drug stores, proprietary stores	31,139	8,130	2,228	10,358	26.1	7.2	33.3
Other retail stores	105,689	26,195	24,612	50,807	24.8	23.3	48.1

[a] U.S. Bureau of the Census, U.S. Census of Business, 1958; Vol. 7, Central Business District Report, Seattle, Washington, Area—BC58-CBD80 (Washington, D.C., 1961), p. 6.
[b] Special tabulations.

Distribution of Sales by Kind of Store

When the distribution of sales by kind of store is examined for the central business district core and frame (see Table 3), some interesting differences are found.

Two major categories of retailers, general merchandise and apparel, account for over 60% of total business in the central business core. These types of stores have high sales volume per square foot and are able generally to pay the highest rentals. In the frame area, these two categories of stores account for less than 20% of the total sales.

In the frame area, retailing is spread among a greater variety of shopping goods stores. While automotive establishments contribute 27.5% of the total sales, only three other categories—general merchandise, other retail stores, and eating-and-drinking establishments—account for more than 10% of the total. Of all of the shopping goods establishments, apparel stores appear to be least important, and contribute only 1.5% of the frame's sales.

Change in Sales Volume

As shown in Table 4, between 1954 and 1958 retail sales in the central business district frame increased 13.3%—over twice the rate of

TABLE 3. Percentage Distribution of Retail Sales by Kind of Business, Seattle Central Business District Core and Frame, 1954–1958

	% of Total Retail Sales	
	CBD Core	CBD Frame
Total retail stores	100.0	100.0
Lumber, building materials, hardware	1.2	6.5
General merchandise group	46.6	17.1
Food stores	3.4	9.1
Automotive dealers	.3	27.5
Gasoline service stations	.9	4.6
Apparel, accessory stores	14.8	1.6
Furniture, home furnishings, equipment	6.6	5.3
Eating, drinking places	10.9	12.9
Drug stores, proprietary stores	3.6	1.3
Other retail stores	11.7	14.1

TABLE 4. Change in Retail Sales by Kind of Business, Seattle Central Business District Core and Frame, 1954–1958

	CBD Core Sales ($1,000)		CBD Frame Sales ($1,000)		% Change, 1954–58	
	1954	1958	1954	1958	Core	Frame
Total retail stores	210,921	223,109	153,644	175,095	5.8	13.3
Lumber, building materials, hardware	2,865	2,783	9,284	11,258	−2.9	21.3
General merchandise group	92,224	103,959	13,892	29,754	12.7	114.2
Food stores	9,372	7,614	15,498	15,880	−18.8	2.5
Automotive dealers	152	649	58,443	47,925	327.0	−18.0
Gasoline service stations	1,950	1,897	8,488	8,037	−2.7	−5.4
Apparel, accessory stores	35,552	32,923	1,839	2,724	−7.4	48.1
Furniture, home furnishings, equipment	12,775	14,714	5,454	9,160	15.2	67.9
Eating, drinking places	24,254	24,245	18,448	22,517	−.1	22.0
Drug stores, proprietary stores	7,577	8,130	2,590	2,228	7.3	−14.0
Other retail stores	24,200	26,195	19,728	24,612	8.2	24.8

increase shown by the central business district core.

While increased sales were registered for five categories in the core area, seven types registered sales increases in the CBD frame. With the exception of automobiles, all types of shopping goods establishments in the frame area registered sales gains.

Two categories, which are important in the core area, general merchandise and apparel stores, registered substantial percentage increases in frame area stores. It appears that the growth in these two categories in the fringe area occurred among low-priced promotional outlets and discount stores.

Eating-and-drinking establishments, another important classification of outlets, also registered above average sales increases during the 4-year period. In addition to declines in fringe area automotive sales, declines were experienced in gasoline service stations and drug outlets; these latter two categories appeal primarily to local residents rather than to city-wide trade.

IMPLICATIONS

It is difficult to generalize regarding the characteristics of the central business district "frame" based on an analysis of retailing areas in one city.

Nevertheless, it appears that the addition of the frame to the downtown core will provide a more comprehensive picture of all retailing facilities attracting business from the entire metropolitan area. In addition, the inclusion of the frame area may make possible more uniform comparisons of downtown retailing facilities in one city as compared with another.

In some cities the boundaries of central business districts include some frame establishments, particularly automotive, while in others present boundaries exclude these outlets. By adding all frame area retailers to present facilities classified as downtown, a more valid comparison of central business district sales between cities will be possible.

DISCUSSION QUESTIONS

The central business district is one of the oldest and still one of the most important "institutions" of American retailing. From the standpoint of analyzing retailing activities and appraising retailing opportunities, The Central Business District is profitably viewed as two basically dissimilar elements—the "core" and the "frame."

1. Table I suggests the principal differences between the CBD "core" and the CBD "frame" concepts. To be sure that you understand some of these differences, provide examples of the following:
   a. Internal "business linkages" and external "business linkages."
   b. Intracity "Transportation Focus" and intercity "Transportation Focus."
2. How would you expect convenience goods to be distributed between the "core", the "frame" and the "rest of the city"? How would you expect shopping goods to be distributed between these three areas? Check your answers with Table 3.

6. Principles of Retail Location

RICHARD LAWRENCE NELSON*

The decision to locate a store may arise in a large variety of situations. The retailer makes this decision every time he signs a new lease, because he is "locating his store" with that signature, even though he may have been in the same place for many years. The retailer who owns his own building "locates" his business every morning when he unlocks the front door. Thus, the decision to select a location is made with great frequency, even though it may be an unconscious decision, manifested merely by an unwillingness to move. The wise retailer analyzes his location periodically with the same care as if he were locating a new store. Many grocery or variety chains re-analyze all of their locations every year or two to find potential gaps in the market saturation pattern, to change some units to better locations, and to eliminate poor locations. Some chains do this work themselves, others use consultants. The principles followed in reaching a decision to remain in a location are the same as those for selecting a new one, and they should be applied continually. Only too infrequently, however, does the "selection" of an existing location involve adequate study.

A much higher percentage of new locations are given thorough analysis. There are two types of site selection procedures. One is to undertake a scientific analysis of the market served and desired to be served, laying out a pattern of areas in which a store should be located or relocated by cataloging all possible sites and preparing volume estimates for each to determine the best. The other procedure is for the retailer to make his interest in a new location known among real estate men or others and to study the proposals submitted. Volume estimate potentials can then be prepared on those locations which appear most desirable,

for the purpose of selecting the best of those proposed.

The first technique, in which the retailer retains the initiative and does an over-all scientific job, is to be preferred from the standpoint of achieving maximum business volume and market saturation. The second has the advantage of leaving the retailer in a better negotiating or bargaining position, as the initiative then rests with the building owner or developer. The most successful of the chains use a combination of these procedures, in order to maximize volume and retain bargaining power at the same time.

The need for relocation may come about because a store requires additional space which cannot be obtained at its current site or because experience has proved that the existing location is inadequate. Sometimes the rent is too high, or the landlord will not renew the lease, or the building is destroyed by fire. All of these come under the heading of "changing location." New locations, on the other hand, involve retailers who are establishing a business for the first time or already own a store or chain but wish to have an additional outlet.

It is not only the retailer who "locates." The realtor or building owner is also responsible for locating a store when he rents store space or sells a building. Much the same sort of site selection technique applies in selecting the kind of occupant who will be the best rent producer and at the same time benefit other tenant stores. The landlord follows the same procedure when he renews the lease of an existing tenant. The developer, in choosing a site and then either selling buildings or selecting tenants, also uses these techniques in order to maximize his own profit.

THE EIGHT PRINCIPLES

Whatever the occasion or motive for locating a store, there are eight principles which must be observed in applying selection criteria to each specific site.

◆ SOURCE: Reprinted by permission from the McGraw-Hill Book Company, in *The Selection of Retail Locations*, 1958, pages 51–56 and 65–68.
* F. W. Dodge Corp.

I. Adequacy of Present Trading Area Potential

The first step in determining the volume of business which can be done at a given location involves counting the people in the trading area and finding out in detail how much money they have to spend and are willing to spend for the type of goods purveyed by the store under study. This step answers the question, "If we secure all the business available in this trading area, how much would it amount to?" The rest of the analysis of a site has principally to do with determining how much of the total business can be captured by an outlet there.

II. Accessibility of Site to Trading Area

One of the chief reasons for choosing a particular site is to secure the maximum accessibility and thereby to have available as much of the business potential as possible. The choice may be positive, in an attempt to put a store in the way of as many people as possible —to try to find a location which people are forced to pass or come near to—or it may be negative, merely involving a site which is not inaccessible. Accessibility must be measured in terms of the source of various types of business. First the potential from various sources must be isolated and then the possible capture estimated for each source.

Generative business (produced by the store itself through heavy advertising, by a reputation for unique merchandise, or in other promotional ways) must be calculated for each segment of the trading area. Public knowledge that a large variety of merchandise is available in one spot is of itself generative. This is a basic factor in the generative power of a department store, which is really a bazaar of departments carrying clothing, jewelry, furniture, appliances, housewares, and other goods —frequently the same type of merchandise carried by other, more specialized, stores nearby. A store that generates all its own business wants to be in the most accessible location commensurate with cost. The automobile showroom or discount house which generates 95 per cent of its business through heavy advertising expenditures might find the most accessible location at the junction of two major streets or highways. The corner at such an intersection, however, is likely to be priced at several times that of an equivalent noncorner piece of land nearby. The slight decline in accessibility of the off-corner location may be more than compensated for by lower costs.

Shared business (secured by a retail store as the result of the generative power of its neighbors) must also be isolated. Loosely speaking, this business is represented by customers who, although making purchases at the store under study, have as their principal purpose in being in the vicinity a visit to a neighboring store. A large part of the business volume of a drugstore located in the heart of the downtown retail district of a large city will come from this source.

Suscipient business (not generated by the store itself or by neighboring retail establishments) can be tabulated. This business comes from people whose principal purpose in being at or near the store is other than buying. As previously mentioned a virtually 100 per cent suscipient business is the newsstand at an airport. It does no advertising, generates no business, is merely a service to travelers. As will be seen later, some downtown stores specifically serve working population and do not generate business—that is, they do not attract people directly from their homes. For stores like these, it is not enough that the location is not inaccessible: the accessibility requirements become so specific that they can perhaps be satisfied only at a single site and at no other.

In most stores, the volume is made up of a combination of all three types of business— generative, shared, and suscipient—and the evaluation of a site's accessibility must take them all into consideration.

III. Growth Potential

It is characteristic of retail business in recent years that profit ratios have declined continually—sometimes gradually, sometimes more rapidly. In order for a retail store, therefore, to maintain dollar profits or to increase them, it must at the same time increase total business volume. It is because of the demanding nature of this trend that many large chains have decided to expand rapidly; frequently this has been accomplished through the purchase of smaller chains or independent stores. Consequently, one of the principles of retail store location is that, as far as possible, the site should be in a trading area of growing population and income.

IV. Business Interception

People tend to continue to go to a traditional source of goods, one to which they have become habituated. In selecting a site according to the principle of business interception, the procedure is to establish oneself between the market (the people in the trading area) and the market place (the traditional source of the same goods), so that the customers will be intercepted on their way in to the market place. Although tending to follow ingrained habits and customs and circulation patterns which may revolve around older stores in established business districts, people will rarely go through a business district or pass by a shopping center or store to get exactly the same product (in as pleasant an atmosphere) farther on. It is much easier to stop them en route, as it were, than to pull them off or away from a beaten path.

V. Cumulative Attraction

In making a site selection, sometimes a choice must be made between taking advantage of the principle of cumulative attraction and that of interception. There are two types of cumulative attraction: one involves similar units which, together, can draw more business than apart; the other, complementary units, that is, compatible units with a high incidence of customer interchange. Both types represent shared business.

VI. Compatibility

In site selection, the principle of compatibility requires that there be no interruption in shopper traffic and that customer interchange be at a maximum. The rules of compatibility indicate that maximum business potential is available in such a location.

The Principle of Compatibility. Some businesses are compatible, others are not. The measure of their compatibility lies in the answer to the questions: "Does Business A next door help Business B? Does it harm Business B, or does it apparently have no effect on Business B?" Sometimes the answer may be the single most important locational factor in the success of a retail business. The experienced shopping center developer takes compatibility carefully into account in planning the placement of stores, and the individual retailer should give it equal attention in selecting his location. Even planning commissions are beginning to consider compatible store groupings when laying out use districts in modern zoning ordinances.

A high degree of compatibility exists between two businesses which, because of their adjacency, do more volume together than they would if separated. This high compatibility may come about because the businesses are complementary in nature or because, though competitive, they carry goods of different styles, lines, and prices, thereby increasing total patronage through cumulative attraction in locations that have a trade area adequate to support two stores. The measure of compatibility is the degree to which the two businesses interchange customers. An analysis by the author of several hundred business districts and shopping centers, and a study of more than 10,000 individual shopping trips, has demonstrated that there is a direct relationship between the rate of interchange in two establishments and their business volume.

The Rule of Retail Compatibility. The rule of retail compatibility may be stated as follows:

Two compatible businesses located in close proximity will show an increase in business volume directly proportionate to the incidence of total customer interchange between them, inversely proportionate to the ratio of the business volume of the larger store to that of the smaller store, and directly proportionate to the sum of the ratios of purposeful purchasing[*] to total purchasing in each of the two stores.

These relationships may be expressed in the equation:

$$V = I(V_L + V_s) \times \frac{V_s}{V_L} \times \left(\frac{P_L}{V_L} \frac{P_s}{V_s} \right)$$

in which: V_L = volume of larger store (total purchasing)

P_L = purposeful purchasing in larger store

V_s = volume of smaller store (total purchasing)

P_s = purposeful purchasing in smaller store

V = increase in total volume of two stores

I = degree of interchange

If there are two retail stores side by side and one customer in 100 makes a purchase in both, the rule indicates that together they will do 1 per cent more business than if separated by such a distance as to make this interchange

---

[*] A purposeful purchase is one made by a shopper who, when interviewed, states that a visit to the store was a major purpose of the shopping trip. Total purchases, of course, include incidentals and impulse purchases as well.

impossible or unlikely. If one customer in ten makes purchases in both stores, their total increase in business will be about 10 per cent. Theoretically, if every customer bought in both stores, their total business volume would double, if both businesses did about the same dollar volume.

However, a very large store and a very small store would not show the same total increase as two stores of equivalent size. For example, if a department store doing $5,000,000 worth of retail volume a year were next door to a variety store doing $500,000 a year, their total would not double even with a 100 per cent interchange of customers. If their customer interchange were on the order of 25 out of 100, the total increase in business for the two establishments would be directly proportionate to the interchange, or 25 per cent, but inversely proportionate to the ratio of their volumes, which is 10:1. Thus the total increase would equal one-tenth of 25 per cent, or 2.5 per cent. If, however, interviews showed purposeful purchasing at the department store and the variety store to be, respectively, on the order of 90 per cent and 15 per cent of total purchasing, the 2.5 per cent increase would have to be multiplied by 105 per cent. Thus, these two stores together would show a business increase of $2.5 \times 1.05 = 2.625$ per cent of the total of $5,500,000, or an additional $144,375. This is not a measure of market potential. All compatibility determinations assume that an adequate market exists.

Two shoe stores are compatible with each other. So are ten. Whether there should be one, two, or ten, however, must be determined by the market potential. Compatibility calculations depend on the theory of cumulative attraction, which, like other aspects of location study, cannot stand independently. Two businesses that are compatible will do better side by side, other things being equal.

VII. Minimizing of Competitive Hazard

The site selection and business volume projections should take into account the location, character, size, and type of existing competitive units, and possible business losses to these units should, of course, be considered. There may, however, also be vacant stores or sites which could be occupied in the future by competitive units. The principle of minimizing competitive hazard should lead the prospective retailer, other things equal, to (1) select a location near which there are as few such competitive sites as possible; (2) consider the feasibility of controlling or earmarking the use of such sites for non-competitive purposes; and (3) select a location in which the competitive sites are in nonintercepting positions.

VIII. Site Economics

The application of the principle of site economics, the final step, involves analysis of the site in terms of the relation of its cost to its productivity. The efficiency of the site, its size, shape, topography, and load-bearing qualities, adjacent amenities like street lighting, availability of utilities, condition of sidewalk and street, and other immediate off-site factors which affect its cost or desirability must be examined in detail. Under this heading also come the effectiveness and cost of any existing building which might be rented or purchased by a retailer. He must study the size and efficiency of the building, the load-bearing quality of its floors, its modernity, the character of its store front, heating and air-conditioning facilities, attractiveness, cost of maintenance and all other factors going into building valuation. (Also to be considered are such items as availability of labor and adequate advertising media.)

IX. Pedestrian Interruptions

In addition to business interchange, there is another group of factors used in measuring compatibility. These are negative and tend to reduce the business of neighboring establishments. For example, it is a principle of trade that interruptions in pedestrian traffic flow harm adjacent retail establishments. Such interruptions may be created by: (1) dead spots where a shopper loses interest in going farther (pedestrians dislike dead frontage); (2) driveways and other physical breaks in the sidewalk; (3) cross traffic, either vehicular or pedestrian; (4) areas that are identified with hazard, noise, odor, unsightliness, or other pedestrian-inhibiting qualities; (5) businesses which generate traffic in the form of trucks, public vehicles, private automobiles, or pedestrians who are not shoppers, and which tend, therefore, to create congestion; (6) businesses whose customers' average parking time is extremely long.

In this connection, it is interesting to observe that the same facility may be compatible in some situations but detrimental in others. In places where parking is short, a parking garage or lot makes a highly desirable neighbor for stores. But if this parking facility has a long "curb cut"—that is, a big driveway lead-in over the sidewalk—it becomes highly incompatible for those retailers who are situated so that the curb cut is between them and the major generators in the shopping center. The effect on pedestrians is similar to that of a street crossing, and in some respects is even worse. The harm done by the driveway can be gaged just by watching mothers clutch the hands of small children as they go past.

DISCUSSION QUESTIONS

The eight principles of location which Mr. Nelson outlines presumably involve a consideration of all of the important dimensions in which a prospective site should be evaluated. Can you identify some element in location which is not expressly considered in one of these eight principles?

1. Can you suggest a simple measure of "growth potential?"
2. Compatibility is measured, Nelson tells us, in terms of "customer interchange." Can you devise a simple measure of customer interchange between two stores?
3. Which of the following types of stores has the greatest latitude in the types of sites upon which it may transact business:
   (a) generative
   (b) shared
   (c) suscipient

7. How Customers Shop the Super Market

Where they go, what they buy, how they act, how much they spend revealed by special report on store traffic.

For a fascinating experience—take time out from your store management duties and follow customers as they shop your store.

You will find, as *Progressive Grocer* editors and advertising salesmen found in following and charting the movements of customers in Dillon super markets, that your shopper friends are alike in many ways—and different in many others.

Differences lie mainly in age, income and composition of shopping groups. They are young married, middleaged and elderly women, some of considerable means, some with modest and some with sub-standard incomes. They are men, some of whom shop alone, many with their wives. And there are children, everywhere there are children, some serious, some playful, some troublesome, some helpful, some funny. Yes, the super market customer is everybody —and to study and watch them as people, rather than as statistics, is something that every operator and employer owes to himself and his store.

Statistics on the movement of customers, their average purchase, time of peak purchases, frequency of purchase by product categories are all shown more clearly and concisely in tables and charts that accompany this article. Interesting and illuminating as these tables are they cannot convey to the reader the impressions, customer habits and attitudes that one observes on watching them as they spend anywhere from a few moments up to as long as thirty to forty minutes in the three, four, and often five super market visits each shopper makes per week.

Perhaps the first impression one gets is that the great majority of customers are "wall shoppers." They travel the perimeter, or at least start with the outside aisles before they stray into the interior. They are drawn into this pattern by two factors—first the wall locations of the perishable departments which are shopped with far greater frequency than the inside grocery aisles and second, the very natural tendency of most of us to travel, stand or sit at the edge rather than the middle of a room.

Most stores today concentrate the often-shopped perishables around the perimeter of the store for operating, maintenance and equipment reasons, but as one watches traffic flow the question arises on whether this is in the interest of better traffic control. Why not locate at least some of the perishable lines in the interior where they can pull people into greater exposure to the whole store?

Another pronounced impression of customers is their intense interest and attention to the process of shopping the super market. So intense are they, in fact, that they are oblivious to such things as flood lights and movie cameras that were used in making motion pictures during The Dillon Study. Yet in spite of their intensity, many do not have a "blue print" for shopping made up or planned in advance. They start along a certain course at relatively high speed, they stop, detour, back-track for certain purchases—but always looking and scanning the aisles and the shelves. They seem anxious for suggestions, for direction, for guide-posts, for assurance, for recommendations.

Customers read and study. They read signs, shelf-talkers, labels. They study prices, compare one brand with another, find out the net weight and ingredients with such earnestness that one cannot help but wonder whether most stores are making the most of this obvious receptive attitude among customers. They want assurance, they want reasons, perhaps even excuses for making certain purchases, and are often influenced by where other shoppers are stopping and what others are buying. Some go so far as to pick up an occasional item from

♦ SOURCE: Reprinted by permission from the editor of *Progressive Grocer*, in the August, 1960, issue, pages D49–D55.

Basic Traffic Flow in a Typical Dillon Store

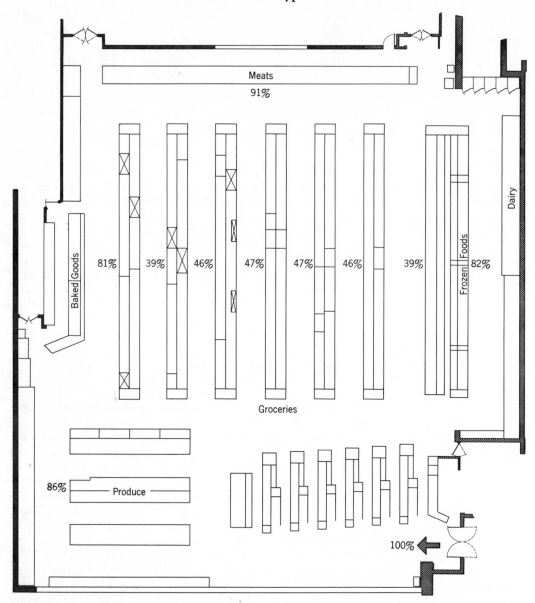

NOTE: Super market customers are, first of all, perimeter shoppers and then interior shoppers as shown by this basic data on store traffic. Of all the customers entering Dillon stores during latter-week periods, approximately 80% travel the perishables aisles compared with only about half that number entering the internal aisles of the grocery department. This, of course, suggests the possibility of spotting one or more perishables departments within the main grocery area in the interest of more thorough traffic circulation. In a special experiment, Dillons also found that full length gondolas increased grocery department traffic circulation and also appeared to increase sales of grocery items as compared with a former arrangement using shorter gondolas with cross aisles. This traffic pattern, probably characteristic of most super markets, points up the need for better ideas and methods of display, merchandise arrangement, product identification and other means to pull shoppers into and through the store's biggest major department, groceries.

Per Cent of Customers Buying from Each Major Category

Category	% Buying
Dairy	63.5%
Meat Department	61.8
Bread Rack	49.3
Produce	45.0
Frozen Foods	27.2
Baked Goods (Service Dept.)	22.4
Paper Products	22.3
Cereals	21.0
Candy	21.0
Canned Vegetables	16.8
Soaps, Detergents, Laundry	14.5
Ice Cream	13.0
Cookies, Crackers	12.8
Soft Drinks, Beer	12.8
Snacks, Chips	12.8
Health & Beauty Aids	12.6
Pet Foods	12.0
Baking Needs, Syrups	12.0
Household Supplies	12.0
Canned Meats, Fish, and Prepared Foods	11.8
Canned Juices	10.8
Macaroni-Spaghetti	10.8
Baby Foods, Milk, Baby Needs	10.7
Jams, Jellies, Spreads	10.5
Sugar	10.5
Soups	8.9
Coffee, Tea, Cocoa	8.7
Magazines	8.5
Canned Fruit	8.5
Cigarettes, Tobacco	8.4
Salad Dressings, Mayonnaise	7.2
Condiments, Sauces	7.0
Desserts	7.0
Canned Milk	6.3
Soft Goods	6.0
Dried Vegetables	5.5
Pickles, Olives	5.2
Salt, Seasonings	5.0
Dietetic Foods	5.0
Dried Fruits	4.5
Housewares	4.0
Stationery	3.7
Toys	3.1
Chinese Foods	2.0

NOTE: Of the people who entered Dillon Super Markets during the busier days of the week and who were "followed" by *Progressive Grocer* researchers—here are the per cents of total customers who bought from each of the major product categories and departments. This table does not indi-cate how much they bought, but merely whether they made a purchase. While not intended as a precise measurement of traffic-pulling power, this analysis can prove useful in store planning, product positioning with a view toward stimulating more thorough shopping patterns.

another shopper's cart in order to see what "other people are buying," then put it back and buy the same thing.

One often hears customers say they spend far more than they intend to in the super market. Yet, in spite of this common yet good-natured complaint, it seems obvious that shoppers would spend even more if store operators paid more attention to ways of making the super market more friendly, more interesting and more helpful. These objectives are easily stated and not easily achieved, yet they are worth striving for in an era of food retailing marked by a growing sameness in store appearance, pricing and type of product offered.

The first thing one notices about shoppers as they enter the store is their cheerfulness. The great majority start their shopping tour in a happy, receptive frame of mind. Coupled with their good nature is an air of receptiveness—a looking forward to seeing what the store has to offer in the way of specials, new items, menu combinations and things particularly appropriate to the season. Shoppers generally start slowly—looking carefully, inspecting, and pausing. However, as the tour progresses, the tempo speeds up somewhat, possibly indicating that the shopper suddenly remembers the magnitude of the super market and perhaps realizes how much ground she must cover, how many items she must locate in the few minutes she can spend before turning to her next duty, possibly picking up the children, meeting her husband, joining friends, returning to her housework. It is at this moment that she seems to be looking for help, directions, suggestions and guidance. It is here that special displays, shelf talkers, the availability of store personnel, talking signs, specials can help to slow her down, to help her find wanted items, to sell her needed merchandise that she has temporarily overlooked.

While the shopper starts out in good humor—she does not always remain that way. A disinterested response to her question by a disinterested employe, an item or two out of stock or out of place, a blocked aisle, or any one of a number of irritants can subconsciously cut her shopping time and her pur-

How Dollar Sales Are Spread by Day of Week

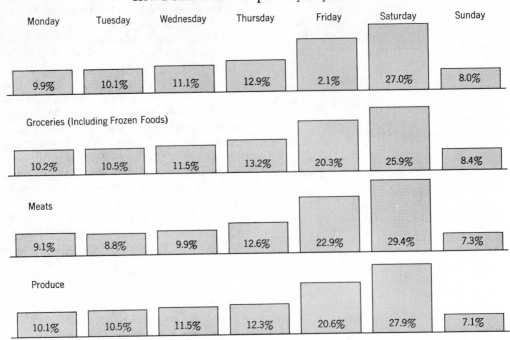

NOTE: Here in general terms is how consumers spread their super market purchases throughout the days of the week. Note the parallels in the shopping pattern for the store as a whole and for major departments within the store. It is particularly interesting to note that meat and produce purchasing follow the same basic trend as in groceries, thus tending to refute the notion that perishables are shopped in higher proportion to total than dry groceries during latter days of the week.

When Customers Shop

	Number of Transactions	Percent of Total Transactions	Average Purchase
By Day of Week			
Monday	1295	13.3%	$2.83
Tuesday	1244	12.7	2.99
Wednesday	1325	13.6	3.09
Thursday	1366	14.0	3.50
Friday	1564	16.0	4.96
Saturday	1952	20.0	5.13
Sunday	1018	10.4	2.91
	9764	100.0%	$3.79
By Period of Day			
8:00 a.m. to Noon	1881	19.3%	$3.95
Noon to 3:00 p.m.	1799	18.4	3.88
3:00 p.m. to 6:00 p.m.	3285	33.6	3.90
6:00 p.m. to 9:00 p.m.	2799	28.7	3.48
	9764	100.0%	$3.79

chases sharply—these irritants are expensive and for the most part unnecessary.

The American woman must shop in all kinds of retail stores, but none has a greater opportunity for friendliness and service than the super market, for in effect—the super market is the woman's store. It offers food, nutrition, affects her family, her budget, her kitchen and her home. It's also quite the social center and certainly not the least important appeal of the super market is the certainty that here she will meet and chat with many, many friends each week.

But the most striking impression an outside observer receives on watching shoppers and their relationship with the super market is this —that super market executives and employes tend to underestimate both the great interest the store holds for its customers, the customers' persistent desire for service, for guidance and for personal recognition and appreciation.

How does one begin to attain these objectives? There are many ways—but perhaps the first step is to take an hour or two each week when one can isolate himself from the routine jobs of store operation and administration and in those hours observe, watch, follow shoppers in an effort to understand their problems and thus develop plans and services that will benefit store and shopper alike.

DISCUSSION QUESTIONS

This article shows that there are some super market shoppers who never travel through the interior of the store layout—these "wall shoppers" or "perimeter shoppers" comprise the majority of customers. Moreover, there is a tendency for the most shopping to occur on Friday and Saturday.

1. What are the causes for "perimeter shopping?" Is it avoidable? How?
2. What are the causes for a time concentration of purchases on Friday and Saturday? Is this pattern avoidable? How?
3. Which of the 8 principles of location which you encountered in an earlier reading have some applicability in the solution of layout problems?

Promotional Competition in Retailing

Promotion includes both written and spoken, personal and impersonal forms of sales efforts. Thus "promotion" includes advertising, personal selling efforts, window and in-store display, and the "silent" salesman—the package. Promotion is important in retailing because it is the means through which the character of the store is made known to prospective customers.

This section includes materials on store or "dealers" brands—a subject which is of growing concern to both manufacturers and retailers. Also included is a discussion of the recent status of trading stamps. Trading stamps represent a form of promotion which many retailers apparently cannot live without, and a form of promotion which many of these same retailers cannot live comfortably with. Stamps are difficult to discontinue without inconvenience to the customer. Another article examines the role of the retailer in the determination of the packaging practices of manufacturers. In addition, an article is included which suggests something about a kind of promotion which may be of greater importance to retailers in the future.

1. The Battle of the Brands

LEON MORSE

NATIONAL BRAND OR PRIVATE LABEL? THE WAR IS GETTING HOTTER.

"We are located in one of the most fiercely competitive markets in the nation," the supermarket executive cried. "The loss leaders in this area are hot enough to scald you. It is not uncommon to take a loss of 20 to 25 cents on every pound of coffee during a weekend special. I think that when the price differential in favor of the private brand reaches the levels I have mentioned, the battle gets too unequal. We cannot even compete by giving away our entire profit on the national-brand label."

No mere special pleader, the man who uttered these words at a recent grocery manufacturers convention is a very significant figure. He is President George W. Jenkins of Florida's 74-unit Publix Super Markets, Inc., and perhaps better than anyone else he put into perfect focus the battle currently raging between the retail (private-label) brand and the national (manufacturer's) brand. Too, Jenkins ably summed up the way the private-label brands have carried the war into the camp of the national brands in the nation's department stores, supermarkets, drugstores and other outlets.

There can be little doubt that the retail brands are indeed on the offensive. "In the last ten years the volume of business done by our 12,000 member stores in private labels has doubled," admits William Burston, manager of merchandising of the National Retail Merchants Association. "The smaller stores do 4% of their volume in private labels. But their greatest impact has been in the larger stores: many of them run as high as 8%—and some 10%—in private brands. And this pie is not a whole one. Many of the department store products are completely unbranded."

The shelves of the supermarkets bear the same marks of invasion. As far back as 1958, a study by the A.C. Nielsen Co. found that supermarkets did 25.6% of their business in brands other than national (included in this figure, of course, were some regional brands too). The record of success of the Great Atlantic & Pacific Tea Co., with 25% of its total volume in private labels, is well known. And private labels have also been proliferating along the aisles of such other major supermarket chains as Safeway Stores, Acme Markets, Food Fair Stores and the Kroger Co.

As alarming as this trend is, one other movement has brought even more concern to national-brand manufacturers: the phenomenal increase in private-label business among the nation's wholesale cooperatives, the companies that deal with grocery outlets. Two examples make the point: in five years, New York's Staff Supermarket Associates has built a $16 million business by servicing member stores with private labels; Chicago's Topco Associates, a buying organization for 29 small and medium-sized supermarket chains throughout the country, has a private-label volume of $200 million in foods, housewares, soft goods and health and beauty aids.

The movement toward private brands in all types of consumer goods is continuing to grow. Although drugs and cosmetics are so universally distributed that it is difficult to estimate private-label volume, clear trends are shaping up here too. Thus Marrud Inc., the nation's largest operator of leased drug and cosmetic departments in discount houses, does 7% of its business in private labels, and expects to do 10% by 1964. So confident is Marrud of the future of retail labels, in fact, it is planning to broaden its operations on a grand scale. From being merely a discount-department operator, Marrud has bought a plant and now intends to make drugs and cosmetics for itself and for other retailers.

To established manufacturers, of course,

* SOURCE: Reprinted by permission from the editor of *Dun's Review and Modern Industry*, in the May 1964 issue, pages 53–54.

such practices smack of what at least one of them has referred to as "piracy." Such charges bother Marrud's balding President Jacob Margolis not at all. "I'll be blunt about it," says Margolis, "it's an accepted practice. As soon as a product proves itself and it's permissible, we take it to one of our suppliers and ask him to duplicate it."

Marrud is not alone. What is worse, from the viewpoint of the manufacturers, is that some of the nation's largest retailers share the views of Jacob Margolis. Moreover, they command sufficient technological muscle among their suppliers to even beat name brands to the punch when the stakes (and the potential volume) warrant it. Just one example: Sears' color television, which the company had ready for market long before many national-brand makers were willing to even attempt the gamble on color.

Why the Rebirth?

All this, of course, only serves to bring up one nagging question: What is behind the present resurgence of private brands? Historically, of course, they are nothing new on the retailing scene, having made their appearance during the 1920s. Then, though, they made hardly a dent in the sales of national brands until the 1930s and the Depression, when price became paramount for the consumer. But even in those dismal days they were of little threat to the "names." One of the few to really hit the dominance of the national brands was A&P's still-active Ann Page label. And a few drugstores, called "pineboards," were hastily set up to discount name brands and sell their own private labels.

But these two diverse examples really constituted the bulk of the private-brand drive; with the exception of Ann Page and a few other products, consumers did not take readily to them. Then they died almost entirely when every spare inch in the nation's plants swung over to defense production during World War II.

Why, then, the return to life? The answer lies in the thin margins that have beset both retailers and manufacturers in recent years. From the retailing point of view, of course, much of today's thin-margined selling came from the discount house. It was this new form of merchandising that wrecked the fair-trade laws by cutting prices on national brands. Bait merchandising became the order of the day; self-service took over virtually everywhere; profit margins went down and volume went up.

Such giant retailing combines as Sears, Roebuck and J. C. Penney (Montgomery Ward had other troubles), armed with their own brands, were more than equal to the challenge. But the sluggish traditional department stores and the variety stores, not quick enough to react to new currents, took the full brunt of this onslaught.

Once the stores did wake up, however, they quickly followed Sears' and Penney's lead in developing the store brand (an old, but effective, weapon that is best described as an "exclusive" private brand). Here, directed by their buying groups, they were able to purchase in sufficient quantity to gain considerable price leverage from manufacturers. In effect, then, the retailers, moving with greater emphasis into the private-brand business, added an impetus all their own. Three of the most adept at this game: Federal Department Stores, R.H. Macy Co. and Allied Stores.

Yet why were they so overwhelmingly successful? Indeed, why have all the private brands succeeded to such a marked degree when the bulk of them went down to such miserable failure even during the 1930s?

In part, it is the consumer himself who has changed. His loss of brand loyalty has been chronicled time and again. So has his lack of respect for a "name." Today's consumer is more sophisticated," explains Professor Malcolm P. McNair of Harvard's Graduate School of Business Administration. "This consumer figures all the angles, looks for the advantageous price, has declining allegiance to brands and institutions, does not necessarily accept any one retailer as his purchasing agent."

Competition, and the thin profit margins that accompany it, has accelerated the movement. "I've seen it happen frequently," observes bespectacled Murray Hillman, senior vice president in charge of planning for top advertising agency McCann-Erickson. "A manufacturer will have a dominant position in the market but then slowly begin to add to the price of his product without creating additional consumer benefits. A few such small increases add up, and when the product gets high enough it becomes vulnerable. Then the private label moves in and undercuts him. There is a difference in price that the market can tolerate—in many cases as much as 20%—but it must be justified by product improvement."

Added to these factors is still another consideration. Nobody has studied the failure-and-success cycle of the private brands more closely than the men who make them today, and they have put their finger on the quality that, along with lesser consumer sophistication, spelled their doom during that earlier marketing period. Simply put, that quality was the retail brands' lack of quality. With the exception of a few reputable brands like Ann Page, the private label on all too many of the products was simply a mask for their lack of quality.

By and large, this mistake has not been repeated in the 1960s. "We've got a better iron than General Electric," claims Frederick L. Devereux, own brands marketing manager of Allied Stores. "We know. We tested them both at the United States Testing Laboratory."

While General Electric undoubtedly would contest that point, there is no doubt that the private-brand makers have learned their lesson on quality. Says George Doherty, vice president of Topco Associates: "We've got to have a strong quality base to our sales effort. We say, and we can prove, that well over 90% of the products we buy from manufacturers are modified to our specifications to get better quality. We tell them what we need to satisfy our customers. We're not content to sit back and just order."

Cooperative wholesalers and buying organizations are even going so far as to make something of a fetish of testing. Topco Associates has 25 people in its testing laboratory. Hundreds of products are tested at the Boston laboratories of Dr. Herbert Shuster for Staff Supermarket Associates. And quality insignias are to be found on a wide variety of private-label products.

There is also, of course, the stature of the companies that now manufacture private brands. "Gone are the days when the private-label supplier was a small manufacturer in a loft," says Benjamin Abrams, president of Emerson Radio & Phonograph Corp. "Retailers these days can count on getting the brands from major manufacturers. Private label is a growing business. We've got to face the reality and come to terms with it."

There is little doubt that the private-label manufacturers have moved out of the loft. When J.C. Penney went into hard goods, for example, its vice president of distribution, William L. Marshall, took particular note of the men soliciting his company's business. "What impressed me," he noted, "was the caliber of the men who made the presentations to us. They were all part of the top management group. It was plain that management was driving for our business. They were leading their aces and giving us the full treatment."

And though there remains notable holdouts, some of the most respected names in manufacturing are now in private brands. These include the Hotpoint division of General Electric, the Hoover Co., SCM Corp., Goodyear Tire & Rubber, the Kelvinator division of American Motors, Westinghouse Electric, Magnavox, Union Carbide, Bell & Howell, Eastman Kodak, Genesco, Norwich Pharmacal and Rexall Drug & Chemical.

Indeed, the retail brand business has grown so large that the past decade has witnessed the emergence of major manufacturers whose sole function it is to produce for this market. One of these companies, the Franklin Manufacturing Co. division of Studebaker Corp., is shooting for a volume of $75 million in 1964; another, Colonial Corp. of America, is aiming at $100 million.

Part of the reason for the increase of "name" manufacturers is that they have learned how to vary the product mix. "We make certain that our products sold through our distributors are distinct from those with the retail label," says Charles J. Gibson Jr., president of the Gibson Refrigerator division of the Hupp Corp. "Take the 'air sweep' feature of our air conditioners: it isn't available to retailers."

The Holdouts

There are, as noted, a few holdouts who stoutly refuse to produce private-label goods. In this group are Maytag Co. and Frigidaire division of General Motors. Claire Ely, vice president in charge of sales and marketing for Maytag, sums up the case for the holdouts. "We do not believe," says Ely unequivocally, "in offering competitors the same merchandise under a different name. We believe dual manufacture is distasteful to our dealers, and we will not manufacture for this market."

Many executives put their objections in far, far stronger language. Not long ago, President Edgar M. Bronfman of Joseph E. Seagram & Sons issued a raging indictment of the private branders. "Roaming the seas of free enterprise," he cried, "they use the precious charts which our national brands have plotted. Muscling in under their price flag, they maraud the markets which you and we and all the others have developed with untold billions of dollars in product improvement and research. They free-load from our hard-won franchise—and drain from our costly advertising."

The Brand Names Foundation is the official spokesman for this point of view. Its budget in 1963 was increased to $750,000, and it has stepped up its numerous promotions, including Brand Names Week. In various speeches, Albert Messer, its president, echoes Bronfman. "Who will do the preselling?" asks Messer. "Who will create the traffic and product development? Who will develop such money-saving devices as palletizing and traypacking if the private label continues to proliferate?"

The retailers have their own answer. "They call us parasites," snorts George Doherty of Topco Associates. "Yet what does a manufacturer do when his competition comes out with a new product? He does the same thing as us: he hurries out and has it copied. That's the way American business works—unless you can protect your product legally."

Nevertheless, some of these charges do have merit. Retailers do use cooperative advertising funds furnished them by manufacturers to advertise their own retail brands. And while manufacturers pay retailers the national rate for cooperative advertising, the retailers pay the local rate. The difference in the two rates is frequently used by the retailers to advertise their own label.

And retailers have contributed little to product innovation. Yet it must be pointed out that this gradually is changing. Sears, for example, has already placed the first thermoelectric refrigerator on the market. Franklin Manufacturing calls its Avanti refrigerator the first with any significant design changes. J.C. Penney claims to have pioneered the first washers with baked-enamel finishes and the first mothproof blankets.

When they face each other across store aisles, of course, both private and national brands have their own weapons. The manufacturer's brand has at its command the high-powered national media of television and magazines that presumably presell the consumer. But the retailer's brand has control of the store and that all-important shelf placing and the use of local advertising—as well as standing in the community, no mean factor in closing many sales.

In truth, the private brand has been adding to its array of weapons. Private-label packaging, for example, has shown dramatic improvement in recent years. Marrud's hair-spray container recently competed against top aerosols at the annual packaging show of the Chemical Specialty Manufacturers Association. Allcolor Co.'s "open-end" slot makes it possible to select any number of tissues from its package—an improvement, asserts the company, over similar national brand packages.

Marrud has also added more sophisticated marketing techniques to its packaging; for example, before new store labels are introduced, they are tested with shoppers. Too, the company offers coupons (discount slip inside a product) and "cross ruffs" (two related products, such as a toothbrush and toothpaste, packaged together and priced particularly low to encourage sales). A favorite ploy of United Whelan Corp. is to create a comparison display of name brands against its own private brands, showing the already great price discount; then to offer an additional 10% discount for purchasing two or more of its store brands.

A Few Problems

Yet marketing the private label in retail stores is not without its difficulties. One of the most critical points, not unnaturally, is the sales clerk. Not only is he more familiar with manufacturers' labels, he is proselytized by the manufacturers' representatives who repeatedly stress the advantages of their products. Moreover, the manufacturer's brand generally has been presold through advertising; as a result, it usually is an easier sale for the clerk, as he well knows.

"Several people in my department do nothing but visit stores trying to stimulate our sales clerks to sell *our* brands," says Fred Devereux of Allied Stores. R. H. Macy makes its house brands even more enticing for the clerk: prizes go to those who are particularly successful merchandisers of Macy's brands. The Frederick Atkins buying office publishes a newsletter to highlight the achievements of those of its stores with the largest increase in store-brand sales.

Can there, though, be such a thing as a winner in the battle of the brands? On the face of it, there cannot. Certainly, both have grown so large that neither need fear disappearing from the marketing scene entirely. But it seems quite clear that the battle between them is growing in intensity. Indeed, both sides have taken to the Government in their zeal for victory.

Thus a major attack on retail branding is being mounted in the United States Congress through the recently introduced Quality Stabilization Bill. This bill, in effect, would reinstitute fair trade by providing that if names and trademarks are used on a product, the seller must abide by the price the manufacturer puts on it; if the retailer wishes to discount the product, he must replace the manufacturer's label. If such a bill should be passed, of course, the discounter could not cut prices on name brands and the traditional retailer's need for retail brands might lessen.

The manufacturers, on the other hand, have been handed a jolt by several decisions made by the Federal Trade Commission. In the first case, the FTC held that the Borden Co. discriminated illegally by selling brand evaporated milk at a higher price than the same milk marketed under other labels. The Borden defense was that advertising added value to the product.

In the second case, the FTC required that Procter & Gamble Co. dispose of the Clorox Co., which it had acquired. The FTC maintained that P&G would only bring greater efficiencies in marketing and advertising to Clorox. Where products are similar, it declared, such efficiencies do not result in benefits to the consumer who pays for them in higher prices.

The FTC, in these cases, evidently took the position that once a product reaches a certain level of acceptance, advertising does not become a benefit to the consumer, but an expense. Both cases take strong positions against advertising. With the power of advertising minimized, however, manufacturers would be gravely handicapped; so both companies are appealing these cases.

Thus the cold war between manufacturer and retailer seems destined to continue without a winner. It appears that the private brand is here to stay, and the manufacturer's brand will just have to make a place for it on the shelf—and learn how to compete with it.

DISCUSSION QUESTIONS

In an earlier article, "vertical" competition between manufacutrers and retailers was identified as one form of competition in American retailing. The "battle of brands" is the popular phrase which describes one aspect of this vertical type of conflict.

1. Is it wrong to copy a product for production and sale under another name? Legally? Morally?
2. Why do manufacturers so often provide the manufacturing facilities for private brands which will, in some measure, compete with their own brands?
3. Why do you see fewer private brands in some merchandise lines than in others? Detergents and soaps, for example!

2. What's Going On in Trading Stamps?

Stamps have just rung up their biggest year in history. Premium Practice magazine estimates 1962's stamp sales at $671 million, 8½% or $53 million more than the $618 million sales recorded during the previous year.

This growth, unexpected because of the already high saturation of stamps, was occasioned in part by the 7% overall increase in retail sales, the rapid growth of E. F. Mac-Donald Plaid stamps ($35 million increase last year) and growth of incentive plans employing stamps.

Consumer interest in stamps nevertheless remained high. During 1961 stamps were distributed with 12.9% of sales—or $30.3 billion of the nation's $235 billion total. In the past two years stamp sales have increased by almost one-third. And roughly two-thirds of all stamps are offered in the food field.

✦ SOURCE: Reprinted by permission from the editor of *Progressive Grocer,* in the August 1963 issue, pages 64–67, 134, 138.
NOTE: Kroger captured an estimated 9% of the market in 1962 with 6% of the super markets, thus capturing fourth position. Kroger was the first food chain to move in with stamps, has since used them in combination with hard-hitting specials, but with decreasing effectiveness as far as increasing its share of market. Fisher's discontinuance of S&H gave Kroger opportunity to advertise to customers, "Don't worry, we won't take away your Top Value stamps—and we'll still keep giving you lowest prices, too." A number of talented division heads have had an opportunity to improve Kroger's position in the market without success.

STOP-N-SHOP with 2.9% of the county's stores rang up 8% of 1962's sales and are counted the hottest group in the area. Really a co-op, Stop-N-Shop had 15 stores operated by 7 independents in 1962, now has 17 stores, 8 owners. Average volume of $3 million per store has been achieved through aggressive "1800 everyday low prices" theme consistently played up in large, well-organized ads which list many items showing "old prices and new." Stop-N-Shop buys through Seaway Foods which also supplies five other co-ops in the county, none of which uses stamps. Stop-N-Shop officials claim they have supplanted Kroger as fourth largest retailer in the area.

All told, more than a quarter million retail outlets offer the trading stamps of some 300 companies to their customers, and the stamp most offered is the ubiquitous S & H Green Stamp. While the Sperry & Hutchinson Company is notoriously tight-lipped about sales figures, it is generally accepted that the 67-year-old company commands 40% of the business, on which, S & H says, it nets about 5%. How much this is in terms of dollars remains problematical, for S & H reckons stamp volume at $780 million, the Trading Stamps Institute pegs it at $800 million, and as already stated, Premium Practice places it at only $671 million.

Whatever the volume, S & H has about 90,000 retailers enrolled in its program for periods ranging from one to ten years, and depending upon the nature of the business, they pay the customary two to three per cent of sales for an exclusive franchise. Some 800 redemption centers and mail-order facilities distribute the 1633 items which are promoted through 35,000,000 S & H catalogs.

95% REDEMPTION CLAIMED

S & H has maintained through the years—and has been able to convince the Internal Revenue Service—that 95% of its stamps are redeemed by consumers, a figure that is roughly disputed by stamp opponents as being too high. In its promotional material S & H stresses that a 12% increase in sales is required to make a stamp program pay off for a super market operator. This, too, is disputed, with 15% considered the minimum by many food retailers.

The largest supplier of stamps is also the largest supplier of statistics in the stamp industry. S & H's survey for 1962, conducted by Benson & Benson, Inc., places 84% of the nation's families in the stamp-saving category, up from 76% for 1961. With 54,600,000 households in the U.S., this amounts to 45,864,000 families that saved one or more kinds of stamps in 1962. This new high represents the fifth year in a row stamps have increased in acceptance.

It wasn't always so, of course. When Thomas A. Sperry and Shelly B. Hutchinson started S & H in Jackson, Michigan, after having observed the success of Shuster's Department Store's stamps in Milwaukee, the budding company numbered mainly New England dry goods dealers among its accounts. One of their few large customers in the early days, oddly enough, was A & P, the last of the recent big holdouts against stamps.

Inevitably, S & H's success attracted a host of imitators, many of them "quick buck" specialists; and just as inevitably stamps began to run into strong opposition. What really eclipsed stamps was World War I, however. With goods in short supply, retailers saw no reason to lure shoppers and abandoned the plans by the thousands. Stamps thereafter existed mainly in the dry goods and department store fields.

1951—YEAR OF BOOM

The boom in stamps never got rolling again until 1951. King Soopers of Denver, now part of the Dillon chain of Kansas, installed S & H stamps in one store in June, then quickly added them in their other three stores. Competing chains countered with their own plans, and the war was on. Within two years Denver became infamous for its stamp wars as five of Denver's six chains and a number of independents fired first "double stamp days," then triple, and in a final fling of merchandising madness, quadruple stamps, at each other. The stamp companies themselves, recognizing the threat to the stamp concept, put an end to the war by announcing jointly that they would enforce their contracts which stipulated that retailers give only one stamp with each 10-cent purchase. King Soopers never did drop stamps and the other chains, some of them thoroughly disenchanted by the war, nevertheless had to stick, too. Denver is still a "stamp town."

Stamp wars notwithstanding, chains in other cities took note of the 15 to 40% sales increases often generated by the plans and moved in with their own. After a quick, successful tryout of S & H, Grand Union launched its Triple-S company; Kroger followed not long after with its Top Value stamps.

With only minor pauses since then, chain after chain has taken on stamps until, among the top twenty, Jewel Tea alone remains stampless. (At that, the 42-store Eisner Division still gives S & H stamps, as it did when it was acquired by Jewel.)

Independents by the thousands took on stamps as well.

How saturated the stamp picture is today for larger stores is revealed by the Super Market Institute's findings among its member companies' stores, all of which have sales of at least a million dollars a year. Of the 353 companies reporting on 5963 stores, 59% now offer stamps—compared with 56% the year previously. About 5% of the companies—generally the smaller organizations—introduced stamps while at the same time 5% of the members dropped stamps. But two-thirds of these companies did so in some of their stores, while continuing to offer stamps in other stores. In terms of super markets, stamps were discontinued in 1.3% of all stores reported on.

90% OF CHAINS ISSUE STAMPS

About 77% of SMI member stores give stamps, down from 78% the previous year. Progressive Grocer's annual survey of food retailing places stamps in 90% of chain and 40% of independent super markets.

The high state of stamps in food retailing has not been reached without rancor. Before A & P took on Plaid Stamps and before his retirement, President Ralph W. Burger, when asked about the company's long-time resistance to use of stamps snapped: "These stamps are a drag on civilization." Lingan Warren, President and general manager of Safeway stores before his company took on Blue Chip stamps, was a bitter antagonist, once threatened to "break" S & H if it didn't stay out of Safeway's trading areas. His successor, Robert Magowan, in reporting good profits for the past year declared, "It certainly wasn't due to stamp activities. They are a drag on profits." Retailers' private comments about stamps are often unprintable.

Kroger's Chairman, Joseph Hall, falls back on the real reason that even anti-stamp retailers have taken them on. "Nobody, says he, loves stamps except the customers."

Efforts to block stamps through legislation have been about as successful as efforts to ignore them. By the end of 1955 alone the stamp companies, led by S & H, had defeated 47 out of 50 attempts to impede or tax stamps. The struggle is similar to that of fair trade, however, in that it is a continuing thing and

S & H's superb legal talent can count on fighting anti-stamp brush fires in a dozen state legislatures at least this year. Even in Great Britain, the House of Lords reverberates these days with the pros and cons of stamps.

The final decision as to whether stamps will stick on a broad scale lies not with legislatures, of course, but with the customer. It is she who has the final vote by bestowing—or withholding—her patronage. In spite of a variety of giveaways, games and gimmicks, food retailing today offers her two basic appeals—stamps and low-prices. Which will she choose?

Many observers look to A & P to supply the answer. It is common knowledge that the giant retailer's Plaid Stamp program has been less than a whirlwind success since its inception in late 1961. Despite a record year in both sales and profits for fiscal 1962, trading stamps get not a single mention, good or bad, in the annual report to stockholders. This silence is in marked contrast with the previous report and coupled with the fact that A & P has completely halted introduction of stamps, after installing them in about half of its 4475 outlets, is considered by observers to be significant.

Will A & P get out of stamps this year? Not likely, say other retailers, and in the manner of baseball fans, they advise "Wait till next year." If profits don't hold up, the reasoning goes, stamps will be discontinued. Board Chairman John D. Ehrgott is leaving the tea company free to go either way; at the annual meeting he avowed that "We are neither chained to the past nor committed to change in the future . . ."

RECENT WITHDRAWALS

Whether A & P drops stamps or not, there have been many recent examples of "selective withdrawals" from stamps. Among the most notable:

- Acme in Buffalo, N.Y., has withdrawn its National Red stamps from 42 area stores in the face of fierce price competition chiefly from affiliated independents.
- Liberal Stores of Dayton, Ohio stopped issuing stamps in seven of its southern Ohio stores—but continued them in Dayton.
- Kroger's Washington, D.C. division has abandoned its Top Value program.
- Thriftway Food Stores of Kansas City

halted distribution of S & H stamps in its 17 stores.
- Universal Food Stores discontinued Sterling Stamps in its 130 units in New England.
- Loblaw's Pittsburgh division cut loose its S & H program in 43 area stores.
- Food Town of Toledo, now a 17-store chain, dropped its own stamp plan, has waxed prosperous ever since.

Meijer's of Grand Rapids, Put & Take of Phoenix are also numbered among the many who successfully stopped issuing stamps.

Trial balloons are not uncommon. Thus we see an "isolated" Grand Union super market in Methuen, Mass., operate without stamps while its sister store seven miles away dispenses the company's Triple-S stamps. Food Fair has experimented along similar lines with three nonstamp stores in the Philadelphia area.

Another method of "getting out" of stamps is to change the corporate name of the store, then operate under a "food discount banner." Penn Fruits' Big Value, National Tea's Big D and Loblaw's Star Discount Food Stores are typical conversions.

Occasionally a chain has "got out of stamps" coincidentally with going into bankruptcy; the Dilbert episode, where its Yellow Stamp discontinuance was so ineptly handled that the state's Attorney General was considering prosecution for fraud, is perhaps the prime example of dropping stamps the hard way.

Those companies that have divorced themselves from stamps usually have managed to promote their new merchandising approach by spending far less than they did under stamps; more often than not gimmicks and giveaways are eschewed altogether in favor of newspaper advertising and circulars only, with money thus saved going into more and more "everyday low prices."

Stamp enthusiasts have rightly trumpeted—and the high rate of acceptance by customers has proved—that the little stickers are indeed accepted, appreciated, expected and even loved; and that they are a selling tool at once sound, stimulating, continuing and effective.

Stamp detractors have countered that the little stickers are oversold, overpriced, and overdue for a fall. Says one operator, "The trading stamp fad has had it." Adds another "Everybody's got 'em—nobody's got the edge here anymore."

Yet the "right" decision to discontinue must

be a local one. For Liberal Markets, it was right to drop them in Cincinnati, right to keep them in Dayton. For Foodtown of Toledo it was right to drop them entirely. What was right for Fisher remains to be seen.

With 90% of chain and 40% of independ-ent super markets already giving them, the great increases posted by stamps are a thing of the past. While the coming year will not be the "Year of the Great Divorce," selective withdrawals will continue at a steady pace in food retailing.

DISCUSSION QUESTION

Trading stamps have been, from their very beginning, a controversial promotional means. Note, for example, that the Internal Revenue Service has a real interest in the percentage of stamps which are redeemed. Why? Note also that there is some argument about the percentage increase in sales required to "make a stamp program pay off" for a super market operator. Why is this figure so important?

Why are trading stamps so attractive to consumers? Why have they been so attractive to resellers? What is the future for trading stamps?

3. A Shift in the Point-of-Purchase?

GEORGE M. NAIMARK

The physical spot at which the customer makes his purchase—the point-of-sale—is of transcending significance. It is at this location that the culmination, successful or otherwise, of all prior advertising and selling effort occurs. This is the last time to appeal to the customer, the moment at which the final decision is made and acted upon.

Since the point-of-purchase is the "test tube" in which the purchase reaction occurs, it represents the final opportunity to enter into or influence the reaction. Further, it is often the time of greatest influence because it represents the most propitious moment: the customer is now ready to buy. This immediacy, coupled with the fact that the customer does not have an opportunity to forget the seller's promotional message, increases the leverage and importance of the point-of-purchase.

This is the critical point; in a sense, all previous marketing endeavors function only to precondition the customer for this moment. As an additive factor, in many cases the purchaser's choice of purchase location itself plays an important part in governing *what* is purchased. For example, the decision to go to Montgomery Ward & Co. for a refrigerator automatically excludes all non-Ward brands of refrigerators. Similarly, if a customer turns to the *Yellow Pages* (which in a sense then *becomes* the point-of-purchase) specifically to choose a Chinese restaurant, he automatically eliminates from consideration the Chinese restaurants that are not listed.

WHAT GOVERNS THE CHOICE OF POINT-OF-PURCHASE?

In significant (though certainly not *total*) measure, the customer's choice of location for consummating his purchase is based upon *his need for information* about the product. The kind and amount of the information he needs, *plus his degree of willingness to rely on others for it,* help to determine his point-of-purchase.

When a customer feels that he must relate his purchase decision primarily to his own *personal* reactions or evaluations (usually of such nonquantifiable characteristics as appearance, smell, heft, sound, and feel), his point-of-purchase must of necessity be at some location at which the merchandise is displayed.

However, when the consumer is willing to base his decision primarily upon the evaluations *or* claims *of others,* his point-of-purchase can well be remote from the store. Under those circumstances, home or office can be the purchase point, with the transaction completed by telephone, by mail, or through a salesman.

This away-from-the-store purchase must in large measure be dependent upon the customer's willingness to rely on information provided by others, whether it be:

(1) *objective quantitative assessment* by qualified, "disinterested" people (for example, actual testing of thermometers by the National Bureau of Standards);

and/or (2) *subjective evaluation* of nonmeasurable characteristics by authoritative disinterested parties, including friends (for example, blindfold taste and smell appraisal of brandies by experts);

and/or (3) *seller's claims* (advertisements or salesmen's statements) that are *believed* by the customer to be reliable.

In all these circumstances, the customer's confidence in others is the dominant factor. With trust, he can remain in his home or office and spend his money; without trust, he must go to investigate personally before he buys.

To be sure, many buying decisions are based on a combination of the personal, subjective reactions of the customer *along with* the evalu-

✦ SOURCE: Reprinted by permission from the American Marketing Association, in the *Journal of Marketing,* January, 1965, pages 14–17.

ations or claims of others. Nevertheless, this basic premise appears generally applicable: the customer's choice of point-of-purchase for many kinds of merchandise (admittedly not all) is based upon his degree of reliance upon others for information and guidance. The corollary premise would then be: as his degree of reliance upon others increases, the need for in-person evaluation by the customer decreases, and the location of the point-of-purchase *can* shift away from the store.

IS THE CONSUMER RELYING MORE ON OTHERS FOR GUIDANCE?

The rapid expansion of knowledge in all fields has forced the nonspecialist to depend upon the specialist, and there is ample evidence that this is increasingly understood by consumers. The result is that we are becoming a guidance-conscious nation. We are learning that authorities are available to guide us in making many of our buying decisions. This manifests itself in a proliferation of information and testing services. Consumer-testing organizations such as Consumers Union and Consumers Research have become shopping bibles for many.

More and more consumers are transferring their reliance to trusted sources (both commercial *and* noncommercial) and basing more and more of their buying decisions on the appraisal of sophisticated information. In a sense, it might be said that the consumer is beginning to function as an efficient purchasing agent might function.

There are many reasons for this, of course. Perhaps the basic point is that the educational level of the population is increasing, and education often improves ability to recognize that which is relevant to the choice of a product or an "authority."

The pattern seems clear, and perhaps the businessman needs only to examine his own business buying procedures to have some insight into this evolution in consumer buying practices. Ideally the industrial purchasing agent relies on specifications, standards, product analyses, references, and guarantees of performance and product characteristics. Such sophistication in business purchasing must slowly spread to the consuming public.

One of the major implications of this reliance on others for buying guidance has been emphasized previously: it minimizes the need for in-person evaluation of merchandise, and

permits the shift of the point-of-purchase away from the store and into the home or office. Since buying guidance information is, in fact, increasingly available from books, magazine articles, consumer testing services, schools, government agencies, and so forth, the means often exist for reaching buying decisions without viewing the merchandise in person.

OTHER FACTORS ENCOURAGING THE SHIFT IN POINT-OF-PURCHASE

While reliance upon others for buying guidance *permits* away-from-the-store shopping, several other factors are serving to encourage the practice. Foremost among these are disenchantment with retail establishments, the growth and acceptance of private and house-brand merchandise, and the expansion of mail order and telephone shopping from catalogs.

The Retail Store

Although the retail store continues as the major outlet for goods (and certainly will continue to be so for the foreseeable future), there is growing evidence of consumer disenchantment. The traffic and parking problems, the time involved in getting served and in checking out, the physical burden of handling and transporting one's purchases—all these inconveniences decrease the charm of in-store shopping for many people.

Further, the inadequate performance of retail sales personnel is now part of our national folklore. The disinterest of automobile salesmen, for example, is a familiar subject of numerous articles. "The most bitter charges are concerned with rudeness, arrogance, vulgarity, indifference, and a strong penchant for misrepresentation." [1]

The inadequacy of many retail personnel contributes to the consumer's desire to avoid the retail establishment. A summary of a survey of retail outlets provides dramatic reinforcement of this view: [2]

1. Many sales clerks are indifferent to customers.

2. Few clerks know much about the merchandise they are selling, and many are of no help at all to customers seeking information.

---

[1] Editorial, "Service? What's That?" *Printers' Ink*, Vol. 281 (October 26, 1962), p. 75.

[2] E. J. McCarthy, *Basic Marketing: A Managerial Approach* (Homewood, Illinois: Richard D. Irwin, Inc., 1960.), p. 515.

3. Most sales people apparently assume that a customer is presold.

4. If a store does not have an item a customer asks about, rarely does the salesman try to sell the prospective buyer anything else.

5. The ratio is one alert, interested clerk to every ten who are lackadaisical and unconcerned.

Private Brands

Strong consumer acceptance of a brand (be it "national" or "private") serves to simplify away-from-the-store shopping. Therefore, growing consumer acceptance of private and house-brand merchandise is another of the major influences encouraging the shift in the point-of-purchase to home or office.

It is becoming increasingly difficult for the consumer to reject private-brand merchandise. This was not always so. Previously lack of confidence regarding its origin, quality, replacement, or repair served as major deterrents. National brands seemed safer, more dependable. The consumer knew the name of the organization that made the product and stood behind it.

Now, however, we are watching an interesting evolution based on three factors. First among these is the more frequent consumer awareness of the fact that private brands are often made by national brand manufacturers to the same or similar specifications as their own nationally advertised brands. Inevitably, this knowledge increases the consumer's confidence in the quality of the private brand, and removes the *basic* consumer uncertainty in accepting such merchandise.

The second important element concerns the growth of the quality and dependability image of the *retailer* of private brand merchandise. Many (not all) major private brand merchandisers are effectively saying to the consumer: "Don't worry about the manufacturer—it was a famous company whose name you know, and they made it to our rigid specifications anyway. Besides, we guarantee the product and your subsequent satisfaction with it. You can shift your confidence to us, the seller." There is evidence that many persons are finding this transference of trust from manufacturer to retailer an easy one to make.

The third factor of no small significance is the frequency of a lower price structure for comparable private brand merchandise.

Returning briefly to the increasing consumer awareness of the manufacturing origin of much private brand merchandise: here are some examples of the frequent public proclamations to that effect.

The *Wall Street Journal* makes this point: "All this should be good news to the consumer because many times private brands offer quality comparable to well-known brands but at substantially lower prices. In fact, some private brand goods roll off the same production lines as their competing prestige products and are identical in every way except for name plate and price." [3] The article goes on to offer specific examples of identical national and private brands with their respective prices.

Changing Times magazine told its readers: "Actually, the 'private' brands are turned out by the nation's biggest companies . . . the products are cheaper than national brands . . . and they can be every bit as satisfactory." [4]

Sales Management magazine announced in 1962 that "Goodyear will sell J. C. Penney its entire supply of private-brand tires." [5]

The private brand merchandisers themselves also educate the consumer to the "equivalence" of private and national brands. Finally, consumer testing organizations often stress the similarity of private and national brands, while emphasizing the disparity in price. Totally, it is becoming more difficult for the consumer to be unaware of the origin of much of the private label merchandise, or to continue to remain wary of its quality.

In other words, the consumer's increasing confidence in private and house brand merchandise is another important factor in the shift of his point-of-purchase to home or office. This is especially true because some of the largest sellers of private brands use every possible means to encourage the consumer to shop at home by mail or telephone from catalogs.

Reference Book Shopping: Catalogs and Directories

The primary mechanism that finally enables the point-of-purchase to shift away from the store and to the home or office is the catalog or

---

[3] David H. Kelsey, "Brand Battle. Rise of Private Labels Cuts Deeply into Sales of 'Name' Merchandise," *Wall Street Journal* (July 30, 1962), p. 1.

[4] Editorial, *Changing Times*, Vol. 16 (October, 1962), p. 4.

[5] Marketing Newsletter, *Sales Management*, Vol. 89 (October 5, 1962). p. 34.

directory. These reference books, when coupled with convenient means for implementing the purchase decision by the use of mail or telephone ordering, are helping to shift the point-of-purchase in a dramatic way.

Present federal estimates indicate that catalog volume for 1963 was up nearly 9% from the previous year, whereas over-the-counter department store volume was gaining at a slower 6.4% rate. Sears Roebuck & Company, for example, reported that telephone orders originating from catalog shopping represent the fastest growing portion of its retail business. Similarly, Sears' mail-order volume is also expanding faster than its retail store volume.

The recent major entry into catalog retailing of J. C. Penney and others suggests that this growth of away-from-the-store shopping is more than an artifact or a temporary pattern. What are the major advantages to the consumer (in addition to those previously emphasized) that account for this shift in the point-of-purchase? Catalog shopping provides several meaningful advantages:

1. Catalogs available when needed (24 hours a day, seven days a week) and endurable.

2. Convenient general source of information, providing shopping and use guidance (usually more than do retail clerks).

3. Provision of comparative specifications and prices.

4. Frequent provisions of unambiguous guarantees of satisfaction.

5. Large merchandise selection (for example, major Sears' catalogs carry about 170,000 items, whereas their largest stores carry about 80,000 items).

6. Usually lower prices (companies with both catalogs and retail stores often charge 5% to 10% less for catalog-purchased merchandise—even after shipping charges are added).

7. Simplified credit shopping.

8. Stable, clearly indicated prices.

9. Expansion of convenient, always available telephone shopping services.

10. Increased availability of catalogs in catalog order offices; and frequent provision of excellent servicing of the merchandise (traditionally dependable in the stocking of repair parts).

A point about catalog shopping deserves emphasis: the major catalog retailers have usually made every effort to merit the confidence of the shopper. By guaranteeing merchandise unconditionally, by providing service facilities, and by detailed, accurate descriptions of goods and services they often gain the trust of the shopper. This has been the touchstone to success that enables the point-of-purchase to shift.

The remarkable fact is that even such lines of merchandise as fur coats and diamond rings are now successfully retailed through catalogs as a result of the consumer's willingness to rely on the representations made (and his knowledge that the transaction is readily "reversible" if he is less than satisfied!). Consider the recent success of Sears in selling fairly expensive *objets d'art*. Persons who had *never* made significant art purchases spent $300 to $400 per item, and were willingly accepting the seller's allegations as to the value of objects that they themselves could not assess! Can there be a more valuable business asset than such consumer willingness to rely on seller's claims?

CONCLUSION

The consumer's willingness to rely on others (authoritative "disinterested" parties such as the consumer testing service, or the claims of sellers) decreases his need for in-person evaluation of merchandise and permits the point-of-purchase to shift away from the store and to the home or office.

Such reliance upon others appears to be increasing, although in a selective and highly sophisticated manner.

Disenchantment with retail store shopping, coupled with the growth and acceptance of private and house brand shopping, is providing further impetus to the shift of the point-of-purchase away from retail store shopping.

Finally, the ready availability of catalogs and directories, and the expansion of mail order and telephone shopping, provide the practical essential mechanism for in-home or in-office purchasing.

The result of all this is the rapid growth of shopping at a point remote from the store, and the expansion of "reference book purchasing" from catalogs and directories. This pattern appears to be the forerunner of a major shift in the point-of-purchase away from the store and into the home. The merchandising implications of this shift are enormous, and will have far-reaching and enduring significance for all manufacturing and retailing organizations.

DISCUSSION QUESTIONS

When the customer is willing to base his decision primarily upon the evaluations or claims of others, his point-of-purchase can well be shifted from the store. With the increasing integrity of manufacturers and their products, the customer needs less of the in-store reassurances which have been a significant part of retailing in the past. The point of purchase may shift toward the home for many types of goods.

1. What implications does this apparent tendency have for retail services?
2. Is it only the large multi-unit retail operation that might use this shift in point-of-purchase to advantage? Or can the single proprietorship find competitive advantage in this shifting P.O.P.? How?

4. Packaging and Super Markets: The Package in the Market Place

CURT KORNBLAU

While the package has been a significant factor in the growth of the super market, the growth of the super market has in turn stimulated the growth in packaging. Manufacturers and retailers both seeking the same goal—greater sales and greater profits—must work together in developing packages which not only meet the needs of the consumer but also enhance greater efficiency and reduce costs in food distribution.

Packaging has been a vital link in the growth and development of the super market. At the same time, the super market has given great impetus to the concept of the package as a basic and indispensable marketing device, the silent salesman of self-service retailing—not only for food and grocery products, but for other consumer goods as well. In effect, the super market has been the testing ground, the research laboratory for the self-service package.

In a sense, the super market business may be described as a continuous process of materials handling. Merchandise is received, price-marked and placed on display. From the many thousands of products displayed, the customer assembles her (or his) order and takes it to the checkstand, where it is paid for, bagged and taken to the customer's car. Turnover is fast. A great number of packages pass through the super market in quick procession.

This paper is concerned principally with the materials handling involved in the movement of merchandise from the manufacturer to the consumer—with the needs and requirements of the food retailer. I will be dealing mainly with merchandise prepackaged into consumer units by the supplier, both food and non-food, although the same principles apply also to foods which require processing and packaging at the store or warehouse level.

Since the retailer's first requirement is to sell, I will also touch on aspects of packaging pertaining to consumer wants and needs. My remarks will cover only those aspects on which the retailer considers himself knowledgeable —on customers' conscious desires and practical needs, as expressed in customer complaints directly voiced. The food retailer does not consider himself an expert on psychology or physiology, on psychic traumas or the rate of eye blinks. Nor is he an expert on layout, art work, color schemes and other elements of package design.

The food retailer also cannot give professional opinions on packaging materials and production techniques. He knows that he wants to sell, at a profit, and he expects the package to help him achieve this goal and purpose for being. For technical details, he defers to the experts who serve the manufacturer in staff or consultant capacities.

Let me give you a specific example of where the super market operator was ignorant enough to ask for the impossible. This particular example relates to a product which is prepackaged at the store level, meat.

Several years ago, the Super Market Institute Meat Productivity Committee met with manufacturers of meat boards and trays to discuss possible improvements in meat backing materials. Here is what the retailer asked for: greater rigidity, greater absorbency, more wet strength and less weight—all at the same time, plus more visibility. Complete transparency would do fine, and no increase in cost, please.

♦ SOURCE: Reprinted by permission from the American Marketing Association, in *Effective Marketing Coordination*, George L. Baker, editor, 1961, pages 296–306.

The manufacturers nodded sympathetically and related that they had already licked a host of technical problems to give us the fine boards and trays then available. As to complete transparency, they told us, in a very nice way, that the suggestion was a pipe dream. The retailers' position was simply that, as customers of meat backing materials, they were stating a problem —and pointing out an opportunity.

Well, the food retailer isn't expert enough to know whether complete transparency is a pipe dream, but I do know that at this very moment a super market company and a packaging material supplier are jointly experimenting with transparent trays made out of a clear synthetic material, ridged on the bottom for greater strength and better cold air circulation around the packaged meat. This material stands up under the heat of a wrapping machine and the cold of a freezer, and it does not affect the taste of the contents. When frozen, it is said, a flick of the wrist separates the meat and the tray. Customer reaction is reported to be highly favorable, and the super market personnel are enthusiastic. It remains to be seen whether this particular tray will sweep the food industry, but super market operators cannot fail to be impressed with this effort to serve the wants to the retailers and consumers.

FACTS ABOUT THE SUPER MARKET INDUSTRY

For a broad perspective about the super market business, here are some relevant facts, based largely on the continuing research studies of Super Market Institute.

First, what is a super market? SMI defines a super market as a complete, departmentalized food store with a minimum sales volume of one million dollars a year and at least the grocery department fully self-service. In 1960, super markets averaged sales of $1,850,000.

Basic principles of super market merchandising include low markup, fast turnover, self-service, cash-and-carry, quality, variety, pleasant shopping atmosphere, low net profit. Self-service prevails not only in the grocery department. As of a year ago, virtually all dairy departments are completely self-service, as are 87 per cent of the meat departments and 64 per cent of the produce departments— with most of the remainder partially self-service. Some 38 per cent of the super markets sell all or nearly all fresh fruits and vegetables prepackaged. Complete bakery departments

(i.e., more than just a commercial baked goods section or meat cold cuts, which are found in every super market and are general self-service) are fully self-service in about six out of ten super markets.

Practically every super market does some prepackaging on the premises. As of two years ago (our latest available figures on this subject), fresh meats are prepackaged in 96 per cent of the super markets, cheese in 67 per cent, fresh fruits and vegetables in 55 per cent, and meat cold cuts in 54 per cent. Many of the larger companies do some central prepackaging.

As of a year ago, the typical super market sells 6,000 different items (each brand, size, flavor, variety, etc. being counted as a separate item). The typical company handles 4,300 dry grocery items. On the average, it took on 200 new grocery items during the previous year and dropped 150. (With shelf space limited, super markets cannot possibly take on all the new products coming on the market. The retailer looks for items that provide a service to the consumer; are truly new, not just "me, too," i.e., a carbon copy of existing items or an additional size not justified by consumer demand; expand the market for the retailer; not merely replace sales of other items; possess adequate profit potential; are backed with a sound promotion program; and are not too burdensome and costly to handle physically.)

Super markets opened in 1960 average 13,400 sq. ft. of selling area, 21,300 sq. ft. of total area, an investment of about half a million dollars. The typical new super market faces direct competition from three other super markets, plus numerous smaller food stores. Sales per square foot in these new units amounted to $2.62 a week, as reported to us late in 1960. For all super markets, including both old and new, sales per square foot averaged $3.69 a week in 1960.

Super market sales are concentrated toward the end of the week. Friday and Saturday account for close to 60 per cent of the week's business. This presents obvious problems in keeping the shelves full and the checkout lines moving. Nearly half of the store employees (45 per cent) are part-timers, often with limited training.

Operating expenses have been rising at a faster rate than sales. This rise has been gradual and persistent. Major store expense items include labor (about half of the total store operating expense), rent and costs relating to equipment. Typical gross profit in 1960 was less than 19 per cent. With gross profit rising less than operating expense, net operating profit before taxes fell to less than 2 per cent.

Here is what all this adds up to: 1. Super market operators are concerned, continuously and increasingly, with operating efficiency as well as with building and maintaining sales. 2. Display space is at a premium.

More specifically now, what does the super market operator expect in a package?

WHAT RETAILERS WANT IN SHIPPING CARTONS

To begin with, the retailer is concerned with the shipping carton, the package around the package, so to speak. It goes without saying—at least it should—that the case must be strong enough and so designed as to prevent damage to the contents in transit, in handling, and while the case is being cut open. The shipping case should lend itself to palletizing, preferably on pallets $40'' \times 32''$ or $40'' \times 48''$, and it should fit onto conveyors. It should be rectangular, not square, and it should not be too bulky or heavy.

The contents should be clearly described, including the brand, variety, quantity, size and color. Markings should be on at least four sides, in bold large print to permit easy reading—no stencils or pasted-on labels. The box should be easy to open and it should have clear instructions as to the method and place of opening. Case pack, the number of units in the shipping carton, should correspond to turnover—neither too big nor too small.

How the product is packed in the shipping case is also important. Retailers want the packages placed in the carton in such a manner that they are ready for price-stamping when the carton is opened—nothing has to be turned over.

WHAT RETAILERS WANT IN PACKAGES

Again, we start with protection of the contents. The package must be strong enough to prevent damage to the product. The retailer fully expects the package to safeguard the quality of the contents. It should keep food at its nutritious best, and it should meet all legal requirements, including the food additives regulations of the Food and Drug Administration. (While on the subject of FDA, we have been advised by the Commissioner of Food and Drugs that his agency is about to commence an aggressive enforcement program to assure compliance with the law regarding prominent and conspicuous appearance of information required to be shown on food labels.)

By all means, there should be a "white spot" for price-marking. This "white spot" should be large enough and it should be on top of the package. The advantages of the "white spot" are so obvious, and retailers have been clamoring for it so long, that a manufacturer who neglects to provide it may automatically be considered uninterested both in the problems of the retailer and the desire of the consumer for price information and speedy checkout. Let me quote on this subject from "Trade Practice Recommendations for the Grocery Industry," a booklet published by Grocery Manufacturers of America in cooperation with the major food retailer and wholesaler groups: "(The white spot) has such labor-saving advantages that decisions on what brand to stock are sometimes influenced by the package with proper marketing facilities." Needless to say, the package must be so constructed that it will not cave in, crack, or break when the price-marking stamp is applied.

Incidentally, the tops of bottles and jars are most suitable for price-marking—i.e., unless they are covered with printing. Manufacturer codes or messages should never interfere with the "white spot," and code numbers should be inconspicuous so that it is impossible to confuse them with the price. Retailers appreciate a simple, understandable date code on perishable and semiperishable products that will enable them to do a proper job of rotation and selling foods at top quality. A code which requires the services of the FBI or CIA to break fools not only the customer and the retailer, but in the long run it can hardly serve the manufacturer's best interests.

The package must stack well on the shelves. It should stand without support and lend itself to attractive display. It should be designed realistically, with the dimensions of shelving and display cases in mind. To the extent possible, packages should be of standard size. If the product is multiple-packaged, the pack should be strong enough to keep the individual packages together even under tough handling, and it must lend itself to easy shelf-stocking. Also, deposit bottles are high on the list of costly nuisances.

A package should give all the necessary information, easy to read. Illustrations of the product, especially eye-catching pictures of the finished (cooked) product can add greatly to package appeal. The package should display the contents to best advantage. Does it make sense, for example, to place so much printing on a transparent package that the contents are hidden? This is not to overstate the case for pretty pictures. Basically, the super market operator is interested in selling and making a profit rather than running an art gallery (although some super markets have been known to hang and even sell paintings).

In general, the modern package should reflect the image of the super market—convenience, value and care in the handling of food, i.e., keeping the contents fresh, sanitary, nutritious and appetizing. Package designers should keep in mind that packages are sometimes displayed with the ends or sides showing, not the face.

The package should be large enough to adequately house the product, but no larger! Shelf space is hard to come by in a super market, and the operator resents packages which take up unnecessary space—especially when he feels that the package has been so designed as to force him to give it additional shelf space. Emphasis should be on reducing the package size, not building it up. A smaller package means more units on display and higher sales per square foot.

As space allocation studies are becoming more widespread, and retailers are learning more about effective shelf space utiltization, let the package designer think about the story of the waiter who served a $3.75 meal, was given a five dollar bill with the check, and brought the change in two pieces: a quarter and a dollar bill. The customer looked at the change, he looked at the waiter, and he pocketed the dollar and left the quarter on the plate as his tip. The waiter took the quarter, smiled and told the diner, "That's all right, sir, I gambled and I lost." A package designer inclined to gamble on the size of the package may find that it will not even get the reduced amount, as did the waiter.

A few special words on a special problem— promotions, deals and premiums. I have already mentioned the need for multiple-unit packages to fit readily on super market shelves —and to stay together. Consumer premiums attached to merchandise are a problem to retailers. They are often stripped off the packages, particularly by children, leaving the

packages unsaleable. Nor are the retailers any happier about many premiums contained inside the package. Too often, they substantially increase the weight or affect the size of the package, making for more difficulty in stocking.

Price-off package deals can be very troublesome. They are acceptable only if the wording makes it crystal clear that the price as marked has already deducted the special reduction from the regular price. For example, "This Special Price (   ) Cents is 15 Cents Less Than Regular Price" is greatly preferable to just "15 Cents Off;" the latter practically invites customers to ask the checker to deduct 15 cents from the price as marked—which already reflects the special reduction. Such practices as printing "10 Cents Off" in large type, with small type reading "on your next purchase," or labels that say "25 Cents Refund" in large type, and in small type require complicated customer compliance are strongly discouraged.

WHAT CUSTOMERS WANT IN PACKAGES

One of the principal requirements of efficient movement is customer acceptance. Let us take a brief look, therefore, at the role of the package in satisfying the wants of the consumer. The comments which follow are based on reports from super market operators, the men in the market place, and on published consumer surveys conducted by various organizations. Interestingly enough (although perhaps not too surprisingly), many consumer desires and complaints parallel those of the super market operator.

The beauty of a package is accepted and appreciated, just like the music and air conditioning and all the other pleasant surroundings in today's super markets, but above all the consumer seems to want convenience and utility. On the whole super market operators respect their customers as rational, intelligent people who cannot be hoodwinked by a package—at least not for long.

Consumers expect the package to protect the contents and keep them at their flavorful best. They want packages that are easy to open, easy to use and easy to close. They are less than happy with pry-off tops, set-in lids, cans that open with a key, packages that leak, deposit bottles, pouring spouts which don't work or no spouts where they should be, "Press here to open" directions which seem entirely unrelated to the facts.

Consumers want packages that will fit on the shelves of the average home and won't topple over because of poor design. They want information on the package that will help them decide whether to purchase the product and, having purchased it, how to use it. This might include descriptive information of the contents, serving suggestions and number of servings, price (here is where the "white spot" comes in again, and proper wording of "cents off" deals), instructions on cooking, storing and shelf life in the pantry. Parenthetically, is the information legible and understandable and will the instructions be destroyed as soon as the package is opened?

Consumers want honest value. They are not favorably impressed, for example, with misleading information as to the number of servings in a package. And in the survey on "Food Packages As Housewives See Them," published recently by *Sales Management,* in a list of fourteen statements designed to probe a variety of consumer attitudes, the following drew the strongest agreement: "Wish manufacturers wouldn't try to fool me by packing a small amount of product in an over-size package." The consumer may be sufficiently attracted by a package to purchase it, and the product itself may fully meet all expectations, but if the package seems deceptive or is a source of irritation while in use, the chances of a repeat purchase are surely diminished.

FOLLOW SUPER MARKET OPERATIONAL DEVELOPMENTS

Let us assume that the manufacturer is already doing everything possible in the way of package construction and design and that his packages and shipping cartons meet all the requirements enumerated earlier. There is one more thing which the retailer would urge upon his manufacturer friend: Constantly keep in touch with operational developments at the super market, as well as with consumer wants and technological packaging advances.

A number of leading retailers are using the tray pack method of stocking grocery shelves, which they consider a more satisfactory technique in many ways—in effecting time and labor savings, fast restocking during peak periods, full shelf appearance, reduced breakage, cleaner shelves, improved rotation, and (given proper design) an opportunity for good point-of-sale advertising.

In a nutshell, the tray pack method involves handling merchandise by the trayful instead of a handful. Top and bottom of the original shipping case (this would apply to a two-layer carton) are cut to form two trays, most commonly 1¼" high, which are then used to move a full layer of packages at a time. Some shipping cartons feature inner trays ready to be taken out along with the contents. While there are still some questions as to just how widespread this practice will become, manufacturers and their package designers should closely follow developments in the use of this method. Just how will the tops and bottoms of the shipping cartons look when they have been cut off to form trays for the packages? Will the lip flash a crisp message for the product, in attractive colors, or will it be unintelligble gibberish—and half the time upside down? Will the lip cover up an important part of the package label?

Not all products qualify for tray pack display. A product with turnover which justifies no more than, say, two facings will not automatically get four facings by being delivered in a carton suitable for tray pack. Another key factor is the type of package—items susceptible to damage in cutting, such as cereals, cake mixes, soap and paper products, cannot be tray packed unless they have tear strips or some other safety device to protect the packages.

Earlier I spoke about the use of pallets. Pre-palletization from the manufacturing plant can mean savings in handling and reduced damage. A Midwestern super market operator recently cited the example of canned pineapple being palletized in Hawaii, loaded into freighters and later railroad cars, and delivered to his warehouse—all on the original pallets. More manufacturers, he urged, should look to palletized shipments as a means of cutting costs to themselves as well as their customers. Again, a need and a trend to be kept in mind by the shipping case designer.

Another development in super market operations is the introduction, at long last, of multideck frozen food cases. Changes in display fixtures and equipment always deserve the attention of the package designer.

And for my final example, I would just like to mention briefly that several manufacturers are working on an automated checkout which would electronically record prices and perhaps complete information on product movement. Adoption of such equipment could affect marketing methods.

SUMMARY

The package has played a significant role in the development of the super market and self-service in general. Super market operators recognize the tremendous contribution made by packaging, but too often they feel that the manufacturer and his package designer ignore the needs and wants of the retailer and also of the consumer.

The food retailer operates on a narrow margin. His costs of doing business are increasing, and so is the severity of competition. He is continually looking for ways to cut expenses and reduce waste. A package which adds to his cost or takes more space than is really needed does not build good will with the retailer. It does not create the incentive to give the product unstinted retailer support.

Packaging is only one element of a good product, of course, but it is an important one. It could be the determining one. Just as you should never underestimate the power of a woman, so in today's competitive market it is not wise to underestimate the depth of feeling of the retailer.

Essentially, the interests of the manufacturer and the retailer are the same. To be sure, the manufacturer is concerned mainly with his own product, the retailer more with his over-all operation. Nevertheless, their common interests far outweigh the areas of potential conflict. Super market operators ask manufacturers to consider the retailer's needs in planning a product and designing the package to help the retailer cut costs and preserve space; to follow operational developments; to take a look now and then at the product in a railroad car or truck, in a grocery warehouse and in a super market backroom as well as on the supermarket shelf. Food retailers are glad to work with manufacturers, individually and through their established trade associations, to further good product handling methods.

My association, Super Market Institute, has taken part in many meetings with other trade groups. Our Information Service and library have been used by many individual manufacturers to study relevant industry recommendations and published literature. Our reports on industry trends are widely circulated and available to anyone concerned with efficient food distribution.

I do not mean to give the impression that the fault lies always with the manufacturer. Retailers are fully aware of the need to educate their own employees on good materials handling methods—including the proper use of the white spot, the tear strip and the tray pack method. Efficient marketing is the responsibility of all the elements involved—manufacturers, distributors, carriers, package designers, container companies, etc.

Yes, efficient marketing requires the continuous and wholehearted cooperation of everyone concerned, but the end result is worth the effort: greater consumer value, greater customer satisfaction, and increased sales, at a profit—in the words of the SMI motto, "more for all."

DISCUSSION QUESTIONS

The "package" and most decisions relating thereto, are generally assumed to fall within the jurisdiction of manufacturers and processors. This article indicates an interest in and sensitivity to packaging matters on the part of retailers.

1. What is the tray-pack method of shelf stocking?
2. Several years ago, one of the large manufacturers of facial tissues "squeezed all of the air out" of their package and, in effect, got twice as many boxes as in a comparable space previously. This probably delighted retail operators. Unless other manufacturers of facial tissue similarly reduce the size of their package, the first product to do so may suffer irreparable damage. How does this damage occur?

5. Customer Types and Salesman Tactics in Appliance Selling

ALFRED OXENFELDT[*]

Appliance customer types—each seeking different product features and varied kinds of services—have helped to segment appliance dealers into different types. Any given dealer sells to all customer types, but in very different proportions, for each type finds that certain kinds of stores match his desires best. Retail stores are, increasingly, adapting their operations to cultivate particular types of customers; consequently, retail institutions and methods of operation are changing.

On the firing line with the customer is the retail salesman. He faces the task of diagnosing differences among individual customers and of finding ways of coping with them. In addition, he must also perform other functions for the retail store of a fairly routine administrative character. Increased understanding of customers can be made to produce benefits for the retailer only if he can transmit it to his salesmen. They must implement it in the actual sales situation.

This article is concerned primarily with explaining retailers' perceptions of their customers and the way that their salesmen deal with customers and perform their other duties. It should help to explain some of the ferment that exists today in retailing and might suggest the direction in which retailing institutions are likely to develop in the near future.

This article draws heavily on intensive studies of two suburban (Long Island, New York) markets for television sets. Although these markets are hardly representative, they do include diverse types of retailers. The findings of those studies have been supplemented from other sources.

VARIED CUSTOMER DESIRES

Customers seek different product features and desire dissimilar kinds of service. In the retailing of such things as clothing, drugs, appliances, and hardware, consumers were offered essentially the same blend of service at essentially the same price until relatively recently. The customer who placed overriding emphasis on low price "had no place to go." He would have been willing to forego such niceties as spacious and attractive premises, convenient locations, ample parking, numerous and attentive salesmen, and speedy delivery service in order to effect a saving. But no retail institution met his desires.

Other customers place heavy emphasis on pleasant surroundings, attentive and informative salesmen, ironclad guarantees, etc. Clearly, the same kinds of shops do not meet the needs and desires and whims of these dissimilar types of customers. Accordingly, new types of retailers—in particular, the "mass" or "volume" retailer now called the "discount house"—emerged. This type of retailer essentially applies the same principles to the sale of such things as appliances and clothing that had been applied for decades to the sale of food products in supermarkets.

We can hypothesize, then, that the activities of appliance dealers represent adaptations to the nature and behavior of their customers. Similarly, distributors and manufacturers of major appliances pick their marketing strategies, methods of display, hours of operation, salesmen, etc., on the basis of the number, location, and expressed or implied preferences

◆ SOURCE: Reprinted by permission from the editor of the *Journal of Retailing*, in the winter 1963–64 issue, pages 9–15.
* The author expresses his deep gratitude to Sperry and Hutchinson for a research grant that made these studies possible and to Mr. Sidney Bloom, who conducted most of the personal interviews on which they rest.

and actions of their customers. To understand, then, why and how appliance dealers and their salesmen do the things they do, one must study the ultimate consumer and determine how the retailer sees him.

Every appliance dealer does business with varied consumers, even though customers of a given type tend to be attracted to a particular kind of retail outlet. At one extreme, there is a substantial and apparently growing class of consumers regarded by retailers and their salesmen as "the enemy." These are aggressive and well-informed but extremely shrewd customers who consider a major purchase a challenge to outsmart the retailer. They place an unreasonably high value on tiny monetary savings because for them it is a matter of pride and principle to make purchases at the lowest possible price. These consumers are found mainly in large cities. They have no store loyalty or personal friendship with a retailer or salesman and buy wherever they can "get the best deal." The notion that the dealer is "entitled" to make a profit is foreign to their thinking; if they were able to buy an appliance below the dealer's actual cost, they would ordinarily boast of it rather than feel compassion for the dealer. Many do not hesitate to invent stories about the low prices they have found in competing stores.

At the opposite extreme are consumers that salesmen call "gentlemen." These customers feel and show genuine concern for the retailer's interests. They would not beat down a price even if they believed that they could. These consumers regard retailers as basically honest and as a general rule trust their advice.

Another important type of consumer, as viewed by appliance dealers and their salesmen, is the "lamb." "Lambs" are very uninformed and unsophisticated buyers; moreover, they are gullible and malleable. Ordinarily they are anxious to own the item for which they are shopping and welcome any advice and sales arguments that facilitate their purchase.

As indicated, every salesman meets all types of customers, though "the enemy" gravitates to the discount houses and appliance chains; he comes out in greatest numbers when those stores are running special promotions. "Gentlemen" and "lambs" are found in all kinds of retail stores. The former tend mainly to patronize local shops and become acquainted, if not friendly, with the retailer and some of his salesmen. "Lambs" are attracted to stores that claim to offer bargains.

Appliance salesmen who have had numerous contacts with "the enemy" tend to become wary. Until they have conducted a reconnaissance to form an estimate of the enemy's intentions and capabilities, they withhold their fire. Once they find an "enemy," most appliance salesmen expect and offer no "quarter." All tactics are considered fair in what they regard as a no-holds-barred struggle—on both sides. Whatever qualms of conscience they might have felt if they used shady tactics with "gentlemen" never arise. They regard their behavior as more than justified—indeed, they consider it necessary for survival—by the nature of the enemy they face.

It is not clear whether all appliance salesmen modify their behavior when they meet, not an "enemy" but a "lamb" or a "gentleman." Doubtless there are substantial differences among salesmen in this regard, with many matching customer consideration if a large financial sacrifice is not involved. On the other hand, some seem to be motivated solely by short-term gain and try to get their customer's name on a contract by any device that might work, regardless of the customer's demeanor.

It is impossible to explain the low ethical standards one finds among metropolitan salesmen of appliances unless one recognizes the aggressiveness and unscrupulousness of many consumers. Consumer avarice certainly reinforces seller deceitfulness.

On the other hand, the aggressiveness and avarice of many consumers can be explained in large measure by the unenviable position they occupy when they come to the marketplace. They confront an enormous variety of similar items among which they must choose. The most important attributes of the product are far too technical for them to appraise. Many of them, moreover, have lost any personal ties with the retailer, for more and more of them buy from department stores or large chains that are impersonal and characterized by rapid turnover of sales personnel.

Moreover, their purchase involves a sizable outlay, so that the penalties of a mistaken choice are substantial. Then, too, every consumer gets to meet the "sharp salesman" who deals loosely with the truth, and finding a trusting consumer, will take outrageous advantage of him. From this strange mixture of dependence, mistrust, insecurity, feelings of inadequacy, and strain because of the large expenditure comes strange and varied consumer behavior. And that is precisely what one finds in the market for major appliances. Consumers vary at least as much as do the stores in which they buy and the salesmen with whom they deal.

THREE CUSTOMER APPROACHES TO PURCHASE SITUATION

Customers have been divided into three broad types on the basis of their approach to the purchase situation and the way they relate to retailers. Within these broad classes of customers are many and very important differences to which skilled retail salesmen are sensitive. Customers differ in income, in education, and in the number and condition of their present television sets. Some are interested in auxiliary equipment (like hi-fi or stereo), some are brand loyal, some are "regular customers," etc. Many salesmen consciously try to identify the types of customers their stores attract and study how best to serve them, as well as other types. No salesman meets only one type. The adaptable salesman is able to serve many classes of customers, even while concentrating his efforts on certain selected types.

CHIEF FUNCTIONS OF APPLIANCE SALESMEN

The appliance salesman performs several distinct functions, often concurrently, that should be distinguished to understand his contribution to the distribution process. First, he communicates product information and frequently demonstrates and displays merchandise in the process. Second, he is a persuader, another form of communication. Third, he participates in record-keeping. Finally, he helps to "manage merchandise," including the floor arrangement of merchandise and some movement from rear spaces to the sales floor; occasionally he also participates in arranging window displays.

Communication of Product Information

Some distribution specialists would describe retail salesmen as purveyors of misinformation rather than as sources of information. This observation partly is a slur on the honesty of the average salesman, who is careless with the truth when he has reason to believe that a fib (whether small, medium, or large, white, grey, or black) would mean the difference between a sale and a lost customer. It attests also to the very limited amount of product informa-

tion that the average salesman possesses and the dubious sources from which he draws it. Especially retail salesmen who sell a wide variety of technical products of varied brands, all of which change frequently, cannot keep informed about the products they sell even if they have had some technical product training. For the usual kinds of people engaged in retail selling the task is overwhelming. Consequently salesmen of appliances tend to substitute glibness for solid fact. Most of them get by because of the even greater ignorance of the customers and their ability to deceive themselves and most others into believing that they really know what they are talking about.

The retail salesman's communication function has altered greatly in recent years. This change has affected the major appliance salesman almost as much as most others. Although self-service and self-selection date far back to the early Woolworth stores, if not before, arrangements for reducing the participation of the salesman in the purchase transaction have been so extended that they have created a new species of salesman-customer relationship. The salesman's communication function has changed dramatically as customers have been brought in direct contact with merchandise. The merchandise itself, plus point-of-sale printed materials, packages, etc., communicate much of the product information formerly supplied by the salesman.

Other Duties

Television set dealers vary widely in the communication duties they assign to their salesmen. Some relegate their salesmen to the role of the salesman in a food supermarket—to virtual nonexistence. At the opposite extreme, other appliance retailers assign a salesman to accompany each customer while he inspects merchandise. Most retailers fall between these two extremes, displaying their merchandise so that customers can inspect it and narrowing down the range of alternatives without personal assistance. At some point, however, a salesman is summoned or volunteers his services.

Retail salesmen have been criticized harshly by some retailing specialists, such as E. B. Weiss, on the grounds of incompetence, low effort, and limited intelligence. Some salesmen no doubt merit this harsh assessment. On the other hand, most of the major appliance salesmen studied by the author over an extended period deserve the highest praise for skill, effort, and intelligence. The proportions of salesmen who belong in these two opposing classes cannot be assessed reliably on the basis of available information. The author's investigations, which were intensive rather than extensive, suggest that talented appliance salesmen represent a large majority in metropolitan centers and their suburbs, particularly in the appliance chains. The caliber of individual salesmen varies enormously, sometimes within the same store.

The Persuasive Function

The salesman provides information, combined with puffery, allegation, falsehood, implication, and innuendo, mainly in an effort to persuade. He also discusses product attributes when customers ask questions of him. But whatever the proportion, the salesman definitely uses the communication process in order to persuade. He relies almost entirely on words and gestures, combined with occasional demonstration of the product. Consequently, persuasion and communication are inextricably intertwined, even though in intent and effect they are quite different.

Beyond the variety of techniques common to retail salesmen generally, appliance salesmen have some special strategies for their attempts to sell a *particular item*. A favorite is the "bait and switch" stratagem by which the customer is persuaded to buy, not the item advertised, but a more expensive one.

The appliance dealer generally sees his main objective—to make sales at a profit—as having two distinct stages: first, he must lure potential customers into his premises; second, he must induce them to make a purchase. And his assumption is that there is no necessary connection between the item used to lure customers into the store and the item that is ultimately sold. In its extreme form, "bait and switch" involves "loss-leading."

"Switching" should not be confused with the related sales tactic of "trading-up." This tactic is planned by the manufacturer at the time the line of products is designed for the market. Specifically, "stepping up the consumer" consists of leading the customer from the model in the line in which he showed greatest original interest to more costly models by stressing, step by step, the features that may be obtained for "modest" added cost. (These added charges seem even more modest when expressed in terms of payments per month.)

Each feature added to a television set ordinarily commands a price that is significantly above the added cost of the feature to the retailer (and to the distributor and manufacturer as well). Consequently, the manufacturer, and the various middlemen through whom he sells, has a strong financial inducement to "step up" the customer to more expensive models. And the number and magnitude of the "step-ups" as well as "switches" he engineers is a major measure of a salesman's skill.

These sales tactics can be evaluated from many standpoints. They can be evaluated simply on the basis of effectiveness. On that score they must be rated in the case of television sets very high. Salesmen (with the conscious or unconscious collaboration of consumers) do succeed in "switching" or trading up a very large proportion of their customers. No exact estimate of their number is possible, but the author would venture the guess that at present it exceeds 65 percent of the television sets sold—and it was even higher in years back. (A switch or step-up occurs when the salesman's efforts induce a customer to purchase a set that yields the retailer and/or the salesman a larger margin of profit than the one in which the customer expressed initial interest.)

The social effects of bait-switch selling are not easy to evaluate. Although the salesman's motives are clearly self-interested, some general consumer benefits may still result from the practice. Judged from the standpoint of consumers who seek merchandise at minimum *price* (which may mean high *cost)*, the bait-switch stratagem increases the supply of attractive goods available.

In rare cases, a customer literally cannot persuade the retailer to sell him the "lure" merchandise, no matter how strong his determination to do so; such "lure" items usually are called "nailed down models." Likewise, some customers cannot be switched. They know their own minds, are not easily intimidated or persuaded by salesmen, and will not buy an item unless they believe its worth to them exceeds its cost. However, "bait" merchandise often leads other consumers to make an unproductive visit to a store in the expectation of finding offerings that are not available or were misrepresented in the store's advertising. Frequently, the "bait" item is advertised in a manner that conveys a false impression to the customer; it often does so by withholding information from the prospective customer— like the fact that it does not include some essential feature, or that it is a model about to be superseded or even a model from a previous year. Occasionally, the "bait" item is made in a style so unattractive that the consumer would consider his home disfigured by its presence; the large black square box type of table model television set is a relatively familiar example from the recent past.

When some misrepresentation or nondisclosure about the "lures" induces the consumer to make an otherwise unplanned shopping trip, then the bait-switch tactic hurts even the consumer who knows what he wants and will not be diverted. Not only has he made an unnecessary and frustrating shopping trip, but in addition he may be subjected to sales pressure of an unpleasant and embarrassing sort. Or he may make a purchase he will regret— hardly a goodwill builder for the firm! And similar harm to the store image may result if consumers discover that a certain store advertises sets that are "new" in the sense that they have not been used but are not "new models" because they were introduced one or more years earlier.

Record-Keeping and Merchandising Functions

Salesmen are expected to give their employers and their suppliers information as well as to inform their customers about products. Manufacturers, store owners, or managers want information on the following aspects of the market: customer reactions to individual brands and models and specifically to particular product features, such as performance, aesthetic appeal, customers' apparent impressions of the value of the guarantees and service facilities offered by different manufacturers.

Many retailers ask their salesmen to keep a written record of such observations which they collect and analyze and then transmit to their suppliers. The vast majority of retailers do not systematically gather such data, however. They require only that their salesmen do the paper work involved in effecting a sale. Especially when the transaction involves installment credit, this element of salesmen's duties can be burdensome. If the salesmen carry it out inefficiently or ungraciously, it can itself become an important source of lost sales.

SALES MANAGEMENT

In considering the functions performed by retail salesmen of television sets, one must take account of the activities of the store owner or executive of an appliance chain who is responsible for managing the retail sales force. Many retailers do not consider it their responsibility to train salesmen. Apparently they feel that their job has been done when they hire someone who seems to be a good salesman. If they find by examining actual sales records that they were mistaken, they will hire a replacement. What training salesmen get comes primarily from manufacturers' or distributors' representatives and is concerned mainly with product information rather than with sales methods.

There are some exceptions, of course. A few appliance chains describe themselves as "fanatics" on the subject of sales training. Inspection of what they actually do suggests outright neglect far more than fanaticism. The retail salesmen who sell television sets ordinarily constitute a very small group. Perhaps the smallness of their number discourages the owner or store executive from designing and carrying out a program of training. The most common method of preparing a new retail salesman for his assignment is to put him under the wing of a senior salesman for a few days. Just what senior salesmen do at such times is difficult to determine. Although the guidance they give new salesmen can scarcely qualify as rigorous sales training administered by a training specialist, it does familiarize the new salesman with the way that store handles its paper work and with the sales approaches of at least one salesman—who may not be very capable as a salesman, let alone as a teacher. The substantial number of capable people among the ranks of appliance salesmen may be better explained by a selective process—self-selection by individuals who undertake this work and skilled employment practices or quick weeding out of the untalented by owners and managers—than by the conscious development of latent sales talent.

Appliance salesmen must, of course, serve all categories of customers. The best salesmen have always classified customers. Mainly, they divide them by two basic questions: first, "do they have the money to buy?" Second, are they "really interested in buying or just looking?" These days, in addition to such criteria, appliance salesmen divide customers into three personality types: the "enemy," the "gentleman," and "lambs." In turn, customers now perceive a much wider range of retail institutions that they might patronize. They accordingly attempt to match their desires and needs against the offerings of the different types of retail establishment. As customers become more discriminating, retailers will be forced to adapt their operations even further to win the favor of the kinds of customers they wish to serve and further segmentation of the retail effort will result.

DISCUSSION QUESTIONS

Oxenfeldt identifies three classes of appliance customers—"the enemy," "the gentleman," and "the lamb."

1. Would your sales approach vary with each of these types of customers? Why?
2. Is the "switching" procedure which is discussed in this article ethical?

VIII

Price Competition
in Retailing

Price competition at the retail level of distribution is characterized by contradiction. On the one hand, we are told that the effectiveness of price competition is dulled by efforts to "maintain" resale prices—whether those efforts be formal or informal. On the other hand such "maintained" prices provide the incentive for new institutions which pay little respect to such prices. Similarly, we contradict ourselves by espousing strong, nondiscriminatory pricing practices on the one hand and legislating against such practices on the other.

This section includes an examination of the most well-publicized price war in the history of American retailing and an analysis of some of the factors which produced the war. In an excellent article, Harkrader identifies some of the hanky-panky in price competition which one may encounter. Deception in the description of retail sale prices is common and, in some instances, unwitting. Guides are presented which will aid in the selection of nondeceptive pricing terms. Another article presents the minority view regarding resale price maintenance—most students find this article an open invitation to debate. Professor Hollander's fine article provides historical perspective for some of the retail price practices and policies which are common today.

1. The New York Department Store Price War of 1951:[1] A Microeconomic Analysis

RALPH CASSADY, JR.

Intensive competition among department stores has prevailed in the New York market for 100 years or more. From time to time over a long period of years, price warfare has broken out among firms determined to prevail in the struggle for business. These "wars" typically involved R. H. Macy & Company and this firm's various rival concerns as opponents.[2]

For a number of years following the enactment of resale price maintenance or "fair trade" legislation in the mid-1930's,[3] competitive struggles involving deep price cutting and undercutting were infrequent in New York as elsewhere. Then came the United States Supreme Court's Schwegmann decision in May, 1951,[4] which freed nonsigner retailers from certain restrictions in the pricing of their goods, assuming interstate commerce was involved, and allowed aggressive sellers to follow their own individual policies in pricing their

merchandise.[5] A bitterly fought price war ensued.

INCEPTION OF THE "WAR"

The key factors in this price war were R. H. Macy & Company—long a champion of free pricing and perennially an aggressive element in the New York market—and Gimbel Brothers, almost, if not quite, as aggressive and located just across the street from Macy's on Herald Square. The Macy slogan, "We endeavor to save our customers at least 6% for cash, except on price-fixed goods," [6] was at

♦ SOURCE: Reprinted by permission from the American Marketing Association, in the *Journal of Marketing*, July 1957, pages 3–11.

[1] Adapted from a section of a general study of price wars to be published later.

[2] For accounts of earlier price struggles, see, for example, Ralph M. Hower, *History of Macy's of New York, 1858–1919* (Cambridge: Harvard University Press, 1943). See, particularly, pp. 21, 168, 288, 291–94, and 349–60.

[3] This included (a) state laws (in most states) legalizing the issuance of contracts by manufacturers which bound distributors within that state to any prices set by manufacturers and (b) a federal law legalizing contracts between manufacturers and distributors located in different "fair trade" states.

[4] See *Schwegmann Bros.* v. *Calvert Distillers Corp.*, 314 U. S. 384 (1951).

[5] In the Schwegmann decision, the Court said in effect that the federal Tydings-Miller law applied only to signers of state "fair trade" contracts and not to nonsigners (who are purportedly bound by the terms of the law). The result is that nonsigner firms such as Macy's were freed from "fair trade" restrictions on all merchandise which had been transported in interstate commerce.

However, the nonsigner clause in "fair trade" contracts continued to apply in any transactions which were neither in nor affected by interstate commerce. Moreover, the law presumably was still enforceable in the case of signatories of interstate contracts. It is interesting that an attempt was made to enjoin Macy's from undercutting "fair trade" prices on certain drug items which were supposed to have originated in New York State and remained in intrastate commerce but with little, if any, effect on the course of the "war."

[6] The store explains its 6-per cent policy in a pamphlet entitled "Here's How Macy's 6% Cash Policy Saves You Money," as follows: "This policy begins with the endeavor to price every article in Macy's *originally* at 6% less than identical or comparable merchandise in charge account stores (except those items price-fixed by law). . . . To back

least theoretically offset by the Gimbel motto, "Nobody—but nobody—undersells Gimbel's." This "war" was not a duel, however. Other important competitive factors in the 1951 "war" were Abraham & Straus (a Brooklyn concern),[7] Bloomingdale's (a Manhattan firm),[8] and Namm's (a Brooklyn store)[9]—all large departmentalized retail institutions. Even the stores which did not actively participate in the struggle were affected by it.

There have been all kinds of explanations of the New York department store price war of mid-1951. It has been suggested that the stores were heavy with inventory and were happy to

have the opportunity of unloading.[10] Some have felt that the stores in Herald Square— Macy's, Gimbel's, and Sak's-34th Street, which were somewhat isolated by a shift in the center of shopping—might have used the price war as a strategic device to draw customers to their establishments. Others have thought, perhaps correctly, that Macy's was simply attempting in a dramatic way to implement the impression that the store's prices were generally lower than those of competitors.

It is difficult to evaluate these factors. It is not difficult, however, to recognize the key factor leading to the initial reductions. It was simply that R. H. Macy, for many years committed (or at least ostensibly committed) to a policy of underselling credit-store competition, suddenly found itself freed by the Schwegmann decision to reduce prices of products which had been price fixed. The store management felt that, in order to be consistent in its policy, it had no alternative but to reduce prices when permitted by law to do so.[11]

Competitive stores, particularly Gimbel's, felt that the Macy policy was invalid[12] and that the move from their points of view was intolerable, especially when made with so much fanfare. This would suggest that the basic cause of the "war" was the Macy policy of purporting to sell for less combined with a highly antagonistic attitude toward Macy's competitive activities on the part of the store's New York competitors which caused them to challenge the Macy move.[13] Fundamentally,

---

up this policy . . . Macy's maintains the largest staff of comparison shoppers in the world to 'police' the correctness of our prices. They make an average of 35,000 shoppings a week. Before any Macy advertisement appears the Comparison Office has shopped stores in the Metropolitan area of New York to check that the Macy price is at least 6% less. . . . If you find the price of any article in Macy's (not price-fixed by law) is not 6% less than that charged by a credit store, we would appreciate your reporting it either to the Comparison Office . . . or to any salesclerk in the department where this merchandise is carried. Or, if you bought an article at Macy's and then discover it is being sold for less in a charge account store, notify us at once. . . . The Comparison Office will check immediately and as soon as your report is confirmed, Macy's will refund the difference plus 6%."

[7] Abraham & Straus reportedly was a tougher competitor than Gimbel's, possibly because it felt that it had to provide attractive enough prices to prevent an exodus of Brooklyn shoppers to Herald Square. The result is that: (1) this institution reduced its prices on a wider list of items than did other competitors, and (2) this store was not always satisfied to just meet Macy's price but would often undercut Macy's quotations.

[8] Bloomingdale's indicated early in the "war" that it was reluctantly entering the conflict but would "meet competition." According to one of the store's executives, in a conversation with the author some time after the "war's" end, it reduced prices in all departments without fanfare and, in some instances, for harassment purposes evidently, suddenly undercut its own reductions with the result that Macy's "did not know what was going on" and consequently was unable to meet the reductions.

[9] Namm's reportedly assumed a passive role in the "war" and followed the policy of placing price-cut merchandise out of sight so that the customer had to ask for it. "Price War Widens . . . ," *The New York Times,* June 5, 1951, p. 34.

[10] For example, Mrs. Sara Pennoyer, then Vice President and Sales Promotion Manager of James McCreery and Company in New York, said in an address made before the Advertising Association of America in St. Louis ("Price War in City Laid to Ad Failure," *The New York Times,* June 11, 1951, p. 34) that the New York price war could be ascribed, in part at least, to failure of advertising to move inventories that were heavier than the merchants liked to carry.

[11] See the first sentence of the Macy policy, footnote 6 above.

[12] A top executive of a large retail competitor of Macy's told this author in strongest possible terms that the Macy policy is unsound because (1) cost savings amount to much less than the highly publicized 6 per cent and that in any case (2) no firm can consistently undersell rivals on tens of thousands of items no matter how much effort they expend in shopping competitive institutions.

[13] On a basis of conversations with executives of Macy competitors after the "war," this author con-

this "war" appears to have resulted from the change in market conditions occasioned by the Supreme Court decision rather than from the existence of freedom of pricing *per se*.

It is difficult to decide with any degree of firmness who was responsible for initiating the conflict. One must, of course, distinguish between a finding as to who initiated a series of competitive moves and the fixing of the responsibility for an ensuing price war. The fixing of responsibility depends on whether Macy's can be said to have been justified in offering its merchandise at a 6-per cent saving on a basis of its cash operation. If so, the responsibility is on the shoulders of those who met or undercut Macy's prices; if not, the responsibility must be borne by Macy's.

There is little question, however, as to the actual sequence of events leading to the conflict: The Schwegmann decision was handed down by the United States Supreme Court on Monday, May 21, 1951, and a little over a week later—on Tuesday, May 29, 1951— R. H. Macy & Company ran a two-page advertisement in the New York papers announcing 6-per cent price reductions on 5,978 items which were formerly price fixed under "fair trade" legislation.[14] This advertisement also carried the price-fixed and the price-free quotations on over 100 of the almost 6,000 branded merchandise items.[15]

On a basis of the type of rivalry prevailing in the New York department store trade in 1951 and the nature of the merchandise offered, it is not at all surprising that prompt retaliatory action was taken by Macy competitors. Actually, one hour after the opening of Macy's store on the morning the Macy advertisement appeared, Gimbel's began to meet the cut.[16] By noon, Abraham & Straus in Brooklyn not only met but undercut prices by 10 per cent or even more on some of the items offered by Macy's.[17] Macy's soon learned of rivals' retaliatory action through its comparison shoppers and reduced its prices to 6 per cent under the competitors' quotations in line with its traditional cash-saving policy.[18] Gimbel's again matched Macy's. Hearn's, Bloomingdale's, Namm's, and other stores soon became involved in the battle, albeit reluctantly. Before the day was out, most of the leading New York department stores were engaged in a full-scale price war.

SUBSEQUENT DEVELOPMENTS

It is clear from the record that the 1951 price war involved well-known branded items and that, unlike most price wars, many of these were high-unit-value durable consumption products. Among the most publicized items on which deep cuts were made during the "Macy-Gimbel" price war were *Toastmasters, Mixmasters, Lewyt* vacuum cleaners, *Palm Beach* suits, *Underwood* typewriters, *Coffeematic* percolators, *Bayer* aspirin, *Ronson* lighters, *Webster* three-speed record players, *Waterman* pens, *Regina* waxers, and *Swank* jewelry as well as current best-seller books. All except two of these items—*Regina* waxers and *Webster* player attachments—were on the original list published by Macy's in its opening barrage. New items added later included *Astral* refrigerators, *Dormeyer* mixers (which were featured when *Mixmasters* were sold out), *Scott-Atwater* outboard motors, *Sunbeam* hedge trimmers, *RainKing* sprinklers, and Goodrich *Koroseal* hoses.

Of the almost 6,000 items on which prices were originally reduced 6 per cent by Macy's, only a small percentage became involved in

---

cluded that the emotional attitude toward Macy's must have had some effect on the outbreak of hostilities, although it could be that the antipathy toward R. H. Macy & Company resulted from rather than caused the "war."
[14] See, for example, the two-page advertisement entitled "Now You Can Buy 5,978 'Price-Fixed' Items at Less Than Price-Fixed-Prices—at Macy's," *The New York Times*, May 29, 1951, pp. 6 and 7. See also the *Wall Street Journal* of May 29, 1951, pp. 6 and 7.
[15] These included bedspreads, books, branded drugs, candy, children's clothing, cigars, cosmetics, fountain pens, games, garden equipment, ginger beer, home appliances, kitchenware, men's clothing, movie cameras, pocket lighters, portable typewriters, smoking equipment, toothbrushes, etc.

[16] "Price War Set Off in Stores; Some Goods Reduced 30%," *The New York Times*, May 30, 1951, p. 1. Meeting price cuts was inevitable if only for the reason that customers played one store against the other. ("Customers Scheme to Get Best Buys," *The New York Times*, January 1, 1951, p. 16.)
[17] "Price War Set Off in Stores . . . ," *op. cit.*, p. 1.
[18] The Macy policy during a price disturbance, as explained to the author by store executives, is to endeavor to keep under the competitors' prices by 6 per cent until invoice cost is reached and after that point to simply match whatever reductions are made by rivals.

the downward spiraling developing out of intensive price competition and were deep cut.[19] Of those which were deep cut, only a very few went substantially below cost.[20] If it had not been for the relatively narrow list of deep-cut items, the solvency of participating stores might have been endangered.[21] As it was, Macy's stated in its 1951 annual report that the "war" had been "expensive." [22]

Prices of many of the items on which price competition was focused dropped very rapidly. This was true, for example, of *Toastmaster*, *Mixmasters*, and *Palm Beach* suits. Prices of such items were about as low on May 31, the second day of the price war,[23] as they ever went (that is, approximately at invoice cost). Others did not drop as fast and were considerably lower a week or so later than they were the second day of the "war." Such items included *Underwood* typewriters, *Waterman* fountain pens, and *Ronson* pocket lighters.

It is difficult to provide a completely satisfactory explanation as to why there was such a marked difference in the tempo of the reductions. It might, of course, have been due to variations in consumer preference for individual items or brands and that antagonists would try to outdo each other on popular items at the outset of the struggle.

In the initial stage of the conflict, the opening prices of warring vendors were only points of departure for further cuts during the day.[24] But soon a measure of stability was reached, although, of course, at considerably lower than normal levels. Because of nonperfect market conditions (for example, absence of prompt and complete information about competitors' quotations), prices of fast-changing items were not necessarily identical in particular stores at any one moment of time, although they were for the most part closely similar.

The consumer response to the price battle was tremendous. Even on the first day of the "war," there were crowds of customers on hand despite publicity limitations and inclement weather. Much of this abnormal sales activity was concentrated on a relatively small list of items. For example, at one time early in the "war," Gimbel's sold 5,100 *Palm Beach* suits in three days when normal sales were about 150 garments per day and 5,280 *Toastmasters* when the daily norm was 40.[25] "Warring" stores were distributing a large proportion of certain makes of appliances sold in the New York market. In fact, Macy's alone was doing a substantial share of the New York business in *Mixmasters* and other Sunbeam appliances.[26]

---

[19] These included *Palm Beach* suits price-fixed at $29.95 and reduced to $16.95, *Mixmasters* price-fixed at $46.60 and reduced to $26.59, *Lewyt* vacuum cleaners price-fixed at $89.95 and reduced to $58.63, etc.

[20] These included the best seller *From Here to Eternity*, ultimately reduced from $4.50 to $1.44, and *Bayer* aspirin, which slipped from 59 cents to 4 cents. It is interesting that prices would sink to such low levels in view of Macy's policy set forth in footnote 18 above. Assuming that Macy's adhered to its policy, we must conclude that at least one competitor undercut Macy's prices after invoice was reached.

[21] Mr. Fred Lazarus, Jr., president of Federated Department Stores, Inc., said at one point during the "war" ("Lazarus Predicts Steady Fall Prices," *The New York Times*, June 8, 1951, p. 43) that there was no evidence that the price war was spreading to all store merchandise and that "should that happen, the stores would be bankrupted."

[22] *The Annual Report for the Fiscal Year Ended July 28, 1951—R. H. Macy & Co., Inc., and Subsidiaries*, p. 8.

[23] As will be recalled, the "war" started on Tuesday, May 29, but Wednesday, May 30, was Memorial Day, a holiday.

[24] In the early stages of the "war," prices of many items were changed at frequent intervals. As an indication of the rapidity of price changes, the Dow-Jones stock ticker carried certain New York department store prices during one phase of the price war.

[25] "Stocks Exhausted by Price War Here," *The New York Times*, June 2, 1951, p. 22. This tremendous sales activity must have adversely affected store efficiency. For example, at one time when *Bayer* aspirin was being offered at 4 cents per hundred, there was a line a half a block long leading into the Macy drug department. Somewhat the same situation occurred with other merchandise items. Under such circumstances, not only is the store out of pocket on each sale (about 32 cents in this instance) but very possibly (a) costs are increased by such operations—in clerk's time, for example—and (b) sales of other items are adversely affected because of the disrupted service.

[26] There is some evidence of the impact of the price war on the sales by various competitors, at least in certain types of items. Sunbeam Corporation—manufacturer of *Mixmasters* and other appliances—has for many years inserted in each appliance carton a so-called guarantee-registration card, which the customer is asked to fill out and

Within a few days after the inception of the "war," heavy selling activity resulted in temporary out-of-stock conditions in popular items.[27] Unusually heavy selling activity in deep-cut items had the effect of enhancing total sales of participating stores (or at least some of them). Survey results show that sales of such stores during the month of June, 1951, were substantially higher than those of the previous June.[28]

The New York price war was confined to relatively few retailing institutions, mostly department stores in downtown Manhattan. Fifth Avenue retail institutions did not participate in the conflict, although they probably

were not unaffected,[29] and representatives of several Fifth Avenue stores stated that it was not their policy to meet price-cutting competition.[30] However, the "war" did extend to the Bronx—one outlying store advertised that it would cut prices to meet or beat downtown competition on such well-known items as *Toastmasters*, *Mixmasters*, and *Lewyt* cleaners. This move resulted in tremendous consumer response in that area.[31]

A survey of neighborhood hardware, appliance, and household-goods stores indicated that their prices were affected by the intensive price competition of downtown stores. Reports indicated that prices in such outlying institutions were often made on a negotiated basis between buyer and seller, prompted by deep-cut quotations downtown.[32] Later in the "war" the merchants of Jersey City cooperated in attempting to dissuade Hudson County shoppers from taking advantage of the low prices prevailing in the New York department stores by offering offsetting bargains in their own community. Specifically, these sellers staged a defensive three-day "war" of their own, during

---

return. One datum on this card is the name of the retailer from whom the item was purchased. Through experience, Sunbeam knows that there is a reasonably constant percentage of returns to sales. As a result, the company is able to determine (a) how many of its appliances have actually moved into the hands of consumers and (b) what stores made the sales.

According to Sunbeam data (*Sunbeam Corporation v. R. H. Macy & Co., et al., Complaint* [October, 1951], p. 40), less than 3.5 per cent of the New York *Mixmaster* business was done by Macy's during the 11 weeks preceding the price war, while over 56.0 per cent of the New York sales of *Mixmasters* were made by Macy's during the 10 weeks following the beginning of the "war." The experience of Abraham & Straus in Brooklyn was similar (*ibid.*, pp. 41–42)—in the 11 weeks preceding the price war, this store sold 2.5 per cent of the *Mixmasters* distributed in that community; but during the 10 weeks after the start of the "war," it sold almost 60.0 per cent.

[27] Some suppliers made it difficult for price cutters to obtain merchandise. Certain manufacturers (including the makers of *Bayer* aspirin and *Eversharp* pens) refused to accept orders for merchandise from price cutters. It is interesting that the makers of *Palm Beach* and *Springweave* suits reportedly cut off supplies to Macy's only on the ground that this firm was the initiator of the "war" and the others were only "acting defensively."

[28] A survey of 13 New York and Brooklyn department stores made by *The New York Times* revealed a 14-per cent gain in June sales over those of a year before. Sales varied, of course, among stores. The sales volume of one retail institution was up 33.4 per cent. As one might expect, the largest increase appeared in major appliances and housewares. Men's clothing, books, toiletries, furniture, floor coverings, and radios and television sets showed increases also. See "Price War Spurs June Store Sales," *The New York Times*, July 3, 1951, p. 34.

[29] It is interesting to find in the same issues of *The New York Times* which reported deep-cut prices on *Palm Beach* suits at $16.95 or thereabouts, identical merchandise advertised by certain Fifth Avenue retailers at the "fair trade" price of $29.95. In at least one instance, this was not as incongruous as it appeared because the three leading antagonists in the price war were all momentarily out of *Palm Beach* suits. In at least one other instance, however, the suits evidently were available in both types of stores at widely divergent prices.

There are several possible explanations for this: (a) Fifth Avenue stores cater to a somewhat different market than the mass-selling institutions; (b) some consumers undoubtedly would consciously avoid the crowded conditions in a "warring" store; and (c) the stores which are not involved in the price war have a better selection of sizes, colors, and styles. However, there are no data indicating the extent to which the participants in the price war made inroads on sales of the Fifth Avenue establishments.

[30] "Macy's Cut Prices 6% on 'Fixed' Items; A 'War' Is Foreseen," *The New York Times*, May 29, 1951, p. 1.

[31] "Price War Widens; 3 Injured in Bronx," *The New York Times*, June 1, 1951, p. 1.

[32] "Small Shops Rock in Price-War Wake," *The New York Times*, June 1, 1951, p. 16. Most merchants granted price cuts when the buyer was able to prove (usually by a newspaper item) that a lower price was obtainable elsewhere. (*Ibid.*)

which *Toastmasters* and *Mixmasters,* among other items, were reportedly offered at deep-cut prices.[33]

Price cutting in the "Macy-Gimbel" engagement appears to have followed a fairly regular pattern.[34] Generally speaking, Macy's instituted the price cuts, which were met or exceeded by competitors, and then Macy's again cut under the competitors' price by 6 per cent. This pattern was repeated, in some instances at least, until the price of the item was reduced to invoice cost level. According to Macy's, any

---

[33] "Jersey Stores Organize Own 3-Day Price 'War,'" *The New York Times,* June 21, 1951, p. 12.

[34] There had been for some time, however, what one might term a "cold war" being waged in New York City between discount houses and regular merchandising institutions. There is little question that a great deal of price cutting on price-maintained, durable-consumption merchandise occurred in the New York market even before the Schwegmann decision. For example, shopping of retail stores handling G. E. appliances from March 7 to June 3, 1950—undertaken by R. H. Macy and by General Electric—revealed that well over 70 per cent of the stores were selling G. E. appliances below "fair trade" prices. (See *General Electric Co. v. R. H. Macy & Co., Inc., Brief on Behalf of Appellant,* original action instituted March 28, 1950, p. 58.) There was, in fact, so much price cutting in these lines, in Macy's opinion, that in March of 1950 the store reduced prices of two G. E. appliances 20 per cent below "fair trade" quotations, although the firm did not advertise the reduction. (*Ibid.,* p. 32.)

There is considerable legal precedent indicating that the courts should not enforce "fair trade" laws against one violator if the market is demoralized. (See, for example, *Calvert Distillers Corp. v. Nussbaum Liquor Store, Inc.,* 166 Misc. (N.Y.) 342 (1938); *Ray Kline, Inc. v. Davega-City Radio, Inc.,* 168 Misc. (N.Y.) 185 (1938); *Automotive Electric Service Corp. v. Times Square Stores Corp.,* 175 Misc. (N. Y.) 865 (1940); and *Carstairs Distillers Corp'n v. Morris Heights Liquor Shop, Inc.,* N.Y.L.J., July 23, 1941, p. 179, col. 2.)

However, in an action directed against the Macy move under the "fair trade" law of New York, the store was enjoined from selling appliances below the minimum price fixed by G. E. in its "fair trade" agreements despite the existence of considerable price cutting by the discount houses on the grounds that the existing price cutting did not constitute a breakdown of the price structure! (*General Electric Co. v. R. H. Macy & Co., Inc.,* 199 Misc. (N.Y.) 87, 97–98, 1951.)

---

further cuts which were initiated by their competitors were met by Macy price makers.[35]

It should be noted that the original cuts made by Macy's applied to almost 6,000 items and that presumably some selection of the particular items on which head-on conflict would be focused was made by Macy's competitors by the process of either meeting or ignoring Macy reductions. It would be reasonable to assume that the size of inventories in various lines carried by these retail institutions had some influence on the choice of the items which were reduced in price, although the popularity of the item was perhaps of paramount importance.

One final point: The stores involved in the struggle used relatively little newspaper advertising to publicize the cut-price offerings, although a limited amount was used.[36] However, news of the battle was by no means lacking. On the contrary, word of the encounter spread rapidly by means of front-page stories in the New York newspapers,[37] commentaries presented over the radio, and word-of-mouth advertising. In fact, stories of the price battle were of great national interest.

TERMINATION OF PRICE WAR

It is very difficult to make a clear-cut statement with respect to the length of the New York department store price war of 1951. The severe price cutting evidently was largely over in early August, six weeks after the "war" started. It is true, however, that some "guerilla warfare" continued for a considerable time,

---

[35] See footnote 18 above.

[36] For example, *The New York Times* for June 14, 1951, carried a large advertisement on p. 11 reading ". . . Nobody beats Gimbel prices . . . Bottle of 100 *Bayer Aspirin* 8¢ COMPARE . . ." and then there followed a list of 90 or so items giving the former fixed price and the much lower price then in effect at Gimbel's.

[37] One retailer not involved in the "war" complained that the price cutters were getting advertising free which cost him $1.50 a line. (See "Macy's Is Assailed on Price-War Role," *The New York Times,* June 8, 1951, p. 41.) It is true that front-page stories appeared in *The New York Times* May 29, May 30, June 1, June 2, June 3, June 4, June 5, June 6, June 7, June 8, and June 10, not to mention the other New York papers, while the *Times* carried numerous other stories on other days and on other pages.

even into early 1952, and certain prices were not restored until many months later.[38]

There is little question that before long the department store price war began to lose consumer appeal and, further, that profits of participants were seriously affected.[39] Consequently, there was undoubtedly a desire on the part of those engaged in the conflict to bring the struggle to an end as quickly as possible without losing face. However, there were practical difficulties in implementing such a desire.[40] One of these certainly was the strong

position each principal had taken with respect to the soundness of his own original move. And hence each presumably would have some hesitation in retreating from the position taken because of loss of face.

First-hand intensive investigation by the author failed to provide a clear-cut explanation of how this "war" was terminated. Because of the hostile attitude of the antagonists toward one another, it is unlikely that any of the retail firms "gave in" with a resulting restoration of prices or that participants agreed to raise prices simultaneously. And certainly the passage of the McGuire Act and the re-establishment of the constitutionality of "fair trade" contracts in interstate commerce had no effect on termination. Actually this law was not enacted until mid-July 1952, long after the conflict was ended.

As was mentioned earlier, the "war" did not end suddenly; rather, the process of restoration of prices to former levels was gradual.[41] There is evidence that the methods by which prices were restored differed considerably. For example, some merchandise (such as *Palm Beach* suits) was seasonal in nature, and obviously the price cutting ended when the merchandise was finally closed out for the year. The manufacturers of other items on which prices were cut refused to supply the merchandise unless an agreement to maintain prices was reached or a "fair trade" contract was signed.[42]

Moreover, as stores exhausted their stocks of price-cut merchandise, or pretended they

---

[38] Even in the fall of 1953, over two years after supposed termination of the 1951 price war, some items reportedly were still being deep cut. This included *Decca* records, which normally sell for 89 cents but which were being sold at that time for 58 cents.

[39] While it would be theoretically possible to maximize net revenue (gross margin minus expenses) by substantially increasing sales on a short-margin basis (see Ralph Cassady, Jr. and Wylie L. Jones, *The Nature of Gasoline Distribution at the Retail Level,* Berkeley, University of California Press, 1951, pp. 129 and 166), it is not likely to eventuate in a price-war situation. There are several reasons for this: (1) margins become very narrow and even nonexistent during price wars, (2) bargain-conscious customers concentrate their purchasing power on price-cut merchandise and buy little regular-priced goods, and (3) crowds tend to disrupt normal store activities and create operating inefficiencies.

[40] There is some evidence of an attempt to restore former prices by at least one of the participants early in the "war." For example, on May 31 Bloomingdale's reportedly attempted to restore prices on *Palm Beach* suits (to the price-fixed level) after its comparison shoppers reported that Macy's stock was exhausted. ("Price War Goes on at a Rising Tempo," *The New York Times,* June 1, 1951, p. 16.)

Later in the price war Macy's, in at least two instances, made moves toward restoring prices to their previous levels. One of these involved summer suits. In the June 10, 1951 issue of *The New York Times* (pp. 18 and 19) there were two half-page ads listing three dozen or more items, all of which were price cut to some degree. Among the items were men's *Palm Beach* and *Springweave* suits. The former, originally priced at $29.95 and early in the "war" at $16.95, were now being offered for $28.14 which is almost exactly 6 per cent less than the fixed price. Most of the other items were deep cut in varying degrees. This suggests that Macy's may have made this move in an attempt to lead prices back up.

The other item on which there was a partial

restoration in price was *Bayer* aspirin. In late June *Bayer* aspirin, which had been offered earlier for as low as 4 cents per hundred, was priced at Macy's at 36 cents. It is interesting that (a) Macy's own brand of aspirin was selling for 11 cents per hundred at this time and (b) Gimbel's had none of the *Bayer* brand in stock ("Some Levels Raised by Price War Stores," *The New York Times,* June 27, 1951, p. 31).

[41] According to a statement made to the author by an executive of one of the participating stores: "Prices 'inched up'—it was a gradual return to normal levels."

[42] Macy's assertedly would not sign a "fair trade" contract, but would write a letter to the manufacturer indicating that it intended to adhere as long as competitors refrained from cutting prices. But see "Macy's Reportedly Signs First 'Fair Trades' Contract with Simmons Co.; . . ." *The New York Times,* June 29, 1951, p. 29.

were out of it,[43] competitors took advantage of the situation to restore prices to original levels. Reportedly, certain merchants entered into arrangements with manufacturers to be ostensibly out of stock for a day or so during which time competitive sellers would restore prices. This would provide the aggressor with an excuse for increasing his prices.

One wonders how the issue of the 6-per cent differential, which finally had to be faced when the prices reached the original level, was resolved. The statements by representatives of the stores are in conflict on this point.

CONCLUSIONS

It has been argued that Macy's erred badly in initiating the price reductions which led to the 1951 department store price war. Some observers contend that the company foolishly entered an engagement that it could not win.[44] They argue, further, that by precipitating the conflict the concern contributed to the victory of the "fair trade" forces in the Congressional battle involving the passage of the new "fair trade" legislation which was being considered at that time.[45]

At least two Macy executives have contended that the company was obliged in good faith to reduce prices in accordance with its policy when free to do so. However, it might be argued that strategically it was not necessary for Macy's to disrupt the whole price structure even when adhering to its policy. Not one but three courses of action were open to Macy's: (a) making an all-out and well-publicized effort to undercut the market on items which were formerly price fixed under the Feld-Crawford ("fair trade") Act—the plan that was followed, (b) disregarding the opportunity of legally reducing prices and failing to make any move in this direction, or (c) reducing prices 6 per cent on previously price-fixed items without any special fanfare.

Some feel that the last-mentioned move would have been preferable. In following this procedure, the store would have at once lived up to its obligation to its customers and avoided becoming involved in a costly struggle with its competitors. It may be thought by some that the cost of this "war" to society was too high—that it not only strengthened the hand of "fair traders" but caused Macy's, a former champion of aggressive price competition in the New York area, to adopt a less aggressive attitude in pricing matters.

In longer run terms, however, it may be that little harm has been done to our competitive structure by the Macy move—even assuming the results indicated. For one thing, latest reports suggest that "fair trade" laws are repeatedly meeting reversals in the courts of the various states on constitutional and other grounds.[46] For another, this freeing up of com-

---

[43] There is no question that in some instances New York stores actually withdrew merchandise from forward stock just for the purpose of providing a basis for the restoration of prices.

[44] The Macy Board of Directors evidently was not satisfied with the strategy which led to the conflict because the top executive of the New York store at the time of the "war" was very shortly deposed.

[45] Adherents of "fair trade" have stated that from one standpoint the price war was "welcome," especially if it became nation-wide ("Price War Flares Among City Stores," *The New York Times,* May 30, 1951, p. 13). The point is that a price war of this type might suggest the *need* for "fair trade" legislation to those having legislative responsibility.

[46] Until a year or so ago and for a considerable period prior thereto (except for the hiatus of federal control between the striking down of the Tydings-Miller Act and the enactment of the McGuire law), the legal status of resale price maintenance was relatively clear and generally stable. "Fair trade" laws were in effect in 45 of the 48 states—all except Missouri, Texas, and Vermont —and in the main there seemed to be little question about their interpretation.

At this writing (August 1956), considerable change has taken place in the price-maintenance picture because of the recent invalidation of some of the "fair trade" laws by state courts. Thus, according to Professor William F. Brown, the state courts of Arkansas, Colorado, Florida, Georgia, Indiana, Kentucky, Louisiana, Michigan, Nebraska, Oregon, South Carolina, Utah, and Virginia have rendered unfavorable decisions in cases involving "fair trade" laws.

These invalidations have resulted mainly from findings that the "non-signer" clauses of these laws (by which a price may be legally maintained if one signer negotiates a contract and notice is given the others) violate the due-process clauses of the constitutions of these states. However, one enactment was struck down, interestingly enough, because of the primacy of an antimonopoly law with which it was found to be in conflict (Virginia). While some of these adverse decisions handed down by lower courts remain untested in higher courts (those in Colorado, Indiana, Kentucky, South Carolina, and Utah), most have been affirmed by state Supreme Court decisions (those

petitive activities in pricing matters will accentuate opportunities for those who are willing to vigorously strive for business and this should have a salutary effect on competitive intensiveness.

One may conclude that the competition of those who do not rely for success on legislative crutches promises to make increasingly serious inroads on the business of those who do. If a merchandising institution is to avoid disaster, it must consider competitive forces in deciding how it will operate its business. If the aggressive vendors of yesteryear (or any one of them) decide to assume a more passive role in the "battle" for business than they have previously taken, other "warriors" undoubtedly will be happy to snatch up the discarded mantle of aggressive market leadership and carry on the fight for patronage on a basis of lowest price offerings.[47] Society has no interest in what institution assumes this role just so long as the function is performed.

---

in Arkansas, Florida, Georgia, Louisiana, Michigan, Nebraska, Oregon, and Virginia). For further information on this matter, see "Legislative and Judicial Developments in Marketing" (W. F. Brown, Editor) in recent issues of this journal.

[47] This role of aggressive leadership, of course, may be divided among many institutions carrying different lines of merchandise (for example, appliances, drugs, soft goods, etc.) rather than concentrated in any one store.

DISCUSSION QUESTIONS

This is an account of one of the most well-publicized retail price wars ever to occur. Much of the "color" of the price war is buried in lengthy footnotes—to appreciate how deep "deep-cut" prices were cut, see footnotes 19, 20, 25, 38.

1. What is "resale price maintenance?"
2. What *logic* is there for "fair trade" or resale price maintenance?
3. Why might retailers, in general, have some reluctance to use price aggressively as a competitive weapon in view of a reaction of this kind?

2. Fictitious Pricing and the FTC: A New Look at an Old Dodge

CARLETON A. HARKRADER[*]

The consumer's understandable desire to buy at a bargain price prompts him to spend money he might otherwise save or spend for something else. It is the vendor's long-time goal to convert this all-too-human trait into the sale of his goods. Yet theoretically, the market price in a competitive economy is set by supply and demand to afford an optimum return to the manufacturer and others in the distribution system for their efforts and capital. Inducing further sales by lowering prices below this point means a loss for some along the line. To solve this dilemma, sellers over the years have hit upon the device of creating illusory bargains in the minds of purchasers, thus playing upon the purchasers' cupidity without sacrificing profits. The infinite variety of techniques for accomplishing this paradox is a tribute, if not to the "morals of the market place,"[1] at least to the inventive genius of businessmen. Such schemes have given rise to a new economic and legal concept: fictitious pricing.[2]

The Federal Trade Commission, throughout its nearly half-century of existence, has condemned many different methods of "fictitious" pricing as injurious to competition or misleading to consumers.[3] Most have involved retail-

[*] SOURCE: Reprinted by permission from the editor of the *St. John's Law Review*, in the December, 1962, issue, pages 1–28.

[*] A.B., Virginia Military Institute, LL.B., Yale University; partner, Wald, Harkrader & Rockefeller, Washington, D. C. The author acknowledges the invaluable assistance of his colleague, Phillip D. Bostwick, and the forebearance of his partners, Robert L. Wald and Edwin S. Rockefeller, during preparation of this article.

[1] Cardozo, J. in Meinhard v. Salmon, 249 N.Y. 458, 464, 164 N.E. 545, 546 (1928).

[2] "Fictitious" prices may result not only from businessmen's efforts to mislead bargain hunters, but may be implied even where the manufacturer or retailer acts in good faith, but objective circumstances result in some unintended "fiction." In FTC matters it is ordinarily immaterial whether the respondent knows his representation is false. Gimbel Bros. v. FTC, 116 F.2d 578 (2d Cir. 1941). *But see* Regina Corp., 3 CCH TRADE REG. REP. ¶ 15936, at 20745 (FTC June 13, 1962).

[3] The FTC was created in 1914 by the Federal Trade Commission Act, 38 Stat. 717 (1914), 15 U.S.C. § 41 (1958). Whereas the Sherman Act, 26 Stat. 209 (1890), as amended, 15 U.S.C. § 1 (1958), had been passed in an effort to *maintain* competition by prohibiting the ends that eliminate it (monopoly and monopolistic practices) and the means by which these are achieved (contracts, combinations and conspiracies in restraint of trade), the FTC Act was passed to *regulate* competition by insuring that competitive practices meet a certain acceptable standard. Section 5 declared that "unfair methods of competition in commerce" were unlawful, and was later amplified by the Wheeler-Lea Amendment, 52 Stat. 111 (1938), 15 U.S.C. § 45 (1958), to include "unfair or deceptive acts or practices." This language was added to nullify the effect of the Supreme Court's holding in FTC v. Raladam Co., 283 U.S. 643 (1931), requiring proof of injury to competition under section 5; it became necessary to show only substantially injurious effects upon the consuming public. See generally Moore, *Deceptive Trade Practices and the Federal Trade Commission*, 28 TENN. L. REV. 493 (1961); note, 36 ST. JOHN'S L. REV. 274 (1962). The FTC has the power to curb acts in their incipiency which, if full blown, would constitute violations of the Sherman Act, but which cannot yet be proceeded against by the Department of Justice. FTC v. Cement Institute, 333 U.S. 683 (1948). (For a discussion of the division of functions in antitrust enforcement see Rockefeller, *Antitrust Enforcement: Duopoly or Monopoly?*, 1962 WIS. L. REV. 437.) Fictitious pricing may violate Section 5 of the FTC Act as an unfair method of competition, as deceptive of consumers, or both. If fur products are fictitiously priced, there is also a violation of the Fur Products Labeling Act, 65 Stat. 175 (1951), 15 U.S.C. § 69 (1958). Mandel Bros. v. FTC, 254 F.2d 18 (7th Cir. 1958), *rev'd on other grounds*, 359 U.S.

ers,[4] but several have attacked manufacturers.[5] The nub of the retailer cases, despite shifting phraseology used by different respondents, has been the actual or implied comparison of two prices: a fictitious higher or "usual" price and a lower or "reduced" actual selling price.[6] The core of the manufacturer cases has been the promulgation of a "normal" retail value for the product through methods such as retail price lists, price tags or marks on the product, which is in fact greater than the price at which the product usually sells.[7] An impressive volume of precedent in both lines of cases had evolved by 1958, when the Commission promulgated its Guides Against Deceptive Pricing.[8] But since that time there have been several important new decisions not anticipated in the Guides. The implications and overtones of these cases pose significant pricing problems for those engaged in the manufacture and distribution of consumer goods.

BACKGROUND

The Revolution in Retailing

Since 1920, when the FTC first held that a piano manufacturer had violated Section 5 of the Federal Trade Commission Act by stencilling his instruments with prices "grossly in excess of the prices at which such pianos . . . are usually sold at retail," [9] an increasing number of Commission cases have dealt with the problem of fictitious pricing. Today it is the leading type of deception practiced in violation of the FTC Act.[10] The upswing in cases can be traced to one paramount factor—the "Revolution in Retailing" of the 1950's.[11]

From the turn of the century until after World War II, retail trade revolved around the downtown department stores. These stores were generally operated on a large (usually forty percent) retail markup over cost, whether on a handkerchief or a refrigerator. Stores were designed to provide the shopper with a large selection of merchandise, each item available at two or three different qualities, brands or prices. Regular customer services included floor clerks, wrapping, packaging, delivery, credit terms and acceptance of returned goods. During this period the manufacturers' suggested retail prices simply reflected the prevailing forty percent markup, hence were clearly not fictitious.

The post-World War II climate, however, produced a new brand of merchandiser: the low-markup, high-volume, quick-turnover discount retailer who dispensed with expensive frills associated with the traditional department store.[12] The birth of the discount house brought a wave of unprecedented competition in selling in an industry already vigorously competitive. "Discounters" cut the retailers' traditional forty percent markup in half, compensating for loss of revenue by holding operating expenses to a minimum. Stores were opened in buildings that were often little more than warehouses, located in the suburbs to take advantage of low rentals and the population migration; employees reduced by self-service techniques; usual customer services ruthlessly eliminated. Because their lower prices meant cold cash savings to consumers when compared with competitive department store prices, and the discount houses specialized in flamboyant advertising of this fact, they flourished.

In many cases aggressive discount house competition brought about the demise or "modification" of department stores. Some failed altogether; others fought back by reduc-

---

385 (1959); De Gorter v. FTC, 244 F.2d 270 (9th Cir. 1957); The Fair v. FTC, 272 F.2d 609 (7th Cir. 1959).

[4] See, *e.g.*, Niresk Indus., Inc. v. FTC, 278 F.2d 337 (7th Cir.), *cert. denied*, 364 U.S. 883 (1960).

[5] See, *e.g.*, Clinton Watch Co. v. FTC, 291 F.2d 838 (7th Cir. 1961), *cert. denied*, 368 U.S. 952 (1962).

[6] *E.g.*, "The use by the respondents in this case [electrical appliance retailers] of manufacturers' suggested list prices and other higher prices in comparison with lower advertised sales prices were misrepresentations as to usual and customary prices and as to savings afforded purchasers . . . ." George's Radio & Television Co., 3 CCH Trade Reg. Rep. ¶ 15691, at 20526 (FTC Jan. 19, 1962).

[7] This theory stems from language of Mr. Justice Brandeis in FTC v. Winsted Hosiery Co., 258 U.S. 483, 494 (1922): "That a person is a wrongdoer who so furnishes another with the means of consummating a fraud has long been a part of the law of unfair competition."

[8] Guides Against Deceptive Pricing, FTC, 23 Fed. Reg. 7965 (1958), 2 CCH Trade Reg. Rep. ¶ 7835.48 (1961).

[9] Holland Piano Mfg. Co., 3 F.T.C. 31 (1920).

[10] In a typical recent year, over thirty per cent of the FTC's cease and desist orders dealt with fictitious pricing. U.S. FTC Press Release, Aug. 22, 1958.

[11] See generally Silberman, *The Revolutionists of Retailing*, Fortune, April 1962, p. 99.

[12] For a discussion about Eugene Ferkauf, originator of the first discount house, New York's E. J. Korvette, Inc., see *Retailing: Everybody Loves a Bargain*, Time, July 6, 1962, p. 57.

ing their prices on competitive items.[13] This in turn triggered a chain reaction of extravagant pricing claims by both kinds of merchants, often abetted by inflated manufacturers' retail price lists and tickets.

But since the department stores could seldom advertise that their new low prices afforded a saving over discount house prices, they had to compare them either with their own former prices or with the manufacturers' suggested retail prices, which generally reflected the traditional forty percent markup. On the other hand, as department store prices dropped to approach discount house prices, the discounters could no longer compare prices with department stores so dramatically. Thus, they too began to compare their prices with the manufacturers' suggested retail prices.[14] As time went on, there came to be little or no difference in the price of many comparable items between discount houses and department stores,[15] and the manufacturers' list prices had become meaningless because very few retailers continued to use the traditional forty percent markup.[16] Yet, whether businessmen might have preferred to operate otherwise or not,[17] price competition forced them to advertise comparatively as their competitors did. The consumer became confused, critical and skeptical.[18] By 1958, there was a sizable agitation for reform.[19]

---

[13] See Silberman, *The Department Stores Are Waking Up*, Fortune, July 1962, p. 143.

[14] Compare Silberman, *The Discounters Choose Their Weapons*, Fortune, May 1962, p. 118.

[15] For a survey comparing the variation between list prices and retail prices of automatic washing machines sold by four groups of retailers (discount houses, department stores, large volume outlets, and small volume outlets) in nine major United States cities, see Jung, *Price Variations Among Discount Houses and Other Retailers: a Re-Appraisal*, 37 J. OF RETAILING 13 (1961).

[16] See Weiss, *The Decline of the List Price*, Advertising Age, No. 13, 1961, p. 140.

[17] See FOY, MANAGEMENT'S PART IN ACHIEVING PRICE RESPECTABILITY 7 (1958): "The roll call of those in favor of sound pricing would be almost as impressive, I am sure, as the classical census of those in favor of motherhood. For as surely as he votes against sin on an open ballot, every good business man decries cutthroat pricing."

[18] *Phoney Price-Cutting: Threat to Advertising Confidence*, Time, No. 10, 1958, p. 78: "More and more customers are becoming suspicious of price cuts. A study by Pittsburgh's Duquesne University shows that buyers strongly suspect claims of price

Fictitious Pricing Case Law to 1958, As Reflected in the Guides

The FTC issued its Guides Against Fictitious Pricing on October 2, 1958.[20] The Guides were intended to spell out in layman's language the requirements of trade regulation law applicable to price advertising. They also served the purpose of "spotlighting persistent violations." Thus, they reflected the Commission's informal experience in this field, as well as the accumulated case precedent. Perhaps, also, in ambiguous areas they projected the FTC staff's view, with some blessing by the Commission, of what the law ought to be. Although the Guides state that they were adopted by the FTC "for the use of its staff in the evaluation of pricing representations in advertising," they also note that they were released to the public "in the interest of obtaining voluntary, simultaneous and prompt cooperation." [21]

The Guides set forth nine principles which the Commission uses to evaluate price repre-

---

cuts above 27.5%." See ZELOMEK, THE INTERRELATIONSHIP OF MERCHANDISING AND PRICING III (1958).

[19] This agitation for truth in advertising was not a new phenomenon. In 1911 the trade magazine Printer's Ink published a Model Statute which many states subsequently adopted. Revised in 1945, some forty-three states had passed the Printer's Ink Model Statute or a variation of it by 1957. See Day, *Ad Ethics Are Higher Today Because Honest Ads Work Best*, Printer's Ink, June 14, 1957, p. 21.

[20] The Guides Against Fictitious Pricing were issued as a part of the FTC's Guide Program, begun several years earlier. See address by John P. Sullivan, Legal Adviser on Guides, FTC Bureau of Consultation, Federal Trades Commission Conference on Public Deception, December 21, 1959: "The Guide Program had its beginning on September 15, 1955 with the issuance of Cigarette Advertising Guides. This was followed on August 27, 1958 by Advertising Guides for the Tire Industry. On October 10, 1958, the Commission launched a new approach in issuing Guides against a practice that was common to many industries. Trade Practice Rules and prior Guides were issued to particular industries, but the new Guides against Fictitious Pricing cut across all industry lines."

[21] "In issuing Guides, it was neither the intent nor purpose of the Commission to inform the adventuresome how far they can skate on thin ice. Rather, they may be likened to caution signs on the highway, warning the motorist where he must slow down to take other action to avoid mishap." *Ibid.*

sentations in advertising. These principles were distilled from past cases and represented an informal "codification" of the law as reflected in those cases. Also included in the Guides were examples of specific words and phrases the Commission had previously held to be deceptive. Thus, it may serve as a useful review of the fictitious pricing methods used up to 1958 briefly to examine the Guides seriatim.

The three most common pre-Guide advertising dodges used by retailers were: (1) advertising an article for sale at a low price when the specific article available for sale was not the one advertised, but a similar or comparable one; [22] (2) quoting a bargain price below a purported regular retail price which was not in fact the regular retail price for the article in the trade area where the statement was made; [23] and (3) quoting a bargain price below the advertiser's recent selling price when in actuality he had made no recent sales

at that price.[24] Guide I proscribes those three types of representations by stating that a savings claim should not be used unless it applies to the specific article offered for sale and is either a saving from the usual and customary retail price [25] of the article in the trade area when it is advertised or from the advertiser's usual retail price of the article in the recent, regular course of business.[26] In addition, the advertisement must clearly show which of these two types of discount applies.

Guide II states some specific limitations on

---

[22] E.g., Mandel Bros. v. FTC, 254 F.2d 18 (7th Cir. 1958), rev'd on other grounds, 359 U.S. 385 (1959) (respondent advertised in a newspaper that fur products offered at a price of $244 were "Usually $299 to $399"; evidence showed that the specific garments advertised had never retailed at those prices, having instead a usual and regular retail price of $244 or $288).

[23] E.g., Awon Film & Supply Co., 54 F.T.C. 1144 (1958); Maxwell Distrib. Co., 54 F.T.C. 260 (1957); Charlet Undergarment Corp., 52 F.T.C. 924 (1956); Benjamin & Edward J. Gross Co., 51 F.T.C. 1248 (1955); Household Sewing Mach. Co., 52 F.T.C. 250 (1955); Robert Hall Clothes, Inc., 50 F.T.C. 196 (1953); Plaza Luggage & Supply Co., 44 F.T.C. 443 (1948); Firestone Tire & Rubber Co., 33 F.T.C. 282 (1941); Goodyear Tire & Rubber Co., 33 F.T.C. 398 (1941); B. F. Goodrich Co., 33 F.T.C. 312 (1941); Sears, Roebuck & Co., 33 F.T.C. 334 (1941); Western Auto Supply Co., 33 F.T.C. 356 (1941). Post Guide cases: e.g., Niresk Indus., Inc. v. FTC, 278 F.2d 337 (7th Cir.), cert. denied, 364 U.S. 883 (1960); Harsam Distrib., Inc. v. FTC, 263 F.2d 396 (2d Cir. 1959); Gimbel Bros., 3 CCH Trade Reg. Rep. ¶ 16020 (FTC July 26, 1962); Giant Foods, Inc., 3 CCH Trade Reg. Rep. ¶ 15937 (FTC June 13, 1962); George's Radio & Television Co., 3 CCH Trade Reg. Rep. ¶ 15691 (FTC Jan. 19, 1962); Bond Stores, Inc., 56 F.T.C. 716 (1960); Filderman Corp., 56 F.T.C. 685 (1959); Hutchinson Chem. Corp., 55 F.T.C. 1942 (1959). For a case dismissing such a charge on grounds that the evidence was insufficient to establish what the usual and regular retail price of the advertised product was, see Sun Gold Indus., 56 F.T.C. 1368 (1960).

[24] E.g., FTC v. Standard Educ. Soc'y, 302 U.S. 112 (1937); Mandel Bros. v. FTC, supra note 22; Consumer Sales Corp. v. FTC, 198 F.2d 404 (2d Cir. 1952), cert. denied, 344 U.S. 912 (1953); Thomas v. FTC, 116 F.2d 347 (10th Cir. 1940); Awon Film & Supply Co., supra note 23; Southern Piano Co., 54 F.T.C. 640 (1957); Walside, Inc., 54 F.T.C. 572 (1957); Artistic Modern, Inc., 54 F.T.C. 225 (1957); Rena-Ware Distrib., Inc., 54 F.T.C. 94 (1957); American Albums, Inc., 53 F.T.C. 913 (1956); Approved Photographer's Ass'n, 53 F.T.C. 610 (1956); American Broadloom Carpet Co., 53 F.T.C. 239 (1956); George's Radio & Television Co., 50 F.T.C. 580 (1953); Zlotnick The Furrier, Inc., 48 F.T.C. 1068 (1952); The Camera Man, 42 F.T.C. 393 (1946); United Art Studios, 36 F.T.C. 977 (1943); Erwin Feather Quilt Co., 30 F.T.C. 1079 (1940); M. E. Moss Mfg. Co., 19 F.T.C. 467 (1934); Perfolastic Inc., 16 F.T.C. 157 (1932); Domino House, Inc., 14 F.T.C. 432 (1931); School of Applied Art, 11 F.T.C. 431 (1927). Post-Guide cases: e.g., Niresk Indus., Inc. v. FTC, supra note 23; Basic Books, Inc. v. FTC, 276 F.2d 718 (7th Cir. 1960); Gimbel Bros., supra note 23; Encyclopaedia Britannica, Inc., 3 CCH Trade Reg. Rep. ¶ 15246 (FTC, June 16, 1961). For a case dismissing such a charge on grounds that the evidence was insufficient to establish the respondent had never sold at the advertised price, see City Stores Co., 3 CCH Trade Reg. Rep. ¶ 15805 (FTC March 27, 1962).

[25] Guide I(b) lists as examples the following phrases used in advertisements which have been held to be interpreted by the consumer to mean the usual and customary retail price: "Maker's List Price," "Manufacturer's List Price," "Manufacturer's Suggested Retail Price," "Sold Nationally At," "Nationally Advertised At" and "Value."

[26] Guide I(c) lists as examples the following phrases used in advertisements which have been held to be interpreted by the consumer to mean the retail price charged by the advertiser in his recent, regular course of business: "regularly," "usually," "formerly," "originally," "reduced," "was —now—," "made to sell for," "woven to sell for," "our list price," "—% off," "save up to $ —," "special," "you save $— " and "$50 dress—$35."

"reduction" or "savings" claims. Some advertisements had compared a low "bargain" price with a higher "retail" price, on the theory that the comparison was justified by a few isolated sales at the higher price, even though the majority of previous sales had been made at the lower price.[27] Savings claims, according to this Guide, should not be made if based on an artificial markup, infrequent or isolated sales, or on a past price that was not in use in the recent, regular course of business, unless this fact is adequately disclosed.

Other advertisements claimed that the price of an article affords the buyer a saving when in fact the article advertised is compared pricewise with a different article of superior quality.[28] Guide III attempts to discourage this type of advertising without forbidding honest savings claim on truly comparable products. It thus requires the advertiser to disclose that the low price of the advertised article is not being compared with the former or with the usual and customary price of that same article, but rather with similar but comparable merchandise of like grade and quality. Furthermore, the more expensive merchandise mentioned in the advertisement must in fact be generally available in that trade area at the comparative price stated, or its unavailability must be stated.[29]

A favorite trick of advertisers is to represent that prices are reduced because of alleged special events such as "clearance" or "manufacturer's close out," which in fact never occur.[30] Guide IV declares that advertisements should not imply that an article was offered for sale at a saving because of some "unusual event or manner of business" unless the statement is true.[31] Some advertisements have represented that two articles could be purchased for the price of one when in fact the price charged for both articles was twice the usual price of one such article.[32] Guide V states that no claim to sell two articles for the price of one should be made unless the price for both is the usual and customary retail price in the recent, regular course of business for the single article. Similarly, Guide VI governs the announcement of an offer of a "1¢ sale" or "half-price sale," when the offer of an article at this special price is conditioned upon the purchase of another article at the same time. Purchasers may be misled if the price charged for the additional article required to be purchased is not the usual and regular price but rather a higher price which will afford the seller a profit on the combined sale.[33] When an advertisement states that an article can be purchased for 1¢ or at half-price, this Guide requires that it be accompanied by a disclosure of the conditions of the offer and that the stated price for the additional article not be inflated.

Mail-order sellers often represent to consumers that they are wholesalers, and are able to offer their merchandise to those on a special mailing list at wholesale prices. In fact, the price offered in such cases has sometimes been higher than the wholesale price paid by retailers, and the price quoted in the catalog has been the usual retail price for the article.[34] To deter this type of advertising, Guide VII prohibits claims that a price is a "factory" or "wholesale" price when it is not the same as that paid by retailers.

In fact, most fictitious price advertisements have originated with retailers. But one common method of fictitious pricing is peculiar to

---

[27] *Cf.* Harsam Distrib., Inc. v. FTC, *supra* note 23. For a case dismissing such a complaint on grounds that respondent had disposed of the business in which the practice occurred, see Chester H. Roth Co., 55 F.T.C. 1076 (1959).

[28] *E.g.,* Mandel Bros. v. FTC, *supra* note 22; Miss Youth Form Creations Corp., 52 F.T.C. 413 (1955).

[29] Guide III(c) states: "An example of a statement which would be proper within the provisions of Guide III if based on facts is: 'Dacron suit $20.00—Comparable suits $25.00.'"

[30] *E.g.,* Kay Jewelry Store, Inc. 54 F.T.C. 548 (1957); Del Mar Sewing Mach. Co., 49 F.T.C. 1257 (1953); Illinois Merchandise Mart, 45 F.T.C. 58 (1948).

[31] Guide IV sets forth the following phrases as illustrative of those which so imply: "Special Purchase," "Clearance," "Marked Down From Stock," "Exceptional Purchase," "Manufacturer's Close-Out," "Advance Sale" and "Sale."

[32] *E.g.,* Thomas v. FTC, *supra* note 24.

[33] *E.g.,* Electrical Center, 48 F.T.C. 726 (1952); Firestone Tire & Rubber Co., 33 F.T.C. 282 (1941); Goodyear Tire & Rubber Co., 33 F.T.C. 298 (1941); B. F. Goodrich Co., 33 F.T.C. 312 (1941); Sears, Roebuck & Co., 33 F.T.C. 334 (1941); Western Auto Supply Co., 33 F.T.C. 356 (1941); *cf.* Kalwajtys v. FTC, 237 F.2d 654 (7th. Cir. 1956), *cert. denied,* 352 U.S. 1025 (1957).

[34] *E.g.,* Progress Tailoring Co. v. FTC, 153 F.2d 103 (7th Cir. 1946); L. & C. Mayers Co. v. FTC, 97 F.2d 365 (2d Cir. 1938); Brown Fence & Wire Co. v. FTC, 64 F.2d 934 (6th Cir. 1933); Macher Watch & Jewelry Co., 32 F.T.C. 763 (1941).

manufacturers and arises out of the practice of preticketing. Many manufacturers affix retail price tags or labels to their products at the factory, thus "suggesting" the retail value to the retailer and, ultimately, to the consumer. If retailers generally sell this pre-priced article for less than the price on the preticket, fictitious pricing problems arise.[35] The Federal Trade Commission has held that the preticketed price constitutes a representation to the consumer of the usual and regular retail price.[36] Thus the retailer who uses the preticket while the product is generally selling for less engages in a deceptive act or practice by holding forth a nonexistent saving to the consumer.[37] But in the same situation the manufacturer has also been held to have engaged in deceptive practices because he supplied the means used to deceive the consumer.[38] The Commission states in Guide VIII that an article should not be preticketed with a price figure which is greater than the usual and customary retail price of that product, and a manufacturer who puts erroneously marked products in the hands of retailers will himself be guilty of deception; furthermore, it is no defense to say that he thought the preticketed price was the usual retail price since he is legally charged with knowledge of the merchandising "facts of life"[39] about his products after they leave the factory.[40]

Present Status and Effect of the Guides

The Guides close with the statement that they "do not constitute a finding in and will not affect the disposition of any formal or informal matter before the Commission." Read in conjunction with their opening sentence—i.e., that the Guides have been adopted "for the use of [the Commission's] staff in the evaluation of pricing representations in advertising" —it is apparent that the original purpose for which the Guides were promulgated did not necessarily contemplate their use as substantive law.[41] A recent decision of the FTC, Gimbel Bros.,[42] however, has apparently raised their status as legal guideposts for pricing practices.

Gimbel's had used the words "list price," "usually," "regularly" and "originally" in advertisements which the Commission alleged were fictitious because of implied false representations about the prices at which the goods had actually been selling in the area.[43] The hearing examiner's initial decision dismissed the complaint on the ground that there was no evidence in the record to prove what meaning the public attached to these particular words despite the specific meaning given to them in the Guides; therefore, since the Guides could not be looked to as substantive law or as a substitute for evidence, the Commission's burden of proving customer deception had not been sustained.

On appeal, the Commission reversed the hearing examiner's initial decision. Recognizing

---

[35] E.g., Ma-Ro Hosiery Co., 53 F.T.C. 862 (1957); Neuville, Inc., 53 F.T.C. 436 (1956); Orloff Co., 52 F.T.C. 709 (1956); Trade Labs., Inc., 25 F.T.C. 937 (1937); Mills Sales Co., 23 F.T.C. 518 (1936); FTC v. Holland Piano Mfg. Co., 3 F.T.C. 31 (1920). Post Guide cases: Baltimore Luggage Co. v. FTC, 296 F.2d 608 (4th Cir. 1961), cert. denied, 369 U.S. 860 (1962); Clinton Watch Co. v. FTC, 291 F.2d 838 (7th Cir. 1961), cert. denied, 368 U.S. 952 (1962); Rayex Corp., 3 CCH TRADE REG. REP. ¶ 15823 (FTC April 2, 1962); Helbros Watch Co., 3 CCH TRADE REG. REP. ¶ 15654 (FTC Dec. 26, 1961).

[36] E.g., Mills Sales Co., supra note 35.

[37] See, e.g., Niresk Indus., Inc. v. FTC, 278 F.2d 337 (7th Cir.), cert. denied, 364 U.S. 883 (1960); see note 6 supra.

[38] E.g., Clinton Watch Co. v. FTC, 291 F.2d 838 (7th Cir. 1961), cert. denied, 368 U.S. 952 (1962); see note 7 supra.

[39] Orloff Co., supra note 35.

[40] Guide IX deals with the relatively infrequent practice of advertising price savings on "imperfect, irregular, seconds" items. It provides: "No comparative price should be quoted in connection with an article offered for sale which is imperfect, ir-

regular, or a second, unless it is accompanied by a clear and conspicuous disclosure that such comparative price refers to the price of the article if perfect. Such comparative price should not be used unless (1) it is the price at which the advertiser usually and customarily sells the article without defects, or (2) it is the price at which the article without defects is usually and customarily sold at the competitive price in the trade area, or areas, where the statement is made, or if such article is not so available, that fact is clearly disclosed."

[41] See address by John P. Sullivan, Federal Trade Commission Conference on Public Deception, December 21, 1959; "Guides are exactly what their name purports them to be. They are not law."

[42] 3 CCH TRADE REG. REP. ¶ 16020 (FTC July 26, 1962).

[43] These words are found in Guide I(c) as examples of words which have been held to be representations of the usual and customary price. See note 26 supra.

that the Guides are "not substantive law in and of themselves," Commissioner MacIntyre's opinion declared that "this does not mean that they may be completely ignored and rejected in the fashion herein accomplished." [44] The opinion then explained the function of the Guides in these significant words:

What, then, is the proper status of the "Guides" with respect to a Commission proceeding? When viewed as a compilation and summary of the expertise acquired by the Commission from having repeatedly decided cases dealing with identical false claims, the role of the "Guides" becomes apparent. *They serve to inform the public and the bar of the interpretation which the Commission, unaided by further consumer testimony or other evidence, will place upon advertisements using the words and phrases therin set out.* It is our view that words and phrases of the type set out in the "Guides" must be consistently dealt with by the Commission or its decisions will have no meaning or value. Only by consistent interpretation can some order be brought to the semantic jungle of advertising.[45]

The Commission then went ahead to hold that Gimbel had engaged in deceptive advertising and entered its order to cease and desist.

Such emphasis on the Guides by the Commission in its decisions makes it increasingly important that they reflect accurately the current thinking of the Commission. At this writing, FTC staff attorneys are in fact engaged in the preparation of a revised version of the original Guides [46] which may be adopted by the Commission in the next few months. If they follow past precedent, the revised Guides will incorporate the most recent case law developments as well as the FTC's administrative experience since promulgation of the original Guides in 1958.

RECENT FICTITIOUS PRICING CASES INVOLVING MANUFACTURERS

Predictably, the merchandising world has shown an avid interest in the Guides Against Deceptive Pricing. A half-million copies were distributed in the first year after their issuance.[47] Moreover, they stimulated state and local action. On January 1, 1959, for example,

the Better Business Bureau of New York City issued its "Standards for Retail Advertising of Price Reduction, Comparison and Saving Claims," which were based upon the FTC's Guides. But the dynamics of retail merchandising defy any static solution; new and even more perplexing problems have arisen to plague the Commission since 1958.

The recent cases point up four common practices of manufacturers not clearly or adequately covered by the Guides. In each instance the Commission has nonetheless claimed that the manufacturer is guilty of placing in the hands of a reseller an instrument of price deception. The practices, to be described in detail, are: (1) a manufacturer's purposeful promoting of periodic reduced-price sales by retailer-customers to insure that a significant proportion of the manufacturer's total sales will be at below-normal sale prices; (2) his supplying of mail-order houses with catalog insert sheets listing both a purported "retail" price and a so-called "wholesale" price at which the goods are actually sold; (3) the preticketing of nationally-distributed products with a uniform price when the regular retail price varies in different parts of the country; and (4) the furnishing of retailers with "suggested" list prices.

Manufacturer-Sponsored Sales

The periodic or seasonal sale is a traditional and effective method by which retailers seek to stimulate business. These sales are frequently promoted by the manufacturer-supplier, who temporarily cuts his own price to facilitate the retailer's price reduction. Seemingly, no deception occurs if the retailer's sale price is actually lower than the usual price charged during the rest of the year. The *Kreiss* [48] case stands as a warning, however, that such sales cannot be depended upon to mask fictitious pricing schemes.

Kreiss involved department store sales of women's hosiery which the manufacturer advertised in cooperation with its retailers at a stated retail price. But twice each year, for periods of two to four weeks, the manufacturer offered the hosiery to retailer-customers at fifty percent off the regular wholesale price on condition that the retailers, in turn, would sell hosiery at half the advertised price during corresponding sale periods. Although the advertised price was maintained throughout

---

[44] Gimbel Bros., 3 CCH Trade Reg. Rep. ¶ 16020, at 20858 (FTC July 26, 1962).

[45] *Ibid.* (Emphasis added.)

[46] Interview with William D. Dixon, Attorney, FTC Bureau of Industry Guidance, Sept. 5, 1962.

[47] U.S. FTC, Annual Report 67 (1961).

[48] 56 F.T.C. 1421 (1960).

the year except during the sale periods, ninety-five percent of all the manufacturer's sales to the retailers were at the lower sale price. In a three-two decision, the Commission dismissed the complaint, finding decisive the fact that the higher price was actually maintained throughout the year except for the two brief sale periods. But the two FTC members dissenting were convinced that the sale price at which such a large percentage of the hosiery was sold was in reality the "customary and usual" retail price and the advertised price was a fictitious one.[49]

On the basis of the close split in the *Kreiss* case and changes in the Commission membership since it was decided,[50] it would be surprising if the FTC did not challenge similar types of promotional schemes, particularly where the sales price is far below an advertised or preticketed price and the sales endure for unusually long periods of time or recur at frequent intervals.[51]

Catalog Insert Sheets

In addition to their "regular" line of merchandise sold through traditional retail outlets, many manufacturers also market a "special," "promotional," or "jobber" line. This merchandise, which is frequently of distinctive design and may be of lower quality than the regular line, is marketed through a relatively new type of distributor known as the "catalog jobber."

Though methods vary considerably, the typical catalog jobber is essentially a retailer.[52] He purchases merchandise from a number of manufacturers and solicits prospective customers through a handsome color catalog. His clientele ranges from individual consumers to business and fraternal organizations and a few small town retail merchants. Some catalog jobbers also maintain display rooms where they sell some merchandise to all comers.

Each manufacturer supplying the catalog jobber customarily furnishes printed "insert sheets" or, more recently, a "color positive" from which the catalog jobber may print such insert sheets, illustrating the manufacturer's products. Two prices are given in the catalog for each item. In some instances they are stated as "retail price" and "your cost," the latter being half the stated "retail price." Other catalogs use "coded prices" and instruct the manufacturers to make up the insert sheets accordingly. Here the "retail price" is preceded by a series of letters and numbers, such as "20 K 0169 TG 525 Necklace $10.50."[53] The catalog contains an explanation that the cost of the item is concealed in these numbers and sets forth the decoding procedure. The price when decoded is typically exactly half the "retail price." For example, the coded price of the "$10.50" necklace above is found in the numbers 525, being $5.25 or half of $10.50. All of this so-called jobber merchandise is sold to all customers at the "coded" or "your cost" price rather than at the higher "retail price."

Oddly, the FTC's first case on this method of pricing did not involve a catalog jobber, but a manufacturer which had furnished catalog insert sheets. In *Leeds Travelwear, Inc.,*[54] the Commission found that supplying such insert sheets was deceptive because the generally prevailing retail price of the manufacturer's merchandise was not the price stated as "retail," but rather the coded price.

In *Leeds,* however, it would seem the Commission has attacked the wrong end of the dragon. There are many more manufacturer-suppliers than catalog jobbers, and the pressure for two-price insert sheets comes from the catalog houses. The Commission's pending cases against catalog jobbers, on the other hand, obviously are more sensible in terms of effort and prospective results.[55] When and if

---

[49] "In my opinion the price at which 95% of respondent's merchandise is sold is the regular price as indicated by this record." *Id.* at 1431 (dissenting opinion of Commissioner Secrest).

[50] Four of the members who participated have been replaced (only Commissioner Anderson remains). This makes the precedential value of the *Kreiss* case doubtful, especially since the majority relied mainly on a narrow pleading ground—*i.e.,* that it was not false, as alleged in the complaint, for Kreiss to represent that the amount charged ten or eleven months a year was "customary and usual." Compare the Commission's more recent use of the phrase "generally prevailing" in Rayex Corp., 3 CCH TRADE REG. REP. ¶ 15823 (FTC April 2, 1962).

[51] See Chester H. Roth Co., 55 F.T.C. 1076 (1959).

[52] For a complete discussion of a catalog jobber's operation, see Coro, Inc., No. 8346, FTC, June 1, 1962 (Initial Decision).

[53] *Ibid.*

[54] 3 CCH TRADE REG. REP. ¶ 15997 (FTC July 20, 1962).

[55] Majestic Elec. Supply Co., 3 CCH TRADE REG. REP. ¶ 15972 (FTC Aug. 13, 1962). A complaint was issued against another catalog jobber (Continental Products, Inc., No. 8517) on June 29, 1962.

this method of doing business is clearly condemned in a catalog-jobber case, the way will be cleared for an industry-wide reform of the two-price catalog insert sheet.

Nationwide Preticketing

Preticketing cases were routine long before 1958 [56] and Guide VIII covered the standard technique up to this time. The cases generally involved extremely exaggerated price tickets where the manufacturer, actually or in effect, informed the retailer that his product could be advertised at the preticketed figure, sold for a much smaller sum, and still provide an adequate profit. The more recent case of *Baltimore Luggage Co.,*[57] however, involved much less extreme facts which were in a legal limbo under the standards laid down in the Guides.

The respondent sold its product to 1,276 retailers located in 46 states and the District of Columbia. It preticketed the merchandise with tags bearing the price of $12.95. The record indicated that 70 percent, or 889, of its retailer-customers, located in 34 states, sold the luggage at the preticketed price. The remaining 30 percent, or 387 retailers, located in 12 states, including the metropolitan trade areas of New York, Philadelphia and Washington, D. C., sold the luggage for approximately $2.00 less. In dollar-volume terms, 62.5 percent of the merchandise was sold at the preticketed price.

On those facts, the Commission held that the preticketed price could mislead consumers in the trade areas in which it did not correspond with the usual and regular retail price.[58] This conclusion was affirmed by the Court of Appeals for the Fourth Circuit. The Commission rejected the Baltimore Luggage Company's argument that its pretickets should be judged on the basis of the entire national retail market,[59] reasoning that the consumer is not interested in bargains available in another section of the country, but only "in the

trade area in which he is making his purchase." [60]

Manufacturers' List Prices

Many manufacturers furnish retailers with illustrative literature containing "suggested list prices" or "suggested retail prices." [61] These are purportedly for the retailer's use, to aid him in pricing the product to consumers at a competitive, yet profitable, figure. If this were the only use made of price lists, they would occasion no fictitious pricing problems for the retailer or the manufacturer.[62] Retailers, however, sometimes display "list" or "suggested retail" prices directly to consumers or use them in comparative advertising as the basis for price-saving claims.[63] Thus, representations such as "G. E. Automatic Toaster $13.27, Mfg. List $19.95" have been held to be deceptive on the part of a retail seller unless $19.95 is in fact the usual and regular retail price, because they misleadingly imply that the consumer can save $6.68 by buying the article at the advertiser's store.[64] Moreover, the FTC has emphatically held that this particular deception was not cured by a disclaimer elsewhere in the advertisement, obviously based upon a reading of the 1958 Guides, stating that the use of the

---

[56] See note 35 *supra.*

[57] Baltimore Luggage Co. v. FTC, 296 F.2d 608 (4th Cir. 1961), *cert. denied,* 369 U.S. 860 (1962).

[58] Baltimore Luggage Co., No. 7683, FTC, Mar. 15, 1961.

[59] See Brief for Petitioners in Court of Appeals, pp. 5–7, Baltimore Luggage Co. v. FTC, *supra* note 57.

[60] Baltimore Luggage Co., *supra* note 58, at 3. In affirming this holding, the Court of Appeals' opinion commented that "no authorities have been cited to us, nor do we find any, which hold that, before the Commission may proscribe a deceptive practice on the part of a manufacturer which is widespread, it must be shown that the practice is not only widespread but universal." 296 F.2d at 611.

[61] *E.g.,* Morris Lober & Associates, 55 F.T.C. 209 (1958); National Silver Co., 27 F.T.C. 596 (1938).

[62] There can be no deception to the consumer if he does not see the price the manufacturer has suggested as a retail price. In a preticketing case, the Commission said: "There is, of course, no convention requiring manufacturers and distributors to use preticketing as a means for 'suggesting' resale prices to their dealers. They could as well simply enclose a list of suggested prices with each shipment. That procedure would involve no possibility of the sort of deception with which we are concerned, assuming the price list information was not passed on to the public." Rayex Corp., 3 CCH TRADE REG. REP. ¶ 15823 (FTC April 2, 1962).

[63] *E.g.,* Giant Foods, Inc., 3 CCH TRADE REG. REP. ¶ 15937 (FTC June 13, 1962).

[64] *Ibid.*

term "manufacturer's list" does not imply that the advertiser has ever sold the products at that price or that the products are for sale generally in the area for that price.[65]

Despite the earlier retailer cases, it was not until the recent decision in *Regina Corp.*[66] that a manufacturer was held responsible for furnishing deceptive price lists to retailers.[67] The Commission found that Regina's "suggested list prices" were higher than the usual and customary prices at which its floor polishers and vacuum cleaners sold at retail, and that Regina was aware that this was so when it made up the lists. Emphasizing the respondent's knowledge, the Commission ordered Regina to cease and desist from supplying distributors or retailers with price lists or other literature when it "knows or has reason to know" that such prices are in excess of the usual and customary retail price of the product.[68]

THE MANUFACTURER'S DILEMMA

Functions of Manufacturer-Suggested Retail Prices

The *Regina* case pinpoints a basic dilemma faced by any manufacturer who wants to use either suggested list prices or pretickets as part of his distributional mechanism. Any discussion of the legal and policy considerations involved in these practices should be preceded by understanding what functions they serve in the commercial world.[69] It would be gross error to assume that most manufacturers who preticket their products or distribute price lists to their customers do so to promote deception, when in fact those practices are traditional in many lines and are thought to serve legitimate business ends.[70] Therefore, the question arises, "Why attempt to price the product at all at the primary level of distribution?"

---

[65] *Id.* at 20746. The disclaimer stated in part: "The manufacturer's list prices referred to in this advertisement are inserted to assist you in identification of the products and to allow you to compare accurately the selling prices offered here and elsewhere. The use of the term manufacturer's list or similar terminology in our advertising is not to imply that Giant has ever sold the advertised products at such list prices or that the products are being offered for sale generally in the area at such list prices. . . . Giant includes these manufacturer's list prices so that you may make simple, intelligent comparisons between our selling prices and those of others."

[66] 3 CCH TRADE REG. REP. ¶ 15936 (FTC June 13, 1962).

[67] *Regina* was perhaps foreshadowed by National Silver Co., 27 F.T.C. 596 (1938), which held a wholesaler (which had falsely represented itself to be a manufacturer) for publishing price lists greatly in excess of the "reasonable or normal" retail value of its products. See also three cases involving manufacturers which sold their goods through company-owned outlets: Firestone Tire & Rubber Co., Goodyear Tire & Rubber Co. and B. F. Goodrich Co., *supra* note 23.

[68] Regina Corp., 3 CCH TRADE REG. REP. ¶ 15936 (FTC June 13, 1962). A reading of the *Regina* opinion raises the additional question whether the Commission considered the manufacturer's knowledge or reason to know that its list prices would be used as part of the retailer's advertising campaign. Price lists themselves vary greatly and may provide clues to their intended use. Some are attractively illustrated and printed, and thus easily adapted for sales promotion at the retail level. On the other hand, simpler printed or mimeographed lists,

especially if they reveal "dealer's cost" as well as the suggested retail price, are unlikely to be shown to customers. But prices from any kind of list are equally usable as the basis for price comparisons in media advertisements.

[69] Although the FTC has never proceeded in any case involving only a manufacturer's nationally advertised price, this practice would appear to have at least as much potentiality for deception as preticketing—*i.e.*, the manufacturer's statement of the item's retail price is directly communicated to the consumer; if it overstates the generally prevailing price in any area, prospective buyers may be deceived. Nationally advertised prices were indirectly involved in Niresk Indus., Inc. v. FTC, 78 F.2d 337 (7th Cir.), *cert. denied*, 364 U.S. 883 (1960) (mail-order firm unsuccessfully attempted to justify "list" price advertisement on ground that manufacturer advertised product in "Life" at that price), and Harsam Distrib., Inc. v. FTC, 263 F.2d 396 (2d Cir. 1959) (manufacturer advertised White Christmas perfume in "Vogue" at $18.50, then furnished retailer with store display, "Advertised in Vogue at $18.50—save 90%").

[70] *But cf.* Baltimore Luggage Co. v. FTC, 296 F.2d 608 (4th Cir. 1961), *cert. denied*, 369 U.S. 860 (1962). Although the evidence in that case showed that seventy percent of the respondent's retail dealers sold the manufacturer's products at the preticketed price, the Court of Appeals quoted with approval the Commission's language: "Respondent's purpose is self-evident—to make it appear to the store customers that the store was selling the luggage at approximately two dollars less than the regular retail price, and the customer would believe that he or she was getting a reduced price." 296 F.2d at 611.

Wouldn't it be simpler and safer for the manufacturer simply to set the price he charges others for the product, based on his cost plus a margin of profit, and then leave other members of the distributional hierarchy free to determine the markup necessary to cover their own cost and profit? [71]

One answer is that the manufacturer does it to meet competition. It is a commercial fact of life that pretickets and price lists are customary concomitants of many kinds of merchandise. When retail merchants demand them for their own competitive use, any manufacturer who refuses to comply places himself at a disadvantage to other manufacturers who are willing to oblige.[72] A second reason for such devices is that, despite the spate of fictitious pricing cases, many—perhaps most—preticketed or price listed items are actually sold at their indicated prices.[73]

Thus manufacturers are impelled by the same kind of motives that lead them to support fair trade laws. They are unconvinced by the apparent economic paradox that a manufacturer should be able to increase sales and profits by lowering retail prices rather than maintaining them. Indeed, it has been suggested that manufacturers who favor fair trade probably already have some degree of monopoly power over their products, so that they will not lose sales and profits by maintaining a higher price.[74]

Attempts to justify manufacturer-suggested prices have also relied upon their claimed usefulness to retailers and consumers in providing a price norm or standard of comparison. It has been contended, for example, that retailers carry so many goods in such varying levels of quality that they have no way of knowing that $29.95 is the "proper" retail price for an automatic coffeemaker—that only the manufacturer has sufficient knowledge to predict what consumers will pay.[75] This argument may have some validity for inexperienced retailers or ones in small towns. Similarly, it is contended that manufacturers' prices aid the consumer by protecting him against being overcharged [76] and also by giving him a method of identifying the particular item that is more comprehensible than model numbers or product names.[77] The FTC's position, however, is that the utility of manufacturers' prices as a superior means of identification is more than offset by the greater possibility of deception inherent in their use if they do not accurately reflect the generally prevailing retail price.[78]

---

[71] For a discussion of the premise that some manufacturers determine first the retail price at which a planned product will sell and work backward from that figure to see how much can be spent for production costs, see the testimony of Lannon F. Mead, president of Regina Corporation, in Regina Corp., *supra* note 68, reproduced in Electrical Merchandising Week, Sept. 25, 1961, p. 9. For an indication that one large retailer also operates in this manner, supervising the manufacture and transportation of the product to its stores, see Silberman, *The Department Stores Are Waking Up,* Fortune, July 1962, p. 143, at 251.

[72] It might appear that if such conduct were flatly declared illegal in one case, all other manufacturers would then discontinue it; but experience teaches otherwise. *Cf.* FTC v. C. E. Niehoff & Co., 335 U.S. 411 (1958).

[73] Many low cost items have the price printed on the product itself or upon the container in which it comes at the request of the retailer because such printing adds nothing to the manufacturer's costs, whereas a retailer may devote as much as twenty-two percent of its total man-hours to having retail prices stamped on its inventory, much of which is sold at the price that the manufacturer would print on it. See *The Price-Marking Problem,* Modern Packaging, Sept. 1959, p. 99. See generally *Sounding Board: What Do You Think of Pre-Pricing By Packagers?—Part I,* Modern Packaging, Dec. 1959, p. 65; *Part II,* Modern Packaging, Jan. 1960, p. 57. Anent products that are sold below premarked prices, see S. 3745, 87th Cong., 2d Sess. (1962), the "Truth in Packaging" bill that would prevent manufacturers from making any "cents-off" markings on labels. See Advertising Age, Oct. 1, 1962, p. 70.

[74] Telser, *Why Should Manufacturers Want Fair Trade?,* 3 J. of L. & ECONOMICS 86 (1960).

[75] See the testimony of Neil H. Borden, Professor of Marketing, Graduate School of Business Administration, Harvard University, before the hearing examiner in Regina Corp., *supra* note 68, reproduced in Electrical Merchandising Week, *supra* note 71.

[76] This argument generally includes a reference to the Automobile Information Disclosure Act, 72 Stat. 326, 15 U.S.C. § 1232 (1958), which requires manufacturers to "preticket" automobiles with a suggested list price. In Baltimore Luggage Co. v. FTC, 296 F.2d 608 (4th Cir. 1961), *cert. denied,* 369 U.S. 860 (1962), the court rejected this argument by noting that the policy behind this Act was the protection of the public against "price packing"—a phenomenon peculiar to the automobile industry.

[77] Regina Corp., *supra* note 68.

[78] Id. at 20835.

The Legal Distinction Between Pretickets and Price Lists

For whatever reason the manufacturer decides to influence the retail price, his next problem is whether to use pretickets, list prices, or both. His choice may be governed by the differing legal standards applicable to the different categories.

Although preticketing is not yet illegal per se,[79] it has become a very dangerous activity. In the first place, this practice often occurs in highly competitive lines where prices fluctuate from one trade area to another and even in the same trade area, often making the concept of a "generally prevailing" retail price virtually meaningless.[80] Moreover, while lack of knowledge of the inaccuracy of the "list prices" cited in the retailer-advertisements appears to be a defense in price list cases,[81] the Commission has held in *Leeds,* which involved both preticketing and catalog insert sheets, that it would look to only two factors: the generally prevailing price in the area and the preticketed price. If they are different, there is a violation of the FTC Act.[82] This means that once a manufacturer pretickets his product he may be at the mercy of market fluctuations.[83] Thus the national manufacturer honestly attempting to print the "generally prevailing" price on his pretickets has little chance of finding the magic figure at which all retailers throughout the nation will sell his product. While there might be no violation if only a few dealers cut this price, there is clear warning that missing the mark by $2.00 in thirty percent of the trade areas is a violation.[84] The fact that the manufacturer's purpose may have been beyond reproach and that the preticket may have been followed in seventy percent of the trade areas will be immaterial.

Supplying retailers with price lists involves many of the same prediction problems as preticketing. A difference between the two practices, however, is that the preticket is clearly intended to be seen by the consumer, whereas, at least arguably, the price list may only be intended to assist the retailer in setting his resale price. This difference has been suggested as the reason why *Regina,* a price list case, requires proof that the manufacturer "knew or ought to have known" that its list prices were fictitious, whereas *Leeds,* a preticketing and catalog sheet case, holds that such knowledge is immaterial in its circumstances. The Commission's opinion in *Regina,* however, does not illuminate this aspect of the problem.

Antitrust Implications

But even if the manufacturer makes an accurate future prediction of the sale price of his product and pretickets it or furnishes suggested list prices that all retailers thereafter follow, he faces the possible accusation of violating another statutory antitrust provision. As Commissioner Elman pointed out in *Rayex:*

Such conduct would not necessarily be immune from scrutiny under other statutory provisions regulating business activity. For example, it might in some circumstances suggest the existence of illegal anti-competitive pricing conditions in the industry. Compare, e.g., *United States v. Parke, Davis & Co.,* . . . 362 U.S. 29. . . . It may be, for example, that the industry in which the practice is undertaken is characterized by price rigidity or uniformity. That is to say, all dealers in a particular product may be content to sell at the

---

[79] Baltimore Luggage Co. v. FTC, *supra* note 76. "The Commission does not contend that for the manufacturer to place tickets on its products before delivering them to retailers indicating the retail purchase price, a practice known as 'preticketing,' is illegal or deceptive *per se.* But the Commission does maintain, and Baltimore agrees, that manufacturers who preticket their products fictitiously are guilty of engaging in an unfair trade practice in violation of the Act." *Id.* at 610.

[80] See, *e.g.,* Rayex Corp., 3 CCH TRADE REG. REP. ¶ 15823 (FTC April 2, 1962).

[81] See note 67 *supra.*

[82] Leeds Travelwear, Inc., 3 CCH TRADE REG. REP. ¶ 15997, at 20835 (FTC July 20, 1962): "Where, as here [the amounts designated as 'retail' in the catalog sheets] . . . are in excess of the generally prevailing retail prices, the practice has a tendency or capacity to deceive. This is the test of legality under Section 5. Knowledge on the part of respondents is not a material consideration under these circumstances."

[83] This is consistent with the provision of Guide VIII that "they (who preticket) are chargeable with knowledge of the ordinary business 'facts of life' concerning what happens to articles for which they furnish 'pre-ticketed prices.'" See note 39 *supra* and accompanying text. Quaere, however, whether the FTC would rigidly follow the Leeds

standard where a precipitous market drop occurred *after* the manufacturer had distributed the preticketed merchandise.

[84] Baltimore Luggage Co. v. FTC, *supra* note 76.

same price. If a manufacturer of such a product pretickets it at what is in fact the uniform retail price in the area, he is not engaging in false or misleading pricing. Of course, rigidity and uniformity of price may make preticketing even more suspect as a manifestation of some form of illegal restraint of trade, but in such circumstances the practice is not vulnerable as deceptive to consumers.[85]

This is a warning to manufacturers of another danger awaiting them once the decision to preticket is made: they may be accused of violating the Sherman Act and, consequently, Section 5 of the FTC Act, by entering into an illegal resale price maintenance agreement with the conforming retailers.[86] This danger is acute if the manufacturer attempts to coerce recalcitrant retailers to sell at the preticketed or suggested price.[87]

---

[85] *Supra* note 80, at 20627.
[86] *But see* Sidney J. Kreiss Inc., 56 F.T.C. 1421 (1960). Apparently oblivious of any vertical price-fixing problem, a differently-constituted Commission recited that a manufacturer "required" retailers to sell at prescribed prices and "permitted" them to reduce these prices by half during special sales.
[87] In United States v. Colgate & Co., 250 U.S. 300 (1919), the Supreme Court decided that no Sherman Act offense was charged by an indictment alleging only that a manufacturer specified resale prices to wholesalers and retailers and told them he would refuse to deal with those who did not adhere to such prices. "In the absence of any purpose to create or maintain a monopoly," the Court stated at 307, "he may announce in advance the circumstances under which he will refuse to sell." Subsequent decisions, however, narrowly confined the *Colgate* doctrine. United States v. A. Schrader's Son, 252 U.S. 85 (1920); Frey & Son v. Cudahy Packing Co., 256 U.S. 208 (1921); FTC v. Beech-Nut Packing Co., 257 U.S. 441 (1922); United States v. Bausch & Lomb Optical Co., 321 U.S. 707 (1944); United States v. Parke, Davis & Co., 362 U.S. 29 (1960). The *Parke, Davis* case involved a manufacturer who told wholesalers he would not deal with them if they supplied retailers who cut prices below the manufacturer's suggested retail prices. Because the wholesalers had acquiesced and withheld supplies from price-cutting retailers, the manufacturer was found to have entered into an illegal combination with them in violation of the Sherman Act. "When the manufacturer's actions . . . go beyond mere announcement of his policy and the simple refusal to deal, and he employs other means which effect adherence to his resale prices . . ." the Court said, "he has put together a combination in violation of the Sherman Act." 362 U.S. at 44.

But *Klein v. American Luggage Works, Inc.*,[88] indicates that conduct falling short of coercion may still be illegal. There a manufacturer preticketed its luggage and announced to its three retailer-customers in one trade area that it would refuse to supply retailers who undercut the preticketed price—a seemingly logical course for a manufacturer interested in avoiding fictitious pricing problems. Yet, when the manufacturer refused to sell to a price-cutting retailer, the court held that the manufacturer *and* the two price-conforming retailers had violated the Sherman Act.[89]

It is implicit in the *Klein* decision that, where a manufacturer sets a retail price for a product, announcing in advance that he will not supply retailers who sell below that price, and some retailers accept the manufacturer's goods, if the manufacturer acts on the prompting of those retailers to refuse to sell to a price-cutter, he may be a candidate for a price-fixing charge.[90]

Thus the manufacturer who makes the decision to place a preticket on his product or to suggest the retail price for it sails henceforth in perilous waters. If he has misjudged the "going" price, a fictitious pricing charge may be forthcoming; if some retailers actually sell at the preticketed price and, at their urging, he cuts off others who do not, he is in peril of being charged with a Sherman Act violation; if *all* retailers sell at the manufacturer's

---

[88] 206 F. Supp. 924 (D. Del. 1962).
[89] The court admitted there was no precedent in the authorities for this part of the decision but reasoned that the two price-conforming retailers and the manufacturer were co-conspirators by drawing analogies to Interstate Circuit, Inc. v. United States, 306 U.S. 208 (1939) and United States v. Masonite Corp., 316 U.S. 265 (1942).
[90] *Quaere* whether the Supreme Court, when and if it reviews the *Klein* case, will find that American Luggage Co. used sufficient "other means" to forfeit protection of the *Colgate* doctrine.

In holding the three defendants liable to the plaintiff the court paid homage to the *Colgate* doctrine, but noted: "The conceptual difficulty which inheres in this seemingly forthright line drawing process [of the *Colgate* Doctrine] is the element of agreement which attends a seller's adherence to a manufacturer's schedule of resale prices. In the face of an advance announcement by the manufacturer that price-cutters will be denied supply, a seller's compliance with prices suggested strongly infers a tacit or implied resale price maintenance agreement." 206 F. Supp. at 937.

price, even though no one complains, there may be a clear-cut Sherman Act violation. This may well cause the manufacturer to decide against any preticketing or price listing at all .

CONCLUSION

A genuine bargain, something-for-nothing, is the utopian dream of many consumers. Since the end of World War II, sellers have fed the public appetite for bargains with a growing variety of phony comparative-price sales appeals. In the fierce competitive infighting for the consumer dollar, fictitious pricing has become a common vice of the market place.

The persistence of these schemes has generated stepped-up regulatory efforts by the Federal Trade Commission. In 1958, the Commission promulgated its Guides Against Fictitious Pricing, which memorialized the considerable body of Commission fictitious price rulings since 1914. The Commission's more recent decisions have reinforced the Guides and, in important cases, have gone beyond the Guides to extend the businessman's periphery of hazard.

The standard of care which the Commission applies to retail comparative price advertising has been drawn with relative precision. Generally speaking, the higher price (however described) against which the retailer lays his "bargain" price must be truthfully told: it must either be an actual immediately-precedent price of the advertiser or a prevailing current price in the relevant trade area. The Commission's test—ordained and largely inflexible— imposes no unconscionable burden on the retailer. The Commission's Guides and adjudicative rulings have defined the terms used by the retailer and have fixed the retailer's responsibility to predetermine the factual truth of his comparative claims.

While the retailer's road, however rough, is traversable, the manufacturer who involves himself in the pricing process through preticketing or list price suggestions runs a considerably more perilous course. If a manufacturer pretickets his product, he will run afoul of the Federal Trade Commission Act wherever the retail price of the product does not substantially conform to the ticketed price. Since preticketed merchandise almost inevitably emerges into competitive markets where retail prices may be highly volatile, it is incumbent upon the manufacturer to ascertain that the ticketed price is actually the price at which the retailers are selling the product to consumers. Short of an automated ticketing program, instantly responsive to shifting market trends, the preticketing manufacturer avoids involvement in deception at the risk of conduct courting antitrust involvement.

The perils of list price suggestion may be even more severe. While the *Regina* doctrine is not yet secure, its gloomy premonitions can already be felt. At the very least, a manufacturer is implicated where he has knowledge that his suggested list prices are in excess of prevailing retail prices (and hence "fictitious"); at the most, he may be vulnerable, with or without knowledge, whenever his list prices, in fact, exceed retail prices. Here, too, the manufacturer assures against deception, reinforces truth, only at a risk of antitrust offense through efforts to stabilize retail prices.

The Federal Trade Commission has raised storm signals in clear view of the businessman determined to use pretickets or suggested list prices. He must now frankly appraise the hazards of such activities in the light of the Commission's newly sensitized alertness to possible deception. At the same time, he must avoid the antitrust implications of too-scrupulous retailer adherence to his ticketed or suggested list prices. In the glare of official scrutiny, ordinary prudence may require extraordinary care.

DISCUSSION QUESTIONS

Selecting and promoting prices is an increasingly complex task. This article indicates some common deceptive practices in pricing, and provides the guides which will minimize usage of phrases and procedures which have been held to involve some element of deception.

1. What causes underlie the widespread use of "fictitious" prices?
2. What is preticketing? What forces have encouraged the use of this pricing practice?
3. What is a "catalog jobber"?

3. Price Maintenance or Price Cutting

FRANK A. FRIDAY

Superficially, the case against resale price maintenance is overwhelming. It is quite simple. Some retailers are willing to sell price-maintained branded goods at retail prices below those prescribed by owners of the brands. This must be a good thing. However, the law allows a brand-owner, if he wishes, to enforce uniform resale prices on any distributor, whether or not that distributor bought the goods under direct contract with the brand-owner. Since this prevents retailers from price cutting, the law should be altered. The emotional appeal of this kind of argument is undoubtedly strong.

In fact, resale price maintenance—the setting and enforcement of uniform prices by the brand-owners (usually manufacturers) in outlets which they do not own—is only one form of price maintenance. There is also direct price maintenance, which is a similar fixing of uniform prices of branded goods in outlets owned by the brand-owners. Indeed, there are many examples of brands being sold at uniform prices under both forms of price maintenance. Resale price maintenance accounts for about 20 per cent of total consumer spending; direct price maintenance represents nearly another 20 per cent.

The practice of enforcing resale prices has arisen from the many different methods of distribution and the growth of branding. Ideally the manufacturer of a consumer product would prefer to sell his own brand direct to final customers himself. With a large proportion of goods this is impossible because a manufacturer would not be able to maintain locations for the sale of his own brands alone; he would have to handle the products of other manufacturers also in order to make the shops pay and then he would become an ordinary retailer.

All manufacturers cannot, therefore, own the outlets stocking and selling their brands; they have to deal in different ways with distributing organisations which they do not own, according to the nature of the product and the number of outlets which the manufacturer considers desirable for the maximum distribution of his range of goods. Under English common law, a manufacturer can establish conditions of sale for his goods by having direct contracts with appointed dealers. This is not always appropriate for a large proportion of consumer goods and many manufacturers find it more convenient to distribute through wholesaling organisations which canalise the products of hundreds of manufacturers and so reduce considerably the number of retailers' orders and the cost of meeting them. Under Section 25 of the Restrictive Trade Practices Act of 1956, the enforcement of resale price maintenance on "non-signers" leaves a manufacturer free to select the most efficient method of distribution for his goods, with the same right to uniform retail prices, if he wants them, as the brand-owner who has direct contracts with appointed retailers or who owns his outlets.

Much has been made by opponents of resale price maintenance of the support which these uniform prices get from the large body of independent retailers. This, itself, is regarded as a form of condemnation, because these retailers are equated with "non-aggressiveness" and "high costs" so they must, by definition, be standing in the way of "progress" and "lower prices." Yet, support for resale price maintenance in the distributive trade is understandable, for it is based on fear of the destructive effect of undercutting as a result of predatory competition. Countries also object to cut pricing which arises from the dumping of goods at specially low prices and they often have anti-dumping laws to stop it. The present law on resale price maintenance puts the onus of enforcement squarely on to the individual man-

♦ SOURCE: Reprinted by permission from the editor of *The Statist*, in the April 13, 1962, issue, pages 115–117.

ufacturer who prescribes the retail prices for his goods and it is the manufacturer, therefore, who has to decide whether or not he wishes to have uniform prices.

"PRICE-CUTTING" DOES NOT LOWER PRICES

The purpose of resale price maintenance is to prevent price cutting. This does not mean that the average level of retail prices of price maintained goods is necessarily any higher than it otherwise would be. Prices go up as well as down when price maintenance is removed. Moreover, gross margins under resale price maintenance are often lower than for similar freely priced goods and, since distributive costs tend to rise gradually as a percentage of retail prices, and the margins set by manufacturers are stable over very long periods, the cost of living may go up as a result of any ban on resale price maintenance; it is most unlikely to go down.

Price cutting, then, must not be taken as being synonymous with a general reduction in prices. Indeed, it is often sporadic and confined to the well-known brands. Whether a manufacturer will wish to prevent it depends on the nature of his range of branded goods, the number and kind of selling locations and the size of gross margin required to stock and sell those goods. Costs in distribution are quite different from costs in manufacturing. The main costs of wholesaling and retailing (rent, rates, maintenance, and labour) are relatively fixed in the short run and cannot easily be allocated to the many hundreds of different lines handled in a single establishment. The percentage relationship of these total expenses to turnover depends not only on the expected sales of each individual line but also on the mix of products. In truly competitive conditions, retail prices of identical articles ought to settle at some uniform figure with the same gross margin in all outlets for goods purchased on similar terms. Because of differences in the wealth and tastes of neighbourhoods and in the geographical densities of their populations, each shop has a different ratio of expenses to turnover and a different average gross margin.

Because of the overhead character of distribution costs and the importance of product mix, the retail prices of individual products can be fixed quite arbitrarily. If price cuts on certain well-known manufacturers' brands successfully divert trade from other retailers, the cost of making the cuts will be much more than offset by the gross margin earned on the additional sales of other articles. The initial effect is to decrease the shop's ratio of expenses to turnover and increase its net profit; but as soon as other retailers follow suit the advantage is lost. Then, all dealers have a higher expense ratio (because the value of sales is down) unless they can restore the ratio by raising the prices of other lines, or by poaching goods with higher margins from other trades. As a weapon for diverting trade, price cutting is often self-defeating. When everybody in a crowd stands on stools, nobody sees any better.

GILDING THE LILY

Similar considerations apply with services. The idea frequently expressed by opponents of resale price maintenance that margins on these goods are so high that retailers have shamefacedly to give away their "excessive" profits by increasing services (delivery, credit, wrapping, and even "elaboration of shop design") is quite fallacious. Extra services are given for the same reason that prices are cut—in expectation that the gross margins obtained on additional sales will exceed the cost of the added services, thus decreasing the ratio of expenses to turnover and *increasing* profits. But, as with price cutting, others adopt the same policy, so the expense percentage is pushed upwards. It is doubtful, however, whether consumers get too much service as a result. With the steady rise in the standard of living people usually want more service, not less. And the same amount of service is not taken by all customers of a shop all the time.

The difference between these two methods of retail competition is that price cutting singles out an individual brand-owner's products for "bait" whereas the general services given by a shop do not. When caught in the quicksands of intermittent price cutting, the manufacturer's concern is that other outlets will cease stocking and displaying his products and so reduce his total sales in the market. It is not just a question of "placating" other dealers. The brand-owner's distribution system can be disrupted and his range of products completely upset. He cannot be indifferent to this. Moreover, once resale price maintenance is eliminated and price cutting becomes prevalent, we lose, as consumers, our standard of realistic retail prices and we get, instead, a higher level of "usual" and "suggested" prices from which discounts can be given. This was the practice in the book trade before resale price maintenance was introduced. When publishers began enforcing a "net" price, customers often paid less for a book than when they got a discount off the published price, because the published price had to be fixed nominally high in order to make the discounts possible. Professor Marshall's *Principles of Economics* was the first book made subject to resale price maintenance. The unenforced published price would have been 16s. and the "lucky" customer who got three shillings in the pound off his purchases (the usual discount) would have paid 13s. 6d. for it; the enforced net price was 12s. 6d.

FREEDOM TO BROWSE

The brand-owner's concern, however, goes beyond this. Price cutting arises also from the poaching of fast-selling lines from other trades where the gross margins are higher. Some measure of poaching trade from trade, and some conflict between shops which concentrate on having a wide stock of fast-moving lines and those which concentrate on a wide choice within a particular field, is inevitable. With the main expenses relatively fixed, product mix and stockturn have a large influence on the ratio of shop expenses to turnover. The cost of distribution is the price we pay for freedom of choice and vacillation, as Professor Taussig pointed out long ago. People want available to them a stock of all consumer goods from which a selection can be made and delivery taken, on the spur of the moment if need be. Distribution is not amenable to the kind of productivity increase obtainable in manufacturing. Economies in absolute costs amount to very little. Differences in rent per square foot reflect differences in expected business per square foot, and the relationship of rents to turnover may not differ very much for premises in a shopping centre and out of town. If, by price cutting, actual sales and profits considerably exceed the expectation on which the rent was based, the value of the property and its rent will go up. Low rents do not "cause" low prices, but to say so creates the right impression for successful trade diversion. Percentage costs can only be reduced by increasing sales faster than any increase in absolute cost. Apart from price cutting and additional services (for example, providing a car park), other methods are aimed at raising stockturn by increasing impulse sales.

Despite improvements in display and handling, and in the ratio of staff to customers, the room for manoeuvre in distribution is really very small. Differences in the gross margins of different articles are largely explained by differences in the value of stocks per square foot of space, stockturn, and the staff needed to handle the goods. Poaching is rarely justified on grounds of efficiency. The upward pressure of costs on margins has its influence in all trades, and supermarkets are not the only places with self-service and check-out points. Because a grocer can work to a margin of 15 per cent and a furniture dealer has 25 per cent does not mean that the grocer could sell furniture more efficiently than the furniture dealer. Yet this is often implied. In fact, if grocers came to stock the same range of articles as furniture dealers, the chances are that the gross margin would also be about 25 per cent. The expense ratio and prices are likely to be lower with the grocer only if the furniture is restricted to the more popular lines with a higher-than-average stockturn.

This poses a problem for the manufacturer of branded goods carrying a normal gross margin above that of the would-be price cutter. Piracy always pays when others are made to play the game; but the others here are outlets willing to handle a full range of slow-moving as well as fast-moving articles, and abandonment of resale price maintenance cannot help them to lower prices and remain solvent. Free pricing is likely to alter the brand-owner's distribution system and the character of his range of products. Although this may result in lower prices for the fast-moving lines taken over, it can also mean fewer specialist outlets and higher prices for the rest of the range. Then the sales of many lines would be severely curtailed and some would disappear altogether. It is sometimes argued that high stockturn articles are made to subsidise the low stockturn under resale price maintenance. This is not true, for manufacturers (and distributors) often do not know *in advance* which will be which. They find out after the goods have been marketed. In these circumstances, the brand-owner's inclination is to support the specialist dealers who carry the risk and cost of holding a full range, rather than the distributor who wants only to have the winners. Development of special low price brands for a restricted range may be preferable to price cutting (like the successful St Michael brand of Marks and Spencer).

It is surely right that a manufacturer should be allowed to decide on the methods of distribution needed for his own brands in the light of his assessment of the genuineness, and the long-term costs, of any new form of retailing. The present law is permissive only, with the onus of enforcement on the individual brand-owner. This is as it should be; and the brand-owner who sells through outlets he does not own should continue to have the same right to uniform prices, and exclusive trading, if he wants it, as the brand-owner who sells only through his own outlets.

DISCUSSION QUESTION

The great majority of professional economists have condemned the concept of resale price maintenance. This article presents the minority view—and though one wants badly to raise some interim questions as Mr. Friday's analysis develops—the argument is, in part, persuasive.

At what points in the argument would further documentation with fact be helpful?

4. Entrepreneurs Test the Environment: A Long Run View of Grocery Pricing

STANLEY C. HOLLANDER*

A review of grocery store pricing and merchandising practices, based upon examination of trade magazines for the period 1869–1949 reveals patterns of repetition, experimentation, and adaptation. Changes in prevailing industry practices seem to result from environmental conditions that lead to acceptance of previously rejected experiments.

Personnel specialists sometimes say that a man is quite likely to be in error when he claims to have had twenty or thirty years' experience in a particular activity. Often, they say, he has really had only one year's experience, repeated twenty or thirty times. This paper is supposedly a report on eighty years' vicarious experience of the retail grocery trade derived from reading consecutive issues of trade magazines (mostly weeklies) from 1869 through 1949.[1] In many ways, although not entirely, that experience is much the same thing as reading one year's issues over and over again eighty times. The language and the writing style change. Perhaps somewhat surprisingly, the editor of the 1870 grocers' magazine assumed a higher level of vocabulary and

literacy in his audience than his current counterpart does. Also if choice of type face and page makeup is any indication, nineteenth century grocers were expected to have keener eyesight than twentieth century ones.

REPETITIVE PROBLEMS

But one of the striking things about the eighty-year run of magazines is the extent to which the editorial content of one period—the indication of the trade's interests, problems and practices—echoes or augers the content of earlier and later periods. Except for minor differences in terminology and expression, we have to check the date of publication to tell whether the authors of the following paragraphs are talking about current problems or old ones.

In these days of hurry and push, people do not like to have to go into six different shops for six different articles; they prefer to buy the lot at one shop and the trader who gives them this facility will get their business.[2]

A price list is one of those advertisements that appeals to nearly all classes of buyers.[3]

For some reason chain stores everywhere seem to have drifted into using the same style of advertising . . . Big black type, a few leaders, with a little explanatory matter, but not much, and the balance straight price list.

---

* SOURCE: Reprinted by permission from the American Marketing Association, in *Marketing and Economic Development*, Peter D. Bennett, editor, 1965, pages 516–527.

* Professor of Marketing, Michigan State University. The author wishes to acknowledge support from The Sperry and Hutchinson Company to Michigan State University for research in grocery and price history.

[1] The principal publications used were *The American Grocer* (sometimes entitled *The American Grocer and Dry Goods Chronicle*), 1869–1898, *Grocery World* (also at times called *Grocery World and General Merchant* and *Modern Merchant and Grocery World*) 1898–1922, and *Progressive Grocer*, 1923–1949. In the interests of brevity, only the short title for *The American Grocer* and *Grocery World* are used in the footnotes below.

[2] "The Sell-Everything System," *The American Grocer*, Vol. 47, January 20, 1892, p. 9.

[3] "Retailers' Advertising," *ibid.*, Vol. 31, January 31, 1884.

It is the circus poster style, the sensational cut price style.[4]

Some of the old and large houses engaged in manufacturing grocers' goods seem to be of the opinion that the trade are obliged to handle their goods and claim that they can compel them to do so by creating a demand among consumers.[5]

. . . up to eight or ten years ago the practice of giving premiums to purchasers was of rare occurance. During the war it revived and has continued to increase until in some localities it has become an almost universal practice.[6]

. . . [grocers] at last awoke to the realization that quick sales and small profits spell success in canned goods.[7]

The comment on scrambled merchandising, then called "the sell-everything system," is dated 1872; the notes on price-list advertising come from 1884 and 1917; the complaint about manufacturers' forcing practices and low margins appeared in 1873; while both the criticism of premiums and the recommendation for low markup-high turnover policies were published in 1878. Similar comments emerged at frequent intervals throughout the eighty year run. Moreover, many other topics that disturb the grocery trade today were equally burning issues, either constantly or at fairly frequent intervals, during the entire eight decades. Sunday and night openings, trading stamps, the proliferation of brands, discount competition (from "cutters" and "economy stores" before the term "discount house" was coined), invasions of the retail grocery trade by outsiders (including department stores, mail order houses, direct selling "wholesalers," wagon vendors, and others), co-operative buying, packaging and labeling problems, and above all, the erosion of margins were standard subjects for discussion in the trade press.

EXPERIMENTS

Merchandise Assortments

The eighty year record, however, is by no means entirely a matter of repetition. It in-

cludes reports of many institutional types, merchandising plans and pricing arrangements that either never caught on, or that once having succeeded eventually withered away. The emergence of various types of specialized retailers, at least for a time, and the shedding of merchandise lines contrast with the tendency towards scrambled merchandising. For example, dairy shops that sold better quality eggs, butter, cream and cheese apparently took considerable business away from the general food stores towards the end of the nineteenth century.[8] The great growth of specialized tea, coffee and spice dealers during the same century rested upon a number of factors, including ingenious and appealing premium schemes, technical knowledge and large assortments at a time when consumers regarded tea blending as a personal art, and price umbrellas provided by high markups for these items in conventional grocery stores.[9] "Package stores," *i.e.* groceries that sold only prepacked merchandise created a considerable stir, partially as a merchandising approach and partially as a stock promotion, in several eastern cities between 1912 and 1918. They were anticipated by at least a few earlier retailers who attempted to specialize in case lots at cut prices.[10] In a sense, the mail order grocery merchants and the "box car merchants" who sent canvassers through the midwest at the turn of the century to solicit orders for subsequent group delivery were also specialists in prepacked and/or dry commodity lines.[11] Five and ten cent grocery stores, in which nothing sold for more than ten cents, appeared from time to time but especially in the years 1927 to 1929.[12] The frozen food store, with its entire stock in freezers, was a short-lived manifestation of the post-World

---

[4] "The Science of Advertising," *Grocery World*, Vol. 63, June 25, 1917, p. 18.

[5] Editorial comment, letters page, *The American Grocer*, Vol. 9, August 2, 1873.

[6] "Gifts to Consumers," *ibid.*, Vol. 21, December 26, 1878, p. 6.

[7] "The Economy of Canned Goods," *ibid.*, Vol. 19, March 7, 1878, p. 667.

[8] "The Sell-Everything System;" Artemas Ward, "Straight Talks to the Trade," *The American Grocer*, Vol. 53, January 23, 1895, p. 7.

[9] "The Prize Goods Case," *ibid.*, Vol. 39, June 13, 1888, pp. 11–13; "The Stroller's Column," *Grocery World*, Vol. 39, February 20, 1905, p. 26.

[10] "The New York Letter," *Grocery World*, Vol. 59, May 10, 1915, p. 14; *ibid.*, Vol. 65, March 4, 1918, p. 14; "Correspondence," *ibid.*, Vol. 63, May 21, 1917, p. 12; "New Canned Goods Scheme in Town," *ibid.*, Vol. 30. February 9, 1905, p. 12.

[11] "Mail Order and Scheme Priced Always High," *ibid.*, Vol. 40, November 13, 1905, p. 9.

[12] "Enter: The Five and Ten Cent Grocery Chain," *Printers' Ink*, Vol. 140, August 11, 1927, p. 142; *Progressive Grocer*, Vol. 7, July, 1928, pp. 66–70; August, 1928, pp. 24–27.

War II period.[13] There are indications that our current prosperity provides some support for the specialized gourmet food shop (translation: imported desserts and confections—usually stale or indigestible) as a replacement for the disappearing old fashioned fancy grocer with his fetish for steamer baskets (translation: imported desserts and confections—usually stale or indigestible).

The American Grocer reported in 1880 that soda fountains had ceased to be profitable additions to grocery stores, and subsequent wavelets of experimentation with grocery store lunch counters, tea rooms and (in San Francisco) bars had little long run impact on the trade.[14] The full scale retreat of department store and mail order firms from the grocery business during the relatively early 1900's proves that merchandising, unlike eggs, can be unscrambled.[15]

Gifts, Premiums, and Rebates

In the late 1880's and 1890's, the grocers of one city after another found themselves involved, much to their consternation, in the practice of giving their customers Christmas gifts. They worried about this for a decade or two, and asked the trade magazines whether they should give every customer the same thing, or whether they should try to adjust the gift to the customer's purchases and needs. Then the custom seems to have died out in most places.[16] But numerous other gift and premium plans emerged. One of the more unusual schemes was a health insurance plan developed by a Dayton, Ohio firm, in which the customers received vouchers that could be redeemed for free groceries in case of illness. Even this plan does not seem as striking as those of the British tea retailers who reportedly offered their regular customers free medical services and widows' pensions, presumably in an attempt to demonstrate the healthfulness of their products.[17]

Numerous co-operative, quasi co-operative and spurious co-operative organizations also appeared during the eighty year period to promise and, sometimes, to provide rebates and allowances to their customer-members.[18] Commissary stores that offered bulk groceries, little service and low prices were operated by many industrial, public utility and governmental employers during the pre- and post-World War I inflationary periods. Several labor unions tried to operate similar stores after World War II.[19] A number of attempts to lower food costs were based on the idea of direct farmer to consumer sales. Many municipalities established or re-established public markets during the years immediately preceding World War I. At about the same time the Post Office and the express companies competed fruitlessly in attempts to develop direct farm to home business. Earlier the Grangers had tried to circumvent the middleman in reaching the consumer, while today the Farm Bureau Federation talks of buying its own retail chain.[20]

Service Variation

The service, convenience and amenities provided for the customer varied widely. The so-called fancy grocers vied in providing carpeted waiting rooms, Italian mosaic and mahogany walls, hand painted gold and silver trimmed

[13] "Frozen Foods: Interim Report," *Fortune*, Vol. 34, August, 1946, p. 180, "Dewey Hails Ex-G.I.'s for Trade Venture," *New York Times*, June 26, 1947, p. 26.

[14] "Stocks and Profits of Country Store," *The American Grocer*, Vol. 23, March 25, 1880, p. 795; "Saloon Grocery Stores," *Grocery World*, Vol. 30, August 13, 1900, p. 12; "The Grocery Restaurant Fad," *ibid.*, Vol. 41, May 7, 1906, p. 13.

[15] Boris Emmet and John E. Jueck, *Catalogues and Counters*, Chicago: University of Chicago Press, 1950, pp. 228–29.

[16] "Grocers' Holiday Gifts," *The American Grocer*, Vol. 40, November 21, 1888, p. 9; "Holiday Gifts," *ibid.*, Vol. 42, December 18, 1889, p. 7.

[17] "Just About the Most Unique Scheme Yet," *Grocery World*, Vol. 62, September 25, 1916, p. 21; "The Most Curious Tea Premium Scheme in the World," *ibid.*, Vol. 32, November 18, 1901, p. 20; "A Doctor's Visit with a Pound of Tea, *The American Grocer*, Vol. 54, November 6, 1895, p. 6.

[18] Orin E. Burley, *The Consumers' Cooperative as a Distributive Agency*, New York: McGraw-Hill Book Company, 1939, espec. Chap. I, IV, XIV; S. C. Hollander, The Rise and Fall of a Buying Club (monog.), East Lansing: Michigan State University, 1959.

[19] S. C. Hollander and G. A. Marple, *Henry Ford: Inventor of the Supermarket?* (monog.), East Lansing: Michigan State University, 1960; "Will Union Hall Food Sales Become Big Business?" *Progressive Grocer*, Vol. 26, November, 1946, pp. 282–88.

[20] "With The Editor," *Grocery World*, Vol. 60, October 18, 1915, p. 10; W. E. Fuller, *R.F.D.*, Bloomington: Indiana University Press, 1960, Chap. 10; "Correspondence," *The American Grocer*, Vol. 16, August 5, 1876, p. 156; "Farmers Weigh Plan to Buy Supermarkets," *Washington Post*, November 8, 1964, p. B18.

tea cannisters, and, in at least one instance, a grand staircase copied from that in the Paris Opera House. A Rochester, Minnesota store placed much of its merchandise in comfortably furnished alcoves and sitting rooms, labeled "food for your breakfast," "food for your lunch," "food for your dinner" and "food for your party." A Connecticut grocer installed telephones in the homes of fifty of his best customers in 1908, so that they could more easily order from him. As early as 1928, a Louisville, Kentucky drive-in was reported to have placed its stock on the perimeter of a large circle where customers could select their purchases without leaving their cars. In contrast, some of the early economy stores provided so little service and had so few employees that they regularly closed during the lunch hour, and a supposedly very successful million dollar California Groceteria of the '30's opened only on Wednesdays and Saturdays, when part-time labor was released from the local high school.[21]

Price Statements

There was considerable change and experimentation in pricing methods and price statements. *The American Grocer* lamented in 1890 that any old-time grocer who returned to the current scene would miss the old-fashioned "combination offer" of a bundle of assorted groceries, sold at a single flat price. Only six years later it reported a number of these deals, which it then criticized as "the Philadelphia pirate style" of merchandising. Similar combination prices were reported in subsequent years.[22] In 1937 one enterprising supermarket

operator tried using two completely separate meat counters, *i.e.* an economy section and a full quality department, in emulation of the department store basement-upstairs merchandising split.[23] As is noted below, many grocers experimented at various times with separate charges for services, such as credit and delivery, an idea endorsed by the Twentieth Century Fund's Distribution Committee in the well-known *Does Distribution Cost Too Much?* "Service Charge Merchandising," which was attempted by a few merchants in the 1930's and again in 1947 carried this idea to its logical extreme. The customer paid a weekly subscription fee for the retailing service, and then simply reimbursed the merchant for the wholesale cost of the food. Although similar plans have been very successful at the wholesaler-retailer level, "service charge merchandising" was a retail failure. Nevertheless, somewhat similar principles supposedly operate in some freezer-frozen food plans today.[24]

These are only a few illustrations of the many variations that can be found in the eighty year records of the grocery trade and its pricing practices. The full record amply documents the amazing amount of inventiveness, adaptability, and experimentation that can be found even in what is supposed to be one of the most pedestrian and routine types of business. The French use the term "grocer" as an epithet, as a synonym for dullness and commonplaceness. The record suggests many exceptions to that characterization.

A review of the eighty year experience also indicates the complexity of the price making process and the multi-dimensional nature of price phenomena. The available time does not permit examination here of all the variations in pricing practices encountered over the eighty year run. Temporal variations in price, for example, embrace seasonal price reductions, including a fairly long-lived custom of January canned goods sales borrowed from the department store entrants into the grocery

[21] "The Finest Grocery Store in the World," *The American Grocer*, Vol. 32, October 2, 1884, pp. 10–11, "Retailers' Advertising," *ibid.*, Vol. 54, July 3, 1895, p. 8; "Around Town," *ibid.*, Vol. 47, January 6, 1892, p. 9; "Los Angeles' Finest Store," *ibid.*, Vol. 57; February 24, 1897, p. 9; "These Plans Have Made Trade," *Grocery World*, Vol. 46, August 17, 1908, p. 20; "The Science of Advertising," *ibid.*, Vol. 63, April 9, 1917, p. 16; "A New Kind of Food Store," *Progressive Grocer*, Vol. 17, March, 1938, pp. 32–34; "Business Highlights in Short Paragraphs," *ibid.*, Vol. 7, December, 1928, p. 54; "Open Two Days a Week—Sells a $1,000,000," *ibid.*, Vol. 14, September, 1935, p. 146.
[22] "The Grocer and Domestic Life," *The American Grocer*, Vol. 43, January 15, 1890, p. 8; "Retailers' Advertising," *ibid.*, Vol. 55, March 4, 1896, p. 8; "Helping Gimbel Bros. Fight Retail Grocers,"

Grocery World, Vol. 44, July 29, 1907, p. 12; "Basket of Groceries at $1 Each Sell Fast," *Progressive Grocer*, Vol. 2, March 1923, p. 20; "Deals Put 'Gross' Into Groceries," *ibid.*, Vol. 17, October, 1938, p. 18.
[23] "Chains Go Supermarket," *Business Week*, May 1, 1937, p. 47.
[24] "Meat Clubs Slip," *Business Week*, February 28, 1948, pp. 49–50; "Service Charge Merchandising," *Progressive Grocer*, Vol. 27, May, 1948, p. 205.

business, as well as various patterns of adjustment between the days of the week or the hours of the day, as in the case of "early bird" specials. Varying quantity discount patterns, for half dozens, dozens and case lots can be discerned. A number of interesting questions center around the selection of price points, the influence of small coins and fractional currency on pricing techniques, and the psychological significance of particular price endings. Another aspect of pricing, to which we shall briefly return, concerns the basis or unit of sale, *i.e.* the question of whether the item being sold shall be measured by unit count, weight, or volume, trimmed or untrimmed, dressed or total, and with or without container. Other pricing issues can be found for example in the relationships between items, product categories, brands, or between advertised and non-advertised lines.

Another way in which the record can be reviewed is as a demonstration of the persistence and the futility of the idea of direct farmer-consumer sales. Public markets, mail order and a variety of institutional arrangements have been tried as substitutes for the middleman, over and over again, without much success. But instead of observing only the things that have not taken root, we should also look at what now seem to be the more persistent trends.

THREE TRENDS

One of the most clearcut tendencies has been toward increased clarity and rigor in communicating the price statement to the consumer. Many critics would argue that the industry has not gone far enough, but comparison clearly indicates that more, and better, price data are now made available to the consumer than was the case in 1870. Another tendency, which may ultimately be reversed, has been toward the reduction of credit and delivery services. A third, obviously, has been the increasing importance of large, self-service stores, *i.e.* supermarkets, in food distribution.

Price Communications

Price information has improved in many respects. Even at the beginning of the period under study, some merchants were sending their customers rather clear messages about their prices. An Indianapolis grocer, for example, wrote to his trade magazine in 1876 to report considerable success with advertise-ments that mentioned specific prices, such as "20 bars of German soap for $1; 12 lbs of Ragoon rice for $1; 11 lbs of New Orleans sugar for $1." Yet even as late as 1889, the same magazine was urging its subscribers to price mark their goods. This practice, it pointed out, was clearly superior to the methods of a New York grocer who expected his clerks to remember the unit and dozen prices for each of over 500 items. Three years later, in 1892, it was still lamenting weaknesses in price information, in this instance on the part of a Little Rock store which sent its customers a 32 page catalog that did not mention a single price.[25]

Although price posting is neither a necessary nor a sufficient condition for a one-price policy, price marking does facilitate and encourage such a policy. In turn, the elimination of differences in the amounts charged different customers for the same item tends to increase the clarity of the store's price messages. Even though the one price system has probably never been quite as widespread and uniform as the myth would have it, this system certainly does characterize most of American grocery retailing today. But its introduction and adoption was hesitant and uncertain. Norris found early evidence on one-price policies on grocery staples, but not necessarily on textiles and other articles, when he examined the pre-Civil War ledgers of seven widely separated country stores. Tonning has reported considerable hesitancy and experimentation with the policy before its final adoption by dry goods merchants in the Champaign-Urbana area during the period 1833–1880. One correspondent, writing to *The American Grocer* in 1893, commented on how many grocers would reply, "Who is it for?" when their clerks asked them the price of some unmarked item. The question of whether prices should be adjusted for good, for prompt paying, or for close bargaining customers was debated in magazine columns in 1884, 1893, and 1908. As late as 1917 one grocers' association voted to abolish special discounts being given to pastors, physicians, and fellow merchants.[26]

---

[25] "Correspondence," *The American Grocer*, Vol. 15, January 15, 1876, p. 62; "System in a Retail Store," *ibid.*, Vol. 42, November 5, 1889, p. 7; "Retailers Advertising," *ibid.*, Vol. 48, November 30, 1892, p. 8.

[26] J. D. Norris, "One-Price Policy Among Antebellum Country Stores," *Business History Review*, Vol. 36, Winter, 1962, pp. 455–458; W. Tonning, "The Beginnings of the Money Back Guarantee

Changes in technology and marketing practices eliminated some of the variations in what different customers received for their money, although they also tended to eliminate some of the over-weights and over-measures that those customers formerly enjoyed. The replacement of the old fashioned balance-and-weights scale by the modern platform computing scale meant that the grocer could charge for small fractions of the pound without going through the miserly-looking process of adding and throwing off one and two ounce pieces from the balance. Similarly the producers of packaged sugar, of packaged flour and of other packaged items that once were sold in bulk argued that the grocers gained, even if the nominal retail margins on the packed goods were lower than for bulk, since the grocer no longer had to throw in a "heaping" or extra measure to prove his generosity. One editorial also suggested that prepackaging reduced the amount of extra weight and measure that the clerks usually gave the "attractive and flirtatious" customer, in preference to the "aged and angular" one.[27]

The story of the long and arduous battle for more accurate grading and labeling is too well known to need rehearsal here. However, a much less heralded change has been a movement toward selling fish, vegetables, fruit and other unstandardized natural products on the basis of actual weight, instead of by simple numerical count. Selling mackerels at 10 or 15 cents each, oysters at 70 cents per 100, or prunes at 20 cents per dozen, as was frequently reported as late as the 1910's, results in far less precise and rigorous determination of what the consumer will get per dollar than does selling the same items on the basis of actual poundage. The rough and ready nature of sale by count was compounded by what seems to have been a widespread practice of leaving many commodities unsorted for size. *Grocery World* noted in 1910 that most merchants usually sold both large and small eggs at the same

per dozen price. An editorial writer for the same magazine commented in 1912 that a prominent butcher had two prices for some meats, one if the customer took it as it came and a higher price if the customer selected the cut. He wondered why grocers couldn't do the same thing with apples, a regular price for random selection and a premium price if the customer wanted to pick out the larger and better fruit.[28] Retail grocers' associations in New York City, and presumably elsewhere, advocated weight as the basis of vegetable and produce sales through the 1880's and 1890's. Dealer organizations in New Jersey, Ohio, Missouri, Illinois and up-state New York took a similar position in the early 1900's. There were some experiments with the sale of eggs by the pound in the U. S. and Canada between 1900 and 1920. State laws began to require sale by weight, or in some jurisdictions by measure, instead of by count. By the 1930's some suppliers, such as United Fruit Company, were urging dealers to sell fruit by the pound instead of by the piece. Yet in 1940 Safeway Stores Los Angeles division considered a switch to selling produce by weight sufficiently newsworthy to warrant full page ads, with series of questions and answers about the novel method, and the trade press gave equal attention to the change. The general transformation, to a predominantly weight basis of sale and to the sorting of unit items on the basis of weight or size, is today apparent in almost any modern supermarket. But the transformation was neither easy, smooth, rapid nor consistent.[29]

Cash, Carry, Self-Service and Supermarkets

The same uneven and hesitant pattern of change can be discerned in the service trends, toward cash and carry and toward self-service supermarkets. The trade journals constantly and monotonously debated the relative merits

and the One-Price Policy in Champaign-Urbana, Illinois, 1833–1880," *Business History Review,* Vol. 30, June, 1956, pp. 196–210; *The American Grocer,* Vol. 50, November 15, 1893, p. 4; December 13, 1893, p. 13; Vol. 31, April 24, 1884, p. 20; May 8, 1884, p. 23; *Grocery World,* Vol. 46, July 20, 1908, p. 8; Vol. 63, May 28, 1917, p. 10.

[27] "Department of Store Management," *Grocery World,* Vol. 30, July 23, 1900, p. 10; Advertisements, Franklin Sugar Company, *ibid.,* Vol. 38, 1904, *passim.;* "The Stroller's Column" *ibid.,* September 5, 1904, p. 24.

[28] Advertisement, Leonard A. Treat, *The American Grocer,* Vol. 55, January 22, 1896. p. 13; *Grocery World,* Vol. 50, August 8, 1910, p. 10; Vol. 54, July 1, 1912, p. 22; November 11, 1912, p. 18; Vol. 70, November 8, 1920, p. 4.

[29] Typical comments appeared in *The American Grocer,* Vol. 28, September 14, 1882, p. 597; Vol. 42, November 20, 1889, p. 8; *Grocery World,* Vol. 28, July 31, 1899, p. 34; Vol. 46, July 27, 1908, p. 12; Vol. 50, August 15, 1910, p. 28, Vol. 56, July 7, 1913, p. 17. For Safeway's program see *Progressive Grocer,* Vol. 19, July, 1940, pp. 83–87, or "Safeway Stores," *Fortune,* Vol. 22, October, 1940, pp. 60–64.

of cash vs. credit, issue after issue. *The American Grocer,* which had reported growing tendencies toward cash in 1877 and 1883 among other years, summarized its discussions with these words in 1895:

One effect of hard times is to increase the number of retailers who decide to change from a credit to a strictly cash basis of conducting trade. A great deal has been said upon this subject throughout the history of *The American Grocer.* Every phase of the subject has been discussed, and, at times, a lively debate carried on by subscribers. And yet the question is one of never failing interest to subscribers, and of permanent or vital interest to some few dealers at some particular time.[30]

Grocers tried all sorts of experiments: discounts for cash, redeemable scrip sold in advance at a discount, stores divided into separate cash and credit departments, imposition of credit charges. There is ample evidence of attempts to get away from the standard pattern of open book credit. Yet a 1919 Harvard report, at a time when the chains were important but certainly not dominant, showed only about 10% of the independents on a strictly cash basis.[31]

Apparently in many communities competitive pressure to provide delivery service did not develop until the latter part of the nineteenth century. Then the merchants longed for the good old days, and at the same time, carried the service to extremes. Some grocers gave their customers pads of order blanks which the deliverymen would collect in the morning and fill before afternoon. The telephone increased the demand for delivery. Yet, by 1906, *Grocery World* noted: "Among the large retail grocery stores, especially in the larger cities . . . there is a unmistakable movement in the direction of abolishing free delivery, or in fact, any delivery on certain articles."[32] The chains were fully involved in their experiments with cash and carry "econ-

omy" stores by 1915. Clarence Saunders created his fully self-service Piggly-Wiggly chain in 1916, and was soon followed or accompanied by a number of similar operations with equally repulsive names: "Jitney Jungle, Handy Andy, Helpy Selfy, Savey Wavey, and Hoggly Woggly."[33] The anti-delivery movement gained momentum and was the subject of increasing discussion throughout the twenties and the thirties. But certainly it is impossible to ascribe the long-run oscillation from predominantly non-delivery to any one individual or to any very specific moments in time. Similarly, although supermarket history often is presumed to have started with King Kullen in New York in 1930 and Big Bear in Elizabeth, New Jersey in 1932, these stores were preceded, as Charvat points out, not only by Saunders and the other small "groceteria" operations, but also by large self-service, cash and carry markets in Los Angeles and elsewhere in the Southwest.[34] Some "warehouse" stores also seem to have anticipated King Kullen and Big Bear, perhaps even as early as the 1910's.[35]

IN SUMMARY

Of course, the marketing experiments and adaptations cited above are only part of the total eighty year record. The picture that emerges even more clearly from the total record is of an industry that is never quite in equilibrium. Instead the trade quivers and stirs with a constant restless probing of its environment. Most often that environment rejects the adjustments that are offered. But occasionally some minor or major market segment is ready for some particular change. The adaptation, perhaps previously rejected a hundred times over, now flourishes to greater or lesser degree, and we then begin to read of a "new" trend in grocery retailing. Parenthetically, this is why attempts to determine the exact date and location of grocery innovations are about as controversial and fruitless as attempts to determine the first department store, or for that matter, the point of introduction

[30] Vol. 18, October 11, 1877, p. 964; Vol. 29, February 22, 1883, p. 389; Vol. 53, January 23, 1895, p. 10.

[31] "Management Problems in the Retail Grocery Stores," *Grocery World,* Vol. 68, November 3, 1919, p. 9.

[32] "1869—The Retail Business—1889," *The American Grocer,* Vol. 42, September 11, 1889, p. 12; "Correspondence," *ibid.,* Vol. 49, February 1, 1893, p. 18; "Grocery Stores Abolishing Deliveries," *Grocery World,* Vol. 42; September 4, 1906, p. 10.

[33] See G. Lebhar, *Chain Stores in America,* 1859–1962, New York: Chain Stores Publishing Co., 1963, pp. 32–34.

[34] F. J. Charvat, *Supermarketing,* New York: The Macmillan Co., 1961; pp. 11– 18.

[35] "Editor's Mail," *Progressive Grocer,* Vol. 11, August, 1932, p. 74; Hollander and Marple, p. 37.

of the marketing concept. But more importantly, if one may be permitted a value judgment, this record of constant change and experimentation is the strongest possible argument for a system that maximizes freedom.

DISCUSSION QUESTIONS

This article provides historical perspective for some competitive experimentation on the part of retailers. Some of the practices described are so very old that they will doubtless seem wholly "new."

1. What is the "one-price" policy? What are the economic ramifications of such a policy:
   (a) for the consumer?
   (b) for the retailer?
2. Of the practices which Professor Hollander describes, which might warrant further experimentation in today's retail markets?

"Service" Competition in Retailing

"Service" competition in retailing includes efforts to distinguish the total offering of the store from that of other stores through the extension of credit, delivery-installation-repair, telephone shopping, gift mailing and wrapping, merchandise return privileges, and so forth. Even in the case where two stores sell identical merchandise they can nevertheless differ significantly in terms of the nature and quality of the services they offer their customers.

Another meaning of the term "service" in retailing suggests the relative importance of the inventories carried by the store. A retail concern may deal exclusively in services in the sense that it may carry few if any merchandise inventories and it may not contemplate the sale of merchandise as an important part of its revenue. An important number of retail operations are essentially service stores in this latter sense. Thus barber shops, beauty shops, and repair shops are "service" retailers.

This section includes articles which deal with "service" in both of the senses indicated above. Of particular interest is the discussion dealing with the pricing of retail services. The different practices of several large retailers are examined in this latter regard. In another article, Professor Regan argues that we might expect more not fewer services from retailing in the future.

1. Full Cycle for Self-Service

WILLIAM J. REGAN

In the post-World War II period the use of self-service has spread horizontally to practically all types of retail stores on the minimum-service level. Whether labeled "self-selection," "display merchandising," "selective open selling," "simplified selling," or something similar, all of these represent variously lesser degrees of the supermarket concept of self-service. Whatever it is called, it refers to a still rapidly developing technology co-ordinating the merchandise-presentation efforts of retail stores.

This article summarizes the pressures that have been exerted upon retail stores to adopt self-service in greater measure and then identifies the main reasons why some stores prefer to extend more personalized service.

Managements of most stores have faced and continue to face unremitting pressures to adopt increasing degrees of self-service or impersonal selling. These pressures may be classified into three types:

1. Self-service orientations of ancillary interests
2. Expectations and preferences of customers
3. Increased competition of self-service stores

Self-Service Orientations of Ancillary Interests

Manufacturers of display fixtures, lighting equipment, cash-register equipment, packaging materials, and most consumer commodities have accepted the concept of impersonal selling and have designed their products accordingly. Advertising agencies and the publishers of trade periodicals have continuously pointed out the impact of advertising in pre-selling goods and the successes of self-service techniques.

As a consequence, fixtures have been designed, emphasizing the cubic dimensions, compartmentalization, and flexibility necessary to implement self-service. Cash-register systems have been devised to simplify the payment procedure for both charging and cash-paying customers. Packaging manufacturers have de-signed their services to maximize the promotional and protective benefits of packaging and to minimize retail repackaging requirements and customer pilferage. Product manufacturers themselves have designed their products to capitalize upon these changing conditions.

These efforts to help direct the retailing process are independently conceived and promoted. Their advantages must be sold to retailers who decide what elements will be co-ordinated in their store systems.

Expectations and Preferences of Customers

Rising standards of living and changing living patterns have helped to change the attitudes with which consumers regard goods. One scholar has advanced five criteria as means to determine the aggregate-characteristics profile of any goods which changes over time. They are: (1) the rate at which a product is purchased and consumed; (2) the gross margin of the product; (3) an adjustment factor representing the amount of services applied to goods to meet needs of consumers; (4) time of consumption during which the product gives up the utility desired; and (5) searching time or the measure of average time and distance from the retail store.[1]

---

[1] Leo Aspinwall, "The Characteristics of Goods and Parallel Systems Theories," in *Managerial Marketing: Perspectives and Viewpoints*, Eugene J. Kelley and William Lazer, editors (Homewood, Illinois: Richard D. Irwin, Inc., 1958), pp. 437–441.

♦ SOURCE: Reprinted by permission from the American Marketing Association, in the *Journal of Marketing*, April, 1961, pages 15–21.

Mere listing of these criteria is sufficient to make it clear that the mass-characteristics profile for each product changes through time. The general trend in the United States has probably been to modify luxury and "near-luxury" goods in the direction of semi-necessity and necessity classifications.

This ungrading in consumption patterns has altered the set of product characteristics for each product in consumers' minds. Distribution channels and store-merchandising practices have also changed in the attempt to distribute goods more econmically. Self-service has become an important way to retail goods, especially those with a relatively high replacement rate, and relatively low values for gross margin, adjustment, time of consumption, and searching time.

Merchandise made for mass market is typically widely advertised and highly standardized. It is designed for customers who want utility, dependable performance, and acceptable or "modern" styling. Much of the merchandise in the nondurable, repetitively purchased category can often be sold by the effective display, full accessibility, and explanation techniques of the well-integrated impersonal selling program. Even much of the durable goods designed for the mass market requires little personal sales assistance beyond competent credit-extension clerks when the goods have been largely pre-sold and are well-presented for self-service appraisal. Indeed, William H. Whyte, Jr., asserts that the consumer, by selling himself on "big-ticket" items has earned a price cut, and that ". . . whether manufacturers like it or not, he is going to get it." [2]

Increased customer familiarity with goods of all descriptions has tended to make a widening variety of goods eligible for self-service attention. Thus, in stores aiming at the mass markets, traditional store merchandise assortments have been reoriented in response to the more compelling classification criterion of "self-service salability." Customers support this change of assortment character whenever they feel that a better combination of convenience, other services, and price are offered.

Modern supermarkets, drug stores, and discount department stores have proved that the range of items that customers consider "com-plementary in purchase" is far wider than assortments that are "complementary in use." [3] By maintaining the traditional assortment emphasis upon merchandise items that are complementary in use, some stores deny themselves whatever advantages are inherent in assortments that are complementary in purchase and capable of being sold on a more impersonal basis. In some large department and departmentized specialty stores, departmental interselling is only a partial remedy to overcome the big inconvenience to consumers of too frequent financial accountings. These transactions bear the correlative risk of psychologically and physically tiring the customer by: (1) repetitively reminding her that she is spending money, (2) loading her with bulky packages unless she requests delivery, and (3) distracting her from concentration upon solving the problems of her household and family.

To a considerable extent, consumers act as "pollinizing agents" in transferring their preferences from one store to another. What they find and like in one retail store they want to find in other stores. Consumers in practically all economic groups have been exposed to self-service buying in supermarkets. They have taken with them some of the characteristics of self-service buying when patronizing other stores, such as increased initiative in finding items wanted, greater willingness to read signs and labels, and closer merchandise inspection. Most stores have responded to such aggressive tactics by evolving toward more open accessible displays, toward more specification-differentiated fixturing, toward more complete merchandise signing, etc.

Increased Competition of Self-Service Stores

The trend toward increased impersonalization in retailing has received considerable impetus from the apparent successes of those stores which have adopted self-service. Indeed, the trend toward the adoption of self-service borders on the revolutionary.

In 1948, 75 per cent of grocery-store volume was clerk-serviced, whereas in 1958 some 84 per cent was done on a self-service basis. [4] The

---

[2] William H. Whyte, Jr., *The Organization Man* (Garden City, New York: Doubleday and Company, Inc., 1956), pp. 348–349, footnote.

[3] F. E. Balderston, "Assortment Choice in Wholesale and Retail Marketing," *Journal of Marketing*, 21 (October, 1956), pp. 175–183, p. 178.

[4] *25th Annual Nielsen Review of Retail Grocery Store Trends*, 1959, p. 15.

1959 Directory of Drug Chains showed over 60 per cent of chain drug stores in the United States to be operated with some form of self-service, compared to 55 per cent in the 1958 Directory and 49 per cent in 1957.[5] Nearly two-thirds of new chain drug stores opened since 1954 have been self-service outlets equipped with checkout lanes.[6] Experience in variety stores is similar with all the major chains engaged in conversion to self-service programs.

Limited-service department and specialty stores of all types have also embraced self-service. This includes the "Quick Service" program of Sears, Roebuck and Company and the practices of most latter-day "discount" or "progressive" department stores. Hardware, stationery, toy, and other type stores have also engaged in self-service to an increasing degree.

Stores retaining personal check service and the traditional store layout, fixturing, display, etc., thus have been faced with an aggressive enterprise differentiation form of competition in self-service. In addition to this competition in service, price competition has been accentuated.

The service policy of most self-service stores is based upon providing only competitively desirable or necessary services above the common service of assortment assembly. When additional services such as credit or delivery are added, the attempt is usually made to offset these costs by charging for them as directly as is competitively possible. Lower personal selling costs engendered by self-service enables them to enhance an already favorable price spread when compared with stores committed to absorbing more of the traditional retailing amenities. As a result, clerk-service stores are faced with increasing price competition for the merchandise items that both types of stores carry and perhaps increasing difficulty in retaining exclusive lines.[7]

REASONS FOR PREFERRING PERSONALIZED SERVICE

Against the mounting pressure from these fronts, some store managements hesitate to adopt self-service where possible for the following reasons:

1. Honest doubts that self-service is wanted or that it can reduce expenses
2. Inability of self-service to satisfy all customers
3. Difficulties of applying self-service to all merchandise items
4. Possible aversion to competitive practices that self-service evokes
5. Other reasons for resistance to self-service

Doubts that Self-Service is Wanted or Able to Reduce Expenses

Most store managements probably recognize that, for the great bulk of consumer goods, the range of necessary selling service has shifted noticeably on the continuum from personalized service toward more impersonal service or self-service. Nevertheless, the managements of many prestige department and departmentized specialty stores, the remaining strong bastion of individual selling attention, believe that more lasting and profitable enterprise differentiation can be achieved by fighting the impersonalization of retailing which supermarkets have nearly made their trademark.

With the view that customers want more intimate personal relationships with stores, some take the position that better and more personal salesmanship is needed, not the abolition of it. These managements tend to accept only peripheral features of impersonal selling programs and consciously work to assimilate as much of the cost-reduction features as possible without compromising the character of their full and individualized services.

Other managements regard self-service more favorably but doubt that it can substantially reduce costs in their operations. They agree that perhaps staple stock will sell, but fear that the newer styles, "ensemble," and impulse purchases will not; that customers will consistently buy the lowest-priced goods; that pilferage will increase; that salespeople will have to be replaced by equally expensive stockpeople.

Cost comparisons with self-service operations usually begin with a direct item-for-item examination of comparative selling costs. The next step may be realization that other costs, such as training, pilferage, returned goods, credit, and delivery may also be affected. Conjecture as to the relative change that self-

[5] Chain Store Age, Vol. 34 (December, 1958), p. 10.
[6] 25th Annual Review of Retail Drug and Proprietary Store Trends, 1959, p. 18.
[7] Victor Lebow, "The Crisis in Retailing," Journal of Retailing, 33 (Spring, 1957), pp. 17–26, 55.

service might induce in these expenses is further complicated by the possibility of changing sales levels.

Perhaps not widely recognized yet is the notion that regrouping of departments according to relative degrees of item self-service-ability may contribute to increased economies through a larger average departmental scale of operation. That is, departmentalization by function rather than by merchandise purpose may permit an increase in the number of items serviced by the same or only slightly increased departmental input effort.

Something like this seems to have taken place in food distribution where the number of items carried in the average modern supermarket has grown from about 1,000 items in 1933 to about 6,000 items in 1956 and where average sales per store in 1934 were $42,000 compared to $893,000 in 1956.[8] According to the same authority, food chains have reduced their margins from 22½ per cent to 18 per cent on the sales dollar in the 21 years prior to 1957 ". . . because of self-service innovations and the development of modern supermarkets where increased volume has made practical the introduction of time- and cost-saving machinery."[9] It was during this period also that meats and produce became "undepartmentized" from the customer's viewpoint and joined the swelling of both food and non-food items in being available on a self-service basis.

Inability of Self-Service to Satisfy All Customers

Competition and the drive to be successful have encouraged retailers to strive for yearly increases in sales and profits. To achieve these increases, many clerk-service stores have expanded beyond the prestige market that they were originally designed to serve and now straddle two markets: the prestige or "class" market, and the volume or "mass" market. In this position, they need to stock and sell enough goods in the mass market to reach their rising breakeven points, and yet carry the proper merchandise and personalized services

to retain the exclusive atmosphere acceptable to the class market.

Many full-service managements recognize that self-service for the mass market and personal sales service for the prestige market would be desirable. However, they resist changing their operational set-ups to provide sales service compatible to the merchandise and customer needs of both markets. Having spent thousands of dollars and many years in the patient development of full-service reputations, most managements hesitate to jeopardize these reputations with innovations that are associated with limited-service stores.

Difficulties of Applying Self-Service to All Merchandise Items

Supermarkets are able to apply self-service exclusively to all items in their assortments. This is because the items sold are typically in the relatively scrutable, repetitively purchased, lower-priced category. Much of the merchandise sold in department and specialty stores has opposite characteristics. In addition, some merchandise has a large number of variable specifications such as styles, sizes, colors, or price lines which make full exposure of goods for customer accessibility difficult.

For example, in a recent year one manufacturer of men's shirts made 42 different collar-and-cuff styles in the white shirt alone. The company made 51 different collar styles and sleeve-length combinations. This combination of collar styles and sizes alone made a total of more than 2,000 different shirt specifications. In addition to this basic white-shirt stock, other shirts were made in different fabrics, stripes, patterns, and solid colors. Most men's furnishings departments and stores carry selections from several different manufacturers' lines and often one under their own label. Clearly it would be uneconomical, if not impossible, to display in open arrangement such a wide variety of shirts. Stores emphasizing wide selections, the new or novel in merchandise, and custom-fitting items have additional problems in the implementation of self-service.

Possible Aversion to Competitive Practices That Self-Service Evokes

It is probable that the continued impersonalization of selling in retail stores and especially supermarkets has contributed to a weakening in customers' institutional loyalty. Part of the

---

[8] National Association of Food Chains, *Progress in Food Distribution*, a statement by John A. Logan, President, National Association of Food Chains, to the Consumers Study Subcommittees of the Committee on Agriculture, House of Representatives, May 8, 1957, pp. 15, 24.

[9] Same reference as footnote 10, p. 15.

strong patronage accorded trading stamps, premium plans, etc. may be explained in the transference of customer loyalty from the retail institution *per se* to the merchandising attraction or appendage that accompanies purchase of goods.

In lieu of traditional store services, supermarkets have tended to compete by offering differential trading-stamp plans, premium offers, coupon plans, lotteries, and other variations for which external product differentiation has been suggested as a classification.[10] Whether many store managements that resist impersonal selling do so partly in order to protect themselves from the possibility of engaging in this kind of competition is doubtful. It is also questionable whether they fully appreciate the magnitude of the market that they are losing to trading stamp and premium redemption plans. In some cases at least it is conceivable that neither the stamp-dispensing retailer nor the consumer is paying for the stamp operation but that would-be retailers of premium merchandise are supporting it by allowing their normal markons to be given away.

Other Reasons for Resistance to Self-Service

Several other reasons support those managements which prefer clerk service. In some cases, stores have experimented with self-service and received adverse results. Although the quality of these experiments has varied widely, adequate tests to provide "before" and "after" comparative results have been nearly impossible to design. Large, multi-unit chains like Sears have an advantage in this respect in that they can judge an innovation in well-designed test stores before applying it to all. According to a Sears official, self-service was initially installed in "about 125" stores in 1953 to determine its effectiveness.[11]

In other cases, managements may be unusually sensitive to the feelings or preferences of salespeople who naturally fear the inroads of impersonal selling upon their livelihoods.

This paternalism for their employees in some cases may be an influence combining with others to make self-service less desirable. In still other cases, store managements committed to the personal selling approach prefer to wait and see how effective their suburban department or specialty stores are before submitting to further degrees of self-service. In these newer suburban stores, fixtures incorporating full exposure and open accessibility of goods have been widely used. The commonly experienced peaking of sales in many branch stores might encourage further experimentation with impersonal selling in time.

INCREASED IMPERSONALITY IN RETAILING

Despite these very real objections and difficulties in accepting further degrees of self-service, evidence of increased acceptance in full-service stores is not hard to find. Under a host of modified titles, such as "self-selection," "selective open selling, or SOS," "simplified selling," "open selling," "display merchandising," self-service or impersonal selling is being applied to ever more heterogeneous assortments.

Increasing degrees of self-selection are employed in many departments of these stores, such as notions, stationery, housewares, records, drugs and cosmetics, toys, and others. Indeed, some full-service department stores have successfully tried the supermarket version of self-service in such departments as toys, greeting card and trimming supplies, and books at peak-selling periods such as Christmas. Macy's in New York uses it for stationery and greeting cards, books, garden supplies, hardware and paints on a regular basis.

Other influences affecting the impersonality trend should be mentioned. The increased encouragement that customers receive to use automatic vending machines, mail-order catalogs and Christmas supplements, newspaper order coupons, and telephone ordering facilities is presumably based on the interpretation that more customers might want this more impersonal service. It is also quite possible that today's face-to-face personal selling in stores lacks some of the warmth or genuine concern that it possessed in days when "regular customers" were more common.

Realization that self-service in full-service stores need not and cannot parallel exactly the development in supermarkets has caused the

---

[10] E. T. Grether, "External Product and Enterprise Differentiation and Consumer Behavior," *Consumer Behavior and Motivation*, Robert H. Cole, editor (Urbana, Illinois: Bureau of Economic and Business Research, The University of Illinois, 1955).

[11] Personal letter from G. R. Berger, Manager, Research and Development Division, Sears, Roebuck and Company, Chicago, Illinois, May 15, 1957.

institution of modified checkout systems in some cases. This modified checkout system offers customers the option of buying goods either through conveniently located cashier checkout stations or through salespeople. There are some control problems in this dual approach. However, offering customers the option of sales service or self-service might be considered the addition of another service. Moreover, it sets up a choice situation in which customers can decide the issue so well phrased in *The Lonely Crowd;* ". . . how much the slow progress toward automation in the tertiary trades is due to . . . consumer demand to buy personalization along with a product, and how much to the needs of the work force itself to personalize . . . whether the customer asks for it or not." [12]

THE SOURCE OF RETAIL INNOVATIONS

Since self-service originated in food retailing, it is easy to understand why full-service managements emphasizing personal sales attention might consider it dubiously. Most of these managements regard it as antithetical to their own more personalized services. This is the customary reception accorded a marketing innovation that has been introduced and successful at the opposite-service level.

Retailing innovations have usually entered

------

[12] David Riesman, Nathan Glazer, and Reuel Denney, *The Lonely Crowd* (Garden City, New York: Doubleday and Company, Inc., 1950), pp. 310–311.

the marketplace from two levels: (1) the prestige or full-service level where new conceptions of service are usually emphasized, and (2) the minimum service level where new cost-cutting concepts yielding ultimate price benefits to customers are emphasized. After suitable test periods, the dynamics of enterprise differentiation compel tests on other retail-service levels. Thus, credit plans were introduced on the upper-service levels, proved acceptable to growing numbers of consumers, and eventually were added to the service components of many limited-service stores. Just as the stronger full-service stores hesitate to accept self-service which they consider to be a service of an unwanted nature, limited-service stores hesitate to accept innovations that they consider to be of a service character. The J. C. Penney Company, for instance, has just in recent years been converting its stores to credit.

Self-service gained its acceptance as a price-reducing innovation. It is now in the "dressing-up" or adaptive stage where variations on the basic theme are being devised to make it more suitable for appropriate merchandise in stores on higher-service levels. Diversity in retail service patterns will surely continue. Some merchandise items may always need personalized sales attention and it is to be hoped that some stores will continue to serve this need.

It seems clear, however, that the range of selling service applied to consumer goods generally has shifted perceptibly in the direction of increased impersonality. Store managements should continue to be alert to the significance of this shift.

DISCUSSION QUESTIONS

Self-service—the merchandising technique in which the bulk of the buying function is shifted to the consumer—is always identified as one of the important elements in modern retailing methods. This article examines some of the reasons for the widespread use of self-servcie techniques, and some of the reasons why self-service has not had much impact on "prestige department stores and departmentalized specialty stores."

1. What is the most important single element underlying the popularity of self-service?
2. Can we expect, as the title of this article **implies**, a retreat from the extensive use of self-service to more personalized services? Why, or why not?

2. Three Concepts of Retail Service

MASTERS' COSTS AND SERVICES

The operating costs of Masters, Inc., the discount store chain, "are slightly more than 12 per cent, and going even lower as our newer units get into full operation," according to Stephen Masters, the company's president, in a paper presented at the Store Management Group Workshop at Harvard last month.

Apparently neither the management structure required by the many-store expansion of this chain along the Eastern seaboard nor its entry into soft goods lines in the past few years has pushed up its costs. As further indication that the Masters stores after 22 years in business will maintain fully their advantage over the traditional department store in respect to inventory investment and costs, it was reported that Masters' Rockefeller Center unit in New York produces sales of $1,000 a square foot; that the company-wide inventory turnover is eight times a year; that payroll costs represent less than seven per cent of sales (although salaries are typically higher than the department store's and that 92 per cent of the employees are selling personnel).

Services and Policies

In a speech read for him by John Haizen, executive vice president of the company, Masters said that his economical operation is not achieved at the expense of services customers want; in fact, he argued, Masters offers services "equal to, and often better than, those offered by many department stores." He listed some of them:

We allow a refund or exchange at any time up to 30 days with no questions asked.

We maintain on our own premises a large, dependable repair service department—we believe we are the only store in the country rendering such a service. We run our repair department not as public benefactors but to

---

◆ SOURCE: Reprinted by permission from the editor of *Stores,* in the July-August, 1959, issue, pages 18–21, 24.

save money. Our studies showed that the tortuous procedure of taking back a product, giving a receipt, sending the product to the manufacturer with proper papers and forms, waiting, picking it up, notifying the customer —all cost us more in man-hours, money, administration and frustration (especially customer frustration) than the system was worth.

We do make home deliveries, charging the customer who demands this service just what it costs us. Our service organization also installs and services major appliances in the customer's home. On major appliances, installation and service is built into the cost of the item whether Masters buys it or Macy's buys it. So here we all operate alike.

On advertising this past year the Masters Chain spent about $1.5 million. We don't use bait advertising or loss leaders; we don't nail any appliance down to the floor. We don't advertise an item when we have only a half dozen in stock. If we advertise it we have it in quantity and we advertise the quantity.

We have a well-established time payment plan worked out with local banks who take our customer's paper at a very good rate. In this way our operating costs don't go up because the only people who pay for this service are the people who want it. We are also working on a charge account system for our customers. It will be done in a new way, much more economical than that of the department stores, a way in which only the participating customers will pay for the service.

Displacing Department Stores?

Some have agreed that discount houses as they grow will become more like department stores in their costs and structures, but Masters took the contrary point of view. "Instead of the discount house being on the defensive as an illegitimate upstart, a fly-by-night," he said, "it is the department store that now seems to be on the defensive. In fact, as the department store adopts more and more of the discount house methods, it may soon be the discount house that is the orthodox method of retail distribution."

In 1955, Masters, Korvette and Two Guys from Harrison had a combined annual volume of $67 million. In 1958 they had grown to $200 million. "No wonder," said Masters, "the Wall Street community is looking with a great deal of interest at our low-margin type of retailing."

Stressing efficiency rather than limited service or price-cutting as the distinguishing characteristic of the discount house, Masters said:

"The secret of the successful discount house is efficient operation, with management able to make quick and intelligent decisions, plus hard work by everyone up and down the line. We make decisions in minutes, not in months. In the old days a department store buyer was a man who could make quick decisions. Those were days of profit and high unit volume for department stores. Today, the department store buyer too often acts merely as a glorified office boy for his merchandising manager and buying committee."

Where the Savings Are

Examining more closely some of the lower costs of his operation, Masters said:

"We have eliminated costly displays and display departments . . . fashion coordinators, unnecessary merchandising men, superfluous vice presidents. Our rental cost per square foot of selling space is about one-third that of the average department store, not because we operate in lower rent areas (the majority of discount houses are in high-traffic, high-rent areas) but because we eliminate costly display space and keep our non-selling space down to a minimum.

"All of our stores are modern and up to date, but our demands for store structures are not as rigid or elaborate as those of department stores. Incidentally, we will never open a store that is on more than one level, because only by having a one-floor operation can we operate the low-cost system we have pioneered.

"While our advertising costs are about equal in percentage to those of the department store, our delivery costs are zero compared to their 1½ per cent. Those who want delivery pay for it. Those who carry their packages save the delivery cost.

"We at Masters do not employ salesclerks in the sense you normally give to this term. The merchandise we sell is already pre-sold to the consumer. Over $10 billion of advertising last year has thoroughly educated the customer to product value and brand recognition. We do employ what I prefer to call 'educated order takers.' These are people who will quickly write up a customer's order. They are very well trained in the merchandise they sell—usually far better trained than a department store salesperson. . . . We forbid 'switch selling.'

"Our merchandise . . . is displayed for easy selection, in orderly product classifications indicating sizes, colors, uses, voltage, horsepower and other technical details, as well as price."

Pricing Formulas

Some of these techniques are now being adopted by department stores, Masters pointed out; he said they are on the right track with self-selection, self-service, delivery charges, prepacks, and accounting in terms of profit dollars rather than percentages. But on the subject of merchandise management accounting and its concept of pricing according to profitability of the individual item, he said this is not his company's practice.

"We use," he reported, "a set formula of markup from cost which applies to all types of merchandise. As a matter of fact, I will hold back from you only one thing about our operation, our exact markup formula. This is my only secret."

As to the future of discount retailing, Masters predicted that it will take an increasingly larger share of total retail volume. These were his reasons:

"1. We are ever improving our technique of operating at low margins.

"2. We are taking on additional categories of consumer goods such as furniture, more soft goods, and even drugs.

"3. We will go increasingly into new types of distribution, such as shopping centers and highway outlets.

"4. More manufacturers will change their policies and pricing schedules to fit into our high velocity operation."

Masters concluded with a bitterly eloquent attack upon the federal fair trade bill approved by the House Commerce Committee, which he called "the most flagrant abuse of consumer trust in congressional history."

ALEXANDER'S SELECTIVE ECONOMIES

The point of view of a successful low-margin fashion retailer was brought to the symposium by R. Duffy Lewis of Alexander's Department Store, who reported that this four-store company will do a volume of $100 million in fashion merchandise this year. Speaking directly to the question, "What does the customer really want in the way of service?" Lewis said:

"In mass distribution, we concentrate mostly on the merchandise, trying to eliminate as many of the expendable services as possible. We eliminate what we consider the fringes, something that the average customer may desire but would prefer to go without if she has to pay for it."

Alexander's limited service policy means, in Lewis's words: "No mail or telephone orders; no charge accounts or credit in any form; no delivery; no superfluous sales or administrative help; no fancy trimmings, such as luxurious chairs, carpets, etc."

"We are," he claimed, "the only mass distributors of fashion merchandise who have been so dedicated to the founding principles of our business that we have stuck to them from our inception through changing times of temptation and stress. No other mass distributor, to our knowledge, has absolutely eliminated mail or telephone orders, deliveries and credit. Some may do without one or two of these services, but not one does without all three as does Alexander's. Also, because we so intensely believe in our policy of never selling a customer an item unless we can save her money, we have never handled an article that must be price-maintained."

The services that Alexander's considers fundamental are these:

1. *Well-Merchandised Assortments.* Big, fresh assortments of wanted merchandise are carried in both the regular and promotional classifications. Alexander's does not try to economize by skimping on the merchandising skills or merchandising tools and records that are needed for this purpose.

"It is not by chance," Lewis said, "that those mass distribution stores which are 'figure hounds' have increased their volume and profit to the point where they are outstanding in the field of retailing. It is because they have put science into their merchandising operations by setting up complete records of their transactions. Because we recognize the importance of this information and the necessity for the buyer to get it on the day following the sales, we make use of electronic equipment, such as I. B. M. When you realize that we sell several hundred thousand units a day you can understand the vastness of this project. We are con-

stantly spending money experimenting on how to get more information more quickly, so that we can service our customers better."

2. *A Modern Plant.* "The mass customer," said Lewis, "wants the value concentrated in the merchandise, but still wants to maintain her dignity and not feel like a basement buyer." The store, he said, should be near subways and buses as well as within walking distances for residents of the area: if possible it should have parking space. Parking space is not easily or cheaply come by in a metropolitan area, but Alexander's has it.

Besides being large enough to hold a big assortment in depth, the store must be spacious to facilitate self-selection, comfortable to shop in, and attractive so that it both pleases customers and enhances the eye appeal of the merchandise. "Our Queens store," said Lewis, "has 260,000 square feet devoted only to soft fashion goods. It is climate-conditioned throughout, and is the brightest in its illuminating capacity of any in the city. The color palette is unique: 41 different colors have been used, to give a welcoming gaiety to the total effect and to set off the various areas."

3. *Consistently Low Prices.* "We will never knowingly be undersold by any store," said Lewis. "Many stores say that, but we try not just to give lip service to the theory but actually to operate that way. That means we will recognize as price competition the big store, the little store, the peddler and the discounter. . . . We will always sell for as low a price as possible, even if there is no competition. . . . Alexander's never holds a sale. We never put a special sale price on merchandise temporarily, only to mark it up later. We want the customer to know she can get the same price any day. . . . The price is clearly shown, never in code nor accompanied by a crossed-out, marked-down price. . . . When irregular merchandise is presented for sale, the display sign, advertising and price ticket must clearly state this. . . . We will not handle any merchandise that has tears, mends, fades or any defect, however minor, that will deprive the customer of the ultimate in satisfaction."

4. *Liberal Returns Policy.* Merchandise may be returned within seven days with no questions asked. The only "not returnable" merchandise which is so identified on the price ticket, is of the sanitary or fragile type. Refunds are in cash; no credit slips are issued. As to the store's adjustment policy, Lewis described Alexander's adjustment manager as

"the store representative appointed to take the customer's point of view."

"There are very few thoroughbreds in the underselling fashion field," Lewis concluded. "Few will build a successful *big* business because with bigness there comes an absolute need for organization, merchandising know-how and competitively large assortments of merchandise. In the last analysis, it's the merchandise that counts."

DEPARTMENT STORE SERVICE COSTS

Of all the services that a department store offers customers, said Howard Davis, general manager of Jordan Marsh, the most appreciated and the most expensive is the simple fact it *is* a department store. That means it carries the slow-moving and hard-to-handle items as well as the choice and profitable ones. Completeness is what gives the department store its character; this is the store where the shopping customer knows she can buy needles and buttons as well as a hi-fi installation; where she can outfit the children and also pick up a part for her pressure cooker; where she can select $500 worth of slipcovers and a 50-cent dress pattern and then meet a friend for lunch in a pleasant restaurant.

But it is also a basic condition of department store operation that price competition must be met. "The penalty for not meeting competition," warned Davis, "is certain—you are allowing your limited service competitors to select your choice items while you continue to service complete assortments."

Remain a Department Store!

"Many department stores," he said, "have discontinued appliances. We haven't; and we meet all competition. But we have changed our delivery policy on appliances, reorganized our appliance service and taken many other steps to get a return from appliance sales. As you might expect, our margins in these departments are not what was once considered proper for department stores. But we have the sales and we have a contribution towards overhead expenses. Isn't this better than not having the sales and not having a contribution towards overhead expenses?"

The pressure of these competitive situations is not the worst thing in the world for department stores, Davis pointed out; because of it, they are learning to examine and control service and handling costs on an item-by-item basis.

"This," he said, "helps us in two ways. First, by understanding the service costs of particular items, we can find ways to reduce these costs. In lamps, for example, the costs of unpacking, storing, repacking and breakage have been very high. As a result, most of us are now insisting that we purchase lamps prepacked by the manufacturer. Second, the understanding of service costs creates better harmony between the buyers of merchandise and those who service it.

"This understanding of the service and handling costs for each item as it is purchased is really merchandise management accounting. Because of the great variety of items carried by department stores I suspect that merchandise management accounting will not become a general *accounting* procedure, but as a philosophy of merchandising and operating, it is inevitable.

"My boss once gave me some good advice which applies to this profit problem. He said, 'Never do the obvious!' An obvious way to improve profits would be to reduce delivery service drastically, revise a returns policy to prevent returns (and perhaps incidentally prevent sales) or set up self-service in all selling departments. Such obvious general solutions would be self-defeating. *We must seek relief in a tough, thorough reappraisal item by item and operation by operation.*"

Service at Lower Cost

Granted that the department store is not going to imitate the limited service store by becoming in fact a limited merchandise store, are there superfluous services it can eliminate or curtail? Davis said there's plenty of water to be squeezed out of the expense sponge, but again warned stores not to fall into the trap of the obvious. He examined individually the five expense centers into which most of the traditional "free services" of the department store fall.

"Miscellaneous Customer Services" in the Harvard Report for 1957, accounted for 0.06 per cent of store expenses. The services included here are trivial, yet their cost or number is not necessarily a measure of their importance to the store. "Perhaps," said Davis, "a doorman is a symbol of many happy shopping experiences for some of the store's customers. This could be as important as the store's advertising in the continuing patronage of these customers."

"Delivery," accounting for 1.45 per cent of expenses, represents to some extent costs that are inherent in the store's merchandise policy: it carries merchandise that the cash-and-carry store does not. But delivery costs should be studied, said Davis, in relation to items. Certain reductions of free delivery service have met with no adverse reaction from Jordan Marsh customers.

"Selling Services," accounting for 1.40 per cent, largely wrapping and packing costs and a necessary part of a free delivery policy. They offer considerable scope for cost reduction, Davis said, without compromising the service policy of the store in any way.

"Direct Selling" costs, amounting to 6.90 per cent, could, in theory, be eliminated by a self-service, turnstile operation. But with the costs would go a lot of volume: the complete department store, selling furniture, better ready-to-wear, men's clothing, etc., cannot dispense with selling service. What is needed is intensified research on how best to sell specific items. Said Davis:

We must study each department and each classification to find out how best to sell it. This is a gruelling, detailed job. There is no *one* way out.

"Accounts Receivable and Credit" cost, 1.95 per cent, is actually offset "on the average about half" by carrying-charge income. Cost and quality controls can reduce it further. "I can assure you," said Davis, "that it's easy but unnecessary to accept high credit losses and high billing costs."

Finally, Davis referred briefly to the con-venience departments and items that are carried entirely for the purpose of making customer service complete. They are part of the department store's "service personality." So too are the special events and community activities that furnish information and entertainment; the civic activities and contributions that make the store an important factor in the life of the community. "It seems to me," said Davis, "that we have been much too defensive and apologetic about our position. We do have a good solid constructive customer and community service to sell and we should sell it with great enthusiasm."

The Quality of Service

It is not in giving service but in giving *poor* service that the department store becomes vulnerable to both criticism and competition, Davis concluded. He advised managements to ask themselves not only how expensive their service is but how good it is:

How do your customers feel about your quality of service? How many go to limited service stores because your salespeople stand between them and the merchandise, whereas in the store that doesn't try to give selling service they can at least get to the merchandise? The basic answer to the question, "What does the customer really want in the way of service?" is that first she wants good quality service. She doesn't want to be frustrated by salespeople who don't sell: wrappers who wrap badly; adjusters who don't call back, or servicemen who don't arrive on time. We must be sure we are actually giving quality service, not just paying for it.

DISCUSSION QUESTIONS

This "article" is sub-divided into three parts: (1) a discussion of the service policy of Masters Inc., a leading discount operation; (2) a discussion of the service policy of Alexander's Department Store—a low-margin fashion retailer and, (3) a discussion of the service policy of Jordan Marsh's—a "full-service" type of department store. These three views represent the extremes from little service to "full" service—or do they?

    1. Is Masters Inc. actually a "serviceless" operation? How then is it different from the package of service offered by the department store?

    2. What do you think the "traditional" type of department store should do to combat "low-margin" competition?

3. Consumer Purchase-Costs—Do Retailers Recognize Them?

WESLEY C. BENDER

As the competition of shopping centers diverted business away from the central business district, concern with barriers to downtown shopping emerged. The parking problem downtown is a difficult barrier to overcome. Other barriers, perhaps less difficult, but nonetheless important, have brought forth various antidotes, some of them merely "gimmicks" to attract customers downtown. But since similar devices were used to attract customers to the suburbs, the flow of the competitive tide was not turned. Thus it may help to view the barriers to shopping in a particular place, or in a particular store, by understanding these in terms of consumer purchase-costs.

The business firm has long recognized that there is a "cost of purchasing" beyond payment of "the price" for a commodity. The price of an item and the cost of obtaining it are not necessarily, or even often, the same thing. When the question is asked, "What did a particular purchase cost the firm?," it is clear that attendant prices such as "freight-in" or the buyer's trip to market are elements of purchase-cost although accounting practice may treat these dissimilarly.

By contrast, the ultimate consumer, some assume, is a purchaser who does not incur purchase-costs beyond the price paid for a commodity. With relatively few exceptions, however, such an assumption is not based on fact.[1] Thus we will explore the concept of consumer purchase-cost as it relates to the consumer's choice among competing stores or shopping centers vs. downtown, and indicate how this concept ought to affect decisions of retail-store executives.

WHAT ARE THE CONSUMER'S PURCHASE-COSTS?

In a purchase and sales transaction the parties to the exchange obtain something from each other with a cost to each. Manifestly, the retailer making a sale does so at a cost. So does the consumer who pays the retailer's price for a commodity. The price of the commodity is a "prime" cost but not the sole cost. A number of "secondary" purchase-costs are necessary to achieve the purchase of the prime or target commodity. Together, prime and secondary purchase-costs comprise total purchase-costs.

Secondary purchase-costs may be defined as all the costs, both monetary and nonmonetary, exclusive of the price directly paid for the target commodity or service, required to effect the purchaser's acquisition of the target commodity or service.

The nature of secondary purchase-costs can be illustrated by the events surrounding the purchase of a lawn sweeper in a downtown store. In order to emphasize the secondary cost elements, we shall rule out the kind of customer who enjoys shopping and who gets a "kick" out of demonstrating his mechanical ability by assembling "knocked-down" gadgets. Some people may enjoy the drive to town but not the potential buyer in this illustration! In the normal order of events, he must bear the costs of time and travel from home to downtown, and if the family car is used he will pay a parking fee. On the downtown streets, this shopper will expend time and effort in search-

♦ SOURCE: Reprinted by permission from the *Journal of Retailing*, in the Spring 1964 issue, pages 1–8.

[1] E. B. Weiss, *Planning Merchandise Strategy for 1961–65* (Doyle Dane Bernbach, Inc., 1960), pp. 6–8. Also, Baumol and Ide, "Variety in Retailing," *Mathematical Models and Methods in Marketing* (Homewood, Illinois: Richard D. Irwin, Inc., 1960), pp. 129–30.

ing. Even after the purchase decision is made there are secondary costs: waiting time—waiting for a salesclerk, waiting while payment is arranged, and waiting to receive the merchandise. Since the box containing the lawn sweeper is a large one, the buyer's time, effort, and aggravation will accompany the box to the parked car—and perhaps all the way home. In any case, travel time from downtown to home, the additional time and frustration costs of unpacking the sweeper, locating the "Instructions for Assembly" sheet, and the attempt to assemble the sweeper—all these are costs incurred before the buyer can use the lawn sweeper in his yard.

Any particular purchase situation, such as a lawn sweeper purchase, is unlikely to involve *all* possible types of secondary costs. Consequently the retailer need not be concerned with an exhaustive list of them. A more meaningful approach—one which relates categories of secondary purchase-costs to consumer behavior—is suggested.

CONSUMER BEHAVIOR: CHOICE OF STORE OR STORE GROUP

Studies of shopping practices indicate that purchase costs, both prime and secondary, affect consumer choices among competitive stores or store groups. This is not to imply that the choices are made with scientific precision!

But presupposed are at least two important behaviorial activities: one, that secondary purchase-costs related to one store or store group are compared with those related to competing stores or store groups—allowing the consumer, if she so desires, to optimize her purchase-cost position. Two, that consumers make decisions involving these comparisons. For were the position taken that consumers cannot compare purchase-costs and that even were they able to do so, their choice of store would not be influenced, there would be no point in carrying forward this discussion.

Few will argue that consumers are unable to compare the prices of identical "prime" or target items (or that sometimes these comparisons involve merely similar but not really *identical* items!). By contrast, however, when the whole range of secondary purchase-costs is considered there *appears* to be no common denominator upon which comparisons can be based. This does not deter the consumer. She simply groups together those secondary purchase-costs that *are* comparable. Thus the whole gamut of these costs can be arranged into three groups and comparisons are made within each of them.

THREE TYPES OF SECONDARY CONSUMER COSTS

In one group containing all "*price*" type secondary purchase-costs, such as parking fees, installation charges, credit charges, sales taxes, and the like, there is easy comparison on a store-by-store basis or a shopping center versus downtown basis in the same way as for the prices of "target" items. In a second category are the "*time*" type secondary purchase-costs, such as waiting time, travel time, or searching time. These may be compared as time units, or they can be converted to money units by using some money value per unit of time.

The third group of secondary purchase-costs is comprised largely of "*psychological*" type factors, such as inner conflict, frustration, depression, anxiety, tension, annoyance, and the like because of human relations, store temperature and humidity, store layout, and physical features of stores, or these in combination with human relations. Within this latter group there is comparability, but this area is more complex than the other two groups.

Consumers who make comparisons among the psychic factors related to purchases appear to do so in many ways. Some ignore purchase-costs of this type, particularly when they are relatively small. At the other extreme, some consumers indicate that they weigh heavily these psychological costs. They are considered more significant than substantial money type secondary purchase-costs.

PSYCHOLOGICAL COSTS VERSUS SATISFACTIONS

Psychological costs can be offset by psychological satisfactions. Moreover, the psychological satisfactions may overcome some or all of the monetary costs. For undoubtedly some consumers do derive pleasure from "searching," from shopping in a store with an "upper crust" image, from "recognition" by the store personnel, or even from assembly of a knocked down appliance. Yet what is pleasurable for one person may be distasteful to another, and what is pleasurable at one time may be distasteful for that person another time. As the psychologists put it, "the cognitive behavior of an individual is a reaction to stimuli as he apperceives them." Thus, although secondary purchase-costs may be balanced out, perhaps, on occasion, leaving a surplus of satisfaction, studies of shopping practices indicate consumer emphasis on the cost elements rather than on the satisfactions when a choice is made of store or shopping center.

As a matter of fact, not all secondary purchase-costs are potentially able to engender satisfactions in ordinary persons. Here a different classification of secondary purchase-costs is helpful. Most individuals are rarely susceptible to the joys, if any, of paying out money. In general, price type secondary-costs such as charges for auxiliary services, taxes, fees, and even "tie-in" deals are in the positive cost category. Along with these are noncompensated losses to property due to risks associated with the buying trip, such as damage to one's automobile, theft of one's purse, and the like. Also included are some psychological costs like frustration, discomfort, depression, anxiety, annoyance, and mental fatigue. Plain physical fatigue should also be added. These constitute a category unlikely to produce satisfaction for *anyone*.

On the other hand, some secondary purchase-costs belong in the category of "sometime" producers of satisfaction. Such buying activities as searching, shopping, looking at displays, travel, assembly of gadgets, meeting people, talking to friends, or even jostling in crowds—all ordinary secondary purchase-costs —can be enjoyable experiences for some people on some occasions.

This dichotomy of the various secondary purchase-costs is significant for the retailer action that we shall examine later.

PURCHASE-COST DECISIONS

The consumer is neither solely a creature of habit nor does he make scientifically precise decisions. In considering him, therefore, we assume neither total "naiveté" nor total "rationality." And while research on "choice of commodity" indicates that habit is important,[2] it is not so important for "choice of store."[3] Moreover, wherever found, habit is not un-

changeable. Consumers, sooner or later, will examine their shopping practices in response to some stimuli or other and act to adjust these practices so as to minimize subjectively perceived costs. Lack of precision and individual sluggishness may make measurement difficult, but this does not deny the existence of the phenomenon, nor make it less important.

Prime Cost vs. Secondary Purchase-Cost

The decision process—choosing among competing stores—involves some "weighing" of the various elements of purchase-cost. This implies the existence of a hierarchy of these elements and asks, *initially*, which is more important to the consumer: prime cost or secondary cost?

That consumers are influenced strongly by reductions in prime prices in their store choice is not to be denied without vitiating much local advertising. However, prime price comparisons per se are fraught with difficulty. And, except where the consumer is comparing equal "commodity packages" or branded merchandise, errors are likely to be made. Where, for example, major gasoline stations in a particular market quote identical prices per gallon for the "same" grade of gasoline and give equal service, motorists may assume that those dealers giving trading stamps do so without increasing the motorist's prime purchase-cost.

Unfortunately, few purchase events enable the consumer to make as neat a comparison of prime prices as does the gasoline situation. Differences in the "commodity package," the multiplicity of commodities in any one store, each commodity with its own price, the use of loss-leaders where legal and the like, reduce the opportunity for consumers to buy efficiently on the sole basis of prime price comparison. Often in choosing among alternative purchase sites consumers can more easily compare secondary purchase-costs than prime prices.

Some consumers, however, are not strongly influenced by secondary purchase-costs. The "do-it-yourself" customer, whose attention seems to focus upon prime price comparisons, whose income is low, and whose evaluation of his marginal time is low, may prefer to bear secondary purchase-costs when he thinks their shifting to him relieves the retailer of this cost—thereby causing a lower prime price. The rise of self-service stores in the 1930's is some evidence of this view. Under conditions of rising family incomes and ample employ-

[2] George Katona, *The Powerful Consumer* (New York: McGraw-Hill Book Company, Inc., 1960), p. 159 *et. seq.*

[3] Russell S. Tate, "The Supermarket Battle for Store Loyalty," *Journal of Marketing*, XXV, No. 6 (October 1961), pp. 8–13.

ment opportunities, a contrary situation tends to prevail.

RELATIVE IMPORTANCE
TO CONSUMERS

It is logical to assume that the consumer attaches more or less importance to the monetary type secondary purchase-cost depending upon the size of the prime expenditure. The larger the prime expenditure, compared to the secondary purchase-cost, the less the importance of monetary type secondary purchase-costs. A consumer seeking to purchase a commodity whose prime price is $100 or more is not likely to be dissuaded by a few dollars of secondary purchase-cost. In a similar situation is the purchaser of a number of articles, each with a small prime price (e.g., grocery items), the aggregate of which is a relatively large sum, say $20. The marginal purchase-cost of adding another item to the group already selected in a particular store is not much more than the prime price of the additional item, since the secondary purchase-costs at the margins are likely to be negligible. Thus the "one stop shopping" appeal has considerable merit.

Within the secondary group, the hierarchy of individual purchase-costs of purely monetary type depends upon the amount of money involved. The larger the amount of money, generally, the more significant to the payer. This seems rather obvious!

More research is needed before much can be concluded about the relative importance of psychological-secondary costs. The impact of a psychological cost depends upon the individual paying it. As mentioned above, "the cognative behavior of any individual is a reaction to stimuli as he apperceives them."

On the other hand, an assay of the relative importance to consumers of psychological cost compared with monetary cost leads to agreement with Katona, who, though writing in a different context, remarks, "The psychological factors do not alone determine the final decision, but under certain conditions they are powerful enough to alter individual as well as mass reactions and thereby influence the entire economy." [4] One observes that some types of consumers put particular emphasis on psychological purchase-cost. Persons in high income brackets, those beyond middle age, those whose sensibility is rather delicately balanced

and for whom marginal tensions and frustrations cause more than ordinary distress, are customers to whom shifts of psychological costs should be avoided if practical.

RETAILER ACTION

The retailer who understands his customer, the nature of consumer purchase-costs, and some marketing principles should have no difficulty—if he has a modicum of ingenuity—in devising appropriate action. A retailer's approach to the kind of consumer behavior in his market should not be generalized on the assumption that it is appropriate for any and every market. Here the utmost care must be exercised. Thus it may be imprudent to attempt specific recommendation of particular devices. Yet, the retailer may find useful some evidence that consumers—perhaps in other markets—do react to efforts to cut their secondary purchase-costs. Consider, for example, the appeal of the "one stop" buying trip of shopping centers, as well as the increase in automatic vending machine sales and telephone selling.[5] Noticeable, too, is the increase in branch banking and auto-banks. Surveys show that congested shopping centers are losing business to less congested shopping centers where parking is easier and dress more casual.[6]

REDUCING CONSUMER
PURCHASE-COST

In general, there are four approaches to a reduction in consumer purchase-cost: (1) lower the prices of prime or target commodities; (2) shift secondary purchase-costs away from the customer; (3) a combination of (1) and (2); and (4) provide offsets to secondary purchase-cost.

Lower Prime Prices

Since as a basic principle, retailer action should aim at minimizing customer total purchase-cost, manipulation of prices on target commodities can be effective where secondary purchase-costs are about equal among com-

---

[4] George Katona, *op. cit.*, p. 6.

[5] "Supermarkets Where the Customers Stay Home," *Business Week*, November 22, 1957, pp. 66–68.

[6] Charles Hindersman, "The Evolving Downtown-Suburban Retail Pattern," *Journal of Marketing*, XXV (October 1960), pp. 59–62. Also, same reference, Samuel Pratt and Lois Pratt, "The Impact of Some Regional Shopping Centers," pp. 44–50.

peting stores. The dangers of this kind of price competition are well known. The advantages lie in the store-traffic building aspects and in the lower marginal secondary purchase-cost where it is normal to purchase a number of target commodities. Also, the additive effect may produce a relatively large prime purchase dwarfing the total secondary purchase-cost, a point mentioned earlier.

Shifting Secondary Purchase-Costs

Every exchange, every purchase and sale, involves a relationship between the parties to the exchange that may conveniently be called a buyer-seller relation. Within this relation, at the retail level, are performed a number of marketing functions and customer services. It is clear that the cost of performing a function or service can be eliminated only when the function or service is eliminated. By definition, marketing functions cannot be eliminated. When they are not retained by the retail vendor, they are shifted—sometimes back to the wholesaler, sometimes forward to the customer. Customer services are difficult to eliminate; they too are shifted between the retailer and the customer. Customer delivery service, for example, when discontinued by the retailer vendor, is shifted to the customer along with its cost.

Both from a social and an individual point of view, costs tend to be optimized when a function is performed by the most efficient performer. An obvious example relates to retailer-paid store air conditioning. The customer is not likely to perform efficiently within the store the task of keeping his body comfortable during the summer heat! An interesting and less obvious illustration relates to shifting the task of assembly of the customer's order from retail clerk to the customer, as self-service stores do. Perhaps few customers really believe that this decreases total waiting time when they must wait at the check-out queue!

COMBINATION OF LOWER PRICES AND SHIFT OF SECONDARY PURCHASE-COSTS

Emphasis here is on total purchase-cost manipulation, so that "on balance" customer purchase-costs are reduced. Suppose, for instance, both prime price and parking expense are lowered for the consumer but searching time is increased because of lack of assortment

(other costs unchanged). If for the consumer the increase in the cost of searching time more than offsets the decrease in the cost of parking and prime price, purchase-cost is increased. Contrariwise, if the customer's cost of searching is increased less than the decrease in the cost of parking and prime price, her total purchase-cost is decreased. *What the customer thinks* about this is crucial, and it should be clear that the retailer must know his customer.

Offsets

Inasmuch as shopping "satisfactions" provide offsets to secondary purchase-costs for some people, retailers may succeed in reducing purchase-costs for their customers by employing satisfaction-giving devices. Many stores and shopping centers have done this, using trading stamps, premiums, give-a-ways, entertainment, and other so-called "attractions" and special promotions. Some of these, like most "one-shot" efforts, have fleeting results. Some others, like trading stamps, have their effect dimmed by competitors' similar action.

No retailer should assume he will retain his present customers from habit alone. Just as competitors are actively soliciting each other's customers, there is a continuing requirement that each retailer provide the stimuli necessary to retain present customers as well as to attract others.

SOME OTHER CONSIDERATIONS FOR RETAILERS

Several important factors related to consumer purchase-costs are worthy of retailer consideration. One such factor concerns pri- should the retailer first give attention? The effect of shifting a secondary purchase-cost from the consumer also should be analyzed.

Priority

It would be most helpful to retail executives to have at hand a continually updated checklist of secondary purchase-cost elements arranged on the basis of some certain knowledge of the importance of each purchase-cost element to each customer. Such a list is not available. But where certain costs are known to be heavily weighted by the customer, early action is demanded.

Secondary purchase-costs, however, can be classified on the basis of the frequency with which they are likely to be encountered by the customer. Those of high frequency should get priority in action to shift them away from the consumer. In the high occurrence group are parking fees, travel time and expense, in-store waiting time, searching time, a host of psychological costs due to store personnel, store layout, lack of assortment of goods, store temperatures, humidity, and the like. But other secondary purchase-costs—such as correspondence costs related to ordering, paying and such, credit charges, installation charges, even delivery charges—are not likely to occur with every shopping trip or purchase event. Action on these can be deferred until those with high priority are dealt with.

SOME EFFECTS OF SHIFTING SECONDARY PURCHASE-COSTS

When a cost, ordinarily a consumer secondary purchase-cost of the purely monetary type, like parking expense, is assumed by a retailer, the cost to the customer may be more or less than what it was prior to the shift—again depending upon the efficiency with which it is performed. When the retailer performs a service, like customer parking, its cost might be included in "prime" prices. But an increase in sales volume may so spread the cost per customer that the impact upon the customer of an increase in prime price, if any, is negligible. Then this type of retailer action, in terms of customer purchase-cost effects, has much to recommend it.

On the other hand, retail vendors may be well advised to proceed cautiously when a shift of function or service—previously a dollar cost to the retailer—becomes a psychological cost to the customer. Suppose a store were to curtail its check-out cashier personnel, causing an increase in customer aggravation and tension. Such augmenting of customer's psychological cost, even with a simultaneous decrease in prime prices, may be shortsighted on the retailer's part, for many customers weigh heavily their psychological purchase-cost. Notable, also, is the increased impact on the consumer of additional increments of psychological cost owing to the cumulative effect associated with pyramiding psychological factors.

CONCLUSION

Sellers, long ago, recognized and reacted to consumer's purchase-cost problems then associated with certain types of goods, such as convenience goods, shopping goods, and specialty goods. "Consumers," writes Aspinwall, "cannot easily be forced to expend an amount of time and energy that is disproportionate to the satisfaction they expect to receive from the goods in question." [7] In other words, unless the want is more than normally urgent, a consumer is unlikely to make a sole purchase of a pack of cigarettes if this entails a 35¢ parking fee! Contrariwise, a consumer may be willing to devote considerable time and energy along with other secondary purchase costs when he is buying a $3000 automobile.

The concern of retailers about consumer reaction to purchase events requiring higher purchase-cost is particularly noticeable in store location research efforts, in participation in outlying shopping centers, in financing parking surveys, in downtown rehabilitation, and in attempts to improve store services. Retailers have sought help from experts ranging from psychologists to economic geographers. Obviously, it is believed that shoppers find no satisfaction in paying parking fees, traveling long rather than short distance to a store, and in fact, incurring any avoidable purchase-cost. It is no accident that retail trading area maps indicate that segments close to a shopping center contain a larger percentage of the center's customers than do segments more distant from the center. Nor is the apprehension and alarm of downtown retailers decreased by loss of customers to shopping centers with more ample parking areas. In the final analysis, retailers cannot disassociate themselves from consumer decisions designed to minimize their secondary purchase-costs. Nor can these be completely offset by sole attention to offering slight concessions in prime cost.

Alternative purchase events continually present themselves for consumer choice. The logical basis for making a choice consistent with consumer goals requires purchase-cost considerations. The manner in which consumers may be expected to approach the choice is a function of three elements: (1) the importance attached to minimizing purchase-costs; (2) individual perception of stimuli suggesting an opportunity to decrease purchase-costs; and

---

[7] Leo Aspinwall, "The Characteristics of Goods and Parallel Systems Theory", in *Managerial Marketing: Perspectives and Viewpoints,* William Lazer and Eugene J. Kelley, Editors, Richard D. Irwin, Inc., Homewood, Illinois, 1958.

(3) the consumer's propensity to make decisions.

The retailer's considerable familiarity with cost analysis and the flexibility of the purchase-cost approach should commend it to the executive who sees the need to target his activity for the consumers in his market.

DISCUSSION QUESTION

Consumer purchase costs are both "primary" and "secondary." Professor Bender argues that secondary purchase costs—those exclusive of the price of the commodity itself—should be the conscious focus of more attention than they are.

> What services can a retailer offer which will reduce or simplify customer's perception of:
> (a) "price" type secondary purchase-costs?
> (b) "time" type secondary purchase-costs?
> (c) "psychological" secondary purchase-costs?

4. Customer Services:
A New Look at an Old Technique

ROBERT D. ENTENBERG

Customers want services and prefer to deal with stores which offer them. The closer department and specialty store management can come to a total service concept, the better the chances are of attracting new customers and holding existing customers who don't mind paying for services and the merchandise that is for sale with them. An over-all service concept permits stores to offer customers a total "package" of satisfactions rather than just a locale where a purchase can be made.

Thus, the continuing boom in service sales is a new conceptual market consideration for department and specialty stores. Regardless of the manner in which service sales are expanded, or which particular types of services are offered, the introduction and promotion of service sales will help improve over-all sales volume and customer patronage motives.

One of the more important facets of expanding service sales are the personal face-to-face relationships which they involve. This would go a long way to help reverse the trend toward sameness which has grown alarmingly at the retail level. By reemphasizing a quality-service image as "the place to shop," more consumers would be willing to go longer distances to shop.

Regardless of how it's done—in dead spaces or other non-productive areas—selling more services can help in several ways. For instance, one distinctive feature of selling services is that, unlike tangible goods, the product cannot easily be separated from the producer—or the store.

A second feature is that services are usually created and sold as wanted. So there is little, if any, problem of physical inventory handling and storing.

A third feature is that alert management is provided the means for maintaining a more continuous, personal and direct contact with customers.

BASIC CHANGES

The desire for prestige and status has always been a culturally acceptable trait of most American consumers. In the past, to satisfy such desires, consumers in upper-income levels purchased exclusive, generally high-priced merchandise. In such cases status was translated in terms of being "different" in goods and/or purchasing habits.

In recent years, however, increasing numbers of consumers have been financially able and willing to conform with the "taste-makers" of the community. As a result, style leaders and community pace-setters have had to turn to other areas in which to differ in their shopping and consumption patterns.

These individuals, and their number is increasing, no longer seek prestige and snob appeal satisfactions solely through the purchasing of differing commodities. As one young suburbanite says, "There's no fun in owning a super-duper wagon when everyone in the block has one." In such cases, satisfying the desire to be different has translated itself into buying increased amounts of services.

For example, some parents seek status through the purchase of particular educational services for their children—such as ballet and music lessons. Or they spend more for travel. However, they also want and are willing to pay for services which are easily adaptable to the department and specialty type of operation. And customers don't want the sameness in merchandise offerings which they are getting in too many of the better stores in which they shop. Why go out of your way to shop for the same thing?

♦ SOURCE: Reprinted by permission from the *Department Store Economist,* in the August, 1963, issue, pages 22–25.

JUST WHAT ARE ADAPTABLE SERVICES?

Of course, the purchase of services by consumers runs the entire gamut from cooked dinners to stenographic and duplicating services. Among some of the adaptable services in which tremendous sales increases have taken place are: credit plans; all kinds of decorating services; television and appliance rental and repair services; beauty shop and personal care services (and products); stenographic, duplicating and printing services; miscellaneous rentals such as reducing equipment, dress suits, and drive-yourself automobiles. In many cases some of the rental charges can be applied to total purchase price when customers want ownership.

As a matter of fact, the growth in the sale

of services is again presenting department and specialty stores with the renewed opportunity to tie up their customers on a strong patronage basis. For example, chiropodists, optometrists and druggists can create strong patronage motives for the entire store, as well as themselves, when their services can be tied into a total service concept within a store.

In 1962, consumers spent more than $147.1 billion for services of all kinds. In 1947 the comparable figure was only $67 billion. An increase of 196% occurred in the 15-year period from 1947 to 1963. This means that the average consumer allocates almost 42¢ of every dollar he spends for services (See Table I).

Further, a growing number of consumers are not so price conscious as they once were—a trend which started shortly after World

TABLE 1ᵃ

	Consumer Expenditures by Type (Billions of Dollars)								Changes in Consumer Expenditure Allocations
	1956		1958		1960		1962		(1956–1963)
	$	%	$	%	$	%	$	%	Percent Change
Goods and Services, Total	269.9	100.0%	293.2	100.0%	328.5	100.0%	356.7	100.0%	+32.2%
Durable Goods	38.5	14.3	37.3	12.7	44.8	13.6	47.5	13.3	23.4%
Non Durable Goods	131.4	48.7	141.6	48.3	151.8	46.2	162.0	45.4	15.5%
Services	100.0	37.1	114.3	39.0	131.9	40.2	147.1	41.2	47.1%

ᵃ Surveys of Current Business, July, 1961, and February, 1963.

War II when many consumers moved into a higher scale of living. This large and expanding middle majority group is apparently more willing to pay for quality and services in all expenditure areas.

One of the principal reasons for this change is that most American consumers feel that they own a sufficient amount of "goods," with the result that many of them are buying larger amounts of services.

This is true even though most kinds of services are approximately 50% more expensive today than they were in 1947. During this same 1947–1963 period the price levels of durable and non-durable goods rose only 18%. For example, when consumers shop for stenographic and duplicating services, attached to

and an integral part of the store's stationery and office supply sections, a total service concept is generated. This means plus business, not only in the stationery departments but throughout the store.

Individuals are not "doing it themselves" in their "leisure" time. Many spend their so-called leisure time in commuting to and from work, school and community activities. These people are a captive market for service expenditures. This is one of the reasons for the tremendous growth in the sale of landscaping and garden-care services, which bring with them sales of the entire gamut of porch and lawn furniture and summer-use accessories.

There are still sizable income groups, of course, where the marginal rate of substitution for goods is quite high. Food expenditures, accounting for approximately two-fifths of all "goods" expenditures, is one of these relatively firm areas.

In marked contrast to the comparatively slow growth (in relation to population) of the high-priority food expenditure categories has been the rapid increase in spending for personal business. These include expenditures for insurance, bank services, bank charges, foreign travel and private education (See Table II).

Apparel and accessory expenditures, with the exception of furs and millinery, have kept up on a volume basis at a faster pace than population growth. On the other hand, the integral service components of these expenditures have become relatively much more important from both a volume and a service concept standpoint. Such services include fur storage and repair, in-store millinery workrooms, watch, jewelry and optical repair.

Services associated with user-operated transportation, such as automobile repairs, installations and automobile insurance, are largely responsible for the tremendous growth in total transportation outlays. Stores offering car rental and accessory installation services, in conjunction with their battery, tire and automobile accessory departments, have been successful in inducing shopping while waiting. Car rental services are naturals for stores which have their own delivery facilities.

More than 18 million new housing units have been added to the total housing market since 1947; almost 70% of these are owner occupied. The purchase of a home, while generally considered an investment, should be considered as the purchase of a consumer's durable "good."

Services related to household operation account for almost one-half of the total outlays for services and have far outstripped the ex-

TABLE II. Service Sales Grow

Kind of Business[a]	Approximate Percentage Growth in Sales Since 1954
Motels, tourist courts	93
Trailer parks, camps	54
Industrial laundries	47
Linen supply	38
Diaper service	27
Beauty shops (including combination with barber shops)	62
Barber shops	45
Photo studios, and so on	40
Miscellaneous personal services (Turkish baths, massage, reducing salons, dress suit rentals, rug, furniture cleaning on location, checkroom concessions, and so on. (SIC729)	95
Credit bureaus, collection agencies	55
Dupilcating, stenographic, blueprinting, statistical	55
Miscellaneous services to dwellings (Janitorial, floor waxing, maintenance and repair to buildings and homes)	80
Auto repair, services, garages	77
Auto and truck rentals	140
Auto parking	35
Radio, TV repairs	65
Electric repairs (including refrigerator)	73
Reupholstery, furniture repair	25
Dance halls, studio and schools (including children's)	75
Bowling alleys	110

[a] Based on Selected Services, U.S. Summary 1958, U.S. Census of Business, various Surveys of Current Business, Department of Commerce, and the writer's projected estimates.

penditures for household goods in post-war growth. It is difficult to separate the warranty and maintenance service expenditures associated with the sales of appliances for new homes.

Most people want help in beautifying and remodeling their homes. They are buying custom-made draperies, custom-built furniture, interior decorating, landscaping, special home movies. Home improvement products that require installation fall into this category, such as storm windows, electronic garage doors, and so on. When department or specialty store managers can't handle the details of specialized service sales, leasing to specialized service agencies should be considered.

Turning non-productive spaces into pick-up stations associated with coin-operated, self-service, and dry cleaning facilities can increase store traffic.

Paid admissions to motion picture theaters and spectator sports, which tapered off during television's initial stages, are beginning to show marked increases in consumer expenditures. The possibilities of including small motion picture theaters in waste or unproductive areas, either in or adjacent to your stores, should be an important consideration for more productive use of facilities and as an expansion of over-all location appeal.

INTEREST ON INDEBTEDNESS NO DETERRENT

A three-fold rise in interest charges on consumer debt has occurred in the post-war period. This has been one of the fastest growth components in over-all consumer spending. From 1948 to 1960, expenditures for credit and service costs in acquiring durable goods represented almost one-half of all consumer expenditures in these areas.

In 1960, the cost of "forced savings" used in buying durables accounted for almost three-fourths of interest charge expense. Another aspect of this increase in interest expense has been the increase in the average length of consumer loans and the increased use of relatively expensive personal banking services. (*Survey of Current Business*, Nov., 1961, p. 16).

Installation and credit costs have been accepted by the average customer as part of the opportunity costs associated with living in a modern, mechanized society. He rarely complains of needed service expenditures. He tends to keep appliances and other equipment in good repair rather than replacing them at the first sign of wear. Stores servicing what they sell are usually the first to be called.

TO SUMMARIZE

Specialized selling and the personal service element in sales is of growing importance once again in retail competition.

Should present expenditure trends continue, the purchase of services will eventually be the largest single component of consumer spending.

Consumers are spending more for service because of increased incomes, a growing sufficiency of goods and a growing sameness of goods. The declining ability of fashion merchandisers and fashion stores to create shopping excitement and sufficient motivational appeal for customers' discretionary spending is also a factor.

Approximately 48% of all families and unattached individual consuming units are earning above $6,000 annually. In 1947, the $6,000-and-up groupings totaled only 17% of all income units. It is obvious that the majority of American families has sufficient income for discretionary spending.

More importantly, the personal service and service sales potential of retail sales is the fastest growing area of competition—cut-price discounters notwithstanding. Competitive factors along these lines are becoming more important because there has been a tremendous increase in sameness of goods, especially at the all-important fashion levels where non-price competition has always been important.

As cut-price competition becomes less effective, more and more discount houses are turning to income-producing services for volume expansion. Thus we have today not only a trend toward "scrambled merchandising" but a trend to "scrambled services," some of these seemingly unrelated.

As the increasing trend toward sameness in merchandise offerings becomes more widespread, real product differentiation will rest with the stores offering services where individuality is still a must. And effective demand for services will continue to increase although consumers, in most cases, are paying more for less services. The market potential is there and even discount house management has found that they are often bypassed by consumers who feel more inclined to shop for service and less inclined to shop for price only.

DISCUSSION QUESTION

Professor Entenberg is primarily concerned with "services" which do not normally involve a concomitant sale of "goods." The "services" examined in earlier articles were "services" which normally attend the sale of some physical product. The opportunity in this strictly "service" retail establishment is both excellent and growing.

> How does a purely "service" retail establishment differ in terms of cost and expense structure and in terms of the skills required of the operator?

Competition Through Internal Control

Successful retail management is well-informed retail management. One of the dimensions in which retail management must have continuous and accurate information concerns the progress that the firm is making toward profit goals. In the same sense that medical doctors use pulse rate, blood pressure, and a host of other indications of the state of a persons health, retail management employs a number of "indicators" which reflect the position of the retail enterprise. This section includes articles which identify and discuss techniques through which the "health" of the firm may be appraised.

Specifically, articles are included which suggest (a) a technique for the determination of the profitability of individual items of inventory, (b) the preferences of different levels of retail management for particular diagnostic measures, (c) a new measure of performance, and (d) a simple technique for the determination of changes in required sales volume necessitated by changes in price and cost.

1. A Simplified Capital Budgeting Approach to Merchandise Management

RICHARD H. HOLTON

Perhaps the traditional Controllers Congress measures of a good merchandising operation need re-examining. For, after all, profits are more precious than markup and a stock turn based on loss leaders puts no black ink on anybody's books. Capital budgeting based on contribution-return on inventory investment provides a new approach which could maximize profits.

The rationalization of decision-making in the manufacturing sector of the economy in recent years has advanced at a pace which most retailers have apparently been unable to match. Manufacturers have been making increasing use of such devices as mathematical programming of production to make optimum use of equipment; application of the theory of inventory controls to give the economic order quantity and optimum stock levels; and capital budgeting to assure optimal use of funds.

Although a handful of large retailers are experimenting with the application of modern control techniques, these advances are clearly neither so numerous nor as significant in retailing as in manufacturing. It may not be an exaggeration to say that in the modernization of decision-making techniques, the race between manufacturing and retailing thus far has been a case of the hare and tortoise.

We need not search far for the roots of this disparity. First of all, successful retailing has always called for more artistry than has successful manufacturing. Contrast the manufacturing of a television set with the retailing of that same television set. The manufacturer faces a limited number of alternatives in the design and pricing of the product; and he produces several combinations of design and price so that he may meet a high proportion of the consumers' preferences. Once this decision is made, he then produces to specification in the most economical way (until the next model change). Thus, there is great emphasis on cost control.

The retailer of television sets, on the other hand, attracts customers to his television department not simply because of the price and design of the sets he displays, but because of countless other features of the store. Customers are attracted by other departments, by special promotions, by the nature of the advertising, by the appearance of the store, by the courtesy of the clerks, credit plans, delivery service and so forth. Just what combination of all these features will prove most appealing to consumers is very largely a matter of insight developed from experience.

MANAGEMENT BY HUNCH

The effect of changes in any of these policies is difficult to quantify, and the effect of any such change may be different from one month to the next. The number of relevant variables and the difficulty of quantifying them seems, in the case of retailing, to have led to management largely by hunch and intuition. Furthermore, the retailer in so many instances handles such a huge number of items (10,000 or more, for example, in many supermarkets) that careful application of quantitative techniques to each item would be prohibitively expensive.

A second reason for the lag in the application of more modern methods to retailing often rests on the simple fact that the number of employees per firm is so much greater in manufacturing than in retailing. One of the virtues

♦ SOURCE: Reprinted by permission from the *California Management Review*, in the Spring, 1961, issue, pages 82–99.

of greater size is, after all, the specialization of managerial talent which it permits.

So in manufacturing we would expect to find, as a rule, more specialists in different phases of management than would be the case in retailing. Of course, the largest retailers in the country are large even by manufacturers' standards. But, even in large-scale retailing, size is achieved in a relatively unique manner, namely by joining together comparatively small units (branch stores or departments) which are in many respects autonomous managerial entities in which managerial specialization is limited.

The retailer's stress on merchandising tactics can in part be explained by the cost conditions he faces. His expenses are largely fixed in the short run, so his profit position is determined primarily by his sales. The manufacturer, on the other hand, faces quite different cost conditions. If his sales slow down he can reduce his work force or close down completely for a few weeks while he sells from inventory. But the retailer's work force produces a service, viz., the service of waiting on customers, and this service cannot be produced for inventory if people happen not to come into the store on some days.

RETAILER HAS HIGH FIXED COSTS

True, the retailer may vary his sales force so that it fits the expected pattern of sales, but the point is that the retailer first decides on the size and distribution of his sales force, then he hopes that customers will come in so that his clerks can produce service. Little wonder, then, that the retailer historically has been somewhat more volume conscious than has the manufacturer. The manufacturer, who can match costs to output much more readily than can the retailer, has laid more stress than the retailer on cost control.

The far greater density of trained engineers in manufacturing is probably another part of the explanation. The engineer, accustomed to a rational, pragmatic approach to manufacturing problems, is predisposed to work with quantitative information and with production, rather than sales, problems. But in the mind of the merchandiser or salesman, by contrast, customers take precedence over costs. Retailing, involving almost no physical transformation of the goods handled, is rarely in need of an engineer. The merchandiser's outlook, rather than the engineer's, obviously prevails, and for good reason.

"THE CUSTOMER COMES FIRST"

This contrast may be overdrawn a bit, but surely it exists nonetheless. It is true, however, that retailers have been taking certain steps in recent years to narrow this gap. After the war the Controllers' Congress of the National Retail Dry Goods Association, now the National Retail Merchants Association, appears to have taken the first major steps toward a more rational approach to retail management procedures.

The downtown department stores' postwar difficulties with the discount house on the one hand and the suburbanization of retailing on the other unquestionably were influential in motivating major metropolitan retailers to sharpen their pencils and examine their costs and operating methods more carefully. The result was the now famous Standard Expense Center Accounting technique for allocating costs to centers within the store.

The individual in charge of each center could then be charged with the responsibility for keeping his controllable costs in hand. More recently, at least one version of merchandise management accounting has been built on the expense center cost approach to give a means of allocating controllable costs to individual shipments of goods so that the contribution to overhead and profit can be ascertained for that item, assuming various prices.[1]

In both expense center accounting and merchandise management accounting one finds a heavy emphasis on the allocation only of controllable costs, i.e., costs which would not have been incurred if the decision in question had not been made. For example, in merchandise management accounting a shipment of goods is allocated only those costs which would not have been incurred if that shipment were not bought.

The difference between this incremental cost and the net sales value of the item in question yields the contribution to overhead and profit associated with the shipment being considered.

[1] For a more detailed discussion of the predecessors of merchandise management accounting, see Malcolm P. McNair and Eleanor G. May, "Pricing for Profit," *Harvard Business Review*, Vol. 35 (May–June 1957), pp. 105–122.

This is nothing more than an application of the incremental (or, to the economist, marginal) analysis. The emphasis on the contribution to overhead and profit has been developing gradually over the years and now seems to be reasonably well established in the thinking of at least the more progressive retail store operators.

GROSS MARGINS AND PROFITS

Despite the growing acceptance of the contribution to overhead and profit as a basis for certain types of merchandising decisions, there can be little doubt, as McNair and May point out, that retailers still lean primarily on other indices of performance.[2] Too often these indices are gross margin percentages or other ratios to sales, which ratios of course have only an indirect relationship to dollar profits.

Information on "typical" ratios for different types of retailing is rather widely circulated via the trade journals and of course the firm will have its own historical ratios. Retailers often then find themselves using the historical ratios, qualified a bit by the industry-wide ratios, as goals. The possibility that the historical or "typical" ratio may not be the best one seems to be examined less often than one might expect it to be.

There can be little question that the practice of applying set mark-ups almost automatically left some types of retailers very vulnerable to new competition which was taking another look at cost and demand conditions. But this is a complaint against nearly all automatic means of computing mark-ups, not just the particular one which has been employed historically by so many retailers.

How might the performance of a department be evaluated and compared with other departments? How might the performance of one line within a department be compared with other lines? These are clearly two of the most troublesome questions for the retailer as he considers his control methods. If the weak departments (or lines within departments) could be spotted readily, then they could be contracted or eliminated if improvements in performance could not be achieved by any of the more common merchandising remedies such as alterations in display, promotion and so forth. If the strong departments can be identified

easily, then they might profitably be expanded at the expense of the less successful departments. And perhaps new departments should be introduced.

"WE LOVE THAT MARKUP"

But the usual measures of performance are poor guides for this sort of decision. For example, one food chain executive, clearly perplexed by the problem of deciding whether the firm's supermarkets should introduce soft goods departments, said that the company policy is to leave the decision to the individual store manager since the firm has no answer to the problem. "We love that markup," he said, "but we hate that turnover." The management had not determined a means of reconciling these two measures of performance.

The argument of this article is that these troublesome questions can be answered simply and with tolerable accuracy if the problem of achieving a profit-maximizing balance among merchandise departments is viewed basically as a problem in capital budgeting. Considered in this way, a number of the nagging problems in retail store management are put in a new and, it is hoped, helpful light.

We shall first spell out the argument that the capital budgeting approach calls for maximizing what we will term the "contribution-return on inventory investment." Then this approach to the problem of merchandise management will be applied to an illustrative case. Finally, certain of the policy problems implied by this approach will be discussed.

CAPITAL BUDGETING AN ANSWER

It should be stressed at the outset that the capital budgeting approach to merchandise management is not really new. The idea of viewing the contribution to overhead and profit as a return on inventory investment has been ducking on and off the stage in a non-speaking role for some time. But it is the contention here that it should spend much more time downstage center and be given star billing as well.

For the sake of simplicity, we will assume that the retail firm is interested primarily in maximizing dollar profits. Although in reality the retailer may be interested in certain other goals as well, presumably the rational procedure for the design of marketing policy in this context would call first for identifying the

---

[2] See note 1.

profit-maximizing policy, then altering that policy insofar as is necessary to bring it into conformity with any other goals of the firm which may conflict with profit maximization.

PROFITS ARE BETTER THAN MARKUP

We are concerned here only with the design of the profit maximizing policy. This emphasis on profit maximization is undoubtedly far less common in retailing than it might be. McNair and May have noted the retailer's fondness for achieving a certain realized gross or net profit percentage when they say that attention has been "focused on ratios to sales rather than on dollars, and the convenient percentages have become crutches."[3] In this paper we will keep this goal of maximum dollar profits firmly in mind.

Can any of the well-known measures of departmental performance (or performance of a line within a department) be used by itself as an index of profitability? As every retailer is aware, the answer of course, is "no." If Department A has a higher realized gross margin percentage than does Department B, A's total sales may be so low as to make it far inferior to B.

Conversely, Department B may have a far higher turnover than does A, but whether this makes B the better department depends on the price and the costs in Department B; after all, turnover in many instances could be maximized by selling below cost. Sales per square foot is a measure commonly used to compare departments; but the department with the highest sales per square foot may also have very high costs per square foot. And sales per square foot could be increased almost indefinitely if promotional expenditures for that department were continually increased, but of course at some point these promotional expenditures would exhaust the dollars of margin provided by that department. Obviously, the sales criterion is inadequate.

More recently dollars of gross margin per square foot have been mentioned as a guide. But in some departments the cost of generating a dollar of gross margin per square foot is much greater than in other departments. Surely, selling costs, delivery and credit costs and the like vary substantially among departments in stores of any size, making for "low cost" dollars of gross margins in some depart-

ments, and "high cost" dollars of gross margins in others.

This weakness can be corrected at least in part by deducting from the dollars of gross margin in each department the direct operating costs, giving the contribution dollars ("controllable profit") per square foot. But even this measure is incomplete, for it fails to recognize that different amounts of investment in inventory are required in different department or lines within departments to generate the contribution to overhead and profit. This suggests that the dollars of contribution *expressed as an annual percentage return on the inventory investment,* may be the best available all-purpose criterion of performance of the individual department.

CONTRIBUTION-RETURN

This contribution-return on investment, i.e., the dollars of annual contribution per dollar of average inventory investment, has much to recommend it as a criterion of performance. Its greatest virtue is that it reflects the rate of sale, the turnover rate, the gross profit percentage, the direct costs of handling and the dollars tied up in inventory investment. If the turnover increases, obviously the contribution-return on investment is increased. If the gross margin is increased, and the number of units sold per time period remains unchanged, the contribution-return is increased. If sales are increased, the contribution return will not be altered unless the sales increase proportionally more than the average investment and the direct costs of selling the merchandise. If selling costs rise, the contribution-return on investment falls. If any of the direct operating expenses increase, the contribution-return falls. All of the common criteria of performance, except those including floor area as a factor, are reflected in this one measure. The reason for omitting area considerations from the contribution return on inventory investment will be taken up later.

The full scope of the contribution return on inventory investment can be seen most clearly, perhaps, in symbolic terms.

Let:

C = contribution as a percentage return on inventory investment

S = net sales in the given department

W = net invoice cost of goods sold by the department

[3] See note 1.

D = direct expenses for the department

I = average investment in inventory in the department

Then:

$$C = 100 \times (S - W - D)/I$$

Turnover is W/I; if the percentage markup is held constant and turnover increases, $(S-W)/I$ increases, raising C. Since the realized gross margin percentage is $(S-W)/S$, an increase in this percentage, whether achieved by increasing S or decreasing W, increases C. And of course a reduction in direct expenses decreases the value of D and therefore increases C. Thus it seems apparent that the contribution-return on investment brings these common measures of departmental performance together into a single index.[4]

Is the maximization of the contribution-return on investment for all departments combined, i.e., for the firm, identical with profit maximization? The answer is in the affirmative *if* one assumes that the amount of investment is fixed. If this fixed investment assumption is dropped and the capital invested in the firm is increased, one would expect an increase in profits which is less than proportional to the increase in investment. (This assumes that the most profitable uses of capital have already been exploited.)

Here the dollar profits would be increased while the return on investment would decrease and profit maximization would not yield the same solution as maximizing the return on in-

vestment. But if the investment in the firm is fixed, any increase in dollars of net profit brings a proportional increase in the percentage return on investment.

MAXIMIZING RETURN

Therefore the retailer may choose to focus on maximizing return on investment, if he wishes, without departing from the profit maximizing goal *if* he realizes that this proposition holds only if investment funds are taken as given. The analysis which follows can easily be extended to fit the case in which the investment funds are not fixed.

Is maximizing the return on the firm's investment in inventory consistent with profit maximization? A retailer's investment funds might be shifted out of buildings, say, by means of a sale and lease-back arrangement, the funds being put into inventory. This could result in greater dollars of net profit but a lower return on investment in inventory. In other words, the dollars of net profit might increase by a smaller proportion than the investment. But if the investment in inventory is given, profit maximization is in fact identical with maximizing return on inventory investment.

With a given investment in inventory, then, profit maximization calls for maximizing return on that inventory investment. Since the retailer's fixed (unallocable) costs are a constant in the short run, maximizing profit can be achieved by maximizing the contribution to overhead and profit expressed as a percentage return on inventory investment. Thus with a given investment in inventory, those investment funds should be allocated among departments and among goods within departments so as to maximize the contribution to overhead and profit per dollar of inventory investment.[5]

AN ILLUSTRATIVE CASE

We can now proceed to apply this criterion to an illustrative firm and to compare it with the other criteria commonly used. The firm,

---

[4] To be conceptually accurate, I in the equation above should be computed on the basis not only of the purchase price of the goods but also the cost of getting the goods into selling position. Professor McNair has suggested (in correspondence) that one should, in order to be completely accurate, compute the average investment to include the investment in the accounts receivable generated by the merchandise in question. Because we are interested in the return on the investment of cash in the merchandise, we should compute the turnover by dividing into 360 the estimated number of days between the outlay of cash and the collection of cash from the sale. This turnover figure would, therefore, reflect not only the length of time cash may be tied up in accounts receivable but also the credit terms on which the purchase was made. (I am indebted to Prof. S. C. Hollander for calling my attention to the problem of the credit terms.) Use of this adjusted turnover figure rather than the more common turnover measure may yield quite different results, particularly for goods with high turnover (as usually defined) rates.

[5] Robert I. Jones, one of the initiators of merchandise management accounting, has emphasized the importance of the return on inventory investment in retailing, but he has not explicitly noted that maximizing the contribution return on inventory investment maximizes profits assuming a given investment in inventory. See his *Merchandise Management Accounting—A Further Discussion*, an address before the NRGDA Controllers' Congress Convention, May, 1957.

a student book store, offers an excellent case for the purpose of exploring the problems of applying the capital budgeting approach for several reasons. Not only are the accounting records readily available; the store is also big enough to have the departmental balance problem without being so large that compilation of the data is troublesome. Also, the fact that it is primarily a book store focuses attention on the familiar problem of the treatment of the department which appears to be performing poorly when viewed by itself but which may be the primary reason for the store's existence or in some degree a "leader" or "traffic-builder" department.

Selected operating data for the store are given in Table I. Let us assume that the direct expenses are allocated correctly to the various departments; Table II, computed from Table I, simply shows the rank of each department by the various criteria of performance.

Two major points are immediately apparent in Tables I and II. First, by any of the criteria shown, the performances of the various departments vary widely. Secondly, no individual department is consistently best or worst among the six.

Needless to say, the department which ranks high in turnover rate is also likely to rank high

in sales per square foot, dollars of gross margin per square foot, contribution per square foot and contribution per dollar of investment; but all the percentage of sales criteria are correspondingly low. As every retailer recognizes, a department with a relatively high turnover shows a relatively low percentage gross margin in part because the turnover is high.

The contribution-return on inventory investment is highest for the candy, tobacco and magazines department, turnover being great enough to offset easily the low gross profit percentage. Books also carry a low gross profit margin, but the turnover, though second among the six departments, is nevertheless so low that the contribution as a percentage return on investment is also very low. The wide variation among the common criteria of performance underscores the necessity for a simple measure which combines the usual criteria into one.

POLICY IMPLICATIONS

One's initial reaction to Tables I and II is that this book store should abandon the book business and concentrate on candy, tobacco and magazines if it wishes to maximize the contribution as a percentage return on inven-

TABLE I. Selected Operating Data for Illustrative Store, by Department

	Unit	Total	Books	Loose Leaf	Social Stationery	Sporting Goods	Candy, Tobacco and Magazines	Fountain Items
Sales	$	966,332	662,762	97,889	72,340	51,667	50,786	30,888
Percent of total	%	100.0	68.6	10.1	7.5	5.3	5.3	3.2
Gross profit	$	244,277	138,157	43,026	25,304	14,977	12,583	10,275
Direct expense	$	128,720	86,367	17,601	13,087	2,940	5,851	2,874
Contribution	$	115,557	51,790	25,425	12,217	12,037	6,687	7,401
Overhead expense	$	34,010	57,960	14,843	10,076	3,584	4,356	3,191
Net profit (loss)	$	21,547	(6,170)	10,582	2,141	8,453	2,331	4,210
Square foot	sq. ft.	6,483	2,999	2,084	1,700	800	200	500
Average investment	$	219,604	160,876	27,828	28,351	15,244	5,275	10,381
Sales per square foot	$	149.06	220.99	46.97	42.55	64.58	253.93	61.78
Gross profit percentage	%	25.2	20.8	44.0	35.0	29.0	24.7	33.3
Net profit percentage	%	2.2	(0.9)	10.3	3.0	16.4	4.6	13.6
Dollars of gross profit per sq. ft.	$	37.68	46.07	20.65	14.88	18.72	62.69	20.55
Turnover rate	%	3.3	3.3	2.0	1.7	2.4	7.3	2.0
Contribution per square foot	$	17.82	17.27	12.20	7.19	15.04	33.44	14.80
Contribution percentage of sales	%	12.0	7.8	26.0	16.9	23.3	13.2	24.0
Contribution per dollar investment	$	.53	.32	.91	.43	.79	1.27	.71

TABLE II. Ranking of Departments in Illustrative Store, by Various Performance Criteria

Performance Criterion	Books	Loose Leaf	Social Stationery	Sporting Goods	Fountain Pens	Candy, Tobacco and Magazines
Sales per square foot	2	5	6	3	4	1
Gross profit percentage	6	1	2	4	3	5
Net profit percentage	6	3	5	1	2	4
Dollars of gross profit per square foot	2	3	6	5	4	1
Turnover rate	2	4	6	3	4	1
Contribution per sq. ft.	2	5	6	3	4	1
Contribution as percentage of sales	6	1	4	3	2	5
Contribution return on investment	6	2	5	3	4	1

SOURCE: Table I.

tory investment. But of course this recommendation is ridiculous. The contribution-return on inventory investment shown in Table I, although it is better than the other criteria, cannot be used as the basis for policy recommendations without further refinement. In order to consider intelligently the policy implications of the capital budgeting approach to merchandise management, we must first examine in more detail the logic underlying the use of the contribution-return on inventory investment as a criterion of performance.

To simplify the problem we will assume for the moment that the demand for any one item in the store is independent of the demand for all other items. This ignores the problem of the leader or traffic-builder department, a problem to which we will return at a later point.

Before any move is taken to shift inventory investment out of the less profitable departments and into the more profitable ones, the retail manager should ask whether he is allocating his investment funds as efficiently as possible within any single department.

Here a variation of merchandise management accounting can be brought into play. If the merchandise management accounting method suggested either by Jones or by McNair and May is altered slightly to show for individual types of goods the contribution in the form of the equivalent annual return on inventory investment, merchandise management accounting can be used to make optimum use of funds within any single department.

This point calls for some amplification. In his original discussion of merchandise management accounting, Jones noted that the objective of merchandise management accounting is to estimate the prospective profit contribution of any item of merchandise.

He then stated, "From an economic standpoint, this requires the ultimate expression of such information in terms of rate of return on inventory investment as the true criteria of profitability." [6] Yet his suggested procedure detours away from that ultimate objective, for he expresses the dollars of controllable profit as a percentage of sales. It is apparently this controllable profit by itself or as a percentage of sales which he would suggest the department buyer use as a guide in selecting merchandise. It would be much more appropriate for the controllable profit to be expressed as an annual percentage return on the investment.

PURCHASE RETURN OVER OUTLAY

McNair and May in their discussion of merchandise management accounting suggest that the contribution to overhead and profit be expressed as a "return on purchase outlay," i.e., as a percentage of the net invoice price of the shipment of goods being evaluated. But this measure fails to give adequate weight to the rate of turnover.

Two shipments of goods may each show a purchase return over outlay of 25 per cent by

---

[6] See note 5.

the method suggested by McNair and May although one may have a rate of stock turn twice as great as the other. The percentage return on purchase outlay in this instance makes the two items appear equally attractive investments, although in fact one is clearly preferable to the other.

To convert this return on purchase outlay to an annual rate of return equivalent, three steps are necessary. First, the average investment in the goods and the accounts receivable arising from the sale of the goods should be substituted for the purchase outlay. As soon as the goods begin to sell, and the accounts receivable collected, the retailer is recouping his investment; therefore as a first approximation, one can assume that the items in the shipment are drawn down at a constant rate over time so that the average investment in the goods is roughly one-half the funds invested in these goods at the time the first unit is sold.

Secondly, the purchase outlay does not represent the retailer's total investment in the item. The firm has paid out not only the purchase price but also the direct costs of selling the item, or at least the direct costs of processing the item and putting it into selling position. So the initial investment is the purchase outlay plus those direct selling costs incurred prior to the actual sale. To say that the initial investment is only the purchase outlay can be compared with the argument that the manufacturer's investment in finished goods consists only of the raw material costs, exclusive of direct processing costs.

STOCK TURN

The third step is equally simple. The contribution percentage must be expressed in terms of an annual return on investment. Thus, the dollars of contribution, divided by the average investment, in the given item, should be multiplied by the estimated number of stock turns per year for the item in question to yield a contribution-return on average inventory investment. This permits sensible comparisons of items with different turnover rates. For more accurate estimates, the length of an average stock turn for an item should be computed from the date cash is actually paid out for the merchandise to the date when cash is collected for it.

How might this procedure be applied in practice? Jones has noted that it is possible to separate the direct costs into two categories. One of these categories consists of those direct costs which vary with the number of physical units handled; the other category consists of those direct costs which vary with the dollar value of sales. Jones indicates that there are relatively few of these cost patterns, i.e., relatively few combinations of the two types of direct costs, in a given store. For each pattern he suggests that a chart be constructed showing the controllable profit (as a percentage of net sales) resulting from any given selling price, assuming different percentage markups.

The Jones approach, though certainly attractive in that it focuses on controllable profit, still falls short of providing the information he says we really want, namely information on the contribution as a rate of return on inventory investment.

This drawback can be overcome rather simply. On any single item being considered for purchase by a department buyer, the contribution-return on inventory investment equals the contribution (in dollars) divided by the average investment (computed as one-half of the purchase price plus one-half of the cost of getting the merchandise into selling position) the whole expression being multiplied by the expected turnover rate and then by 100 to give a percentage figure.

Let

C = contribution percentage return on inventory investment

C' = contribution per unit in dollars

T = turnover rate [7]

S = selling price per unit

W = net purchase price per unit

I = average inventory investment

D_1 = direct cost, in dollars, per unit handled

D_2 = direct costs which vary with dollar sales, expressed as a percentage of selling price

Then

$$C = \frac{C'}{I} \cdot T \cdot 100$$

but since

$$C' = S - (W + D_1 + D_2 S)$$

and

$$I = 1/2(W + D_1 + D_2 S)$$

---

[7] Strictly speaking, the turnover should refer to the turnover of the funds invested in the inventory in question. Thus a highly refined approach to this solution would call for an estimate of average investment which would be corrected for deferred billing and for the fact that accounts receivable are not immediately converted to cash.

then

$$C = \frac{100T[S - (W + D_1 + D_2S)]}{1/2(W + D_1 + D_2S)}$$

which reduces to:

$$C = 200T \left(\frac{S}{W + D_1 + D_2S} - 1 \right)$$

For any given cost pattern, the above expression can be put into tabular form for various probable values of T, W and S.

Table III is a very limited version of such a table, with the costs pattern being one in which D_1 equals $4.00 and D_2 equals 10 per cent. The invoiced cost is $10.00 in this example. Similar tables, including more values of T and S, could be easily computed for other costs. The department buyer could enter the table at the selling price of the item under consideration and then read off directly the contribution return on investment permitted by the expected turnover rate. Of course, the higher prices would presumably be associated with lower turnover rates. By means of this table the contribution-return on investment approach can be used as a basis for pricing policy.

Table III is only illustrative of the end-product of the capital budgeting approach and should not be taken as the only means of presenting the return on investment for the buyer's prospective purchases. If the firm's policy is to use strict price lines in a given department, the return on investment table might show only these price lines as values for X.

Not every conceivable combination of price and turnover rate a buyer might face needs to be included in such a table, of course, since crude interpolation is simple. And, of course, such a table designed for actual use would not carry values for S or T which give negative

values for C. Such values are left in Table III so that the full pattern of C-values can be seen.

It is critical to emphasize that a table such as that illustrated is only a guide to judgment, for the buyer applying the table must estimate what turnover is likely to result from each possible retail price. If he wishes to price the item in question to earn, say, a 165 percent contribution-return, Table III shows that to earn such a contribution-return at a price of $17.00 requires a turnover rate of 10, whereas an $18.00 price requires a turnover rate of only 6.

Let us presume that the retailer does utilize this modified version of merchandise management accounting to estimate the contribution-return on inventory investment for the individual items stock within each department. Furthermore, we will temporarily retain the assumption that the demand for each item is independent of the demand for all other items. From among the items that might be bought for each department, the rational retailer would attempt to select those which he estimates would bring the greatest contribution-return on investment.

If we conceive of a single department which is being expanded in terms of inventory investment and space and facilities devoted to it, there must be some size beyond which increments of investment are associated with smaller and smaller contribution percentage returns on investment. In other words, the incremental or marginal contribution percentage return on investment surely must begin to fall at some level of investment.[8]

---

[8] Here $\frac{C'}{I}$ is the dollars of contribution per dollar of investment; multiplying by T converts the return to an *annual* rate; and multiplying by 100 converts the expression to a *percentage* annual rate.

TABLE III. Contribution to Overhead and Profit Expressed as an Annual Rate of Return on Inventory Investment, for Selected Turnover Rates and Selling Prices, Assuming $D_1 = \$4$, $D_2 = .10$, and $W = 10$

T	$13.00	$14.00	$15.00	$16.00	$17.00	$18.00	$19.00	$20.00
6	−180.36	−109.08	−38.76	30.72	99.36	167.04	234.00	300.00
8	−240.48	−145.44	−51.68	40.96	132.48	222.72	312.00	400.00
10	−300.60	−181.80	−64.60	51.20	165.60	278.40	390.00	500.00
12	−360.72	−218.16	−77.52	61.44	198.72	334.08	468.00	600.00
14	−420.84	−254.52	−90.44	71.68	231.84	389.76	546.00	700.00

MARGINAL CONTRIBUTION-RETURN

Within this framework of assumptions, it is clear that if profits are to be maximized, investment funds should be allocated among departments so as to equate the *marginal* contribution-return on investment.[9] In other words, the departments are in balance if the next $100 invested in Department A would result in the same additional contribution as would an additional $100 invested in Department B or an additional $100 invested in Department C, and so on. If the marginal contribution-return in Department A is greater than that in Department B, profits would be increased if funds were shifted out of Department B and into Department A. Since the lines bringing the lowest contribution-return would be dropped from B, the marginal rate in that department would thereby be increased.

In Department A, the addition of inventory would decrease the contribution at the margin. This sort of reallocation of funds would result in increased profits; but when the returns are equated at the margin, further shifts would only decrease profits. Needless to say, this hairline adjustment can never be made with complete accuracy because of space limitations, inadequate data, shifting demand, and so forth. But the capital budgeting approach calls for the firm always to attempt to move toward this profit-maximizing position.

If the marginal contribution-return on investment is the same in each department, the average contribution-return can, of course, differ greatly from one department to another. In Table I, for example, the contribution-return on investment in the candy, tobacco and magazines department is 127 per cent compared with 71 per cent in the fountain pens department.

At first glance one might conclude that investment funds should be shifted out of fountain pens and into candy, tobacco and magazines. Such a move would increase the marginal contribution-return on fountain pens and reduce it in the candy department. But

here the familiar distinction between the average and the marginal or incremental figure is critical. It is conceivable that the next most profitable use of inventory investment funds in the fountain pens department would be the addition of an item which would bring a contribution-return on investment of 60 per cent whereas the next most profitable item which might be added to the candy department would be some obscure candy bar which would yield only 30 per cent.

If this were the case, the contribution-return on investment would be greater at the margin in the fountain pen department than in the candy department even though the *average* contribution is larger in the latter department. Under these circumstances, inventory investment funds could be profitably shifted out of the candy department and into the fountain pens department, thus actually increasing the disparity between the two *average* contributions.

"OK IN THEORY, BUT . . ."

To summarize to this point, it has been argued that, assuming (1) that funds available for investment in inventory are given, (2) that the demand functions for the items in each department are independent of each other and of the demand functions for items in other departments, and (3) that in each department investment in inventory is at or beyond the point of diminishing marginal returns, then profits are maximized in the retail firm if the contribution-return on investment is equated at the margin among items and among departments.

But there is the ancient complaint, "That's OK in theory, but in practice . . ." In the paragraphs which follow certain aspects of the application of the suggested procedure will be taken up.

LOSS LEADERS

First, is it realistic to assume that the investment in inventory is fixed? Since this is assumed only for the short run, it is probably not unrealistic. If it does appear in the short run that the contribution-return on inventory investment is greater than the cost of capital, an expansion of the investment in inventory is called for. But once the funds are in hand or budgeted in total, the allocation among department and items can be carried out as though

---

[9] It is possible that the investment in a department could be so small that customers would overlook the department entirely; under these circumstances increments in investment might be associated with increases in the contribution percentage return on investment over a certain range. See F. E. Balderston, "Assortment Choice in Wholesale and Retail Marketing," *Journal of Marketing*, **21** (October, 1956), 182.

that total were fixed. This is surely not a serious departure from reality.

The second assumption is probably justified also. It is undoubtedly true that as the investment in a given department increases from zero, up to some point the contribution-return may increase. This is saying only that a retailer is motivated to establish a department of some minimum size or else not establish it at all. We assume here that the retailer senses with reasonable accuracy what this critical investment level is for each department and that he operates any given department only if his investment in that department is going to be beyond this minimum size.

The third assumption of course cannot be dismissed so easily. The existence of the interdependence of demand among departments, which gives rise to sales in Department A to the customer who came into the store primarily to buy something in Department B, is widely recognized. How can the capital budgeting approach be adjusted to take this feature of retailing into account?

One approach, often found in practice, is to insist that each department "stand on its own two feet," since it is so difficult to determine to what extent demand for the item in Department B really influences the sales in Department A. This presumes, in effect, that all departments benefit to the same degree from the joint demand conditions. More precisely, it presumes that sacrificing a given contribution per dollar of investment in Department B has the same effect on sales in all other departments as does a sacrifice of the same contribution per dollar of investment in any other department.

A second approach, which might be of some use in this context, views the leader department as a type of advertising. The total dollar contribution sacrificed because a given department exists rather than the best alternative use of that space is the cost of generating greater sales in other departments than would otherwise be the case. If the amount of contribution sacrificed can be estimated, then this means of advertising can be evaluated as would other types of advertising.

TESTS FOR DEMAND

To learn which of these approaches is justified, a number of tests of cross-elasticity of demand might be attempted. First, the historical scales might possibly indicate whether the department sales, e.g., the annual "white sale," have any effect on the sales of other departments. A crude estimate of the dollar of contribution generated in other departments per dollar of contribution lost in the "sale" department would give some notion as to the promotional effect of the margins lost. Or charge accounts could be checked during the period of such sales to ascertain what else was bought on the day of the sale by people whose accounts show purchases in the sale department.

As a first approximation, it could be assumed that an account showing, say, $20 of purchases in other departments on the day a $4 purchase was made in the sale department, indicates $20 of sales which would not have been made had it not been for the sale. The illustrative customer in this case might have bought some if not all of the $20 worth of purchases even if there had been no sale. And some sales in other departments may have been directly traceable to customers who came into the store to look at the sale items even though they did not buy them. Whether the bias of the first sort is greater than or less than the bias of the second sort is difficult to say.

If the sale is one such that a high proportion of people who came to look at the sale item buy something on sale, then the bias of the first sort is likely to be greater than the bias of the second type. It is apparent that these interrelationships are of the most complex sort. But they are interrelationships which must be considered by the retailer regardless of his use of the contribution-return on investment as an index of performance. They are not complexities which arise because of the use of the contribution index. Rather the use of the contribution-return on investment merely exposes to brighter light a problem which has actually been there all the time.

Suppose that application of the direct costing technique to individual lines of merchandise in the illustrative book store were to reveal, as it well might, that the marginal contribution-return on investment in books is far below the marginal contribution-return in the candy and other departments. What should be done about it? In this particular case, undoubtedly the management would reason that since it is a student-owned book store it should carry sufficient books to meet some stipulated and presumably high proportion of student book needs even though this may not be definitely consistent with short-run profit maximization for the store.

WHAT ABOUT CUSTOMER SERVICE?

This service criterion, then, rather than the marginal contribution-return on investment criterion, should set the size of the book department investment. The remaining departments, however, could be balanced by means of the contribution-return on inventory investment criterion. This policy would be based on the assumption that these other departments support each other and that no single department is a greater traffic builder than is any other.

If it is felt strongly that the existence of the candy, tobacco and magazines department causes greater sales in the other departments, then investment in this department might be pushed beyond the point at which its marginal contribution rate would be equated with that of the other departments.

This leaves one main question unanswered: Should not the dollars of contribution per square foot play some role in the decision to increase or to decrease investment in a department? The answer is in the negative if the retailer has a justifiable and rigid rule setting the inventory density per square foot in each department. But presumably this is generally not the case, and this introduces a complication into the capital budgeting solution to the merchandise management problem.

SPACE BUDGETING

The emphasis on the dollars of contribution per square foot of floor space no doubt arises because some retailers recognize that it is floor space, and not capital, which is the really limiting factor in their operations. The problem of merchandise management is, then, a two-fold one; space budgeting as well as capital budgeting is involved. If a retailer does not wish to consider changing the space allocated to various departments in the given planning period, then the square budgeting problems are set aside and the capital budgeting approach can be employed.

But suppose the retailer is willing to consider changes in the amount of space alloted to various departments. Ignoring for the moment the restrictions on changes in sizes of departments, how might the problem be viewed? Assume that Department A is estimated to be earning $100 contribution on the marginal square foot while Department B is earning only $50. If it were practical to shift one square foot out of

Department B (thus reducing B's total contribution by $50) and into Department A (thus increasing A's total contribution by $100), the whole operation would be generating an additional $50 contribution just because of this shift in space. But presumably this contribution from the marginal square foot of space falls off in any department as it is increased in size, while the contribution of the marginal square foot increases in any department is reduced in size. The shifting of floor space, ideally, between Departments A and B in the above example, would continue until Department A is so large relative to B that the dollars of contribution from the marginal square foot in the two departments are roughly equal.

Let us assume for the sake of argument that these are equated at $70 per square foot in each of the two departments in question. Assume further that Department A shows an average inventory investment per square foot of $140 while Department B's average inventory investment is only $70. A's marginal contribution percentage return on investment is only 50% compared with B's 100%. This would suggest that if the nature of the merchandise and store policy permit the density of merchandise, i.e., the inventory investment per square foot, should be increased in Department B and decreased in Department A. If this is done, the dollars of contribution of the marginal square foot would be reduced in Department A and increased in Department B, thus warranting a shift of some space from A to B.

It appears that under apparently reasonable assumptions about the shape of the contribution function, both space and capital can be allocated among departments in such a manner as to yield a single optimum solution, at which point the marginal contribution percentage returns are equated for all departments and the dollars of contribution of the marginal space are also equated for all departments.[10]

In actual cases, of course, one finds that retailers are faced with certain restrictions on the allocation of space among departments. Furthermore, they may have certain well-founded policies which restrict the possibilities for varying the inventory investment per square foot in a given department. One would scarcely expect to find the application of the

---

[10] I am indebted to Saul H. Hymans of the University of California, Berkeley, for working out the formal solution to this problem. His work appears in the Mathematical Appendix.

logic of this paper to an actual case to result in equality of the estimated marginal returns.

However the reasoning suggested here, if applied to a firm's present operations, might well reveal certain departments which are clearly far short of or far beyond optimum size. The objective of the capital budgeting approach to merchandise management is not to identify for any given retailer an exact, pinpoint optimum solution to the problem of balance among departments, but rather to provide a guide for avoiding really bad decisions and for moving toward the optimum.

CONCLUSIONS

The usual measures of performance of individual lines of merchandise and of departments, such as percentage gross margin, sales per square foot and rate of stock turn, are all inherently inadequate when used alone. The contribution return on inventory investment, however, is a much more inclusive and therefore useful measure. Assuming (1) fixed inventory investment, (2) independence of demand among departments and among lines within departments, and (3) that investment in any one department or line of merchandise is pushed at least to the point of diminishing marginal returns, then profits are maximized if the contribution return, expressed as a percentage of investment, is equated at the margin. The first and third assumptions are not unrealistic, at least for the short run. The second one causes difficulties which cannot easily be surmounted. These difficulties, however, do not arise because of the use of the contribution return on investment as a criterion of performance, but rather have been a headache for retail managers all through the years.

It appears that the problem of capital budgeting can be solved simultaneously with the problem of space budgeting, although precise solutions involving equality at the margin will presumably never result because of restrictions arising from the nature of the store layout and of the firm's merchandising policies. Nevertheless the capital budgeting point of view would appear to be a worthwhile point of departure for consideration of the nagging problem of balance among departments.

DISCUSSION QUESTION

The reader should compare the discussion in this article with that in Professor Dalrymple's article (Part X, Article 3). The myopic result of concentrating on "gross margins" as an evaluative criterion has never been more effectively stated than in the quotation Professor Holton cites, "We love that markup—but we hate that turnover." The position taken is that "contribution" dollars expressed as "an annual percentage return on the inventory investment, may be the best available all-purpose criterion of performance of the individual department."

Professor Holton develops the simple formulation:

$$C = 100 \times \frac{(S - W - D)}{I}$$

Identify the following elements in this formula:
(a) stock turnover
(b) cost of goods sold
(c) gross margin percentage.

2. Departmental and Item Profitability for Retailers

WILLIAM H. HOFFMAN, JR., and DONALD E. VAUGHN

Expense center accounting, developed a few years ago, is being refined and expanded into a technique called merchandise management accounting, which offers new possibilities in the management services field.

The worth of the certified public accountant's advice in rendering managerial services for a client-manufacturer must be predicated upon sound historical financial information and the realism with which it is applied to present and future situations. If the data are unavailable or inaccurate in substance, or if the over-all approach of the client is misguided or impractical, the resulting product may possess questionable value. Fortunately, improvements in cost accounting techniques have enabled practitioners to guide manufacturers in arriving at broader and more effective managerial decisions.

Yet there remains in the business world of today one area where the accountant has just barely begun to show his full potential. Several reasons exist as to why retailers, particularly department stores, have tended to lag behind manufacturers in the refinement and application of more meaningful accounting techniques. First, the wide variety and number of products handled by most retail outlets serves as a deterrent to unit cost computations. Second, too much emphasis continues to be placed upon the calculation of departmental net profit or loss. Under conventional accounting procedures most widely in use, the departmental income statement involves the troublesome and frequently arbitrary allocations of fixed store-wide expenses. Third, inadequate attention is paid to an accurate determination and use of item profitability. When the individual product is considered in making merchandising decisions, all too often the costs projected are based

upon percentage figures derived from departmental averages. Fourth, the grouping and affixing of responsibility for service expenses has not always followed the course that would lay stress upon productivity and maximum control.

The foregoing problems are not subject to quick and easy solutions. In fact, the uniqueness of the retail industry seems to indicate that managerial decisions based upon accounting data will never achieve the certainty or the degree of reliability possible in manufacturing operations. Yet the past decade has seen the formulation of three related innovations which, when properly understood and applied, will greatly enhance the value of accounting to the retailer.

EXPENSE CENTER ACCOUNTING

The first major change in expense accounting came with the introduction of the *Standard Expense Center Accounting Manual* released by the Controllers' Congress of the National Retail Dry Goods Association in 1954. In this new work the functional classification of expenses (viz., administrative, occupancy, publicity, buying and selling) was eliminated and a natural division of expenses was substituted. The seventeen natural expenses considered essential under the revised system are as follows: payroll, property rentals, advertising, taxes, imputed interest, supplies, services purchased, unclassified (e.g., cash shortages, supper money, travel allowances given job applicants), traveling, communications, pensions, insurance, depreciation, professional services, donations, losses from bad debts, and equipment rentals. Further subdivision of expenses is recom-

♦ SOURCE: Reprinted by permission from the *Journal of Accountancy,* in the August, 1963, issue, pages 50–58.

mended where the problems of the retail establishment would dictate a need for greater detail in accounting information.

Once the reclassification of expenses along suggested lines is accomplished, expense centers can be created which will serve to accumulate costs relating to one principal job of work. Expenses are now to be charged to specific expense centers on a controllable cost basis. As a rule, the cost of doing a job of work consists principally in the allocation of payroll, supplies, services purchased and unclassified.

The number of expense centers to be used by any one particular retailer would depend upon the size of the concern and the desired expense control. Smaller stores would probably have no need for expense centers at all and would place principal reliance upon the natural classification of expenses. For any larger group the *Manual* suggests from fourteen to seventy-one expense centers. These are arranged in three combinations, designated Group B (fourteen expense centers), Group C (thirty-six expense centers), and Group D (seventy-one expense centers). As an example of the greater detail provided by Groups C and D, the expense center, control and accounting, fan out in the manner illustrated in Chart I.

CHART I

Group B		Group C		Group D	
E. C. No.	Account	E. C. No.	Account	E. C. No.	Account
200	Control & Accounting	210	Control & Office Management	211	Control & Office Management
				215	Mail & Messenger Service
		220	Accounting and Payroll	221	General Accounting and Statistical
				225	Timekeeping & Payroll
		230	Accounts Payable	230	Accounts Payable
		240	Cash Office	240	Cash Office
		250	Sales Audit	250	Sales Audit

Table I shows the fourteen expense centers established for Group B and the recommended allocations of natural expenses.

PRODUCTION UNIT ACCOUNTING

By itself expense center accounting offers little help in controlling expenses or in providing a measure of the efficiency of the service departments. The main objective is to reclassify these expenses into more meaningful control accounts. Once this has been accomplished a further refinement may be introduced which will aid in measuring the productivity of these centers by identifiable and controllable units. This refinement is designated production unit accounting and is also set forth in the *Standard Expense Center Accounting Manual*. Single and multiple production units are suggested for certain work centers, depending on the center's complexity and upon the local situation in the subject store. This permits maximum expense control by providing a useful measure of productivity.

Not all expense centers can be subject to the application of production unit accounting. Thus, under the Group D classification of expense centers, only thirty-nine out of seventy-one centers appear to offer a means of measuring productivity. As applied to the previous illustration of the control and accounting classification, the *Manual* makes the following suggestions:

Expense Center	Recommended Measuring Unit
211—Control and Office Management	None
215—Mail and Messenger Service	None
221—General Accounting and Statistical	None
225—Timekeeping and Payroll	Payments made
230—Accounts Payable	Merchandise and expense invoices handled
240—Cash Office	Cash received
250—Sales Audit	Gross sales transactions

TABLE 1—Group B. Chart of Natural Divisions by Expense Center

Expense Center	Payroll	Property Rentals	Advertising	Taxes	Imputed Interest	Supplies	Services Purchased	Unclassified	Traveling	Communications	Pensions	Insurance	Depreciation	Professional Services	Donations	Losses from Bad Debts	Equipment Rentals	Contra Credits
110—General Management	01					06		08	09					14				
120—Real Estate Costs		02		04	05							12	13					19
130—Furniture, Fixture and Equipment Costs				04	05							12	13				17	
140—Other Fixed and Policy Expenses				04				08				12			15			
200—Control and Accounting	01					06	07	08	09	10								
300—Accounts Receivable and Credit	01				05	06	07	08		10						16		
400—Sales Promotion	01		03			06	07	08	09	10				14				
500—Superintendency and Building Operations	01					06	07	08	09	10				14				
610—Personnel	01					06	07	08	09					14				
620—Employee Welfare	01					06	07	08										
630—Supplementary Benefits	01			04				08			11	12						
700—Material Handling	01			04	05	06	07	08				12	13				17	
800—Direct and General Selling	01					06	07	08		10								
900—Merchandising	01				05	06	07	08	09					14				

Source: *Standard Expense Center Accounting Manual.*

Assuming the activity of the expense center is subject to measurement, the results desired can be predicated upon the simple arithmetic formula of work load ÷ productivity (= hours used) × pay rate = payroll expense.

The use of expense center accounting does not require the adoption of production unit accounting. The latter process merely utilizes the information accumulated within expense centers to measure productivity by means of output per man-hour for the purpose of reducing and controlling expenses.

THEORY OF CONTROLLABLE PROFIT

To secure the information necessary by which merchandising decisions can be effectively accomplished, expenses should be analyzed in terms of fixed and variable categories.[1] Variable is defined as those costs resulting from the fact that an item is sold; fixed are those costs that are incurred irrespective of whether or not a specific item is sold. However, no expense is either fixed or variable under all conditions. Thus, if a department manager decided to hire space in an outside warehouse to handle a large shipment of goods, a variable cost would be incurred for the storage of those particular goods. Conversely, if the company owned its own warehouse the amortization costs from the investment in such facilities would constitute a fixed expense.

Dangerous as generalizations may be, the following expenses are usually fixed: real estate costs, furniture, fixture and equipment costs, superintendency and building operations, personnel, employee welfare, professional services, and selling supervision. With like warning, and after certain fixed elements such as supervision and depreciation are removed, the following expenses are usually classified as variable: receiving, warehousing, delivery, selling, advertising, alterations, wrapping and packing, sales audit, and accounts payable. Once these distinctions between fixed and variable expenses are carried out, the variable group will be deducted from gross profit to arrive at a result termed "controllable profit."

The controllable profit concept applied at the departmental level becomes the key to practical application of accounting information. Since fixed expenses are not taken into consideration, the need for difficult and frequently artificial allocation procedures is thereby circumvented. By assigning to the departmental manager only those expenses within his control,[2] a means for establishing meaningful responsibility is made available. Most important of all, introducing controllable profit at the departmental level formulates the predicate necessary for placing increased emphasis upon the individual product. Item profitability, popularly designated merchandise management

accounting, involves the utilization of the individual product's controllable profit to resolve pressing merchandising decisions. This last objective can be accomplished more easily if store personnel and management can be taught to think in terms of controllable profit rather than conventional net profit results.

Table 2 reflects the controllable profit principle as applied to the music department of a department store. Wherever possible, costs have been assigned to the department on the basis of charges actually incurred (direct expenses). In other cases, some means of allocation was necessary. The distribution from the expense centers of account information was accomplished in the following manner:

Merchandising. Includes payroll and expenses of department manager and buyers and 4 per cent imputed interest per annum on the cost value of merchandise inventories at the beginning of each month.

Material Handling. Includes receiving, checking, marking, transfer hauling and delivery of

**TABLE 2. Music Department Departmental Distribution Form
For the Month of July, 19___**

Expense Center Number*		Departmental Total
	Gross Sales	$40,000.00
	Customer Returns	1,200.00
	Net Sales	38,800.00
	Purchases (less discounts)	$ 30,000.00
	Freight In	800.00
	Beginning Inventory	90,000.00
	Goods Available for Sale	120,800.00
	Less Ending Inventory	94,200.00
	Cost of Goods Sold	26,600.00
	Gross Profit on Sales	12,200.00
	Controllable Expenses	
900	Merchandising (Buying and Imputed Interest on Merchandise)	1,100.00
200	Control and Accounting (accounts payable)	150.00
400	Sales Promotion (advertising)	1,280.00
800	Selling	3,880.00
	Alterations and Workrooms (Maintenance)	350.00
700	Material Handling	400.00
300	Accounts Receivable and Credit	400.00
	Total	7,560.00
	Controllable Profits	$ 4,640.00

* Based upon the Group B classification of expense centers as set forth in the *Standard Expense Center Accounting Manual* of the Controllers' Congress of the National Retail Dry Goods Association.

goods held for resale. The expense center records should be maintained in such a way that the average cost of handling different classes of materials can be ascertained and allocated to the appropriate departments.

Control and Accounting. That portion of this expense center which relates to the processing of accounts payable was considered a variable charge. Production unit accounting will establish the necessary cost information based upon the measuring unit of the number of invoices handled. The inclusion of an allocation of sales audit expenses on the basis of the number of sales transactions for the department may also be permissible.

Sales Promotion. Only that portion of advertising and display expense is distributed which directly benefits the department concerned.

Accounts Receivable and Credit. This should be assigned on the basis of the number of charge transactions within the department. Production unit accounting facilitates this distribution by providing the cost per credit sale transaction.

ITEM PROFITABILITY

One of the prime deterrents preventing the calculation of controllable profit of specific products has been the large preponderance of different items that any one department store must carry. Yet, two factors exist that prevent this obstacle from being as formidable as might appear. First, there is no compelling need to determine the profitability of all stocked merchandise. In the absence of the labor- and time-saving procedures of electronic data processing equipment, controllable profit analysis can be limited to the higher priced lines. Second, it is possible to develop within any particular department categories of merchandise sufficiently uniform to show similar experience for such variable costs as receiving, checking and marking, credit, delivery, and others. Thus, there might exist no more than ten or twelve differing costs for a function such as delivery. The range of such unit costs would be established in accordance with the nature of the goods delivered (e.g., bulk, weight, fragile quality). Different products possessing almost identical delivery characteristics could then be assigned the same unit delivery cost. In this manner, the number of available unit costs can be considerably narrowed without any serious sacrifice of accuracy.

Unit costs for variable expenses will be derived from the accounting data provided by expense center and production unit accounting, supplemented by stop-watch observations and reference to specific arrangements such as commission plans and delivery contracts. Once formulated, care must be exercised to see that these costs are periodically revised to enhance their value for projection purposes.

To illustrate the development of item profitability, Table 3 brings together the cost pattern data for four big-ticket products of the music department of a department store. Table 4 then uses the information from Table 3 to determine the controllable profit for each product. As will be noted from Table 4, all products yield some controllable profit, thereby adding to the surplus available for the absorption of storewide fixed expenses. Taken by itself, Table 4 indicates that Product D, because of its high yield, might warrant increased sales effort on the part of management.

REFINEMENTS DETERMINING ITEM PROFITABILITY

In arriving at product controllable profit, certain factors will always be present that defy standard classification and require special attention. Markdowns can prove particularly troublesome in this regard. Departmental averages may prove satisfactory where the indications are that the product will not be accorded unusual treatment. Otherwise, such as in the case of special merchandise intended for discount, separate estimates must be made. Another example where standard cost computations might prove inappropriate would be in the case of determining advertising allowances for special promotional merchandise.

Wherever possible the unit costs that provide the cost patterns for determining item profitability should be expressed in dollar amounts rather than as a percentage of sales. Any other approach might well result in an unnecessary loading of costs among higher priced lines. As an example of what might otherwise occur, the unit delivery expenses listed in Table 3 can be further analyzed. A departmental average for this particular department shows a delivery expense of approximately 1 per cent of retail price. Applying this rate to Product D results in an estimated dollar cost of $17 or approximately three times the amount actually incurred. Further variations among other expenses compound this inaccuracy to the point where management is no

TABLE 3. Music Department Basis for Allocating Controllable Expenses
(Percentages refer to per cents of selling prices)

Expenses	Product A	Product B	Product C	Product D
Purchase Price	65.0%	65.0%	65.0%	65.0%
Freight—in	$ 5.50	$20.00	$20.00	$25.00
Buying	2.0%	2.0%	2.0%	2.0%
Imputed interest (4% per year on cost)				
Control and Accounting	$ 3.00	$ 3.00	$ 3.00	$ 3.00
Sales Promotion	3.2%	3.2%	3.2%	3.2%
Selling	10.0%	10.0%	10.0%	10.0%
Alterations & Workrooms	$32.00	$15.00	$15.00	$20.00
Accounts Receivable & Credit	$ 6.00	$ 6.00	$ 6.00	$ 6.00
Delivery	$ 5.50	$ 5.50	$ 5.50	$ 5.50

longer capable of rendering effective pricing decisions.

The importance of merchandise turnover in retail operations cannot be overemphasized. To be truly significant as a guide to management action, item profitability must be related to the velocity factor. Otherwise, undue importance may be placed upon the higher priced lines that usually tend to yield larger controllable profits. Interjecting the turnover factor to the controllable profit, results derived in Table 4 would produce the following additional information:

	Product A	Product B	Product C	Product D
Annual Turnover	3 times	6 times	4 times	2 times
Annual Contribution to Controllable Profit				
In Dollars	$71.19	$632.58	$568.00	$510.00
As a % of Sales	5.93%	13.18%	14.20%	15.00%
As a % of Initial Investment	27.38%	121.65%	87.38%	46.15%

Evaluation of the velocity rate reveals that Product B, rather than Product D, now possesses the more promising potential for future development.

PRACTICAL APPLICATIONS

The information collected and correlated on cost patterns can be arranged in such a manner as to provide the store buyer with a quick and ready reference for use at the various markets that he may visit. These worksheets, often called "buyers' guides," enable the buyer to make spot decisions on whether or not a particular markup will cover all of the many variable expenses that will be involved in such a purchase. It should be added that the buyers' guide provides the buyer with an excellent weapon for bargaining purposes if in fact the guide reflects that a particular product cannot be profitably handled. The buyer may also be able to secure from the manufacturer or wholesaler any one of the following concessions in lieu of or in addition to price reductions:

1. Freight adjustments (e.g., FOB destination, direct shipments to customers, shipments in carload lots)

2. New or increased advertising allowances

3. Demonstration of the product by the manufacturer's representative

4. Prepackaging or premarking

One form of a buyer's guide, based upon the facts accumulated by Tables 3 and 4, is presented in Table 5. Note that only the first pair of columns would be prepared before the buyer goes to market. The information contained therein is derived from the latest available cost data on the product actually ex-

TABLE 4. Music Department Computation of Controllable Profit

	Product A (Used)	Product B	Product C	Product D
Selling Price	$400.00	$800.00	$1,000.00	$1,700.00
Expenses:				
Purchase Price	260.00	520.00	650.00	1,105.00
Freight—in	5.50	20.00	20.00	25.00
Buying	8.00	16.00	20.00	34.00
Imputed Interest	3.47	3.47	6.50	22.10
Control and Accounting	3.00	3.00	3.00	3.00
Sales Promotion	12.80	25.60	32.00	54.40
Selling Commission	40.00	80.00	100.00	170.00
Alterations and Workrooms	32.00	15.00	15.00	20.00
Accounts Receivable and Credit	6.00	6.00	6.00	6.00
Delivery	5.50	5.50	5.50	5.50
Total Variable Expenses	376.27	694.57	858.00	1,445.00
Controllable Profit	$ 23.73	$105.43	$ 142.00	$ 255.00

perienced by the retailer. The center column would be filled in by the buyer and would serve as his guide for further purchases of this product. The last set of columns will be completed by management once the results of the new acquisition have been determined and will become the basis for a subsequent buyer's guide.[3]

Item profitability has also found use in helping to resolve the following managerial decisions:

1. Arriving at product prices
2. Determining the items to advertise
3. Setting stock quantities
4. Discontinuance of old or acceptance of new products or manufacturer's lines
5. Expense control

Since the quality of the cost data to be used in the various applications of item profitability (i.e., merchandise management accounting) will often spell the success or failure of the particular undertaking, it is imperative that the basic accounting system be examined with great care. If some form of expense center and production unit accounting has already been installed, the war can be considered more than half won. With only slight modification, these accounting systems become the ideal foundation for every conceivable utilization of merchandise management accounting. In fact, it has been said that merchandise management accounting cannot live without expense center and production unit accounting.[4]

Assuming expense center and production unit accounting are in operation, what can be done to convert the cost data available for effective use in merchandise management accounting? In general terms, the conversion process will entail a shifting of controllable costs accumulated on a store-wide basis to the individual products chosen for merchandise management accounting analysis. An ideal step in this transfer of costs would utilize the existing financial reporting procedures of the various selling departments. Thus, the departmental income statement should be modified to reflect controllable profit. Table 2 shows the various expense centers that would be involved (under a Group B classification) in making this assignment of variable expenses to the department. Once a department's controllable costs are determined, analysis and assignment of such costs to the products within that department provide the raw materials necessary for computing item profitability.

CRITICAL ASPECTS

Merchandise management accounting is not an answer for all retailing ills. No one thing can be a cure, considering the complicated facets of the current distribution process. From this standpoint, much of the criticism that is heaped upon this management device is unwarranted. For example, it has been maintained that one of the weaknesses of this concept is that it does not provide a final inventory.[5] This clearly shows a misconception of the true purpose of merchandise management accounting. It is not intended as a sub-

TABLE 5. Estimated Controllable Profit

Dept._____

Item_____

No. of Units_____

List Price_____

	Historical		Buyer's Estimate	Actual	
Merchandise Margin	$280.00	35.0%	$—	$—	—%
Less:					
Freight—In	20.00	2.50	—	—	—
Buying Expense	16.00	2.00	—	—	—
Imputed Interest	3.47	.43	—	—	—
Control of Accounting	3.00	.38	—	—	—
Sales Promotion	25.60	3.20	—	—	—
Sales Commission	80.00	10.00	—	—	—
Alterations and Workroom	15.00	1.87	—	—	—
Accounts Receivable and Credit	6.00	.75	—	—	—
Delivery Expense	5.50	.69	—	—	—
Total	$174.57	21.82%	—	—	—
Controllable Profit	$105.43	13.18%	—	—	—

Date Historical Cost Compiled_____   Buyer_____

Date of Buyer's Estimate_____

Date Actual Cost Compiled_____

stitute for the retail inventory method, and it was therefore never designed to perform the function of providing a final inventory figure.

Valid justification can be found for the criticism that the name "merchandise management accounting" is not really descriptive of what is involved in the concept.[6] Some feel that the emphasis on accounting in the title might restrict the use of this valuable tool to the controller's office. Merchandise managers might thereby be dissuaded from recognizing the full potential of the technique. Some of the recommendations that have been offered for a more descriptive name are as follows: merchandising cost analysis, controllable profit merchandising,[7] item costing, item contribution accounting,[8] and item profitability. Despite the inescapable merit in these suggestions, this process has come to be known as merchandise management accounting, and the likelihood of change seems remote.

One of the greatest alleged faults of merchandise management accounting. In fact, it ness of its cost patterns. First, some have contended that the cost pattern is not an accurate compilation. For example, it has been said that the use of these patterns is "analogous to

measuring tree trunks with micrometers: an interesting but costly procedure with somewhat dubious prognosis for practical application of the results." [9] Granted that if incorrect information is fed into a system, it will produce incorrect results. The fault lies, not with merchandise management accounting, but with the users of the technique. Providing the proper cost information for a proper foundation is not the job of merchandise management accounting but of cost procedures such as expense center and production unit accounting. Second, the critics maintain that there is danger that the cost pattern will become rigid and will not be modified with changing conditions.[10] This is a real possibility, but one that can be avoided by diligent and cautious supervision. Cost patterns should always remain flexible and should be revised whenever unit costs change. Third, complaints are made that item profitability cannot be carried far enough. Unquestionably, unit costs lend themselves better to the handling of staple goods rather than promotional merchandise. Similarly, the large numbers of items that a department store carries generally mean that the setting up of cost patterns has to be limited to hard goods of a big-ticket nature. There exists considerable hope that the installation of modern electronic computers may solve the problem for all kinds of merchandise. The experience of those few stores that have adopted MMA techniques seems to bear out these predictions.[11]

It should be emphasized that MMA is not a neatly wrapped package that can be purchased and easily put into effect. Not only will it require a certain amount of modification for any one particular store, but the basic principles themselves are still in a state of change. The processes that are involved are too new to be kept inflexible. For this reason further experimentation by the individual retailer is urged and can be expected. The fact that the principles of MMA can be introduced to a store on a selective department basis rather than on a store-wide basis will aid in stimulating the aforementioned experimentation.

CONCLUSION

The whole trend of thinking in retailing is on how to curtail distribution costs without impairing profits. When handled properly, expense center accounting, production unit accounting and MMA promise to have great value in improving the efficiency of the retail unit. This desirable objective will be accomplished by:

1. Adopting the natural classification of expenses

2. Establishing expense centers with clear lines of responsibility

3. Formulating units of measurement with which to judge the productivity of expense centers

4. Assigning to sales departments only those variable expenses within the control of the department manager

5. Placing increased emphasis upon the accurate determination of item profitability

6. Effectively utilizing the concept of item profitability to resolve key management decisions

Though several accounting firms have already recognized the potential of applying cost accounting techniques to retail concerns, the value of this approach remains largely unrecognized. Truly, then, this area must be considered as one with the brightest prospects for the future extension of management services by the CPA.

NOTES

[1] Considerable confusion has arisen in differentiating between various classifications of expenses. Thus, expenses have been termed "controllable-noncontrollable," "fixed-variable," "escapable-inescapable," or "direct-indirect." The authors have proceeded upon the assumption that variable expenses are largely controllable, consequently, these two terms are used interchangeably. The classifications of "direct-indirect" and "escapable-inescapable" are not quite as clear and have usually been avoided. However, one must recognize that the directness of an expense unquestionably facilitates its assignment to a particular department or product.

[2] Each store will have to make its own determination as to which expenses can be considered as controllable. Practice varies widely in this regard and the authors' selections are merely suggestions.

[3] To encourage buyers to make effective use of these guides, their performance should be judged through a comparison of the various columns on the buyers' guide. At least one author has further suggested that some or all of the incentive compensation of these buyers be based upon the improvement in controllable profit that can be brought about at the wholesale market. See comment by John I. Gotlinger in *Retail Control*, Vol. 26, No. 1 (September, 1957), p. 151.

[4] Kenneth P. Mages, "M. M. A. Should Supplement Expense Center Accounting," *Journal of Retailing*, Vol. 34, No. 1 (Spring, 1958), p. 52.

[5] William S. Darrow, "Some Practical Restrictions on an M. M. A. Program," *Retail Control*, Vol. 26, No. 6 (February, 1958), p. 64.

[6] Mages, *op. cit.*, p. 30.

[7] Gordon B. Cross, "A Critical Analysis of Merchandise Management Accounting," *Journal of Retailing*, Vol. 34, No. 1 (Spring, 1958), p. 22.

[8] Malcom P. McNair and Eleanor G. Mag, "Pricing for Profit: A Revolutionary Approach to Retail Accounting," *Harvard Business Review*, Vol. 35 (May-June, 1957), p. 111.

[9] Joseph S. Friedlander, "Perspectives on Merchandise Management Accounting," *The New York Retailer*, Vol. 10, No. 5 (December, 1957), p. 3.

[10] Cross, *op. cit.*

[11] The results of favorable experience with furniture can be found in R. E. L. Johnson's comments in *Retail Control*, Vol. 26, No. 6 (February, 1958),

p. 45. For the results of experience with soft goods lines see the comments of Edward B. Cagle in the same issue of *Retail Control*, p. 52. For an interesting discussion of the utility of item profitability in food stores see the address by Robert I. Jones, "Manufacturer and Distributor Brands In Food Stores—A Proposed Study on the Evaluation of Profit Performance," delivered before the Grocery Manufacturers of America, Midyear Meeting— White Sulphur Springs, June 10, 1959.

DISCUSSION QUESTIONS

Expense center accounting, production unit accounting and the concept of "controllable" profits comprise "merchandise management accounting." This technique offers great promise in both the planning of merchandise assortments and in the diagnosis of "troubled" operations.

1. What are the practical applications of merchandise management accounting?
2. What are the weaknesses of MMA?

3. Quantitative Methods of Measuring Merchandising Performance in Selected Department Stores

DOUGLAS J. DALRYMPLE

The effective design and operation of merchandising control systems are essential to the profitable operation of retail organizations. Retailers have used and are using many different measuring devices to evaluate their merchandising performance. Stock turnover, sales per employee, gross margin, sales per square foot, markon, controllable margin, and profits as a percent of sales are only a few of the many ratios that can be used to guide the efforts of retailers.

The extreme variety of measures available and the subtle differences among them have raised several pertinent questions. Are some of the measures more important than others? Are some measures more appropriate to particular situations or firms? What are the factors that influence the choice of measures? Is the buyer who obtains the highest gross margin percentage doing a better job than the buyer who obtains a high contribution in gross margin dollars? Further, how should the buyer balance markon against stock turnover to achieve his sales and profit objectives?

This study was designed to answer these and other questions relating to the measurement of merchandising performance in department stores. The primary concern of this study was to provide some basic information on what control factors were being used and how these factors function in a department store environment.

HYPOTHESES

An analysis of published materials on merchandising performance measurement and pre-liminary interviews with department store buyers led to the development of a set of hypotheses. These hypotheses do not represent an exhaustive listing of all unsolved problems in the area of performance measurement, but they do represent a list of statements worthy of research effort. The first hypothesis suggested that although retail firms may have similar goals, the unique character of each firm produces differences in the utilization of merchandising control factors. A second hypothesis proposed that the utilization of retail performance measures changes with the job level of the executive due to differences in responsibilities. Additional hypotheses were concerned with the extent to which the more recently developed control factors have been integrated into retail operations and how the emphasis on performance factors has changed over time. Two other hypotheses dealt with the impact of salary systems and centralization of buying on the utilization of merchandising control factors.

RESEARCH PROCEDURE

Empirical data to test the hypotheses were collected during personal interviews with department store executives. The individual firms that participated in the study were obtained through contacts made by the National Retail Merchants Association. A total of 111 executives from 11 firms cooperated in the study. The sample was characteristic of California department stores and included firms from the San Francisco, Los Angeles, and San Diego metropolitan areas. The firms ranged in size from about $5 million to over $100 million in annual sales and 10 of the 11 firms operated more than one store.

♦ SOURCE: Reprinted by permission from the American Marketing Association, in *Reflections in Progress in Marketing*, L. George Smith, Editor, 1964, pages 119–131.

DEPARTMENT STORE GOALS

The issue of homogeneity of department store goals was examined by asking the executives what they felt were the most important overall objectives of their companies and tabulating their answers by individual firms (Figure 1). This analysis showed that there was fairly close agreement among executives of different firms with regard to their perception of company objectives. This was particularly true with respect to profits. This factor ranked as the most frequently stated goal by executives of six firms and was the second most frequently mentioned goal in four other firms.

DIFFERENCES IN THE UTILIZATION OF CONTROL FACTORS

Possible differences in the utilization of control factors were studied by asking the executives what control factors were being used and tabulating their responses by separate companies (Figure 2). This analysis showed that there were few differences among the eleven firms with regard to the ranking of sales volume. It was the most frequently mentioned factor in five firms, it was second in five other firms, and it ranked third in one firm. There was also considerable agreement among the firms on the general importance of the factors which ranked

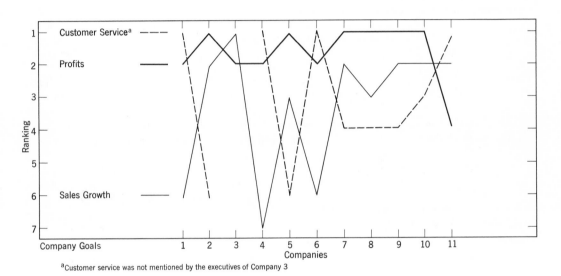

FIG. 1. Rankings of department store goals by company.

second through sixth, yet exact positions in the rankings varied somewhat among firms. It is interesting to note that while profit was the most important overall goal as seen by merchandising executives, sales volume was the most frequently mentioned factor used to control merchandising operations. Profits ranked fifth behind sales volume, stock control, promotions, and markdowns. This result may be related to the frequency with which profit and sales data are made available for use by merchandising executives.

UTILIZATION OF CONTROL FACTORS AT DIFFERENT JOB LEVELS

The survey results indicated that three levels of merchandising executives exhibited fairly

close agreement concerning the use of merchandising control factors (Figure 3). The seven most frequently mentioned control factors reported by buyers were also the seven most frequently mentioned by divisional merchandise managers. Also these same seven factors occupied seven out of the first eight rank positions mentioned by the general merchandise managers. This uniformity in control factor usage was substantiated by data from another question where the executives were asked to choose from matched pairs of performance factors (Table 1). In general, the buyers agreed with the divisional and general merchandise managers on the relative importance of the control factors. Buyers' preferences corresponded with their superiors' choices in seven of the eight pairs of performance measures.

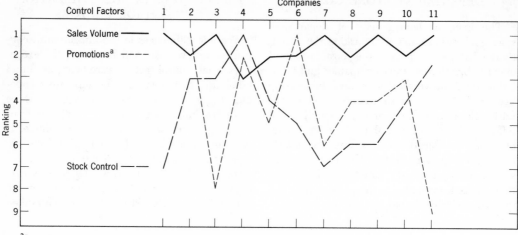

^aPromotions were not mentioned as a control factor by the executive of Company 1

FIG. 2. Rankings of merchandising control factors by company.

The only difference occurred in the third pairing, where buyers showed a slight preference for stock turnover, and the divisional and general merchandise managers picked sales growth 70 percent of the time.

THE IMPORTANCE OF STOCK TURNOVER

It was clear from the survey that stock turnover was only of secondary importance to merchandising executives in department store organizations. Although stock turnover appeared as an answer in eight questions, it received so few mentions it could not be considered an essential control factor. In a question concerning duties and responsibilities, turnover ranked fifteenth among the answers given and it was mentioned by only twelve executives. In a question on control factor usage, stock turnover ranked seventh and was mentioned by only 23 of the 111 executives interviewed in the study. Among changes in performance measures reported by the executives "more emphasis on stock turnover" ranked sixth with nine mentions. In another question stock turnover ranked twentieth among the organizational goals stated by the merchandising executives. When stock turnover was compared directly with sales growth, gross margin, and the profit ratio, it was not preferred by the executives in any of the pairings. In fact,

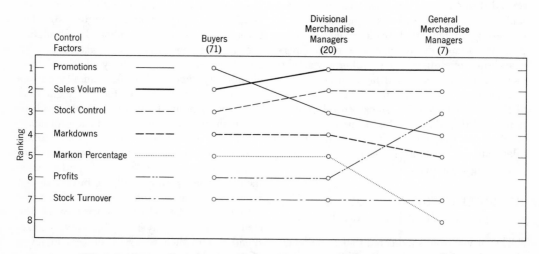

FIG. 3. Rankings of merchandising control factors by different managerial levels.

TABLE 1. Executive Preferences for Paired Control Factors

Pair Number	Paired Merchandising Control Factors	Numbers of Executives Preferring Each Factor			
		Buyers (71)	Divisional Merchandising Managers (20)	General Merchandising Managers (7)	Total All Executives (98)
1	Realized Gross Margin Percentage	22	5	3	30
	Net Profits as a Percent of Sales	44	14	4	62[a]
	No Preference	1	1	0	2
	No Answer	4	0	0	4
2	Net Profits Per Sq. Foot of Selling Area	19	5	3	27
	Net Profits Per Dollar of Inventory	47	14	4	65[a]
	No Preference	1	1	0	4
	No Answer	4	0	0	2
3	Sales as a Percent of Previous Year	31	14	5	50
	Stock Turnover	35	6	2	43
	No Preference	1	0	0	1
	No Answer	4	0	0	4
4	Net Profits as a Percent of Sales	37	17	6	60[b]
	Net Profits as a Percent of Invested Capital	29	3	1	33
	No Preference	0	0	0	0
	No Answer	5	0	0	5
5	Realized Gross Margin Percentage	44	12	7	63[a]
	Stock Turnover	21	6	0	27
	No Preference	2	2	0	4
	No Answer	4	0	0	4
6	Net Profits Per Dollar of Inventory	44	13	5	62[b]
	Controllable Profits Per Dollar of Inventory	23	6	2	31
	No Preference	0	1	0	1
	No Answer	4	0	0	4
7	Stock Turnover	15	4	1	20
	Net Profits as a Percent of Sales	50	14	6	70[a]
	No Preference	2	2	0	4
	No Answer	4	0	0	4
8	Net Profits as a Percent of Invested Capital	34	10	4	48
	Net Profits as a Percent of Total Capital	22	8	3	33
	No Preference	1	0	0	1
	No Answer	14	2	0	16

[a] The chance that this factor was not significantly preferred to the paired control factor is one in a thousand.

[b] The chance that this factor was not significantly preferred to the paired control factor is one in two hundred.

gross margin and the net profit ratio were significantly preferred to stock turnover (Table 1). The subordinate status of stock turnover was also shown by the fact that when department stores were confronted by higher expenses, the great majority of the executives emphasized higher markons rather than increased stock turnover. The typical attitude was shown by the remarks of one buyer who said he found stock turnover too difficult to use in making merchandising decisions. He felt that markon was more dependable than stock turnover in controlling merchandising operations.

Some support for the importance of stock turnover was provided by the remarks of nine buyers who said they would buy low markon merchandise if the item had a potential for high turnover. Nine other executives said that turnover is where you make your money. One indicated that competitors prevented increases in markons and that turnover was the only way to increase profits. It would appear that a small minority of the merchandising executives interviewed in this study believed that stock turnover was an important control factor, but to most executives it was only a vague concept of secondary consequence.

The fact that stock turnover was not important to merchandising executives suggests that additional research is needed to determine exactly how this factor influences profits. Department store executives' preoccupation with markon may be entirely justified, but increased emphasis on stock turnover might increase the rate of return on capital for the firm. It is entirely possible that stock turnover is not important to the successful operation of department stores, but the validity of this statement should be established by research rather than by the accidental design of the retail system of merchandise accounting.

THE MARKON PERCENTAGE

The merchandising executives interviewed in this study placed considerably more emphasis on the markon percentage than they did on stock turnover. This was shown by the many executives who mentioned markon in response to questions on pricing procedures. The importance attached to this factor would seem to be related to the stress it receives in the retail system of merchandise accounting. This system focuses on the production of a planned gross margin percentage and markon

percentages are therefore useful control devices to assure that the desired gross margin will be attained. The importance of the markon percentage was also strengthened by the practice of requiring buyers to put the planned markon percentage on all orders so that the merchandise manager could check the markon when he signed the orders.

So great was the emphasis on markon that the amount of markon available determined which items were bought, promoted, or eliminated. Fourteen buyers indicated that if an item did not allow an average or better markon they did not buy it. Several indicated that they wanted a high profit as a percent of sales and low markon merchandise would not help them. One buyer said that low markon merchandise was not promoted and three other buyers said that they dropped low markon merchandise. Two buyers did not buy volume items at less than average markon percentages and several others pushed high markon merchandise. The drive for markon prompted fifty-five buyers to take higher markons on confined, imported, or private label merchandise where customers lacked pricing knowledge. The effects of stressing markon were also reflected by buyers who had items redesigned to allow more markon and other buyers who asked manufacturers to raise suggested list prices so that more markon could be obtained. Fifteen other buyers indicated they try to get all "the traffic will bear" and one buyer said that department stores had not approached an upper limit as far as markon was concerned. These results clearly indicate that the markon percentage was one of the most important control factors used by the executives in this study.

CHANGES IN PERFORMANCE MEASURES

It was anticipated that department stores would be currently stressing different measures of merchandising performance than have been emphasized in the past. This proposition was evaluated with data gathered from a question which asked the executives if they had observed any changes in performance measures. While a majority of those interviewed believed that changes had occurred, the only response that received a significant number of mentions was that higher markons were needed. Thirty-four executives followed this answer with the remark that expenses of doing business had increased as a percent of sales. This response supports the need for higher markon percentages, but it does not prove that a change has occurred in the use of this control factor. It appeared that this quest for more markon did not represent a change in control factor emphasis, but merely reflected a change in the *amount* of markon that was acceptable. In general the study was unable to detect any significant changes in the emphasis on merchandising control factors.

SALARY SYSTEMS AND MERCHANDISING CONTROL

The relationship between methods of compensation and merchandising control was studied by examining the performance measures stressed by executives and the payment systems used in different firms. The eleven firms in the study all employed salary plus bonus plans for their merchandising executives. The three factors emphasized in the bonus plans were frequently mentioned as merchandising factors. Sales, for example, was the most frequently mentioned response to a question on control factor usage. Profits ranked fifth and gross margin tenth as answers to this same question. In addition executives in the firms that emphasized profits and gross margin in their bonus plans ranked these factors higher as measures of merchandising performance than the average of the eleven firms. These data suggest that the factors used in calculating executive bonuses were also important control measures employed by merchandising executives in the execution of their jobs.

UTILIZATION OF RECENTLY DEVELOPED CONTROL FACTORS

The executives' responses to the survey questions failed to indicate any appreciation for some of the more recently developed control factors that emphasize item contributions or contribution returns on inventory investments. Further when the executives were asked to choose between eight pairs of performance factors, the traditional measures were preferred in six of seven test pairs (Table 1). The merchandising executives appeared to be well satisfied with the present system of merchandising control. When they were asked to suggest changes to improve the system, almost all of the answers called for improved stock control methods and for better physical handling of the merchandise. None of the executives suggested a change to Merchandise Management Accounting or to the use of the ratio of contribution profits to inventory investment. Despite the widespread discussion of Merchandise Management Accounting for the past seven years, there was no evidence that any of the ideas from this system have been accepted by merchandising executives. It would appear that the retail system of merchandise accounting is firmly embedded in the thinking of department store executives and that any basic changes in the system are apt to be accepted slowly.

CENTRALIZATION AND MERCHANDISING CONTROL

A study of the impact of decentralization on merchandising control was hampered by the fact that only one firm used decentralized buying. All of the other organizations used a centralized system of merchandise acquisition. When the survey results for the decentralized firm were compared with those for the centralized firms, it was obvious that virtually the same performance factors were being used by both groups. Because of the limited data available, a more complete analysis of this issue was not possible.

CONCLUSIONS

This research project was designed to study the utilization of quantitative merchandising control factors in department stores. It was expected that the investigation would show that different performance measures were being used by different firms and that executives at different job levels emphasized separate factors. It was found, however, that the department stores in this study all used the same control factors and the factors were employed at all three levels of management studied. Differences in the size of the firms, the type of merchandise, and in the sex of the buyers had little influence on the use of merchandising control factors.

It was anticipated that the factors emphasized by the salary system would influence executive behavior and the research data supported this hypothesis. It was also believed that some of the newer control factors would not be widely used by merchandising executives. The study showed the newer measures were not used at all and that traditional control factors dominated the thinking of merchandising executives. The data revealed an almost universal reliance on the markon percentage as the most discriminating guide to executive action. Even though the executives said that profits and sales volume were important, markon was clearly one of the most frequently used factors in making merchandising decisions. The amount of markon available determined what items were bought, what items were promoted, and what items were dropped. Markon also influenced the proportions of private-label and imported merchandise that was included in the merchandise mix. Stock turnover, in comparison, was almost completely ignored in making merchandising decisions.

The widespread use of traditional merchandising control factors in department stores may indicate that these factors are the most important considerations in the achievement of retail profit goals. This study suggests that conformity in the use of these factors is produced by the retail accounting system, but there is not enough information to draw a firm conclusion on this issue. It should, therefore, be the objective of future research to identify precisely the role and importance of all merchandising performance factors. Only when the merchandise executive knows the relationship between the various control factors and his company's profit objectives, will he be able to produce an optimum solution to the problem of how to utilize effectively quantitative decision criteria.

DISCUSSION QUESTIONS

This article indicates the preferences of different management levels in department stores for particular merchandising control factors. The preferences of buyers, divisional merchandise managers, and general merchandise managers are observed. The merchandise control factors involved are:

(a) realized gross margin percentages
(b) net profits on a percentage of sales
(c) net profits per square foot of selling area
(d) net profits per dollar of inventory
(e) sales as a percentage of previous year
(f) stock turnover
(g) net profits as a percentage of invested capital

1. Since this article involves a sample of department stores, would you expect the executives who were respondents to place great or little emphasis on stock-turnover as a control device? Why?
2. How would you expect department store executives to feel regarding the importance of the amount of gross margin? Why?

4. Determining Compensating Sales Quantities for Price and Cost Changes

ALAN M. FROMMER

It is surprising how often decisions regarding changes in sales volume are made on an intuitive basis, rather than on derived data. Usually decisions caused by a change in market conditions are thought of as distinct from those caused by internal conditions, yet they are both very much related to the same factors. These are price, cost and sales volume (quantity). Clearly what is needed by anyone intending to make a price or a cost-change decision is an understanding of the effects of this change. They can be described by two double-barreled questions:

1. If my unit cost increases (decreases), how many more (less) units must (can) I sell and still keep my total dollar contribution constant?

2. If I increase (decrease) my unit price, how many less (more) units can (must) I sell and still keep my total dollar contribution constant?

In dealing with these factors we are talking only about variable costs. Fixed costs are extraneous to the analysis. It is to be remembered that the method is for short-run decisions. Therefore, fixed costs are assumed not to change. No attempt is made here to cover the long-run effects that always have the implication of the "human element" and thus are always hard to measure or, for that matter, impossible to predict with any accuracy.

The relationships derived in this paper are true and serve as a meaningful basis for marketing decisions. It would be an overstatement to say that they provide answers. No one piece of information can do that. Yet the analysis defines the limits to our range of decisions. In

this respect, a basis is provided for marketing decision making. Such a basis is needed. Usually we find ourselves thinking of a loss or a gain in volume without specifics.

All too familiar is the situation in which a salesman will say that he can boost sales 15 percent if the home office will cut the price 5 percent. This sounds good on the surface but is the increase enough to cover the lower realization on each sale? Where will the total profits of the company be in comparison to where they are now? Another common proposal is to increase price. There are the arguments that more revenue will result and that people will still buy the product. In contrast, there are the arguments against, such as that people will switch brands. Arguments on both sides have merit, but only analysis will decide the question at hand. For example, if we are contemplating a price increase, we must know how many fewer units can be sold at the increased price without changing our present profit position. Anything sold beyond our allowable drop in volume will then be to our advantage.

THE EQUATIONS

Two equations are presented below, from which three cross reference tables have been prepared. The quantity needed to sustain profit margins after a change in price or cost can be described by the equations:

Change in price

$$\frac{Q_2}{Q_1} = \frac{\mu}{\mu + (1 - \gamma)\kappa}$$

Change in cost

$$\frac{Q_2}{Q_1} = \frac{\mu_1}{\mu_2}$$

The symbols represent:

• SOURCE: Reprinted by permission from the *N. A. A. Bulletin,* in the May, 1963, issue, pages 35–42.

Q_1 = Original quantity sold at one price. This is the average or standard price where different prices exist for the same product

Q_2 = New quantity at which total dollar contribution for the item described by Q_1 will be the same at the new profit margin as at the old.

μ_1 = Original profit margin percent (contribution) of the item at the standard price.

μ_2 = New profit margin percent (contribution) of the item at a new standard price or cost.

γ = Percentage to sales of costs (cash discounts and allowances) variable with sales.

κ = Percentage change in price.

Any reader of this article who would rather do so may, without loss to the practical value of the presentation, skip the next section, which deals as compactly as possible with the derivation of the equations. When that has been taken care of for the benefit of those interested, we go on to the tables which the equations permit us to construct and the use of these tables to assist in solution of practical problems of cost and price change, especially those of planning.

DERIVATION OF THE EQUATIONS

We want to determine the relationship between a new quantity to be sold and the quantity now being sold (Q_2/Q_1). This ratio will tell us what must happen to compensate for the gain or loss in contribution due to a price or cost change. We can state the underlying relationship as follows, where P is selling price and C is cost:

$$(P_1 - C_1)Q_1 = (P_2 - C_2)Q_2$$

We will now set up the four underlying equations we need. Rearranging the foregoing terms we get the first equation:

$$(1) \qquad \frac{Q_2}{Q_1} = \frac{P_1 - C_1}{P_2 - C_2}$$

Before proceeding we must derive certain relationships between P_1, C_1, P_2 and C_2. First, it is known that the percentage change in price (κ) is a function of P_1 and P_2. Thus the second equation is:

$$(2) \qquad \kappa = \frac{P_2 - P_1}{P_1}$$

(express as percent)

Second, the profit margin (μ) for any product is a function of P and C. Thus we have:

$$(3) \qquad \mu = \frac{P - C}{P}$$

(express as percent)

The last relationship to be derived is between the original cost and the new cost when price changes. This is derived from direct manufacturing expense, plus expense for cash discounts and general allowances, with these latter items expressed as a percent of gross sales, designated as percent gamma (γ). Thus the magnitude of this expense per unit will vary with the change in price per unit. Hence the equation relating C_1 and C_2 will be:

$$(4) \qquad C_1 = C_2 + \gamma(P_1 - P_2)$$

Change in price. Our objective is to develop from equation (1) a relationship expressing Q_2/Q_1 when price changes, by stating the relationship in the knowns of percent present margin and percent price change. In equation (1) we can substitute values obtained from equations (2) to (4) by rearrangement. Substituting equation (2) for P_2, equation (3) for C_1, and equation (4) for C_2 we have:

$$\frac{Q_2}{Q_1} = \frac{P_1 - (P_1 - P_1\mu)}{(P_1\kappa + P_1) - [C_1 - \gamma(P_1 - P_2)]}$$

$$\frac{Q_2}{Q_1} = \frac{P_1\mu}{(P_1\mu + P_1) - [C_1 - \gamma(P_1 - P_2)]}$$

The next substitution is equation (3) for C_1:

$$\frac{Q_2}{Q_1} = \frac{P_1\mu}{(P_1\kappa + P_1) - (P_1 - P_1\kappa) + \gamma(P_1 - P_2)}$$

or

$$\frac{Q_2}{Q_1} = \frac{P_1\mu}{P_1\kappa + P_1\mu + \gamma(P_1 - P_2)}$$

The last substitution is equation (2) for P_2:

$$\frac{Q_2}{Q_1} = \frac{P_1\mu}{P_1\kappa + P_1\mu + \gamma P_1 - \gamma(P_1 + P_1\kappa)}$$

or

$$\frac{Q_2}{Q_1} = \frac{P_1\mu}{P_1\kappa(1 - \gamma) + P_1\mu}$$

We get our price-change equation, already presented:

$$\frac{Q_2}{Q_1} = \frac{\mu}{\mu + (1 - \gamma)\kappa}$$

Thus, to keep the total contribution constant when price changes, the ratio of the new quantity to be sold (Q_2) to the present quantity being sold (Q_1) must be at least as much as the present margin percentage (μ) is to itself, plus the percent change in price (κ) times one minus the factor (γ) representing costs variable with sales price.

Change in cost—In the foregoing development price was a variable. It is now a constant, and cost changes. We can again start with equation (1). Because price is constant we can drop the subscripts from P_1 and P_2, with the following result:

$$\frac{Q_2}{Q_1} = \frac{P - C_1}{P - C_2}$$

But we know from equation (3) that:

$$C = P - P\mu$$

Substituting:

$$\frac{Q_2}{Q_1} = \frac{P - (P - P\mu_1)}{P - (P - P\mu_2)}$$

or

$$\frac{Q_2}{Q_1} = \frac{\mu_1}{\mu_2}$$

Thus, the change in sales quantity required to keep total dollar contribution constant, due to a change in cost, must be as the ratio of the original margin (μ_1) is to the new margin (μ_2).

THE TABLES

Having the equations describing the effect on volume (keeping profit constant) when price or cost changes, what is needed is to put them into a quick reference form. Exhibits 1 to 3 are tables similar to those used on road maps for finding the distance between two points. Exhibits 1 and 2 are, respectively, increase-in-price and decrease-in-price schedules. Exhibit 3 is the change-in-cost schedule. All figures on the tables are percentages.

For the change-in-price schedules I have chosen the original percent of profit margin for one axis. The other is the percent change in price. The readings are to the new quantity to be sold in relation to the quantity now being sold expressed as a percent (Q_2/Q_1). Inasmuch

EXHIBIT 1. PERCENT NEW QUANTITY TO OLD (Q_2/Q_1) TO MAINTAIN TOTAL CONTRIBUTION WHEN PRICE INCREASES

Percent Increase in Price

Q_2/Q_1	1	2	3	4	5	6	7	8	9	10	11	12	13	14	15	16	17	18	19	20
30	97	94	91	89	86	84	81	79	77	76	74	72	70	69	67	66	64	63	62	61
29	97	94	91	88	86	83	81	79	77	75	73	71	70	68	67	65	64	62	61	60
28	97	93	91	88	85	83	80	78	76	74	72	71	69	67	66	64	63	62	60	59
27	97	93	90	87	85	82	80	78	76	74	72	70	68	66	65	63	62	61	59	58
26	96	93	90	87	84	82	79	77	75	73	71	69	67	66	64	63	61	60	58	57
25	96	93	90	87	84	81	79	76	74	72	70	68	66	65	63	62	60	59	57	56
24	96	92	89	86	83	80	78	76	73	71	69	67	65	64	62	61	59	58	56	55
23	96	92	89	86	83	80	77	75	72	70	68	66	65	63	61	60	58	57	55	54
22	96	92	88	85	82	79	76	74	72	69	67	65	63	62	60	59	57	56	54	53
21	96	92	88	84	81	78	76	73	71	68	66	64	62	61	59	57	56	55	53	52
20	95	91	87	84	80	77	75	72	70	67	65	63	61	59	58	56	55	53	52	51
19	95	91	87	83	80	76	74	71	68	66	64	62	60	58	57	55	53	52	51	49
18	95	90	86	82	79	76	73	70	67	65	63	61	59	57	55	54	52	51	49	48
17	95	90	85	81	78	74	71	69	66	64	61	59	57	56	54	52	51	49	48	47
16	94	89	85	80	77	73	70	67	65	62	60	58	56	54	52	51	49	48	46	45
15	94	88	84	79	75	72	69	66	63	61	58	56	54	52	51	49	48	46	45	44
14	94	88	83	78	74	71	67	64	62	59	57	55	53	51	49	47	46	44	43	42
13	93	87	82	77	73	69	66	63	60	57	55	53	51	49	47	46	44	43	41	40
12	93	86	80	76	71	67	64	61	58	55	53	51	49	47	45	44	42	41	39	38
11	92	85	79	74	69	65	62	59	56	53	51	49	47	45	43	41	40	39	37	36
10	91	84	77	72	67	63	59	56	53	51	48	46	44	42	41	39	38	36	35	34
		85			70					50										

ORIGINAL MARGIN PERCENT

Exhibit 2. Percent New Quantity to Old (Q_2/Q_1) to Maintain Total Contribution When Price Decreases

Percent Decrease in Price

Q_2/Q_1	1	2	3	4	5	6	7	8	9	10	11	12	13	14	15	16	17	18	19	20
30	103	107	111	115	119	124	129	135	141	148	155	164	173	183	195	208	223	240	261	285
29	103	107	111	115	120	125	131	137	143	150	158	167	177	190	201	216	233	252	276	304
28	104	107	112	116	121	126	132	138	146	153	162	172	182	196	209	225	244	267	294	328
27	104	108	112	117	122	128	134	140	148	156	166	176	188	203	218	236	258	285	317	358
26	104	108	113	118	123	129	135	143	151	160	170	182	195	212	228	249	275	306	346	398
25	104	108	113	118	124	130	137	145	153	164	175	188	202	222	240	265	296	334	384	451
24	104	109	114	119	125	132	140	148	157	168	180	195	211	233	255	285	322	370	436	529
23	104	109	115	120	127	134	142	151	162	173	187	203	222	248	274	309	356	419	510	650
22	105	110	115	121	128	136	145	155	166	179	195	213	235	265	297	342	403	490	627	866
21	105	110	116	123	130	139	148	159	172	186	204	225	251	288	328	387	471	602	837	1364
20	105	111	117	124	132	141	152	164	178	195	215	240	272	318	370	451	578	803	1325	3704
19	105	111	118	126	134	144	156	169	186	205	229	260	299	360	432	554	772	1275	3725	
18	106	112	119	128	137	148	161	176	195	218	247	285	336	421	529	741	1233	3673		
17	106	113	121	130	140	152	167	184	206	234	270	320	391	518	708	1189	3696			
16	106	114	122	132	144	157	174	195	221	255	302	370	478	702	1143	3721				
15	107	115	124	135	148	164	183	208	240	285	349	452	638	1172	3750					
14	107	116	126	138	153	172	195	225	267	328	424	603	1037	3684						
13	108	118	129	143	160	182	210	249	307	398	565	985	3714							
12	109	119	132	148	168	195	231	284	370	529	923	3570								
11	110	122	136	155	179	213	263	342	491	866	3667									
10	111	124	141	164	195	240	313	450	806	3704										
		115	130	150							∞									

Left axis: Original Margin Percent

as Q_1 is known, Q_2—the new quantity to maintain total margin—can be readily found. The change-in-price tables are for a merchandising margin from ten to thirty percent and a change in price from plus twenty to minus twenty percent. These limits may be varied to fit the particular situation. Once a table is established for the appropriate ranges, one need never refer to the equation.

In like manner, a table has been constructed from the basic cost equation for cost changes. This time the axes are the new and original profit margins expressed as percentages. The readings are again the ratio, Q_2/Q_1. One table serves both for increases and decreases in cost or, what is the same thing, increases and decreases in profit margin. The downward sloping diagonal is the null case. To the left of the diagonal, the readings are for a decrease in cost, conversely to the right.

The change-in-price tables shown in Exhibits 1 and 2 must be constructed for each company for itself, as the solution of the underlying equation is affected by the value assigned to gamma. In the determination of the values in

the exhibits, gamma was set at 2.7 percent of sales (and hence of change in sales). The readings in Exhibit 3, the change in cost schedule, are not so conditioned and may be considered generally applicable.

APPLICATIONS TO CHANGE IN PRICE

If a 10-percent price decrease is contemplated for an item which currently has a margin of 25 percent, what must our increase in sales be so that total profit remains constant? Employing the decrease-in-price table, Exhibit 2, we find that the relationship of new quantity to be sold (Q_2) to the quantity presently being sold (Q_1) is as 164 is to 100. Stated succinctly, an increase of 64 percent in present unit sales is required, so that there will be no change in profit if the price is decreased 10 percent. Although we have not fully answered the question as to whether to drop the price or not, we have found the main criterion, i.e., can sales be increased at least 64 percent over the present volume?

A company has two items, A and B, similar

Exhibit 3. Percent New Quantity to Old (Q_2/Q_1) to Maintain Contribution When Cost Changes

New Margin Percent

Q_2/Q_1	30	29	28	27	26	25	24	23	22	21	20	19	18	17	16	15	14	13	12	11	10
30		103	107	111	115	120	125	130	136	143	150	158	167	176	188	200	214	231	250	273	300
29	97		104	107	112	116	121	126	132	138	145	153	161	171	181	193	207	223	242	264	290
28	93	97		104	108	112	117	122	127	133	140	147	156	165	175	187	200	215	233	255	280
27	90	93	96		104	108	113	117	123	129	135	142	150	159	169	180	193	208	225	245	270
26	87	90	92	96		104	108	113	118	124	130	137	144	153	163	173	186	200	217	236	260
25	83	86	89	93	96		104	109	114	119	125	132	139	147	156	167	179	192	208	227	250
24	80	83	86	89	92	96		104	109	114	120	126	133	141	150	160	171	185	200	218	240
23	77	79	82	85	88	92	96		105	110	115	121	128	135	144	153	164	177	192	209	230
22	73	76	79	81	85	88	92	96		105	110	116	122	129	138	147	157	169	183	200	220
21	70	72	75	78	81	84	88	91	95		105	111	117	124	131	140	150	162	175	191	210
20	67	69	71	74	77	80	83	87	91	95		105	111	118	125	133	143	154	167	182	200
19	63	66	68	70	73	76	79	83	86	90	95		106	112	119	127	136	146	158	173	190
18	60	62	64	67	69	72	75	78	82	86	90	95		106	113	120	129	138	150	164	180
17	57	59	61	63	65	68	71	74	77	81	85	89	94		106	113	121	131	142	155	170
16	53	55	57	59	62	64	67	70	73	76	80	84	89	94		107	114	123	133	145	160
15	50	52	54	56	58	60	63	65	68	71	75	79	83	88	94		107	115	125	136	150
14	47	48	50	52	54	56	58	61	64	67	70	74	78	82	88	93		108	117	127	140
13	43	45	46	48	50	52	54	57	59	62	65	68	72	76	81	87	93		108	118	130
12	40	41	43	44	46	48	50	52	55	57	60	63	67	71	75	80	86	92		109	120
11	37	38	39	41	42	44	46	48	50	52	55	58	61	65	69	73	79	85	92		110
10	33	34	36	37	38	40	42	43	45	48	50	53	56	59	63	67	71	77	83	91	

(Row labels at left: Original Margin Percent)

in the fact that their sales react alike to price changes. As profits are being reduced due to increased costs, it is felt that the price must be raised for each item by five percent. The marketing department's best estimate is that, with such an increase in price, approximately one fifth of the firm's customers will discontinue using A and B. What should the company do? Since both products react alike to price changes, it is decided to raise the price of one item first to test the market reaction. The problem is which one to choose. It is known that, under present conditions, the products have profit margins of 14 percent and 28 percent respectively. Using the price-increase table, (Exhibit 1), it is seen that, for a 5 percent increase in price, we can sustain a loss in physical volume of 26 percent for A and only 15 percent for B without affecting the total profit adversely. As our best estimate, is a 20 percent loss in volume, then we should experiment with item A.

1. The smaller the original profit margin, the greater the increase in sales needed to keep the total dollar contribution constant as price is reduced. Conversely, when the price is increased, the smaller the original margin, the greater the loss in sales quantity the item can sustain, without diminishing over-all contribution.

2. The heavy lines on the tables are drawn to divide them into broad areas of needed sales increase or decrease, as the case may be. These areas are: up to ±15 percent, ±30 percent, ±50 percent and ± more than 50 percent. If the charts are visualized as constructed to the left and right of the same axis, in ascending percentage of price change, it can be seen that these areas would take the shape of an inverted isosceles triangle. What is of particular interest is that the wedge shape of the areas becomes narrower and approaches a splinter (e.g., the area representing necessary quantity increases or decreases up to 15 percent). Scrutiny of the price-change scale at the top of the charts in relationship to the areas marked off by the heavy lines, shows that three such areas (to 50 percent needed quantity increase) are involved in price decreases up to 10 percent while only two (to 30 percent needed quantity increase) are involved in price increases up to 13 percent. Hence price declines quickly require marked quantity increases to equalize contribution.

APPLICATIONS TO CHANGE IN COST

A company has a product that sells for $1.50 and which presently costs $1.20 to manufacture. The product, therefore, has a margin of 20 percent. Cost has risen 5¢ per unit, making the new margin 17 percent. As it is undesirable to raise the price, how many more units must now be sold so that total profit contribution remains constant? By using the cost-change chart (Exhibit 3), we cross reference the two margins to find that an increase in unit sales of 18 percent is needed.

A sales promotion in which 21 units will be shipped to the customer for the price of 20 is proposed by the sales department. The managing director asks whether the increase in sales volume will cover the free twenty-first unit or not? An analysis tells us that units one through twenty are sharing equally the cost of the twenty-first unit. To illustrate the point and conclusion, some numbers are substituted.

Sales price	$100
Cost per unit	80
Gross profit margin	$ 20

The cost added to each of the first twenty units is 80/20=4. Thus the new cost is 84 and the new margin is 16 percent. Using the increase-in-cost table, it is found that, for an original margin of 20 percent, and a new margin of 16 percent, the quantity sold must be 125 percent of the quantity now being sold, if the total dollar contribution is to remain constant. Will unit sales increase 25 percent to cover the cost of the promotion?

SERVICES OF CHARTS

From these illustrations, both of the change-in-price charts and of the change-in-cost chart, the point is clear that we can measure marketing decisions or proposals in light of a company's profit picture, related to the products involved. No doubt there will be counter-arguments based on nonmeasurable factors but, by using the formulas, one can see if the company can afford to make a particular decision, and by how much. Again, no equation can give the answer but, from it, one can establish a firm basis and limits for making marketing decisions.

DISCUSSION QUESTION

Working toward target margins or profits in the face of changes in cost, price, or both, is a common enough problem in retailing. This article develops the solution for and, for those who prefer, tables which accomodate a typical range of cases for price increases, price decreases, and cost changes.

> If the old gross margin on a product was 25% and a price increase of 10% occurs, what percent of the previous level of sales would have to be realized to maintain the same contribution?